THE LAW OF CORPORATIONS, PARTNERSHIPS, AND SOLE PROPRIETORSHIPS

The West Paralegal Series

Your options keep growing with West Publishing.
Each year our list continues to offer you more options for every course, new or existing, and on-the-job reference materials. We now have over 140 titles from which to choose.

We are pleased to offer books in the following subject areas:

Administrative Law	Family Law
Alternative Dispute Resolution	Federal Taxation
Bankruptcy	Intellectual Property
Business Organizations/Corporations	Introduction to Law
Civil Litigation and Procedure	Introduction to Paralegalism
CLA Exam Preparation	Law Office Management
Client Accounting	Law Office Procedures
Computer in the Law Office	Legal Research, Writing, and Analysis
Constitutional Law	Legal Terminology
Contract Law	Paralegal Employment
Criminal Law and Procedure	Real Estate Law
Document Preparation	Reference Materials
Environmental Law	Torts and Personal Injury Law
Ethics	Will, Trusts, and Estate Administration

You will find unparalleled, practical teaching support.
Each text is enhanced by instructor and student supplements to ensure the best learning experience possible to prepare for this field. We also offer custom publishing and other benefits such as West's Student Achievement Award. In addition, our sales representatives are ready to provide you with needed and dependable service.

We want to hear from you.
The most important factor in improving the quality of our paralegal texts and teaching packages is active feedback from educators in the field. If you have a question, concern, or observation about any of our materials or you have written a proposal or manuscript, we want to hear from you. Please do not hesitate to contact your local representative or write us at the following address:

West Paralegal Series, 3 Columbia Circle, P.O. Box 15015, Albany, NY 12212-5015.

For additional information point your browser to
http://www.westpub.com/Educate and **http://www.delmar.com**

West Publishing — *Your Paralegal Publisher*
an imprint of Delmar Publishers

an International Thomson Publishing company

THE LAW OF CORPORATIONS, PARTNERSHIPS, AND SOLE PROPRIETORSHIPS

SECOND EDITION

Angela Schneeman

WEST PUBLISHING

an International Thomson Publishing company I(T)P®

Albany • Bonn • Boston • Cincinnati • Detroit • London • Madrid
Melbourne • Mexico City • Minneapolis/St. Paul • New York • Pacific Grove
Paris • San Francisco • Singapore • Tokyo • Toronto • Washington

NOTICE TO THE READER

Cover Background: Jennifer McGlaughlin
Cover Design: Linda DeMasi

Delmar Staff

Acquisitions Editor: Christopher Anzalone
Editorial Assistant: Judy A. Roberts
Developmental Editor: Jeffrey D. Litton

Project Editor: Eugenia L. Orlandi
Production Coordinator: Linda J. Helfrich
Art & Design Coordinator: Douglas J. Hyldelund

Printed in the United States of America
5 6 7 8 9 10 XXX 02 01 00 99

For more information, contact Delmar, 3 Columbia Circle, PO Box 15015, Albany, NY 12212-0515; or find us on the World Wide Web at http://www.westlegalstudies.com

International Division List

Japan:
Thomson Learning
Palaceside Building 5F
1-1-1 Hitotsubashi, Chiyoda-ku
Tokyo 100 0003 Japan
Tel: 813 5218 6544
Fax: 813 5218 6551

Australia/New Zealand:
Nelson/Thomson Learning
102 Dodds Street
South Melbourne, Victoria 3205
Australia
Tel: 61 39 685 4111
Fax: 61 39 685 4199

UK/Europe/Middle East:
Thomson Learning
Berkshire House
168-173 High Holborn
London
WC1V 7AA United Kingdom
Tel: 44 171 497 1422
Fax: 44 171 497 1426

Latin America:
Thomson Learning
Seneca, 53
Colonia Polanco
11560 Mexico D.F. Mexico
Tel: 525-281-2906
Fax: 525-281-2656

Canada:
Nelson/Thomson Learning
1120 Birchmount Road
Scarborough, Ontario
Canada M1K 5G4
Tel: 416-752-9100
Fax: 416-752-8102

Asia:
Thomson Learning
60 Albert Street, #15-01
Albert Complex
Singapore 189969
Tel: 65 336 6411
Fax: 65 336 7411

Library of Congress Cataloging-in-Publication Data
Schneeman, Angela
      The law of corporations, partnerships, and sole proprietorships/
Angela Schneeman.—2nd ed.
          p.   cm.
      Includes bibliographical references and index.
      ISBN 0-8273-7568-9
      1. Sole proprietorship—United States. 2. Partnership—United
States. 3. Corporation law—United States. 4. Legal assistants—
United States—Handbooks, manuals, etc. I. Title.
KF1355.Z9S36   1997
346.73'066—dc20   96-24674
[347.30666]   CIP

DEDICATION

To my parents, Al and Anna Lutterman

CONTENTS

CHAPTER 2:   Partnerships 16

CHAPTER 3:   Limited Partnerships 72

CHAPTER 4:   Limited Liability Companies 114

CHAPTER 5:   Corporations 158

CHAPTER 6:   Formation of the Corporation 184

CHAPTER 7:   The Corporate Organization 236

CHAPTER 8:   The Corporate Financial Structure 294

CHAPTER 9:   Public Corporations and Securities Regulations 326

CHAPTER 11:   Qualification of a Foreign Corporation 410

CHAPTER 12: Corporate Dissolution 432

CHAPTER 13: Employee Benefit Plans 460

Appendices

PREFACE

The purpose of this book is to educate the paralegal student with regard to the law of business organizations, and to prepare the student to work in the area of corporate law as a paralegal. It gives an overview of the law and the theory behind the law, as well as practical information that the paralegal can use on the job.

Each chapter includes a general discussion of the law concerning the pertinent topic, often using model or uniform acts and case law as examples. The heavy use of model and uniform acts in this book is intended to give the student an understanding of the model laws that state legislatures commonly follow, as well as to give the paralegal familiarity with statutory research. Tables of state law refer the student to the law of his or her home state.

Cases are included throughout this text to illustrate the application of the laws being discussed. Corporate case law tends to be very complex, and the cases included in this text have been edited to simplify them as much as possible. Although it is important for the student to grasp the main point being made by each case, a complete understanding of all of the procedural formalities included within each case is not necessary. Terms that may be unfamiliar have been defined to help eliminate any confusion, and those marked with a dagger are from *Ballentine's Legal Dictionary and Thesaurus* (Delmar/LCP, 1994).

Review questions at the end of each chapter require that the student review and summarize the key points learned throughout the chapter. In addition, hypothetical questions require the student to apply that knowledge to a practical situation.

Forms and a discussion of pertinent procedures that often must be followed by paralegals are included throughout this text wherever practical. Each chapter also contains a section that specifically discusses the role of the paralegal as it relates to that chapter's topic.

The discussions of available resources to assist the paralegal serve as a useful reference to working paralegals.

Although the main focus of this text is on corporate law, it also contains chapters on sole proprietorships, partnerships, limited partnerships, and limited liability companies. These topics have been included with the aim of giving the paralegal student an understanding of the alternate forms of business organizations. Each of these chapters includes a discussion of the advantages and disadvantages of doing business in that format.

The discussions of corporate law include an in-depth analysis of the nature, formation, dissolution, and financial structure of the corporation. Mergers and acquisitions, securities, and employment agreements are covered in separate chapters.

Probably the most significant addition to the Second Edition is a chapter on the limited liability company. As recently as 1993, when the First Edition of this text was published, the limited liability company was a new entity that was recognized in just eight states. Now every state has adopted or is considering limited liability company legislation. Chapter 4 is an in-depth introduction to the law of limited liability companies. The recently-adopted Model Limited Liability Company Act is also included as Appendix E.

The partnership chapter of the Second Edition now includes an in-depth discussion of the new Uniform Partnership Act, which was adopted subsequent to the publication of the First Edition. This new Uniform Act is included as Appendix C.

One topic covered here that is rarely found in introductory corporate law texts is employee benefit plans. I have included this chapter because many paralegals are employed in the benefits area, and there is seldom a separate course offered on employee benefit plans.

Finally, because corporate law is not always considered to be the most stimulating topic—and students cannot learn anything from a text if it puts them to sleep—there are several features included within the chapters to pique the student's interest in corporate law. As much as possible, I have tried to include discussions relating to corporate law that may be of particular interest to the paralegal student. These "features" are written in a magazine-article style and include discussions of current news topics and items that may be of special interest to working paralegals.

I would like to give my thanks to several people for the assistance they have given me on this project, including Chris Anzalone, Jeff Litton, and Judy Roberts at Delmar and Jehanne Schweitzer and Mark Arnest at Graphics West.

I would also like to thank my family, friends and co-workers for their advice and encouragement. A very special thanks to my husband, Greg, and my children Alex and Katherine for their patience and support.

Lastly, I acknowledge the contributions of the following reviewers, whose suggestions and insights have helped me enormously:

Randi Ray
Des Moines Area Community College
Des Moines, Iowa

David Hardy
University of Charleston
Charleston, West Virginia

Claudia Clinton
McMurry University
Abilene, Texas

Jim Hodge
International College
Naples, Florida

Charles DeWitt
University of Memphis
Memphis, Tennessee

Anthony Piazza
David N. Meyers College
Cleveland, Ohio

Angela Schneeman

ABOUT THE AUTHOR

A resident of suburban St. Paul/Minneapolis, Angela Schneeman received her paralegal certificate from the University of Minnesota. She completed her internship at the law firm where she had been working as a legal secretary. Subsequently, Schneeman convinced the attorneys of that firm to hire her on a full-time, permanent basis as a paralegal. "I was the first paralegal the law firm had ever hired, and when I first started, neither the attorneys nor I had a very clear idea of how my time and skills could best be utilized by the firm. Fortunately, the attorneys I worked for were very busy and willing to delegate any work that could possibly be done by a paralegal," Schneeman says. Within two years there were two other paralegals working for the firm, and the attorneys were very convinced of the benefits of working with paralegals.

The firm Schneeman worked for specialized in corporate law, mergers and acquisitions, qualified plans, estate planning, probate, and real estate. Originally she worked in all of those areas, but corporations became her specialty. Most of her workdays were fast-paced and unpredictable. On a "typical" day, she would spend most of her time meeting with several attorneys, calling and/or meeting with clients, and drafting legal documents and correspondence. Some of the legal documents that she prepared were articles of incorporation, bylaws, and other corporate documents. It was also her responsibility to keep the clients' corporate-minute books up to date by preparing the necessary annual minutes and other documentation.

One of the most interesting and exciting aspects of Schneeman's job involved mergers and acquisitions. She was often responsible for drafting and organizing the numerous documents required for large closings, which she usually attended. "It was very exciting and rewarding to me to be an integral part of a multi-million dollar transaction," Schneeman says. Although she found that working on mergers and acquisitions was very interesting, it also involved working long hours under a lot of pressure. It was not uncommon for her to work late into the night, and in some cases, early into the next morning, to prepare for a large closing.

The group of attorneys who employed Schneeman understood the importance of a good team effort and recognized that every member of the law firm staff is essential. Typically, when the firm was about to undertake a large project, the attorneys would decide on a team to handle the work. This team would usually consist of a partner of the firm, an associate attorney, a paralegal, and a secretary. The team would meet to discuss how the project would be handled, and then work together to see the project through to its successful conclusion.

"My advice to anyone considering a career as a paralegal is to explore several different opportunities. The field is very diverse, and job descriptions and position qualifications can vary greatly depending on the size of the firm or corporation and the type of law being practiced. I think it is important to find a position with the challenges and rewards that will match your personality," Schneeman advises.

Currently, Schneeman is a free-lance paralegal, working directly with small corporations and their attorneys. She is also the corporate columnist for *Legal Assistant Today*.

TABLE OF CASES

CHAPTER 1

SOLE PROPRIETORSHIPS

In industry, it is never the industry leader who makes the big leap. On the contrary, it is the inventor or small guy who makes the big leap.
— ***Burton Klein***

Introduction

Before we begin our in-depth discussion of corporations in this text, we will investigate the characteristics of some simpler forms of business organizations and determine how those business organizations compare to corporations.

This chapter focuses on **sole proprietorships**, the most prevalent form of business in the United States. We begin by defining the term *sole proprietorship* and taking a look at the role of sole proprietorships in the United States. We then consider the advantages and disadvantages of doing business as a sole proprietorship, in contrast to the other types of business organizations. Next we focus on what it takes to form and operate a sole proprietorship, the role of the paralegal working with a sole proprietorship, and the resources that are available to paralegals whose work involves sole proprietorships.

§ 1.1 Sole Proprietorship Defined

The sole proprietorship is the simplest type of business organization. A **sole proprietor** is the sole owner of all of the assets of the business and is solely liable for all the debts of the business.

Unlike a corporation, the business of the sole proprietor is not considered a separate entity. Rather, it is considered an extension of the individual. The sole proprietor is personally responsible for all legal

TERMS

sole proprietorship [†] Ownership by one person, as opposed to ownership by more than one person, ownership by a corporation, ownership by a partnership, etc.

sole proprietor The owner of a sole proprietorship.

debts and obligations of the business and is entitled to all of the profits of the business.

The sole proprietor may delegate decisions and management of the business to agents, but all authority to make decisions must come directly from the sole proprietor, who is responsible for all business-related acts of employees.

§ 1.2 Sole Proprietorships in the United States

The small business owned by a sole proprietor is the most common form of business in the United States. Although sole proprietorships make up the majority of business enterprises in this country, they account for a much smaller portion of gross business receipts than corporations do. For example, income tax returns for 1991 indicated that there were over 15 million sole proprietorships in the United States and only 3.8 million corporations. However, those 3.8 million corporations showed business receipts of over $9.9 trillion, while the sole proprietorships accounted for receipts of only $712 billion (see Figure 1-1).[1]

§ 1.3 Advantages of Doing Business As a Sole Proprietor

The small businessperson can find several advantages in doing business as a sole proprietor. This section focuses on some of the more important advantages of operating as a sole proprietorship, in contrast to operating as a corporation or partnership, including the sole proprietor's full management authority of the business, the minimal formalities and reporting requirements associated with sole proprietorships, the low cost of organizing sole proprietorships, and the income tax benefits offered by sole proprietorships.

Full Management Authority

The sole proprietor has the advantage of having full authority to manage the business in any way he or she sees fit, without having to obtain permission from a partner or a board of directors. Because the sole

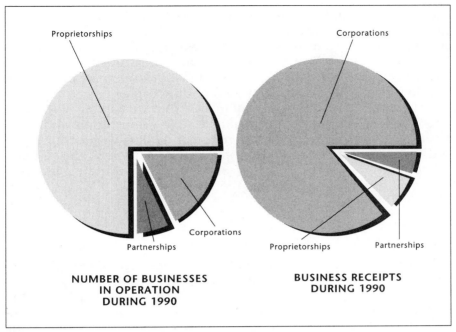

FIGURE 1-1 Comparison of Business Types and Receipts

proprietor is not required to document decisions or obtain permission from others, the sole proprietorship is not subject to the bureaucracy and delays in the decision-making process that are often associated with partnerships and corporations.

Any number of employees or agents may be hired by a sole proprietor, and any authority the sole proprietor chooses may be delegated. However, as the only owner of the business, the sole proprietor is always in command. If the sole owner of a business chooses to grant an ownership interest in the business to an employee in exchange for the employee's services, the business is no longer a sole proprietorship, but rather a partnership.

Minimal Formalities and Regulatory and Reporting Requirements

Sole proprietorships are not created or governed by statute, so there are very few formalities that must be followed by a sole proprietor. A sole proprietor must, however, comply with licensing and taxation regulations that are imposed on all forms of businesses. A sole proprietor must be aware of and obtain any necessary licenses, sales tax permits, and tax identification numbers before commencing business. Also, if the business is transacted under a name other than the sole proprietor's personal name, the state where the business is transacted will probably require that an application for **certificate of assumed name, trade name, or fictitious name** be filed. Assumed names, trade names, and fictitious names are discussed in § 1.5 of this chapter.

There are no qualification requirements for transacting business in a foreign state as a sole proprietorship. Unlike a corporation, a sole proprietor may transact business in a neighboring state without having to qualify and pay a fee to the appropriate state authority. The sole proprietor must, however, be sure to comply with any licensing and taxation requirements peculiar to that foreign state.

Low Cost of Organization

Formalities and regulatory requirements for beginning and operating a sole proprietorship are minimal. As a result, the costs for starting and maintaining a sole proprietorship are relatively low. There are no minimum capital restrictions and few, if any, state filing fees. Some possible startup expenses include attorneys' fees for legal advice and filing and publishing fees for a certificate of assumed name, trade name, or fictitious name.

Income Tax Benefits

The income of the sole proprietorship is reported on a schedule to the sole proprietor's individual income tax return. The profit or loss of the business is added to the sole proprietor's other income, if any, and taxed at the individual rate of the taxpayer. This can be particularly advantageous for new businesses, which often incur a loss in the first year or so. If a sole proprietorship experiences a net loss during a particular year, the sole proprietor can use that loss to offset other income.

Another income tax benefit to the sole proprietor is that there is no double taxation, which is often a drawback to corporate ownership. *Double taxation* refers to a situation whereby the income of the business is taxed twice: income taxes are paid once at the corporate level and

---

TERMS

certificate of assumed name, trade name, or fictitious name   A certificate granted by the proper state authority to an individual or an entity that grants the right to use an assumed or fictitious name for the transaction of business in that state.

Dividends

Sole Proprietors on the Information Superhighway

Sole proprietors have always been a driving force in our economy and in our culture. In the mid-1990s an estimated 20 million individuals in this country consider themselves to be sole proprietors. Approximately one out of every five new jobs is created by a sole proprietorship.

In years past, the term *sole proprietor* would often bring to mind the man or woman who owned and operated the local corner store or barber shop. In the 1990s sole proprietors have taken on a new identity. The new sole proprietor is more likely an entrepreneur who runs a computer-based business from his or her home office.

The sophisticated, yet affordable, home office equipment that is now available means that many individuals are able to offer high-quality services from their home offices at an affordable price. No single factor has played a larger role in the success of the home-based entrepreneur than the personal computer and the Internet. Technology that was only imaginable a few short years ago is now available, affordable, and easy to use.

The Internet began in 1969, as an experiment by the United States Department of Defense with the goal of linking remote computers to large data bases and computer systems. Since then the Internet has grown into a virtual network of networks, connecting millions of computers world wide. Sole proprietors who are savvy in the ways of the Internet make use of its vast banks of information and other resources, its communication abilities, and the unique marketing opportunities it presents.

Writers, consultants, and others who offer information-based services now have the ability to access library and data banks throughout the world almost instantly and at a minimal cost. A financial consultant can offer clients information concerning the New York Stock Exchange or the Tokyo Stock Market in minutes. A travel agent can access a road map of a particular area of Paris while the client is still on the telephone. Writers and researchers can access information in libraries throughout the world to provide their clients with the most up-to-date information available.

The sole proprietor who transacts business over the Internet has the ability to communicate interactively with clients all over the world—either one-on-one or via an electronic conference. In addition to improved communications, the Internet allows small businesses to offer their clients electronic billing and information transfer. The sole proprietor may now, from his or her home office, transfer files to clients that include documents, graphics, photos, charts, tables, and even sound. Billing done via the Internet can save both time and paperwork.

One of the newest and most exciting features of the Internet for the small business owner is the ability to attract new customers. The Internet can introduce the sole proprietor's business to the world. According to the Internet Society (ISOC), as of the spring of 1994, the Internet reached seventy-five countries directly and 146 countries indirectly. It consisted of 35,000 networks and 3 million computers.[1] The number of Internet users is growing at an unbelievable pace. Potential customers surfing the Internet can access information concerning a company or a product 24 hours a day. An advertisement may range from a short introduction to a single product to an entire catalog of products, complete with photographs. Being able to reach such numbers of people throughout the world via home computer access is having a dramatic effect on the sole proprietor's business. The creative use of the Internet for marketing purposes is still in its infancy. The future is promising, but unpredictable.

Another valuable Internet resource for the sole proprietor is the ability to network. The individual who works alone can combat the feeling of isolation by communicating with others in similar situations via the bulletin boards on the Internet. Those owning and operating home-based businesses can offer each other support and advice on numerous topics.

The Internet has connected the sole proprietor to the entire business world, and its impact is only beginning to be felt.

[1] LaQuey, Tracy, *The Internet Companion* 3 (1994).

again as the income flows through to the individual shareholders in the form of a salary or dividend.

§ 1.4 Disadvantages of Doing Business As a Sole Proprietor

Along with the advantages of doing business as a sole proprietor, there are several disadvantages. Operating as a sole proprietorship can significantly restrict the growth of the business under many circumstances. Many sole proprietors eventually incorporate to achieve their business's full growth potential.

The disadvantages discussed in this section include the unlimited liability of the sole proprietor, the sole proprietorship's lack of business continuity, and the fact that there is no diversity in the management of a sole proprietorship. Next, we examine the difficulty in transferring the proprietary interest of a sole proprietorship and the limitations on raising capital for a sole proprietorship. This section concludes with a brief look at the circumstances under which the income taxation of a business could be a disadvantage to a sole proprietor. All of these disadvantages must be weighed against potential advantages before a sound business decision can be made as to the most advantageous business format.

Unlimited Liability

One of the most significant disadvantages of doing business as a sole proprietor is the unlimited liability faced by the owner of the business. The owner is solely responsible for all debts and obligations of the business, as well as any torts committed personally by the sole proprietor or by employees acting within the scope of their employment, without any protection of the sole proprietor's personal assets. Creditors may look to both the business and personal assets of the sole proprietor to satisfy their claims.

Insurance can help to prevent a personal catastrophe to the sole proprietor, but insurance is not available to cover every potential type of liability. Individuals who operate businesses that have a high, uninsurable liability risk will almost always do best to incorporate or form a limited liability company.

Lack of Business Continuity

Because the sole proprietorship is in many ways merely an extension of the individual, when the individual owner dies or ceases to do business, the business itself often terminates. Although the sole proprietor may have employed several employees or agents, the agency relationship terminates upon the death of the sole proprietor. In most states, the sole proprietor may direct the personal representative of the estate to oversee the continuance of the business until the estate has been settled and the business is passed to the **legatee**. However, if the business was dependent upon the sole proprietor for its management, it may be difficult to maintain the business. If all of the assets of the business are transferred to another individual and the business is kept intact, another sole proprietorship is formed.

No Diversity in Management

Although it may be very appealing to an individual starting a new business to be able to make all the business decisions, there are many instances in which diversity in management can be advantageous. The sole proprietor does not have the experience and expertise of other partners, directors, or shareholders to rely on.

Difficulty in Transferring Proprietary Interest

When it comes time to sell the business, transferring the full interest of a sole proprietor may be difficult. Because the business is linked closely with the identity of the owner, the business may be worth much less when broken down by tangible assets. If no buyer is available for

---

TERMS

legatee[†]   A person who receives personal property as a beneficiary under a will, although the word is often loosely used to mean a person who receives a testamentary gift of either personal property or real property.

the business, the sole proprietor may have to take a loss by selling off the assets of the business.

The sale of a sole proprietorship also may be expensive. Unlike the shareholder of a publicly traded corporation, who can sell shares of stock on an exchange for a broker's fee, selling a sole proprietorship can be a difficult, time-consuming, and expensive ordeal. Many sales require extensive appraisals of the assets of the business. It may be difficult to place a fair dollar value on several assets of the business, including the **goodwill** and name of the business.

Limited Ability to Raise Capital

A wealthy entrepreneur starting a second or third business may not have a problem with lack of capital to start a sole proprietorship. However, to most individuals a barrier is created by the limitations of their own financial wealth. The funds they are able to borrow based on their personal assets and their business plan may not be sufficient to fund the type of business they desire to run.

Tax Disadvantages

The sole proprietorship's income is taxed at the sole proprietor's personal income tax rate. Individuals who run very profitable businesses or who have a large income from other sources will pay taxes at a higher tax rate.

§ 1.5 Formation and Operation of the Sole Proprietorship

Very few formalities must be followed for an individual to commence business as a sole proprietorship. Because a sole proprietorship is not considered to be a separate entity, but rather an extension of the individual owner, one need do nothing to "form" the sole proprietorship.

TERMS

goodwill [†] The benefit a business acquires, beyond the mere value of its capital stock and tangible assets, as a result of having a good reputation and the respect of the public. Goodwill is intangible property. However,

The formalities that must be followed are not unique to sole proprietorships, but are required of all types of business organizations. These may include filing a certificate of assumed name, trade name, or fictitious name and applying for tax identification numbers, sales tax permits, and licenses.

Using an Assumed Name, Trade Name, or Fictitious Name

Most states allow a sole proprietor to transact business under a name other than his or her own name, provided that the purpose for doing so is not a fraudulent design or the intent to injure others.[2] The statutes of most states set forth certain requirements that must be followed before an individual may transact business under an **assumed name**, **trade name**, or **fictitious name**, as it may variously be called.

Typically, if the proposed name is available and otherwise complies with state statutes, an application for certificate of assumed name, trade name, or fictitious name, or similar document, is filed with the Secretary of State of the state in which the sole proprietor intends to do business. State statutes often require publication of a notice of intent to transact business under an assumed name. The intent of these statutes is to protect the public by giving notice or information as to the persons with whom they deal, and to afford protection against fraud and deceit.[3]

The appropriate state statutes should be carefully reviewed to ascertain the state requirements for assumed names, trade names, or fictitious names, and the Secretary of State or other appropriate state official should be contacted. Often the Secretary of State's office will provide its own forms to be completed to apply for a certificate of assumed name. Figure 1-2 shows a fictitious or assumed name certificate that may be used by a sole proprietor.

TERMS

goodwill is a function only of a going concern, and therefore can be assigned a value for accounting purposes only in connection with the sale of a business that is a going concern.

assumed name [†] A fictitious name or an alias.

trade name [†] The name under which a company does business. The goodwill of a company includes its trade name.

fictitious name [†] An artificial name that a person or a corporation adopts for business or professional purposes.

[From 14 AM. JUR. 2d Legal Forms (Rev)]

CERTIFICATE

It is hereby certified:

1. The undersigned is, or will be, transacting business at _____ [address], City of [_____], County of [_____], State of _____ , _____ [zip code] under the _____ [fictitious or assumed] name of _____ .

2. The real name of the undersigned is _____ , and the residence address of the undersigned is _____ , City of _____ , County of _____ , State of _____ , _____ [zip code].

3. The undersigned is of full age, and no other person is interested as a partner, part owner, or otherwise in the business or the conduct of it.

4. The nature of the business is _____ .

This certificate is executed and filed pursuant to _____ [cite statute] relating to the conduct of business under _____ [a fictitious or an assumed] name.

Dated: _____ , 19___ .

[Signature]

[Acknowledgment]

FIGURE 1-2 Fictitious or Assumed Name Certificate—By Individual

Hiring Employees and Using Tax Identification Numbers

If a sole proprietor will be hiring employees, a federal employer identification number (EIN) must be obtained. This number is obtained by completing and filing an Application for Employer Identification Number (Form SS-4). See Figure 1-3. The application and a complete set of instructions can be obtained by contacting your local IRS office or calling the IRS at 1-800-829-1040. The instructions include information on obtaining the EIN over the telephone through the IRS Tele-TIN service and for submitting the application by fax and through the mail.

Some states require employers to have a state tax identification number separate from the federal tax identification number. The appropriate state authority should be contacted to ensure that the sole proprietor is in compliance with all requirements for tax identification numbers.

The sole proprietor must also be aware of and comply with all requirements concerning state and federal withholding and unemployment taxes.

Form **SS-4**
(Rev. December 1993)
Department of the Treasury
Internal Revenue Service

Application for Employer Identification Number

(For use by employers, corporations, partnerships, trusts, estates, churches, government agencies, certain individuals, and others. See instructions.)

EIN

OMB No. 1545-0003
Expires 12-31-96

Please type or print clearly.

1 Name of applicant (Legal name) (See instructions.)

2 Trade name of business, if different from name in line 1

3 Executor, trustee, "care of" name

4a Mailing address (street address) (room, apt., or suite no.)

5a Business address, if different from address in lines 4a and 4b

4b City, state, and ZIP code

5b City, state, and ZIP code

6 County and state where principal business is located

7 Name of principal officer, general partner, grantor, owner, or trustor—SSN required (See instructions.) ▶

8a Type of entity (Check only one box.) (See instructions.)
☐ Sole Proprietor (SSN) _____
☐ REMIC   ☐ Personal service corp.
☐ State/local government   ☐ National guard
☐ Other nonprofit organization (specify) _____
☐ Other (specify) ▶ _____

☐ Estate (SSN of decedent) _____
☐ Plan administrator-SSN _____
☐ Other corporation (specify) _____
☐ Federal government/military   ☐ Church or church controlled organization
(enter GEN if applicable) _____

☐ Trust
☐ Partnership
☐ Farmers' cooperative

8b If a corporation, name the state or foreign country (if applicable) where incorporated ▶

State

Foreign country

9 Reason for applying (Check only one box.)
☐ Started new business (specify) ▶ _____
☐ Hired employees
☐ Created a pension plan (specify type) ▶ _____
☐ Banking purpose (specify) ▶ _____

☐ Changed type of organization (specify) ▶ _____
☐ Purchased going business
☐ Created a trust (specify) ▶ _____
☐ Other (specify) ▶

10 Date business started or acquired (Mo., day, year) (See instructions.)

11 Enter closing month of accounting year. (See instructions.)

12 First date wages or annuities were paid or will be paid (Mo., day, year). Note: If applicant is a withholding agent, enter date income will first be paid to nonresident alien. (Mo., day, year) ▶

13 Enter highest number of employees expected in the next 12 months. Note: If the applicant does not expect to have any employees during the period, enter "0." ▶

Nonagricultural | Agricultural | Household

14 Principal activity (See instructions.) ▶

15 Is the principal business activity manufacturing?   ☐ Yes   ☐ No
If "Yes," principal product and raw material used ▶

16 To whom are most of the products or services sold? Please check the appropriate box.   ☐ Business (wholesale)
☐ Public (retail)   ☐ Other (specify) ▶   ☐ N/A

17a Has the entity ever applied for an identification number for this or any other business?   ☐ Yes   ☐ No
Note: If "Yes," please complete lines 17b and 17c.

17b If you checked the "Yes" box in line 17a, give applicant's legal name and trade name, if different than name shown on prior application.
Legal name ▶   Trade name ▶

17c Enter approximate date, city, and state where the application was filed and the previous employer identification number if known.
Approximate date when filed (Mo., day, year) | City and state where filed | Previous EIN

Under penalties of perjury, I declare that I have examined this application, and to the best of my knowledge and belief, it is true, correct, and complete.

Business telephone number (include area code)

Name and title (Please type or print clearly.) ▶

Signature ▶   Date ▶

Note: Do not write below this line.   For official use only.

Please leave blank ▶ | Geo | Ind. | Class | Size | Reason for applying

For Paperwork Reduction Act Notice, see attached instructions.   Cat. No. 16055N   Form **SS-4** (Rev. 12-93)

FIGURE 1-3 IRS Form SS-4, Application for Employer Identification Number

Sales Tax Permits

Most states require businesses to obtain a sales tax permit before sales are made. Again, the appropriate state authority must be contacted to ensure that the proper procedures are followed.

Licensing

Many types of businesses are required to obtain licenses of one form or another. The proper city and state authorities must be contacted to ascertain whether a license is required for the type of business that the sole proprietor proposes to commence.

§ 1.6   The Role of the Legal Assistant in Sole Proprietorship Matters

The involvement of legal assistants in working with attorneys who advise sole proprietors varies greatly, depending on the circumstances and the client. If the client is an experienced businessperson who perhaps has started a business before, he or she may need little legal assistance from the attorney and the legal assistant. Legal services may be confined to legal advice given by the attorney to the sole proprietor. An experienced businessperson may decide to personally handle all formalities connected with the sole proprietorship.

Other clients, however, because of inexperience or lack of time, may decide to ask more assistance of the attorney and the legal assistant. The attorney may meet with the client to give legal advice as requested, and then ask the legal assistant to directly assist the client by seeing that all of the necessary formalities are complied with.

The legal assistant may prepare for the client, or assist the client in preparing, all necessary documents, including tax identification number applications and a certificate of assumed name. For this reason, it is important for legal assistants working in the area to be familiar with state and local requirements and procedures that must be followed to form and operate a sole proprietorship.

Following is a checklist that may be used to ensure that the client is given all the necessary information and assistance to begin his or her own sole proprietorship.

CHECKLIST FOR STARTING A SOLE PROPRIETORSHIP

- ☐ Contact proper state and federal agencies to request information regarding taxation, unemployment insurance, workers' compensation insurance, etc. (The law firm may keep extra state and federal information and forms on hand for clients.)
- ☐ Complete and file necessary applications for employer identification numbers—both federal and state if necessary.
- ☐ File application for certificate of assumed name, trade name, or fictitious name with Secretary of State or other appropriate state agency (if necessary).

☐ Publish notice of transacting business under assumed name in local newspaper (if necessary).

☐ Secure necessary business licenses and permits—state and local.

☐ Obtain sales tax permits, if necessary.

§ 1.7 Resources

Many resources are available to the legal assistant who is working with a sole proprietorship. Much of this information is published by the government and is free for the asking. Some of the most valuable resources to assist the legal assistant in this area include United States Small Business Administration publications, publications and information available from state and local government offices, state statutes, and the Secretary of State's office.

United States Small Business Administration

The United States Small Business Administration (SBA) has offices in nearly every major city in the country. The local SBA office can often provide a wide variety of free information on federal requirements for forming and operating small businesses, including sole proprietorships. The SBA's Office of Advocacy's toll-free "Answer Desk" number is 1-800-827-5722.

State and Local Government Offices

Licensing and taxation requirements vary by state and locality, and it is important that the appropriate authorities be contacted to obtain information relating to all state and local licensing and taxation matters, including unemployment insurance, withholding for employee income taxation, and sales tax permits and licenses. Again, the information obtainable from your local Small Business Administration can help direct you to the appropriate offices that must be contacted.

State Statutes

The appropriate state statutes must be consulted for information regarding use of assumed names, trade names, or fictitious names, if applicable, as well as for any requirements or regulations related to sole proprietorships.

Secretaries of State

The Secretary of State or other appropriate state authority should be contacted for procedural information regarding filing of an application for use of assumed or fictitious name, if applicable. See Appendix A of this text for a directory of Secretaries of State.

Review Questions

1. What form of business ownership is the most prevalent in the United States? What form of business entity generates the most income?

2. Explain why doing business as a sole proprietor can be an income tax advantage to some individuals but an income tax disadvantage to others.

3. Suppose that the Johnson Grocery Store is a sole proprietorship owned by Jill Johnson. If her store manager, Ben, in the ordinary course of business, orders too many tomatoes, can Jill Johnson refuse the order? Why or why not?

4. Explain why an individual with limited financial resources might choose to incorporate rather than form and operate a sole proprietorship.

5. Jim is contemplating going into business for himself as a general contractor specializing in apartment complexes. For what reasons may Jim choose to operate as a sole proprietorship? What factors may cause him to consider incorporating?

Notes

1 The Reference Press, *The American Almanac Statistical Abstract of the United States: 1994–1995,* 114th ed. (Austin, Texas 1994), 835, 840.

2 57 AM. JUR. 2d *Name* § 64 (1988).

3 *Id.* § 66.

CHAPTER 2

PARTNERSHIPS

Introduction

Although partnerships are not as prevalent as sole proprietorships or corporations, they are a common form of business organization. Partnerships necessarily involve two or more people and are naturally somewhat more complex than sole proprietorships. However, for many of the reasons discussed in this chapter, the formation of a partnership is often a viable alternative to incorporating.

In this chapter, we define the term *partnership* and take a look at the rights and responsibilities of the individual partners. We then investigate the specific advantages and disadvantages of doing business as a partnership. Next we examine the organization and management of the partnership, including the partnership agreement. We then focus on the financial structure of a partnership; the dissolution, dissociation, winding up, and termination of the partnership; and special types of partnerships. This chapter concludes with a discussion of the role of the paralegal working with partnerships and the resources available to assist in that area.

§ 2.1 An Introduction to Partnerships

The **partnership** is a unique type of business organization that creates a unique relationship among its members. In this section, we define *partnership*, discuss the role of partnerships in the United States, and review the law that governs partnerships. This section concludes

TERMS

partnership [†]   An undertaking of two or more persons to carry on, as coowners, a business or other enterprise for profit; an agreement between or among two or more persons to put their money, labor, and skill into commerce or business, and to divide the profit in agreed-upon proportions. Partnerships may be formed by entities as well as individuals; a corporation … may be a partner.

with a look at the interpretation of partnership law with regard to the aggregate and entity theories of partnerships.

Partnership Defined

A *partnership* is an "association of two or more persons to carry on as co-owners a business for profit."[1] The five essential words or phrases in this definition, which are considered to be the elements of a partnership, are "two or more persons," "carry on," "co-owners," "business," and "for profit."

The "two or more persons" element differentiates the partnership from the sole proprietorship. The word "persons," as used in this definition, includes "individuals, partnerships, corporations and other associations."[2]

The "carry on" element implies that the partners must actively carry on the partnership business together, in addition to possessing co-ownership of the business or of property.

The "co-ownership" element refers to ownership of the business of the partnership and requires that the business be a single business entity owned by more than one person. Co-ownership also means that the partners have a right to participate in the management of the partnership and to share in the profits (and losses) of the partnership.

The "business" element of the definition includes "every trade, occupation, or profession."[3]

The "for profit" element refers to the intention of the partnership. Obviously, not every partnership earns a profit, but earning a profit must be an objective of the partnership. Nonprofit organizations may not be partnerships.

A **general partnership** differs from a limited partnership in that all partners to a general partnership are considered **general partners**. In contrast, a **limited partnership** consists of general partners and limited partners. General partners have unlimited personal liability for the debts and liabilities of a partnership, whereas limited partners risk no more than their investment. Limited partnerships are discussed in Chapter 3 of this text.

TERMS

general partnership[†]   An ordinary partnership, as distinguished from a limited partnership. "General partnership" is synonymous with "partnership."

general partner[†]   A partner in an ordinary partnership, as distinguished from a limited partnership. "General partner" is synonymous with "partner."

limited partnership[†]   A partnership in which the liability of one or more of the partners is limited to the amount of money they have invested in the partnership.

Partnerships in the United States

Partnerships in the United States are fewer in number and earn less than either sole proprietorships or corporations. During 1991, there were over 1.5 million partnerships in the United States, with business receipts totaling $539 billion. During the same period, there were over 3.8 million corporations and 15.1 million sole proprietorships, with business receipts of approximately $10 trillion and $712 billion, respectively.[4] The number of partners in these partnerships ranged from two partners to several hundred partners.

United States partnerships are formed for a wide variety of business purposes. During 1991, there were 804,000 partnerships in existence in the finance, insurance, and real estate category, which is by far the largest category of existing partnerships in the United States. The services category ranked second, with 260,000 partnerships, and the wholesale and retail trade category ranked third, with 171,000 partnerships.[5] (See Figure 2-1.)

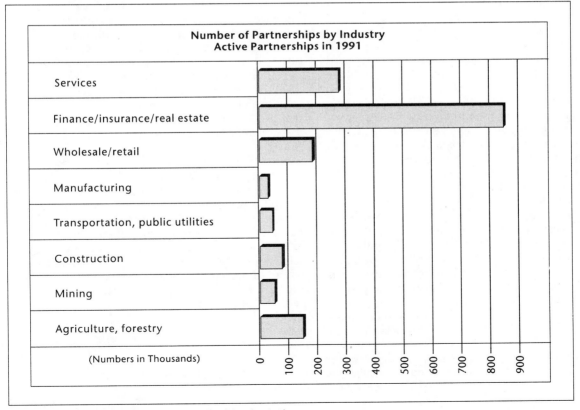

FIGURE 2-1 Number of Active Partnerships by Industry

Dividends

These Judges Can Be Bought (or at Least Rented)

Although corporate attorneys work for their clients with the aim of preventing involvement in litigation, even the best laid plans can go wrong. Each year thousands of partnerships and corporations are involved in litigation that may take years to resolve and be very expensive. The annual cost of litigation in this country has been estimated to be in excess of $50 billion.

The attempt to thwart the high cost of litigation through the use of alternative dispute resolution, or ADR, has recently received much attention in the legal community, and ADR is becoming increasingly popular. ADR involves the resolution of disputes through means other than litigation and offers the parties involved in a dispute the chance to settle their differences quickly, usually at a significantly reduced cost. The two most common means of ADR are *mediation,* which involves a third party who works to help both sides resolve their dispute, and *arbitration,* which involves a third party or a panel that hears evidence from both parties to the dispute and renders a binding judgment. The American Arbitration Association, which has offices in almost every major city in the country, currently has over 57,000 trained arbitrators, including lawyers, businesspersons, engineers, and other trained specialists.[1] In addition to traditional mediation and arbitration, many new forms of ADR are becoming popular, including *minitrials,* which involve the top managers from two disputing companies, and *rent-a-judge,* which involves hiring a private judge to decide a dispute.

Most partnership agreements and commercial contracts entered into by partnerships and corporations contain ADR clauses that specify a means other than litigation for resolving any dispute arising from the contract. An ADR clause in a contract may restrict the parties' rights to sue the other party for breach of contract.

Management of several of the larger corporations in the United States is demanding that their attorneys follow strict procedures to attempt ADR prior to initiating lawsuits. These procedures often require in-house counsel to attempt to resolve disputes through various means before resorting to litigation. In fact, over 600 major corporations have signed the ADR pledge drafted by the Center for Public Resources, a New York nonprofit group that promotes litigation alternatives. That pledge promises, among other things, that in the event of a business dispute, the pledgor will attempt to negotiate and use ADR methods to resolve that dispute.[2] Other pushes for ADR have come from both the government and the judicial system itself. More than 1,200 courts in the United States are currently offering various alternatives to trial.

The increasing popularity of ADR to thwart litigation does not necessarily mean a lost business for attorneys. In fact, many law firms are cashing in on this new trend. According to a recent survey by the CPR Institute for Dispute Resolution, several firms now bill more than $1 million a year in mediation and arbitration-related fees.[3] Many larger firms that are looking to the future have designated ADR partners to increase their business and their involvement in the ADR practice.

[1] "Got a Beef? Call in a Peacemaker," *Businessweek*, Sept. 23, 1991, at 122.
[2] "Guilty! Too Many Lawyers and Too Much Litigation. Here's a Better Way," *Businessweek*, Apr. 13, 1992, at 60.
[3] *Arbitration and the Like Attract More Converts and Revenue at Firms,* The Wall Street Journal, Feb. 24, 1995, at B8.

Law Governing Partnerships

In 1914, the National Conference of Commissioners on Uniform State Laws approved the Uniform Partnership Act and recommended it for adoption by all state legislatures. The American Bar Association approved the Uniform Partnership Act in 1915. Prior to that time, partnerships had been governed by common and civil law. The Uniform Partnership Act was designed to codify existing statutory and common law.[6] After the adoption of the Uniform Partnership Act by nearly every state in the country, partnership law remained largely unchanged until August 1992, when the Revised Uniform Partnership Act was adopted by unanimous vote of the National Conference of Commissioners on Uniform State Laws. Adoption of a uniform law by this committee does not constitute the passing of a law. Rather, uniform laws are laws which are recommended by the National Conference of Commissioners on Uniform State Laws for adoption by each state in the country. State legislatures *may* adopt uniform laws in whole or in part, or they may not adopt them at all. Even though the Revised Uniform Partnership Act has not been adopted in every state in the country, uniform laws tend to have a great influence on the future of related legislation. For that reason, our focus in this chapter is on the Revised Uniform Partnership Act as amended in 1993 and adopted in 1994.

Partnerships are governed mainly by the provisions of the Uniform Partnership Act or the Revised Uniform Partnership Act, as modified by the state of domicile, but are also affected by contract law, common law, and civil law.

The Partnership As a Separate Entity

Whereas the sole proprietor's business is considered an extension of the individual, and the corporation is considered to be a separate entity, the exact nature of the partnership is not so readily defined. There are arguments to support both the **aggregate theory**, which suggests that a partnership is the totality of persons engaged in a business, rather than an entity in itself, and the **entity theory**. Under common law the partnership was not considered to be a separate entity, but rather an extension of its partners.

TERMS

aggregate theory Theory regarding partnerships that suggests that a partnership is the totality of the persons engaged in a business rather than a separate entity.

entity theory Theory that suggests that a partnership is an entity separate from its partners, much like a corporation.

The Uniform Partnership Act recognized a partnership as a separate entity for certain purposes. For example, there are specific provisions in the Uniform Partnership Act for property ownership and transfer in the name of the partnership, and for the continuance of the partnership after the assignment of a partner's interest. Also, under the Uniform Partnership Act, partners are charged with a **fiduciary duty** to the partnership itself, in addition to their fiduciary duty to each other. Partnerships are also considered legal entities for purposes of taxation, attachment, licensing, garnishment, liability for tortious injury to third parties, and enforcement of judgments against partnership property.[7]

The aggregate theory applies in many sections of the Uniform Partnership Act relating to substantive liabilities and duties of the partners. Most importantly, the Act provides that partners are jointly and severally liable on certain obligations.

Unlike its predecessor, the Revised Uniform Partnership Act specifically states that, "[a] partnership is an entity distinct from its partners."[8] This appears to be the modern view, as noted in several recent court cases.

It is important to note that both the Uniform Partnership Act and the Revised Uniform Partnership Act serve only as models for the states that have adopted them. State statutes and common law are the final authority on whether a partnership is considered a separate entity or an aggregate of its partners in a particular state.

§ 2.2 Partners' Rights and Responsibilities

Partners have a unique relationship, both among themselves and in dealings with third parties on behalf of the partnership. This section examines the rights of partners with regard to the partnership property and in dealing with each other and third parties. We also look at the duties of partners in dealing with each other and with third parties on behalf of the partnership, including the fiduciary duty that partners owe to each other. We then investigate the agency nature of the partnership, the liability of partners, and the relationship between partners and others. This section concludes with a discussion of partnership powers and partnership property.

TERMS

fiduciary duty[†]   A relationship between two persons in which one is obligated to act with the utmost good faith, honesty, and loyalty on behalf of the other. A fiduciary relationship is often loosely but inaccurately considered to be the equivalent of a confidential relationship.

Partners' Rights in Partnership Assets

Under the Uniform Partnership Act, each partner was considered a co-owner with the other partners of specific partnership property. Partnership property was held in a **tenancy in partnership**. Each partner had an equal right to possess specific partnership property for partnership purposes, but had no right to possess such property for any other purpose without the consent of the other partners.[9]

Because the Revised Uniform Partnership Act treats a partnership as a separate entity, it does not recognize the concept of tenancy in partnership. The Revised Uniform Partnership Act states specifically that a partner "is not a co-owner of partnership property and has no interest in partnership property which can be transferred, either voluntarily or involuntarily."[10] This restriction on transfers refers only to partnership property, not to each partner's right to receive income or profits or losses from the partnership property.

A partner's right in specific partnership property is not assignable except in connection with the assignment of rights of all the partners in the same property, nor is the right in specific partnership property subject to attachment or execution, except on a claim against the partnership. For example, if a partnership has three equal partners and its specific partnership property consists of three identical apartment buildings, no single partner has the right to sell or assign any one of the apartment buildings to a third party. A partner may not split up the specific partnership property and sell his or her proportionate share.

Partners' Rights in Dealing with Each Other

Many partners' rights are prescribed by state statute. Many statutory rights granted to partners apply unless altered in the partnership agreement. The partnership agreement must be carefully drafted to address any desired deviations from the applicable statutes regarding the partners' rights in dealing with each other, to avoid any potential conflicts. Section 401 of the Revised Uniform Partnership Act grants partners the following rights in relation to dealings with each other, unless altered by mutual agreement of the partners:

1. The right to have a separate account that reflects the partner's share of the gains and losses in the partnership assets

---

TERMS

tenancy in partnership Form of ownership for property held by a partnership, subject to the pertinent statutory provisions regarding partnership property.

2. The right to an equal share of the partnership profits
3. The right to reimbursement for certain money spent by the partner on behalf of the partnership
4. The right of each partner to share equally in the management and conduct of the business
5. The right of access to the books and records of the partnership
6. The right to reasonable compensation for services rendered in winding up the partnership affairs.

Partners' Rights to a Separate Account

Pursuant to § 401(a) of the Revised Uniform Partnership Act, each partner is deemed to have a separate account in an amount equal to the partner's contributions and share of the partnership profits, less the partner's distributions received and the partner's share of partnership losses.

Partners' Rights to an Equal Share of the Partnership Profits

Pursuant to § 401(b) of the Revised Uniform Partnership Act, each partner is entitled to an equal share of the partnership's profits and is chargeable with an equal share of its losses. It is important to note, however, that this is a right that can be—and often is—revised in a Partnership Agreement. To offer the partnership maximum flexibility, it is common for partners to make contributions to the partnership in unequal amounts. In that event, it is common that profits and losses are not shared equally among all partners, but rather in proportion to their contributions. Any arrangements which suit the partners with regard to sharing the profits and losses of the partnership can be made in the partnership agreement.

Partners' Rights to Reimbursement

Certain partners may be called on to spend their own money on behalf of the partnership. In almost every instance the partner has the right to be reimbursed for these expenditures. Most of these expenditures are considered to be loans to the partnership made by the partner and must be repaid with interest, which accrues from the date of the payment or advance. The Revised Uniform Partnership Act specifically provides for reimbursement when a partner has put forth his or her own money for payments made by a partner (1) in the ordinary course of business of the partnership or for the preservation of its business or property, or (2) as an advance to the partnership beyond the amount of the partner's agreed contribution. Details regarding repayment of loans made to the partnership by a partner generally are set forth in the partnership agreement.

Partners' Rights to Participate in the Management of the Partnership

Each partner is granted by statute the right to participate in the management of the partnership. Because full participation in the management by every partner is often not practical or desirable, the partnership agreement may appoint a managing partner or a managing partnership committee. However, partners may not be denied the right to join in the management of the partnership if it is their desire to do so and if there are no contradicting terms in the partnership agreement. The right to participate in the management of the partnership must be specifically waived by any partner giving up that right.

Partners' Rights to Access to the Books and Records of the Partnership

Pursuant to § 403 of the Revised Uniform Partnership Act, the partnership must keep its books and records, if any, at its chief executive office, and these books and records must be available to each partner and his or her agents and attorneys, within reason.

Partners' Rights to Compensation for Winding Up the Affairs of the Partnership

Whereas partners are typically not entitled to receive payment for their services rendered to the partnership, when a partnership dissolves, any partner who is charged with the duty of **winding up** the affairs of the partnership is entitled to receive fair compensation for this service.

Partners' Duties in Dealing with Each Other

Partners' duties are also prescribed by statute. The Revised Uniform Partnership Act provides that partners have the following duties, unless otherwise indicated in the partnership agreement:

TERMS

winding up [†]   The dissolution or liquidation of a corporation or a partnership.

1. The duty of partners to contribute toward losses sustained by the firm according to each partner's share in the profits
2. The duty of partners to work for the partnership without remuneration
3. The duty of partners to submit to a vote of the majority of the partners when differences arise among the partners as to any ordinary matters connected with the partnership affairs
4. The fiduciary duty to all partners and the partnership.

Partners' Duties to Contribute to Partnership Losses

Unless the partnership agreement specifically states otherwise, each partner has the duty to contribute equally to any losses and liabilities incurred by the partnership.

Partners' Duties to Work for Partnership Without Remuneration

Pursuant to § 401 of the Revised Uniform Partnership Act, partners are not entitled to remuneration for services performed for the partnership, except for reasonable compensation for services rendered in winding up the partnership business. This, of course, can be revised in the partnership agreement in the event that the participation of the partners is unequal. Often, one partner contributes only capital or other resources to the partnership and another may devote his or her full time services to the partnership business. In such an event the partnership agreement could be worded so that the working partner could receive compensation from the partnership business.

Partners' Duties to Submit to a Vote of the Majority of the Partners

Unless the partnership agreement states otherwise, the vote of the majority of the partners will be the deciding factor in resolving a disagreement among the partners.

Partners' Fiduciary Duties to the Partnership and Other Partners

Under the Uniform Partnership Act and common law, partners have always owed a fiduciary duty to each other. Exactly what is meant by a fiduciary duty is now specifically set forth in § 404 of the Revised Uniform Partnership Act, which states that partners owe to the partnership and other partners the duty of loyalty and the duty of care set forth in subsections (b) and (c), which follow:

(b) A partner's duty of loyalty to the partnership and the other partners is limited to the following:

(1) to account to the partnership and hold as trustee for it any property, profit, or benefit derived by the partner in the conduct and winding up of the partnership business or derived from a use by the partner of partnership property, including the appropriation of a partnership opportunity;

(2) to refrain from dealing with the partnership in the conduct or winding up of the partnership business as or on behalf of a party having an interest adverse to the partnership; and

(3) to refrain from competing with the partnership in the conduct of the partnership business before the dissolution of the partnership.

(c) A partner's duty of care to the partnership and the other partners in the conduct and winding up of the partnership business is limited to refraining from engaging in grossly negligent or reckless conduct, intentional misconduct, or a knowing violation of law.

Each partner is granted by statute an equal right to manage the partnership affairs.   **SIDEBAR**

Partners As Agents

Partnership law has always considered partners to be agents of the other partners and of the partnership. The Revised Uniform Partnership Act clarifies this by stating that "[e]ach partner is an agent of the partnership for the purpose of its business."[11] The statutes of most states follow the Revised Uniform Partnership Act, which further provides that any acts of a partner will be binding upon the partnership so long as the partner's act is apparently undertaken for the purpose of carrying on the ordinary course of the partnership business or business of the kind carried on by the partnership.

There are three important exceptions to the rule that acts of the partner are binding on the partnership:

1. An act of a partner that is apparently not undertaken for the purpose of carrying on in the ordinary course of the partnership business is not considered binding on the partnership unless that act was approved by the rest of the partners

2. An unauthorized act undertaken with a third party who has knowledge that the act is not authorized is not considered binding on the partnership

3. An act of a partner that is contrary to a Statement of Partnership Authority that has been duly executed and filed for public record is not considered binding on the partnership.

Liability of Partners

Although the exact degree of a partner's liability may vary somewhat from state to state, partners generally are **jointly liable** for all debts and obligations of the partnership, and creditors may look to the personal property of partners in the event that partnership assets are insufficient to cover a debt. In addition, partners are **jointly and severally liable** for any loss or injury caused to any person, or for any penalty incurred due to the wrongful act or omission of any partner acting in the ordinary course of the business of the partnership or with the authority of co-partners. Joint and several liability means that a creditor may sue the partners either individually or together. In the event of any such wrongful act or omission, the partnership is liable to the same extent as the partner so acting or omitting to act.[12] Furthermore, the partnership is bound to make good on any loss incurred from the misappropriation of funds of one or more partners.

Because partners have personal liability for the obligations of the partnership, the partnership's creditors may look to the individual partners for payment after the partnership's assets have been exhausted. The following case demonstrates that the partners are each personally liable for the entire obligation of the partnership, not just a pro rata portion.

Relationship Between Partners and Others

Except as otherwise specified in the partnership agreement, a recorded statement of partnership authority, or by statute, each partner acts as an agent of the partnership when dealing with others concerning

========== TERMS ==========

joint liability[†]   The liability of two or more persons as if they were one person so that, in the absence of statute providing otherwise ... , if one of them is sued the other or others liable with her must be joined as defendants.

joint and several liability[†]   The liability of two or more persons who enter into an agreement promising, individually and together, to perform some act. Thus, there are joint and several notes, bonds, mortgages, and other contracts. The legal effect is that if default or breach occurs, the promisee can sue either or both promissors. However, such liability is always based upon express language in the agreement ... or upon language from which severalty can be implied.

THOMPSON
v.
WAYNE SMITH CONSTRUCTION COMPANY, INC.,
Court of Appeals of Indiana,
Second District
640 N.E.2d 408 (Ind. App. 1994)
September 20, 1994
Sullivan, Presiding Judge

Suit on South Carolina judgment against partnership was brought against individual partner in Indiana. Judgment against partner individually was rendered by the Marion Superior Court ... and partner appealed. The Court of Appeals ... held that: (1) fact that South Carolina Court of Appeals had vacated judgment against individual partners on ground that there was no separate contract with the individual partners did not preclude, on the ground of full faith and fair credit and **res judicata**, Indiana court from reaching partner's individual assets after partnership assets had been exhausted, and (2) decision of the Ohio Supreme Court, in suit on the same South Carolina judgment, that individual partners were liable only for a pro rata share was not entitled to full faith and credit since it was not a decision on the merits of the South Carolina judgment.

Affirmed.

... In 1986, Wayne Smith Construction Company, Inc. (Wayne Smith), procured a judgment on a contract against the partnership of Wolman Duberstein and Thompson, (the Partnership). During the intervening time, Wayne Smith has tried to collect on the judgment in South Carolina, Ohio, and Indiana. The South Carolina Court of Appeals, the Supreme Court of Ohio, and now the Court of Appeals of Indiana all have been involved in this dispute.

... The genesis of this dispute arose in South Carolina when the Partnership hired Wayne Smith to build two homes on Hilton Head Island. After a dispute arose between the parties regarding payment, Wayne Smith sued the Partnership and the individual partners for breach of contract in the South Carolina Court of Common Pleas. The South Carolina trial court entered judgment against the Partnership and each partner individually. The court calculated the damages plus interest at $107,381.65. On appeal, the South Carolina Court of Appeals affirmed the judgment against the Partnership but vacated the judgment against the individual partners. ...

Two years later, Wayne Smith registered the South Carolina judgment in Ohio, where it believed partnership assets existed. After recovering $2,582.31, the Partnership assets were exhausted. Wayne Smith then instituted a new action in Ohio against the Partnership and the partners individually for the balance of the judgment. The partners defended the suit, claiming that because the South Carolina appellate court vacated the judgment against the individual partners, the doctrines of full faith and credit and res judicata dictated that Ohio could not enter a judgment against them. Nevertheless, the Ohio trial court entered judgment for the balance against the partners individually. The Partnership and the individual partners eventually appealed to the Ohio Supreme Court.

While the Ohio judgment was on appeal to the Ohio Supreme Court, Wayne Smith filed suit against Kenneth E. Thompson (Thompson), a resident of Marion County. At all times relevant times Thompson was a general partner of the Partnership. The Indiana trial court granted Wayne Smith's motion for a summary judgment and entered judgment against Thompson for the

---

TERMS

res judicata [†] Means "the thing (i.e., the matter) has been adjudicated"; the thing has been decided. The principle that a final judgment rendered on the merits by a court of competent jurisdiction is conclusive of the rights of the parties and is an absolute bar in all other actions based upon the same claim, demand, or cause of action.

full amount of the unpaid South Carolina judgment, $155,703.01. Almost six months after the Indiana trial court's decision, the Ohio Supreme Court handed down its decision, which affirmed the judgment against the individual partners, but limited each partner's total liability to a pro rata share. As there were three partners in the Partnership, the Ohio court held that each partner was liable only for one-third of the South Carolina judgment. Thompson now appeals the Indiana judgment against him individually, and alternatively the judgment against him for the full amount of the debt.

I. Partnership Assets

Thompson contends that because the South Carolina appellate court vacated the judgment against the individual partners, full faith and credit and res judicata prevent either Ohio or Indiana from reaching the partners' individual assets. We disagree.

The South Carolina court held that a partnership is its own entity, separate and distinct from the individual partners. ... This is consonant with the modern view of partnership law. ...

... Under South Carolina law, a partnership creditor must try to satisfy his judgment from partnership property before reaching individual property; whereas an individual creditor may attach any property the partner owns at any time. ... This exhaustion rule is recognized in most jurisdictions in which the partnership liability is joint. Once partnership assets have been exhausted, however, a partnership creditor becomes a creditor of the individual partner with the same rights and upon the same level as the partner's other individual creditors. ... By vacating the judgment against the individual partners,

the South Carolina appellate court merely established that, at the time judgment was entered, Wayne Smith was still a creditor of the partnership and not of each partner individually.

... Regardless of whether a partner's joint liability is actually transformed into several liability, the law is clear that once partnership assets are exhausted, each partner becomes individually liable for the debt.

II. Share of Liability

Thompson argues that if he is personally liable for the judgment, he is only liable for a one-third share. Although this issue was never presented in the Ohio litigation or the subsequent appeal, the Ohio Supreme Court ... determined that because Thompson is a joint debtor, he is liable only for a pro rata share of the judgment. ... Thompson argues that this holding must be given full faith and credit. Again, we disagree.

... The Ohio Supreme Court cites no authority for its proposition that a joint debtor is liable only for a pro-rata share. We have found no such authority. Such limitation is not an incident of joint liability. The authorities agree that each joint debtor is responsible for the entire amount of the debt. ... under joint liability, once all of the joint debtors are named in the suit and judgment is entered against them, the creditor may force any one of the debtors to pay all of the judgment. This rule has long been recognized in South Carolina and in Indiana.

In reviewing a grant of summary judgment, we must determine whether the record reveals a genuine issue of material fact and whether the trial court correctly applied the law. ... We hold that the trial court correctly applied the law.

The judgment of the trial court is affirmed.

partnership business and has **actual authority** to bind the partnership to contractual relationships with third parties. That authority may be

TERMS

actual authority [†] In the law of agency, the power of an agent to bind his principal. Although such authority must be granted by the principal

express authority stemming from the partnership agreement, or it may be **implied authority** based on the nature of the partnership relationship. In addition, partners have **apparent authority**, which allows them to bind the partnership in a contractual relationship so long as the partner *appears* to be acting on behalf of the partnership in accordance with the usual business of the partnership, and so long as the party outside the partnership has no knowledge that the partner is not acting on behalf of the partnership.

The act of one partner is sufficient to bind the partnership, even if that partner is not acting in good faith, and the signature of one partner is sufficient to execute any instrument in the name of the partnership, so long as the instrument is executed for the apparent purpose of carrying on, in the usual way, the business of the partnership. Any outsider dealing with a partnership is reasonable in assuming that a partner has the authority to enter into a contractual agreement on behalf of the partnership, so long as the agreement to be entered into appears to be in line with the usual business of the partnership.

Certain acts, however, specifically those that are not within the normal course of business, require unanimous consent of the partners. Whereas the Uniform Partnership Act listed five such acts as specifically requiring the unanimous consent of the partners, the Revised Uniform Partnership Act remains silent on the issue. Although this allows more flexibility for the partnership, it can also be a cause of ambiguities. Ideally, the partnership agreement will outline the types of transactions that require the unanimous consent of the partners. Such acts may include:

1. Assigning the partnership property in trust for creditors or on the assignee's promise to pay the debts of the partnership
2. Disposing of the goodwill of the business
3. Anything that would make it impossible to carry on the ordinary business of a partnership

TERMS

to his or her agent, authority will be deemed to have been granted if the principal allows the agent to believe that the agent possesses it. Further, actual authority may be implied from the circumstances and need not be specifically granted.

express authority [†]   Authority expressly granted to or conferred upon an agent or employee by a principal or employer.

implied authority [†]   The authority of an agent to do whatever acts are necessary to carry out his or her express authority.

apparent authority [†]   Authority which, although not actually granted by the principal, he or she permits his or her agent to exercise.

4. Confessing a judgment on behalf of the partnership
5. Submitting a partnership claim or liability to **arbitration** or reference.

The execution of one of the foregoing by an unauthorized partner is not considered an act of the partnership.

Any one partner can generally transfer partnership property to third parties. There are, however, set guidelines for effecting such a transfer of property. Unless otherwise stated in a statement of partnership authority, partnership property that is held in the name of the partnership may be transferred by an instrument of transfer executed by a partner in the partnership name.

If the partnership property is held in the name of one or more partners, with or without an indication that it is owned as partnership property, the property may be transferred by an instrument of transfer executed by the persons in whose name the property is held.

Under some circumstances the partnership can recover partnership property wrongfully transferred by one or more of its partners if it can prove that the partner or partners transferring the property had no authority to do so.

Statement of Partnership Authority

A new trend in partnership law, which has been adopted by the Revised Uniform Partnership Law, is the option of filing a **statement of authority** with the Secretary of State or other appropriate state official. The statement of authority gives public notice of the authority granted or denied certain partners. Pursuant to § 303 of the Revised Uniform Partnership Act, the statement of authority must include:

- The name of the partnership;

TERMS
---

arbitration [†]   A method of settling disputes by submitting a disagreement to a person (an arbitrator) or a group of individuals (an arbitration panel) for decision instead of going to court. If the parties are required to comply with the decision of the arbitrator, the process is called *binding arbitration;* if there is no such obligation, the arbitration is referred to as *nonbinding arbitration.* Compulsory arbitration is arbitration required by law, most notably in labor disputes.

statement of authority   A statement filed for public record by the partners of a partnership to expand or limit the agency authority of a partner, to deny the authority or status of a partner or to give notice of certain events such as the dissociation of a partner or the dissolution of the partnership.

- The street address of its chief executive office and of one office in this State, if there is one;

- The names and mailing addresses of all of the partners or of an agent appointed and maintained by the partnership for the purpose of subsection (b); and

- The names of the partners authorized to execute an instrument transferring real property held in the name of the partnership.

In addition, the statement of authority may set forth the authority, or limitations on the authority, of some or all of the partners to enter into other transactions on behalf of the partnership and any other matter.

A statement of authority which is in full force and effect supplements the authority of a partner to enter into transactions on behalf of the partnership as follows:

1. Except for real estate transfers, a grant of authority in the statement of authority is conclusive in favor of a person who gives value without knowledge to the contrary, so long as and to the extent that a limitation on that authority is not then contained in another filed statement.

2. A grant of authority to transfer real estate held in the name of the partnership contained in a certified copy of a filed statement of partnership authority recorded in the office for recording transfers of that real estate is conclusive in favor of a person who gives value without knowledge to the contrary.

In general, persons transacting business with the partnership are not deemed to know of a limitation on the authority of a partner merely because the limitation is contained in the filed statement.

Although the filing of a statement of authority is optional, partnerships that routinely transact business such as buying and selling real estate may be required to file a statement by those who wish to transact business with the partnership.

Statement of Denial

In addition to the statement of authority, another new document, entitled the statement of denial, may also be filed at the state level on behalf of the partnership. A **statement of denial** can be filed by a

---

TERMS

statement of denial   A statement filed for public record by a partner or other interested party to contradict the information included in a statement of authority.

partner or other interested party to contradict the information included in a statement of authority. For example, a withdrawing partner may file a denial of his or her status as a partner.

Partnership Powers

Under state statutes, certain powers may be granted to the partnership as a separate entity. The Uniform Partnership Act set forth specific acts that partnerships have the authority to conduct, including the powers necessary for it to conduct business, including entering into contracts, borrowing money, acting as agent for others, becoming a member of another partnership, becoming a shareholder of a corporation, and entering into a joint venture with a third party. Because the Revised Uniform partnership recognizes the partnership as a separate entity, these powers may be assumed under the revised act.

Partnership Property

Typically, all real or personal property that is initially contributed to the partnership by the partners, all subsequent contributions, and all property acquired with the funds of the partnership is considered partnership property and not property of the individual partners. Accurate partnership records must be kept so that there is no question as to which property is considered partnership property and which property is the personal property of a partner.

Acquisitions of significant partnership property should be approved by unanimous written consent of the partners to alleviate any possible problems in the future. Following is § 204 of the Revised Uniform Partnership Act which discusses when property is partnership property:

§ 204. WHEN PROPERTY IS PARTNERSHIP PROPERTY

(a) Property is partnership property if acquired in the name of:
(1) the partnership; or
(2) one or more partners with an indication in the instrument transferring title to the property of the person's capacity as a partner or of the existence of a partnership but without an indication of the name of the partnership.

(b) Property is acquired in the name of the partnership by a transfer to:
(1) the partnership in its name; or
(2) one or more partners in their capacity as partners in the partnership, if the name of the partnership is indicated in the instrument transferring title to the property.

(c) Property is presumed to be partnership property if purchased with partnership assets.

§ 2.3 Advantages of Doing Business As a General Partnership

In many respects, the advantages of doing business as a partnership are similar to the advantages offered by the sole proprietorship, yet partnerships offer some unique advantages as well. In this section, we discuss some of those unique advantages, including the flexibility of the management of the partnership, the minimal formalities and regulatory and reporting requirements, and the low cost of organizing a partnership. We also examine the unique income tax benefits available to partners and the expanded base from which capital may be raised for the partnership.

Participation and Flexibility in Management

Unless one or more partners waive their rights, every partner has equal power and authority to manage the partnership affairs. Partners of smaller partnerships may find this appealing if the partners have varied backgrounds and areas of expertise and all wish to actively participate. All partners are allowed to act freely on behalf of the partnership, with few restrictions.

Larger partnerships, on the other hand, are allowed the flexibility of putting the management of the partnership into the hands of the best individual or group of individuals for the job.

Minimal Formalities and Regulatory and Reporting Requirements

Although partnerships are governed by statute, the required statutory formalities are few. A concise written partnership agreement is a good investment in almost any circumstance. However, it is not required, and a partnership may be formed by a verbal agreement between two or more people and can be implied by behavior.

State statutes vary with regard to partnership filing requirements and other formalities, and the pertinent state statutes must always be reviewed and complied with. Most states do not require partnership registration with the Secretary of State or other state official before commencing business. However, a certificate of assumed name or other similar document is usually required when the partnership is going to transact business under an assumed name, trade name, or fictitious name. If the partnership name consists of the names of the partners, it usually is not considered a fictitious name that must be recorded in compliance with a statute requiring registration of fictitious partnership names. However, some state statutes provide that the name of a partner followed by "& Co." or "Co." may require the filing of an application for certificate for assumed name, trade name, or fictitious name, or other similar document.[13]

A number of states require the registration of every partnership with the appropriate state official, regardless of whether the partnership is using a fictitious name. Typically, a certificate setting forth the name of the partnership, its principal place of business, and the names of all partners is filed with the Secretary of State or the county clerk of the county in which the partnership's principal place of business is located.

Whereas a corporation must qualify to do business as a foreign corporation in any state other than its state of domicile, in which it transacts business, historically it has not been necessary to register to do business as a foreign partnership. Recently, however, New Hampshire enacted a requirement for foreign partnerships to qualify to do business in that state.[14] Again, a thorough review of the pertinent statutes must be made to ensure that all statutory requirements with regard to fictitious name filings, partnership registrations, and qualification of foreign partnerships are complied with.

Although it is an option rather than a requirement, a partnership in a state that follows the Revised Uniform Partnership Act closely may find it advantageous to file a Statement of Partnership Authority with the Secretary of State or other designated state authority that specifies which partners are authorized to execute real estate transfer documents, and which contains other information concerning the authority of individual partners to act on behalf of the partnership.

Any business carried on by a partnership that requires licensing must be licensed by the partnership or by the individual partners. Typically, no special licensing requirements are imposed on a partnership because it is a partnership; rather, the licensing requirements are imposed because of the nature of the business transacted by the partnership.

Partnerships are required to file a United States Partnership Return of Income, which reports the income and distributions of the partnership. A tax return also may be required at the state level.

Low Cost of Organization

There are no minimum capital requirements for starting a partnership, and the startup costs, including any required state filing fees, tend to be significantly lower than those for corporations.

Income Tax Benefits

The partners of a general partnership are taxed in much the same way as sole proprietors. The net income or loss of the partnership is passed through to the partners, according to the partnership agreement or statute. The individual partners then report their partnership income on a schedule filed with their personal tax returns and pay income tax based on their personal income tax rates. The principal tax benefit to the partners over doing business as a corporation is that a corporation is subject to a first tax on its income, and then a second tax is paid by the shareholders when corporate after-tax income is distributed to them. A partnership, on the other hand, is not taxable, so that only a single tax is paid by the partners on income derived from the partnership. Partnerships are required to file only an informational tax return with the Internal Revenue Service.

Also, because the income of the partnership flows through to the individual partners, if the partnership experiences a net loss, each partner's share of that loss may be written off on the partner's individual income tax return, offsetting any other income. The partnership allocation of profits and losses must, however, comply with the substantial economic effect requirements of the Internal Revenue Service.

Diversified Capital Resources

Although partnerships are generally restricted to the personal capital of the partners and the capital that they are able to borrow based on their personal wealth, the partnership does have an advantage over a sole proprietorship, in that there is a broader base from which to obtain capital. Simply put, more than one person is contributing to the business; therefore, more is potentially available.

§ 2.4 Disadvantages of Doing Business As a Partnership

Some of the same partnership characteristics that present advantages to the partners, in certain circumstances, can be considered disadvantages under other circumstances. This section discusses the disadvantages of doing business as a partnership. We start with the partnership characteristic that is often considered to be the most significant disadvantage—the unlimited liability exposure of the partners. Next, we look at the loosely structured management of the partnership, the partnership's lack of business continuity, and the difficulty in transferring a proprietary interest in a partnership. We also investigate the possible hardships in raising capital for a partnership and the possibly substantial legal and organizational expenses. This section concludes with an examination of the potential income tax disadvantages to partners.

Unlimited Liability

One of the strongest arguments against doing business as a general partnership is the unlimited liability characteristic of the partnership. Partners are personally liable for the debts, obligations, and torts committed by or on behalf of the partnership. This disadvantage is compounded by the fact that all partners are liable for the acts of any one partner who is acting on behalf of the partnership. Wealthy partners may be at a disadvantage when the liabilities of the partnership exceed the partnership assets and creditors turn to the individual partners for payment.

There are ways to reduce the probability that the partners will have to personally cover the debts and liabilities of the partnership. The partnership may, for instance, purchase insurance to cover many potential liabilities, and third parties may agree in their contracts with the partnership to limit their recovery to partnership assets. However, not all liabilities are insurable, and lenders may not work with a partnership without the personal guarantees of the partners.

Loosely Structured Management

Although the loosely structured management of a partnership may be an advantage under certain circumstances, it may also work as a definite disadvantage to other partnerships. The number and personalities of the partners can greatly affect the success, or failure, of the loosely structured management prescribed for partnerships by statute. Because the majority rules, in the event of disagreement regarding management decisions, a stalemate can result if the partnership consists of an even number of partners. This, in turn, can lead to the partnership's inability to act. The fact that each partner can act on behalf of the partnership can also cause problems when partners disagree on fundamental issues.

A carefully constructed partnership agreement that delegates the authority to make management decisions can alleviate some of these problems when there is disagreement among the partners, but the partnership agreement cannot account for all possible contingencies.

Lack of Business Continuity

Under the Uniform Partnership Act, unless otherwise specified in the partnership agreement or other written agreement among the partners, the partnership dissolves whenever one partner ceases to be a partner, for whatever reason. This can be a definite disadvantage for a going concern, as the dissolution may be untimely and costly to the remaining partners.

Upon the death of a partner, the deceased partner's right to specific partnership property will pass to the remaining partners, who have the right to possess the property for partnership purposes. However, the deceased partner's interest in the partnership passes to the deceased partner's heirs. Unless addressed in a carefully worded agreement, the remaining partners often have to liquidate the partnership assets to distribute the deceased partner's interest to his or her heirs.

Under the Revised Uniform Partnership Act, it is much easier for the partnership to continue after the death or withdrawal of one partner. However, if the partnership is a **partnership at will**, the partnership may be dissolved whenever one of the partners decides to withdraw and dissolve the partnership.

Difficulty in Transferring Proprietary Interest

Unlike corporate shareholders, who may generally sell their shares of stock without restriction, a partner's entire right to the partnership is not freely transferable. Although a partner may sell or assign his or her rights to receive profits and losses from the partnership business, the right to specific partnership property may not be sold or assigned unless sold or assigned by all partners. In addition, a partner's right to participate in the management of the partnership is not assignable. Therefore, a partner's share of the partnership may not simply be sold to another individual who will become a partner.

Limited Ability to Raise Capital

Unlike a corporation, a partnership may not sell shares of stock to raise capital to run its business. The capital of the partnership usually

---
TERMS
---

partnership at will A partnership formed without designated a date for its termination, or without stating a condition under which the partnership will terminate.

consists of contributions from the partners and any loans obtained based on the partners' personal wealth and the partnership assets. This can be a great deterrent to businesses that have substantial initial capital requirements.

Legal and Organizational Expenses

Although the legal and organizational expenses involved in forming and operating a partnership are usually significantly less than those involved in forming and operating a corporation, these costs can still be substantial. In addition to any necessary state filing fees for the partnership certificate and a certificate of assumed or fictitious name, there are typically significant legal fees associated with the drafting of the partnership agreement. Because of the diverse nature of partnerships, a good partnership agreement will usually require significant and specific drafting, and the initial legal fees can be considerable.

Tax Disadvantages

Again, as with the sole proprietorship, partnership income flows through to the partners, to be taxed at each partner's personal income tax rate. If the partnership is earning a substantial income, partners with other income who are already in a high income tax bracket may be at a disadvantage.

§ 2.5 Organization and Management of a General Partnership

The organization and management of partnerships can vary significantly depending on the partners of the partnership and other circumstances. The parameters of the organization and management are defined by the statutes of the state of domicile and by the partnership agreement.

This section focuses on the agreement among the partners, beginning with a look at the management and control of the partnership and a brief discussion of oral partnership agreements. It then discusses the essential elements of the partnership agreement, and includes specific examples of partnership agreement provisions.

Management and Control

Although all partners have equal rights to manage the partnership, this is not always a practical or desirable method of management, and these rights may be altered in the agreement among the partners. Often, especially with larger partnerships, the partners will delegate the management of the partnership to one or more partners. This delegation of the right to manage must be granted by all partners, and no partner can be denied the right to manage the partnership unless that right is waived.

When one partner is delegated to see to the management of the partnership, that partner is usually referred to as the *managing partner.* Management also may be delegated to a management committee, a senior or voting partner, or one or more other partners named in the partnership agreement.

Often, the partners each agree to be responsible for a different area of partnership management. For example, one partner may be in charge of the partnership accounting, while another takes care of public relations and promotion. Regardless of the style of management decided upon by the partners, it is highly desirable that the management duties of each partner be fully described in the partnership agreement.

The general rule regarding a dispute in the internal management affairs of the partnership is that the decision is made by a majority of the partners.[15] There are, however, many exceptions to that rule. For example, acts taken outside of the ordinary course of business of the partnership require the unanimous consent of all partners, as do acts not in accordance with the partnership agreement and acts amending the partnership agreement. Acts not in accordance with the partnership agreement and amendments to the partnership agreement also require the unanimous consent of all partners.

Another circumstance in which the majority does not rule is when the partnership agreement provides an alternate method for resolving disputes among the partners. For instance, the managing partner or partners may be given authority to make the final decision in the event of a disagreement among the partners. The partnership agreement may also prescribe arbitration for certain disagreements among the partners.

References to a majority of the partners generally do not take into account the disproportionate percentages of interest that the partners may hold. The partnership agreement may contain provisions fixing a different method for determining what is the majority of the partners, such as the contributors of a majority of the partnership capital.

Managing partners and other partners who are often required to spend a significant amount of their time managing the business and assets of the partnership are usually compensated by way of a salary and paid expenses by the partnership. This salary is over and above any profits to which the managing partner is entitled pursuant to the other terms of the partnership agreement. Any salaries paid to partners for their management of the partnership should be specifically designated as such on the books and records of the partnership.

Oral Partnership Agreements

Although the partnership agreement is fundamental to the partnership, the agreement may be oral, or a partnership may exist with no express agreement between the parties whatsoever, so long as all the elements of a partnership are present. Although an oral partnership agreement may be legal and binding, it is inadvisable, because it is difficult to prove the terms of an oral partnership agreement—or even that a partnership exists—when there is no written agreement.

Certain types of oral partnership agreements may be prohibited by law. For instance, under the **Statute of Frauds**, it is impossible to form an oral agreement for a period longer than one year.

Although it is possible to have a binding oral partnership agreement, attorneys almost always advise their clients to put their agreement into a formal, written contract to avoid future disputes. In the following case, we see what happened when a group of attorneys did not follow that advice.

Partnership Agreements

The partnership agreement, or *partnership articles,* as that document is sometimes referred to, is the contract entered into by all partners setting forth the agreed-upon terms of the partnership. The partnership agreement is considered the "law of the partnership" and will be enforced as such, unless any of the terms of the partnership agreement are contrary to law. The partnership agreement is a contract among the partners and thus is subject to contract law.

Following is a discussion of some of the various matters that should be contained in a partnership agreement. The sample paragraphs used here are only a small representation of the types of clauses that may be included in a partnership agreement. See § 2.9 of this text for a checklist

---

TERMS

statute of frauds [†]   A statute, existing in one or another form in every state, that requires certain classes of contracts to be in writing and signed by the parties. Its purpose is to prevent fraud or reduce the opportunities for fraud.

of items to be considered when drafting a partnership agreement, and Appendix G-1 for a partnership agreement form.

Names and Addresses of Partners

The full name and address of each partner should be included in the first section of the partnership agreement.

Name of Partnership

This section of the partnership agreement should set forth the full name of the partnership. The name of the partnership may, but need not, include any or all of the names of the partners, or it may be a totally fictitious name. If a fictitious name is used, a certificate of assumed or fictitious name may be required.[16]

Purpose of Partnership

A specific purpose may be set forth in this agreement section, or a general purpose, such as the one shown in the following example, may be stated. This section may also set limitations on business activities and on partners' competitive business activities.

EXAMPLE: *Partnership Purpose*

To have and to exercise all the powers now or hereafter conferred by the laws of the State of _____ on partnerships organized pursuant to the laws of that state.[17]

Address of Principal Place of Doing Business

In addition to setting forth the address of the principal place of business of the partnership, this section may also contain a provision designating the governing law under which the terms of the partnership agreement must be applied and construed.

Term of Partnership Agreement

This section of the partnership agreement may designate a date upon which the partnership will terminate, such as in the following example, or it may designate a condition upon which such termination shall occur. For instance, if a partnership is formed for the development and sale of several specific pieces of real estate, the partnership

WILLIAMS
v.
TRAPOLIN LAW FIRM
Court of Appeal of Louisiana,
Fourth Circuit
641 So. 2d 673 (La. Ct. App. 1994)
July 27, 1994
Barry, Judge

... Williams sued Miles and Ivor Trapolin and the Trapolin Law Firm for breach of contract. Williams alleged that between March 18–20, 1992, they entered into a partnership agreement with him. According to Williams, the agreement was not reduced to writing but it was orally agreed: that all income except personal injury, collection and succession cases already begun would be pooled; that Williams would have a draw of $60,000 (including a $10,000 bonus if he averaged at least 35 billable hours a week); that profits would be shared according to a stated formula; that Williams' performance would be reviewed after six months. The firm name would remain the same and Williams' status as a partner would be reviewed after one year. Williams claimed the agreement raised reasonable expectations of employment for at least a year and probably more. By July 13, 1992, Miles Trapolin informed Williams that his continued association with the firm was not possible. Williams alleged that on July 14, 1992 he and Miles Trapolin reached an agreement on the separation but Miles Trapolin reneged on the agreement. By November, 1992 the Trapolins threatened to sue if Williams did not remit $17,325.03. Williams sought payment for his billings from March 23, 1992 to July 13, 1992, or $42,000, and his projected billings for 1 year, $136,875, minus his $17,000 salary plus 12 months of office expenses, $24,000, a net of $95,375.

The Trapolin Law Firm filed an answer and claimed ... that Williams was its employee from March, 1992 to July 1992 when his employment was terminated. On August 12, 1992 the firm entered into a contract with Williams to "divide fees and repay costs from various files." The

Trapolin Law Firm claimed that Williams owed $17,325.03 and costs associated with its Williams Blvd. office. ...

Ivor Trapolin (Miles had not been served) filed an exception of no right or cause of action. Williams filed a first amendment in which he alternatively contended that Miles and Ivor Trapolin, acting on their own behalf, entered into a partnership contract with him to form the new Trapolin Law Firm. The trial court maintained Ivor Trapolin's exception of no cause of action.

Miles Trapolin answered that he and Ivor acted only in the capacity of an officer and a director of the Trapolin Law Firm, a PLC. In that capacity he entered into an employment contract with Williams in March, 1992 and terminated that contract with Williams on July 13, 1992. ...

The defendants' motion for summary judgment was granted and it was ordered that the proceedings be dismissed. ...

... Williams appeals the judgment which maintains Ivor Trapolin's exception of no cause of action. ...

THE LAW

... To be considered a partnership, a business relationship must meet the following criteria; the parties must have mutually consented to form a partnership and to participate in profits in determined proportions which may accrue from property, skill or industry furnished to the business; parties must share in losses as well as profits; the property or stock must form a community of goods in which each party has a proprietary interest. ... There are no hard and fast rules in the determination of whether a partnership exists. Each case is considered on its own facts. Consent to form a partnership may be inferred from circumstantial evidence.

ANALYSIS

... The defendants' memorandum requested a partial summary judgment as to Williams' status as an employee. The defendants claimed that Williams' status was a material fact that would insure or preclude his recovery. Williams sued for damages resulting from a breach of contract and the defendants had reconvened. When the trial court granted summary judgment and dismissed the proceedings ... the defendants filed a motion to amend in order to save their reconventional demand. Using a partial summary judgment to obtain a determination that Williams was an employee was improper.

Regardless, the defendants were not entitled to summary judgment. The defendants supported the motion with their affidavits that they did not intend to bring Williams into the Trapolin Law Firm as a partner or to create a new Trapolin Law Firm with him as a partner. They declared that he was hired as an employee ...

... Williams countered with his affidavit that they intended by verbal contract to be partners. He submitted several handwritten documents to show negotiations which evidenced an intent to form a partnership and invoices to show the purchase of office furniture.

There remain genuine issue of material fact as to whether the parties created or intended to form a partnership and whether there was a breach of a verbal contract.

The summary judgment and amended judgment are reversed and the matter remanded for further proceedings.

REVERSED: REMANDED

agreement may designate that the partnership will terminate when all of the designated real estate has been sold.

A partnership that is formed without designating a date for termination of the partnership, or without stating a condition under which the partnership will terminate, is a *partnership at will*. This type of partnership continues as long as the parties give their mutual consent. The partnership at will may be terminated when agreed to by the partners, or upon the withdrawal of any one partner.

When a partnership for a fixed term or particular undertaking is continued after the termination of such term or particular undertaking without any express agreement, the partnership continues as if it were a partnership at will.

EXAMPLE: Duration of Partnership

The partnership shall commence on _____, 19___, and shall terminate on _____, 19___, unless sooner terminated by operation of law or by the occurrence of a condition precedent specified in the agreement as cause for termination, as follows: _____.[18]

Contribution of Partners

This section should be drafted with care, because it may be crucial to the division of the profits and losses of the partnership and the distribution of assets upon the partnership's termination. This section may include the amount of contribution made by each partner, the date the contribution is made to the partnership, the form of contribution, and valuation of contributions other than cash. In addition, provisions for any interest to be paid on contributions, adjustments in contributions required from each partner, and provisions for loans to the partnership by the partners may be included in this section.

EXAMPLE: Contribution to Partnership Capital—Parties and Shares

The capital of the partnership shall be _____ dollars ($_____), which shall consist of the estimated value of the combined real and personal assets contributed to the business as of _____, 19___. _____ shall contribute _____ percent (___%) of this value, and _____ shall contribute _____ percent (___%) of this value. Partners shall share in the profits and losses of the business in the above proportions.[19]

EXAMPLE: Contribution to Partnership Capital—Real Property

The initial capital contribution to the partnership shall be _____ dollars ($_____). This total shall consist of _____ dollars ($_____) in cash contributed by _____ , and real property contributed by _____. The real property has an assessed valuation of _____ dollars ($_____) and a market value of _____ dollars ($_____), and shall be accepted by the partnership at a value of _____ dollars ($_____). It is described as follows:

[insert legal description]

The cash contribution shall be deposited in the partnership account at _____ [bank], located at _____ [address], City of _____ , County of _____ , State of _____ , on or before _____ , 19___. The real property contribution shall be accomplished by _____ executing a [grant] deed conveying the real property to _____ [the partnership or as the case may be] on or before _____ , 19___.[20]

Additional Contribution Requirements

This section should set forth the procedure for establishing the necessity of additional capital contributions, the amount of those contributions required from each partner, the notification requirements for additional contribution, and the redistribution of partnership interest for nonproportional contributions.

Assets of Partnership

This section should identify the assets of the partnership, including a valuation of the assets, the manner for handling the control of assets and accountability therefore, and the distribution of assets. Following is an example of a paragraph that may be used with an attached schedule, which may be updated from time to time.

EXAMPLE: *Description of Assets by Attached List*

All property, both personal and real, specifically set forth in Appendix A attached to this agreement and made a part of it, is deemed by the partners to be partnership property and shall be and constitute the assets of the partnership as of the date of this agreement. The items of partnership property set forth in the attached Appendix A are set forth by way of specification and not by way of limitation, and may be added to subsequently at the discretion of the partners.[21]

EXAMPLE: *Distribution of Assets in Proportion to Investment*

On the termination or reorganization of the partnership, the assets of the partnership shall be used to discharge all outstanding indebtedness of the partnership, and the balance of the assets shall be distributed among the partners in proportion to their respective interests in the partnership.[22]

Goodwill Evaluation to Be Considered on Distribution of Assets

The goodwill of a partnership may be considered a sizable asset to a continuing business. However, it may be no asset at all to a partnership that is terminating. This section should set forth the conditions under which the goodwill of the partnership will be considered as a part of the evaluation of the assets of the partnership, and set forth the formula to be used in that evaluation of goodwill when applicable.

Liability

This section may restate and amend many of the provisions for partner liability found in the statutes. It may also be used to address more specific conditions regarding liability among the partners. It should address the partners' liability to one another, the partners' liability to third parties, and the liability of the partnership.

Distribution of Profits and Losses

This is another crucial section of the partnership agreement, which should address all matters regarding distribution of the profits and losses of the partnership, including how the division of profits and losses is to be made. In this section the partners may also specifically guarantee profits to any one partner and set forth how salaries may be an element of profits for distribution. The partners may also set forth a schedule for distribution, establish reserve funds for partnership expenses prior to distribution, and set limitations on distribution of profits or liability for losses by one partner and distributions made to the partnership.

Following are examples of paragraphs that may be used when equal distribution among all partners is desired or when proportional distribution is desired, respectively:

EXAMPLE: *Equal Distribution of Profits and Losses*

The partners shall be liable and shall discharge equally among them all expenses required for the maintenance and operation of the partnership business at all times. All profits that shall arise from the partnership business shall be divided equally among the partners, and all losses that the partnership shall incur by bad debts or otherwise shall be borne and paid equally by all partners.

The net profits or losses shall be determined within _____ days after the close of the partnership fiscal year and distributed or assessed within _____ days thereafter.[23]

EXAMPLE: *Proportionate Distribution of Profits and Losses*

_____ has contributed _____ dollars ($___) to the capital of the partnership, which is equal to ___ percent (___%) of the partnership interest, and _____ has contributed _____ dollars ($_____) to the capital of the partnership, which is equal to ___ percent (___%) of the partnership interest. Each partner shall be entitled to a share of the partnership net profits or shall be assessed for his share of the partnership losses in direct proportion to his partnership interest.[24]

Indemnity Provisions

This section should set forth the partners' agreement for indemnification of their obligations on behalf of the partnership.

EXAMPLE: *Indemnity by Partnership—Obligation of Existing Partners*

Each partner shall be indemnified by the partnership on all obligations incurred by that partner in the normal course of conducting partnership business. The partners are limited by the provisions of Section ___ of this agreement in the scope of obligations they shall incur on behalf of the partnership.[25]

Duties of Partners

This section should set forth the duties of the partners in as much detail as practical, and address the specific responsibilities of each partner and the approximate amount of time required of each partner.

EXAMPLE: *Duties of Partners—Division of Duties*

The duties of the partners shall be divided to provide for the economical and timely conduct of the partnership business. _____ shall manage the office, fiscal, customer relations, and sales portions of the partnership. _____ shall manage the purchasing, designing, manufacturing, and shipping portions. Each partner shall have sole responsibility for the personnel policies and internal operating procedures within those areas of responsibility assigned to her. Partners shall consult with each other in establishing and determining overall business policies that will affect the partnership business.[26]

Powers of Partners and Limitations Thereon

This section of the partnership agreement should set forth the powers of the partners and any limitations on those powers. It should also address the engaging of partners in acts outside the scope of partnership business, partnership employee policies, contractual rights and limitations, and patents and trade secrets.

Compensation and Benefits for Partners

This section may address any compensation and benefits that will be given to the partners in any form, including salaries, drawing accounts, vacations, holidays, retirement, and other benefits.

EXAMPLE: *Salary—In General*

In consideration of their business experience, _____ shall receive from the partnership a salary of _____ dollars ($_____) per week, and _____ shall receive a salary of _____ dollars ($_____) per week. Salaries shall be paid on _____ of each week, and these salaries shall be charged to an expense account as part of the cost of conducting the partnership business. These salaries shall be payable whether the partnership earns a profit or not.

No other partner shall be entitled to any salary from the partnership, but shall receive a proportionate share of the partnership net profits only.[27]

EXAMPLE: *Drawing Account—In General*

Each partner shall be authorized to draw _____ dollars ($_____) per week from the funds of the partnership to meet that partner's personal expenses. Any draw shall be chargeable against that partner's share of partnership net profits, and the total amount of draw taken by each partner during the fiscal year shall be deducted from his share of the net profits prior to distribution of net profits.[28]

Provisions for Expenses of Partners and Partnership

This section should address all matters concerning the expenses of the partners and the partnership. It should designate a depository for the partnership funds, name the party responsible for controlling income and distribution, designate the authorized signators on checks and drafts, and authorize partners to negotiate loans. In addition, it should set forth a method and time for disbursing payments on indebtedness and set limitations on indebtedness of partners.

Management and Control of Business

This section should set forth all partnership policies for the management and control of the business. It should appoint any desired managing partner or committee and should specify the management rights and duties of each partner, to the extent practical.

The partnership agreement should also specify a designated time for partnership meetings to discuss various management matters concerning the partnership business. This section may also specify who will keep the books and records of the partnership and what types of books and records should be kept.

EXAMPLE: *Management and Control—In General*

Each partner shall have an equal role in the management and conduct of the partnership business. All decisions affecting the policy and management of the partnership, including compensation of partners and personnel policies, may be made on behalf of the partnership by any active partner. In the event of a disagreement among the partners, a decision by the majority of them shall be binding on the partnership. All partners shall be authorized to sign checks and to make, deliver, accept, or endorse any commercial paper in connection with the business and affairs of the partnership.

The partners shall conduct a _____ [weekly] meeting at the principal office of the partnership to discuss matters of general interest to the partnership. A vote of partners representing _____ percent (___%) of the partnership interest shall be necessary to implement any policy or procedure introduced at a partnership meeting, except for any change in this partnership agreement, which shall require a unanimous vote.[29]

EXAMPLE: *Management and Control—Consent of Both Partners Required*

Each partner has an equal voice in the management of the partnership business. Either partner has the right to make decisions relating to the day-to-day operations of the partnership in the normal course of its business, provided that the consent of both partners is required to do any of the following:

1. Borrow or lend money on behalf of the partnership, other than purchases made on credit in the normal course of business or the partnership not exceeding $___ each, or make, execute, deliver, or endorse any negotiable instrument for the partnership, or agree for the partnership to indemnify or hold harmless any other person, firm, or corporation;
2. Assign, sell, transfer, pledge, or encumber any assets of the partnership;
3. Assign, transfer or pledge any debts due the partnership or release any debts due, except on payment in full;

4. Compromise any claim due to the partnership or submit to arbitration or litigation any dispute or controversy involving the partnership;

5. Lease or purchase any property for the partnership except for purchases in the normal course of the partnership's business, or purchases out of the normal course of business not exceeding $___ each;

6. Assign the partnership's property in trust for creditors or on the assignee's promise to pay the debt to the partnership;

7. Dispose of the goodwill of the partnership;

8. Confess a judgment against the partnership; or

9. Commit any other act which would make it difficult or impossible to carry on the ordinary business of the partnership.[30]

Partnership Accounting

This section should set forth all accounting methods and policies of the partnership, including the accounting period and fiscal year of the partnership, the frequency and types of reports to be completed, details regarding the books of accounts, audit provisions, and provision for examination of books.

Changes in Partners

One restriction that is an essential characteristic of the partnership relation is that no person can become a member of a partnership without the consent of all of the partners, unless there is a contrary provision in the partnership agreement. This very important section of the partnership agreement should set forth the partners' wishes regarding the admission of new partners, if allowed, acceptance requirements, and provisions for the redistribution of assets. This section should also address all matters concerning withdrawing partners, including the necessity of the consent of the other partners, notice requirements, valuation of the withdrawing partner's share of the partnership, the option of the remaining partners to purchase the interest, and the assignment of the withdrawing partner's interest to a third party. It should also describe the conditions for expulsion of a partner, notice requirements, and all other matters concerning the expulsion of a partner.

The partnership's policy regarding a retiring partner should also be addressed in this section, including the reorganization of partnership rights and duties.

EXAMPLE: New Partner—In General

The admission of new partners to the partnership is authorized by this agreement, and shall be accomplished by the approval of partners holding at least _____ percent (___%) of the partnership interest.

A supplemental agreement shall be created prior to admission of a new partner to the partnership. This supplemental agreement shall provide, as a minimum (1) the contributions to partnership capital required of the new partner, (2) his percentage interest in the partnership, (3) any special offices or duties the new partner shall have in the partnership, and (4) the adjusted percentage of interests in the partnership of all existing partners based on the new partner's contribution.

All partners, including the new partner, shall execute the supplemental agreement, which shall become effective on the date signed by the last partner. The supplemental agreement shall then be attached to this agreement as an appendix.[31]

EXAMPLE: Withdrawing Partner—Option of Remaining Partners to Purchase Interest

Any partner desiring to withdraw from the partnership prior to termination or dissolution of the partnership shall be allowed to do so only with the consent of the remaining partners. Prior to granting or denying approval of a partner's request to withdraw, the remaining partners shall have the option to purchase a proportionate share of her interest in the partnership. On their election to exercise the option, the withdrawing partner shall immediately be paid the appraised value of her share, and the remaining partners' interests shall be proportionately increased.

If any of the remaining partners approve of the withdrawal of the partner, but do not desire to purchase a portion of her share, the other remaining partners may purchase the additional segment and thereby obtain a larger proportionate share in the partnership.[32]

EXAMPLE: Retirement of Partner—In General

Any partner who has ____ years of service with the partnership and is at least ____ years of age shall have the option of retiring from the partnership, providing he shall have given the remaining partners written notice of his intention so to do at least _____ months in advance of the intended date of his retirement. When a partner shall retire, an inventory shall be taken of all of the firm's assets in the same manner usually employed by the firm, except that all collectible outstanding accounts shall be valued at _____ percent (___%) of their gross amount and the value of all doubtful accounts shall be adjusted by agreement. The retiring partner shall receive from the partnership _____ percent (___%) of his interest in cash within ____ days after retirement and the balance in a note from the firm payable ____ months thereafter with interest at _____ percent (___%) per year. All other interests of the partner in the firm shall cease, and mutual releases, except for the liability of the partnership on the note, shall be exchanged between the partner and the partnership.

The remaining partners shall each be entitled to receive a proportionate share of the retiring partner's interest in the partnership providing they contribute to the payment for the retiring partner's share on a proportionate basis. If any partner shall refuse to contribute, the other partners may purchase that additional portion proportionately.[33]

Death of Partner

The section dealing with the death of any partner should address all aspects of the purchase of the deceased partner's interest, including the valuation of the deceased partner's share, the dissolution of the partnership, and any desired provision for the estate of the deceased to act as a partner.

EXAMPLE: Termination of Partnership on Death of Partner—
at Conclusion of Fiscal Year

The partnership shall terminate at the close of the current partnership fiscal year on the death of any partner during that fiscal year. The estate of the deceased partner shall be paid the full share to which the deceased partner shall be entitled, at the time of distribution of partnership assets, ___ days after winding up the partnership business.[34]

EXAMPLE: Partnership to Continue after Death of Partner—
Estate to Continue as Partner

On the death of any partner, the partnership shall not terminate, but the legal representative of the deceased partner's estate shall immediately be substituted as a partner under this agreement, with all rights, powers, and duties of a partner as provided in this agreement. The legal representative shall execute a supplemental agreement with the surviving partners, agreeing to be bound by all terms and conditions of this partnership agreement.[35]

Sale or Purchase of Partnership Interest

In this section of the partnership agreement, the partners may set forth all desired provisions regarding the potential sale or purchase of the partnership interest, including conditions for right of first refusal in remaining partners, limitations on purchase of interest, terms of sale, and the reorganization of the partnership.

EXAMPLE: Sale of Interest—Other Partner Given First Refusal

Neither partner shall, during her lifetime, sell, assign, encumber, transfer, or otherwise dispose of all or any part of her interest in the partnership without complying with the following procedure:

If one of the partners wishes to dispose of her interest voluntarily, she shall first offer in writing to sell her interest to the other partner at the price determined in accordance with the provisions of Section ___. If the other partner wishes to purchase the partnership interest, she shall notify the offering partner of her decision in writing within ___ days after receipt of the offer and shall pay for the partnership interest in any case within ___ days after giving notice of her acceptance. In the event the offer to sell has not been accepted within such ___-day period, the offering partner shall have the right to take legal steps to dissolve the partnership.[36]

Arbitration of Differences

The partners may provide in their partnership agreement that certain differences between the partners will be settled by arbitration, upon the terms and conditions set forth in the agreement.

Termination of Partnership

The partnership agreement should set forth all matters concerning the termination of the partnership, including the set date of termination, if there is one, events requiring termination, and procedures for terminating the partnership.

Dissolution and Winding Up

This section of the partnership agreement sets forth all of the agreed-upon terms of the partnership for dissolving and winding up the partnership. It should include provisions for an individual or committee who will be responsible for winding up the partnership business, and compensation for that individual or committee.

EXAMPLE: Dissolution—By Unanimous Agreement of Partners

The partnership shall not be dissolved prior to the termination date set forth in Section ___ of this agreement, except by the unanimous consent of all partners to this agreement at least ___ days prior to the intended date of dissolution.

The unanimous consent shall be obtained at a duly constituted business meeting of the partnership, and the proceedings of the meeting shall be properly and accurately recorded.[37]

EXAMPLE: Winding Up—Appointment of Committee

In the event of the dissolution of the partnership, a management committee shall be selected, with the approval of partners owning _____ percent (___%) of the partnership interest, to consist of ___ partners, who shall have the right to wind up the partnership business and dispose or liquidate the partnership's assets. In the event of liquidation, the committee members are appointed as liquidating partners.

Members of the committee shall each be entitled to receive _____ dollars ($_____) per month as compensation for services during the duration of the committee.[38]

Date of Agreement and Signature of Partners

The partnership agreement must be dated and signed by all partners.

§ 2.6 Financial Structure of a Partnership

Partnerships have a unique financial structure that can often be tailored to suit the needs of the partners. This section discusses the capital of the partnership and the allocation and distribution of profits and losses.

Partnership Capital

The partnership capital, which includes all the assets of the partnership, consists of contributions from the partners and the undistributed income earned by the partnership.

Capital Contributions

There are no minimum capital requirements for partnerships under the Uniform Partnership Act or Revised Uniform Partnership Act. The partnership capital is usually contributed by the partners, and it may be in the form of cash, real or personal property, or the personal expertise or services rendered by a partner. The partnership agreement should state the required capital contribution of each partner and the form of that contribution. In addition to the initial capital contribution, the partnership agreement may require each partner to contribute additional capital to the partnership as needed for the continuance of the partnership business.

Generally, no withdrawal of capital from the partnership is permitted until the partnership is dissolved. If this is not desirable, the appropriate provisions should be made in the partnership agreement for the withdrawal of capital prior to dissolution of the partnership.

Partner Loans and Advances

In addition to the capital contribution, partners may provide capital to the partnership in the form of a loan or an advance, which may be repaid with interest on terms provided for in the partnership agreement, or on terms agreed to by the loaning partner and the remaining partners.

Partners' Right to Accounting

Under the Uniform Partnership Act, every partner is entitled to a formal accounting as to the partnership affairs. This right may be exercised whenever a partner is wrongfully excluded from the partnership business or possession of its property by the co-partners; whenever such rights exist under the partnership agreement or other agreement; whenever appropriate because of the fiduciary nature of each partner to the partnership; or whenever other circumstances render it just and reasonable.[39]

The statutory language concerning the partners' rights to a formal account is quite broad, so these rights should be more clearly defined in the partnership agreement.

While the Revised Uniform Partnership Act is silent on the right of a partner to a formal accounting, it does provide for broad rights of inspection of the books and records of the partnership by the partners, their agents, and their attorneys.

Partnership Records

Unless otherwise provided for in the partnership agreement, the partnership books must be kept at the partnership's executive office and are subject to inspection by any partner at any time. The duty to keep the books of the partnership usually falls to the managing partner or another partner, as appointed in the partnership agreement or by oral agreement between the partners.

Profits and Losses

Another of the more important characteristics of a partnership is a sharing of the profits and losses among the partners. Under the Uniform Partnership Act and the Revised Uniform Partnership Act, the partners share the profits and losses of the partnership equally, regardless of each partner's capital contribution to the partnership. The partners may, however, set their own formula for sharing in the profits and losses of the partnership, which may be based on several factors, including (1) the amount of the initial capital contribution by each partner, (2) additional capital contributions, and (3) services rendered on behalf of the partnership by each partner. If partners' contributions to the partnership are unequal, their shares of the profits and losses may be unequal as well.

The Internal Revenue Service (IRS) generally recognizes a profit and loss allocation that is agreed to by all partners, so long as it has "substantial economic effect." If the IRS determines that the profit and loss allocation set forth in the partnership agreement has no economic effect, but has been drafted merely as a means to avoid paying income taxes, the IRS will allocate profits and losses pursuant to each partner's ownership interest in the partnership.

In any event, if it is not desirable for all partners to share all profits and all losses equally, it is crucial that this matter be addressed in the written partnership agreement.

§ 2.7 Dissolution, Dissociation, Winding Up, and Termination of the Partnership

The dissolution of a partnership is more of a process than an event. This section first examines the definition of the terms dissociation, dissolution, and winding up of a partnership. Next, it discusses the events that cause partnership dissociation and the effects of partnership dissociation, the events causing dissolution and the effects of partnership dissolution, the continuation of a partnership after dissolution, wrongful dissociation of a partnership and the use of a dissolution agreement. This section concludes with a look at giving notice to third parties of a partnership dissolution, winding up the partnership, and distributing partnership assets.

Dissociation, Dissolution, and Winding Up

The term **dissociation** is a new term used in the Revised Uniform Partnership Act. It is distinctly different than **dissolution**. Under the Uniform Partnership Act, whenever one partner ceased being a partner for any reason the partnership was considered to be dissolved. Under the Revised Uniform Partnership Act, one or more partners may be dissociated from a partnership without causing its dissolution. As used in the Revised Uniform Partnership Act, the term dissociation is used to denote the change in the relationship caused by a partner's ceasing to be associated in the carrying on of the business.

The term dissolution refers to the commencement of the winding up process. Upon dissolution of a partnership, the partnership relationship terminates with respect to all future transactions and the authority of all partners to act on behalf of the partnership and on behalf of each other terminates, except to the extent necessary for the winding up

TERMS

dissociation   The event that occurs when a partner ceases to be associated in the carrying on of the partnership business.

dissolution of corporation[†]   The termination of a corporation's existence and its abolishment as an entity.

of the partnership. The partnership will cease to exist upon completion of the winding-up process—the disposition of all liabilities and assets of the partnership.

Events Causing Partner's Dissociation

A partner's dissociation can be caused by agreement, by statute, or wrongfully. The Revised Uniform Partnership Act sets forth the following acts that can cause a partner's dissociation:

1. The partner giving notice to the partnership of his or her express will to withdraw as a partner on some specific date
2. The occurrence of an event agreed to in the partnership agreement as causing the partner's dissociation
3. The partner's expulsion pursuant to the partnership agreement
4. The partner's expulsion by the unanimous vote of the other partners if:
   a. it is unlawful to carry on the partnership business with that partner
   b. the partner transfers all or substantially all of his or her transferable interest in the partnership
   c. the partner is a corporation that has filed a certificate of dissolution, had its charter revoked, or its right to conduct business suspended
   d. the partner is a partnership that has been dissolved and its business is being wound up
5. Judicial determination, based on an application by the partnership or another partner because:
   a. the partner engaged in wrongful conduct that adversely and materially affected the partnership
   b. the appointment of a trustee, receiver, or liquidator of the partner's property
6. The partner's death
7. Appointment of a guardian or general conservator for the partner
8. A judicial determination that the partner has otherwise become incapable of performing the partner's duties under the partnership agreement
9. If the partner is a trust, distribution of the trust's entire transferable interest in the partnership
10. If the partner is an estate, distribution of the estate's entire transferable interest in the partnership
11. Termination of a partner who is not an individual, corporation, trust, or estate.

Effect of Partner's Dissociation

Generally, upon a partner's dissociation, the partner's rights to participate in the management and conduct of the partnership business terminate. The dissociated partner will no longer be able to act on behalf of the partnership except to wind up the affairs of a dissolving partnership. Likewise, the dissociated partner will not be liable for any obligations incurred by the partnership after his or her dissociation. The partner's duty of loyalty and duty of care continue only with regard to matters arising and events occurring before the partner's dissociation, unless the partner participates in the winding up of the partnership's business.

The effect a partner's dissociation will have upon the partner and upon the partnership depends on whether the dissociation causes the dissolution and winding up of the partnership and whether the partner's dissociation was wrongful.

Effect of Partner's Dissociation When Partnership Continues

In most instances, a dissociating partner has the right to have his or her interest in the partnership purchased for a buyout price as set forth in the partnership agreement or by statute. The Revised Uniform Partnership defines the buyout price of a dissociated partner's interest as "the amount that would have been distributable to the dissociating partner if, on the date of dissociation, the assets of the partnership were sold at a price equal to the greater of the liquidation value or the value based on a sale of the entire business as a going concern without the dissociated partner and the partnership were wound up as of that date."[40]

In the case of a wrongful dissociation, the damages caused by that dissociation can be used to offset the buyout price paid to the dissociated partner.

In the event of the death of a partner, the deceased partner is considered to be dissociated, and the partner's transferable interest in the partnership will pass to his or her estate. The remaining partners or the partnership typically will then buy out that interest from the estate and continue the partnership business.

Statement of Dissociation

In states where the Revised Uniform Partnership Act has been adopted, either the dissociated partner or the partnership may file with the appropriate state authority a statement of dissociation stating the name of the partnership and that the partner is dissociated from the partnership. The statement of dissociation is a public notice of the dissociated partner's limitation of authority and liability with regard to partnership matters.

Events Causing Dissolution and Winding Up of Partnership Business

Exactly what precipitates the dissolution and winding up of a partnership will be dictated by state statute. In states that strictly follow the Uniform Partnership Act, several acts, including the death, withdrawal or any event that causes a partner to cease being a partner, will cause the dissolution of a partnership.

In states that have adopted the Revised Uniform Partnership Act, only the following events cause a dissolution and winding up of the partnership business:

1. In a partnership at will, the partnership's receiving notice from a partner of that partner's express will to withdraw as a partner
2. In a partnership for a definite term or particular undertaking:
   a. the expiration of a ninety-day period after a partner's dissociation by death or otherwise, or through wrongful dissociation, unless a majority in interest of the remaining partners, agree to continue the partnership
   b. the express will of all of the partners to wind up the partnership business
   c. the expiration of the term or the completion of the undertaking
3. An event agreed to in the partnership agreement resulting in the winding up of the partnership business
4. An event that makes it unlawful for the partnership business to be continued
5. A judicial determination, based on an application by a partner that:
   a. the economic purpose of the partnership is likely to be unreasonably frustrated
   b. another partner has engaged in conduct which makes it not reasonably practicable to carry on the business in partnership with that partner, or
   c. it is not reasonably practicable to carry on the partnership business in conformity with the partnership agreement
6. A judicial determination, based on an application by a transferee of a partner's transferable interest that the term for the partnership

has expired or the undertaking has been completed, or at any time if the partnership was a partnership at will at the time of transfer.

When it is the desire of the partners to plan for the continuation of the partnership after the death of one or more of the partners, life insurance on the life of each partner is often purchased by the partnership or by the partners to fund the buyout of a deceased partner.

The buyout of a dissociated partner is a new concept under the Revised Uniform Partnership Act. Previously, whenever a partner dissociated, the partnership would be dissolved.

Dissolution Agreement

A written dissolution agreement among the partners of a dissolving partnership can help alleviate any disputes as to the method and timing of the dissolution, as well as any disputes that may arise subsequent to the winding up of the partnership due to unforeseen circumstances. In the dissolution agreement, the partners who have the right to wind up the partnership generally appoint a liquidating partner or partners and delegate the authority to liquidate the partnership and settle the partnership affairs.

Notice to Third Parties

Notice of the partnership dissolution or withdrawal of a partner must be given to parties who have previously dealt with the partnership. Creditors who are not given notice and do not know of the dissolution are entitled to hold former partners liable for obligations incurred by continuing partners after dissolution.

A new provision in the Revised Uniform Partnership Act provides for an optional filing of a statement of dissolution by any partner of a dissolving partnership who has not wrongfully dissociated. The statement of dissolution cancels any statement of partnership authority that may have been filed on behalf of the partnership.

Winding Up

Winding up is the process by which the accounts of the partnership are settled and the assets are liquidated in order to make distribution of the net assets of the partnership to the partners and dissolve the partnership. This may include the performance of existing contracts, the collection of debts or claims due to the partnership, and the payment of the partnership debts.

Distribution of Assets

Unless otherwise specified in the partnership agreement, the rules for distribution of the partnership assets are set by statute.

In settling the accounts of the partnership, the partnership property is first used to pay the creditors of the partnership. If the partnership property is insufficient to cover all of the partnership liabilities, then the partners will be required to make contributions to cover the liabilities.

If any, but not all, of the partners are insolvent, or otherwise unable or unwilling to contribute to the payment of the liabilities, the liabilities of the partnership must be paid by the remaining partners in the same proportion as their share of the profits of the partnership. Any partner, or the legal representative of any partner, who is required to pay in excess of his or her fair share of the liabilities to settle the affairs of the partnership, has the right to enforce the contributions of the other partners pursuant to statute and the partnership agreement, to the extent of the amount paid in excess of his or her share of the liability.

The exact method of distribution should be set forth clearly in the partnership agreement. Generally, the partners are entitled to a distribution of the assets in the same percentage as their contribution of capital to the partnership, with adjustments made for subsequent contributions in the form of capital contributions and services rendered on behalf of the partnership. If partners' contributions to the partnership are unequal, their shares of the profits and losses may be unequal as well, so long as the appropriate provision is made in the partnership agreement.

§ 2.8   Other Types of Partnerships and Similar Organizations

Although the general partnership is by far the most common type of partnership, there are other types of partnerships and other organizations that resemble partnerships. This section briefly reviews a few of the other types of partnerships, including partnership associations, joint ventures, and mining partnerships.

Limited liability companies and limited liability partnerships are discussed in Chapter 4.

Partnership Association or Limited Partnership Association

The statutes of a few states provide for the formation of an organization that may be referred to either as a *partnership association* or a *limited partnership association.* This organization is somewhat of a hybrid between a limited partnership and a corporation and is considered a separate entity.

Joint Ventures

Joint ventures and partnerships are governed by the same basic legal principles. A joint venture that meets the definition of partnership may, for certain purposes, be considered a partnership when determining its rights and obligations. However, there are important differences between a partnership and a joint venture. The primary difference is that the joint venture is formed for a single transaction or isolated enterprise, whereas a partnership is formed to operate an ongoing concern. Also, the loss-sharing character of the partnership is not essential to the joint venture.

Mining Partnerships

Certain mining states provide for the statutory formation of mining partnerships, which are special business organizations with some attributes distinguishing them from general partnerships. However, a mining business may also do business as a typical general partnership.

§ 2.9 The Role of the Legal Assistant in Partnership Matters

As with sole proprietorships, the bulk of legal services performed for persons forming and operating a partnership is usually in the form of legal advice given by the attorney. The legal assistant, however, may be instrumental in drafting the partnership agreement and performing research regarding the requirements for forming, operating, and dissolving a partnership, as well as research regarding partnership disputes. Most law firms have partnership agreement forms integrated into their word processing systems. The legal assistant is often responsible for the revising and drafting required to make each agreement fit the unique circumstances of each new partnership.

Form books commonly found in law libraries may help with the drafting of unique language, as will samples of previous work done by the legal assistant or others in the law firm.

The following is a checklist of items that should be considered when drafting a partnership agreement.

PARTNERSHIP AGREEMENT CHECKLIST

- ☐ Names and addresses of partners.
- ☐ Name of partnership.
- ☐ Purpose of partnership.
- ☐ Address of principal place of doing business.
- ☐ Term of partnership agreement.
- ☐ Partner contributions.
- ☐ Requirements for additional contributions.
- ☐ Partnership assets.
- ☐ Goodwill evaluation on distribution of assets.
- ☐ Partners' and partnership liability.
- ☐ Distribution of profits and losses.
- ☐ Partner indemnification.
- ☐ Partners' duties.
- ☐ Partners' powers and limitations thereon.
- ☐ Partner compensation and benefits.
- ☐ Partner and partnership expenses.
- ☐ Management and control of business.
- ☐ Life insurance on lives of partners.
- ☐ Accounting procedures and record keeping.
- ☐ Changes in partners.
- ☐ Death of partner.
- ☐ Sale or purchase of partnership interest.
- ☐ Arbitration of differences among partners.
- ☐ Partnership termination.
- ☐ Dissolution and winding up.
- ☐ Date of agreement.
- ☐ Signatures of all partners.

The legal assistant may also be asked to help with the other formalities associated with forming and operating a partnership, including research regarding filing requirements for partnerships, the actual filing of the partnership certificate, filing and publishing a certificate of assumed or fictitious name, and applying for tax identification numbers.

§ 2.10 Resources

The paralegal has many resources available for researching statutory requirements for partnerships and drafting partnership agreements. State statues provide the statutory requirements for partnerships, and legal form books provide many possible clauses for partnership agreements. For state and local formalities concerning partnerships, the Secretary of State and other state and local government offices should be contacted.

State Statutes

Table 2-1 is a list of the statutory citations of the Uniform Partnership Act or Revised Uniform Partnership Act as adopted by each state:

TABLE 2-1 STATUTORY CITATIONS TO UNIFORM PARTNERSHIP ACT AND REVISED UNIFORM PARTNERSHIP ACT

State	Code	Act
Alabama	Ala. Code § 10-8-1 *et seq.*	Uniform Partnership Act
Alaska	Alaska Stat. § 32.05.010 *et seq.*	Uniform Partnership Act
Arizona	Ariz. Rev. Stat. Ann. § 29-201 *et seq.*	Uniform Partnership Act
Arkansas	Ark. Code Ann. § 4-42-101 *et seq.*	Uniform Partnership Act
California	Cal. Corp. Code § 15001 *et seq.*	Uniform Partnership Act
Colorado	Colo. Rev. Stat. § 77-60-101 *et seq.*	Uniform Partnership Act
Connecticut	Conn. Gen. Stat. § 34-39 *et seq.*	Uniform Partnership Act
Delaware	Del. Code Ann. tit. 6 § 41-101 *et seq.*	Uniform Partnership Act
District of Columbia	D.C. Code Ann. § 41-101 *et seq.*	Uniform Partnership Act
Florida	Fla. Stat. ch. 620.56 *et seq.*	Uniform Partnership Act
Georgia	Ga. Code Ann. § 14-8-1 *et seq.*	Uniform Partnership Act

TABLE 2-1 *(continued)*

State	Code	Act
Hawaii	Haw. Rev. Stat. § 425-101 *et seq.*	Uniform Partnership Act
Idaho	Idaho Code § 53-301 *et seq.*	Uniform Partnership Act
Illinois	Ill. Rev. Stat. ch. 106 1/2, para. 1 *et seq.*	Uniform Partnership Act
Indiana	Ind. Code § 23-4-1-1 *et seq.*	Uniform Partnership Act
Iowa	Iowa Code § 544.1 *et seq.*	Uniform Partnership Act
Kansas	Kan. Stat. Ann. § 56-301 *et seq.*	Uniform Partnership Act
Kentucky	Ky. Rev. Stat. Ann. § 362.150 *et seq.*	Uniform Partnership Act
Louisiana	La. Rev. Stat. Ann. § 9:3401 *et seq.*	Not an adaptation of the Uniform Partnership Act or the Revised Uniform Partnership Act
Maine	Me. Rev. Stat. Ann. tit. 31, § 281 *et seq.*	Uniform Partnership Act
Maryland	Md. Corps. & Ass'ns Code Ann. § 9-101 *et seq.*	Uniform Partnership Act
Massachusetts	Mass. Gen. L. ch. 108A, § 1 *et seq.*	Uniform Partnership Act
Michigan	Mich. Comp. Laws § 449.1 *et seq.*	Uniform Partnership Act
Minnesota	Minn. Stat. § 323.01 *et seq.*	Uniform Partnership Act
Mississippi	Miss. Code Ann. § 79-12-1 *et seq.*	Uniform Partnership Act
Missouri	Mo. Rev. Stat. § 358.010 *et seq.*	Uniform Partnership Act
Montana	Mo. Rev. Stat. § 35-10-101 *et seq.*	Revised Uniform Partnership Act
Nebraska	Neb. Rev. Stat. § 67-301 *et seq.*	Uniform Partnership Act
Nevada	Nev. Rev. Stat. § 87.010 *et seq.*	Uniform Partnership Act
New Hampshire	N.H. Rev. Stat. Ann. § 304-A:1 *et seq.*	Uniform Partnership Act
New Jersey	N.J. Rev. Stat. § 42:1-1 *et seq.*	Uniform Partnership Act
New Mexico	N.M. Stat. Ann. § 54-1-1 *et seq.*	Uniform Partnership Act

TABLE 2-1 *(continued)*

State	Code	Act
New York	N.Y. Partnership Law § 1 *et seq.*	Uniform Partnership Act
North Carolina	N.C. Gen. Stat. § 59-31 *et seq.*	Uniform Partnership Act
North Dakota	N.D. Cent. Code § 45-05-01 *et seq.*	Uniform Partnership Act
Ohio	Ohio Rev. Code Ann. § 1775.01 *et seq.*	Uniform Partnership Act
Oklahoma	Okla. Stat. tit. 54, § 201 *et seq.*	Uniform Partnership Act
Oregon	Or. Rev. Stat. § 68.010 *et seq.*	Uniform Partnership Act
Pennsylvania	15 Pa. Cons. Stat. Ann. § 8301 *et seq.*	Uniform Partnership Act
Rhode Island	R.I. Gen. Laws § 7-12-12 *et seq.*	Uniform Partnership Act
South Carolina	S.C. Code Ann. § 33-41-10 *et seq.*	Uniform Partnership Act
South Dakota	S.D. Codified Laws Ann. § 48-1-1 *et seq.*	Uniform Partnership Act
Tennessee	Tenn. Code Ann. § 61-1-101 *et seq.*	Uniform Partnership Act
Texas	Tex. Rev. Civ. Stat. Ann. art 6132b	Revised Uniform Partnership Act
Utah	Utah Code Ann. § 48-1-1 *et seq.*	Uniform Partnership Act
Vermont	Vt. Stat. Ann. tit. 11, § 1121 *et seq.*	Uniform Partnership Act
Virginia	Va. Code Ann. § 47-8A-1 *et seq.*	Uniform Partnership Act
Washington	Wash. Rev. Code § 25.04.010 *et seq.*	Uniform Partnership Act
West Virginia	W.Va. Code § 47-8A-1 *et seq.*	Uniform Partnership Act
Wisconsin	Wis. Stat. § 178.01 *et seq.*	Uniform Partnership Act
Wyoming	Wyo. Stat. § 17-21-101 *et seq.*	Revised Uniform Partnership Act

Legal Form Books

Legal form books, such as *Am. Jur. Forms 2d., Nichols Cyclopedia of Legal Forms Annotated, Rabkin & Johnson Current Legal Forms,* and *West's Legal Forms Second Edition,* are a good source for general information and sample paragraphs for drafting partnership agreements and other documents related to the formation and operation of partnerships.

Secretary of State or Other Appropriate State Authority

The Secretary of State or other appropriate state authority must be contacted to determine if there is a requirement that partnerships be registered with the state, and to determine what the procedures are for complying with that requirement. (See Appendix A for a Secretary of State directory.)

The Secretary of State should also be consulted for procedural information regarding filing of an application for use of assumed name, trade name, or fictitious name, if applicable.

State and Local Government Offices

Because the formalities for operating a partnership vary by state, it is important that the appropriate state authority be contacted to obtain information relating to all state taxation matters, including unemployment insurance, withholding for employee income taxation, sales tax permits, and licenses.

Review Questions

1. What five elements are necessary to form a partnership?

2. In what ways are partnerships similar to sole proprietorships? In what ways do they differ from sole proprietorships?

3. Suppose that John, Megan, and Alex form a partnership to operate a restaurant pursuant to the Uniform Partnership Act. John decides to buy hamburger buns from the Fresh Bread Bakery. He enters into a contract with the owner of the Fresh Bread Bakery, on behalf of the partnership, for

the delivery of 500 hamburger buns each week, for the price of $70 per week. If Megan and Alex disagree with this decision because they prefer another baker, is the partnership still liable for this contract? Must the Fresh Bread Bakery be paid out of the partnership funds?

4. Suppose again that John, Megan and Alex form a partnership, and John has contributed 50 percent of the capital, Megan has contributed 30 percent of the capital, and Alex has contributed 20 percent of the capital. Who has the right to manage the partnership under the Revised Uniform Partnership Law, assuming the partnership agreement has no contrary provisions? How will decisions be made in the event of a disagreement?

5. What are the three rights that partners have to partnership property? Which, if any, of these rights are assignable?

6. Is it possible for two individuals to form a partnership with an oral agreement to operate a construction business for three years? Why or why not?

7. Kara, Tim, and Anna have formed partnership to purchase and renovate old homes. Kara and Tim have contributed the bulk of the capital for the corporation and Anna's main contribution has been her services. All partners agree that either Kara or Tim should have the authority to sign documents transferring real estate on behalf of the partnership and that Anna should not have that authority. If the partnership is formed in a state that follows the Revised Uniform Partnership Act, what steps must they take to give notice to those dealing with their partnership of their agreement with regard to the authority to transfer real estate?

8. Janet is a partner in a ten-partner partnership located in a state that follows the Revised Uniform Partnership Act. If Janet decides to withdraw from the partnership before its duration lapses, what are the possible outcomes to the partnership and the remaining partners? What if the partnership is located in a state that follows the Uniform Partnership Act?

Notes

1 Uniform Partnership Act § 6.

2 *Id.* § 2.

3 *Id.*

4 The Reference Press, *The American Almanac Statistical Abstract of the United States: 1994–1995, 114 ed. at 835, 837, 840 (Austin, Texas 1994).*

5 *Id.* at 836.

6 59A AM. JUR. 2d *Partnership* § 26 (1987).

7 *Id.* § 7.

8 Revised Uniform Partnership Act § 201.

9 Uniform Partnership Act § 24.

[10] Revised Uniform Partnership Act § 501.

[11] *Id.* § 301.

[12] Uniform Partnership Act § 13.

[13] See § 1.5 of this text.

[14] N.H. Rev. Stat. Ann. § 305-A:1 (Supp. 1973).

[15] Revised Uniform Partnership Act § 401(j), Uniform Partnership Act § 18(h).

[16] See § 1.5 of this text.

[17] 14 AM. JUR. Legal Forms 2d (Rev) § 194:123 (1994).

[18] *Id.* § 194:141 (1994).

[19] *Id.* § 194:162 (1994).

[20] *Id.* § 194:164 (1994).

[21] *Id.* § 194:213 (1994).

[22] *Id.* § 194:242 (1994).

[23] *Id.* § 194:384 (1994).

[24] *Id.* § 194:390 (1994).

[25] *Id.* § 194:312 (1994).

[26] *Id.* § 194:321 (1994).

[27] *Id.* § 194:421 (1994).

[28] *Id.* § 1994:441 (1994).

[29] *Id.* § 194:501.

[30] *Id.* § 194:503.

[31] *Id.* § 194:571.

[32] *Id.* § 194:598.

[33] *Id.* § 194:631.

[34] 14 AM. JUR. Legal Forms 2d (Rev) § 194:631 (1982).

[35] 14 AM. JUR. Legal Forms 2d (Rev) § 194:696 (1994).

[36] 14 AM. JUR. Legal Forms 2d (Rev) § 194:696 (1982).

[37] *Id.* § 194:744.

[38] 14 AM. JUR. Legal Forms 2d (Rev) § 194:811 (1994).

[39] Uniform Partnership Act § 22.

[40] Revised Uniform Partnership Act § 701(b).

CHAPTER 3

LIMITED PARTNERSHIPS

Coming together is a beginning; keeping together is progress; working together is success.
——————————— *Henry Ford*

Introduction

Limited partnerships are a special type of partnership that offers certain partners limited liability. This business organization shares many of the characteristics of general partnerships, with a few important differences. Those differences are highlighted in this chapter.

First, we define the characteristics of a limited partnership. We then discuss the rights and responsibilities of the general and limited partners and the advantages and disadvantages of doing business as a limited partnership. The examination of limited partnerships then continues with a look at the organization and management of a limited partnership, including the contents of a limited partnership agreement. Next, we briefly investigate the financial structure of a limited partnership. This chapter concludes with a discussion of derivative actions, dissolution of a limited partnership, the role of the legal assistant in working with limited partnerships, and resources available to aid the legal assistant.

§ 3.1 An Introduction to Limited Partnerships

This section begins by defining the term *limited partnership*. Next, it discusses the role of limited partnerships in the United States and the laws governing limited partnerships. Finally, it examines the separate entity nature of limited partnerships.

Limited Partnership Defined

A **limited partnership** is a partnership created by statute with one or more **general partners** and one or more **limited partners**. The status of the general partners in a limited partnership is very similar to that of the partners in general partnerships, and they have many of the same rights, duties, and obligations. Limited partners, on the other hand, are in many ways more like investors than partners, as their risk is limited to the amount of their contribution to the limited partnership, and they are not entitled to manage the business of the partnership.

As with a general partnership, a partner may be a "natural person, partnership, limited partnership (domestic or foreign), trust, estate, association, or corporation."[1]

Limited Partnerships in the United States

The popularity of limited partnerships in the United States has been attributed mainly to the unique tax advantages they offer. Because the limited partnership is usually not taxed as a separate entity, that business form offers the opportunity to pass profits, and especially losses, directly to the limited partners. For that reason, and because limited partners are not personally liable for the debts and obligations of the partnership, the limited partnership has become a favored vehicle for investments in this country, particularly in the area of real estate.[2]

With the increasing availability of new types of business organizations that offer both limited liability and partnership taxation treatment, we may see a decrease in the number of new limited partnerships formed each year in the future. Two such entities are limited liability companies and limited liability partnerships, which are discussed in Chapter 4 of this text.

TERMS

limited partnership [†] A partnership in which the liability of one or more of the partners is limited to the amount of money they have invested in the partnership.

general partner [†] A partner in an ordinary partnership, as distinguished from a limited partnership. "General partner" is synonymous with "partner."

limited partner A partner in a limited partnership whose liability is limited to the sum she contributed to the partnership as capital; a special partner. A limited partner is not involved in managing or carrying out the business of the partnership.

Dividends

The Importance of Confidentiality

Attorney-client communications are considered privileged and must be kept strictly confidential. Information communicated to an attorney by the client cannot be revealed to anyone, unless the attorney has been given permission.

This rule of client confidentiality extends to all employees of the attorney as well, including paralegals. Both the National Federation of Paralegal Associations' ethical standards and the National Association of Legal Assistants' Code of Ethics and Professional Responsibility include provisions affirming the confidential nature of communication between the client and the legal assistant.

Most law firms have strict office policies concerning confidentiality that apply to all law firm employees. These policies are usually based on the following three rules:

1. Do not divulge client names or any information regarding a client's case or business to any individual outside the law firm, including the press.
2. Any inquiries regarding a client should be directed to the attorney responsible for the client's file.
3. Do not release any documents from a client's file without permission from the attorney who is responsible for the file.

The confidential nature of the legal professional-client relationship has several applications to legal assistants working in the corporate law area. A Supreme Court decision in 1981 extended the attorney-client privilege to corporations, allowing corporations the right to keep confidential any information passed on to their attorneys. In effect, this ruling prevents attorneys from testifying against their corporate clients in a court of law or from disseminating unauthorized information about the corporation to the press. Special attention to client confidentiality must be given by the paralegal working in the securities or merger and acquisition areas, and by paralegals working for law firms that have been retained to conduct internal investigations on behalf of corporate clients.

Rumors regarding mergers and acquisitions can have a devastating effect on the outcome of the proposed transaction, as well as an effect on the price of the stock of either or both parties involved. Likewise, unauthorized leaks of information from a law firm that represents publicly held corporations, or corporations that are planning public offerings, can have significant financial implications for the client. All information regarding a publicly held corporation must be carefully monitored and released only with forethought. Information passed on to third parties regarding a publicly held corporation may be considered "insider information" and could subject individuals purchasing stock based on that information to civil suits, criminal prosecution, or both.

The confidential nature of the attorney-client relationship is so sacred that corporate management has recently begun to hire outside counsel to perform internal investigations if it suspects wrongdoing within the company. Any information uncovered by such outside counsel is considered privileged information and cannot be used against the corporation in any potential future lawsuits or criminal prosecutions. This allows the corporate management to attempt to put an end to any wrongdoing within the corporation or to attempt damage control before an official investigation begins.

Paralegals working in the corporate law area are advised not to discuss details of their work concerning corporate clients with anyone, even spouses, family members, or close friends. One word to the wrong person can lead to the loss of your job, your firm's client, and possibly even criminal prosecution.

Law Governing Limited Partnerships

The first uniform law concerning limited partnerships in the United States was the Uniform Limited Partnership Act of 1916, which was adopted by the vast majority of the states. In 1976, the Revised Uniform Limited Partnership Act was introduced. In 1985 substantial changes were made to that Act. Over the years, most states have adopted the Revised Uniform Limited Partnership Act with 1985 amendments. At this time, Vermont and the Virgin Islands still follow the Uniform Limited Partnership Act, and the state of Louisiana is governed by statutes based on common law. Section 3.11 of this chapter includes a list of the state limited partnership statutes. (See Appendix C of this text for the Revised Uniform Limited Partnership Act with the 1985 revisions.)

Throughout this chapter, references to the Uniform Limited Partnership Act are to the original act as approved in 1916. References to the Revised Uniform Limited Partnership Act are to the Revised Act with the 1985 amendments thereto, unless otherwise indicated. Uniform laws are not always adopted verbatim, and it is very important, when researching limited partnerships, that the proper state's statutes be consulted, as even seemingly minor variations can be important.

The Limited Partnership As a Separate Entity

Much like general partnerships, a limited partnership may be treated as a separate entity for certain purposes. When dealing with matters such as real estate ownership and the capacity to sue, the limited partnership is considered a separate entity. For other purposes, however, the limited partnership is still considered an aggregate of the individual partners. Under common law, no partnership was ever considered a separate entity, and many states still subscribe to the common law approach when dealing with limited partnerships.[3] The limited partnership is generally not considered a separate entity for income tax purposes.

§ 3.2 Partners' Rights and Responsibilities

Limited partnerships consist of more than one type of partner, and those partners are subject to different statutory rights and responsibilities. This section examines the rights and responsibilities unique to general partners and those unique to limited partners. The section concludes with a discussion of the relationship between general partners and limited partners.

General Partners' Rights and Responsibilities

Except as otherwise provided by statute and the limited partnership agreement, the rights and responsibilities of a general partner in a limited partnership are very similar to the rights and responsibilities of those of a partner in a general partnership. Unlike limited partners, general partners are personally responsible for the liabilities of the limited partnership.

Section 9(1) of the original Uniform Limited Partnership Act limits the powers of the general partners by providing that:

> without the written consent or ratification of the specific acts by all the limited partners, a general partner or all of the general partners have no authority to
>
> (a) Do any act in contravention of the certificate,
> (b) Do any act which would make it impossible to carry on the ordinary business of the partnership,
> (c) Confess a judgment against the partnership,
> (d) Possess partnership property, or assign their rights in specific partnership property, for other than a partnership purpose,
> (e) Admit a person as a general partner,
> (f) Admit a person as a limited partner, unless the right so to do is given in the certificate,
> (g) Continue the business with partnership property on the death, retirement or insanity of a general partner, unless the right so to do is given in the certificate.

No similar restrictions on general partners are enumerated in the Revised Uniform Limited Partnership Act.

Limited Partners' Rights and Responsibilities

The limited partner is often seen as more of an investor than an actual partner to the partnership. The limited partner has few of the rights granted to partners in a general partnership, and correspondingly few of the responsibilities. One of the most important characteristics of limited partners is that they have limited liability. The risk of a limited partner is limited to the amount of that partner's investment in the limited partnership.

The interest of a limited partner in a partnership is considered to be personal property, even if the partnership assets include or consist solely of land. The limited partner holds no title to the assets of the partnership, but has only his or her interest in the partnership.[4]

Unlike the partners in a general partnership, limited partners have no right to participate in the management of the partnership, and may actually be in danger of losing their limited liability status if they do participate in the control of the partnership business. In that event, the limited partner may be held personally liable for the debts and obligations of the limited partnership. Under the Revised Uniform Limited Partnership Act, a limited partner who participates in control of the business is liable only to persons who transact business with the limited partnership reasonably believing, based upon the limited partner's conduct, that the limited partner is a general partner.[5] No such condition is set forth in the original Uniform Limited Partnership Act.

Exactly what constitutes "taking part in control" of the business has been the subject of many a court case, and is still subject to debate. However, under the Revised Uniform Limited Partnership Act, some guidance is given by way of a list of "safe harbor" activities. The Revised Uniform Limited Partnership Act states:

A limited partner does not participate in the control of the business ... solely by doing one or more of the following:

(1) being a contractor for or an agent or employee of the limited partnership or of a general partner or being an officer, director, or shareholder of a general partner that is a corporation;

(2) consulting with and advising a general partner with respect to the business of the limited partnership;

(3) acting as surety for the limited partnership or guaranteeing or assuming one or more specific obligations of the limited partnership;

(4) taking any action required or permitted by law to bring or pursue a derivative action in the right of the limited partnership;

(5) requesting or attending a meeting of partners;

(6) proposing, approving, or disapproving, by voting or otherwise, one or more of the following matters:

   (i) the dissolution and winding up of the limited partnership;

   (ii) the sale, exchange, lease, mortgage, pledge, or other transfer of all or substantially all of the assets of the limited partnership;

   (iii) the incurrence of indebtedness by the limited partnership other than in the ordinary course of its business;

   (iv) a change in the nature of the business;

   (v) the admission or removal of a general partner;

   (vi) the admission or removal of a limited partner;

   (vii) a transaction involving an actual or potential conflict of interest between a general partner and the limited partnership or the limited partners;

   (viii) an amendment to the partnership agreement or certificate of limited partnership; or

   (ix) matters related to the business of the limited partnership not otherwise enumerated in this subsection (b), which the partnership agreement states in writing may be subject to the approval or disapproval of limited partners;

(7) winding up the limited partnership ... or

(8) exercising any right or power permitted to limited partners under this Act and not specifically enumerated in this subsection (b).[6]

ALZADO
v.
BLINDER, ROBINSON & CO., INC.
Supreme Court of Colorado
752 P.2d 544 (Colo. 1988)
Kirshbaum, Justice

In *Blinder, Robinson & Co. v. Alzado,* 713 P.2d 1314 (Colo. App. 1985), the Court of Appeals affirmed in part and reversed in part several judgments entered on jury verdicts in a civil action arising from disputes among promoters of an exhibition boxing match between petitioner Lyle Alzado (Alzado) and Muhammed Ali (Ali) ... .

In the spring of 1979, Alzado, Alzado's former accountant, Tinter, and Alzado's former agent, Ronald Kauffman (Kauffman), formed Combat Promotions, Inc. to promote an eight-round exhibition boxing match in Denver, Colorado, between Alzado and Ali. Ali had agreed to engage in the match on the condition that prior to the event his attorneys would receive an irrevocable letter of credit guaranteeing payment of $250,000 to Ali.

Combat Promotions, Inc. initially encountered difficulties in obtaining the letter of credit. Ultimately, however, Meyer Blinder (Blinder), President of Blinder-Robinson, expressed an interest in the event. Blinder anticipated that his company's participation would result in a positive public relations image for its recently opened Denver office. Blinder-Robinson ultimately agreed to provide the $250,000 letter of credit ... .

On June 25, 1979, an agreement was executed by Combat Promotions, Inc. and Blinder-Robinson creating a limited partnership, Combat Associates. Under the terms of the agreement, Combat Promotions was the general partner and Blinder-Robinson was the sole limited partner. Blinder-Robinson contributed a $250,000 letter of credit to Combat Associates, and the partnership agreement provided expressly that the letter of credit was to be paid off as a partnership expense.

On the same day, June 25, 1979, Alzado executed a separate guarantee agreement with Blinder-Robinson. This agreement provided that if Ali drew the letter of credit, Alzado personally would reimburse Blinder-Robinson for any amount Blinder-Robinson was unable to recover from Combat Associates under the terms of the limited partnership agreement. ... Subsequently, on July 14, 1979, the event occurred as scheduled.

Few tickets were sold, and the match proved to be a financial debacle. Ali drew the letter of credit and collected the $250,000 to which he was entitled. Combat Associates paid Blinder-Robinson only $65,000; it did not pay anything to Alzado or, apparently, to other creditors.

In January of 1980, Blinder-Robinson filed this civil action seeking $185,000 in damages plus costs and attorney fees from Alzado pursuant to the terms of the June 25, 1979, guaranty agreement. Alzado denied any liability to Blinder-Robinson and asserted several **affirmative defenses** to the complaint ... .

Alzado also filed two **counterclaims** against Blinder-Robinson. The first alleged that because of its conduct Blinder-Robinson must be deemed a general partner of Combat Associates and, therefore, liable to Alzado under the agreement between Alzado and the partnership for Alzado's participation in the match ... .

TERMS

affirmative defense   A defense that amounts to more than simply a denial of the allegations in the plaintiff's complaint. It sets up new matter which, if proven, could result in a judgment against the plaintiff even if all the allegations of the complaint are true.

counterclaim   A cause of action on which a defendant in a lawsuit might have sued the plaintiff in a separate action. Such a cause of action, stated in a separate division of a defendant's answer, is a counterclaim.

The jury returned a verdict in favor of Blinder-Robinson and against Alzado in the amount of $185,000 on Blinder-Robinson's complaint. The jury also returned two verdicts in favor of Alzado and against Blinder-Robinson, as follows: $92,500 on Alzado's claim that Blinder-Robinson, as a general partner, was responsible for Combat Associates' debt to Alzado, and $100,000 on Alzado's claim of an oral agreement of waiver and indemnification ... .

Blinder-Robinson also filed a motion for judgment notwithstanding the verdict or, alternatively, for a new trial with regard to the two verdicts entered against it on Alzado's counterclaims. Blinder-Robinson asserted that the evidence failed to establish that it exercised sufficient control of Combat Associates' activities to be deemed a general partner thereof or that it entered into any release and indemnification agreement with Alzado ... .

The Court of Appeals reversed the trial court's denial of Blinder-Robinson's motion for judgment notwithstanding the verdict with respect to Alzado's first counterclaim, concluding that the evidence failed to establish that Blinder-Robinson's conduct constituted control of Combat Associates ... .

Alzado ... contends that the Court of Appeals erred in concluding that Blinder-Robinson's conduct in promoting the match did not constitute sufficient control of Combat Associates to justify the conclusion that the company must be deemed a general rather than a limited partner. We disagree ... .

The record here reflects that Blinder-Robinson used its Denver office as a ticket outlet, gave two parties to promote the exhibition match and provided a meeting room for many of Combat Associates' meetings. Blinder personally appeared on a television talk show and gave television interviews to promote the match. Blinder-Robinson made no investment, accounting or other financial decisions; all such fiscal decisions were made by officers or employees of Combat Promotions, Inc., the general partner. The evidence established at most that Blinder-Robinson engaged in a few promotional activities. It does not establish that it took part in the management or control of the business affairs of the partnership. Accordingly, we agree with the Court of Appeals that the trial court erred in denying Blinder-Robinson's motion for judgment notwithstanding the verdict with respect to Alzado's first counterclaim.

The Revised Act further states that the possession or exercise of any powers not included in the preceding list does not necessarily constitute participation of the limited partner in the partnership business.

In the following case involving a limited partnership formed to promote an exhibition boxing match between Lyle Alzado and Muhammad Ali, who were at the time a professional football player and the world heavyweight boxing champion, respectively, the Supreme Court of Colorado found that a limited partner who was involved in promotional activities was not taking part in the control of the limited partnership.

Although limited partners have no right to manage the business of the partnership, they are granted certain rights under the Uniform Limited Partnership Act and the Revised Uniform Limited Partnership Act, including the statutory right to information regarding the partnership business. Limited partners are generally entitled to inspect the limited partnership records at any reasonable time.[7]

The Relationship Between General Partners and Limited Partners

Because limited partners are prohibited from participating in the control of the business, the relationship between general partners and limited partners differs significantly from the relationship among partners in a general partnership. General partners owe a fiduciary duty to limited partners, and the sole general partner of a limited partnership owes to limited partners an even greater duty than that normally imposed on partners, especially when the general partner holds a majority interest.[8] The duty of a general partner, acting in complete control, has been compared both to the fiduciary duty of a trustee to the beneficiaries of a trust, and to the fiduciary relationship of a corporate director to a shareholder.

One person may be both a general partner and a limited partner in the same partnership. In that event, the partner will have all of the rights and responsibilities of a general partner. However, his or her contribution to the partnership as a limited partner will be protected in the same manner as the contribution of any other limited partner.

§ 3.3 Advantages of Doing Business As a Limited Partnership

Limited partnerships have several unique advantages to offer both general and limited partners. In this section, we look at some of the more important advantages of doing business as a limited partnership, including the limited liability available to limited partners, potential income tax benefits, the relative transferability of partnership interests and continuity of business as compared to general partnerships, and the availability of diversified capital resources.

Limited Liability for Limited Partners

One of the best features of a limited partnership is the limited liability offered to its limited partners. Limited partners can invest money without becoming liable for the debts of the firm as long as they do not participate in the control of the business or hold themselves out to be general partners.

Income Tax Benefits

A limited partnership is usually not treated as a separate tax entity for federal income tax purposes. Therefore, limited partnerships can offer attractive tax advantages to both general and limited partners. The ability of the limited partnership to pass tax profits and losses directly to the limited partners, without the limited partners' risking anything more than their investment, can be a significant advantage over the corporate and general partnership tax structures. Although limited partnerships generally are not subject to federal income taxation, they are subject to state income taxation in many states.

Transferability of Partnership Interest

Although a partner's interest in a limited partnership is not as easily transferred as a corporate interest, the limited partner's interest is generally assignable with fewer restrictions than those imposed on the partners of a general partnership. The assignment of a limited partner's interest in a limited partnership does not necessarily cause a dissolution of the limited partnership. In some situations, the entire interest of the limited partner may be assigned, with the assignee becoming a substitute partner. There may be restrictions on this right, however, and the proper state statutes and limited partnership agreement must be consulted.

General partners also have certain rights to assign their interests in the limited partnership. Under the Revised Uniform Limited Partnership Act, a general partner may have all of the same rights of assignability as a limited partner, although certain assignments may be considered an event of withdrawal. In any event, the limited partnership offers much more flexibility with regard to the transfer of partnership interests than the general partnership.

Business Continuity

The limited partnership does not enjoy the continuity of business to the same extent as does a corporation, but it is not always necessary for a limited partnership to dissolve upon the death, retirement, or withdrawal of a partner. Under the original Uniform Limited Partnership Act, a limited partnership need not dissolve upon the death, retirement, or insanity of a general partner if the business is continued by the remaining general partners with the consent of all members, or if the right to continue the partnership is granted in the certificate of limited partnership.[9]

Under the Revised Uniform Limited Partnership Act, the limited partnership will not necessarily dissolve upon the withdrawal of a general partner if at the time (1) there is at least one other general partner, (2) the written provisions of the partnership agreement permit the business of the limited partnership to be carried on by the remaining general partner, and (3) that partner does so. In any event, the limited partnership need not be dissolved and is not required to be wound up by reason of any event of withdrawal if, "within 90 days after the withdrawal, all partners agree in writing to continue the business of the limited partnership and to the appointment of one or more additional general partners if necessary or desired."[10]

Diversified Capital Resources

In addition to the capital resources that are typically available to the general partnership, the limited partnership has the ability to raise initial capital by attracting passive investors. The limited partnership may raise additional capital when required by adding new limited partners.

§ 3.4 Disadvantages of Doing Business As a Limited Partnership

Although there are several advantages to doing business as a limited partnership, this type of entity also has some serious disadvantages. This section explains the disadvantages associated with operating as a limited partnership due to the unlimited liability of the general partners, the prohibition on control of the business by limited partners, the formalities and regulatory and reporting requirements, and the associated legal and organizational expenses.

Unlimited Liability

Because limited partners put at risk only their investment in the limited partnership, a limited partnership cannot exist without at least one general partner who has unlimited liability for the debts and obligations of the limited partnership. As discussed in previous chapters, there are ways to decrease the impact of unlimited personal liability. However, unlimited liability can still be a significant drawback.

Prohibition on Control of Business

Although every partner is entitled to an equal share of the management of a general partnership, limited partners must relinquish all control over partnership matters in order to maintain their status and enjoy limited liability. Limited partners must place their full trust in the general partners for the successful management and control of the business.

Formalities and Regulatory and Reporting Requirements

The limited partnership is a creature of statute and, as such, must be "created" by documentation filed with the proper state authority. A certificate of limited partnership must be executed, and filed, before the limited partnership's existence begins. Therefore, many more formalities are associated with the creation of a limited partnership than with a sole proprietorship or a general partnership. Limited partnerships are also often subject to many of the same reporting requirements as corporations.

Also, a limited partnership may be required to register or qualify to do business as a foreign limited partnership in any state, other than its state of domicile, in which it proposes to transact business. The registration or qualification requirements are set by the statutes of the state where the foreign limited partnership is proposing to transact business, and are often the same or similar to the requirements for foreign corporations transacting business in that state.[11] These requirements vary greatly from state to state, so the appropriate statutes must be consulted whenever a limited partnership is considering transacting business in a state other than its state of domicile.

Legal and Organizational Expenses

Compared with the sole proprietorship or general partnership, the legal and organizational expenses of a limited partnership can be quite substantial. In addition to the capital required for the ordinary expenses incurred in operating the limited partnership business, the founders of a limited partnership will usually incur significant legal fees for preparation of a limited partnership agreement and certificate, filing fees for the certificate of limited partnership, and possibly for filing a certificate of assumed name.

TABLE 3-1 LIMITED PARTNERSHIPS

Advantages	Disadvantages
▪ *Limited Liability for Limited Partners.* Limited partners have no personal liability for the debts and obligations of the limited partnership.	▪ *General Partners Do Not Have Limited Liability.* Every limited partnership must have at least one general partner who is personally liable for the debts and obligations of the limited partnership.
▪ *Income Tax Benefits.* Not subject to federal income taxation. Income "flows through" to the partners.	▪ *May Be Subject to State Income Taxation.*
▪ *Transferability of Partnership Interest.* Compared with general partnerships, limited partners have much more freedom to transfer their interests in the limited partnership.	▪ *Prohibition on Control of Business.* Limited partners may not be involved in the management of the limited partnership.
▪ *Business Continuity.* In contrast to the general partnership or sole proprietorship, the limited partnership offers much more continuity of business.	▪ *Formalities and Regulatory and Reporting Requirements.* Limited partnerships can not exist until the proper documentation is filed at the state level. In addition, limited partnerships may be subject to various reporting requirements that are not imposed on sole proprietorships and general partnerships.
▪ *Diversified Capital Resources.* Unlike sole proprietorships and general partnerships, limited partnerships have the ability to attract passive investors who accept no personal liability.	▪ *Legal and Organizational Expense.* The legal and organizational expenses associated with forming and maintaining a limited partnership are typically considerably more than those associated with partnerships and sole proprietorships.

§ 3.5 Organization and Management of a Limited Partnership

The organization and management of a limited partnership are unlike that of any other type of entity. This section discusses the management and control of the limited partnership by the general partners, the preparation and filing of the limited partnership certificate, and the contents of the limited partnership agreement.

Management and Control

The management and control of a limited partnership are similar to that of a general partnership, with one important distinction: only the general partners of the limited partnership have control of the partnership business.

Limited Partnership Certificate

The document that is filed with the Secretary of State or other appropriate state authority to form the limited partnership is called the **limited partnership certificate**. This document may include the entire agreement between the partners, but more commonly it contains the minimum amount of information required by state statute, with the full agreement of the partners contained in a limited partnership agreement or in other documents that are not filed for public record.

Under the original Uniform Limited Partnership Act, the limited partnership certificate must contain the following information:

1. The name of the partnership
2. The character of the business
3. The location of the principal place of business
4. The name and place of residence of each member, with general and limited partners being respectively designated
5. The term for which the partnership is to exist
6. The amount of cash and a description and the agreed value of the other property contributed by each limited partner
7. The additional contributions, if any, agreed to be made by each limited partner and the times at which or events on the happening of which such contributions shall be made
8. The time, if agreed upon, when the contribution of each limited partner is to be returned
9. The share of the profits or the other compensation by way of income that each limited partner is to receive by reason of his or her contribution

---

TERMS

limited partnership certificate   Document required to be filed with the Secretary of State or other appropriate state authority to form a limited partnership.

10. The right, if given, of limited partners to substitute assignees as contributors in their places, and the terms and conditions of the substitution

11. The right, if given, of the partners to admit additional limited partners

12. The right, if given, of one or more of the limited partners to priority over other limited partners, as to contributions or as to compensation by way of income, and the nature of such priority

13. The right, if given, of the remaining general partner or partners to continue the business after the death, retirement, or insanity of a general partner

14. The right, if given, of a limited partner to demand and receive property other than cash in return for his or her contribution.[12]

Under the Revised Uniform Limited Partnership Act, many of the provisions previously required to be included in the limited partnership certificate may instead be included in the limited partnership agreement or records kept by the limited partnership. They need not be made public in the limited partnership certificate. In states that have adopted the Revised Uniform Limited Partnership Act, the certificate of limited partnership must include the following:

1. The name of the limited partnership

2. The office address and the name and address of the agent for service of process

3. The name and business address of each general partner

4. The latest date upon which the limited partnership is to dissolve

5. Any other matters the general partners desire to include in the certificate.[13]

The limited partnership certificate in Figure 3-1 is an example of a limited partnership certificate that could be filed in a state following the Revised Uniform Limited Partnership Act.

In addition, under the Revised Uniform Limited Partnership Act, the following records must be kept at a partnership office which has been designated as the office where the partnership records are kept:

1. A current list of the names and business addresses of all partners. This list must identify the general partners, in alphabetical order, and separately list, in alphabetical order, the limited partners.

2. A copy of the certificate of limited partnership and all certificates of amendment thereto, together with executed copies of any powers of attorney pursuant to which any certificate has been executed.

FIGURE 3-1
Limited
Partnership
Certificate

LIMITED PARTNERSHIP CERTIFICATE

1. The name of the limited partnership is _____.

2. The office address of the principal place of business of the limited partnership is: _____.

3. The name and office address of the agent for service of process are: _____.

4. The name and business address of each general partner are as follows:

Name   Address

                                              _____

                                              _____

                                              _____

5. The latest date upon which the limited partnership is to dissolve is _____ , 19___.

Signed this ___day of _____ , 19___ .

GENERAL PARTNERS:

                                              _____

                                              _____

                                              _____

---

3. Copies of the limited partnership's federal, state, and local income tax returns and reports, if any, for the three most recent years.

4. Copies of any effective written partnership agreements.

5. Copies of any financial statements of the limited partnership for the three most recent years.[14]

The following information must be set out in a writing kept at the partnership office, unless it is contained in the limited partnership agreement:

1. The amount of cash and a description and statement of the agreed value of any other property or services contributed by each partner and which each partner has agreed to contribute.

2. The times at which or events on the happening of which any additional contributions agreed to be made by each partner are to be made.

3. Any rights of partners to receive, or of a general partner to make, distributions, which include a return of all or any part of the partner's contribution.

4. Any events upon the happening of which the limited partnership is to be dissolved and its affairs wound up.[15]

These records must be kept and are subject to inspection and copying at the reasonable request and at the expense of any partner during ordinary business hours.

Execution and Filing of the Limited Partnership Certificate

Under the Uniform Limited Partnership Act, two persons desiring to form a limited partnership must sign and swear to the certificate.[16] The Revised Uniform Limited Partnership Act differs from the original Act in that the limited partnership certificate need only be signed by the general partner(s) of the limited partnership. The limited partnership certificate must be filed with the appropriate state authority, with the required filing fee, to be effective. In addition, any other filing requirements set forth in the state statutes must be complied with.

Amendment to Limited Partnership Certificate

The Uniform Limited Partnership Act and the Revised Uniform Limited Partnership Act both set forth events that necessitate the filing of an amendment to the limited partnership certificate and the requirements for the certificate of amendment itself.[17] In general, when any significant information that is included in the limited partnership certificate changes or when an error in the information on the limited partnership certificate is detected, an amendment must be filed. Under most circumstances, any amendment to the limited partnership certificate must be approved and executed by all partners.

Limited Partnership Agreement

The limited partnership agreement should encompass the entire agreement among all partners. This document usually goes into much more detail than the limited partnership certificate, because it is not a document of public record that is filed with the state, and because it is more easily amended than the limited partnership certificate.

Following is a discussion of some of the various matters that should be contained in a limited partnership agreement. The examples used in the following sections are only a small representation of the type of paragraphs and clauses that may be included in a limited partnership agreement. See Appendix G-2 of this text for a limited partnership agreement form.

Name of Limited Partnership

The full name of the limited partnership should be set forth in this section. Special consideration must be given to the name of a limited partnership, for several reasons. First, the name chosen for the limited partnership must be available. A call to the appropriate state authority will usually verify the availability of a proposed name. (See Appendix A of this text for a Secretary of State directory.)

Second, state statutes may require that the name of the limited partnership contain the words "limited partnership" or other specific language. Finally, the name of the limited partnership may not contain the name of a limited partner unless it is also the name of a general partner or the corporate name of a corporate general partner, or the business of the limited partnership was carried on under that name before the admission of that limited partner. The appropriate state statutes must be consulted to be certain that all requirements regarding the name of the limited partnership are complied with.

Names and Addresses of Partners and Designation of Partnership Status

This section of the partnership agreement should contain the names and addresses of all partners and, most importantly, the designation as to which partners are general partners, which partners are limited partners, and which partners (if any) are both.

Purpose of Partnership

Neither the Uniform Limited Partnership Act nor the Revised Uniform Limited Partnership Act places any restrictions on the nature of business that may be carried on by a limited partnership. Both acts simply state that a limited partnership may carry on any business that can be transacted by a general partnership.[18] However, the statutes of some states may prohibit certain regulated industries, such as insurance or banking, from transacting business as a limited partnership.

This section of the limited partnership agreement should set forth the purpose of the limited partnership, without being restrictively specific.

EXAMPLE: *Partnership Purpose—Generally*

The parties do hereby form a limited partnership under the provisions of [the Uniform Limited Partnership Act or the Revised Uniform Limited Partnership Act] of the State of _____ to conduct the business of _____ , and any other lawful activity that the general partners deem advisable, under the business name of _____ .

The above-enumerated purposes shall not be construed as limiting or restricting in any manner the purposes in which this partnership may engage, and the partnership shall always have the power to engage in any purpose incidental to the specific purposes designated above.[19]

Principal Place of Business

This section should set forth the address of the partnership's principal place of business. This is important because certain documents are required by law to be kept at the principal place of business of the limited partnership.

Duration of Limited Partnership Agreement

This section should set forth the intended duration of the limited partnership, as well as certain conditions that may cause the termination of the partnership.

EXAMPLE: *Duration of Partnership—Termination on Notice from a Partner*

The limited partnership shall commence on _____ , 19___ , and shall continue until terminated by ___ months' notice in writing from a partner desiring to withdraw from the partnership and requesting the partnership's termination. Outstanding partnership business shall be consummated and obligations discharged during the period between receipt of notice and the effective date of termination contained therein.[20]

Contributions of Both General and Limited Partners

This very important section of the agreement should set forth the partners' agreement regarding all contributions to the limited partnership, including the form of each contribution, any interest to be paid on contributions, any adjustment provisions for contributions, any additional contribution requirements, and the time when contributions are to be returned to limited partners. This section should also set forth any rights of partners to demand property in lieu of cash for a return of contribution.

EXAMPLE: Contribution to Partnership of Limited Partner

The contribution of _____ , one of the limited partners, shall be the sum of _____ dollars ($_____) in cash. _____ shall contribute no other property in addition to that contribution, and the contribution shall be returned at the termination of the limited partnership as provided below. _____ shall receive from the partnership no share of the profits, but as compensation by way of income _____ shall receive the sum of _____dollars ($_____) per year, to be paid monthly, provided, however, that after such payment is made the partnership assets are in excess of partnership liabilities, except liabilities to limited partners on account of their contribution and liabilities to general partners.[21]

Assets of Limited Partnership

All information regarding the assets of the limited partnership should be included in this section, including identification, valuation, control, and distribution of assets, and accountability therefor.

EXAMPLE: Distribution of Assets—Return of Contribution Plus
Increment on Dissolution

The contribution of each limited partner, increased by any gains and not withdrawn or decreased by losses, is to be returned upon the termination of the partnership in accordance with the terms of Section ___ , or upon any earlier dissolution of the partnership if caused by the death, retirement, or insanity of a general partner, provided, however, that at any such time all liabilities of the partnership, except liabilities to general partners and to limited partners on account of their contributions, shall have been paid, and that there shall then remain property of the partnership sufficient to make such return.[22]

EXAMPLE: Distribution of Assets—Proration if Assets Insufficient

If the property remaining following the payment of all liabilities of the partnership is not sufficient to repay in full all the partners' (general and limited) contributions adjusted to reflect accumulated gains or losses, then each of the partners shall receive such proportion of the remaining property as his, her, or their respective contribution, as adjusted, shall bear to the aggregate of all such adjusted partnership contributions that have not been repaid. In such event limited partners shall not have any further claim against the partners for the return of the balance of their contributions or credited gains.[23]

Liability

This section of the agreement should contain all provisions regarding the liability of general and limited partners to one another and to third parties.

EXAMPLE: Liability of Partner—Absorption of Losses from General Partner's Contributions

As between the parties hereto, all losses incurred by the partnership shall be borne by the general partners to the extent of and until their contributions to the partnership are exhausted. Only in the latter event shall the losses incurred by the partnership be chargeable to the capital contributions of the limited partners.[24]

EXAMPLE: Liability to Third Party—Limitation of Liability

Notwithstanding any other provision contained in this agreement, except to have her capital account charged for losses to be borne by her as provided herein, no limited partner shall have any personal responsibility whatever for or on account of any losses or liabilities of the partnership; and to the extent that losses and liabilities of the partnership exceed its assets such losses shall be borne solely by the general partners.[25]

Distribution of Profits and Losses to General and Limited Partners

This section should set forth the terms and conditions for distributions from the partnership, including restrictions on distributions and distributions made to various classes of partners.

EXAMPLE: Proportionate Distribution of Profits

The following schedule shall govern the distribution of the net profits of the partnership:

1. The first _____ dollars ($_____) of net profits, or such lesser amount as the partnership may earn during any fiscal year, shall be shared by the partners in accordance with the following schedule of allocations:
General Partners _____ percent (___%).
Limited Partners _____ percent (___%).
2. All net profits earned above _____ dollars ($_____) and up to and including _____ dollars ($_____), during any fiscal year, shall be shared by the partners in accordance with the following schedule of allocation:
General Partners _____ percent (___%).
Limited Partners _____ percent (___%).
3. All net profits above _____ dollars ($_____) shall be shared by the partners in accordance with the following schedule of allocation:
General Partners _____ percent (___%).
Limited Partners _____ percent (___%).
4. All sums allocated to the partners as salaries, commissions, and bonuses shall be deducted prior to the computation of net profits for this purpose, it being

deemed that all such salaries, bonuses, and commissions are to be considered as an expense of the partnership before the determination of net profits.

5. The allocation to the limited partners shall be divided among the limited partners ratably in accordance with their ownership as determined from the "Percentage Allocation of Interest Between Special Partners" as set out in Section ___.

6. The allocation to the general partners shall be divided among the general partners in the following proportions [set out names and percentages].[26]

Indemnity

This section should set forth the partners' agreement for indemnification of their expenses on behalf of the partnership.

Duties of General Partners

This section should set forth the duties of each general partner in as much detail as practical.

EXAMPLE: Duties of Partners—Devotion of Efforts to Firm—General Partners

The general partners at all times during the continuance of this partnership shall devote their best endeavors to the partnership business for the joint interest and advantage of the partnership and shall devote to the performance of such duty substantially their entire time, except for such periods as they may be prevented by illness or other emergencies, or as the general partners may agree on inter se.[27]

Duties of Limited Partners

This section should set forth the duties of any limited partners who are employees of the limited partnership. This section should be carefully drafted so that no misunderstanding arises regarding the inability of limited partners to control the partnership business.

Limited Partners' Rights of Substitution

This section should address all of the desired rights of partners to substitution, including the right to admit additional limited partners and priorities of certain limited partners over others.

EXAMPLE: Powers of Partners—Assignment of Limited Partner's Interest

A limited partner's interests shall be assignable in whole or in part. All limited partners shall have the right to confer upon the assignee of their interests or a part thereof the rights of a substituted limited partner as provided by the [Uniform Limited Partnership Act or Revised Uniform Limited Partnership Act] of the State of _____ [cite appropriate statute].[28]

Compensation and Benefits for Partners

This section should set forth all matters concerning the compensation of and benefits for general partners, including salaries, retirement benefits, health and other insurance, etc.

EXAMPLE: Salary—General Partner

Each of the general partners shall receive as a salary for the services rendered the sum of _____ dollars ($_____) per year, payable on the ___ and ___ of each month. The salary shall be treated as a business expense in the ascertainment of profits for distribution among the partners.[29]

Management and Control of Business by General Partners

This section should set forth the management and control policies of the limited partnership.

EXAMPLE: Limited Partners' Participation in Conduct of Business

No limited partner shall have any right to be active in the conduct of the partnership's business, or have power to bind the partnership in any contract, agreement, promise, or undertaking.[30]

Limited Partners' Rights in Review of Business Policies

This section should set forth the limited partnership's policy with regard to the limited partners' rights to review the business policies of the partnership.

Policies of Business

Any policies that the partners desire to set forth in a written agreement may be set forth in this section of the limited partnership agreement.

Accounting Practices and Procedures

This section should set forth all accounting methods, practices, and policies of the partnership, including the accounting period and fiscal year of the partnership, the frequency and types of reports to be completed, details regarding the books of accounts, audit provisions, and provisions for examination of books.

Changes in General or Limited Partners by Withdrawal, Expulsion, Retirement, or Death

In this very important section of the limited partnership agreement, the partners may set forth their desires regarding the admission of new general and limited partners, their acceptance requirements, and the redistribution of assets. This section should also address all matters concerning withdrawing partners, including the necessity of the consent of the other partners, notice requirements, valuation of the withdrawing partner's share of the partnership, the option of the remaining partners to purchase the interest, and the assignment of the withdrawing partner's interest to a third party. Partners may also want to include conditions for expulsion of a partner, notice requirements, and all other matters concerning the expulsion of a partner.

The partnership's policy regarding a retiring partner should likewise be addressed in this section, including the reorganization of partnership rights and duties.

EXAMPLE: New Limited Partner

Amendments to the certificate of limited partnership of the partnership for the purpose of substituting a limited partner will be validly made if signed only by the general partners and by the person to be substituted and by the assigning limited partner. If any one or all general partners resign or are expelled or otherwise cease to be a general partner under the provision of this agreement, and pursuant to this agreement a new general partner or partners are elected, the amendment to the certificate to make the change will be validly made if signed only by the remaining general partner and the new general partner or by the new general partners.[31]

EXAMPLE: Expulsion of Partner by Vote of Limited Partners

Upon the vote of limited partners holding a majority in interest of the partnership, a general partner may be expelled as a general partner of the partnership and a new general partner may be elected by the same vote.[32]

Sale or Purchase of Limited Partnership Interest

This section of the partnership agreement should set forth the partners' desires with regard to the sale of new limited partners' interests, either to replace a withdrawing limited partner or to add new limited partners to raise additional capital for the partnership. It may also contain provisions for the purchase of a withdrawing limited partner's interest by the limited partnership.

Termination of Limited Partnership

This section should set forth the desired provisions regarding termination of the limited partnership.

Dissolution and Winding Up

This section should set forth the desired provisions regarding the dissolution and winding up of the limited partnership, including the settlement and distribution of partnership assets.

EXAMPLE: Winding Up—Distribution of Assets

Upon dissolution or termination of the partnership, after the liabilities shall have been paid, payment shall be made to the partners in the following order: (1) To the limited partners the sums to which they are entitled by way of interest on their capital contributions on their share of profits; (2) to the limited partners the amount of their capital contributions; (3) to the general partners such sums as may be due, if any other than for capital and profits; (4) to the general partners the amount they are entitled to receive as interest on their capital contributions and as profits; and (5) to the general partners for their capital contributions.[33]

Date of Agreement and Signatures

The limited partnership agreement should be dated and signed by all partners, both general and limited.

The following case involves a dispute over the contents of a limited partnership agreement. It illustrates the importance of the contents of the limited partnership agreement, especially with regard to the rights of the limited partners.

§ 3.6 Changes in Partnership

Many types of changes in the limited partnership affect the continuance of the limited partnership. This section examines the effects of common changes on the limited partnership, including the admission of new general partners, the admission of new limited partners, and the withdrawal of both general and limited partners.

DIAMOND PARKING
v.
FRONTIER BLDG. LTD.
Court of Appeals of Washington
864 P.2d 954 (Wash. App. Div. I 1993)
December 30, 1993
Forrest, Judge

... Diamond Parking, Inc., (Diamond) appeals the trial court's order granting Frontier Building Limited Partnership's summary judgment motion, contending that the amendment to the original partnership agreement (1) violated partnership law and the agreement's provisions and (2) material facts exist showing the general partners breached their fiduciary duty in proposing and gaining passage of the amendment.

In 1981, Diamond Parking, Inc., and six other parties signed a partnership agreement (Original Agreement) creating a real estate partnership, Frontier Building Limited Partnership (Frontier). Frontier's purpose was to acquire two adjoining properties in Anchorage, Alaska and develop them as commercial office space in stages labeled Phase I and Phase II.

Diamond provided an initial $1.5 million capital contribution toward the $10 million total capital raised among the other limited partners. In addition, Diamond contributed over $50,000 of additional capital since 1980. Limited Partners received a pro rata interest based on their contributions. Two general partners, John H. Resing (Resing) and Rainier-Associates-Frontier Building (RAFB) were named in the agreement and received approximately 25% interest in the partnership.

The Original Agreement vested the general partners with authority over the management, control of the business and affairs of the partnership. However, to make certain "major decisions," including amending the Original Agreement or admitting new general partners, the general partners had to obtain the prior written consent of the limited partners owning 70 percent of the total limited partner interest.

When the Anchorage real estate market became depressed in 1988, Frontier's expenses began to exceed its income ... . In the spring and summer of 1989, after having investigated additional means of raising the needed funds, and realizing the limited partners were reluctant to make additional capital contributions, the general partners devised an amendment to restructure the partnership.

The proposed restructuring offered those limited partners willing to risk more capital a "substantial profit opportunity" and re-labeled them Class A limited partners. The amendment essentially divided the partnership interest into three groups: Class B limited partners would retain a collective 5 percent interest. Class A limited partners, would receive an 85 percent interest, and general partners were entitled to a 10 percent interest. ...

Four of the limited partners owning approximately 74 percent of partnership units voted in favor of the amendment. Diamond did not vote and refused to purchase Class A units.

Diamond's interest was diluted from approximately 10 percent to 0.65 percent and its capital account was adjusted from $1.5 million to $56,250 ... .

Diamond filed suit in superior court alleging (1) the less than unanimous adoption of the 1989 amendment was wrongful and violated partnership law and/or the Original Agreement, (2) general and limited partners acceding to the amendment breached their fiduciary duty owed to Diamond. ...

Frontier moved for summary judgment, which the superior court granted. The trial court based its dismissal of Diamond's claims on the grounds that (1) the changes effectuated by the restructuring agreement were within the scope of the terms of the Original Agreement ... .

DISCUSSION

... At trial, Diamond's principal contention was that the partnership amendment was so grossly unfair that as a matter of law Diamond was entitled to relief. This contention is essentially abandoned on appeal and correctly so. A partnership agreement is the law of the partnership. Nothing in the amendment violates the partnership act. ... Like all the partners, he was presented with a business decision as to whether to invest more money in hopes of salvaging an investment that was in financial difficulty. Having elected not to make any further investment, he has no legal cause of complaint for the reduction of his interest in the partnership.

... On appeal Diamond's chief contention is that the general partners breached their fiduciary duty to the limited partners because they had a conflict of interest with regard to, and failed to make full disclosure of the material facts concerning, the proposed amendment and that therefore he is entitled to some form of relief.

... We agree that the general partners owe limited partners a fiduciary duty described as *the highest standard of conduct*. ... The main elements of the partners fiduciary duty are well recognized: utmost good faith, fairness, and loyalty. ... However general statements as to fiduciary duty are not very helpful on these facts.

Here the unusual and dispositive fact is that the direct cause of any damage to Diamond flowed from the votes of his fellow limited partners and not from the general partners' unilateral actions. In light of this fact, Diamond's theory that he was damaged by any breach of the general partners' fiduciary duty is peculiar indeed. Diamond cannot claim that he was in any way misled because he abstained from voting which is the equivalent of voting against. So his claim is reduced to assertions that a more complete disclosure including the alleged conflict of interest would have led enough of the other limited partners to oppose the amendment to defeat it. The fatal flaw with this theory is that there is not a shred of evidence to support it. ...

Accordingly, we affirm the trial court's grant of summary judgment, finding that no genuine issues of fact exist as to Diamond's various claims.

GROSSE and AGID, J.J. concur.

Admission of New General Partners

The requirements for admitting new general partners vary from state to state and depend especially upon which form of the Uniform Limited Partnership Act has been adopted by the state in question. In general, in states following the original Uniform Limited Partnership Act, partnerships may admit general partners only by the unanimous written consent of all partners or by consent of all general partners and ratification of the act by all limited partners. Typically, in states following the Revised Uniform Limited Partnership Act, general partners may be admitted with the written consent of all partners, or by another means set forth in the limited partnership agreement.

Admission of New Limited Partners

With regard to the admission of additional limited partners, states following the original Uniform Limited Partnership Act generally require that an amendment to the limited partnership certificate be filed before a new limited partner can be added.[34] This, in effect, requires the approval of all partners, because that approval is required for amending the limited partnership certificate. However, in states following the Revised Uniform Limited Partnership Act, an additional limited partner may be admitted in compliance with the provisions of the limited partnership agreement. If such an event is not provided for in the limited partnership agreement, an additional limited partner may also be admitted by the written consent of all partners.[35] Amendment of the limited partnership certificate is not necessary because the names of the limited partners do not have to be set forth in the limited partnership certificate. The Revised Uniform Limited Partnership Act also provides that the assignee of a limited partner's interest in a limited partnership may become a limited partner to the extent that the assignor gives the assignee that right, or if all other partners consent.

Withdrawal of General Partners

As with the general partnership, the death or withdrawal of a general partner generally causes the dissolution of a limited partnership. However, there are many exceptions to this rule.[36]

A general partner may withdraw from a limited partnership at any time by giving written notice to the other partners. However, if a general partner withdraws from the partnership in violation of the terms of the limited partnership agreement, the limited partnership may recover damages from the withdrawing partner for breach of the partnership agreement, and those damages may be used to offset any distribution to which the withdrawing general partner is otherwise entitled.

Withdrawal of Limited Partners

The limited partnership is not dissolved upon the death or withdrawal of a limited partner. In the event of the death of a limited partner, the executor, representative, or administrator of the deceased limited partner's estate succeeds to all of the decedent's rights for the purpose of settling the estate.

A limited partner may generally withdraw at the time specified in the partnership agreement or in another agreement entered into by the partners. If no definite time is specified in the partnership agreement for the permitted withdrawal of a limited partner, and no event that would cause the withdrawal of a limited partner is specified, a limited partner may generally withdraw at any time with six months' notice to each general partner.[37]

Upon withdrawal, the withdrawing partner is entitled to receive the distribution as set forth in the limited partnership agreement. Pursuant to the Revised Uniform Limited Partnership Act, if the amount of distribution is not provided for in the limited partnership agreement, the withdrawing partner is entitled to receive the fair value of his or her interest in the limited partnership based upon his or her right to share in distributions from the limited partnership.[38] The original Uniform Limited Partnership Act does not set forth the distributive share of a withdrawing partner in the absence of a provision in the limited partnership agreement.

The distribution to which each partner is entitled under the partnership agreement will be in cash, unless otherwise indicated in the partnership agreement.

§ 3.7 Financial Structure of a Limited Partnership

The financial structure of a limited partnership is typically more complex than that of either a sole proprietorship or a general partnership. This section focuses on the capital of the limited partnership, the withdrawal of contributions from the limited partnership, and limited partnership profits and losses.

Partnership Capital Contributions

A basic concept of the limited partnership is that a limited partner must "make a stated contribution to the partnership, and place it at risk."[39] Under the original Uniform Limited Partnership Act, limited partners are allowed to contribute cash or other property, but not services.[40] This restriction was not carried through to the Revised Uniform Limited Partnership Act.

The Revised Uniform Limited Partnership Act specifically states that the contribution may also be in the form of a "promissory note or other obligation to contribute cash or property or perform services."[41] Any promise made by a limited partner to contribute to the limited partnership must be in writing if it is to be enforceable.

Withdrawal of Contributions

Terms and conditions for disbursements and the withdrawal of contributions prior to dissolution of the limited partnership are typically set forth in either the limited partnership certificate or the limited partnership agreement. However, there are certain statutory restrictions on the withdrawal of contributions. Under the Uniform Limited Partnership Act, no disbursements to or withdrawals of contributions by limited partners are allowed unless all liabilities of the partnership, except those to general partners and those to limited partners on account of their contributions, have been paid or there remains sufficient partnership property to pay them.[42] Under the Revised Uniform Limited Partnership Act, distributions to partners are forbidden except to the extent that, after giving effect to the distribution, all liabilities, other than those to partners on account of their interests, exceed the fair value of the partnership assets.

Profits and Losses

The profits and losses of the limited partnership are shared among the partners pursuant to the partnership agreement or certificate. The Revised Uniform Limited Partnership Act provides that the profits and losses of a limited partnership shall be allocated among the partners in the manner provided in writing in the partnership agreement. If the partnership agreement does not specify a manner for allocating profits and losses, they shall be allocated on the basis of the value, as stated in the partnership records, of the contributions made by each partner to the extent they have been received by the partnership and have not been returned.[43]

§ 3.8 Derivative Actions

A **derivative action** is an action brought by a limited partner in the right of a limited partnership to recover a judgment in its favor. Although the original Uniform Limited Partnership Act had no provisions for derivative actions, the Revised Uniform Limited Partnership Act expressly

---

TERMS

derivative action An action brought by one or more stockholders of a corporation to enforce a corporate right or to remedy a wrong to the corporation, when the corporation, because it is controlled by wrongdoers or for other reasons, fails to take action.

grants limited partners the right to bring an action on behalf of the limited partnership if the general partners with authority have refused to bring an action or if an effort to cause those general partners to bring the action is not likely to succeed.[44] A derivative action may be needed when the general partner to the partnership has a conflict of interest that would prevent or discourage the general partner from bringing an action on behalf of the limited partnership.

Derivative actions are not accepted or permitted in all states. A few jurisdictions apply a strict interpretation of the original Uniform Limited Partnership Act, holding that only a general partner may maintain an action on behalf of the partnership, leaving the limited partner to pursue redress of any wrong through dissolution or individual action against the wrongdoer.[45]

The plaintiff to a derivative suit must be a partner at the time the action is brought and must have been a partner at the time of the transaction of which the plaintiff complains, or the plaintiff's status as a partner "must have devolved upon him by operation of law or pursuant to the terms of the partnership agreement from a person who was a partner at the time of the transaction."[46]

§ 3.9 Dissolution, Winding Up, and Termination of the Limited Partnership

The process of terminating a limited partnership involves several steps. This section investigates the termination process, including the distinction between limited partnership dissolution and winding up, the causes of dissolution, cancellation of the limited partnership certificate, winding up the affairs of the limited partnership, and settlement and distribution of the assets of the limited partnership.

Dissolution Versus Winding Up

As with the general partnership, once a limited partnership has been dissolved, the partnership does not terminate until the affairs of the limited partnership have been wound up.

Causes of Dissolution

The original Uniform Limited Partnership Act states that dissolution of the limited partnership occurs on the retirement, death, or insanity of a general partner, unless the business is continued by the remaining general partners under a right to do so stated in the certificate of limited partnership, or with the consent of all members.[47]

The Revised Uniform Limited Partnership Act provides that a limited partnership is dissolved, and its affairs must be wound up, when the first of the following events occurs:

1. The time period specified in the certificate expires
2. Specific events specified in writing in the certificate occur
3. All the partners consent in writing to dissolve the partnership
4. An event of withdrawal of a general partner occurs
5. A decree of judicial dissolution is entered.[48]

An *event of withdrawal,* as that term is used in the Revised Uniform Limited Partnership Act, refers to:

1. The general partner's voluntary withdrawal
2. Assignment of the general partner's interest
3. Removal of the general partner in accordance with the partnership agreement
4. Unless otherwise provided in the certificate of limited partnership, any one of several specified occurrences indicative of the general partner's insolvency (the filing of a voluntary bankruptcy, for instance)
5. Unless otherwise provided in the certificate of limited partnership, the fact that any of several specified conditions indicative of insolvency has endured longer than a specified time (for instance, a proceeding to liquidate the general partner has not been dismissed within 120 days or the appointment of a receiver has not been vacated or stayed within 90 days)
6. In the case of a general partner who is an individual, her death or an adjudication that she is incompetent to manage her person or estate
7. In the case of a general partner acting as such by virtue of being the trustee of a trust, the termination of the trust
8. In the case of a general partner that is a separate partnership, its dissolution and the commencement of its winding up
9. In the case of a general partner that is a corporation, the filing of a certificate of its dissolution (or the equivalent) or the revocation of its charter
10. In the case of an estate, the distribution by the fiduciary of the estate's entire interest in the partnership.[49]

However, the Revised Uniform Limited Partnership Act also states that an event of withdrawal does not cause dissolution if there is at least one other general partner and there is permission in the certificate for the business to be carried on, or if, within ninety days after such an event, all partners agree in writing to continue the business. If all partners agree to continue the business, they may appoint one or more additional general partners if necessary or desirable.

Under the original Uniform Limited Partnership Act, a limited partner has the right to have the partnership dissolved and wound up by court decree when the limited partner's rightful demand for return of contribution is not met, or when the limited partner would be entitled to its return by the fact that the liabilities have not been paid and the partnership property is insufficient for their payment. Under the Revised Uniform Limited Partnership Act, the limited partner may apply for a court decree to dissolve a limited partnership whenever it is not reasonably practicable to carry on the business of the limited partnership in conformity with the partnership agreement.

Cancellation of Certificate of Limited Partnership

Because a limited partnership is created by the certificate of limited partnership that is filed with the Secretary of State or other state authority, the certificate of limited partnership must be canceled before the limited partnership is terminated. The certificate of limited partnership is canceled upon the dissolution of the limited partnership and the commencement of its winding up, or at any other time that there are no limited partners. The certificate is canceled by means of a certificate of cancellation, which is filed with the Secretary of State and must contain:

1. The name of the limited partnership
2. The date of filing of the certificate of limited partnership
3. The reason for filing the certificate of cancellation
4. The effective date of cancellation, if not effective upon filing the certificate
5. Any other information determined by the general partners filing the certificate.[50]

The certificate must be signed by all general partners.

Winding Up

Under the Revised Uniform Limited Partnership Act, "the general partners who have not wrongfully dissolved a limited partnership or, if none, the limited partners, may wind up the limited partnership's affairs."[51] Any partner or any partner's legal representative or assignee may also make application to an appropriate court to wind up the limited partnership's affairs.

Settlement and Distribution of Assets

Under § 23 of the original Uniform Limited Partnership Act, the accounts of the partnership are settled in the following order after a dissolution:

1. Those to creditors, in the order of priority as provided by law, except those to limited partners on account of their contributions, and to general partners
2. Those to limited partners in respect to their share of the profits and other compensation by way of income on their contributions
3. Those to limited partners in respect to the capital of their contributions
4. Those to general partners other than for capital and profits
5. Those to general partners in respect to profits
6. Those to general partners in respect to capital.

Unless the certificate or a subsequent agreement provides otherwise, limited partners share in the partnership assets in respect to their claims for capital. In respect to their claims for profits or compensation, limited partners share by way of income on their contributions.

Under § 408 of the Revised Uniform Limited Partnership Act, the assets of the limited partnership are distributed in the following order upon dissolution:

1. To creditors, including partners who are creditors, to the extent permitted by law, in satisfaction of liabilities of the limited partnership other than liabilities for distributions to partners under §§ 601 or 604; otherwise permitted by law, in satisfaction of liabilities other than interim distributions and distributions on withdrawal
2. Except as provided in the partnership agreement, to partners and former partners in satisfaction of liabilities for distributions under §§ 601 or 604
3. Except as provided in the partnership agreement, to partners first for the return of their contributions and secondly respecting their partnership interests, in the proportions in which the partners share distributions.

§ 3.10 The Role of the Legal Assistant in Limited Partnership Matters

The role of the legal assistant in working with limited partnerships is very similar to that in working with general partnerships, with a few additions. The legal assistant may be asked to help draft the limited partnership agreement, usually with the aid of office forms and examples of previously drafted limited partnership agreements. Following is a checklist of items to be considered when drafting a limited partnership agreement.

LIMITED PARTNERSHIP AGREEMENT CHECKLIST

- ☐ Name and address of each limited partner and each general partner and a designation of partnership status.
- ☐ Name of the limited partnership.
- ☐ Purpose of the limited partnership.
- ☐ Address of principal place of business of the limited partnership.
- ☐ Duration of limited partnership agreement.
- ☐ Contributions of both general partners and limited partners.
- ☐ Limited partnership assets.
- ☐ Liability of general partners and limited partners to each other and third parties.
- ☐ Distribution of profits and losses to general and limited partners.
- ☐ Indemnification of partners.
- ☐ Duties of general partners.
- ☐ Duties of limited partners.
- ☐ Limited partners' rights of substitution.
- ☐ Limitation on powers.
- ☐ General partner compensation.
- ☐ Partnership expenses.
- ☐ Management and control of business by general partners.
- ☐ Limited partners' rights in review of business policies.
- ☐ Business policies.
- ☐ Accounting practices and procedures.
- ☐ Changes in general or limited partners by withdrawal, expulsion, retirement, or death.
- ☐ Sale or purchase of limited partnership interest.
- ☐ Arbitration provisions.
- ☐ Termination of limited partnership.
- ☐ Dissolution and winding up.
- ☐ Date of agreement.
- ☐ Signatures of all general and limited partners.

The legal assistant may also be responsible for filing the limited partnership certificate pursuant to state statutes. If there are any publication or county recording requirements for the limited partnership certificate, it will often be the legal assistant's responsibility to see that those requirements are complied with as well.

The legal assistant must be well acquainted with the state statutory requirements for limited partnerships, as well as the procedural requirements at the state level. In addition, the legal assistant must be aware of any requirements for qualifying the limited partnership as a foreign limited partnership in other states in which the limited partnership intends to transact business.

§ 3.11 Resources

Numerous resources are available to the legal assistant working with limited partnerships. This section lists some of the more crucial resources, including state statutes, legal form books, and information available from the office of the Secretary of State, state and local government offices, and the Internal Revenue Service.

State Statutes

It is always important to be familiar with the state statutes of the limited partnership's state of domicile, especially since the provisions of the limited partnership acts vary greatly, depending on which version is followed. Here is a list of the statutory citations of the uniform partnership acts that have been adopted in each state, as well as an indication of which uniform act is followed by each state.

Ala. Code § 10-9A-1 *et seq.*	RULPA
Alaska Stat. § 32.11.010 *et seq.*	RULPA
Ariz. Rev. Stat. Ann. § 29-301 *et seq.*	RULPA
Ark. Code Ann. § 4-43-101 *et seq.*	RULPA
Cal. Corp. Code § 15611 *et seq.*	RULPA
Colo. Rev. Stat. § 7-62-101 *et seq.*	RULPA
Conn. Gen. Stat. § 34-9 *et seq.*	RULPA
Del. Code Ann. tit. 6, § 17-101 *et seq.*	RULPA
D.C. Code Ann. § 41-401 *et seq.*	RULPA
Fla. Stat. Ann. § 620.101 *et seq.*	RULPA
Ga. Code Ann. § 14-9-100 *et seq.*	RULPA
Haw. Rev. Stat. § 425D-101 *et seq.*	RULPA
Idaho Code § 53-201 *et seq.*	RULPA

Ill. Rev. Stat. ch. 106 ½, para. 151-1 *et seq.*	RULPA
Ind. Code § 23-16-1-1 *et seq.*	RULPA
Iowa Code § 545.101 *et seq.*	RULPA
Kan. Stat. Ann. § 56-1a101 *et seq.*	RULPA
Ky. Rev. Stat. Ann. § 362.401 *et seq.*	RULPA
Me. Rev. Stat. Ann. tit. 31, § 401 *et seq.*	RULPA
Md. Corps. & Ass'ns § 10-101 *et seq.*	RULPA
Mass. Gen. L. ch. 109, § 1 *et seq.*	RULPA
Mich. Comp. Laws § 449.1101 *et seq.*	RULPA
Minn. Stat. § 322A.01 *et seq.*	RULPA
Miss. Code Ann. § 79-14-101 *et seq.*	RULPA
Mo. Rev. Stat. § 359.011 *et seq.*	RULPA
Mont. Code Ann. § 35-12-501 *et seq.*	RULPA
Neb. Rev. Stat. § 67-233 *et seq.*	RULPA
Nev. Rev. Stat. § 88.315 *et seq.*	RULPA
N.H. Rev. Stat. Ann. § 304-B:1 *et seq.*	RULPA
N.J. Rev. Stat. § 42:2A-1 *et seq.*	RULPA
N.M. Stat. Ann. § 54-2-1 *et seq.*	RULPA
N.Y. Partnership Law § 121-101 *et seq.*	RULPA
N.C. Gen. Stat. § 59-101 *et seq.*	RULPA
N.D. Cent. Code § 45-10.1-01 *et seq.*	RULPA
Ohio Rev. Code Ann. § 1782.01 *et seq.*	RULPA
Okla. Stat. tit. 54, § 301 *et seq.*	RULPA
Or. Rev. Stat. § 70.005 *et seq.*	RULPA
15 Pa. Cons. Stat. Ann. § 8501 *et seq.*	RULPA
R.I. Gen. Laws § 7-13-1 *et seq.*	RULPA
S.C. Code Ann. § 33-42-10 *et seq.*	RULPA
S.D. Codified Laws Ann. § 48-7-101 *et seq.*	RULPA
Tenn. Code Ann. § 61-2-101 *et seq.*	RULPA
Tex. Rev. Civ. Stat. Ann. art. 6132a-1	RULPA
Utah Code Ann. § 48-2a-101 *et seq.*	RULPA
Vt. Stat. Ann. tit. 11, § 1391 *et seq.*	RULPA
Va. Code Ann. § 50-73.1 *et seq.*	RULPA
Wash. Rev. Code § 25.10.010 *et seq.*	RULPA
W. Va. Code § 47-9-1 *et seq.*	RULPA
Wis. Stat. § 179.01 *et seq.*	RULPA
Wyo. Stat. § 17-14-201 *et seq.*	RULPA

Louisiana limited partnerships are governed by La. Rev. Stat. Ann. § 9:3401 *et seq.*

Legal Form Books

Because a limited partnership is formed only by the filing of a certificate of limited partnership, the drafting of a suitable certificate and the limited partnership agreement are vital. As well as limited partnership certificates and agreements previously drafted by the law firm, legal form books can be an excellent resource for finding appropriate forms and optional language to use in limited partnership documents.[52]

Secretary of State or Other Appropriate State Authority

Because the limited partnership certificate must be filed with the Secretary of State or other appropriate state authority, the appropriate state office must be contacted to inquire as to the proper filing procedures and fees. Often, the appropriate state office will also have forms and guidelines available. See Appendix A of this text for a Secretary of State directory.

Government Tax Offices

As when working with a general partnership, it is important that the appropriate state offices be contacted regarding state income taxation matters. It is also advisable to contact the local Internal Revenue Service office to request information regarding the income tax filing requirements for limited partnerships.

Review Questions

1. Is a limited partnership treated as a separate entity for all purposes? If not, give an example of an instance in which a limited partnership is treated under the aggregate theory.

2. Why is the fiduciary duty between the general partner and limited partners even greater than the fiduciary duty between partners in a general partnership?

3. Suppose that Beth Henderson is a limited partner of the ABC Limited Partnership, a limited partnership formed for the purpose of purchasing and developing real estate. Beth wanted to be a limited partner because she has considerable personal assets that she wants to protect. Soon after the formation of the limited partnership, Beth becomes concerned about its management by the general partners. She starts attending the general partners' meetings and participating in all major decisions concerning the limited

partnership. However, the partnership becomes insolvent anyway. Creditors are left with thousands of dollars' worth of unpaid bills. The limited partnership and the general partners have no substantial cash or other assets. Might creditors prevail in a lawsuit against Beth Henderson to recover their losses? Why or why not?

4. Brian, Jeanne, and William have formed OakRidge Limited Partnership, a limited partnership for shopping center development and management. William is the general partner and Brian and Jeanne are limited partners. The limited partnership is about to enter into an agreement to purchase a new shopping center; however, the bank that is lending them the money wants personal guarantees from each partner. If the limited partnership is governed by the laws of a state that follows the Revised Uniform Limited Partnership Act, would Brian and Jeanne be able to guarantee the obligation of the OakRidge Limited Partnership without risking their limited liability status?

5. Suppose that Jake, Bryan, and Jill decide to form a limited partnership for the purpose of owning and operating a liquor store. They are all concerned about their personal liability, so they decide that they will all be limited partners. Would this be possible? Why or why not? What if Jill agreed to be both a general partner and a limited partner?

6. Why might a limited partnership want to put only the minimum required information in the limited partnership certificate and go into more detail in the limited partnership agreement or other documents?

7. What is one advantage the limited partnership has over the general partnership with regard to raising capital for the business?

8. Who may initiate a derivative action?

9. Why have limited partnerships become popular as tax shelters?

Notes

1 Revised Uniform Limited Partnership Act § 101(11).

2 59A AM. JUR. 2d *Partnership* § 1240 (1987).

3 *Id.* § 1246.

4 *Id.* § 1345.

5 Revised Uniform Limited Partnership Act § 303(a).

6 *Id.* § 303(b).

7 *Id.* § 105; Uniform Limited Partnership Act § 10.

8 59A AM. JUR. 2d *Partnership* § 1333 (1987).

9 Uniform Limited Partnership Act § 20.

10 Revised Uniform Limited Partnership Act § 801.

11 See chapter 12 of this text.

12 Uniform Limited Partnership Act § 2.

13 Revised Uniform Limited Partnership Act § 201.

14 *Id.* § 105.

15 *Id.*

16 Uniform Limited Partnership Act § 2.

17 *Id.* § 24; Revised Uniform Limited Partnership Act § 202.

18 Uniform Limited Partnership Act § 3; Revised Uniform Limited Partnership Act § 106.

19 14A Am. Jur. Legal Forms 2d (Rev) § 194:1101 (1994).

20 *Id.* § 194:1111.

21 *Id.* § 194:1121.

22 *Id.* § 194:1133.

23 *Id.* § 194:1134.

24 *Id.* § 194:1141.

25 *Id.* § 194:1151.

26 *Id.* § 194:1191.

27 *Id.* § 194:1165.

28 *Id.* § 194:1172.

29 *Id.* § 194:1211.

30 *Id.* § 194:1231.

31 *Id.* § 194:1251.

32 *Id.* § 194:1255.

33 *Id.* § 194:1293.

34 Uniform Limited Partnership Act § 8.

35 Revised Uniform Limited Partnership Act § 704.

36 See § 3.9(b) for more information on causes of dissolution.

37 Uniform Limited Partnership Act § 16; Revised Uniform Limited Partnership Act § 603.

38 Revised Uniform Limited Partnership Act § 604.

39 59A Am. Jur. 2d *Partnership* § 1354 (1987).

40 Uniform Limited Partnership Act § 4.

41 Revised Uniform Limited Partnership Act § 501.

42 Uniform Limited Partnership Act § 16.

43 Revised Uniform Limited Partnership Act § 503.

44 *Id.* § 1001.

45 59A Am. Jur. 2d *Partnership* § 1395 (1987).

46 Revised Uniform Limited Partnership Act § 1002.

47 Uniform Limited Partnership Act § 20.

48 Revised Uniform Limited Partnership Act § 801.

49 *Id.* § 402.

50 Uniform Limited Partnership Act § 24; Revised Uniform Limited Partnership Act § 203.

51 Revised Uniform Limited Partnership Act § 803.

52 See § 2.10(b) of this text for a list of selected form books.

CHAPTER 4

LIMITED LIABILITY COMPANIES

People who want to stay in business should learn how to cope with change.

Barbara Morgenstern
Corporate Consultant

§ 4.1 An Introduction to Limited Liability Companies

The newest and fastest growing type of business entity in the United States is the **limited liability company.** The limited liability company (LLC) is a type of non-corporate entity that is something of a cross between a partnership and a corporation. It offers many of the benefits of both a partnership and a corporation.

In this chapter, we define the term *limited liability company,* look at their unique characteristics, and examine the history and status of limited liability companies in the United States. Our discussion then turns to the law governing limited liability companies and the rights and powers limited liability companies possess. Next, we focus on members' rights and responsibilities, the organization and management of the limited liability company, its financial structure, and the dissolution of the limited liability company. After a discussion of the advantages and disadvantages of doing business as a limited liability company, especially as compared with other types of business entities, this chapter concludes with a look at the foreign limited liability company, other types of unincorporated limited liability entities, and the role of the legal assistant working with limited liability companies.

Limited Liability Company Defined

The limited liability company has many of the characteristics of a corporation, including limited liability for all owners or members; yet it meets specific Internal Revenue Service requirements that allow it to be

---

TERMS

limited liability company A type of non-corporate entity that offers limited liability to its owners, as well as partnership taxation status.

taxed as a partnership rather than a corporation. State statutes dictate the exact requirements for the formation and operation of limited liability companies. However, to be taxed as a partnership and have the income flow through the limited liability company to its members, the limited liability company must meet certain tests prescribed by the IRS. If a limited liability company possesses too many corporate characteristics, it may lose its partnership taxation status and be taxed like a corporation. Section 4.3 of this chapter discusses the rule used by the Internal Revenue Service for determining whether a limited liability company should be considered a corporation for taxation purposes.

Limited liability company documents must be carefully drafted and must follow state statutes and IRS guidelines precisely to obtain the desired tax status.

Limited Liability Company Characteristics

The limited liability company is an unincorporated entity based on the concept of freedom of contract. It is a legal entity distinct from its members.

The characteristics of any limited liability company will depend on its members' objectives and the statutes of the state in which it is formed. However, most limited liability companies have common characteristics, including limited liability, flexible management, limited duration, restricted transferability of interest, and partnership taxation status.

Limited Liability

Like a corporation, the owners of a limited liability company typically have no personal liability for the debts and obligations of the limited liability company.

Management

Management of the limited liability company is very flexible. All members of the limited liability company are granted the right to manage its business unless otherwise provided for in the limited liability company's **articles of organization.**

State statutes typically permit the owners of a limited liability company to allocate the management authority among its members in any manner they choose. They may decide to be managed by one individual,

TERMS

articles of organization   Document required to be filed with the proper state authority to form a limited liability company.

Dividends

Choices, Choices, Choices ...

Never before have there been more types of business entities to choose from in the United States. In the not too distant past, an individual or group of individuals wishing to begin business could choose from operating as a sole proprietor, partnership, limited partnership, or corporation. The recent addition of several more new types of business entities has made the selection more appealing, but also more confusing. Organizers of business enterprises in most states may now add to their list of options S corporations, limited liability companies, limited liability partnerships, and a vast array of other business entities that are unique to one or a few states.

Each of these new business entities was designed to fill a void, or a need in the business community. For example, the limited liability company was designed for those individuals who wanted both the tax status of a partnership and the limited liability of a corporation.

It is important to know the major characteristics of each type of existing business entity, and to keep abreast of new developments in the future. The following chart sets forth some characteristics of the most popular types of business entities. It is important to keep in mind that some of these factors may vary by state, and the statutes of the entities' state of organization is the final authority for defining the business enterprise.

	Restrictions on Ownership	Restrictions on Participation in Management	Limited Personal Liability	Continuity of Life
Sole Proprietorship	One owner only	None	None	None
Partnership	Two or more owners	None	None	Very Limited[3]
Limited Partnership	Two or more owners	Limited partners may not participate in management	For limited partners only	Very Limited[4]
Limited Liability Company	Two or more owners[1]	None	Yes. For all owners/members	No
S Corporation	One owner, but no more than 35, several other restrictions on ownership[2]	None	Yes. For all owners/shareholders	Yes
C Corporation	No or few restrictions	None	Yes. For all owners/shareholders	Yes

[1] A few states permit one owner.

[2] S corporations shareholders must all be individuals, estates, or trusts that meet certain prerequisites; nonresident aliens may not be shareholders.

[3] In some states, if the Partnership Agreement so provides, the partnership may continue after the death or dissociation of one or more member.

[4] The limited partnership can usually continue after the death or withdrawal of one or more *limited* partners.

by committee, or by the majority of the owners. Some limited liability companies appoint a **board of managers**, similar to a corporation's board of directors. A written agreement among the members, referred to as an **operating agreement**, sets forth the details concerning the management of the limited liability company.

Decisions of a limited liability company are usually made by the members holding a majority of the limited liability company interest, unless otherwise provided for in the operating agreement or by statute.

Duration of Life

The life of a limited liability company is limited in two ways. First, because under many circumstances it may be dissolved by the desire of any one member, its duration it is said to not have continuity of life. Rather, it is considered an **entity at will**. Second, unlike business corporation statutes, most limited liability company statutes provide that the articles of organization must set forth a period of duration that may not exceed thirty years. If organized in a state that permits perpetual duration, the organizers of the limited liability company must keep in mind that continuity of life is one of the characteristics that the IRS has assigned to corporations.

Transferability of Interest

Much like the interest of partners of a general partnership, the transfer of ownership interest of a member of a limited liability company is restricted. State statutes typically provide that the entire interest of a member of a limited liability company may not be assigned to another individual who will become a new member. Only the financial interest of the member is assignable; the other rights possessed by the member are not.

Ownership

There are very few restrictions on the number or type of owners who may own limited liability companies. Owners in the limited liability company are referred to as members.

═══════════════════════ **TERMS** ═══════════════════════

board of managers   Group of individuals who manage the limited liability company. Similar to a corporation's board of directors.

operating agreement   Document that governs the limited liability company. Similar to a corporation's by-laws.

entity at will   Entity that may be dissolved at the wish of one or more members or owners.

TABLE 4-1 LIMITED LIABILITY COMPANY CHARACTERISTICS

- Unincorporated Entity
- Legal Entity Distinct From Its Members
- Limited Personal Liability for Members
- Flexible Management
- Limited Duration
- Restricted Transferability of Interest
- Partnership Taxation Status

Formalities of Organization

The limited liability company is formed in much the same way that the business corporation is formed. Articles of Organization are filed with the Secretary of State or other appropriate state authority. In addition, a limited liability company may be subject to annual reporting requirements imposed by the state in which it was organized.

Taxation

Under most circumstances, limited liability companies are classified as partnerships by the IRS. Thus, the limited liability company avoids the double taxation associated with business corporations. However, some states have imposed a corporate tax on limited liability companies.[1]

§ 4.2 Limited Liability Companies in the United States

Limited liability companies are the newest form of business entity in the United States and the first new entity to be introduced in several decades. While similar entities have existed in other countries for several years, the first state legislation adopting limited liability companies was not passed in this country until 1977. This first state, Wyoming, was followed by Florida in 1982. These statutes did not receive much national attention until a 1988 IRS Revenue Ruling[2] classified a Wyoming limited liability company as a partnership for federal tax purposes—a decided advantage for many business owners. At this time, nearly every state in the country has either adopted legislation approving the limited liability company or is currently considering such legislation.

§ 4.3 Law Governing Limited Liability Companies

Limited liability companies are governed by the statutes of the state in which they are formed. Many of the state statutory acts resemble the **Uniform Limited Liability Company Act.** To qualify for partnership taxation treatment, limited liability companies must comply with the pertinent sections of the Internal Revenue Code and Regulations. In addition, limited liability companies may be subject to the Securities Act of 1933 and the Securities Exchange Act of 1934.

State Law and the Uniform Limited Liability Company Act

State legislatures have adopted limited liability company acts rapidly, and the statutes have been very diverse. The differences between state acts create difficulties for limited liability companies that transact business in more than one state. To compound that problem, little case law exists because of the relative newness of the limited liability company.

In 1994, the National Conference of the Commissions of Uniform State Law adopted the Uniform Limited Liability Company Act. Its main purpose was to give state legislatures some uniform guidelines for drafting state legislation. The Uniform Act encompasses many of the provisions that have already been adopted by individual states, but it allows for maximum flexibility. Because it is impossible to discuss the laws of each state individually in one chapter, this chapter will focus on the provisions of the Uniform Limited Liability Company Act. (The Uniform Limited Liability Company Act is included in this text as Appendix E.) It is important to remember, however, that the limited liability company act of your state may vary significantly, and state law must always be consulted. Table 4-2 includes a list of state statutes for each state that has adopted limited liability legislation as of August 1995.

TERMS

Uniform Limited Liability Company Act Uniform Act adopted by the National Conference of the Commissions of Uniform State Laws in 1994 to give states guidance when drafting limited liability company statutes.

TABLE 4-2   STATE LIMITED LIABILITY COMPANY STATUTES

State	Limited Liability Company Statute	Effective Date
Alabama	Ala. Code § 10-12-1 *et seq.*	10/1/93
Alaska		
Arkansas	Ark. Code Ann. § 4-32-101 *et seq.*	4/12/93
California	S.B. 469	
Colorado	Colo. Rev. Stat. § 7-80-101 *et seq.*	4/18/90
Connecticut	Public Act No. 93-267	6/1/92
Delaware	Del. Code § 18-101 *et seq.*	10/1/92
District of Columbia	1994 Act 10-243	
Florida	Fla. Stat. § 608.401 *et seq.*	1982
Georgia	O.C.G.A. § 14-11-1 *et seq.*	3/1/94
Hawaii	H.B. 777	
Idaho	Idaho Code § 53-601 *et seq.*	7/1/93
Illinois	Ill. Ann. Stat. Ch. 805, para 180/1-1 *et seq.*	7/1/93
Indiana	Ind. Code § 23-18-1	7/1/93
Iowa	Iowa Code § 490A.101 *et seq.*	9/1/92
Kansas	Kan. Stat. Ann. § 17-7601	7/1/90
Kentucky	S.B. 184, H.B. 255	
Louisiana	La. Rev. Stat. § 12:1301	7/7/92
Maine	H.B. 1123	
Maryland	Md. Ann. Code § 4A-101 *et seq.*	10/1/92
Massachusetts	H.B. 1793, S.B. 72	
Michigan	1993 Mich. H.B. 4023	6/1/93
Minnesota	Minn. St. § 322B.01	1/1/93
Mississippi	Chap. 402, 1994 Miss. Laws	
Missouri	Mo. Rev. Stat. §§ 347.010 *et seq.*	12/1/93
Montana	MCA § 35-8-101 *et seq.*	10/1/93
Nebraska	Neb. Rev. Stat. §§ 21-2601 *et seq.*	9/9/93
Nevada	Nev. Rev. Stat. § 86.010	7/1/93
New Hampshire	N.H. Rev. Stat. Ann. § 304-C:1	7/1/93
New Jersey	1992 N.J. Stat. Ann. §§ 42:2B-1 *et seq.*	1/26/94
New Mexico	1993 N.M. Stat. Ann. §§ 53-19-1 *et seq.*	7/1/93

TABLE 4-2 *(continued)*

State	Limited Liability Company Statute	Effective Date
New York	S.B. 7511-A, AB11317-A	
North Carolina	N.C. Gen. Stat. Chapter 57-C	10/1/93
North Dakota	N.C. Cent. Code § 10-32-01	8/1/93
Ohio	Act 94-74	7/1/94
Oklahoma	Okla. Stat. 18 § 270	9/1/92
Oregon	Or. Rev. Stat. §§ 63.001 *et seq.*	1/1/94
Pennsylvania	H.B. 2474	
Rhode Island	R.I. Gen. Laws § 7-16-1	9/19/92
South Carolina	1994 S.C. Act 448	
South Dakota	S.D. Codified Laws Ann. § 47-34-1 *et seq.*	7/1/93
Tennessee	H.B. 952	6/22/94
Texas	Tex. Rev. Civ. Stat. Ann. art. 1528n-1.01 *et seq.*	8/26/91
Utah	Utah Code Ann. § 48-2b-101 *et seq.*	7/1/91
Vermont	S.B. 314	
Virginia	Va. Code § 13.1-170 *et seq.*	7/1/92
Washington	S.S.H.B. 1235	10/1/94
West Virginia	W. Va. Code § 31-1A-1 *et seq.*	3/6/92
Wisconsin	Wisc. Stat. § 183.0101	1/1/94
Wyoming	Wyo. Stat. § 17-15-101 *et seq.*	1977

IRS Rulings

Limited liability companies are subject to Treas. Reg. § 301.7701-2, which distinguishes corporations from other forms of business. Treas. Reg. § 301.7701-2 recognizes four characteristics that are unique to corporations. Any limited liability company, or other type of entity, that possesses three or more of these characteristics will be considered a corporation for taxation purposes. Those characteristics are:

1. Continuity of life
2. Centralization of management
3. Limited liability
4. Free transferability of interests.

When establishing a limited liability company, the founders must be aware of this rule, and be sure to establish their company with no more than two of the above corporate characteristics. If a limited liability company resembles a corporation by possessing only one or two of the above characteristics, it will qualify for partnership taxation treatment in this regard. For example, a limited liability company can offer both limited liability for all of its members and centralized management and still be considered a partnership for taxation purposes by the IRS. However, if that same limited liability company were also to have continuity of life, the IRS would consider it a corporation and it would be taxed as a corporation.

Some states have designed their statutes with limited flexibility, so that it is impossible to form a limited liability company in that state with more than two of the above characteristics. These statutes are often referred to as **bulletproof statutes.** Other state statutes offer more flexibility to the organizers of limited liability companies, who must be careful not to choose more than two corporate characteristics.

Securities Laws

The applicability of state and federal securities laws to limited liability company interest is still an open question in many respects. If a member's interest is determined to be an investment contract under the Securities Exchange Act, then the interest is considered a **security** subject to state and federal securities laws. For purposes of determining the existence of a security as defined in federal securities law, a security must have the three following elements: It must be (1) an investment (2) in a common enterprise (3) with an expectation of profits to be derived solely from the efforts of others.

A membership interest in a limited liability company will include these first two elements. It is the third element that requires an expectation of profits *to be derived solely from the efforts of others* that will determine

---

TERMS

---

bulletproof statutes   With regard to limited liability company statutes, bulletproof statutes are state statutes that are drafted to make it impossible to form a limited liability in that state that complies with the statutes, unless it also complies with the Internal Revenue Code requirement limiting the limited liability company to two corporate characteristics.

security [†]   Collateral; a pledge given to a creditor by a debtor for the payment of a debt or for the performance of an obligation. With regard to limited liability companies, certificates representing a right to share in the company's profits or in the distribution of its assets, or in a debt owed by a company or by the government.

whether a member's interest is considered a security. In a limited liability company where all members play an active role in the operation of the business, the limited liability company may *not* be considered a security. Whereas, the interest of a member in a limited liability company with very centralized management may be considered a security.

Some states have attempted to answer the question by passing laws that include interests in limited liability companies in their list of securities subject to regulation. However, not all states have taken this step, and even those that have list exceptions to the rule. For example, an interest in a small limited liability company in which all members actively participate is almost never considered a security. An interest in a limited liability company that *is* determined to be a security is subject to both federal securities laws and state blue sky laws, which are discussed in Chapter 9 of this text.

§ 4.4 Limited Liability Company Rights and Powers

Much like a partnership or corporation, the limited liability company as a separate entity is granted certain powers by statute and by its articles of organization. In states that follow § 112 of the Uniform Limited Liability Company Act, limited liability companies have the same powers as individuals to do all things necessary or convenient to carry on business, including the powers to:

- Sue and be sued, and defend in the name of the limited liability company

- Purchase, receive, lease or otherwise acquire and own real or personal property

- Sell, convey, mortgage, grant a security interest in, lease, exchange, or otherwise encumber or dispose of all or any parts of its property

- Purchase, receive, or otherwise acquire and own shares or other interest in any other entity

- Sell, mortgage, grant a security interest in, or otherwise dispose of and deal in and with shares or other interest of any other entity

- Make contracts and other obligations, which may be convertible into or include the option to purchase other securities of the limited liability company

- Secure any of its obligations by a mortgage on, or a security interest in, any of its property, franchises, or income

- Lend money, invest and reinvest funds, and receive and hold real and personal property as security for repayment

- Be a promoter, partner, member, associate, or manager of any partnership, joint venture, trust, or other entity

- Conduct its business, locate offices, and exercise the powers granted by the Act within or without this state

- Elect managers and appoint officers, employees, and agents of the limited liability company, define their duties, fix their compensation, and lend them money and credit

- Pay pensions and establish pension plans, pension trusts, profit sharing plans, and any other type of employee benefit plan for any or all of its current or former members, managers, officers, employees, and agents

- Make charitable donations, and

- Make payments or donations, or perform any other act, not inconsistent with law, that furthers the business of the limited liability company.

Many state statutes are similar to the Uniform Limited Liability Company Act. Others simply state that a limited liability company *has all powers necessary to transact business* in that state.

§ 4.5 Members' Rights and Responsibilities

The owners of a limited liability company are referred to as members. The role of members is similar to that of partners of a general partnership, and, in some instances, the shareholders of a corporation.

Members As Agents

If a limited liability company has no designated manager, its members are considered to be agents of the limited liability company, in much the same way as partners may act on behalf of a partnership. Each member has the authority to bind the limited liability company in actions that are apparently aimed at carrying on the ordinary course of the company's business, or business of the kind that is carried on by the limited liability company. The act of a member that is not apparently aimed at carrying on the ordinary course of the company's business does not bind the company unless such act is authorized by the other members. The authority of members to act on behalf of the limited liability company is a matter that can be amended in the operating agreement of the limited liability company, and also by the statutes of the limited liability company's state of organization.

Transferability of Interest

The interest of a member in a limited liability company is viewed in much the same way as the interest of a partner in a general partnership. The members' ownership consists of two parts, one which is transferable, and one which is not. Members of a limited liability company may transfer their financial interest to receive profits and losses from the company. However, the rights of a member to vote and partake in the management of the limited liability company are not transferable. Therefore, it is not possible to transfer one's entire interest in a limited liability company to an individual who will become a new member.

Because members are unable to transfer their full voting membership, the limited liability company lacks the free transferability characteristic possessed by corporations.

As owners of a limited liability company, members are granted certain rights and responsibilities by statute, by the company's articles of organization, and the company's operating agreement.

Members' Statutory Rights

State statutes may grant several different rights to members of the limited liability company. At a minimum, these rights will include the right to have reasonable access to any records of the limited liability company at reasonable locations and times.

Rights Granted by the Operating Agreement

The vast majority of member rights will be provided for in the limited liability company's operating agreement. The organizers of a limited liability company have numerous options to choose from when granting rights to members. Specific rights granted may include:

- Voting rights
- Rights to profits
- Rights to distributions.

These rights may be granted uniformly to all members of the limited liability company, or they may be granted only to certain classes of members.

§ 4.6 Organization and Management of a Limited Liability Company

A limited liability company is formed when the proper organizer or organizers file articles of organization with the proper state authority. A limited liability company generally can be formed for any lawful business purpose. State statutes may restrict the formation of not-for-profit limited liability companies or limited liability companies formed for providing services by professionals such as doctors or lawyers.

Organizers of a limited liability company must proceed with caution and be aware of all formalities surrounding the formation of a limited liability company. They must plan to organize and operate the limited liability company in a way that will not jeopardize its tax standing as a partnership. That is, they must be sure that the limited liability company is not organized or operated in such a manner that it possesses three or more of the corporate characteristics at which the Internal Revenue Service looks to determine whether an entity is to be taxed as a corporation.

Organizers of the Limited Liability Company

Although the Uniform Limited Liability Act provides that any one or more persons may form a limited liability company, in many states two or more persons are required to form a limited liability company. State statutes must be checked carefully on this point.

Articles of Organization

The limited liability company cannot legally exist until it has been properly formed by filing articles of organization or a similar document with the appropriate state authorities. The limited liability company is then *given its life* by the proper state authority.

The articles of organization must contain the information prescribed by the statutes in the state in which it formed. Typically, the articles of organization will include:

- The name of the limited liability company
- The address of the initial designated office
- The name and address of the initial agent for service of process
- The name and address of each organizer
- The duration of the existence of the limited liability company

- The name and address of the limited liability company's initial managers if the limited liability company is to be managed by managers
- Information concerning the members' liability for any debts, obligations, and liabilities of the limited liability company.

Name of the Limited Liability Company

There are two types of requirements set by state statute with regard to the name of a limited liability company, as set forth in its articles of organization:

1. The name must contain language specifying that the entity is a limited liability company
2. The name must be available for use in the state in question.

The name of a limited liability company must include certain words or abbreviations required by state statute. For example, the names of limited liability companies in states following the Uniform Limited Liability Company Act must include the words *limited liability company* or *limited company* or the abbreviation *L.L.C., limited liability company, LC,* or *LC. Limited* may also be abbreviated as *Ltd.,* and *company* may be abbreviated as *Co.*

The name of a limited liability company must be distinguishable upon the records of the Secretary of State from the names of other limited liability companies, corporations, partnerships, and limited partnerships. State statutes set forth the exact standards to which the names of limited liability companies must adhere.

A paralegal who is responsible for filing articles of organization must first determine that the name the limited liability company wishes to use

TABLE 4-3   TIPS FOR DRAFTING ARTICLES OF ORGANIZATION

- Always begin by checking state statutes for requirements.
- Make sure the name being used for the limited liability company is available, and that it conforms to state requirements.
- Do not use a post office box for the address of the agent for service of process.
- Check to make sure the limited liability company is designed so that it has no more than two corporate characteristics (as defined by the IRS).
- Be sure the articles are signed by the proper individual or individuals.
- Information not *required* to be included in the articles of organization by state statute may be included in the operating agreement, which is not filed for public record.

is available for use in the state of organization. To do this, the Secretary of State's office, or other appropriate office must be contacted. Typically, the office of the Secretary of State will grant a preliminary approval of a name over the telephone, but not guarantee the availability until the Articles of Organization are filed or until the name is formally reserved pursuant to state statutes. See Appendix A of this text for a directory of state Secretary of State offices.

Not only must the name set forth in the articles of organization include words that indicate the entity is a limited liability company, but the company must be sure that the full name with such an indication is used in all correspondence, stationery, checks, and other materials that the company uses to conduct its business. It is important that the company establishes itself as a limited liability company with those with whom the company transacts business. In fact, if the company does not use those specific words in its name when it transacts business, and individuals doing business with the limited liability company are deceived into thinking they are dealing with a partnership, the members of the limited liability company may be held personally accountable for any debts or obligations to such individuals who were so deceived.

Address of the Limited Liability Company's Initial Office

The articles of organization must set forth the complete address of the limited liability company's initial office.

TABLE 4-4 TIPS FOR CHECKING LIMITED LIABILITY COMPANY NAME AVAILABILITY

- The name you are checking should be in compliance with state statute as to format (it must contain the words *Limited Liability Company* or similar words or abbreviations).

- Before you place a call to the Secretary of State or other state authority, have one or two alternate names ready to check.

- Most states will allow you to call for a preliminary check of name availability (see Secretary of State Directory at Appendix A of this text).

- Telephone lines to the Secretary of State offices are notoriously busy—be patient.

- If Articles of Organization will not be filed very shortly after name availability is checked, the name should be reserved with the Secretary of State.

- Clients should be advised *not* to use their new name until (1) Articles of Organization have been accepted for filing, or (2) the name has been reserved.

Registered Agent for Service of Process

Within the articles of organization, a limited liability company must designate the name and address of an agent who is located within the state of organization and who is authorized to accept service of process on behalf of the limited liability company. The address set forth in this section may not be a post office box. It must be a physical location where service of process may be made in person.

Names and Addresses of the Organizers of the Limited Liability Company

The full names and addresses of the organizers of the limited liability company, who may or may not be the original members, must be set forth in the articles of organization.

Duration of the Limited Liability Company

Limited liability companies usually have a limited duration. State statutes must be checked carefully for requirements concerning the permitted life span of the limited liability company. Most state statutes provide that the duration of the limited liability company must not exceed thirty years, or that the duration may not be perpetual.

Names and Addresses of the Managers of the Limited Liability Company

If the limited liability company is formed as a manager-managed limited liability company, the names and addresses of the initial manager or managers must be set forth in the articles of organization.

Information Concerning Personal Liability of the Limited Liability Company's Members

Pursuant to the Uniform Limited Liability Company Act, no member or manager of the limited liability company is personally liable for the debts, obligations, or liabilities of the limited liability company. If, however, the organizers of a limited liability company feel that it is in the best interests of the company for certain managers or members to be held personally liable for certain types of debts, obligations, or liabilities of the company, they can so provide by setting forth those exceptions in the articles of organization. No member or manager can be held personally liable for any debts, obligations, or liabilities of a limited liability company unless they agree to be held personally liable in a written agreement with the company.

Statutory Requirements

Several other requirements for articles of organization are set by state statutes. Some of the more common requirements for inclusion in the articles of organization are:

- Powers of the limited liability company

- Terms and conditions for new members

- Rights of members to continue business after death or withdrawal of one or more members

- Rights of members to withdraw

- Rights of members upon dissolution.

Management and Control of the Limited Liability Company

The management of a limited liability company is generally very flexible. Most details concerning the operation and management of the limited liability company may be set forth in the Operating Agreement. The limited liability company may be either member-managed, or manager-managed.

Member-Managed Limited Liability Companies

In a **member-managed limited liability company**, each member has equal rights in the management of the limited liability company's business. Each member has the right to act on behalf of the limited liability company with regard to most matters. Decisions relating to the business of the company are made by a majority of the members.

Except as otherwise provided by statute or the limited liability company's operating agreement, any matter relating to the business of the company may be decided by a majority of the members.

Much like partners in a general partnership, members of a member-managed limited liability company owe a fiduciary duty to one another. In states that follow the Uniform Limited Liability Company Act in this regard, the members owe each other a duty of loyalty and a duty of care, as prescribed by statute.

═══════════════◖ **TERMS** ◗═══════════════

member-managed limited liability company   A limited liability company in which the members have elected to share the managing of the company's affairs.

Manager-Managed Limited Liability Companies

The organizers of a limited liability company may decide to designate certain individuals to manage the business of the company. In that event, the limited liability company is referred to as a **manager-managed limited liability company.** Such managers are typically named in the company's articles of organization, which must be amended if the managers change. If the limited liability company is manager-managed, the managers are agents of the limited liability company and other members are not considered to be agents. They lack the authority to act on behalf of the limited liability company in most instances. The acts of a limited liability company manager generally bind the limited liability company unless:

1. The manager has no authority to act for the company in that particular matter and the individual with whom the manager was dealing knew or had notice that the manager lacked authority

2. The act of the manager was not apparently aimed at carrying on the ordinary course of the company's business or the business of the kind carried on by the company, and the members of the limited liability company did not authorize such act.

Because managers are given the authority to act on behalf of the other members of the limited liability company, they owe a fiduciary duty to the other members. In states that follow the Uniform Limited Liability Company Act, managers owe the members the duty of loyalty and the duty of care prescribed in that Act.

Matters Requiring Consent of All Members

Certain matters provided for in state statutes or the limited liability company's articles of organization or organization agreement require the consent of all members. Actions that often require unanimous consent of the members include:

- Amendment of the limited liability company's operating agreement

- Approval of acts or transactions by certain members or managers that would otherwise violate the duty of loyalty

- Amendments to the articles of organization

<hr>

TERMS

manager-managed limited liability company   A limited liability company in which the members have agreed to have the company's affairs managed by one or more managers.

FIGURE 4-1
Sample
Articles of
Organization

ARTICLES OF ORGANIZATION
OF
_____

ARTICLE I

The name of the limited liability company is :_____.

ARTICLE II

The address of the initial designated office within this state is:

_____

_____.

ARTICLE III

The name and address of the initial agent for service of process are:

_____

_____

_____.

ARTICLE IV

The Company shall exist from the date of filing of these Articles of Organization with the Secretary of State until _____.

ARTICLE V

No member of this Company shall assume any personal obligation for any debts, liabilities, or obligations of the Company.

IN WITNESS WHEREOF, these Articles of Organization have been executed by the undersigned on _____ , 1996.

_____

Name _____

- The compromise of an obligation to make a contribution
- The compromise, as among members, of an obligation of a member to make a contribution or return money or other property paid or distributed in violation of state statute
- The making of interim distributions
- The admission of a new member

- The use of the company's property to redeem an interest subject to a charging order
- Dissolution of the company
- A waiver of the right to have the company's business wound up and the company terminated
- The merger of the limited liability company with another entity
- The sale, lease, exchange, or other disposal of all, or substantially all, of the company's property with or without goodwill.

When the act of a limited liability company requires the consent of all members, the act may be approved at a meeting of the members or by a written consent signed by all members.

The Operating Agreement

Operating agreements set forth the agreement of the members of the limited liability company concerning the management and operation of the company. Because the operating agreement is not filed for public record, information that may be contained in either the articles of organization or the operating agreement is often contained in the operating agreement. The items that can be included in an operating agreement are numerous and will vary depending on the pertinent state statutes and the particular circumstances. Following is a sample checklist including items that often are included in an operating agreement.

OPERATING AGREEMENT CHECKLIST

- ☐ Formation and Term
- ☐ Nature of Business
- ☐ Accounting and Records
- ☐ Names and Addresses of Members
- ☐ Rights and Duties of Members
- ☐ Meetings of Members
- ☐ Managing Members
- ☐ Contributions and Capital Accounts
- ☐ Allocations and Distributions
- ☐ Taxes
- ☐ Disposition of Membership Interests
- ☐ Dissociation of a Member
- ☐ Additional and Substitute Members
- ☐ Dissolution and Winding Up
- ☐ Amendment
- ☐ Miscellaneous Provisions

Most state statutes allow for maximum flexibility concerning the contents of the operating agreement. The Uniform Limited Liability Company Act sets forth certain restrictions concerning the contents of the operating agreement with regard to the rights and duties of its members. Section 103(b) of the Act provides:

(b) The operating agreement may not:

(1) unreasonably restrict a right to information or access to records under Section 408;

(2) eliminate the duty of loyalty under Section 409(b) or 603(b)(3), but the agreement may:

(i) identify specific types or categories of activities that do not violate the duty of loyalty, if not manifestly unreasonable; and

(ii) specify the number or percentage of members or disinterested managers that may authorize or ratify, after full disclosure of all material facts, a specific act or transaction that otherwise would violate the duty of loyalty;

(3) unreasonably reduce the duty of care under Section 409(c) or 603(b)(3);

(4) eliminate the obligation of good faith and fair dealing under Section 409(d), but the operating agreement may determine the standards by which the performance of the obligation is to be measured, if the standards are not manifestly unreasonable;

(5) vary the right to expel a member in an event specified in Section 601(5);

(6) vary the requirement to wind up the limited liability company's business in a case specified in Section 801(4) or (5); or

(7) restrict rights of third parties under this [Act], other than managers, members, or their transferees

Annual Reporting Requirements

Like corporations, limited liability companies in most states are subject to annual reporting requirements with the Secretary of State or other appropriate state authority. The statutes of the limited liability company's state of organization must be checked carefully to be sure that all annual reporting requirements are complied with. Typically, annual reports must be filed that contain such information as:

- Name of the limited liability company

- State or country where limited liability company is organized

- Name and address of agent within state for service of process

- Address of the limited liability company's principal office

- Names and addresses of any managers.

§ 4.7 Financial Structure of a Limited Liability Company

The financial structure of a limited liability company resembles that of a partnership in many ways. Financing generally comes from member contributions. Members who spend money on behalf of the limited liability company are entitled to reimbursement for expenditures they make on behalf of the company, and members are entitled to receive distributions pursuant to statute and the limited liability company's operating agreement.

Member Contributions

The initial assets of the limited liability company typically consist of the contributions of members. Limited liability company members will be required to make certain contributions to the company as provided for in the company's operating agreement, articles of organization, and agreements of the members. Unless otherwise prohibited by statute or by the limited liability company's articles of organization or operating agreement, the contributions of members may be in the form of cash or tangible or intangible property, including services. For example, if a limited liability company formed for the purposes of developing a piece of property is in need of the services of a general contractor, the members of the company may decide to grant membership to a general contractor in return for his or her services. Other new members may be required to make cash contributions.

Member Reimbursement

From time to time, certain members who are involved in the operation of the limited liability company may make expenditures on behalf of the company. These members are entitled to reimbursement of certain expenses made by them on behalf of the limited liability company, as provided by state statute and the company's operating agreement.

Distributions to Members

Details concerning distributions made to members of the limited liability company should be set forth in the operating agreement of the company. Unless otherwise provided for in the operating agreement or articles of operating agreement, any distributions made by the limited liability company must be made pursuant to state statute. Most state statutes provide that any distributions must be made to the members in equal shares.

Distributions may be prohibited by statute under certain circumstances, such as when the limited liability company would not be able to pay its debts when they are due in the ordinary course of business.

§ 4.8 Dissolution of the Limited Liability Company

Limited liability companies, as a rule, do not have perpetual existence. The duration of a limited liability company may be limited by statute, or by the terms of its articles of organization or operating agreement.

The **dissolution** of a limited liability company may be prompted either by the end of its planned and stated duration, or by some other event that triggers a dissolution. Like partnerships under the Revised Uniform Partnership Act, one or more members may be dissociated from the limited liability company without causing a dissolution of the company.

Member's Dissociation

In states that follow the Uniform Limited Liability Company Act[3] in this regard, dissociation may be caused by several events, including a member's withdrawal (with written notice), death, bankruptcy, or appointment of a guardian for the member. A member may also be dissociated by unanimous vote of the other members under certain circumstances, such as when it is unlawful to carry on the company's business with the member.

Judicial determination on the application by the company or another member may cause a member to be dissociated if the member is engaged in wrongful conduct.

TERMS

dissolution [†] A breaking up; the separation of a thing into its component parts. With regard to a limited liability company, dissolution refers to the termination of the limited liability company's existence and its abolishment as an entity.

Wrongful Dissociation

A member's dissociation may be wrongful, as in instances where the dissociation is in breach of an express provision of the operating agreement; or, under certain circumstances, when the dissociation is before the expiration of the term of a company that has a definite term. If a member wrongfully dissociates from a limited liability company, he or she may be liable to the company and the remaining members for wrongful dissociation.

Effect of Dissociation of a Member

Upon a member's dissociation from a limited liability company:

- The member loses all right to participate in the management of the company's business

- The member is treated the same as a transferee of a member

- The member's duty of loyalty and duty of care continue only with regard to events occurring before the dissociation, unless the member participates in winding up the company's business.

Purchase of the Dissociated Member's Interest

State statutes and the limited liability company's operating agreement typically will provide specific terms and conditions for the purchase of a dissociating member's interest in the limited liability company. Members who dissociate from a limited liability company at-will are typically entitled to have their interest purchased shortly after their dissociation.

When the member's dissociation results in the dissolution of the limited liability company, the dissociating member is generally entitled to a final distribution when the business of the company is wound up.

Dissolution of the Limited Liability Company

The events that cause the dissolution of a limited liability company are provided for by the limited liability company's articles of organization, operating agreement, and by state statute. Most state statutes provide that the death, bankruptcy, or withdrawal of any of its members will dissolve the limited liability company. Many states provide exceptions that allow the business to continue upon agreement of the remaining members or if the articles of organization permit it. In states that follow the Uniform Limited Liability Company Act,[4] the following events cause a dissolution and winding up of the partnership business:

1. An event specified in the operating agreement
2. Consent of the members, as specified in the operating agreement
3. Dissociation of a member under certain circumstances, such as the member's filing for bankruptcy, but only if a majority of the remaining partners do not agree to continue the business of the company within ninety days (if permitted in the operating agreement of the company)
4. An event that makes it unlawful for the business to continue, if such illegality is not cured within ninety days after notice is given to the company of the event
5. Entry of a judicial decree, upon the application by a member, that:
   (i)   the economic purpose of the company is likely to be unreasonably frustrated;
   (ii) another member has engaged in conduct relating to the company's business that makes it not reasonably practicable to carry on the company's business with that member;
   (iii) it is not otherwise reasonably practicable to carry on the company's business in conformity with the articles of organization and the operating agreement;
   (iv) the company failed to purchase the petitioner's distributional interest as required by statute;
   (v)   actions of the managers or members in control of the company are, or have been, illegal, oppressive, fraudulent, or unfairly prejudicial to the petitioner
6. A judicial determination, based on application by a transferee of a member's interest, that it is equitable to wind up the company's business:
   (i)   after the expiration of a specified term; or
   (ii) at any time, if the company is a company at will
7. The expiration of a specified term.

After the limited liability company has been dissolved, it continues only for the purpose of winding up its business.

Winding Up the Limited Liability Company

After a decision has been made to dissolve a limited liability company, its business must be wound up. Any member, except a member who has wrongfully dissociated from the limited liability company may participate in winding up its business. Judicial supervision of the winding up may be ordered upon the application of any member of the company for good cause.

Distribution of Assets

The rules for distribution of the assets of the limited liability company may be set by the articles of organization, or the company's operating agreement. However, state statute may have provisions regarding distribution of the limited liability company's assets that may not be superseded. These rules may provide that the property of the limited liability company may first be used to pay the debts and obligations of the limited liability company, before the members receive distributions.

Articles of Termination

Because the articles of organization are filed with the secretary of state or other state authority to give notice of the company's existence, notice of the company's dissolution must also be filed at the state level. In states that follow the Uniform Limited Liability Company Act,[5] this involves filing **articles of termination** with the secretary of state.

Articles of termination would typically include the following information

1. The name of the company
2. The date of the company's dissolution
3. A statement that the company's business has been wound up and the legal existence of the company has been terminated.

The existence of the limited liability company is terminated when the articles of termination are filed, or on a later date specified in the document.

§ 4.9 Advantages of Doing Business As a Limited Liability Company

There can be several advantages to doing business as a limited liability company. Some of the most important reasons include the limited liability offered to owners of the company, the beneficial tax treatment received by the owners, and the flexible management structure available to the limited liability company.

TERMS

articles of termination Document that must be filed with the proper state authority to dissolve a limited liability company.

Limited Liability for All Owners

The fact that the owners of the limited liability company are not subject to personal liability for the debts and obligations of the company is probably the most significant advantage to doing business as a limited liability company instead of as a limited partnership or general partnership. Whereas general partners of a limited partnership and all partners of a general partnership may be held personally liable for the debts and other obligations of their business, owners of a limited liability company may not. The owners of a limited liability company generally have the same protection from personal liability that is granted to shareholders of a corporation.

The statutes of some states, however, provide that the members may agree to be personally liable for the limited liability company's debts.[6]

Unrestrictive Ownership

S Corporations, which are discussed in Chapter 5 of this text, are very similar to limited liability companies in many respects and offer many of the same benefits. However, there are several statutory restrictions on the ownership of S Corporations. For example, S Corporations may have no more than 35 shareholders and these shareholders must be natural persons (not partnerships, corporations, or other entities). There are fewer restrictions placed on ownership of limited liability companies.

Ability to Raise Capital for the Business

Membership interests in the limited liability company offer maximum flexibility to investors. In general, the details of the membership interests sold in the limited liability company are up to the investors. Unlike S Corporations, investors in a limited liability company may include corporate or foreign investors.

Beneficial Tax Treatment

An unincorporated entity that meets the specific guidelines prescribed by the IRS may be taxed as a partnership. This gives the limited liability company a decided tax advantage over the corporation. When a limited liability company is treated like a partnership for federal income tax purposes, the income earned by the limited liability company *flows through* to the owners of the company and is added to their personal income. The limited liability company's income is taxed once, at the income tax rate of the individual owners. Corporate income, on the other hand, may be subject to double taxation—once at the corporate level when the income is received by the corporation, and once at the shareholder level when dividends are earned.

Flexibility of Management

In comparison with other forms of business, there are generally few statutory restrictions placed on the management of a limited liability company. Unlike the limited partnership, for example, all members of the limited liability company are free to contribute to the management of the company without the threat of losing their limited liability status. In addition, limited liability companies are not subject to the requirements for holding shareholder meetings to which corporations must adhere.

§ 4.10 Disadvantages of Doing Business As a Limited Liability Company

The advantages to doing business as a limited liability company must be weighed against the potential disadvantages. Most of the disadvantages to doing business as a limited liability company are restrictive in nature. The transferability of ownership of a limited liability company is restricted, as is the continuity of the business. Other disadvantages stem from relative uncertainties of transacting business as a limited liability company. There are uncertainties associated with piercing the veil of the limited liability company, as well as income tax uncertainties. In addition, there remains a lack of uniformity in limited liability law between the states.

Limited Transferability of Ownership

As discussed in § 4.5, the members of limited liability companies are not permitted to transfer their entire rights to a limited liability company to another owner. Although they may transfer their financial interest in a limited liability company, other member rights, such as the right to participate in the management of the business of the limited liability company, are untransferable.

No Business Continuity

Most state statutes specifically require that the limited liability company dissolves after a limited amount of time, such as thirty years. This can be a significant disadvantage over the corporation, which can have a perpetual duration. Many limited liability company statutes provide that the limited liability company can exist for no more than thirty years.

In addition, the statutes of most states provide that the limited liability company will dissolve upon the agreement of the members or upon the death, retirement, resignation, expulsion, bankruptcy, or dissolution of a member. However, in many cases the limited liability company may continue with the consent of the remaining members. A limited liability company having a specified term that continues after the expiration of that term is considered an *at-will company,* and the members and managers rights and duties remain substantially the same as they were at the expiration of the term.

Possibility of Piercing the Limited Liability Company Veil

Under certain circumstances, the corporate entity may be disregarded and the directors and shareholders of a corporation may be held personally liable for the debts and obligations of the corporation. This is referred to as *piercing the corporate veil* and is generally done when the corporation is not really being operated as a separate entity, but rather as an extension of the individual owners. Piercing the corporate veil is discussed further in Chapter 5. The statutes of many states have stated that the limited liability company entity may also be disregarded and the owners of the company may be held personally liable under certain unique circumstances. To date there have been no court cases involving piercing the corporate veil of a limited liability company and there is some uncertainty as to how this will be viewed in the courts.

Income Tax Uncertainty

There is little uniformity among states with regard to taxation of limited liability companies. Although most states treat the limited liability company as a partnership for income tax purposes, there are a few states that have treated limited liability companies as corporations for income

TABLE 4-5   TABLE OF STATE STATUTORY PROVISIONS FOR LIMITED LIABILITY COMPANY DURATION

State	Statutory Provision Re: Duration
Alabama	
Arizona	
Arkansas	
Colorado	Duration not to exceed 30 years
Connecticut	
Delaware	Duration not to exceed 30 years
Florida	May be perpetual
Georgia	
Idaho	
Indiana	
Iowa	
Kansas	
Louisiana	
Maryland	
Michigan	
Minnesota	Duration not to exceed 30 years
Missouri	
Montana	
Nebraska	Duration not to exceed 30 years
Nevada	Duration not to exceed 30 years
New Hampshire	
New Jersey	Thirty-year life if organizers fail to state dissolution date
North Carolina	
North Dakota	Duration not to exceed 30 years
Oregon	Thirty-year life if organizers fail to state dissolution date
Rhode Island	
South Dakota	Duration not to exceed 30 years
Texas	May be perpetual
Utah	
Virginia	
West Virginia	
Wisconsin	
Wyoming	Duration not to exceed 30 years

tax purposes, and a few states that have not ruled one way or another. This makes it extremely difficult for tax planning, especially for those limited liability companies that transact business in several states.

Lack of Uniformity in State Laws

Although the whole intent of the Uniform Limited Liability Company Act was to bring uniformity to state law, the Act was written after limited liability company legislation was adopted in most of the states. Thus, there is little uniformity in statutory law between states with regard to limited liability companies. To further complicate matters, there is almost *no* case law concerning limited liability companies published to date. These two factors make it very difficult for limited liability companies that transact business in several states.

§ 4.11 Transacting Business As a Foreign Limited Liability Company

In every state in which a limited liability company transacts business, other than its state of organization, it is considered a **foreign limited liability company.** The foreign limited liability company is subject to the laws of each state in which it transacts business. A limited liability company must be granted a **certificate of authority to transact business as a foreign limited liability company** (or similar document) before it begins transacting business in any state other than its state of organization.

As with corporations, a foreign limited liability company subjects itself to the jurisdiction of the courts of each state in which it transacts business. For that reason, foreign limited liability companies must comply with state statutes that pertain to the transaction of business in the foreign state, and they must comply with statutory formalities regarding foreign limited liability companies.

TERMS

foreign limited liability company   A limited liability company that is transacting business in any state other than the state of its organization.

certificate of authority to transact business as a foreign limited liability company   Certificate issued by the secretary of state, or other appropriate state official, to a foreign limited liability company to allow it to transact business in that state.

TABLE 4-6 ADVANTAGES AND DISADVANTAGES OF DOING BUSINESS AS A LIMITED LIABILITY COMPANY

Advantages	Disadvantages
■ Limited Liability for All Owners	■ Limited Transferability of Ownership
■ Unrestrictive Ownership	■ No Business Continuity
■ Ability to Raise Capital for Business	■ Possibility of Piercing the LLC Veil
■ Beneficial Tax Treatment	■ Income Tax Disadvantages
■ Flexibility of Management	■ Lack of Uniformity in State LLC Law

When the owners of a limited liability company organize their business or expand it, a decision must be made as to what its legal obligations are with regard to states with which the company comes in contact, other than the company's state of organization. First, it must be determined whether the limited liability company is actually *transacting business* within the foreign state, as defined by the statutes of the foreign state. If the limited liability company is in fact transacting business in the foreign state, or if it plans to in the future, the limited liability company must obtain a certificate of authority from the secretary of state of the foreign state and appoint an agent for service of process who is located within the foreign state. If it is determined that the limited liability company is not actually *transacting business* within the foreign state, the limited liability company will not need to apply for a certificate of authority, but the organizers of the company may decide that it would be beneficial to register the name of the limited liability company within that state.

The statutes of each state in which the limited liability company wishes to transact business must be carefully reviewed before the company begins transacting business in that state.

Transacting Business As a Foreign Limited Liability Company

At times, there is no question whether a limited liability company is transacting business in another state; for instance, if the expansion of a limited liability company into another state involves the construction of a factory in that state and hiring employees from that state to work in the factory. In other instances, however, such as when a salesperson occasionally crosses state borders to make a sale, the question requires a closer look at state statutes.

The statutes of most states address the matter either by giving a general definition of what constitutes transacting business in their state or by providing a list of activities that *do not* constitute the transaction of business. The Uniform Limited Liability Company Act addresses the question by providing such a list in § 1003, which follows:

SECTION 1003. ACTIVITIES NOT CONSTITUTING TRANSACTING BUSINESS.

(a) Activities of a foreign limited liability company that do not constitute transacting business within the meaning of this [article] include:

(1) maintaining, defending, or settling an action or proceeding;

(2) holding meetings of its members or managers or carrying on any other activity concerning its internal affairs;

(3) maintaining bank accounts;

(4) maintaining offices or agencies for the transfer, exchange, and registration of the foreign company's own securities or maintaining trustees or depositories with respect to those securities;

(5) selling through independent contractors;

(6) soliciting or obtaining orders, whether by mail or through employees or agents or otherwise, if the orders require acceptance outside this State before they become contracts;

(7) creating or acquiring indebtedness, mortgages, or security interests in real or personal property;

(8) securing or collecting debts or enforcing mortgages or other security interests in property securing the debts, and holding, protecting, and maintaining property so acquired;

(9) conducting an isolated transaction that is completed within 30 days and is not one in the course of similar transactions of a like manner; and

(10) transacting business in interstate commerce.

(b) For purposes of this [article], the ownership in this State of income-producing real property or tangible personal property, other than property excluded under subsection (a), constitutes transacting business in this State.

(c) This section does not apply in determining the contacts or activities that may subject a foreign limited liability company to service of process, taxation, or regulation under any other law of this State.

There can be several negative consequences to the limited liability company that transacts business in another state without first receiving a certificate of authority. Probably the most significant consequence is the lack of access to the courts in that state. For example, if a limited liability company must seek a court action to enforce a contract in a neighboring state, the company will be unable to enforce that contract in the courts of the neighboring state.

Application for a Certificate of Authority

Before a limited liability company begins transacting business in a foreign state, it must obtain a Certificate of Authority from the Secretary of State or other appropriate state official in the foreign state. The Certificate of Authority is obtained by completing an Application for Certificate of Authority to Transact Business as a Foreign Limited Liability Company, and filing it with the appropriate state authority. The application must be completed pursuant to the statutes of the foreign state and further requirements prescribed by the secretary of state. The application typically includes the following information:

- Name of the limited liability company

- State where the limited liability company is organized

- Address of the principal office of the limited liability company

- Address of the initial designated office within the foreign state

- Name and street address of the limited liability company's agent for service of process within the foreign state

- Duration of the limited liability company

- Name and address of the limited liability company's managers if the company is manager-managed

- Statement regarding any personal liability assumed by any managers or members of the limited liability company.

One requirement that is uniform in all states is that any limited liability company that wishes to transact business in a foreign state must designate, in its application for certificate of authority, an agent within that state to accept service of process on its behalf. This ensures that if there is ever a cause of action against a limited liability company that arises within the foreign state, service of process may be made upon that limited liability company by service on its agent within the state.

The Secretary of State may have additional requirements, such as the filing of a copy of the company's articles of organization or a certificate of existence from the limited liability company's state of organization.

Name Registration

One important factor for the organizers of a limited liability company to consider is its name, and its name availability in other states. If a limited liability company plans to expand its business into several states in the future, the organizers must make sure that its name will be

**CHECKLIST FOR FILING APPLICATION FOR
CERTIFICATE OF AUTHORITY
TO TRANSACT BUSINESS AS A
FOREIGN LIMITED LIABILITY COMPANY**

☐ Complete Application for Certificate of Authority in format prescribed by state authority of foreign state (the Secretary of State may require that the application be completed on a form furnished by their office).

☐ Be sure that the application includes a *street address within the foreign state* where service of process may be made on an agent of the LLC.

☐ Be sure the Application is signed by an authorized individual.

☐ Include the appropriate filing fee.

☐ Include copy of the Articles of Organization if required by the foreign state.

☐ Include Certificate of Existence or similar document if required by the foreign state.

available for use in each state. For example, suppose a limited liability company is organized under the laws of Iowa as Peterson Engineering Limited Liability Company. The organizers plan to build their business on the reputation of its founders, and expand it into the entire Midwest region. If their state-by-state expansion begins in three years, they may have a problem if the name *Peterson Engineering Limited Liability Company* is not available for use in any of the surrounding states.

One way around this problem is foreign name registration. In states that follow the Uniform Limited Liability Company Act in this regard, a foreign limited liability company may register its name in a foreign state, provided that name meets with the state's requirements. Names of foreign limited liability companies are typically registered for a one-year period. A registered name will be reserved for future use for the limited liability company if the limited liability company decides to transact business in that state in the future.

§ 4.12 Other Types of Unincorporated Limited Liability Entities

Limited liability companies are not the only form of unincorporated entity that provides limited liability to its owners. State statutes provide for other types of limited liability associations that include professional limited liability companies and limited liability partnerships.

Professional Limited Liability Companies

Many states allow the formation of **professional limited liability companies** by doctors, lawyers, and other professionals. However, the professional members of a professional limited liability company are still personally liable for any acts of malpractice.

Limited Liability Partnerships

Another new form of business entity in this country, the **limited liability partnership**, is very similar to the general partnership, with one important distinction—the partners of limited liability partnerships provide that a partner is not liable for any debts or obligations of the partnership that arise from a wrongful act or omission of another partner or agent of the partnership. This new form of partnership is, therefore, very advantageous to partners of a professional partnership such as doctors or lawyers who no longer have to fear the threat of personal liability for the malpractice of a partner.

There are restrictions on the limitation of personal liability on the partners of this type of entity, however. Partners of this type of entity are personally liable for the contractual obligations of the partnership, such as loans. In addition, partners are personally liable for their own wrongful acts or omissions. Only a few states have adopted this new form of partnership, although many more states may be adopting similar legislation in the near future.

§ 4.13   The Role of the Legal Assistant

Legal assistants can perform a variety of functions to assist with the formation, maintenance, and dissolution of limited liability companies. Many of the services to be performed on behalf of a limited liability company will be procedural in nature, and can easily be performed by

---

TERMS

professional limited liability company   Entity similar to a professional corporation, that allows limited liability and partnership taxation status to its members, who must be professionals.

limited liability partnership   A form of business organization similar to a partnership but that offers limited liability to its partners.

TABLE 4-7 TABLE OF STATE PROFESSIONAL LIMITED LIABILITY COMPANY ACTS

State	Statute
Alabama	Alabama Limited Liability Company Act, Ala. Code § 10-12-45
Arizona	Arizona Limited Liability Company Act, A.R.S. § 29-843
Arkansas	Arkansas Small Business Entity Pass Through Act, Ark. Code Ann. § 4-32-306
Connecticut	Connecticut Limited Liability Company Act, Public Act No. 93-267, § 2(16), 8(b)
Georgia	Georgia Limited Liability Company Act, O.C.G.A. § 14-11-314, 1107(f)
Idaho	Idaho Limited Liability Company Act, Idaho Code § 53-605(2) & 615
Indiana	Indiana Business Flexibility Act, Ind. Code 23-18-2-15
Iowa	Iowa Limited Liability Company Act, Iowa Code § 40A.1501
Kansas	Kansas Limited Liability Company Act, Kan. Stat. Ann. § 17-2708
Louisiana	Louisiana Limited Liability Company Law, La. Rev. Stat. § 12:1302
Maryland	Maryland Limited Liability Company Act, Md. Ann. Code, Corps. & Ass'ns, § 4A-201
Michigan	Michigan Limited Liability Company Act, 1993 Public Acts No. 23, § 901
Minnesota	Minn. St. § 319A.01-22
Missouri	Missouri Limited Liability Company Act, Mo. Rev. Stat. § 359.702(4)
Montana	Montana Limited Liability Company Act, MCA, § 35-8-1307
Nebraska	Nebraska Limited Liability Company Act, 1993 LB No. 121, § 3(15)
New Hampshire	New Hampshire Limited Liability Company Act, N.H. Rev. Stat. Ann. § 304-D:1
North Carolina	North Carolina Limited Liability Company Act, N.C. Gen. Stat. § 57-C-2-01(c)

TABLE 4-7 *(continued)*

State	Statute
Oregon	Oregon prohibits the organization of such an entity
Rhode Island	Rhode Island prohibits the organization of such an entity.
South Dakota	South Dakota Limited Liability Company Act, 1993 S.D. Senate Bill 139
Texas	Texas Limited Liability Company Act, Tex. Rev. Civ. Stat. Ann. art. 1528n-11.01
Utah	Utah Limited Liability Company Act, Utah Code Ann. § 48-2b-104
Virginia	Virginia Professional Limited Liability Company Act, Va. Code, § 13.1-1100
West Virginia	West Virginia Limited Liability Company Act, W. Va. Code, § 31-1A-68

an experienced legal assistant with the proper resources. Most of the functions performed by legal assistants will involve drafting appropriate legal documentation and performing research.

Drafting Limited Liability Documentation

Legal assistants, with the use of current forms and form books, may be responsible for drafting virtually all documents associated with the limited liability company. These documents may include the articles of organization, operating agreement, applications for certificates of authority to transact business as a foreign limited liability company, and others.

The legal assistant may be responsible for attending an initial client meeting to collect information concerning the formation of a limited liability company. With the use of a customized checklist, the legal assistant can collect all of the information required to prepare drafts of the organization documents. The legal assistant may also become the client contact to assist with future needs of the limited liability company client.

TABLE 4-8   STATE LIMITED LIABILITY PARTNERSHIP STATUTES

State	Limited Liability Partnership Statute
Alabama	1994 Ala. H.B. 181 (signed by Governor March 1, 1994)
Alaska	
Arizona	1994 Ariz. S.B. 1012 (signed by Governor April 19, 1994)
Arkansas	
California	
Colorado	
Connecticut	
Delaware	Del. Code Ann. tit. 6, §§ 1544 *et seq.*
District of Columbia	1993 D.C. Stat. 34
Florida	
Georgia	
Hawaii	
Idaho	
Illinois	
Indiana	
Iowa	
Kansas	1994 Kan. S.B. 582 (signed by Governor April 7, 1994)
Kentucky	1994 Ky. S.B. 184 (signed by Governor April 11, 1994)
Louisiana	La. Rev. Stat. Ann. §§ 9:3431 *et seq.*
Maine	
Maryland	
Massachusetts	
Michigan	
Minnesota	1994 Minn. Laws 539 (signed by Governor April 29, 1994)
Mississippi	
Missouri	
Montana	
Nebraska	
Nevada	

TABLE 4-8 *(continued)*

State	Limited Liability Partnership Statute
New Hampshire	
New Jersey	
New Mexico	
New York	
North Carolina	N.C. Gen. Stat. §§ 59-84.2 *et seq.*
North Dakota	
Ohio	
Oklahoma	
Oregon	
Pennsylvania	
Rhode Island	
South Carolina	
South Dakota	
Tennessee	
Texas	Tex. Rev. Civ. Stat. Ann. art. 6132b *et seq.*
Utah	Utah Code Ann. §§ 18-1-42 *et seq.*
Vermont	
Virginia	1994 Va. H.B. 994 (signed by Governor April 5, 1994)
Washington	
West Virginia	
Wisconsin	
Wyoming	

Limited Liability Company Research

Because limited liability company law is so new, and because it varies so much between states, there may be a great need for legal research in this area. Because there is little case law in this area yet, most research will involve state statutes, although research of the Internal Revenue Code to determine the IRS's position issues involving limited liability company taxation may also be required.

§ 4.14 Resources

The main resources legal assistants will use when working with limited liability companies are the state statutes, state authorities, the Internal Revenue Code, and form books and treatises.

State Statutes

The main source for answering questions concerning limited liability companies is the statutes of the state of organization. State statutes will include all basic information regarding the formation, operation, and dissolution of a limited liability company within that state. In addition, state statutes also contain information required by foreign limited liability companies doing business within that state. See Table 4-2 for a list of state Limited Liability Company statutes.

State Authorities

At times, the quickest way to find an answer concerning requirements for forming or operating a limited liability company (especially procedural questions regarding state filings) may be to contact the office of the secretary of state or other appropriate state official. The office of the Secretary of State will often provide the following forms to use for filing in their office:

- Articles of Organization
- Reservation of Name
- Annual Reports
- Name Registration
- Application for Certificate of Authority to Transact Business as a Foreign Limited Liability Company.

In addition, the office of the Secretary of State will often provide filing fee schedules and instructions for filing procedures.

Internal Revenue Code

Questions concerning the taxation of a limited liability company may be answered by researching the Internal Revenue Code (IRC), Treasury Regulations and Revenue Rulings and Procedures.

Form Books and Treatises

In recent years, numerous books have been written on the topic of limited liability companies. These books are a good source for general information, forms, and state-by-state treatment of limited liability companies.

Review Questions

1. In what ways are limited liability companies different from general partnerships?

2. Can a limited liability company that is managed by one member have limited liability for all members and a fixed duration of ten years, qualify for partnership taxation status?

3. If a limited liability company is member-managed, has limited liability for all members and an unlimited duration, could it qualify for partnership taxation status?

4. If Sandy owes Mike $5,000 that she is unable to repay, can she assign to him her rights as a limited liability company member to receive payments as set forth in the company's operating agreement? Can Sandy assign her entire rights in the limited liability to Mike, making him a new member with the right to manage the business?

5. Katherine is a member of a member-managed limited liability company that designs software called K & A Software Ltd. Liability Company. Can she enter the company into a contract for the design of new educational software for a local college? What if the K & A Software Ltd. Liability Company is manager-managed?

6. As a legal assistant for a law firm, you have just been given an attorney's notes from an initial client meeting and asked to draft the Articles of Organization for a new limited liability company. What are some of the steps you might take to determine the requirements and format to use for drafting the Articles?

7. Suppose that you are forming a limited liability company that will own and operate auto dealerships. Your company will only operate one dealership in Missouri to start with, but you want to expand into Illinois, Texas and Arizona. What steps might you take during the organization process to plan for your future expansion?

8. If you are a family practice physician going into business with three other doctors, what options are available in your state for transacting business? Why might a limited liability partnership be an attractive alternative?

Notes

1 Florida and Texas treat the limited liability company as a corporation for income tax purposes.

2 Rev. Rul. 88-76.

3 Uniform Limited Liability Company Act § 601.

4 Uniform Limited Liability Company Act § 801.

5 Uniform Limited Liability Company Act § 805.

6 Texas is one state that provides that members may agree to be personally liable for the limited liability company's debts (1991 Tex. Sess. Law Serv. ch. 901, H.B. 278, § 46, art. 4.03.)

CHAPTER 5

CORPORATIONS

Organizations exist for only one purpose: to help people reach ends together that they could not achieve individually.

Robert H. Waterman
Management consultant and writer
The Renewal Factor *(Bantam, 1987)*

Introduction

The corporation is one of the most complex forms of business organization. There are many types of corporations, most of which are subjects of entire texts of their own. This chapter and the rest of this book focus on the *business corporation,* which is the predominant form of corporation. First we define the term *corporation,* determine the characteristics of business corporations, and discuss the role of business corporations in the United States. Next, we examine the rights and powers of a corporation and consider both the advantages and disadvantages of doing business as a business corporation, in contrast to other types of business organization. This chapter concludes with a discussion of other types and classifications of corporations, a look at the role of the legal assistant working in the corporate law area, and the resources available to assist paralegals working in the corporate law area.

§ 5.1 An Introduction to Corporations

This section defines the term *corporation* and looks at some of the characteristics common to business corporations, including the fact that corporations are considered to be separate entities for most purposes. Next it defines and discusses "piercing the corporate veil" and examines the law governing corporations.

Corporation Defined

An early Supreme Court decision defined the corporation as "an artificial being, invisible, intangible, and existing only in contemplation of law."[1] This definition has been used frequently over the years.

Another definition that is popular in the courts defines the corporation as a "creature of the law, with an identity or personality separate and distinct from that of its owners, and which, by necessity, must act through its agents."[2] Whatever the exact definition, the corporation possesses four characteristics that distinguish it from other types of business organizations:

1. The corporation is an artificial entity created by law.
2. The corporation is an entity separate from its owners or managers.
3. The corporation has certain rights and powers, which it exercises through its agents.
4. The corporation has the capacity to exist perpetually.

The Corporation As a Separate Legal Entity

In contrast to the sole proprietorship and general partnership, which are extensions of the individual owner or owners, the corporation is considered "an entity distinct from its individual members or stockholders, who, as natural persons, are merged in the corporate identity, and remains unchanged and unaffected in its identity by changes in its individual membership."[3] In many respects, corporations are treated as artificial persons under law, unless the law provides otherwise. As an artificial person, a corporation is subject to many of the same rights and obligations under law as a natural person. The courts have found on several occasions that "[w]hile all statutes which speak of persons cannot be construed to include artificial persons—that is, corporations—the term 'person' may unquestionably include a corporation."[4] It is the intent behind the statute that must be considered.

Because the corporation is a separate entity, the corporation itself is liable for any debts and obligations it incurs. The shareholders, directors, and officers of a corporation are generally not personally liable for the debts and obligations of the corporation merely by virtue of their interest in the corporation.

Piercing the Corporate Veil

Although the shareholders of a corporation are generally free from personal liability for the corporation's obligations, there are certain circumstances under which the corporate entity may be disregarded and shareholders may be considered personally liable for its debts and obligations. This is referred to as *piercing the corporate veil*. Courts generally

Dividends

How Do Corporate Paralegal Salaries Rate?

In general, corporate paralegals are paid better and receive better benefits than their colleagues that specialize in other areas of law. According to a 1995 survey by the National Federation of Paralegal Associations (NFPA), corporate paralegals constitute approximately 7.5 percent of all paralegals.

Corporate paralegals work for both private law firms that represent corporations and for corporate legal departments. Approximately 18 percent of all paralegals are employed by corporations. However, many of these may specialize in litigation or other areas of law.

Also according to the NFPA survey, the average salary of paralegals employed by corporations was $36,245, in comparison to the $31,924 average salary of paralegals employed by law firms. The overall 1995 average salary of paralegals who responded to the survey was $32,875.

Paralegals who are employed by corporations also often enjoy some of the following advantages over paralegals who work in law firms:

1. The corporation may enjoy a more relaxed atmosphere than the typical law firm
2. Excessive overtime is not usually required
3. Corporate fringe benefits may be more generous than those offered by law firms
4. Paralegals employed by corporations typically have no minimum billable hour requirements.

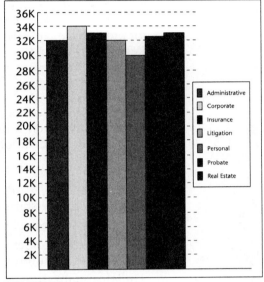

Average Salary by Area of Law

Legend: Administrative, Corporate, Insurance, Litigation, Personal, Probate, Real Estate

1993 NFPA Salary Survey

On the other hand, corporate paralegals who work in law firms often enjoy the fast-paced atmosphere and variety associated with working for several different attorneys and corporate clients.

The future also looks promising for corporate paralegals. Recent hiring trends indicate that corporate paralegals, especially those with specialized experience, are very much in demand, and the demand is increasing rapidly.[1]

[1] Patrick, Diane, "The Latest Hiring Trends," *Legal Assistant Today* 75 (March/April 1994).

---

are reluctant to pierce the corporate veil, but may do so when the corporation is used to avoid a clear legislative purpose,[5] or when it is necessary to preserve, protect, and enforce the rights of others or to prevent an injustice.[6]

The corporate veil of a small or closely held corporation may also be pierced when the corporation is found to be an alter ego of an individual and if such attribution of liability is in the interest of securing a just determination of the action.[7] Courts have found that the "corporate entity may be disregarded where there is such unity of interest and ownership that the separate personalities of the corporation and the individual no longer exist and where, if the acts are treated as those of the corporation alone, an inequitable result will follow."[8]

Keeping in mind that courts will usually seek to pierce the corporate veil only to prevent inequity, injustice, or fraud, other factors are taken into consideration. The corporation is closely scrutinized to determine if it is actually being operated as a corporation and to determine if statutory formalities for incorporating and operating the corporation have been followed. The following factors are often taken into consideration in support of piercing the corporate veil:

1. Improper or incomplete incorporation
2. Commingling of corporate and shareholder funds
3. Failure to follow statutory formalities
4. Failure to hold regular shareholders' and directors' meetings
5. Failure of shareholders to represent themselves as agents of a corporation, rather than individuals, when dealing with outside parties
6. Undercapitalization

To provide an equitable settlement of the corporation's debts, and to preserve the rights of certain creditors, the corporate veil may be pierced and the corporate existence ignored by a bankruptcy court under the Federal Bankruptcy Act. The Internal Revenue Service also may seek to pierce the corporate veil when the corporate entity is used solely for the purpose of income tax evasion.

The fact that it is possible for the corporate veil to be pierced under certain circumstances makes it imperative that all corporate formalities be followed by the corporation and that those formalities be properly documented. In the following case, the corporate defendant was found to be merely an alter ego of its owner, and the corporate veil was pierced.

Law Governing Corporations

As a separate entity, the corporation must be in compliance with all laws concerning it. The source of most laws to which corporations are subject is state statutes, common law, case law, or federal statutes.

LAKOTA GIRL SCOUT COUNCIL
v.
HAVEY FUND-RAISING MANAGEMENT
Eighth Circuit
519 F.2d 634 (8th Cir. 1975)
June 27, 1975
Webster, Circuit Judge

Havey Fund-Raising Management, Inc., and Francis P. Havey appeal from a jury verdict and a judgment awarding damages against them for breach of a contract to provide fund-raising services to the plaintiff, Lakota Girl Scout Council, Inc. They do not challenge the jury's finding that the contract was breached, but contend instead that (1) the District Court lacked personal jurisdiction over Francis P. Havey, founder and chief executive officer of Havey Fund-Raising Management, Inc.; (2) there was insufficient evidence to find Francis P. Havey liable as the alter ego of the corporation, the entity with which plaintiff Lakota Girl Scout Council, Inc., had contracted; and (3) the court erroneously allowed the jury to consider lost profits as a measure of damages and improperly admitted opinion evidence in support thereof. We affirm the judgment of the District Court.

In 1968, the Lakota Girl Scout Council decided to hold a fund-raising drive, the proceeds of which would be used to develop year-around facilities at its 175-acre campsite near Dayton, Iowa. Four professional fund-raising firms, including Havey Fund-Raising, Inc. were considered to coordinate the campaign. Havey Fund-Raising conducted a survey and informed the Council that it was feasible to raise $325,000-$350,000 for the project. The Council thereupon set its goal at $345,000 and selected Havey Fund-Raising, Inc. to assist it.

On October 1, 1968, the parties executed a contract: Havey Fund-Raising was to provide professional assistance to help the Council reach its goal in return for a fee of $28,000; the Havey firm did not guarantee that any money would in fact be raised. When Havey Fund-Raising failed to perform in accordance with the contract and the campaign fell far short of its goal, the Council instituted this action, seeking various enumerated damages.

In the course of discovery, the Council determined to its satisfaction that Havey Fund-Raising, Inc. was the alter ego of Francis P. Havey and accordingly sought to join Havey as a party defendant. The District Court allowed Havey to be joined, pursuant to Fed.R.Civ.P. 20, and later denied Havey's motion to quash service for want of **in personam jurisdiction**.

The case was tried and submitted to a jury, which awarded the Council $35,000 in damages and, in response to a special **interrogatory**, found the corporation to be Havey's alter ego. The District Court entered judgment against

---

TERMS

in personam jurisdiction (or **jurisdiction in personam**) † The jurisdiction a court has over the person of a defendant. It is acquired by service of process upon the defendant or by his or her voluntary submission to jurisdiction. Voluntary submission may be implied from a defendant's conduct within the jurisdiction, for example, by doing business in a state or by operating a motor vehicle within a state (see implied consent statutes). Jurisdiction in personam is also referred to as personal jurisdiction.

interrogatory Written question submitted by one party to a lawsuit to another party in the lawsuit, which must be answered in writing and under oath. The court may also submit written interrogatories upon one or more issues of fact to the jury. The answers to these interrogatories are necessary for a verdict.

both defendants for $35,000, "piercing the corporate veil" of Havey Fund-Raising, Inc. on the basis of the jury's answer to the special interrogatory. ...

[T]he propriety of the District Court's assertion of jurisdiction in the instant case ultimately depends upon the propriety of its decision to pierce the corporate veil of Havey Fund-Raising, Inc.

Evidence was introduced at trial showing that (1) Francis P. Havey is and has always been the sole shareholder of Havey Fund-Raising, Inc.; (2) Havey was the firm's sole incorporator and his capital contribution was $550.00; (3) Havey, and no one else, gave loans to and borrowed money from the corporation; (4) Havey and his wife owned the building where the company was headquartered and received rental payments from the company; (5) the company purchased a Lincoln automobile for Havey's business use which Havey also used for incidental personal business. In short, the evidence was overwhelming that Havey dominated and controlled the business and treated it as his own.

Judge Hanson submitted a special interrogatory to the jury on this subject in which he stated that a corporation's existence is presumed to be separate, but can be disregarded if (1) the corporation is undercapitalized, (2) without separate books, (3) its finances are not kept separate from individual finances, individual obligations are paid by the corporation, (4) the corporation is used to promote fraud or illegality, (5) corporate formalities are not followed or (6) the corporation is merely a sham. In response, the jury found the corporation to be the alter ego of Francis P. Havey.

Judge Hanson's interrogatory properly enumerates the factors that may be considered in determining if a corporation is merely the alter ego of its dominating shareholder. ... There was ample evidence from which the jurors could find that the corporation was Havey's alter ego; their finding is supported by substantial evidence and the determination of the trial judge to hold Havey liable by piercing the veil was not an abuse of his equity power ... .

State Statutes

Corporations are created by and generally governed by the statutes of the **state of domicile** (the state in which the corporation is incorporated). A corporation that is qualified to do business in a foreign state, however, subjects itself to the statutes of that state for certain purposes.

The statutes of every state in the country are derived, at least in part, from the Model Business Corporation Act, first published in 1950, or the 1984 Revised Model Business Corporation Act. These acts were drafted by the American Bar Association Section of Corporation, Banking and Business Law, and the 1984 Revised Model Business Corporation Act continues to be revised through the date of this publication. In this text, all references to the "Model Business Corporation Act" are to the 1984 Revised Model Business Corporation Act, as amended through 1994. (See Appendix E for the 1984 Revised Model Business Corporation Act, as amended.)

TERMS

state of domicile   The home state of a corporation or partnership; the state in which the corporation is incorporated or the partnership is formed.

Unlike the Uniform Partnership and Limited Partnership Acts, the model corporation acts are just *model* acts, not *uniform* acts. The model acts serve only as an aid to the state legislatures in drafting their own statutes, and corporate laws still vary significantly from state to state. The laws of the state of Delaware, which is often referred to as the "incorporation state," also often serve as a model to the legislatures of other states.

Common Law and Case Law

Corporations are created and governed by statute. Therefore, common and case law play a less significant role in governing corporations. However, the number of corporate issues decided in court illustrates that case law is relevant in interpreting the law governing corporations and in ruling on matters not covered by the statutes. Because Delaware has such a disproportionately high number of domestic corporations, much of today's corporate law has been derived from the decisions of the courts of Delaware.

Federal Statutes

Federal law also governs certain aspects of a corporation. For instance, securities matters of public corporations are subject to federal statutes and regulations, as well as the statutes of the state of incorporation. The Securities Exchange Act of 1934 and the Securities Act of 1933 are the major federal laws governing corporations that sell shares of stock or other securities publicly. Corporations are also subject to federal legislation in other areas that govern and regulate corporations, including, among others, the areas of bankruptcy, interstate commerce, and taxation.

§ 5.2 Corporations in the United States

This text focuses on the law of corporations; therefore, a full analysis of the influence of United States corporations on our society is beyond its scope. However, it is important to recognize the magnitude of the role that the corporation plays in the United States economy and in each of our lives. During 1991, United States corporations reported nearly $10 trillion in business receipts—almost ten times that of sole proprietorships and partnerships combined.[9]

Most of us are dependent on a corporation for our livelihoods, be it a small, family-owned corporation or a multimillion-dollar corporate conglomerate. We also cannot overlook the great influence that corporate marketing has over the consumer purchases we make and the prices we pay for those goods. The most recent figures available indicate that corporations report over $129 billion per year in advertising expenses.[10]

§ 5.3   Corporate Rights and Powers

As a separate entity, the corporation enjoys certain rights and powers separate from those of its shareholders, directors, or officers. Corporations, as artificial persons, are entitled to many of the same rights as natural persons, including many of the same constitutional rights. There are, however, many exceptions to this rule. For instance, the Fourteenth Amendment to the Constitution, which guarantees liberty, and the Fifth Amendment, which protects persons from self-incrimination, apply to natural persons only. Additionally, corporations are generally not considered to be "citizens" as that word is used in the federal constitution.

Many powers are granted to corporations by state statute, and may be limited or enhanced by the corporation's **articles of incorporation**. The following section from the Model Business Corporation Act enumerates the powers granted to corporations under that Act:

3.02   GENERAL POWERS

Unless its articles of incorporation provide otherwise, every corporation has perpetual duration and succession in its corporate name and has the same powers as an individual to do all things necessary or convenient to carry out its business and affairs, including without limitation power:

(1)   to sue and be sued, complain and defend in its corporate name;
(2)   to have a corporate seal, which may be altered at will, and to use it, or a facsimile of it, by impressing or affixing it or in any other manner reproducing it;

TERMS
---

articles of incorporation [†]   The charter or basic rules that create a corporation and by which it functions. Among other things, it states the purposes for which the corporation is being organized, the amount of authorized capital stock, and the names and addresses of the directors and incorporators.

(3) to make and amend bylaws, not inconsistent with its articles of incorporation or with the laws of this state, for managing the business and regulating the affairs of the corporation;

(4) to purchase, receive, lease, or otherwise acquire, and own, hold, improve, use, and otherwise deal with, real or personal property, or any legal or equitable interest in property, wherever located;

(5) to sell, convey, mortgage, pledge, lease, exchange, and otherwise dispose of all or any part of its property;

(6) to purchase, receive, subscribe for, or otherwise acquire; own, hold, vote, use, sell, mortgage, lend, pledge, or otherwise dispose of; and deal in and with shares or other interests in, or obligations of, any other entity;

(7) to make contracts and guarantees, incur liabilities, borrow money, issue its notes, bonds, and other obligations (which may be convertible into or include the option to purchase other securities of the corporation), and secure any of its obligations by mortgage or pledge of any of its property, franchises, or income;

(8) to lend money, invest and reinvest its funds, and receive and hold real and personal property as security for repayment;

(9) to be a promoter, partner, member, associate, or manager of any partnership, joint venture, trust or other entity;

(10) to conduct its business, locate offices, and exercise the powers granted by this Act within or without this state;

(11) to elect directors and appoint officers, employees, and agents of the corporation, define their duties, fix their compensation, and lend them money and credit;

(12) to pay pensions and establish pension plans, pension trusts, profit sharing plans, share bonus plans, share option plans, and benefit or incentive plans for any or all of its current or former directors, officers, employees, and agents;

(13) to make donations for the public welfare or for charitable, scientific, or educational purposes;

(14) to transact any lawful business that will aid governmental policy;

(15) to make payments or donations, or do any other act, not inconsistent with law, that furthers the business and affairs of the corporation.

§ 5.4 Advantages of Doing Business As a Corporation

The advantages of doing business as a corporation are both numerous and unique. Most of the advantages stem from the separate entity characteristic of the corporation. This section discusses the corporation's advantages over partnerships and sole proprietorships. The advantages we focus on include the limited liability available to the shareholders of the corporation, income tax benefits, the continuity of the business of a corporation, and the increased opportunities to raise capital for corporations. We also examine the benefits of the centralized management structure of a corporation and the relative ease with which corporate ownership can be transferred.

Limited Liability

Probably the most prevalent reason for forming a corporation is the limited liability that the corporate structure offers to its shareholders, directors, and officers. Theoretically, the corporation is responsible for its own debts and obligations, leaving the shareholders, directors, and officers free from personal liability.

This can be a benefit to an individual or group of individuals wanting to start a business in several ways. Most obviously, the founders of the corporation put at risk only their initial investment in the corporation and protect their personal assets. Also, the ability to raise capital to start and operate the business is increased, because potential investors may own a piece of the corporation and put at risk no more than their investment to purchase shares of stock.

The limited liability benefit of incorporating does have its boundaries, however. As discussed previously in this § 5.1, the corporate veil may be pierced under certain circumstances, leaving the individual shareholders exposed to personal liability for the corporation's debts and obligations. Also, as a practical matter, shareholders of a new or small corporation are often required to give their personal guarantees to obtain financing on behalf of the corporation. If the corporation has few assets in its own name, banks and other lenders often refuse financing to the corporation without the personal guarantee of individual shareholders who have an adequate net worth to secure the corporation's loan.

Beneficial Tax Treatment

With the exception of S corporations, which are discussed in § 5.6, corporations are taxed as separate entities, and a corporate income tax is payable on the net income earned by the corporation. This can be an advantage under certain circumstances.

Corporate Expenses

Many corporate expenses, including employees' salaries, can be itemized and subtracted from the earnings of the corporation to reduce the taxable profits of the corporation.

Employee Benefit Plans

The owners of a corporation may be in a position to take advantage of several employee benefit plans that can be used both to compensate employees and to reduce the income tax liability of the corporation. These benefits may be in the form of contributions to qualified pension and profit-sharing plans, group-term life insurance, medical care insurance, medical reimbursement plans, and other employee benefits. Many of these benefits constitute nontaxable income to the employee-shareholders of the corporation and can be used as a means to pass tax-free income through to the shareholders of the corporation, while giving the added bonus of a tax deduction to the corporation.

In recent years the Internal Revenue Service (IRS) has put several restrictions on plans that are designed for the benefit of highly compensated key employees/shareholders and discriminate against lesser-paid employees. Many types of employee benefit plans must be qualified by the IRS to ensure the full deduction to the corporation. In general, qualified plans must not be designed to favor highly compensated employee/shareholders while discriminating against the average employee. Qualified retirement plans are discussed in Chapter 13.

Choice of Tax Year

With the exception of S corporations, corporations may freely choose their fiscal tax year, which may be different from the calendar year. The corporation can choose the tax year that is most advantageous to its business and that best fits its natural business cycle.

Business Continuity

Another important advantage of doing business as a corporation is that the corporation has the ability to exist perpetually. Unlike the sole proprietorship or partnership, the corporation does not dissolve upon the death or withdrawal of any of its shareholders, officers, or directors. Shares of stock may be sold, given, or bequeathed to others without affecting the continuity of the corporation or its business.

Ability to Raise Capital

Compared to sole proprietorships or partnerships, the corporation has an increased potential for raising capital. Investors may be enticed by the tax benefits and limited liability offered by corporations. The flexible nature of the corporate capital structure allows corporations to appeal to a wide variety of investors with varying needs; for example, the corporation may sell shares of stock of different classes. The financial structure of a corporation is discussed in Chapter 8 of this text. Securities are discussed in Chapter 9.

Centralized Management

Although the shareholders of a corporation have the right to vote for directors of the corporation, they generally do not have an automatic right to participate directly in the management of the business, as general partners do. Shareholders participate in management of the corporation through their votes for the directors of the corporation. The directors, in turn, are given the right to elect the officers of the corporation—the individuals they feel are the best people to operate the day-to-day business of the corporation. The officers are given the authority to operate the business as they see fit, with little interference from the board of directors or shareholders. Shareholder or director approval, or both, must be given to certain extraordinary actions taken by the officers on behalf of the corporation, however.

In small, closely held corporations, the shareholders often elect themselves to be the directors and officers of the corporation. In effect, the small corporation is often run by the owners of the corporation. In contrast, directors and officers of larger corporations may own little or no stock in the corporation they work for. Corporate management and the roles of the officers, shareholders, and directors are discussed in more detail in Chapter 7 of this text.

Transferability of Ownership

In contrast to the sole proprietorship, limited liability company, and partnership, the ownership interest of a corporation is easily transferred. Barring a prohibitive agreement among the shareholders, or restrictions in the corporation's articles of incorporation or bylaws, shares of stock may be bought and sold freely. Because a shareholder's interest in the corporation is represented by stock certificates, the transfer of unrestricted stock may be as simple as an endorsement by the shareholder, on the back of the certificate, to the purchaser or transferee of the stock.

In many situations, however, restrictions are placed on the transfer of shares of closely held corporations, either by statute, the articles of incorporation, bylaws, or in an agreement between the shareholders. These agreements often give the corporation or existing shareholders the first option to purchase the shares of a shareholder who would like to sell stock in the corporation. An agreement of the shareholders may also provide for purchase of shares of a deceased shareholder by the corporation or the other shareholders. Unless addressed in a written agreement, a deceased shareholder's shares of stock are passed on to his or her heirs, just like any other asset. Shareholder agreements restricting the transfer of stock are discussed in more detail in Chapter 7 of this text.

§ 5.5 Disadvantages of Doing Business As a Corporation

The many advantages of doing business as a corporation must be weighed against the disadvantages before a determination can be made as to whether to incorporate. Figure 5-1 summarizes both sides of the question. In this section we explore some of the disadvantages of doing business as a corporation, including the formalities and reporting requirements that must be followed by corporations, and the income taxation disadvantages.

Corporate Formalities and Reporting Requirements

The corporation is the most complex type of business entity, and there are numerous formalities and reporting requirements associated with its formation and maintenance.

First, because the corporation is a creature of statute, it does not exist until formed by the proper documentation filed with the designated state authority in accordance with state law. Articles of incorporation must be filed, and all other statutory requirements for incorporating must be complied with before the corporate existence begins. Corporate formation is discussed in detail in Chapter 6 of this text. Also, unlike sole proprietorships and most partnerships, for a corporation to transact business in any state other than its state of domicile, it must qualify with the proper state authority in the foreign state.

Once the corporation is formed, several ongoing statutory requirements must also be complied with. Annual meetings of the shareholders and directors may be required, and annual reports often are required by the state of domicile. In addition, corporations may be subject to securities regulations that include securities registration and annual and quarterly reporting.

The corporation, as a separate entity, must file a separate corporate income tax return and pay income tax each year to the Internal Revenue Service, its state of domicile, and states in which it transacts business.

All of the foregoing requirements can be time-consuming and costly. However, as mentioned previously in this chapter, it is important that a corporation comply with all corporate formalities to ensure that there is no cause for the corporate veil to be pierced.

Taxation

Although the corporate structure can offer advantages under certain circumstances, in other instances the tax disadvantages may be enough reason to choose another form of business organization.

Double Taxation

The most serious corporate tax drawback is double taxation of the corporate income. Unlike sole proprietorships, partnerships, limited liability companies, and S corporations, most corporations are taxed as entities separate from their shareholders, and must pay income tax on their earnings. In addition, the shareholders of the corporation must pay income tax on income or dividends received from the corporation. The income of the corporation is, in effect, taxed twice.

Taxes Peculiar to Corporations

In addition to income tax, corporations may be subject to special state taxes, including incorporation taxes and franchise taxes. Corporations

---

ADVANTAGES AND DISADVANTAGES OF DOING BUSINESS AS A CORPORATION

Advantages

- Limited liability for shareholders
- Beneficial tax treatment
- Business continuity
- Ability to raise capital
- Centralized management
- Transferability of ownership

Disadvantages

- Corporate formalities and reporting requirements
- Double taxation
- Legal expenses

FIGURE 5-1   Corporation's Advantages versus Disadvantages

are also subject to fees and taxes in any foreign states in which they transact business.

§ 5.6 Types and Classifications of Corporations

There are many types and classifications of corporations, stemming from their financial structure, ownership, and purpose. This section deals only with the more common types and classifications of corporations, to give a general understanding of their nature and purpose, including business corporations, professional corporations, nonprofit corporations, S corporations, statutory close corporations, and parent and subsidiary corporations.

Business Corporations

Business corporations, which include large, publicly held corporations and smaller, closely held corporations, are by far the most common type of corporation in this country. This is the type of corporation that this text focuses on, unless otherwise indicated. As discussed previously in this chapter, business corporations generally may be formed for the purpose of engaging in any lawful business, unless a more limited purpose is desired.

Professional Corporations

Under common law, professionals were allowed to practice only as individuals or partners. In recent years, most states have adopted statutes providing for the formation of *professional corporations,* or *professional service corporations,* as they are sometimes called. These corporations are treated in much the same way as a business corporation, with a few important distinctions.

Typically, state statutes provide that the professional corporation is subject to all the provisions of that state's business corporation act, except to the extent that it is inconsistent with the professional corporation act of that state. Many professional corporation acts are based on the Model Professional Corporation Act, which provides that professional corporations may be formed "only for the purpose of rendering professional services and services ancillary thereto within a single profession."[11] An exception to the single profession rule permits one or more professions to be combined to the extent permitted by the licensing laws of the state of domicile.

Some state statutes enumerate the types of professions that may be incorporated under the professional corporation statutes. These lists typically include many of the following professions: physicians and surgeons, chiropractors, podiatrists, engineers, electrologists, physical therapists, psychologists, certified public accountants and public accountants, dentists, veterinarians, optometrists, attorneys, and licensed acupuncturists. Often the statutes provide that professional corporations may be formed for the performance of any type of service which may be rendered only pursuant to a license issued by law.

Many types of professionals have the option as to whether to incorporate as a professional corporation or a business corporation. Given a choice, it is usually advantageous to incorporate under the business corporation laws of the state in question, as the professional corporation laws are generally more restrictive.

The enactment of professional corporation acts has allowed professionals to realize many of the tax and other benefits normally associated with corporations that were not previously available to them as partners or sole proprietors. Of special interest to professionals is the limited liability benefit associated with the corporate structure. Although licensed professionals remain personally liable for their own acts and omissions, professionals practicing in a group may incorporate to provide protection against personal liability for the acts and omissions of their associates, or for torts committed by them.

In addition to the restricted corporate purpose, several other restrictions also apply to professional corporations. For instance, stock ownership of professional corporations typically has statutory restrictions placed upon it. The stock of a professional corporation usually may be owned only by licensed professionals, or partnerships consisting only of partners who are licensed professionals.

Nonprofit Corporations

Another common type of corporation is the *nonprofit corporation,* or *not-for-profit corporation* as it is sometimes referred to, which is formed only for certain nonprofit purposes. Many nonprofit corporations are formed for charitable, civic, educational, and religious purposes. However, nonprofit corporations may be formed for several different reasons.

Nonprofit corporations are generally governed under the nonprofit corporation statutes of the state of domicile. Many states' nonprofit corporation acts were based on the Model Nonprofit Corporation Act.

Incorporating as a nonprofit corporation does not insure exemption from federal income taxation. To qualify for federal tax exemption,

the nonprofit corporation must meet the requirements of the Internal Revenue Code (IRC) and obtain approval from the Internal Revenue Service. IRC § 501(c) lists specifically the purposes that may qualify a nonprofit corporation for tax-exempt status.

S Corporations

The Internal Revenue Service recognizes a special category of corporations, referred to as *S corporations,* for federal income tax purposes. This category is made up of eligible small business corporations that file elections to be treated as S corporations. All shareholders of the corporation must agree to the election. There is usually no distinction between S corporations and other types of corporations at the state level.

Unlike a business corporation, the income of an S corporation generally is not taxed at the corporate level, but is passed through to the shareholders of the corporation, much like income is passed through to the partners of a partnership. S corporation status is often elected by smaller, closely held corporations that are formed with the expectation of incurring a net loss for the first few years. The loss of the corporation is passed on to the shareholders of the corporation, who may use it to offset their other income.

Pursuant to § 1361 of the Internal Revenue Code, S corporations must make an election to be treated as such by filing a Form 2553 (shown in Figure 5-2), and they must meet the following eligibility requirements:

1. The corporation must be a domestic corporation.
2. The corporation must have no more than 35 shareholders. A husband and wife (and their estates) are treated as a single shareholder.
3. The corporation's shareholders must all be individuals, estates, or trusts that meet certain prerequisites.
4. Nonresident aliens may not be shareholders.
5. The corporation cannot issue more than one class of stock.
6. The corporation may not be a member of an affiliated group. Consequently, the corporation may not be a holding company.
7. The corporation may not be a financial institution to which Internal Revenue Code §§ 585 or 593 apply.
8. The corporation may not be an insurance company taxable under Subchapter L by the Internal Revenue Code.
9. The corporation may not have elected to come under IRC § 936 concerning the Puerto Rico and possession tax credits.
10. The corporation may not be a domestic international sales corporation (DISC) or former DISC under the Internal Revenue Code.

Form 2553
(Rev. September 1993)

Department of the Treasury
Internal Revenue Service

Election by a Small Business Corporation
(Under section 1362 of the Internal Revenue Code)
▶ For Paperwork Reduction Act Notice, see page 1 of instructions.
▶ See separate instructions.

OMB No. 1545-0146
Expires 8-31-96

Notes: 1. This election, to be an "S corporation," can be accepted only if all the tests are met under **Who May Elect** on page 1 of the instructions; all signatures in Parts I and III are originals (no photocopies); and the exact name and address of the corporation and other required form information are provided.

2. Do not file **Form 1120S**, U.S. Income Tax Return for an S Corporation, until you are notified that your election is accepted.

Part I   **Election Information**

Please Type or Print	Name of corporation (see instructions)	A Employer identification number (EIN)
	Number, street, and room or suite no. (If a P.O. box, see instructions.)	B Date incorporated
	City or town, state, and ZIP code	C State of incorporation

D   Election is to be effective for tax year beginning (month, day, year) . . . . ▶   /   /

E   Name and title of officer or legal representative who the IRS may call for more information   F   Telephone number of officer or legal representative ( )

G   If the corporation changed its name or address after applying for the EIN shown in A, check this box . . . . ▶ ☐

H   If this election takes effect for the first tax year the corporation exists, enter month, day, and year of the **earliest** of the following: (1) date the corporation first had shareholders, (2) date the corporation first had assets, or (3) date the corporation began doing business . . . . ▶   /   /

I   Selected tax year: Annual return will be filed for tax year ending (month and day) ▶ . . . .
If the tax year ends on any date other than December 31, except for an automatic 52-53-week tax year ending with reference to the month of December, you **must** complete Part II on the back. If the date you enter is the ending date of an automatic 52-53-week tax year, write "52-53-week year" to the right of the date. See Temporary Regulations section 1.441-2T(e)(3).

J Name and address of each shareholder, shareholder's spouse having a community property interest in the corporation's stock, and each tenant in common, joint tenant, and tenant by the entirety. (A husband and wife (and their estates) are counted as one shareholder in determining the number of shareholders without regard to the manner in which the stock is owned.)	K Shareholders' Consent Statement. Under penalties of perjury, we declare that we consent to the election of the above-named corporation to be an "S corporation" under section 1362(a) and that we have examined this consent statement, including accompanying schedules and statements, and to the best of our knowledge and belief, it is true, correct, and complete. (Shareholders sign and date below.)*		L Stock owned		M Social security number or employer identification number (see instructions)	N Share-holder's tax year ends (month and day)
	Signature	Date	Number of shares	Dates acquired		

*For this election to be valid, the consent of each shareholder, shareholder's spouse having a community property interest in the corporation's stock, and each tenant in common, joint tenant, and tenant by the entirety must either appear above or be attached to this form. (See instructions for Column K if a continuation sheet or a separate consent statement is needed.)

Under penalties of perjury, I declare that I have examined this election, including accompanying schedules and statements, and to the best of my knowledge and belief, it is true, correct, and complete.

Signature of officer ▶   Title ▶   Date ▶

See Parts II and III on back.   Cat. No. 18629R   Form **2553** (Rev. 9-93)

FIGURE 5-2   IRS Form 2553, Election by a Small Business Corporation

S corporation status may be revoked only if shareholders holding a majority of the shares of stock of the corporation consent to the revocation. If the corporation ceases to meet these requirements, and all other requirements set forth in the Internal Revenue Code, the business may lose its S corporation status.

Form 2553 (Rev. 9-93) Page **2**

Part II Selection of Fiscal Tax Year (All corporations using this part must complete item O and one of items P, Q, or R.)

O Check the applicable box below to indicate whether the corporation is:
   1. ☐ A new corporation adopting the tax year entered in item I, Part I.
   2. ☐ An existing corporation retaining the tax year entered in item I, Part I.
   3. ☐ An existing corporation changing to the tax year entered in item I, Part I.

P Complete item P if the corporation is using the expeditious approval provisions of Revenue Procedure 87-32, 1987-2 C.B. 396, to request: **(1)** a natural business year (as defined in section 4.01(1) of Rev. Proc. 87-32), or **(2)** a year that satisfies the ownership tax year test in section 4.01(2) of Rev. Proc. 87-32. Check the applicable box below to indicate the representation statement the corporation is making as required under section 4 of Rev. Proc. 87-32.

   1. Natural Business Year ► ☐ I represent that the corporation is retaining or changing to a tax year that coincides with its natural business year as defined in section 4.01(1) of Rev. Proc. 87-32 and as verified by its satisfaction of the requirements of section 4.02(1) of Rev. Proc. 87-32. In addition, if the corporation is changing to a natural business year as defined in section 4.01(1), I further represent that such tax year results in less deferral of income to the owners than the corporation's present tax year. I also represent that the corporation is not described in section 3.01(2) of Rev. Proc. 87-32. (See instructions for additional information that must be attached.)

   2. Ownership Tax Year ► ☐ I represent that shareholders holding more than half of the shares of the stock (as of the first day of the tax year to which the request relates) of the corporation have the same tax year or are concurrently changing to the tax year that the corporation adopts, retains, or changes to per item I, Part I. I also represent that the corporation is not described in section 3.01(2) of Rev. Proc. 87-32.

Note: If you do not use item P and the corporation wants a fiscal tax year, complete either item Q or R below. Item Q is used to request a fiscal tax year based on a business purpose and to make a back-up section 444 election. Item R is used to make a regular section 444 election.

Q Business Purpose—To request a fiscal tax year based on a business purpose, you must check box Q1 and pay a user fee. See instructions for details. You may also check box Q2 and/or box Q3.

   1. Check here ► ☐ if the fiscal year entered in item I, Part I, is requested under the provisions of section 6.03 of Rev. Proc. 87-32. Attach to Form 2553 a statement showing the business purpose for the requested fiscal year. See instructions for additional information that must be attached.

   2. Check here ► ☐ to show that the corporation intends to make a back-up section 444 election in the event the corporation's business purpose request is not approved by the IRS. (See instructions for more information.)

   3. Check here ► ☐ to show that the corporation agrees to adopt or change to a tax year ending December 31 if necessary for the IRS to accept this election for S corporation status in the event: (1) the corporation's business purpose request is not approved and the corporation makes a back-up section 444 election, but is ultimately not qualified to make a section 444 election, or (2) the corporation's business purpose request is not approved and the corporation did not make a back-up section 444 election.

R Section 444 Election—To make a section 444 election, you must check box R1 and you may also check box R2.

   1. Check here ► ☐ to show the corporation will make, if qualified, a section 444 election to have the fiscal tax year shown in item I, Part I. To make the election, you must complete **Form 8716,** Election To Have a Tax Year Other Than a Required Tax Year, and either attach it to Form 2553 or file it separately.

   2. Check here ► ☐ to show that the corporation agrees to adopt or change to a tax year ending December 31 if necessary for the IRS to accept this election for S corporation status in the event the corporation is ultimately not qualified to make a section 444 election.

Part III Qualified Subchapter S Trust (QSST) Election Under Section 1361(d)(2)**

Income beneficiary's name and address	Social security number
Trust's name and address	Employer identification number

Date on which stock of the corporation was transferred to the trust (month, day, year) . . . . ► / /

In order for the trust named above to be a QSST and thus a qualifying shareholder of the S corporation for which this Form 2553 is filed, I hereby make the election under section 1361(d)(2). Under penalties of perjury, I certify that the trust meets the definitional requirements of section 1361(d)(3) and that all other information provided in Part III is true, correct, and complete.

Signature of income beneficiary or signature and title of legal representative or other qualified person making the election   Date

**Use of Part III to make the QSST election may be made only if stock of the corporation has been transferred to the trust on or before the date on which the corporation makes its election to be an S corporation. The QSST election must be made and filed separately if stock of the corporation is transferred to the trust after the date on which the corporation makes the S election.

♻ *Printed on recycled paper*   *U.S. Government Printing Office: 1995 — 387-095/20123

FIGURE 5-2 *(continued)*

Statutory Close Corporations

Statutory close corporations are generally considered to be corporations having no more than 50 shareholders (or some other number specified by statute) that have elected to be treated as a statutory close corporation. Statutes applying to statutory close corporations take into consideration the nature of these smaller corporations, which are often operated in a manner similar to partnerships. Courts have recognized that a statutory close corporation often "has a small number of stockholders, there is no ready market for its stock, and all or a substantial majority of the stockholders participate in the management, direction and operations of the corporation."[12]

Statutory close corporations are usually governed by specific statute provisions within the business corporation act of the state of domicile, or in a separate act similar to the Close Corporation Supplement to the Model Business Corporation Act (MBCA), which states, "The ... Business Corporation Act applies to statutory close corporations to the extent not inconsistent with the provisions of this Supplement."[13] Pursuant to the Close Corporation Supplement, a statutory close corporation must include a statement in its articles of incorporation specifically stating that it is a close corporation.[14] Any corporation electing to become a statutory close corporation after its incorporation typically must have the approval of at least two-thirds of the corporation's shareholders. In addition, the stock certificates representing shares of stock of statutory close corporations must contain specific language on their face to indicate to the shareholder that the corporation is a statutory close corporation and that the rights of a shareholder of a statutory close corporation may differ from those of other corporations. State statute provisions may vary from the requirements in the MBCA's Close Corporation Supplement. However, all state statutes have some type of provisions regarding the notification of an election to become a statutory close corporation.

Typically, statutory close corporations are allowed to place certain restrictions on the transfer of shares of the corporation. There may be provisions within the articles of incorporation or another, separate document that provide for such transfer restrictions. The Close Corporation Supplement provides that shares of a close corporation may not be transferred, except as permitted by the articles of incorporation or without first giving the corporation the right of first refusal pursuant to the Close Corporation Supplement, except as follows:

1. A transfer may be made to the corporation or to any other holder of the same class or series of shares.[15]

2. A transfer may be made to members of the shareholder's immediate family.[16]

3. A transfer may be made if it has been approved in writing by all of the holders of the corporation's shares having general voting rights.[17]

4. A transfer may be made to an executor or administrator, upon the death of a shareholder, or to a trustee or receiver as the result of a bankruptcy, insolvency, dissolution, or similar proceeding brought by or against a shareholder.[18]

5. A transfer may be made by a merger or share exchange or an exchange of existing shares for other shares of a different class or series in the corporation.[19]

6. A transfer may be made by a pledge as collateral for a loan that does not grant the pledgee any voting rights possessed by the pledgor.[20]

7. A transfer may be made after termination of the corporation's status as a statutory close corporation.[21]

Statutory close corporations are generally allowed to operate without all of the statutory formalities imposed on other types of corporations. Recognizing that the shareholders and directors of small corporations are often the same individuals, statutory close corporations are usually permitted to operate without a board of directors, leaving the management and operation to the shareholders.

Another formality imposed on other types of corporations that may be waived for statutory close corporations is the necessity of having bylaws. Under § 22 of the MBCA's Close Corporation Supplement, "A statutory close corporation need not adopt bylaws if provisions required by law to be contained in bylaws are contained in either the articles of incorporation or a shareholder agreement authorized by section 20."

In the broadest sense, § 25 of the Close Corporation Supplement grants the close corporation the right to transact business without complying with all of the usual corporate formalities imposed on other types of corporations. Section 25 reads as follows:

> The failure of a statutory close corporation to observe the usual corporate formalities or requirements relating to the exercise of its corporate powers or management of its business and affairs is not a ground for imposing personal liability on the shareholders for liabilities of the corporation.

Parents and Subsidiaries

The parent and subsidiary classifications given to corporations refer to a relationship between corporations, depending on the ownership and control of the corporations. A *parent corporation* is a corporation that owns stock in a subsidiary corporation which is sufficient to control the subsidiary corporation.

§ 5.7 The Role of the Legal Assistant in Corporate Law Matters

In the fast-growing paralegal field, the number of paralegals employed in the corporate area of law is second only to the number working in litigation. In addition to paralegals employed in the corporate law departments of law firms, approximately 10 percent of all paralegals work for corporations, typically in their legal departments.

Short of giving legal advice to corporate clients, corporate paralegals are allowed to assist with almost all areas and aspects of corporate law. Typically the paralegal's duties will be dominated by document drafting and research.

The paralegal working in the corporate law area often specializes in one or more areas within that field, including incorporation and organization of business corporations or nonprofit corporations, corporate mergers and acquisitions, securities law, or qualified retirement plans. Specific duties in each of these areas are discussed in the pertinent chapters of this text.

§ 5.8 Resources

Many resources are available to assist the paralegal working in the corporate law area. In addition to the statutes that the paralegal must be familiar with, there are several sources that may provide useful information, including legal encyclopedias, form books, and state agencies.

State Statutes

The primary source of information on business corporations is the business corporation act (or similar act) in the statutes of the corporation's state of domicile. Information regarding special types of corporations can be found in the pertinent state's close corporation act or supplement, its professional corporation act, and its nonprofit corporation act, any or all of which may be part of the state's business corporation act.

Federal Statutes

Although state law is the primary source of law for corporations, corporations are also subject to special federal statutes and regulations in specific areas, such as interstate commerce, income taxation, bankruptcy, and securities. The paralegal should be aware of the corporation's business focus and alert for possible applications of such federal statutes.

Legal Encyclopedias

Legal encyclopedias, such as *American Jurisprudence 2d* and *Corpus Juris Secundum*, can be a good place to begin research regarding a specific topic concerning corporations that you are unfamiliar with. These references can give you a good background on the topic and refer you to pertinent case law.

Forms and Form Books

For drafting corporate documents, most law firms and corporate law departments have systems and forms to follow. Standard forms and previously drafted documents can be invaluable resources and save the paralegal from having to reinvent the wheel every time a corporate document is to be drafted. However, it is crucial that these resources not be used without careful consideration. All pertinent information must be gathered and appropriately adapted whenever it might be used in newly drafted corporate documents.

Numerous form books are available in the public law libraries and in most in-house law libraries. These may include state-specific form books as well as more generic form books. Some of the more popular form books are *Am. Jur. Forms 2d., Nichols Cyclopedia of Legal Forms Annotated, Rabkin & Johnson Current Legal Forms,* and *West's Legal Forms Second Edition.*

Secretary of State or Other State Corporation Agency

For procedural information regarding incorporations and annual reporting, contact the Secretary of State of the business's state of domicile. (See Appendix A for a Secretary of State directory.)

Review Questions

1. What are four characteristics of a corporation that distinguish it from the sole proprietorship and the partnership?

2. If a corporation defaults on its debts, may the creditors typically look to the shareholders for payment? Under what circumstances might the shareholders become personally liable for the debts of the corporation?

3. Suppose that John's Appliance, Inc., is a corporation formed by John Miller. John Miller is the only owner and employee of John's Appliance, Inc., an appliance repair service business. John Miller has formed the corporation to shelter his personal assets. He has put title to the repair truck (which he often uses for his own personal enjoyment), all of his equipment and tools, and his workshop in his own name, although he leases these items back to the corporation. What are some of the potential problems with this arrangement? What can John Miller do to decrease the risk that the corporate veil of John's Appliances could be pierced in the event of a lawsuit?

4. Dave Breen and Sue Martin would like to start a business involving themselves and D&S Equipment, Inc., a corporation that holds certain of their assets. Could they form a regular business corporation with Dave Breen, Sue Martin, and D&S Equipment, Inc., being the shareholders? Could they form an S corporation?

5. Who elects the directors of a corporation? Who elects the officers? Could an individual be a shareholder, director, and officer all at the same time?

6. Could a group of attorneys and physicians form a professional corporation? Why or why not?

7. Are all corporations incorporated as nonprofit corporations automatically exempt from paying income tax?

8. Explain the general differences between a regular business corporation and an S corporation.

9. What are some of the practical differences between regular business corporations and statutory close corporations?

10. Suppose that Mike and Sandy want to start a business to market a new food product they have invented. Limited liability is important to them because of the potential product liability problems associated with manufacturing and selling food products. Initially, Mike and Sandy will be the only investors, and they may not see a profit in their business for a few years. What types of business organizations are available to Mike and Sandy? What type of organization would you suggest? Why?

Notes

[1] Trustees of Dartmouth College v. Woodward, 17 U.S. (4 Wheat.) 518 (1819); 18 AM. JUR. 2d *Corporations* § 1 (1985).

[2] 18 AM. JUR. 2d *Corporations* § 1 (1985).

[3] *Id.* § 42.

[4] United States v. Union Supply Co., 215 U.S. 50 (1909); 18 AM. JUR. 2d *Corporations* § 65 (1985).

[5] 18 AM. JUR. 2d *Corporations* § 43 (1985).

[6] *Id.* § 44.

[7] *Id.* § 45.

[8] Flynt Distrib. Co. v. Harvey, 734 F.2d 1389 (9th Cir. 1984); 18 AM. JUR. 2d *Corporations* § 45 (1985).

[9] The Reference Press, *The American Almanac Statistical Abstract of the United States: 1994–1995,* 114th ed. at 835, 837, 840 (Austin, Texas 1994).

[10] *Id.*

[11] Model Professional Corporation Act § 3.

[12] 18 AM. JUR. 2d *Corporations* § 36 (1985).

[13] Statutory Close Corporation Supplement § 2(a).

[14] *Id.* § 3(a).

[15] *Id.* § 11(b)(1).

[16] *Id.* § 11(b)(2).

[17] *Id.* § 11(b)(3).

[18] *Id.* § 11(b)(4).

[19] *Id.* § 11(b)(5).

[20] *Id.* § 11(b)(6).

[21] *Id.* § 11(b)(7).

CHAPTER 6

FORMATION OF THE CORPORATION

Introduction

The corporation is an entity that cannot exist unless it has been properly incorporated. Articles or a certificate of incorporation must be filed with the Secretary of State or other appropriate state official, who will give the corporation its life and its right to transact business. This chapter discusses the formation of the corporation, from preincorporation matters through the organizational meeting following incorporation. Special attention is given to preincorporation concerns, the incorporator, the articles of incorporation, organizational meeting, bylaws, and the formation of special types of corporations. This chapter concludes with a look at the role of the paralegal in corporation formations and the resources available to assist paralegals in that area.

§ 6.1 Preincorporation Matters

The life of the corporation does not begin until the proper documentation is filed with the appropriate state authorities. Therefore, some actions that concern the incorporation must necessarily be taken before the corporation actually exists. In this section, we examine the preincorporation matters that are often dealt with by the incorporators of a business corporation, including the decision to incorporate and the choice of a domicile for the corporation. We also discuss the actual promoters of the corporation, preincorporation agreements, and stock subscription agreements. The section concludes with a look at the important task of gathering client information prior to incorporation of a business.

Deciding on the Corporate Structure

When an attorney meets with clients to advise them concerning the formation of a business organization or the expansion of an on-going business, one of the first things they must decide on is the proper format for the business. The attorney and client will consider the advantages and disadvantages of each type of available business organization, as discussed in previous chapters. Then, taking all factors into consideration, including income tax implications, capital requirements, applicable statutory requirements, and desired management structure, and weighing the importance of limited liability, transferability of ownership, ease of forming and dissolving the business entity, and business continuity, a decision will be made as to whether to incorporate.

This chapter investigates the process of forming a business corporation, assuming that the corporation is being created based on an informed consideration of all possibilities.

Choosing a Domicile

The state in which a corporation's articles or certificate of incorporation are filed is considered the corporation's home state or the *state of domicile*. Although it may seem obvious that incorporators should incorporate their businesses in the state in which they live and intend to operate, this is not necessarily true, and should not be taken for granted. Persons forming a corporation usually have their choice of the domicile or state in which they wish to incorporate, and their actual home state may not be the most advantageous for the business. The nature of the state's corporate law is usually the primary consideration, although there are several others. Following is a list of factors to be considered when choosing a state of domicile:

1. Does the law of the state being considered allow the corporation to be operated in the manner desired?
2. What costs are associated with incorporating in the state being considered?
3. What is the state's judicial policy toward corporations?
4. Is the proposed corporate name available in the state being considered?
5. May shareholder meetings be held out of state?
6. What is the statutory treatment of shareholder and director liability?
7. Must any corporate records be kept in the proposed state?
8. What are the annual reporting requirements in the proposed state (tax and informational)?

Dividends

Why Incorporate in Delaware?

Over 200,000 businesses have chosen to incorporate in the state of Delaware. Why is the second smallest state in the country the state of domicile for nearly half of the corporations listed on the New York Stock Exchange? For years Delaware has attracted corporations by adopting corporate laws that are among the most liberal in the country. In addition, the Delaware Department of State, Division of Corporations, is one of the most user-friendly in the country.

The state of Delaware places a high priority on attracting corporations. The Delaware Corporate Law Council of the Delaware State Bar Association works closely with the legislature to keep their state laws among the most attractive in the country. Some of the laws that Delaware has passed to attract corporations include the following features:

- Maximum protection against hostile takeovers
- Limited personal liability of directors and shareholders
- No minimum capital requirements
- No corporate state income tax for corporations that do not conduct business in the state
- Anonymous ownership of a corporation, if desired
- Unanimous written consents and conference calls are permitted in lieu of directors' meetings
- Mergers and acquisitions can be completed with a minimum of red tape
- Directors may determine what part of consideration received for stock is capital
- Corporations may purchase shares of their own stock and hold, sell, or transfer those shares
- No limitations are set on the amount of stock held by the corporation, either inside or outside the state.

Furthermore, the judicial system of Delaware has proven that it can handle an incredible volume of corporate law cases quickly, efficiently, and consistently.

In addition to offering attractive corporate laws and an efficient judicial system, the Delaware Department of State, Division of Corporations, has been set up to handle an enormous number of incorporations in an easy and efficient manner. Some of the special features offered by the Delaware Division of Corporations include the following:

- The division will provide the names and addresses of over fifty professional registered agents that may be retained to act as the corporation's representative in Delaware
- Most documents filed with the division need not be notarized or witnessed
- Professional registered agents in Delaware are allowed direct access to the division's corporate databases
- Corporate names may be reserved by telephone
- Name availability can be checked by telephone free of charge
- Corporate documents are filed on the same day they are received by the division
- The certificate of incorporation and other forms required to incorporate are provided free of charge by the division, upon request
- Many documents can be submitted to the division by facsimile transmission.

Incorporation can be big business, and Delaware has reaped substantial revenues as a result of that business. Currently, many other states are attempting to compete with Delaware to attract more incorporations. It remains to be seen what effect the stiff competition will have on the state of Delaware, and on corporate law in the United States. ▥

In addition to the foregoing factors, the incorporators must be aware of the foreign corporation requirements in states other than the state of domicile. The corporation will be required to qualify to do business as a foreign corporation in any state, other than the state of domicile, in which it transacts business. Each state's statutes set requirements for qualifying as a foreign corporation. These requirements should be researched carefully before deciding where to incorporate.

Historically, many incorporators have chosen to incorporate in the state of Delaware, which is known for its liberal corporate laws and favorable judicial treatment of corporations. In recent years, however, many states have revised their corporate laws to conform more closely to the current Model Business Corporation Act, and the advantages to incorporating in Delaware have diminished somewhat. One clear advantage to incorporating in Delaware remains, however, in that the corporate law of Delaware has been interpreted numerous times in that state's courts, whereas many newer corporate laws of other states have yet to be tested in court.

Promoters

The individual or individuals initiating the incorporation may serve as the **promoter** or promoters of the proposed corporation. A *promoter* is generally considered to be "one who actively assists in creating, projecting, and organizing a corporation."[1]

Any transactions made by the promoter on behalf of the corporation before the actual incorporation are considered to be **preincorporation transactions**. The corporation does not legally exist until its articles of incorporation are properly filed. Therefore, any preincorporation transactions must be ratified by the corporation after it is formed if they are to be valid. Promoters may be liable for contracts entered into on behalf of the future corporation, until the contracts are ratified by the corporation, unless the contracts specifically state that the promoter is acting only on behalf of the future corporation and assumes no personal liability. In the following case, a promoter was held personally liable for expenses incurred on behalf of the future corporation.

When there is a significant amount of planning and organizing before the incorporation of the business, the promoter may have a substantial

---

TERMS

promoter [†] A person who organizes a business venture or is a major participant in organizing the venture.

preincorporation transactions Actions taken by promoters or incorporators prior to the actual formation of the corporation.

TABLE 6-1 1992 INCORPORATIONS BY STATE

State	Number of Incorporations in 1992
Florida	86,037
New York	67,503
California	36,973
Texas	34,011
Delaware	33,582
Illinois	30,928
New Jersey	29,983
Michigan	24,726
Georgia	21,046
Ohio	18,730
Maryland	17,201
Pennsylvania	16,947
Virginia	16,936
Colorado	14,876
Nevada	12,610
North Carolina	12,580
Washington	12,500
Massachusetts	12,197
Indiana	11,119
Louisiana	10,839
Missouri	10,020
Minnesota	10,002
Arizona	9,148
Oregon	8,861
Tennessee	8,514
Connecticut	7,339
Wisconsin	7,289
Oklahoma	7,207
Kentucky	7,155
Alabama	7,087
South Carolina	6,189
Arkansas	6,078
Iowa	4,918
Utah	4,582
Kansas	4,305

TABLE 6-1 *(continued)*

State	Number of Incorporations in 1992
Hawaii	3,792
Mississippi	3,758
Nebraska	3,302
New Mexico	2,843
New Hampshire	2,577
Rhode Island	2,553
Maine	2,431
District of Columbia	2,256
West Virginia	2,236
Idaho	2,127
Montana	1,948
Wyoming	1,707
Vermont	1,589
South Dakota	1,218
North Dakota	984
Alaska	102

role in bringing interested persons together, procuring subscriptions for the stock of the corporation, and seeing to the actual formation of the corporation. However, under most circumstances, the role of the promoter, if there is one, is negligible.

Preincorporation Agreements

Because the incorporation process can usually be completed within a matter of a few days at most, a formal **preincorporation agreement** (an agreement to incorporate) is generally not necessary. However, under any of the following circumstances, a formal preincorporation agreement setting forth the agreement of interested parties may be desirable:

1. When a considerable amount of time will lapse between the decision to incorporate and the actual incorporation

TERMS

preincorporation agreement Agreement entered into between parties setting forth their intentions with regard to the formation of a corporation.

2. When extensive financial contributions in advance of incorporation are required

3. When it is desirable to bind participants to make future financial contributions that may be essential to the business venture

4. When one or more participants are being induced to participate in the venture by promises of employment or other business advantage

5. When it is necessary to protect a trade or business secret.

CLINTON INVESTORS COMPANY, II
v.
WATKINS
Supreme Court, Appellate Division,
Third Department
536 N.Y.S.2d 270 (A.D. 1989)
January 5, 1989
Yesawich, Justice

... Appeal (1) from that part of an order of the Supreme Court (Brown, J.), entered December 1, 1987 in Saratoga County, which *inter alia*, granted a cross-motion by defendants Berne Watkins and Francis White for summary judgment dismissing the complaint against them, and (2) from the judgment entered thereon.

Plaintiff, as landlord, entered into a three-year lease with "The Clifton Park Learning Center" (hereinafter the learning center), as tenant; the lease, which expressly declared throughout that the tenant was "continuing occupancy", was executed on behalf of the tenant by defendant Berne Watkins, who represented himself to be the treasurer of the learning center. On May 31, 1984, the day before the lease term commenced, Watkins signed a rider to the lease, again as treasurer of the learning center, but the rider identified the tenant as "The Clifton Park Learning Center, Inc."

The learning center thereafter occupied the leased premises, procured utilities, conducted business in the corporate name, and paid rent and other expenses by corporate checks. However, Watkins and defendant Francis J. White, who had not consulted an attorney regarding the formation of this corporation, allegedly mistook their reservation of a business name with the Secretary of State for the filing of a certificate of incorporation. There is no mention in the record as to when the name (presumably, the Clifton Park Learning Center, Inc.) was reserved and it was not until February 11, 1985 that a certificate of incorporation, dated January 25, 1985, was filed.

By March 1986, the learning center had become delinquent in its rental payments. Plaintiff's management company requested that White, president of the learning center, sign a promissory note guaranteeing payment of the corporate rent, but White refused. Plaintiff then initiated this action for past rent, maintenance charges, real estate taxes, insurance, late fees and replacement of fixtures, all totaling $18,103.62, plus counsel fees. Thereafter plaintiff moved for summary judgment, prompting Watkins and White to cross-move for summary judgment dismissing the complaint against them. Supreme Court granted plaintiff's motion only as against defendant Clifton Park Learning Center, Inc. and dismissed the action with respect to Watkins and White. Plaintiff, as limited by its brief, appeals from the dismissal of its complaint against Watkins.

... Because no corporation existed when Watkins signed the lease with plaintiff, his legal status was that of a promoter of the learning center ... Generally, a promoter who executes a preincorporation contract in the name of the proposed corporation is himself personally liable on the contract unless the parties have otherwise agreed. ... Watkins asserts that because the learning center corporation subsequently adopted the lease he is therefor no longer liable on the lease. However, corporate adoption of a contract "gives rise to corporate liability in addition to any individual liability" ... so that the promoter nevertheless remains obligated unless there has been a **novation** between the corporation and the plaintiff, which is not the situation here. Nor does the record disclose any explicit or implicit agreement by plaintiff to hold Watkins personally liable on the lease. ... Furthermore, for Watkins to be relieved of his personal liability it must appear that in dealing with him plaintiff knew it was contracting with an as yet nonexistent principal. But the proof is that plaintiff was led to believe by Watkins that the corporation was indeed in existence at the commencement of the lease term. ...

Order and judgment modified, ... motion granted and cross motion denied to the extent that plaintiff is awarded summary judgment against defendant Berne Watkins on the issue of liability, and the matter remitted to the Supreme Court to determine damages; and, as so modified, affirmed.

A preincorporation agreement should, in general, include the agreement of the future corporation's shareholders regarding the terms for formation of the corporation. The preincorporation agreement should address such matters as the content of the articles of incorporation and bylaws, the identity and initial term of the first board of directors, and the identity of the statutory agent of the corporation, if one is to be appointed. The preincorporation agreement may also include the subscription agreement of the future shareholders of the corporation who are entering into the preincorporation agreement.

Stock Subscriptions

A *stock subscription* is an agreement to purchase a stated number of shares of a corporation or a future corporation at a stated price. Often a promoter may aid in the acquisition of preincorporation stock subscriptions to finance the corporation. Once the corporation is actually formed, the subscription agreement is ratified by the corporation and then executed as shares of stock are issued to the subscribers pursuant to the agreements.

TERMS

novation [†] The extinguishment of one obligation by another; a substituted contract that dissolves a previous contractual duty and creates a new one. Novation, which requires the mutual agreement of everyone concerned, replaces a contracting party with a new party who had no rights or obligations under the previous contract.

Stock subscription agreements may be used at any time during the life of the corporation to add new shareholders to the corporation, or to document the purchase of additional shares by existing shareholders. Following is a checklist of matters to be considered when drafting a stock subscription agreement[2]:

- Name and address of each subscriber

- Name of corporation to be formed

- Other identification of corporation, in the event the proposed name is not available

- Class and number of shares subscribed

- Statement of consideration for subscription

- Conditions on subscription, if any

- Date on or before which subscription is to be executed by issuance of stock and payment of subscription price

- If stock is to be paid for other than in cash, description and value of property to be exchanged

- Identification of subscriber as incorporator or promoter, in appropriate case

- Date of subscription agreement

- Special provisions regarding stock subscribed to, such as redemption of preferred stock.

Figure 6-1 shows an example of a stock subscription agreement form to be used by incorporators.

Gathering Client Information to Incorporate

Once the decision has been made to incorporate, the attorney or legal assistant must gather the necessary information from the client to begin the incorporation process. This can be done at an initial meeting between the client, attorney, and the legal assistant. Collecting this information is extremely important for two reasons. First, the information is necessary to correctly prepare the initial incorporation documents and subsequent documents that may be prepared on behalf of

---

stock subscription agreement   Agreement to purchase a specific number of shares of a corporation.

Subscription—By Incorporators
[From 6 AM. JUR. Legal Forms 2d (Rev.)]

SUBSCRIPTION AGREEMENT

The undersigned, as incorporators of the corporation to be known as _____ [corporate name], in accordance with the agreement to incorporate, dated and executed by them this date, and in consideration of the mutual subscriptions hereby made, do agree among themselves, each with the others, and with the corporation, to subscribe to and purchase from the corporation, at _____ [par or book] value, the class and number of shares of the corporation set forth opposite their respective signatures below. Each of the undersigned hereby subscribes for the kind and number of shares set opposite his or her name, and his or her obligation hereunder shall not be dependent upon performance by any of the other signatories.

The respective subscription prices shall be due and paid after the formation and organization of the corporation substantially in accordance with the agreement to incorporate, and upon issuance to and receipt by the corporation of a stock permit from _____ [the Secretary of State, or the Corporation Commission, or as the case may be] of the State of _____.

In the event that such stock permit is not received by the corporation on or before _____ , 19___ , or such later date as may hereafter be agreed upon by all the subscribers below signed, then this agreement and the obligations of the respective subscribers shall be null and void and of no further force and effect.

In witness whereof the subscribers have executed this subscription at _____ [place of execution] this _____ day of _____ , 19___ .

Subscribers' Signatures	Class of Shares	Number of Shares
_____	_____	_____
_____	_____	_____
_____	_____	_____
_____	_____	_____

FIGURE 6-1   Sample Stock Subscription Agreement Form

the corporate client. Second, the collection of this information may lead to discussions that cause the client or clients to consider and discuss facets of the business that have not previously been contemplated. Following is a list of information that typically must be obtained from the client to begin the incorporation process[3]:

- Is the corporation the appropriate business organization? Has the client considered:
  — A partnership?
  — A limited partnership?
  — A limited liability company?

- What is the proposed corporate name?
  — What is the client's first choice?
  — What are possible alternatives?

- What business is to be conducted?
  — What is the corporation's primary business?
  — Is the corporation to be authorized to conduct other businesses?
  — Are any limits to be placed on the business the corporation is to be allowed to conduct, if state law allows corporations to engage in any lawful business?
  — Should specific business purposes be set out in the articles of incorporation, if not required by state law?

- Will the corporation's business be conducted in the state of incorporation?

- Will the corporation's business be conducted in other states?
  — Through offices or branches in the other states?
  — By making sales through independent contractors?
  — By soliciting orders by mail or through employees, agents, or otherwise, if such orders must be accepted outside the state before becoming binding contracts?
  — Through sales made wholly in interstate commerce?
  — As isolated, nonrepetitive business only?

- How much total capital is needed to begin business?

- How much of the capital do the founders plan to contribute?
  — What amount is to be treated as equity?
  — What amount will be loaned and on what terms?

- Is any public financing planned?
  — Through sale of stock?
  — By debt financing?
  — If debt financing is planned, what interest would the corporation be willing to pay and what loan period is contemplated?
  — Are the investors' equity interests to be protected against dilution?

- Do the founders want corporate income taxed directly to stockholders (i.e., should election to be treated as an S corporation be made if the corporation is eligible)?
  — What are the tax brackets of the stockholders?

- — What is the projected income of the corporation?
- — Does the corporation need to accumulate capital?

- Who is to have control of the corporation?
  - — If public financing is not needed, but there is to be more than one stockholder, is each founder to have a veto over corporate actions, or will one of the founders or a group of founders have effective control of the corporation?
  - — If public financing is needed, is effective control, to the extent possible, to be kept in the hands of the founders?

- How many initial directors of the corporation are planned and what are their names?

- What officers will the corporation have?
  - — Who are they?
  - — What are the proposed salaries for each officer, including bonuses?
  - — What is the term of office?
  - — Will the corporation have power to remove officers without cause, or only for cause?

- Where is the principal office to be located?

- Where is the annual meeting of stockholders to be held?

- What will the corporation's fiscal year be?

§ 6.2 Incorporators

The *incorporator* is the individual who actually signs the articles or certificate of incorporation to form the corporation. The actual role played by the incorporator is usually very minor, and the involvement of the incorporator typically ceases after the articles or certificate of incorporation are filed or after the organizational meeting electing the first board of directors is held. At times, the attorney for the corporate client will serve as the incorporator so that the attorney can sign and file the articles of incorporation on behalf of the client.

Qualifications for incorporators are usually set forth in the statutes of the state of domicile. The Model Business Corporation Act states only that "One or more persons may act as the incorporator or incorporators of a corporation by delivering articles of incorporation to the secretary of state for filing."[4] *Persons*, as defined by the Model Business Corporation Act, means individuals and entities, including other profit or not-for-profit corporations, whether foreign or domestic, as well as business trusts, estates, partnerships, trusts, unincorporated associations, and governments. State statutes with more restrictive provisions may require that the incorporators be natural persons,[5] or may require more than one incorporator.[6]

§ 6.3 Articles of Incorporation

The document that is actually filed with the Secretary of State or other appropriate state authority to form the corporation is typically called the *articles of incorporation,* although in some states that document may be referred to as the *certificate of incorporation* or **charter**. For ease in discussion, we refer to the incorporation document as the "articles of incorporation" throughout the rest of this chapter. The articles of incorporation contain essential information regarding the corporation and must comply with statutory requirements of the state of domicile.

The articles of incorporation must be filed with the Secretary of State or other designated state official in order to be valid. For ease in discussion, here we refer to every state official responsible for accepting the articles of incorporation for filing as the Secretary of State. In some states, the Secretary of State may supply forms, upon request, to be used when preparing articles of incorporation. Other states require the use of an official form that is available from the Secretary of State. Statutes regarding the articles of incorporation vary from state to state. However, most states have provisions similar to the Model Business Corporation Act, which is discussed later in this chapter.

This section examines the mandatory articles of incorporation provisions required by most state statutes, the articles of incorporation provisions that are usually considered optional, and the statutory provisions that apply to all corporations unless contrary provision is made in the articles of incorporation.

Mandatory Provisions

The mandatory provisions for articles of incorporation vary from state to state and depend upon the type of corporation to be formed.

TERMS

charter[†] A corporation's articles of incorporation, together with the laws that grant corporate powers.

Under the Model Business Corporation Act, the only four provisions that are required to be set forth are:

1. A corporate name for the corporation that satisfies all statutory requirements[7]
2. The number of shares the corporation is authorized to issue[8]
3. The street address of the corporation's initial registered office and the name of its initial registered agent at that office[9]
4. The name and address of each incorporator.[10]

Name

The name chosen by the corporation must comply with the statutes of the state of domicile. Basically, there are three aspects of name availability that the incorporators must comply with. First, the name must include at least one of a number of specific words that may be required by statute, and must not contain any prohibited words. Second, the name of the corporation must not be the same as, or deceptively similar to, the name of another corporation or entity of record in the office of the Secretary of State of the state of domicile. Third, most state statutes require that the name of the corporation not mislead as to the purpose of the corporation.

Most state statutory requirements provide that the name of the corporation must contain a word or words indicating that the corporation is a corporate entity, as opposed to a partnership or other type of business entity. The names of corporations domiciled in states following the Model Business Corporation Act must include the word *corporation, incorporated, company,* or *limited,* or the abbreviation *corp., inc., co.,* or *ltd.,* or words or abbreviations of like import in another language.

The proposed name of the corporation must not already be in use in the state of domicile. Although name availability standards vary from state to state, § 4.01(b) of the Model Business Corporation Act addresses name availability in a typical manner, as follows:

(b) Except as authorized by subsections (c) and (d), a corporate name must be distinguishable upon the records of the secretary of state from:

(1) the corporate name of a corporation incorporated or authorized to transact business in this state;

(2) a corporate name reserved or registered under section 4.02 or 4.03;

(3) the fictitious name adopted by a foreign corporation authorized to transact business in this state because its real name is unavailable; and

(4) the corporate name of a not-for-profit corporation incorporated or authorized to transact business in this state.

Subsections (c) and (d) of § 4.01 of the Model Business Corporation Act, which follow, provide some remedies for names that may otherwise be unavailable:

(c) A corporation may apply to the secretary of state for authorization to use a name that is not distinguishable upon his records from one or more of the names described in subsection (b). The secretary of state shall authorize use of the name applied for if:

(1) the other corporation consents to the use in writing and submits an undertaking in form satisfactory to the secretary of state to change its name to a name that is distinguishable upon the records of the secretary of state from the name of the applying corporation; or

(2) The applicant delivers to the secretary of state a certified copy of the final judgment of a court of competent jurisdiction establishing the applicant's right to use the name applied for in this state.

(d) A corporation may use the name (including the fictitious name) of another domestic or foreign corporation that is used in this state if the other corporation incorporated or authorized to transact business in this state and the proposed user corporation:

(1) has merged with the other corporation;

(2) has been formed by reorganization of the other corporation; or

(3) has acquired all or substantially all of the assets, including the corporate name, of the other corporation.

The Secretary of State or other appropriate state official of most states will check the apparent availability of a proposed corporation name over the telephone. See appendix A of this text for a Secretary of State directory.

Authorized Stock

The articles of incorporation must set forth the number of shares of each class of stock that the corporation is authorized to issue in accordance with the statutes of the state of domicile. When there is only one class of stock, that class is typically referred to as **common stock.**

The state statutes may require additional information regarding the corporation's authorized stock as well, such as the par value of the stock and the rights and preferences of all classes of stock. Capitalization of

---

TERMS

common stock[†] Ordinary capital stock in a corporation, the market value of which is based upon the worth of the corporation. Owners of common stock vote in proportion to their holdings, as opposed to owners of other classes of stock that are without voting rights. By contrast, however, common stock earns dividends only after other preferred classes of stock.

the corporation is discussed in further detail in Chapter 8 of this text. The following examples show articles of incorporation paragraphs setting forth the number of shares of stock of the corporation.

EXAMPLE: Authorized Stock

The corporation is authorized to issue _____ shares (_____) of common stock of the corporation.[11]

EXAMPLE: Capitalization

The total number of shares of all classes of stock which the corporation shall have authority to issue is _____ divided into _____ [number] shares of common stock at _____dollars ($_____) par value each and _____ [number] shares of preferred stock, at _____ dollars ($_____) par value each. _____ [State designations and powers, preferences, and rights, and the qualifications, limitations, or restrictions of the classes of stock.]

This corporation will not commence business until it has received for the issuance of its shares consideration of the value of _____ dollars ($_____), consisting of money, labor done, or property actually received, which sum is not less than _____ dollars ($_____).

This Article can be amended only by the vote or written consent of the holders of _____ percent (_____%) of the outstanding shares.[12]

Registered Office and Registered Agent

This section of the articles of incorporation must set forth the corporation's **registered office** and its **registered agent**, or statutory agent, as it is sometimes referred to (if one is required and appointed).

Under the Model Business Corporation Act, each corporation must appoint and maintain both a registered office and a registered agent. The registered office of the corporation may be the same as any of the corporation's places of business within the state of domicile. The registered agent required by the Model Business Corporation Act may be an

---

TERMS

registered office   Office designated by the corporation as the office where process may be served. The Secretary of State or other appropriate state authority must be informed as to the location of the registered office. Corporations are generally required to maintain a registered office in each state in which the corporation is qualified to transact business.

registered agent   Individual appointed by a corporation to receive service of process on behalf of the corporation and perform such other duties as may be necessary. Registered agents may be required in the corporation's state of domicile and in each state in which the corporation is qualified to transact business.

individual resident of the state of domicile whose business office is identical with the registered office, or a domestic corporation or qualified foreign corporation with a business office identical to the registered office of the corporation. This requirement is typical of most states, although there are some deviations regarding it. For example, not all states require the appointment of a registered agent.

Following is an example of an articles of incorporation paragraph in which the registered office and registered agent of the corporation are appointed.

EXAMPLE: Registered Office and Registered Agent

The street address of the corporation's initial registered office and the name of its initial registered agent at that office are as follows:

Registered Office: _____

_____

Registered Agent: _____.[13]

Name and Address of Incorporators

The name and address of each incorporator must be set forth in the articles of incorporation. The incorporators also must sign the articles of incorporation in the method prescribed by state statute. Figure 6-2 illustrates a form that may be used for articles of incorporation in states that follow the Model Business Corporation Act.

Optional Provisions

The articles of incorporation may basically contain any information that the incorporators choose to include regarding the management and administration of the corporate affairs. The Model Business Corporation Act states that the articles of incorporation may set forth:

1. The names and addresses of the individuals who are to serve as the initial directors[14]
2. The purpose or purposes for which the corporation is organized[15]
3. Provisions regarding the management of the business and regulation of the affairs of the corporation[16]
4. Provisions defining, limiting, and regulating the powers of the corporation, its board of directors, and shareholders[17]
5. Provisions setting a par value for authorized shares or classes of shares[18]

FIGURE 6-2
Sample
Articles of
Incorporation

[In compliance with minimum requirements of the 1984
Revised Model Business Corporation Act]

ARTICLES OF INCORPORATION

The undersigned, acting as Incorporator(s) of a corporation under the
_____ Business Corporation Act, adopt(s) the following
Articles of Incorporation for such corporation:

I. NAME

The name of this corporation is _____.

II. AUTHORIZED STOCK

The number of shares that the corporation is authorized to issue is
_____ shares, all of one class.

III.   INITIAL REGISTERED OFFICE AND AGENT

The name and address of the initial registered agent and office of this
corporation are as follows:

_____

_____.

IV.   INCORPORATOR(S)

The name(s) and address(es) of the Incorporator(s) signing these Articles of
Incorporation [is] [are]:

Name   Address

_____   _____

_____   _____

_____   _____

IN WITNESS WHEREOF, the undersigned Incorporator(s) has/have
executed these Articles of Incorporation this _____ day of _____ , 19___.

_____
Incorporator

_____
Incorporator

STATE OF _____

COUNTY OF _____

FIGURE 6-2
(continued)

> BEFORE ME, the undersigned authority, personally appeared
> _____and_____ , to me known to be the
> persons who executed the foregoing Articles of Incorporation, and [he] [she]
> [they] acknowledged to and before me that [he] [she] [they] executed such
> instrument.
>
> IN WITNESS WHEREOF, I have hereunto set my hand and seal this _____
> day of _____, 19___.
>
>
> _____
> (Notarial Seal)   Notary Public, State of _____
> My Commission Expires:

6. Provisions imposing personal liability on shareholders for the debts of the corporation to a specified extent and upon specified conditions[19]

7. Any provision that is required or permitted by statute to be set forth in the bylaws[20]

8. Provisions eliminating or limiting the liability of directors of the corporation or its shareholders for money damages for any action taken, or any failure to take any action, as a director, except under certain circumstances.[21]

Initial Board of Directors

In the past, most statutes have required that the initial board of directors be appointed in the articles of incorporation. The Model Business Corporation Act, and several state statutes that are following suit, now give incorporators the option of including this information. However, the directors are still often appointed in the articles of incorporation to relieve the incorporators of any further responsibility.

Purpose

The purpose of the corporation is often set forth in the articles of incorporation, and the statutes of most states require it. The purpose of the corporation must be a lawful purpose in compliance with state statutes. The purpose clause in the articles serves to notify both the public and its own shareholders of the corporation's general business purposes. Courts have found that "the corporate purpose stated in the articles of incorporation serves to inform the public of the nature of the organization, thus benefiting those with whom it deals, and serves to inform its members of the scope and range of its proper activities and to assure them that they will not be involved in remote and uncontemplated lines of activity."[22]

State statutes may require at least one specific purpose, or merely a vague statement that the purpose of the corporation is "any lawful business." Section 3.01 of the Model Business Corporation Act, which follows, is typical of the purpose provisions under many state statutes.

§ 3.01 PURPOSES

(a) Every corporation incorporated under this Act has the purpose of engaging in any lawful business unless a more limited purpose is set forth in the articles of incorporation.

(b) A corporation engaging in a business that is subject to regulation under another statute of this state may incorporate under this Act only if permitted by, and subject to all limitations of, the other statute.

Following is an example of a purpose paragraph that is often used in states that follow the Model Business Corporation Act.

EXAMPLE: Purpose

The purpose of this corporation is to engage in any lawful business or activities permitted under the laws of the United States and the State of _____.

Business organizations with certain purposes, such as the banking or insurance industries, may be prohibited from incorporating or may be required to incorporate under different statutes. Special types of corporations, such as professional service corporations or nonprofit corporations, will be required to incorporate under the pertinent state statutes.

Management of Corporation

The Model Business Corporation Act states that the articles of incorporation may include any lawful provision regarding the management of the business and regulation of the affairs of the corporation. The incorporators may be as specific as they wish in this regard. However, because the articles of incorporation may be amended only with shareholder approval, and because an amendment requires an additional filing at the state level, it may be advisable to include most of the desired specific information regarding management of the corporation in the **bylaws** of the corporation.

═══════════════ TERMS ═══════════════

bylaws Document which is considered the rules and guidelines for the internal government and control of a corporation. Bylaws prescribe the rights and duties of the shareholders, directors, and officers with regard to management and governance of the corporation.

Powers of Corporation

The powers of the corporation, the directors, and the shareholders of the corporation are typically set forth by statute, unless amended by the articles of incorporation. Any desired limitations on the statutory powers granted to the corporation, or the directors or shareholders of the corporation, must be made in the articles of incorporation within the scope of the state statutes.

Par Value of Shares of Stock and Classes of Stock

The **par value** of the shares of stock may be included in the articles of incorporation, if desired. Under the Model Business Corporation Act, this information is not mandatory. However, the statutes of many states require that the par value of each class of authorized stock be set forth in the articles.

Imposition of Personal Shareholder Liability

Any provisions imposing personal liability on the shareholders of the corporation must be set forth in the articles of incorporation, along with the limitations thereto.

Provisions That May Be Required or Permitted in Bylaws

There are many matters that the incorporators may choose to include in either the articles or the bylaws of the corporation. Incorporators should choose the inclusions to the articles carefully, because any item in the articles of incorporation may be amended only by amending the articles of incorporation, which usually involves shareholder approval and an additional filing with the Secretary of State.

Limitation on Board of Director Liability

One relatively recent addition to the Model Business Corporation Act is the inclusion of specific language regarding the limitation of directors' liability in the articles of incorporation. This new provision allows the incorporators to draft the articles to limit the liability of

---

TERMS

par value [†] The value of a share of stock or of a bond, according to its face; the named or nominal value of an instrument. The par value and the market value of stock are not synonymous; there is often a wide difference between them. The issuer of a bond is obligated to redeem it at par value upon maturity.

directors of the corporation for actions arising based on their actions or inactions on behalf of the corporation, except in the event of wrongful financial benefit to the director, intentional infliction of harm, a violation of the director's duty of care, or an intentional violation of criminal law. Director liability is discussed further in Chapter 7.

Statutory Provisions That May Be Amended Only in the Articles of Incorporation

The statutes of most states contain several provisions that govern the internal affairs of corporations, unless the corporation has provisions in its articles of incorporation to the contrary. Depending on the format of the statutes, a specific list of these provisions may be provided, or these provisions may be found under the section of the act relating to the subject matter. Following is a list of some of the provisions that are most often set by statute but that may be amended in the articles of incorporation:

1. Shareholders do not have a right to cumulate their votes for directors.[23] (Cumulative voting is discussed in Chapter 7.)

2. The shareholders may remove one or more directors with or without cause.[24] (Removal of directors is discussed in Chapter 7.)

3. All shares of the corporation are of one class with identical rights.[25] (Share classes are discussed in Chapter 8.)

4. Shareholders have no preemptive rights to acquire unissued shares.[26] (Preemptive rights are discussed in Chapter 7.)

Execution

The articles of incorporation must be properly executed by the incorporators, in accordance with state statutory provisions, to be valid. Many state statutes require that the signature or signatures on the articles of incorporation be witnessed, acknowledged, or notarized.

Filing

The articles of incorporation and the appropriate filing fee must be filed with the Secretary of State within the state of domicile. Statutes regarding filing requirements should be reviewed carefully, and the appropriate state authority should be contacted, to ensure that all filing procedures are complied with. Failure to comply with filing requirements could seriously delay the incorporation of the corporation.

Publication

The statutes of a few states in the country have publication laws requiring that the articles of incorporation, or a notice of incorporation, be published in a legal newspaper in accordance with statutory provisions.[27] It is important that the statutes be consulted to assure that this requirement is complied with, if necessary.

County Filing

Often, state statutes require that the articles of incorporation or a copy thereof be filed with the county recorder or other county official of the county in which the registered office of the corporation is located.[28] Again, the state statutes must be consulted to determine if county recording is necessary.

Effective Time and Date

The effective time and date of the articles of incorporation are important because they are, in effect, the time and date for the commencement of the corporate entity. Again, this matter is addressed by state statute. Most state statutes provide that the articles of incorporation are effective when filed with the Secretary of State or at a different time specified in the articles of incorporation. Most statutes that allow a later effective date and time to be specified limit that time to ninety days.

In the following case, the defendant builders were sued for breach of contract. They were found personally liable for the contract they had entered into, partly because the corporation they formed did not come into existence until two weeks after the contract was signed.

§ 6.4 Organizational Meetings

After the articles of incorporation have been filed, the organizational meeting of the corporation is usually held. The requirements for this organizational meeting and the organizational actions that must be taken vary greatly from state to state. Depending on the statutes of the state of domicile, the incorporators or a majority of the directors named in the articles of incorporation may be required to call the organizational meeting and give notice to the directors and/or shareholders of the corporation.

WELCH
v.
FUHRMAN
496 So. 2d 484 (La. Ct. App. 1986)
Louisiana Court of Appeals
October 15, 1986
Savoie, Judge

Defendant, Robert Fuhrman, appeals from the judgment of the trial court finding him individually liable for breach of building contract.

On August 10, 1982 plaintiffs, Leroy J. Welch and Glynda H. Welch, entered into an oral contract with Capital Builders and Distributors, represented by Leroy Joslin, Sr. for the construction of an addition to their home. At the time of this contract, Capital Builders and Distributors was owned and operated by defendants Robert Fuhrman and Joseph A. Kunstler and Richard Hurt. Mr. Joslin presented plaintiffs with a floor plan and a pier plan drawing of the proposed addition, along with a cost breakdown of work to be performed. The agreed price for the job was $21,979.63. Plaintiffs paid $4,000.00 as a down-payment and financed the balance due of $17,979.63, which was paid upon substantial completion.

After final payment was made, plaintiffs noticed that the job was not fully completed and that numerous faults and defects existed. As a result, plaintiffs secured an estimate of $6,750.09 to complete the job and make the necessary repairs. In addition, defendants had failed to pay an electrical sub-contractor which resulted in a lien in the amount of $1,149.50 being filed against the property by Marshall Electrical, Inc.

Plaintiffs then instituted the present action to recover the sums expended to complete the job along with attorney's fees. Named as defendants were Robert Fuhrman and Joseph A. Kunstler, d/b/a Capital Builders of Louisiana. Defendant Fuhrman answered, filing a general denial, and claimed that any contract plaintiffs entered into was with Capital Builders of Louisiana, Inc., a separate legal entity. It was later determined at trial that the actual name of the corporation was Capital Builders and Distributors, Inc., and that the charter for this corporation had not been issued until August 24, 1982. Listed as directors of this corporation were Robert Fuhrman, Joseph Kunstler and Richard Hurt.

Following trial on the merits, judgment was rendered against defendants Fuhrman and Kunstler individually as well as against the organization known as Capital Builders of Louisiana. In addition to the amounts prayed for, plaintiffs were awarded $500.00 for attorney's fees. From this judgment defendant Fuhrman appeals alleging the following **assignments of error**:

1. The trial court erred in finding the defendant-appellant, Robert Fuhrman, individually, liable for the damages awarded to the plaintiff-appellees.
2. Error was committed in awarding attorney's fees to the plaintiff.
3. Error was committed in not finding that the entity Capital Builders and Distributors, Inc. was and is a corporation existing under the laws of Louisiana.

ASSIGNMENTS OF ERROR
NOS. 1 & 3

By these assignments of error defendant contends that the trial court erred in determining that he, individually, and not the corporation, was liable to plaintiffs. In his reasons for judgment, the trial judge stated:

> Defendants contend that Capital Builders of Louisiana is the only proper party to the suit. The plaintiffs point out that the articles of

<hr>

TERMS

assignments of error [†]   On appeal, a listing of mistakes of law or mistakes of fact alleged to have been committed by the lower court, which are designated by the party complaining of them as grounds for reversal.

incorporation were filed with the Secretary of State's office on August 24, 1982, although they were drafted and executed on July 12, 1982.

The sole issue before the Court, as to the defendants, is whether defendants are liable under the contract, or was the corporate entity legally constituted at the time the contract was confected.

This Court is of the opinion that the plaintiffs were of the opinion that Capital Builders of Louisiana was an organization owned by Robert Fuhrman and Joseph A. Kunstler and were doing business with them and not a corporate entity. ...

This Court must conclude that the plaintiffs are entitled to judgment against Robert Fuhrman and Joseph A. Kunstler, individually and against the organization known as Capital Builders of Louisiana.

We agree with the findings of the trial court. [La. Rev. Stat. Ann. §] 12:25(C) provides as follows:

Upon the issuance of the certificate of incorporation, the corporation shall be duly incorporated, and the corporate existence shall begin, as of the time when the articles were filed with the secretary of state, except that, if the articles were so filed within five days (exclusive of legal holidays) after acknowledgment thereof or execu-

tion thereof as an authentic act the corporation shall be duly incorporated, and the corporate existence shall begin, as of the time of such acknowledgment or execution.

The record clearly indicates that the articles of incorporation, although executed on July 12, 1982, were not filed with the Secretary of State's office until August 24, 1982. Accordingly, the corporate existence did not begin until that date, some fourteen days after entering into the contract with plaintiffs. As such, plaintiffs' contract was not with Capital Builders and Distributors, Inc. but rather was with the organization known as Capital Builders and Distributors which was owned and operated by Robert Fuhrman and Joseph Kunstler.

Additionally, we note that the record is void of any evidence that plaintiffs were put on notice that they were dealing with a corporation. ...

For the above and foregoing reasons, the judgment of the trial court awarding attorney's fees is hereby reversed. In all other respects, the judgment of the trial court is affirmed. All costs of this appeal are to be paid by defendant-appellant, Robert Fuhrman.

AFFIRMED IN PART, REVERSED IN PART.

This section examines the various requirements for organizational meetings, the purpose of organizational meetings, and the resolutions typically passed by incorporators, directors, and shareholders at organizational meetings. The section concludes with a discussion of the use of unanimous written consents in lieu of organizational meetings.

Organizational Meeting Requirements

As a practical matter, the organizational meeting is usually attended by the incorporators, the initial board of directors, and the shareholders, which often total only a very few people. Under certain circumstances, a unanimous written consent in lieu of an organizational meeting may be used to approve the necessary resolutions. Unanimous written consents are discussed in § 6.6 of this chapter.

Requirements for the organizational meeting under the Model Business Corporation Act are set forth in § 2.05:

TABLE 6-2 REASONS FREQUENTLY GIVEN BY STATE AUTHORITIES FOR REJECTING ARTICLES OF INCORPORATION FOR FILING

- Corporate name chosen is unavailable or otherwise unacceptable
- Inclusion of a provision giving authority to the board of directors to change the authorized number of directors, where such provision is contrary to state statute
- Improper execution and/or acknowledgment of the articles of incorporation
- Failure to name a street address for the registered office and/or registered agent of the corporation for service of process. P.O. Boxes are *not* acceptable in most jurisdictions
- Nonpayment of fees and taxes as required by state and local law
- Failure to state the specific number of authorized directors (where required by statute)
- Failure to state the total number of authorized shares
- Failure to state the aggregate par value of all shares of stock having a par value (where required by statute)
- Failure to state the par value, preferences, privileges and restrictions, and number of shares of each class of authorized stock (where required by statute)

§ 2.05 ORGANIZATION OF CORPORATION

(a) After incorporation:
   (1) if initial directors are named in the articles of incorporation, the initial directors shall hold an organizational meeting, at the call of a majority of the directors, to complete the organization of the corporation by appointing officers, adopting bylaws, and carrying on any other business brought before the meeting;
   (2) if initial directors are not named in the articles, the incorporator or incorporators shall hold an organizational meeting at the call of a majority of the incorporators:
      (i) to elect directors and complete the organization of the corporation; or
      (ii) to elect a board of directors who shall complete the organization of the corporation.
(b) Action required or permitted by this Act to be taken by incorporators at an organizational meeting may be taken without a meeting if the action taken is evidenced by one or more written consents describing the action taken and signed by each incorporator.
(c) An organizational meeting may be held in or out of this state.

In any event, the statutes of the state of domicile should be consulted regarding the organizational meeting to determine the following:

1. Who is responsible for giving notice of the organizational meeting?
2. Who is entitled to receive notice of and attend the organizational meeting?
3. What are the notice requirements?
4. What actions must be taken by the incorporators, directors, and shareholders at the organizational meeting?
5. May a written resolution signed by all interested parties be substituted for an actual organizational meeting?

Purpose of Organizational Meeting

The purpose of the organizational meeting is to "organize the corporation," which usually involves the "election of officers, the subscription and payment of the capital stock, the adoption of bylaws and such other steps are as necessary to give the legal entity the capacity to transact the legitimate business for which it was created."[29]

Incorporators' Resolutions

When the first board of directors is not named in the articles of incorporation, the incorporators may hold the organizational meeting.

Election of Board of Directors

Typically, the first and only order of business at an organizational meeting held by incorporators is to elect the first board of directors. Following is an example of a resolution that might be made by the incorporators at the organizational meeting to elect the first board of directors.

EXAMPLE: Election of First Board of Directors

RESOLVED, by the incorporators, that the following individuals, having been duly nominated, are hereby elected as the first board of directors of this corporation, to serve until the first annual meeting of the shareholders, or until their successors are elected and qualified:

_____
_____
_____.

Adoption of Bylaws

In some jurisdictions, the incorporators may adopt the bylaws of the corporation at the organizational meeting. Figure 6-3 is an example of a form of minutes of an organizational meeting of the incorporators.

MINUTES OF ORGANIZATIONAL
MEETING OF INCORPORATORS

The organizational meeting of incorporators of _____ [name of corporation], a corporation duly incorporated under the laws of the State of _____ , was held on _____ [date], at _____ [address] pursuant to the attached waiver of notice.

The following incorporators were present: _____.

On motion duly made, seconded and carried, _____ [name] was chosen chairperson of the meeting and _____ [name] was chosen as secretary.

The chairperson reported that the articles of incorporation had been filed with the Secretary of State of the State of _____ on _____ [date]. The Secretary was directed to file a copy of the certificate of incorporation in the corporate minute book.

On motion duly made, seconded, and carried, the following resolutions were adopted:

RESOLVED, that the number of initial directors of the corporation shall be ___.

FURTHER RESOLVED, that the following individuals shall serve as the initial directors of the corporation, to serve in accordance with the bylaws of the corporation until the first annual meeting of the shareholders and until their successors are elected and shall have qualified:

_____

_____

_____.

FURTHER RESOLVED, that the Board of Directors is hereby authorized to issue the capital stock of this corporation to the full extent authorized by the Articles of Incorporation in such amounts and for such consideration as from time to time shall be determined by the Board of Directors and as may be permitted by law, provided, however, that par value stock shall not be issued for less than par.

There being no further or other business to come before the meeting, on motion duly made, seconded, and carried, the meeting was adjourned.

_____
Chairman

_____
Secretary

FIGURE 6-3 Sample Minutes of First Meeting of Incorporators

Board of Directors' Resolutions

The items discussed in this section are often considered for action by the board of directors at the organizational meeting or the first meeting of the board of directors. Depending on state statute, some of these actions may also require shareholder approval. Figure 6-4 shows a sample of a form of minutes of the first board of directors' meeting, which includes the items discussed in the rest of this section.

Approval and Acceptance of Articles of Incorporation

Often, as a formality, the incorporators will present to the board of directors a copy of the articles of incorporation and report on its filing at the organizational meeting. This action should be noted by a resolution in the minutes of the meeting of the board of directors. Following is an example of a resolution that may be made by the board of directors to approve the articles of incorporation.

EXAMPLE: Acceptance of Articles of Incorporation

RESOLVED, that the articles of incorporation of the corporation, a copy of which is presented by the incorporator, are hereby ratified and approved. The secretary of the corporation is directed to see that the same is filed in the corporate minute book of the corporation, along with the certificate of incorporation issued by the secretary of state, providing evidence of the filing and acceptance of the articles.

Acceptance of Stock Subscriptions

Although the Model Business Corporation Act does not require any paid-in capital before the commencement of business, the statutes of some states require that a certain proportion of the stock be subscribed for, or even paid in, before the commencement of corporate business. Other states may require subscription for, or payment for, a specified amount of stock as a condition precedent to corporate existence.

In any event, it is important that the statutory requirements regarding the subscription and payment for stock of the corporation be complied with at the organizational meeting. This typically involves the acceptance of subscriptions and the issuance of stock of the corporation in accordance with the subscription agreements. The names of the shareholders, number and class of shares received by the shareholders, and the consideration received by the corporation from each shareholder should be noted. A statement regarding the paid-in capital of the corporation, in accordance with state statute, should be agreed on

MINUTES OF THE FIRST MEETING OF THE
BOARD OF DIRECTORS

Minutes of meeting of _____
[corporation]

Pursuant to _____ [notice or call and waiver of notice], the first board of directors of _____ [corporation] assembled and held its first meeting at _____ [address], City of _____ , State of _____ , at _____ o'clock _____.M., on _____ , 19___.

The following, being all of the directors of the corporation, were present at the meeting:

_____   _____

_____   _____

_____ [Name] called the meeting to order. On motion duly made and seconded, she was appointed temporary chairman, and _____ [name] was appointed temporary secretary.

The election of officers was thereupon declared to be in order. The following individuals were elected to the offices set forth opposite their names:

_____President

_____Vice President

_____Secretary and Treasurer.

_____ [Name] took the chair and presided at the meeting.

The chairman then announced that the _____ [articles or certificate] of incorporation had been filed with the _____ [Secretary of State or other appropriate official] on _____ , 19___. The secretary was instructed to cause a copy of the _____ [articles or certificate] of incorporation to be inserted in the front of the minute book of this corporation.

The secretary presented a form of bylaws for the regulation of the affairs of the corporation, which were read, section by section.

On motion duly made, seconded, and carried, it was

Resolved, that the bylaws submitted at and read to this meeting be, and the same hereby are, adopted as and for the bylaws of this corporation, and that the secretary be, and he hereby is, instructed to certify the bylaws, and cause the same to be inserted in the minute book of this corporation, and to certify a copy of the bylaws, which shall be kept at the principal office of this corporation and open to inspection by the stockholders at all reasonable times during office hours.

FIGURE 6-4   Sample Minutes of First Meeting of Board of Directors

On motion duly made, seconded, and carried, it was

Resolved, that the seal, an impression of which is herewith affixed, be adopted as the corporate seal of the corporation.

[Corporate Seal]

The secretary was authorized and directed to procure the proper corporate books.

On motion duly made, seconded, and carried, it was

Resolved, that _____ [bank] of the City of _____ , State of _____ , be, and it hereby is, selected as a depository for the monies, funds, and credit of this corporation and that _____ , _____ _____ , and _____ be, and they are, and any two of them are, authorized and empowered to draw checks (including checks payable to their own order or to bearer) on the above depository, against the account of this corporation with the depository, and to endorse in the name of this corporation and receive payment of all checks, drafts, and commercial papers payable to this corporation either as payee or endorsee.

Further resolved, that the authority hereby conferred above shall remain in full force and effect until it shall have been revoked and until a formal written notice of such revocation shall have been given to and received by _____ [bank] of the City of _____ , State of _____ .

Further resolved, that the certification of the secretary of this corporation as to the election and appointment of persons so authorized to sign such checks and as to the signatures of such persons shall be binding on this corporation;

Further resolved, that the secretary of this corporation be, and he hereby is, authorized and directed to deliver to _____ [bank] of the City of _____ , State of _____ , a copy of these resolutions properly certified by him.

On motion duly made, seconded, and carried, it was

Resolved, that the principal office of the corporation for the transaction of its business be, and it hereby is, fixed at _____ [address], City of _____ , State of _____ .

On motion duly made, seconded, and carried, the following preambles and resolutions were unanimously adopted:

Whereas, this corporation is authorized, in its _____ [articles or certificate] of incorporation, to issue _____ [number] shares of its capital stock without nominal or par value; and

Whereas, this corporation has received stock subscriptions for a total of _____ shares of its authorized stock, and consideration for those shares of stock, in an amount deemed sufficient by the board of directors, has been received, the following number of authorized shares of stock are to be issued to the following individuals:

FIGURE 6-4 *(continued)*

Shareholder	Number of Shares
_____	_____
_____	_____
_____	_____
_____	_____.

A copy of the certificate of stock proposed to be issued by the corporation was considered, and

On motion, duly made, seconded, and carried, it was

Resolved, that the above certificate be substantially in the following form: _____ [set out certificate of stock in full].

There being no further business, the meeting was adjourned.

[Signature of secretary]

FIGURE 6-4 *(continued)*

and noted in the minutes of the meeting. Following is an example of a resolution that could be passed by the board of directors regarding the issuance of stock of the corporation.

EXAMPLE: *Issuance of Stock*

RESOLVED, that the subscriptions for the shares of the corporation filed in the corporate minute book of the corporation are hereby accepted and the amount and fair value of the consideration recited therein are hereby approved. The corporation has received the consideration recited, and the officers of the corporation are hereby authorized to issue to each such subscriber, a certificate or certificates for the shares therein subscribed as follows:

Subscriber	Number of Shares	Consideration Received
_____	_____	_____
_____	_____	_____
_____	_____	_____

The corporation, having received the minimum consideration for the issuance of the shares of the corporation fixed in the articles of incorporation, is duly organized and ready to commence business.

Ratification of Acts of Incorporator(s)

It is usually prudent, even if not required, for the directors of the corporation to approve and ratify the acts of the incorporator or incorporators taken on behalf of the corporation, even if those acts consisted only of filing the articles of incorporation.

Election of Officers

The directors of the corporation will elect the officers of the corporation, which may include a chief executive officer, president, vice president or vice president(s), chief financial officer or treasurer, secretary, and any other or different officers as may be desired by the board of directors and in accordance with the statutes of the corporation's state of domicile and the corporation's bylaws. Following is an example of a resolution that could be passed by the directors to elect the officers of the corporation.

EXAMPLE: Election of Officers

RESOLVED, that the following persons are hereby elected as officers of the corporation to assume the duties and responsibilities fixed by the Bylaws, and to serve until their respective successors are chosen and qualify:

Chief Executive Officer: _____

President: _____

Vice President: _____

Secretary: _____

Treasurer: _____

Assistant Secretary: _____

Adoption of Bylaws

The bylaws of the corporation, which are typically prepared in advance of the organizational meeting and reviewed by all directors, should be approved at the organizational meeting by the appropriate individuals in accordance with state statute. Often, the bylaws are adopted by the corporation's directors and ratified by its shareholders. Following is an example of a resolution that could be passed by the board of directors to adopt the bylaws of the corporation.

EXAMPLE: Adoption of Bylaws

That the proposed bylaws, a copy of which is filed in the corporate minute book of the corporation, are hereby adopted by the board of directors as the bylaws of the corporation, and the secretary of the corporation is hereby authorized to sign said bylaws on behalf of the corporation.

Approval of Accounting Methods

The board of directors should agree upon the general accounting methods to be used by the corporation, including the fiscal year of the corporation, if a fiscal year other than the calendar year is an option.

Authorization of Appropriate Securities Filings

If the corporation will be subject to any securities filings, the board of directors is generally responsible for those filings. Any potential filings should be discussed during the organizational meeting, and a resolution should be passed authorizing the board of directors to prepare and file the necessary documentation.

Approval of Form of Stock Certificate

The board of directors will often approve a form of stock certificate to be used by the corporation, including any necessary restrictive legends. Following is an example of a resolution that could be passed by the board of directors to approve a form of stock certificate for use by the corporation.

EXAMPLE: *Approval of Form of Stock Certificates*

RESOLVED, that the form of stock certificate attached hereto as Exhibit _____ be and hereby is adopted and approved.

Adoption of Corporate Seal

If a corporate seal is required by state statute, or if a seal is desired, the seal should be approved at the organizational meeting. If no corporate seal is to be used by the corporation, that should be so agreed upon and noted.

Banking Resolutions

The directors of the corporation should agree on and establish a corporate bank account or bank accounts, and the terms of the bank account(s) should be determined, including the type of account(s) to be opened, where such account(s) should be opened, and who the authorized signatories on the bank account will be. Following is an example of a resolution that could be passed by the board of directors regarding the designation of a bank for corporate accounts.

EXAMPLE: Banking Resolution

RESOLVED, that the standard form of resolution of _____ Bank, with respect to checking accounts at said bank, is hereby adopted, and a copy thereof is ordered to be filed with the minutes of this meeting. The proper officers are hereby authorized and directed to file the necessary papers with said bank, including the signature authorization card, with respect to said checking account.

Approval of S Corporation Election

The directors should discuss the advisability of electing to be treated as an S corporation for federal income tax purposes. If it is decided that the corporation will elect to become an S corporation, a resolution must be completed and must be approved by the directors and all shareholders. Following is an example of a resolution that could be passed by the board of directors to approve the election of S corporation status for the corporation.

EXAMPLE: S Corporation Election

RESOLVED, that the corporation shall elect to be taxed as an S Corporation in accordance with Section 1372 of the Internal Revenue Code of 1954, as amended. The officers of the corporation are hereby authorized and directed to do all acts and to execute and file all papers, documents, and instruments necessary to cause the corporation to make such election.

Adoption of Employee Benefit Plans

Any employee benefit plans to be adopted by the corporation may be approved by the board of directors at the organizational meeting or the first meeting of the board of directors. These plans may include medical insurance plans, medical expense reimbursement plans, life insurance plans, qualified retirement plans, or any other employee benefit plans.

Shareholder Resolutions

The shareholders may be required by statute to be a part of the organizational meeting or to hold a different meeting referred to as the *first meeting of shareholders*. This meeting is often a part of, or held immediately following, the organizational meeting or the first meeting of the board of directors. The items discussed in this section are often considered for action by the shareholders of the corporation at their first meeting.

Election of Directors

The directors of the corporation must be elected pursuant to the statutes of the state of domicile. The statutes may permit this to be done by the incorporators if not done in the articles of incorporation, or the first board of directors may be elected or ratified by the shareholders of the corporation at the organizational meeting. Following is an example of a resolution that could be used by the shareholders of the corporation to elect the first board of directors.

Example: Election of First Board of Directors

RESOLVED, that the following individuals, having been duly nominated, are hereby elected as the first board of directors of this corporation, to serve until the next annual meeting of the shareholders, or until their successors are elected and qualified:

_____

_____

_____

_____.

Approval of S Corporation Election

The shareholders of the corporation must unanimously approve the adoption of S corporation status and the proper documents must be signed by all shareholders.

Approval of Bylaws

In most states, the directors of the corporation are granted the authority to adopt the bylaws of the corporation. However, this adoption of bylaws may be ratified by the shareholders of the corporation.

Unanimous Writings versus Minutes

Traditionally, formal organizational meetings were required by statutes in most every state. However, two changes in corporate law in recent years have made the formal organizational meeting unnecessary in certain instances.

First, the required minimum number of directors has gone from three to one in almost every state in the country. Previously, an organizational meeting of the directors was considered necessary to have a "meeting of the minds." This is obviously not necessary when there is only one director, who may also be the only shareholder of the corporation.

Second, modern corporate law typically provides for the use of unanimous writings in lieu of meetings. Unanimous writings do away with the necessity of having to give notice of and attend a formal meeting every time an action of the board of directors or shareholders is called for. Especially when there is great geographical distance between the individual directors or shareholders, the use of unanimous writings can be invaluable.

In unanimous writings, the directors, or shareholders, as the case may be, waive their statutory right to notice and attendance at a meeting and agree to set forth the agreed-upon resolutions in the form of a written consent, often referred to as a *unanimous writing*. The unanimous writing must be signed and dated by all individuals entitled to notice and attendance at a meeting of the directors or shareholders. State statutes must be consulted and followed carefully if a unanimous writing is used. Figure 6-5 is a sample form of a unanimous writing in lieu of meeting of an organizational meeting.

§ 6.5 Bylaws

Bylaws are considered the "rules and guidelines for the internal government and control of a corporation."[30] The bylaws, which are typically adopted by the board of directors, prescribe the rights and duties of the shareholders, directors, and officers with regard to the management and governance of the corporation. They are considered to be a contract between the members of a corporation and between the corporation and its members.[31]

Some state statutes specifically address the information to be contained in the bylaws. The Model Business Corporation Act merely states that the "bylaws of a corporation may contain any provision for managing the business and regulating the affairs of the corporation that is not inconsistent with law or the articles of incorporation."[32]

The following paragraphs discuss and show examples of some of the more common matters addressed in corporate bylaws. See Appendix H-4 for a sample bylaws form.

Office of the Corporation

The bylaws typically set forth the principal office of the corporation and any other significant offices to be used by the corporation.

CONSENT TO ACTION TAKEN IN LIEU OF
ORGANIZATIONAL MEETING
of

_____

The undersigned, being all of the incorporators, shareholders, and directors of the corporation, hereby consent to and ratify the action taken to organize the corporation as hereafter stated:

The Certificate of Incorporation filed on _____ , 19___ , with the Secretary of State of this state is hereby approved and it shall be inserted in the record book of the corporation.

The persons whose names appear below are hereby duly appointed directors of the corporation to serve for a period of one year and until their successors are appointed or elected and shall qualify:

The persons whose names appear below are hereby duly appointed officers of the corporation to serve for a period of one year and until their successors are appointed or elected and shall qualify:

President:

Vice President:

Secretary:

Treasurer:

Bylaws, regulating the conduct of the business and affairs of the corporation, as prepared by _____ , counsel for the corporation, are hereby adopted and inserted in the record book.

The seal, an impression of which appears in the margin of this consent, is hereby adopted as the corporate seal of the corporation, and the specimen of certificates for shares in the form exhibited and inserted in the record book is hereby adopted as the corporate stock certificate.

The directors are hereby authorized to issue the unsubscribed capital stock of the corporation at such times and in such amounts as they shall determine, and to accept in payment therefor cash, labor done, personal property, real property or leases therefor, or such other property as the board may deem necessary for the business of the corporation.

The treasurer is hereby duly authorized to open a bank account with _____ , located at _____ , and is authorized to execute a resolution for that purpose on the printed form of said bank.

The president is hereby duly authorized to designate the principal office of the corporation in this state as the office for service of process on the

FIGURE 6-5 Sample Unanimous Writing in Lieu of Meeting

corporation, and to designate such further agents for service of process within or without this state as is in the best interests of the corporation. The president is hereby further authorized to execute any and all certificates or documents to implement the above.

Dated _____

_____

_____

_____

FIGURE 6-5   *(continued)*

EXAMPLE: *Principal Corporate Office*

The principal office of the corporation shall be located at_____ [address], City of _____ , County of _____ , State of _____. The board of directors shall have the power and authority to establish and maintain branch or subordinate offices at any other locations _____ [within the same city or within the same state or as the case may be].[33]

Shareholder Meetings

Requirements for shareholder meetings are sometimes specifically set by state statute. However, details regarding the shareholder meetings are typically left to the corporation. The bylaws often set the time, place, and notice requirements for the annual meetings and the requirements for calling and holding special meetings of the shareholders. In addition, the bylaws should address the question of who is entitled to receive notice of shareholder meetings.

EXAMPLE: *Annual Meetings of Shareholders*

The annual meeting of the stockholders shall be held on the _____ [ordinal number] day in the month of _____ in each year, beginning with the year 19___ , at _____ o'clock _____.M., for the purpose of electing directors and for the transaction of such other business as may come before the meeting. If the day fixed for the annual meeting shall be a legal holiday in the State of _____ , such meeting shall be held on the next succeeding business day. If the election of directors is not held on the day designated herein for any annual meeting of the shareholders, or at any adjournment thereof, the board of directors shall cause the election to be held at a special meeting of the stockholders as soon thereafter as is convenient.[34]

EXAMPLE: Special Meetings of Shareholders

Special meetings of the stockholders, for any purpose or purposes, unless otherwise prescribed by statute, may be called by the president or by the board of directors, and shall be called by the president at the request of the holders of not less than _____ [number] of all the outstanding shares of the corporation entitled to vote at the meeting.[35]

EXAMPLE: Place of Shareholder Meetings

The board of directors may designate any place within [if desired, add: or without] the State of _____ , as the place of meeting for any annual meeting or for any special meeting called by the board of directors. A waiver of notice signed by all stockholders entitled to vote at a meeting may designate any place, either within or without the State of _____, as the place for the holding of such meeting. If no designation is made, or if a special meeting is otherwise called, the place of meeting shall be the principal office of the corporation in the City of _____ , State of _____ .[36]

EXAMPLE: Notice of Shareholder Meetings

Written or printed notice stating the place, day, and hour of the meeting and, in case of a special meeting, the purpose or purposes for which the meeting is called, shall be delivered not less than _____ nor more than _____ days before the date of the meeting, either personally or by mail, by or at the direction of the president, or the secretary, or the officer or persons calling the meeting, to each shareholder of record entitled to vote at such meeting. If mailed, such notice shall be deemed to be delivered when deposited in the United States mail, addressed to the shareholder at his or her address as it appears on the stock transfer books of the corporation, with postage thereon prepaid. [If appropriate, add: Notice of each meeting shall also be mailed to holders of stock not entitled to vote, as herein provided, but lack of such notice shall not affect the legality of any meeting otherwise properly called and noticed.][37]

Number and Term of Directors

The bylaws often include information on the directors of the corporation, including the number of directors required, the term of office, and the qualifications of the directors.

EXAMPLE: Number, Tenure, and Qualifications of Directors

The number of directors of the corporation shall be _____. Directors shall be elected at the annual meeting of stockholders, and the term of office of each director shall be until the next annual meeting of stockholders and the election and qualification of his or her successor. Directors need not be residents of the State of _____ [but shall be stockholders of the corporation *or* and need not be stockholders of the corporation].[38]

Meetings of the Board of Directors

The bylaws should contain information regarding the annual and special meetings of the directors, such as the time and place of the meetings, who may call the meetings, and notice requirements. The bylaws should also set a quorum of directors who may take action at a meeting.

If permitted by statute, the bylaws may also provide that meetings of the board of directors of the corporation may be transacted via telephone, or that meetings may be waived and replaced by a unanimous written consent of the directors in lieu of meeting.

EXAMPLE: Regular Meetings of Board of Directors

A regular meeting of the board of directors shall be held without notice other than this bylaw immediately after and at the same place as the annual meeting of stockholders. The board of directors may provide, by resolution, the time and place for holding additional regular meetings without other notice than such resolution. Additional regular meetings shall be held at the principal office of the corporation in the absence of any designation in the resolution.[39]

EXAMPLE: Special Meetings of Board of Directors

Special meetings of the board of directors may be called by or at the request of the president or any two directors, and shall be held at the principal office of the corporation or at such other place as the directors may determine.[40]

EXAMPLE: Notice of Board of Directors' Meetings

Notice of any special meeting shall be given at least ___ [48 hours or as the case may be] before the time fixed for the meeting, by written notice delivered personally or mailed to each director at his or her business address, or by telegram. If mailed, such notice shall be deemed to be delivered when deposited in the United States mail so addressed, with postage thereon prepaid, not less than _____ days prior to the commencement of the above-stated notice period. If notice is given by telegram, such notice shall be deemed to be delivered when the telegram is delivered to the telegraph company. Any director may waive notice of any meeting. The attendance of a director at a meeting shall constitute a waiver of notice of such meeting, except where a director attends a meeting for the express purpose of objecting to the transaction of any business because the meeting is not lawfully called or convened. Neither the business to be transacted at, nor the purpose of, any regular or special meeting of the board of directors need be specified in the notice or waiver of notice of such meeting.[41]

EXAMPLE: Quorum

A majority of the number of directors fixed by these bylaws shall constitute a quorum for the transaction of business at any meeting of the board of directors, but if less than such majority is present at a meeting, a majority of the directors present may adjourn the meeting from time to time without further notice.[42]

EXAMPLE: Board Decisions

The act of the majority of the directors present at a meeting at which a quorum is present shall be the act of the board of directors _____
[except that vote of not less than _____ (fraction) of all the members of the board shall be required for the amendment of or addition to these bylaws or as the case may be].[43]

Removal and Resignation of Directors

The bylaws should set forth the procedures for removing directors from the board, including who may remove the directors, for what cause directors may be removed, how resignations of directors are to be tendered, and how vacancies on the board of directors are to be handled.

Director Compensation

The compensation of the directors or the means for determining the directors' compensation should be set forth in the bylaws. The bylaws should also address the directors' expense reimbursement and the indemnification of directors.

Director Liability

The liability of the directors may be limited or expanded in the bylaws of the corporation, within the limits imposed by statute.

Officers

The bylaws of the corporation should name the titles of the officers that the corporation will have, define the powers and duties of each officer, and set forth the compensation for each officer, or the means for determining that compensation.

EXAMPLE: Number of Officers

The officers of the corporation shall be a president, one or more vice-presidents (the number thereof to be determined by the board of directors), a secretary, and a treasurer, each of whom shall be elected by the board of directors. Such other officers and assistant officers as may be deemed necessary may be elected or appointed by the board of directors. Any two or more offices may be held by the same person, except the offices of _____ [president and secretary, or as the case may be].[44]

EXAMPLE: Election and Term of Office

The officers of the corporation to be elected by the board of directors shall be elected annually at the first meeting of the board of directors held after each annual meeting of the stockholders. If the election of officers is not held at such meeting, such election shall be held as soon thereafter as is convenient. Each officer shall hold office until his or her successor has been duly elected and qualified or until his or her death or until he or she resigns or is removed in the manner hereinafter provided.[45]

EXAMPLE: Removal of Officers

Any officer or agent elected or appointed by the board of directors may be removed by the board of directors whenever in its judgment the best interests of the corporation would be served thereby, but such removal shall be without prejudice to the contract rights, if any, of the person so removed.[46]

EXAMPLE: Vacancies

A vacancy in any office because of death, resignation, removal, disqualification, or otherwise may be filled by the board of directors for the unexpired portion of the term.[47]

EXAMPLE: Powers and Duties of Officers

The powers and duties of the several officers shall be as provided from time to time by resolution or other directive of the board of directors. In the absence of such provisions, the respective officers shall have the powers and shall discharge the duties customarily and usually held and performed by like officers of corporations similar in organization and business purposes to this corporation.[48]

Stock Certificates

The bylaws should approve a form of stock certificate for the corporation for each class or type of stock to be used, including the required signatures on each stock certificate. The bylaws should also provide the means for transfer of stock and replacement of lost, stolen, or destroyed certificates. If there is any restriction on the transfer of shares, this restriction should be set forth in the bylaws, as well as on each stock certificate.

EXAMPLE: Certificates for Shares

Certificates representing shares of the corporation shall be in such form as shall be determined by the board of directors. Such certificates shall be signed by the president or a vice-president and by the secretary or an assistant secretary. All certificates for shares shall be consecutively numbered or otherwise identified. The name and address of the person to whom the shares represented thereby are issued, with the number of shares and date of issue, shall be entered on the stock transfer books of the corporation. All certificates surrendered to the corporation for transfer shall be canceled and no new certificate shall be issued until the former certificate for a like number of shares shall have been surrendered and canceled, except that in case of a lost, destroyed, or mutilated certificate a new one may be issued therefor on such terms and indemnity to the corporation as the board of directors may prescribe.[49]

Dividends

The bylaws may provide the method for determining the dividends to be paid on the stock of the corporation, and the timing and method for payment of those dividends.

Fiscal Year

The fiscal year of the corporation should be set forth in the bylaws of the corporation.

Corporate Seal

If the corporation plans to use a corporate seal, the seal should be described or reproduced in the bylaws. If the corporation does not plan to use a corporate seal, a statement to that effect should be included.

EXAMPLE: Corporate Seal

The board of directors shall provide a corporate seal, which shall be circular in form and shall have inscribed thereon the name of the corporation and the state of incorporation and the words "Corporate Seal." The seal shall be stamped or affixed to such documents as may be prescribed by law or custom or by the board of directors.[50]

Corporate Records

A statement should be made regarding the corporate records that are to be kept, their location, and the inspection rights of the officers, directors, and shareholders. Corporate records may include the stock certificate book, the stock transfer ledger, the minute book, and records of accounts.

Amendment of Bylaws

Procedures for amending the bylaws of the corporation, congruent with state statutes, should be set forth in the bylaws.

Signatures on Bylaws

The bylaws of the corporation are typically dated and signed by the secretary of the corporation in accordance with statute.

§ 6.6 Formation of Special Types of Corporations

Corporations other than business corporations are often subject to statutory incorporation requirements that differ from those prescribed for business corporations. In this section, we look at the special statutory provisions for incorporating statutory close corporations, professional corporations, and nonprofit corporations.

Statutory Close Corporations

Most states that have statutory provisions for statutory close corporations have different or additional requirements for such an entity's articles of incorporation. If a corporation is to be incorporated as a close corporation, it typically must so state in its articles of incorporation.

Under the Close Corporation Supplement to the Model Business Corporation Act, the articles of incorporation must include a statement that the corporation is a statutory close corporation. Other provisions unique to close corporations may be required as well, and the appropriate close corporation statutes must be consulted.

Special attention must also be paid to the stock certificates and bylaws of a statutory close corporation. Close corporations are typically required to include a statement on each stock certificate indicating that the corporation is a statutory close corporation and including any restrictions on transfer of the stock of the corporation that are typical to close corporations.

Bylaws may be optional for close corporations. Many of the provisions often included in the bylaws of other types of corporations are included in the articles of a close corporation or in resolutions by the shareholders or directors, if the corporation has directors.

Professional Corporations

The professional corporation must be incorporated in accordance with the professional corporation act or the professional corporation supplement to the business corporation act of the state of domicile. The requirements for forming a professional corporation are generally very similar to the requirements for forming a business corporation, with the exception of the restrictions on the officers, directors, and shareholders that were discussed in Chapter 5. The name of a professional corporation often must indicate that it is a professional corporation rather than a business corporation.

Nonprofit Corporations

Incorporation requirements for nonprofit corporations are also set by state statute, usually a state nonprofit corporation act. Requirements will vary, although they typically resemble the business corporation incorporation requirements at least in part. Typically, requirements for the articles of incorporation of a nonprofit corporation differ from those for a business corporation, but the articles must be filed in much the same way.

§ 6.7 The Role of the Legal Assistant in Corporate Formation

The legal assistant can handle almost all aspects of the incorporation process under the direction of an attorney. Given correct and complete information, the legal assistant can prepare all incorporation documents, including the articles of incorporation, bylaws, and first minutes or unanimous writings of the board of directors and shareholders. The specific tasks that can be performed by the legal assistant are numerous and include the following:

1. Attend initial attorney/client meeting to collect information required to complete incorporation process
2. Check name availability and prepare and file application for name reservation, if desired
3. Prepare and file articles of incorporation

4. Check for compliance with any publication or county recording requirements
5. Draft corporate documents, including:
   a. Bylaws
   b. Notices of organizational meetings
   c. Minutes or unanimous writings in lieu of organizational meeting or first meeting of directors and shareholders
   d. Stock subscription agreements
   e. Stock certificates
   f. Banking resolutions

In addition, the legal assistant can make sure that all administrative details are completed, such as ordering the corporate minute book for the corporation and completing stock certificates.

§ 6.8 Resources

The resources that the legal assistant will typically find useful when working on the formation of a corporation include the state statutes, information from the Secretary of State, and legal form books.

State Statutes

As discussed in this chapter, incorporation requirements for business corporations are found in the business corporation act of the statutes of the corporation's state of domicile.

Secretary of State

The articles or certificate of incorporation must be filed with the Secretary of State or other appropriate state official. In addition, the Secretary of State may have forms available for the documents that must be filed with the state. In some instances, use of these forms may be mandatory. The Secretary of State can also answer procedural questions regarding the documents, such as any questions about fees and forms. Although the filing fees are typically set forth in the statutes, they are subject to frequent changes, and it is a good idea to verify the filing fee with the Secretary of State to avoid any unnecessary delays. (See Appendix A for a Secretary of State directory.)

Form Books

In addition to the forms typically found within law firms or corporate law departments, numerous forms and form books are available to assist with the drafting of incorporation documents, including those mentioned in Chapter 5. When using generic forms for incorporating, it is important to use state-specific forms, when available, or to make allowances for specific state requirements when using other forms.

Review Questions

1. Are corporations bound to contracts made by the promoter prior to incorporation?

2. Can two individuals from New York form a Florida corporation?

3. If two residents of Texas file articles of incorporation in New York and transact the majority of their business in Florida, what is their state of domicile?

4. In addition to filing articles of incorporation, what incorporation formalities are imposed by some states before the incorporation process is complete?

5. Can the incorporator also be a director of a corporation?

6. What required provisions must be included in the articles of incorporation in a state following the Model Business Corporation Act?

7. Why is it advisable to gather more information from the client than the minimum required for the incorporation documents?

8. Why might it be preferable to put information in the bylaws, as opposed to the articles of incorporation, when the statute provides that the information could be in either document?

9. Would the name "Johnson Brothers Furniture Store" be a valid corporate name in a state following the Model Business Corporation Act? Why or why not?

10. When must the incorporator(s) attend the organizational meeting?

Notes

1 18 Am. Jur. 2d *Corporations* § 98 (1985).

2 *Id.* § 100.

3 *Id.* § 162.

4 1984 Revised Model Business Corporation Act § 2.01.

5 Alaska, Arizona, Georgia, Hawaii, Iowa, Maryland, Minnesota, Missouri, Nebraska, Nevada, New York, North Dakota, Rhode Island, South Dakota, Utah, Vermont, and Wisconsin have statutory provisions requiring that the incorporator or incorporators be natural persons.

6 Arizona, the District of Columbia, and Utah have statutory provisions requiring more than one incorporator.

7 1984 Revised Model Business Corporation Act § 2.02(a)(1).

8 *Id.* § 2.02(a)(2).

9 *Id.* § 2.02(a)(3).

10 *Id.* § 2.02(a)(4).

11 Minimum required information under 1984 Revised Model Business Corporation Act § 2.02(a)(2).

12 6B Am. Jur. Legal Forms 2d (Rev.) § 74:148.

13 Minimum required information under 1984 Revised Model Business Corporation Act § 2.02(a)(3).

14 1984 Revised Model Business Corporation Act § 2.02(b)(1).

15 *Id.* § 2.02(b)(2)(i).

16 *Id.* § 2.02(b)(2)(ii).

17 *Id.* § 2.02(b)(2)(iii).

18 *Id.* § 2.02(b)(2)(iv).

19 *Id.* § 2.02(b)(2)(v).

20 *Id.* § 2.02(b)(3).

21 *Id.* § 2.02(b)(4).

22 18A Am. Jur. 2d *Corporations* § 204 (1985).

23 1984 Revised Model Business Corporation Act § 7.28(b).

24 *Id.* § 8.08(a).

25 *Id.* § 6.01.

26 *Id.* § 6.30.

27 Arizona, Georgia, Nebraska, Pennsylvania, and Texas all have publication requirements for incorporating in those states.

28 Alabama, Delaware, Illinois, Iowa, Kansas, Kentucky, Louisiana, Maryland, Nebraska, Nevada, New York, Tennessee, West Virginia, and Wisconsin all have requirements for filing the articles of incorporation or a copy thereof at the county level.

29 18A Am. Jur. 2d *Corporations* § 217 (1985).

[30] *Id.* § 310.

[31] *Id.* § 313.

[32] 1984 Revised Model Business Corporation Act § 2.06.

[33] 6 AM. JUR. Legal Forms 2d (Rev.) § 74:991.

[34] *Id.*

[35] *Id.*

[36] *Id.*

[37] *Id.*

[38] *Id.*

[39] *Id.*

[40] *Id.*

[41] *Id.*

[42] *Id.*

[43] *Id.*

[44] *Id.*

[45] *Id.*

[46] *Id.*

[47] *Id.*

[48] *Id.*

[49] *Id.*

[50] *Id.*

CHAPTER 7

THE CORPORATE ORGANIZATION

Introduction

A corporate entity must act through its agents, the most visible agents being its officers and directors. The officers, directors, and shareholders may play very different roles, but each functions as an integral part of the operation of the business corporation. This chapter discusses the role of each type of member of the corporation, beginning with the authority, duties, liabilities, and compensation of the directors of the corporation. It examines how they are elected and how they act through directors' meetings. Next we investigate the officers, who are elected by the directors of the corporation, and follow with a study of the rights and responsibilities of the shareholders of the corporation, and how they participate in the corporate affairs through shareholder meetings. We then take a brief look at the restrictions that may be placed on the transfer of shares of corporate stock. This chapter concludes with a discussion of the paralegal's role in corporate organizational matters and the resources available to assist paralegals working in that area.

§ 7.1 Authority and Duties of Directors

Directors are given the statutory authority to make most decisions regarding the operation of the corporation, and it may appear that they have a free rein to operate the corporation as they see fit. However, it is important to remember that, although directors have full authority in most matters, they are elected by the shareholders of the corporation. The director who does not serve what the shareholders feel to be their best interests could be voted out of office at the next election, or even removed before his or her term expires. In this section we will look at both the authority and the duties of corporate directors.

Directors' Authority

It has been said that the "corporate board of directors, exercising their reasonable and good faith business judgment, possess the paramount right to corporate control and management."[1] The corporation, in effect, acts through its directors.

Section 8.01(b) of the Model Business Corporation Act represents the common statutory grant of authority to a corporation's board of directors:

> (b) All corporate powers shall be exercised by or under the authority of, and the business and affairs of the corporation managed under the direction of, its board of directors, subject to any limitation set forth in the articles of incorporation or in an agreement authorized under section 7.32.

Under § 7.32 of the Model Business Corporation Act, shareholders may enter into agreements that eliminate or restrict the discretion or powers of the board of directors under certain circumstances.

In addition to granting the board of directors the authority to manage the business and affairs of the corporation, the Model Business Corporation Act, like most state business corporation acts, grants the board of directors the authority to delegate the management of the business and affairs of the corporation.

Delegation of Authority to Officers

Directors generally are given the authority to appoint officers and to delegate certain authority to them. Under the Model Business Corporation Act, the business affairs of the corporation may be managed "under the direction of" the board of directors. This recognizes the fact that the directors of the corporation, alone, are often not the appropriate individuals to run the day-to-day business of the corporation. Directors are frequently employed outside the corporation, or have other interests that make demands on their time. Some individuals serve on the boards of several corporations.

There is a difference between the delegation of authority and power and the delegation of responsibility. It is generally accepted that, although the board of directors may delegate authority to corporate officers, the board must continue to "exercise general supervision over the activities of its delegates."[2] Directors are generally responsible for the acts of the officers whom they appoint.

The powers delegated to the officers of the corporation may be very broad, or they may be set forth very specifically in the articles or bylaws of the corporation, or by director resolution. The extent to which the officers are directed and limited in their authority by the board of directors will depend on the statutes of the corporation's state of domicile and the governing instruments of the corporation.

Delegation of Authority to Committees

Directors also commonly delegate authority to one or more committees that are comprised of members of the board of directors. With the complexities of managing a modern business, groups such as executive committees, nominating committees, finance committees, public affairs committees, and litigation committees are often appointed to oversee specific areas of concern.

The authority of directors to appoint committees may come from the statutes of the corporation's state of domicile, or the articles or bylaws of the corporation. Under the Model Business Corporation Act, the board of directors is granted the authority to create committees, unless the articles of incorporation or bylaws of the corporation provide otherwise. The creation of the committee and the appointment of its members must be approved by a majority of the board of directors, unless a larger number is required for a **quorum** under the articles of incorporation or bylaws of the corporation.

The only authority that a committee has to act on behalf of the corporation is the authority delegated to it by the board of directors, or as authorized in the articles of incorporation or bylaws of the corporation. Restrictions on the authority of the committee and the powers that may be delegated to it are often found in the state statutes. Additional restrictions may be imposed by the articles or bylaws of the corporation. The Model Business Corporation Act specifically states that a committee may not do any of the following:

1. Authorize dividends or distributions to the shareholders of the corporation[3]
2. Approve or propose to shareholders action that the Model Business Corporation Act requires to be approved by shareholders[4]
3. Fill vacancies on the board of directors or on any of its committees[5]
4. Amend articles of incorporation pursuant to MBCA § 10.02[6]

TERMS

quorum The minimum number of individuals who must be present or represented at a meeting as a prerequisite to the valid transaction of business.

5. Adopt, amend, or repeal bylaws[7]
6. Approve a plan of merger that does not require shareholder approval[8]
7. Authorize or approve reacquisition of shares, except according to a formula or method prescribed by the board of directors[9]
8. Authorize or approve the issuance, sale, or contract for sale of shares, or determine the designation and relative rights, preferences, and limitations of a class or series of shares, except that the board of directors may authorize a committee (or a senior executive officer of the corporation) to do so within limits specifically prescribed by the board of directors.[10]

Limitations on Directors' Authority

The state statutes generally grant full authority to the board of directors to manage the business and affairs of the corporation. However, that authority may be limited in the articles of incorporation of the corporation. In addition, certain corporate acts, not considered to be within the ordinary business and administration of the corporation, may require approval of the shareholders of the corporation. This restriction on the directors' actions may be either a statutory restriction or a restriction in the corporation's articles of incorporation.

Following is a list of actions that often require shareholder approval:

1. Amendment and restatement of the articles of incorporation
2. Enactment, amendment, or repeal of bylaws
3. Issuance of stock of the corporation
4. Dissolution of the corporation
5. Calling of shareholder meetings
6. Approval of merger and consolidation plans
7. Sale of corporate assets other than in the regular course of business.

Directors' Duties

The duties of a director to the corporation are several and complex. Directors' duties often are based on common law that has been upheld by numerous court cases, as well as specific statutes dealing with the duty of directors to the corporation.

In general, directors owe the following types of duties to the corporation and its shareholders:

1. A director's fiduciary duty to the corporation and its shareholders

Dividends

White Collar Criminals: Trading in Cuff Links for Hand Cuffs

Not all thieves wear ski masks and carry guns. Each year, white collar criminals steal millions of dollars from United States citizens and businesses. White collar crime includes various non-violent crimes such as theft, fraud, embezzlement, bribery, racketeering, and other forms of theft that involve the violation of trust.

White collar crime has been on the rise in recent years. According to recent FBI statistics, between 1989 and 1992 there was a 27 percent increase in white collar crime. During 1992, there were over a half-million arrests for forgery, counterfeiting, embezzlement, and fraud. We are often outraged by stories in the media concerning violent crime. However, the effects of white collar crime can also be devastating. Ordinary people have lost their homes and life savings from white collar crime. In addition, white collar crime costs every one of us with increased insurance premiums and rising taxes and consumer costs. It is estimated that the collapse of the savings and loan industry, which has been attributed largely to fraud and embezzlement, will cost taxpayers nearly $1 trillion.

Public tolerance for white collar crime has been shrinking by the decade. In the 1960s the public became enraged by bid rigging committed by electrical companies. The 1970s saw outrage over illegal payments overseas by giant government contractors. In the 1980s, public fury was once again raised over insider trading and banking abuses that touched the pocketbooks of so many people. The public is becoming even more intolerant as various white collar crimes have made the headlines in the 1990s.

In response to fear and outrage concerning organized white collar crime, state governments and the federal government have passed Racketeer Influenced and Corrupt Organization laws (RICO laws) to investigate, control, and prosecute organized crime. Federal RICO laws specifically prohibit activities affecting interstate

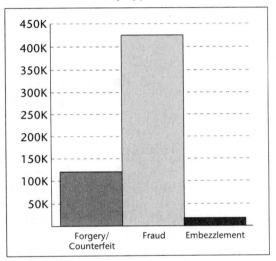

Arrests During 1992 for White Collar Crimes by Type of Crime

or foreign commerce. A RICO claim must allege the existence of seven elements: (1) that the defendant (2) through the commission of two or more acts (3) constituting a pattern (4) of racketeering activity (5) directly or indirectly invests in, or maintains an interest in, or participates in (6) an enterprise (7) the activities of which affect interstate or foreign commerce. 18 U.S.C.A. § 1962. Violation of RICO laws can result in both civil and criminal sanctions.

White collar crime can be doubly dangerous for the corporation and its executives. Not only can corporate executives face personal prosecution for crimes committed by the corporation, but in addition the corporation can be liable for crimes committed by its executives.

Corporate executives who commit white collar crime risk severe penalties, including fines and imprisonment. In recent years, billionaires such as Michael Milken, Ivan Boesky, and Charles Keating have received prison sentences for violation of securities and tax laws.

Corporations that are implicated in white collar crime face new federal sentencing guidelines that provide for corporate fines of up to $500 million under certain circumstances. In August of 1991, Salomon Brothers admitted to violation of rules of government bond trading and agreed to pay $290 million to settle charges.

These severe penalties have contributed to a move among corporations to take an aggressive proactive approach in dealing with white collar crime in their organization. Not only are they taking action against their employees who break the law; many corporations also consider education in business ethics to be a prerequisite for employment.   ▥

2. A director's duty of care to the corporation and its shareholders
3. A director's duty of loyalty to the corporation and its shareholders.

Fiduciary Duty

One duty owed to a corporation and its shareholders by the directors has been compared to a fiduciary duty. It is probably more accurate to refer to the relationship as a quasi-fiduciary relationship—one that has several but not all of the elements of an actual fiduciary relationship.

The duty of the director to the corporation and its shareholders resembles a fiduciary duty in that the entire management of corporate affairs is often entrusted to the directors of the corporation, who are responsible for acting in the best interests of the corporation and the shareholders.

In numerous court cases, courts have defined the directors' "quasi-fiduciary" relationship to the corporation and its shareholders as follows:

> They are required to act in the utmost good faith, and in accepting the office, they impliedly undertake to give to the enterprise the benefit of their care and best judgment and to exercise the powers conferred solely in the interest of the corporation or the stockholders as a body or corporate entity, and not for their own personal interests.[11]

A director who acts contrary to the best interests of the corporation for his or her own personal gain is breaching his or her fiduciary duty to the corporation. Shareholders have the expectation of sharing in the profits of the corporation, and when a director is personally benefited at the expense of the corporation, the director breaches his or her duty to the shareholders of the corporation by depriving them of the full potential profit from the corporation.[12]

Duty of Care

Directors must use "due care" and be diligent in the management and administration of the affairs of the corporation and in the use or preservation of its property.[13] The exact measure of the degree of care that must be exercised is impossible to define, although one test often used is the *ordinarily prudent person test,* which means acting with the diligence and care that would be exercised by an ordinarily prudent person in like circumstances. The following list indicates typical actions of directors who would generally be considered to be acting in the manner of a prudent person:[14]

1. Attend board meetings and committee meetings on a regular basis
2. Read, understand, and act on (when necessary) information received between the meetings of the board of directors, including minutes of past meetings, proposed agendas, proposals, and financial statements
3. Participate in discussions of the board of directors
4. Make independent inquiries when needed
5. Make objections when warranted
6. Review stockholder reports.

The Model Business Corporation Act, which defines the general standards for directors, indicates that the directors must discharge their duties:

(1) In good faith[15]
(2) With the care an ordinarily prudent person in a like position would exercise under similar circumstances[16]
(3) In a manner [they] reasonably believe to be in the best interests of the corporation.[17]

Duty of Loyalty

Numerous times courts have found that a director "must remain loyal to the corporation, acting at all times in the best interests of the corporation and its shareholders and unhampered by any personal pecuniary gain."[18] Directors must at all times act in a manner that serves the best interest of the corporation, as opposed to a director's other interests or the director's personal interests. Often individuals who are directors of related corporations or have interests in related businesses may find themselves in a position of a potential conflict of interest. Directors should abstain from participating in corporate decisions that might give even the appearance of a conflict of interest. Statutes modeled after the Model Business Corporation Act with regard to director conflicts of interest require that directors disclose the existence and nature of potential conflicting interests and all known material facts with regard to the decision as to whether to proceed with the proposed transaction.

Reliance upon Information from Others

Directors cannot reasonably be expected to have first-hand knowledge of all business affairs of the corporation for which they are responsible. For that reason, it is assumed that directors are entitled to rely upon information given to them and statements made to them by those who are in immediate charge of the corporation's business. Under § 8.30(b) of the Model Business Corporation Act, directors are expressly granted the right to rely on information from others:

> (b) In discharging his duties a director is entitled to rely on information, opinions, reports, or statements, including financial statements and other financial data, if prepared or presented by:
>
> (1)   one or more officers or employees of the corporation whom the director reasonably believes to be reliable and competent in the matters presented;
>
> (2)   legal counsel, public accountants, or other persons as to matters the director reasonably believes are within the person's professional or expert competence; or
>
> (3)   a committee of the board of directors of which he is not a member if the director reasonably believes the committee merits confidence.

The director is responsible for ascertaining the validity of the information given to him or her to the extent that any cause for suspicion by the director or any facts that would cause an ordinarily prudent person to become suspicious must be investigated.

§ 7.2   Personal Liability of Directors

The imposition of personal liability on corporate directors for poor business decisions would be an impractical, if not impossible, task. Directors generally cannot be held personally liable for any damages caused to the corporation as the result of decisions made by them in good faith.

However, there are several instances in which personal liability may be imposed. Under certain conditions, personal liability is imposed on the directors of a corporation by statute, unless the corporation's articles of incorporation provide otherwise. It is, therefore, important that the incorporators of a business be well informed regarding the potential for director liability, and that the incorporation documents be drafted accordingly.

This section discusses application of the business judgment rule to corporate directors. It also considers the risk of personal liability to directors under certain circumstances.

Business Judgment Rule

The courts have recognized for years that the decisions made by directors involve a certain amount of risk, and that even an informed, good faith decision can still result in an unfavorable outcome for the corporation.

The *business judgment rule,* which has been followed by courts as a standard in determining the potential personal liability of a director, states that:

> A corporate transaction that involves no self-dealing by, or other personal interest of, the directors who authorized the transaction will not be enjoined or set aside for the directors' failure to satisfy the standards that govern a director's performance of his or her duties, and directors who authorized the transaction will not be held personally liable for resultant damages, unless:
>
> (1) The directors did not exercise due care to ascertain the relevant and available facts before voting to authorize the transaction; or
> (2) The directors voted to authorize the transaction even though they did not reasonably believe or could not have reasonably believed the transaction to be for the best interest of the corporation; or
> (3) In some other way, the directors' authorization of the transaction was not in good faith.[19]

Imposition of Personal Liability on Directors

As we have discussed, personal liability is generally not imposed on corporate directors for their poor business decisions. However, the amount of litigation involving personal liability of directors in recent years is indicative of the many exceptions to that rule.

A director who fails in his or her fiduciary duty, duty of due care, or duty of loyalty to the corporation may be subject to the imposition of personal liability for any damages caused to the corporation or the shareholders of the corporation.

Unauthorized Acts

When directors clearly act beyond the scope of their authority, personal liability may be imposed upon them for losses to the corporation caused by their unauthorized acts. Directors acting beyond the scope of their authority may be required to make good any losses caused by their acts out of their personal assets.

Negligence

Directors are personally liable for their negligent acts that involve injury or loss to the corporation or to third parties. Personal liability of the directors for negligent acts is based on the common law rule "which renders every agent liable who violates his authority or neglects his duty to the damage of his principal."[20]

Fraud or Other Illegal Acts

Directors may also be personally liable to the corporation and to third parties for any fraudulent or other **tortious** acts committed by them, or by the corporation with their knowledge. Corporate directors are not personally liable for fraud involving the corporation that they were unaware of, if they should not have reasonably been expected to be aware of it.

Statutory Imposition of Personal Liability

State statutes or the articles of incorporation of a corporation, or both, may specify that the directors of a corporation are personally liable for certain actions. Under the Model Business Corporation Act, directors may be held personally liable for the payment of distributions in violation of state statutes or the articles of incorporation. Under § 8.33 of the Act, directors can be held personally liable to the corporation for the amount of any distribution that exceeds the permitted distribution under statute or under the articles of incorporation. However, the Model Business Corporation Act also provides that directors can be

---

TERMS

tortious   Wrongful. A tortious act subjects the actor to liability under the law of torts. A *tort* is a private or civil wrong for which the legal system provides a remedy in the form of an action for damages.

EDWARDS
v.
HORSEMEN'S SALES CO., INC.
Supreme Court, New York County
560 N.Y.S.2d 165 (Sup. Ct. 1989)
November 9, 1989
Greenfield, Justice

Plaintiff moves for an order ... granting summary judgment on the third cause of action in the amended complaint alleging that Steve M. Ostrer and Benjamin Ostrer (Collectively the Ostrer brothers), as directors and officers of Horsemen's Sales Co., Inc. misappropriated and converted $49,002 to their own use.

Plaintiff had consigned five horses to Horsemen's Sales to be sold at auction at the August 1985 yearling sales at Saratoga Springs. The sale, after deduction of commissions and expenses, netted $49,002. The proceeds of the sale were never remitted to plaintiff.

On October 7, 1986, plaintiff was awarded summary judgment against Horsemen's Sales and a judgment in the amount of $54,514.73 was entered against that corporation. To date plaintiff has not been paid.

Plaintiff now seeks an order holding the individual Ostrer brothers liable on the ground that they "fraudulently, wrongfully and unlawfully and in violation of their trust and fiduciary responsibilities ... misappropriated and converted the net proceeds of sale of $49,002 for uses other than payment, as legally required to plaintiff."

[1] The individual defendants contend they cannot be held personally responsible for the defaults of the corporation. While this is the general rule, a corporate officer or director may be held personally liable for conversion or misappropriation of trust funds. ... This is true whether or not the individual officer or director was acting for the corporation, so long as he participated in the act. ... There need be no showing of tortious intent or bad faith. ...

Under the Consignor's contract, the net proceeds of the auction received were to be remitted within 45 days. While there was no requirement that the proceeds be segregated in a separate account, and cash is fungible, the proceeds were not to be used for general corporate purposes, but to be turned over to plaintiff, as consignor. According to the contract, the auctioneer was to receive the proceeds of the sale for the consignor's account. ... Instead, the individual defendants caused the proceeds from the sale of plaintiff's horses to be used to pay bills, salaries, and general obligations of the corporation, including their own personal out-of-pocket expenses, rather than turning the funds over to plaintiff.

... Accordingly, the court finds as a matter of law that the individual defendants are liable to plaintiff for the conversion of the proceeds from the sale of plaintiff's horses, together with interest.

Plaintiff's motion for summary judgment on the third cause of action of the amended complaint is granted.

held personally liable for such amount only if they did not exercise the proper standard of conduct as defined by the Act.

Director liability has been the subject of much debate and many court cases in recent years. Many states have amended their state statutes to clarify the state's position on director liability, and many corporations have amended their articles of incorporation, usually to afford their directors the greatest amount of protection available under law. Many of the newer statutes have yet to be tested in court, and the full impact of the new laws regarding directors' liability remains to be seen.

TABLE 7-1   PERSONAL LIABILITY OF DIRECTORS

DIRECTORS MAY BE HELD PERSONALLY LIABLE FOR:

- Unauthorized Acts (acts clearly beyond the scope of their authority)
- Negligent Acts
- Fraud or Other Illegal Acts
- Acts That Are Controlled by State Statute That Provide for Personal Liability by Directors

§ 7.3 Compensation and Indemnification of Directors

Directors are often called upon to serve the corporation in several different ways, and they may or may not be directly compensated by the corporation. This section scrutinizes the compensation of directors and their indemnification for expenses incurred on behalf of the corporation.

Compensation of Directors

Directors may or may not receive compensation specifically for their roles as directors in the corporation. Director compensation is usually set by the board of directors, unless the right to set director compensation is limited to the shareholders in the statutes of the state of domicile, or the corporation's articles of incorporation or bylaws.

Indemnification

A director generally has a right to be reimbursed for advances made or expenses incurred by him or her on behalf of the corporation. A director, however, has no right to be reimbursed for expenses incurred by his or her own wrongdoing.

Indemnification refers to the act by which corporations reimburse directors for expenses incurred by them in defending a lawsuit to which they become a party because of their involvement with the corporation. This type of reimbursement is addressed separately by law and usually by the articles and bylaws of the corporation. Typically, the statutes of the state of domicile will set guidelines directing mandatory indemnification under certain circumstances and prohibiting indemnification of the directors under other circumstances.

Mandatory Indemnification

Statutes typically prescribe certain conditions under which a director must be indemnified, usually when a director is successful in the defense of any proceeding to which he or she was a party because of his or her directorship of the corporation. Section 8.52 of the Model Business Corporation Act addresses mandatory indemnification as follows:

§ 8.52 MANDATORY INDEMNIFICATION

A corporation shall indemnify a director who was wholly successful, on the merits or otherwise, in the defense of any proceeding to which he was a party because he was a director of the corporation against reasonable expenses incurred by him in connection with the proceeding.

Optional Indemnification

Statutes typically address several circumstances under which directors may be indemnified if the articles of incorporation or bylaws of the corporation provide for indemnification under those conditions. Provisions such as these require careful drafting of the articles and bylaws to provide the desired indemnification of directors of the corporation. A corporation normally indemnifies its directors when they conduct themselves in good faith and when they reasonably believed that their actions were in the best interests of the corporation. In the event of criminal proceedings, directors will often be indemnified, pursuant to the corporation's articles of incorporation or bylaws, if the directors had no reasonable cause to believe that their conduct was unlawful. Again, the articles of incorporation or bylaws of the corporation must provide for this type of director indemnification in accordance with statute, if desired.

Prohibited Indemnification

Statutory provisions such as subsection (d) of § 8.51 of the Model Business Corporation Act make it clear that directors are not to be indemnified for expenses incurred for defense in proceedings involving their own wrongdoing:

(d) Unless ordered by a court under section 8.54(a)(3), a corporation may not indemnify a director:
   (1) in connection with a proceeding by or in the right of the corporation, except for reasonable expenses incurred in connection with the proceeding if it is determined that the director has met the relevant standard of conduct under subsection (a); or

(2) in connection with any proceeding with respect to conduct for which he was adjudged liable on the basis that he received a financial benefit to which he was not entitled, whether or not involving action in his official capacity.

Following is a sample paragraph that could be included in a corporation's bylaws, when it is the desire of the directors and shareholders to indemnify the officers and directors of the corporation to the fullest extent permitted by law.

EXAMPLE: Indemnification

The corporation shall hereby indemnify the officers and directors of the corporation and their heirs, executors, and administrators to the full extent permitted by _____ [cite appropriate statute section]. The board of directors and officers of the corporation are hereby authorized to take the necessary and appropriate action to indemnify the officers and directors of the corporation, and their heirs, executors, and administrators to the full extent permitted by the aforesaid statute.

---

§ 7.4 Election and Term of Directors

The board of directors is chosen by vote of the shareholders of the corporation to serve a definite term. In this section we examine the election of directors and the terms they serve.

Election of Directors

The directors of a corporation are elected by the shareholders to operate and manage the affairs of the corporation. With the possible exception of close corporations, all corporations are generally required to elect a board of directors and to have a board of directors at all times.

If the first board of directors is named in the articles of incorporation, those directors serve only until the first meeting of the shareholders. At that time, the initial directors are either reelected or replaced by a vote of the shareholders, as discussed below under "Term of Directors."

Number and Qualifications of Directors

Traditionally, corporations were required by statute to have at least three directors on their boards. Often, those individuals were required to be shareholders of the corporation or residents of the state of the corporation's domicile, or both. With the relaxation of corporate law restrictions and the advent of the one-person corporation, many states amended their restrictions on the number of directors by passing laws that allow the board of directors to consist of one individual, who may or may not be a shareholder of the corporation or a resident of the corporation's state of domicile. Modern corporate law typically allows restrictions on either the number of directors or their qualifications to be made by provisions in the articles of incorporation or bylaws of the corporation.

The Model Business Corporation Act states that the "board of directors must consist of one or more individuals, with the number specified in or fixed in accordance with the articles of incorporation or bylaws."[21] Section 8.02 of the Model Business Corporation Act addresses director qualifications as follows:

§ 8.02 QUALIFICATIONS OF DIRECTORS

The articles of incorporation or bylaws may prescribe qualifications for directors. A director need not be a resident of this state or a shareholder of the corporation unless the articles of incorporation or bylaws so prescribe.

Because the directors typically have the authority to amend the bylaws of the corporation, many state statutes that allow the number of directors to be prescribed by the bylaws of the corporation also place limits on the power of the board of directors to increase or decrease their own number. This may be done by providing that a range in the number of directors be stated in the articles of incorporation of the corporation (which may only be amended with shareholder approval), or by providing that the number of directors may not be increased or decreased by more than a certain amount without shareholder approval.

Special types of corporations may have different statutory requirements for the number and qualifications of directors. As discussed in Chapter 5, certain statutory close corporations are not required to have a board of directors, but may be managed by the shareholders of the corporation instead.

Directors of professional corporations are usually subject to more specific qualifications, such as being license holders of the profession being practiced by the professional corporation.

Term of Directors

Under the Model Business Corporation Act, the term of each director expires at the next annual meeting of the shareholders following their election, when the director's successor is elected and qualifies, or when the number of directors decreases.

The shareholders may decide to ensure the continuity of management of the corporation by staggering the terms of the directors. The Model Business Corporation Act provides that corporations that have nine or more directors may stagger their terms by dividing the total number of directors into two or three groups, as nearly equal in number as possible. These groups may be elected for one-, two-, or three-year terms that will expire in different years. At each annual shareholder meeting, directors will be elected or reelected to fill the positions of the directors whose terms are expiring that particular year.

For example, if a board of directors is eventually to consist of nine directors who will each serve for a two-year term, three of the first directors may be elected for an initial three-year term, three may be elected for an initial two-year term, and three may be elected for an initial one-year term. Annual board of director elections in subsequent years will be required only for the replacement of those directors whose terms are expiring in that particular year.

Resignation

Directors are generally allowed to resign their positions at any time, in accordance with state statute. Courts have generally found that directors "may resign at any time and for any reason if they act in good faith and without personal gain."[22] Resignation is generally given by written notice delivered to the chairman of the board of directors or to the board itself.

Removal of Directors

The board of directors is elected to serve the best interests of the corporation and, more specifically, the shareholders. It is generally the shareholders' right to remove any director or directors with or without cause by a majority vote at a special shareholder meeting called specifically for that purpose. Corporations that allow cumulative voting may provide that the number of votes required to elect a director, if cast in favor of retaining a director, is sufficient to keep the director in office. Cumulative voting is discussed in § 7.8 of this text.

The statutes of a few states protect the directors of the corporation by providing that they may not be removed without cause unless specific provisions for removal without cause are included in the articles of incorporation or bylaws of the corporation. Requirements and procedures for removing a director of the corporation may be set by the articles of incorporation or the bylaws of the corporation, so long as those provisions fall within the boundaries of the statutes of the state of domicile. The Model Business Corporation Act provides for the removal of directors in § 8.08:

(a) The shareholders may remove one or more directors with or without cause unless the articles of incorporation provide that directors may be removed only for cause.

(b) If a director is elected by a voting group of shareholders, only the shareholders of that voting group may participate in the vote to remove him.

(c) If cumulative voting is authorized, a director may not be removed if the number of votes sufficient to elect him under cumulative voting is voted against his removal. If cumulative voting is not authorized, a director may be removed only if the number of votes cast to remove him exceeds the number of votes cast not to remove him.

(d) A director may be removed by the shareholders only at a meeting called for the purpose of removing him and the meeting notice must state that the purpose, or one of the purposes, of the meeting is removal of the director.

Under certain circumstances, when it is desirable to remove a director who is a shareholder with sufficient voting power to prevent his or her own removal, or in larger, publicly held corporations where it is impractical to call a special meeting of the shareholders for the purpose of removing a director, it may be necessary or desirable to remove a director by court order. Pursuant to § 8.09 of the Model Business Corporation Act, which is followed closely by most states in this regard, shareholders of a corporation holding at least 10 percent of the outstanding shares of any class, or the corporation itself, may initiate a court action to request the removal of a director when it can be shown that the director "engaged in fraudulent or dishonest conduct, or gross abuse of authority or discretion, with respect to the corporation,"[23] or when it can be shown that the removal of the director is "in the best interest of the corporation."[24]

Filling Vacancies on the Board

In some states a vacancy on the board of directors may be filled by a vote of the remaining directors. Statutes of other states provide that a special meeting of the shareholders may be called to elect a director to fill a vacancy on the board. In either event, the replacement director serves until the next annual meeting of the shareholders, or until his or her successor is duly elected and qualified.

§ 7.5 Board of Directors Meetings and Resolutions

Most actions of the board of directors are taken through resolutions passed at meetings of the board. This section examines the requirements for board of directors meetings, including requirements for holding annual meetings and for notifying the directors about meetings. It also discusses the requisite quorum for passing a resolution of the board of directors at a board meeting, and the minutes taken to formalize the resolutions of the board of directors. Finally, we focus on the ability of directors to act without a meeting, through the use of unanimous written consents and telephonic meetings.

Board of Directors Meetings

Under common law a corporation could act only through its directors at regularly held meetings. State statutes almost uniformly required annual meetings of the board of directors and dictated the procedures for calling and holding the annual and special board meetings that were necessary for the directors to take action.

The tendency of modern corporate law, however, recognizes the impracticality of mandatory, formal directors' meetings for all board of director actions, and the following three changes to the Model Business Corporation Act have been adopted almost uniformly by the states to make it easier for a board of directors to take action:

1. Annual board of directors meetings are optional
2. Action may be taken by the board of directors by a unanimous written consent, signed by each director
3. Telephonic meetings by the board of directors are generally acceptable.

Notice requirements for board meetings have also been relaxed in most states.

Corporations generally address the issue of directors' meetings in the bylaws of the corporation. If an annual meeting is desired, the date for the annual meeting is typically set forth, as well as the place and time for the meeting and the notice requirements.

Depending on the degree to which directors are directly involved in the day-to-day business of a corporation, the board of directors may meet regularly for monthly or even weekly meetings. Other corporations, especially large and publicly held corporations, may limit their board of directors meetings to annual meetings, which typically are held immediately following the annual meeting of the shareholders of the corporation, as prescribed in the bylaws of the corporation.

The directors of the corporation must be aware of and follow all requirements for annual and special meetings, as prescribed by statute, and by the corporation's articles of incorporation and bylaws.

Annual Meetings of the Board of Directors

Annual board of directors meetings are generally held for several purposes. In almost all instances, an election is held to re-elect or replace the current officers, and the acts of the officers for the past year are ratified. In addition, the board of directors reviews important events that have occurred during the past year and takes actions on those matters requiring action for the upcoming year.

A typical agenda for an annual meeting of a board of directors might include several of the following items:

1. Approve the minutes from the last meeting of the board of directors
2. Approve dividends to be paid to the shareholders of the corporation
3. Approve the annual report, to be filed with the appropriate state authority (if required)
4. Review the financial reports of the corporation
5. Elect officers of the corporation, to serve until the next annual meeting or until their successors are duly elected and qualified
6. Set the compensation of the officers of the corporation for the succeeding year
7. Approve bonuses for the officers and directors
8. Ratify the acts of the officers and directors for the past year
9. Address any other matters of concern regarding the operation and business of the corporation.

Notice of Meetings

Notice of annual and special meetings of the board of directors must be given in accordance with statute and with the articles of incorporation or bylaws of the corporation. Under the Model Business Corporation Act, "Unless the articles of incorporation or bylaws provide otherwise, regular meetings of the board of directors may be held without notice of the date, time, place, or purpose of the meeting."[25] Specific notice requirements for special meetings are often set forth in statutes, as they are in the Uniform Business Corporation Act, which provides that at least two days' notice of the date, time, and place of the meeting must be given. It is common for the statutes or the corporation's articles or bylaws to require that the purpose of a special meeting of the board of directors be included in the notice of the meeting.

Typically, notice requirements set forth in the bylaws of the corporation for annual and special meetings of the board of directors include a statement to the effect that the directors of the corporation may waive any required notice and that a director's attendance at any meeting constitutes a waiver of notice for that meeting. The exception is that it is not considered a waiver of notice for a meeting if a director attends a meeting only to object to the holding of the meeting or the transaction of business at the meeting.

Figure 7-1 shows a form that could be used for a notice of annual meeting of a board of directors.

Quorum

A *quorum* is the minimum number of individuals who must be present or represented at a meeting as a prerequisite to the valid transaction of business. Section 8.24 of the Model Business Corporation Act, which is followed by most states in this regard, sets forth the following quorum and voting requirements for taking action at a meeting of the board of directors:

1. A quorum of the board of directors consists of a majority of the fixed number of directors if the corporation has a fixed board size, or a majority of the number of prescribed directors or the number of officers in office immediately before the meeting begins if the corporation has a variable-range size board.

**NOTICE OF ANNUAL MEETING
OF THE BOARD OF DIRECTORS**

OF THE _____ CORPORATION

You are hereby notified that the 1996 Annual Meeting of the Board of Directors of the _____ Corporation will be held at the registered office of the corporation, at _____ [address], at _____ , on _____ , 19___ , for the purpose of transacting all such business as may properly come before the board.

Dated the ____ day of _____ , 1996.

_____
Secretary

FIGURE 7-1   Sample Notice of Annual Meeting of Board of Directors

2. The affirmative vote of a majority of the directors present is the act of the board of directors if a quorum is present when the vote is taken.
3. A director who is present at a meeting of the board of directors when corporate action is taken is deemed to have assented to the action taken unless:
    a. The director objects at the beginning of the meeting (or promptly upon arrival) to holding it or transacting business at the meeting
    b. The director's dissent or abstention from the action taken is entered in the minutes of the meeting; or
    c. The director delivers written notice of dissent or abstention to the presiding officer of the meeting before its adjournment or to the corporation immediately after adjournment of the meeting.

The Model Business Corporation Act provides that the articles of incorporation or the bylaws of the corporation may provide for the following deviations from statutory requirements:

1. The articles or bylaws may require a greater number for the quorum of a meeting
2. The articles of incorporation may require a lesser number for a quorum of a meeting of the board of directors, so long as the number is no fewer than one third of the number prescribed by statute.

These requirements for quorum and voting are typical of the laws of many states. However, the quorum and voting requirements vary by state, and the corporation's articles of incorporation and bylaws must always be consulted to see that quorum and voting requirements are complied with in order for an action of the board of directors to be valid.

Minutes

Complete and accurate minutes must be taken at every meeting of the board of directors. These minutes of the board of directors typically are taken and signed by the secretary of the corporation, who then places them in the corporate minute book, along with a copy of the notice of the meeting that was sent to all directors, any waivers of notice received from the directors, and any other documents pertaining to the meeting. Figure 7-2 is a form of annual minutes that could be used for an annual meeting of a board of directors.

Board Actions Without Meeting

Modern corporate law in most states recognizes the complexity of assembling a board of directors every time a board resolution is required,

MINUTES OF THE ANNUAL MEETING
OF THE BOARD OF DIRECTORS

OF THE _____ CORPORATION

The annual meeting of the Board of Directors of the _____ Corporation was held on _____ , at the registered office of the corporation at _____ .

Present at the meeting were the following persons:

_____

_____

_____

_____

which constitutes all of the members of the Board of Directors.

The Chairman of the Board of the corporation, _____ , presided as chairman of the meeting, and _____ acted as its secretary.

The chairman called the meeting to order and stated that a quorum of directors was present for the conduct of business.

The secretary presented and read a waiver of notice to the meeting signed by all directors of the corporation, which was ordered to be made part of the minutes of this meeting.

A discussion was had on the corporation's financial statements, salary increases and bonuses for the officers and directors of the corporation, and dividends to be paid on the outstanding stock of the corporation.

After motions duly made, seconded, and carried, the following resolutions were adopted by the Board of Directors:

RESOLVED, that the financial statements, as presented to the Board of Directors at this meeting, are hereby ratified and approved.

RESOLVED, that due to the profitable nature of the business of the corporation during the past fiscal year, the following officers shall be given a bonus in the following amounts:

_____	$ _____
_____	$ _____
_____	$ _____
_____	$ _____

RESOLVED, that the following persons are hereby elected to the following described offices, to serve in such capacities until their successors are elected at the next annual meeting and qualify:

FIGURE 7-2 Sample Minutes of Annual Meeting of Board of Directors

Chairman of the Board   _____

Chief Executive Officer   _____

President   _____

Vice President   _____

Secretary   _____

Treasurer   _____.

Each of the above-named officers accepted the office to which he or she was elected.

RESOLVED, that in consideration of their services to the corporation, the following annual salaries of the officers of the corporation for the fiscal year beginning _____ , 19___ , were approved:

_____ $_____

_____ $_____

_____ $_____

_____ $_____.

RESOLVED, that a dividend is hereby declared out of the capital surplus of the corporation to be payable to the stockholders of the corporation in an amount of $_____ per share. Such dividend shall be payable on the _____ day of _____ , 19___ , in cash, to shareholders of record on the _____ day of _____ , 19___ . The treasurer of the corporation is hereby authorized to set aside the sum necessary to pay said dividends.

There being no further business before the meeting, it was, on motion duly made, seconded, and unanimously carried, adjourned.

_____
Secretary

FIGURE 7-2 *(continued)*

by allowing for such resolutions to be passed by unanimous written consents and by telephonic meetings.

Written Consents

As discussed in Chapter 6, the unanimous writing of the board of directors has become a very popular means for taking a formal action of the board of directors. The unanimous writing can be very useful to corporations whose board of directors may be spread out over a large geographical distance. Unanimous writings are also a useful means of formalizing the agreement of directors of smaller corporations who may work side by side every day without ever going through the formality of holding a "meeting" of the board of directors.

Unanimous writings do have some drawbacks, the foremost being that it is generally required that the consent in fact be *unanimous*. If any one director disagrees with the proposed action, a meeting must be held and a vote must be taken.

The sample in Figure 7-3 demonstrates how the same resolutions that are typically passed at an annual meeting of a board of directors can be passed by the unanimous written consent of the directors.

**UNANIMOUS WRITTEN CONSENT
OF THE BOARD OF DIRECTORS**

OF THE _____ **CORPORATION**

The undersigned persons, being all of the Directors of the _____ Corporation (hereinafter referred to as the "Corporation"), hereby take the following actions by written consent in lieu of an annual meeting of the Board of Directors, pursuant to _____ [cite pertinent statute].

RESOLVED, that due to the profitable nature of the business of the corporation during the past fiscal year, the following officers shall be given a bonus in the following amounts:

_____	$ _____
_____	$ _____
_____	$ _____
_____	$ _____

RESOLVED, that the following persons are hereby elected to the following described offices, to serve in such capacities until their successors are elected at the next annual meeting and qualify:

Chairman of the Board	_____
Chief Executive Officer	_____
President	_____
Vice President	_____
Secretary	_____
Treasurer	_____

FIGURE 7-3 Sample Unanimous Written Consent of Board of Directors

RESOLVED, that in consideration of their services to the corporation, the following annual salaries of the officers of the corporation for the fiscal year beginning _____ , 19___ , are hereby approved:

_____ $ _____

_____ $ _____

_____ $ _____

_____ $ _____

RESOLVED, that a dividend is hereby declared out of the capital surplus of the corporation to be payable to the stockholders of the corporation in an amount of $_____ per share. Such dividend shall be payable on the _____ day of _____ , 19 ___ , in cash, to shareholders of record on the _____ day of _____ , 19___. The treasurer of the corporation is hereby authorized to set aside the sum necessary to pay said dividends.

Dated: _____ .

_____   _____

_____   _____

FIGURE 7-3 *(continued)*

Telephonic Meetings

Another modernization of corporate laws, which is found in the Model Business Corporation Act and has been followed by most states, allows regular or special meetings of the board of directors to be conducted through "any means of communication by which all directors participating may simultaneously hear each other during the meeting"[26]—the conference call.

Corporate Minute Books

The minutes or unanimous written consents of both directors' and shareholder meetings are kept in a corporate minute book, along with other important documents regarding the corporation. The contents of the corporate minute book often include the articles or certificate of incorporation, the corporate charter, the corporate bylaws, the minutes of the organizational meeting, all minutes of meetings of the board of directors or shareholders, and all unanimous written consents of the board of directors and shareholders (see Figure 7-4). Corporate minute

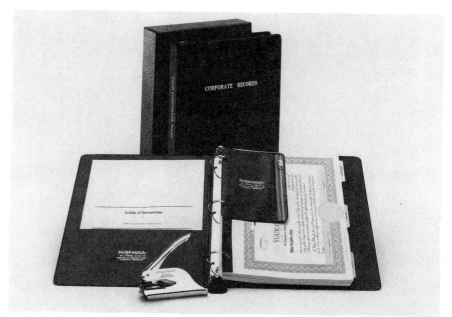

FIGURE 7-4 Corporate minute books contain the corporation's incorporation documents, meeting minutes, and unanimous writings. (Photo courtesy of Liberty Legal, Houston, Texas)

books are often kept in the office of the corporate attorney, and the task of keeping the corporate minute book in order and up to date often falls to the paralegal.

§ 7.6 Corporate Officers

Officers are in the broadest sense considered to be agents of the corporation.[27] They are individuals elected by the board of directors to oversee the business of the corporation, under the authority of the directors. An individual may be an officer and a director at the same time; in small corporations, all of the officers are commonly directors of the corporation as well.

This section examines the titles and typical duties of various corporate officers, and the officers' potential for personal liability. The section concludes with a discussion of the election and terms of office of corporate officers.

Titles and Duties of Officers

Generally, the officers of a corporation have the titles, duties, and responsibilities assigned to them under the statutes of the state of domicile, by the articles of incorporation or bylaws of the corporation, or by resolution of the board of directors. Statutes may be very specific regarding the required officers of a corporation, naming the titles and duties that must be assumed by officers of a corporation. More often, however, in modern corporate law the corporation is given much latitude regarding the officers it chooses and the duties assigned to those officers.

The Model Business Corporation Act addresses the required officers of a corporation in § 8.40:

§ 8.40 REQUIRED OFFICERS

(a) A corporation has the officers described in its bylaws or appointed by the board of directors in accordance with the bylaws.
(b) A duly appointed officer may appoint one or more officers or assistant officers if authorized by the bylaws or the board of directors.
(c) The bylaws or the board of directors shall delegate to one of the officers responsibility for preparing minutes of the directors' and shareholders' meetings and for authenticating records of the corporation.
(d) The same individual may simultaneously hold more than one office in a corporation.

The Model Business Corporation Act also gives further latitude to corporations in assigning duties of the officers. In states following the Model Business Corporation Act, officers have the authority to perform the duties set forth in the bylaws, or prescribed by the board of directors, or at the direction of an officer authorized by the board of directors to prescribe the duties of other officers.

Typically, bylaws of the corporation will set forth:

1. The titles of the officers of the corporation
2. A description of the duties of the officers of the corporation
3. The method for electing the officers of the corporation
4. Any special qualifications for the directors of the corporation.

The following subsections list the officers that are often elected to serve a corporation and describe the duties often assigned to those officers, in terms that might be used in corporate articles or bylaws.

Chief Executive Officer

The chief executive officer of the corporation (CEO) shall actively manage the business of the corporation and directly and actively supervise all other officers, agents, and employees. The chief executive officer shall preside over all meetings of the shareholders and the board of directors.

President

The president of the corporation shall preside at all meetings of the board of directors and shareholders, in the absence of the chief executive officer. The president shall perform all duties incident to the office of the president as may from time to time be assigned by the board of directors, and shall perform the duties of the chief executive officer in the chief executive officer's absence.

Chairman of the Board

The chairman of the board, if elected, shall be a member of the board of directors and, if present, shall preside at each meeting of the board of directors. The chairman of the board shall keep in close touch with the administration of the affairs of the corporation, advise and counsel with the chief executive officer, and perform such other duties as may from time to time be assigned by the board of directors.

Vice President

Each vice president shall perform all such duties as from time to time may be assigned by the board of directors, the chief executive officer, or the president. At the request of the chief executive officer, the vice president shall perform the duties of the president, in the president's absence, and when so acting, shall have the powers of and be subject to the restrictions placed upon the president in respect of the performance of such duties.

Chief Financial Officer

The chief financial officer of the corporation shall be the custodian of the funds, securities, and property of the corporation. The chief financial officer shall receive and give receipts for moneys due and payable to the corporation from any source whatsoever, and deposit all such moneys in the name of the corporation in such banks, trust companies, or other depositories as shall be selected. The chief financial officer shall perform all of the duties incident to the office, and such other duties as may be delegated by the board of directors. If required by the board of directors, the chief financial officer shall give a bond for the faithful discharge of duties in such sum and with such surety or sureties as the board of directors shall determine.

Treasurer

The treasurer of the corporation, if one is appointed, shall have such duties as the chief financial officer and the board of directors may delegate. The treasurer shall give bonds for the faithful discharge of his or her duties in such sums and with such sureties as the board of directors shall determine.

Secretary

The secretary shall be responsible for the prompt and correct recording of all proceedings of the board of directors. The secretary shall further supervise the preparation and publication of reports, studies, and other publications of the board of directors, and shall prepare such correspondence and perform such other duties as may be required.

Assistant Secretary

The assistant secretary of the corporation, if one is appointed, shall have such duties as the secretary and the board of directors may delegate. The assistant secretary may sign, with the president or vice president, certificates for authorized shares of the corporation.

Personal Liability of Officers

Under the Model Business Corporation Act, as in most states, officers are generally held to the same standards of conduct as directors of the corporation. Officers not acting in good faith or breaching their fiduciary duty, duty of care, or duty of loyalty may be subject to personal liability for damages caused to the corporation by them, often in the same manner as directors of the corporation.

Election and Term of Office

Officers are generally elected by a majority of the board of directors at an annual meeting of the board of directors. Traditionally, officers hold their office for one year and are either reelected or replaced at the annual meeting of the board of directors. In recent years, however, key corporate officers have negotiated contracts with the board of directors that extend well beyond the traditional one-year term.

§ 7.7 Shareholders' Rights and Responsibilities

A shareholder, or stockholder, is the owner of one or more shares of the stock of a corporation. The shareholder is, in effect, at least part owner of the corporation itself. The relationship between the shareholder and the corporation is a contractual relationship separate from any other relationship the shareholder may have with the corporation.

There are generally no qualifications that must be met by shareholders of business corporations. A shareholder may be an individual or an entity. There are, however, restrictions on who may be a shareholder of special types of corporations. For example, the shareholders of professional corporations may be required to be licensed professionals; shareholders of S corporations generally must be individuals (and may not be entities). Not-for-profit corporations that do not issue stock may have members instead of shareholders.

This section examines the rights of shareholders, including the shareholder's preemptive right to purchase shares of the corporation and the shareholder's right to inspect the books of the corporation. We also discuss the possibility of shareholders being held personally liable for the debts and obligations of the corporation.

Shareholders' Preemptive Rights

Preemptive rights give shareholders the opportunity to protect their position in the corporation by granting to shareholders the right to purchase newly issued shares of the corporation's stock in an amount proportionate to their current stock ownership.

Traditionally, shareholders were granted preemptive rights as a matter of law. In recent years, however, the tendency is to grant preemptive rights to shareholders only in corporations that specifically grant that right to shareholders in the articles of incorporation. Statutes vary from state to state, however, and many states still provide that preemptive rights are granted unless waived in the articles of incorporation.

Under the Model Business Corporation Act, shareholders do not have a preemptive right unless, and to the extent, granted in the articles of

---

TERMS

preemptive right [†] The right or privilege of a stockholder of a corporation to purchase shares of a new issue before persons who are not stockholders. This entitlement allows a shareholder to preserve his or her percentage of ownership (i.e., his or her equity) in the corporation.

incorporation. The Model Business Corporation Act provides that if a corporation states that its shareholders are granted preemptive rights in its articles of incorporation, they are deemed to have the preemptive rights described in § 6.30 of the Model Business Corporation Act, which reads, in part, as follows:

> (1) The shareholders of the corporation have a preemptive right, granted on uniform terms and conditions prescribed by the board of directors to provide a fair and reasonable opportunity to exercise the right, to acquire proportional amounts of the corporation's unissued shares upon the decision of the board of directors to issue them.

Special consideration must be given to the statutory treatment of preemptive rights in the corporation's state of domicile, and the incorporation documents must be drafted accordingly.

Shareholders' Right to Inspect Corporate Records

The shareholders are the owners of the corporation. As such, they are entitled to certain rights to inspect the corporate records of the corporation. These rights are usually set forth in the statutes of the state of domicile, and may be further elaborated on in either the bylaws or the articles of incorporation of the corporation.

Section 16.02 of the Model Business Corporation Act provides that shareholders are entitled to inspect and copy minutes of meetings, accounting records, and shareholder records. To exercise these rights, the shareholder must give the corporation at least five business days' notice, and the inspection and copying must be done during regular business hours. In addition, the demand for inspection must be made "in good faith for a proper purpose" and the demand must describe the shareholder's purpose for the inspection. Further, the records inspected must be directly connected with the shareholder's purpose.

In the following case, the court found that the shareholder's purpose for inspecting corporate records was not a proper purpose, and the shareholder's demand for inspection was denied.

Personal Liability of Shareholders

One of the greatest advantages of incorporating is that the corporate entity shelters the individual shareholders from personal liability for the corporation's debts and obligations. A shareholder's liability generally consists of no more than the consideration that must be paid for the shareholder's own stock in the corporation.

STATE ex rel. PILLSBURY
v.
HONEYWELL, INC.
Supreme Court of Minnesota
291 Minn. 322, 191 N.W.2d 406,
50 A.L.R.3d 1046 (1971)
October 22, 1971
Kelly, Justice

Petitioner appeals from an order and judgment of the district court denying all relief prayed for in a petition for **writ of mandamus** to compel respondent, Honeywell, Inc., (Honeywell) to produce its original shareholder ledger, current shareholder ledger, and all corporate records dealing with weapons and munitions manufacture. We must affirm.

The issues raised by petitioner are as follows: (1) Whether Minnesota or Delaware law determines the right of a shareholder to inspect respondent's corporate books and records; (2) whether petitioner, who bought shares in respondent corporation for the purpose of changing its policy of manufacturing war munitions, had a proper purpose germane to a shareholder's interest ... .

Petitioner attended a meeting on July 3, 1969, of a group involved in what was known as the "Honeywell Project." Participants in the project believed that American involvement in Vietnam was wrong, that a substantial portion of Honeywell's production consisted of munitions used in that war, and that Honeywell should stop this production of munitions. Petitioner had long opposed the Vietnam war, but it was at the July 3rd meeting that he first learned of Honeywell's involvement. He was shocked at the knowledge that Honeywell had a large government contract to produce anti-personnel fragmentation bombs. Upset because of knowledge that such bombs were produced in his own community by a company which he had known and respected, petitioner determined to stop Honeywell's munitions production.

On July 14, 1969, petitioner ordered his fiscal agent to purchase 100 shares of Honeywell. He admits that the sole purpose of the purchase was to give himself a voice in Honeywell's affairs so he could persuade Honeywell to cease producing munitions. Apparently not aware of that purpose, petitioner's agent registered the stock in the name of a Pillsbury family nominee—Quad & Co. Upon discovering the nature of the registration, petitioner bought one share of Honeywell in his own name on August 11, 1969. ...

During 1969, subsequent to the July 3, 1969, meeting and after he had ordered his agent to purchase the 100 shares of Honeywell stock, petitioner inquired into a trust which had been formed for his benefit by his grandmother. The purpose of the inquiry was to discover whether shares of Honeywell were included in the trust. It was then, for the first time, that petitioner discovered that he had a contingent beneficial interest under the terms of the trust in 242 shares of Honeywell.

Prior to the instigation of this suit, petitioner submitted two formal demands to Honeywell requesting that it produce its original shareholder ledger, current shareholder ledger, and all corporate records dealing with weapons and munitions manufacture. Honeywell refused.

TERMS

writ of mandamus [†]   (Latin) Means "we command." A writ issuing from a court of competent jurisdiction, directed to an inferior court, board, or corporation, or to an officer of a branch of government (judicial, executive, or legislative), requiring the performance of some ministerial act. A writ of mandamus is an extraordinary remedy.

On November 24, 1969, a petition was filed for writs of mandamus ordering Honeywell to produce the above mentioned records. In response, Honeywell answered the petition and served a notice of **deposition** on petitioner, who moved that the answer be stricken as procedurally premature and that an order be issued to limit the deposition. After a hearing, the trial court denied the motion, and the deposition was taken on December 15, 1969.

In the deposition petitioner outlined his beliefs concerning the Vietnam war and his purpose for his involvement with Honeywell. He expressed his desire to communicate with other shareholders in the hope of altering Honeywell's board of directors and thereby changing its policy. To this end, he testified, business records are necessary to insure accuracy.

A hearing was held on January 8, 1970, during which Honeywell introduced the deposition, conceded all material facts stated therein, and argued that petitioner was not entitled to any relief as a matter of law. Petitioner asked that alternative writs of mandamus issue for all the relief requested in his petition. On April 8, 1970, the trial court dismissed the petition, holding that the relief requested was for an improper and indefinite purpose. Petitioner contends in this appeal that the dismissal was in error. ...

2. The trial court ordered judgment for Honeywell, ruling that petitioner had not demonstrated a proper purpose germane to his interest as a stockholder. Petitioner contends that a stockholder who disagrees with management has an absolute right to inspect corporate records for purposes of soliciting proxies. He would have this court rule that such solicitation is per se a "proper purpose." Honeywell argues that a "proper purpose" contemplates concern with investment return. We agree with Honeywell. ...

The act of inspecting a corporation's shareholder ledger and business records must be viewed in its proper perspective. In terms of the corporate norm, inspection is merely the act of the concerned owner checking on what is in part his property. In the context of the large firm, inspection can be more akin to a weapon in corporate warfare. ...

Petitioner had utterly no interest in the affairs of Honeywell before he learned of Honeywell's production of fragmentation bombs. Immediately after obtaining this knowledge, he purchased stock in Honeywell for the sole purpose of asserting ownership privileges in an effort to force Honeywell to cease such production. ... But for his opposition to Honeywell's policy, petitioner probably would not have bought Honeywell stock, would not be interested in Honeywell's profits and would not desire to communicate with Honeywell's shareholders. His avowed purpose in buying Honeywell stock was to place himself in a position to try to impress his opinions favoring a reordering of priorities upon Honeywell management and its other shareholders. Such a motivation can hardly be deemed a proper purpose germane to his economic interest as a shareholder. ...

We do not mean to imply that a shareholder with a bona fide investment interest could not bring this suit if motivated by concern with the long- or short-term economic effects on Honeywell resulting from the production of war munitions. Similarly, this suit might be appropriate when a shareholder has a bona fide concern about the adverse effects of abstention from profitable war contracts on his investment in Honeywell.

TERMS

deposition [†]   The transcript of a witness's testimony given under oath outside of the courtroom, usually in advance of the trial or hearing, upon oral examination or in response to written interrogatories.

In the instant case, however, the trial court, in effect, has found from all the facts that petitioner was not interested in even the long-term well-being of Honeywell or the enhancement of the value of his shares. His sole purpose was to persuade the company to adopt his social and political concerns, irrespective of any economic benefit to himself or Honeywell. This purpose on the part of one buying into the corporation does not entitle the petitioner to inspect Honeywell's books and records. ...

The order of the trial court denying the writ of mandamus is affirmed.

The two most common exceptions to the rule of nonliability occur when the corporate veil is pierced, or when the individual shareholder grants a personal guarantee for some obligation of the corporation. Both of these occurrences are discussed in Chapter 5.

Although, in most cases, the imposition of personal liability stems from disregard of the corporate entity, at times a shareholder can be held personally liable for the tortious acts of the corporation if it can be proved that the shareholder participated in the commission of the action. Certainly, a shareholder who participates directly in the management of the corporation, such as in a statutory close corporation, is exposed to a higher degree of risk for the imposition of personal liability than that commonly associated with shareholders.

§ 7.8 Shareholder Meetings

Shareholder meetings are often the forum for the most important decisions made regarding the future of the corporation (Figure 7-5). This section discusses the requirements for annual and special meetings, including their location and notice. It also examines the use of proxies for voting at shareholder meetings and the necessity of having a quorum to adopt a shareholder resolution. We then focus on the actual voting at shareholder meetings, concentrating on the election of directors and other acts that require shareholder approval. This section concludes with an investigation of the documents that formalize shareholder resolutions, the minutes of shareholder meetings, and the unanimous written consents of shareholders.

Requirements for Annual Meetings

Annual meetings of the shareholders are often required under state statutes, although the statutes generally allow that the time and place

FIGURE 7-5 Shareholders participate in the management of the corporation through participation in annual shareholder meetings. (Photo courtesy of Imcera Group Inc.)

for holding the annual meeting may be set in the bylaws of the corporation. Statutory requirements for holding annual meetings are often similar to the requirement set forth in the Model Business Corporation Act, which requires only that a meeting of the shareholders be held annually at a time stated in, or fixed by, the bylaws. Under the Model Business Corporation Act, shareholder meetings may be held at any place indicated in the corporate bylaws within or without the state of domicile. If no place for the meeting is set forth in the bylaws, the meeting will be held at the corporation's principal office.

Finally, § 7.01(c) of the Model Business Corporation Act provides that "failure to hold an annual meeting at the time stated in or fixed in accordance with a corporation's bylaws does not affect the validity of any corporate action." If a corporation does not hold annual meetings of the shareholders in accordance with its bylaws, shareholders are generally granted the statutory right to move for a court order to compel the corporation to call and hold an annual shareholder meeting. Typically, any shareholder may apply to the appropriate court for an order to compel an annual meeting if an annual meeting was not held within six months, or some other time prescribed by statute.

Requirements for Special Meetings

It is sometimes necessary or desirable to hold shareholder meetings between the regularly scheduled annual meetings of a corporation. These meetings are referred to as *special meetings*. Specific requirements as to who may call a special meeting are prescribed by statute and generally may be further specified in the articles of incorporation or bylaws of a corporation. The Model Business Corporation Act provides that a special meeting may be called by the corporation's board of directors, persons holding at least 10 percent of all the votes entitled to be cast on the proposed matter, or persons authorized by the articles of incorporation or bylaws.

Location

Requirements for the location of both annual and special meetings of the shareholders of a corporation are usually outlined in the state's statutes and set forth in further detail in the corporation's bylaws. Modern corporate law tends to be very liberal regarding the location of both annual and special meetings. Requirements in the Model Business Corporation Act for both annual and special meetings dictate only that the meeting "may be held in or out of this state at the place stated in or fixed in accordance with the bylaws."[28] If no provision is made in the bylaws regarding the location of annual and special meetings of the shareholders, the Model Business Corporation Act provides that such meetings must take place at the corporation's principal office.

Notice

The actual notice given of an annual shareholder meeting will vary, depending on the size and circumstances of the corporation. In small, closely held corporations, the notice may be a telephone call to one or two individuals, followed by waivers of notice signed at the actual meeting. Giving notice to shareholders of corporations that may have hundreds of shareholders is a much more complicated matter.

First, there must be a determination as to which individuals are entitled to receive notice of the meeting. A *record date* for determining the shareholders of the corporation is generally fixed by the bylaws of the corporation or by the board of directors. All shareholders of the corporation on the record date are entitled to notice of the annual meeting and are entitled to vote at the meeting. Because any purchasers of stock subsequent to that date, but before the annual meeting, will not be entitled to receive notice of the meeting, the record date must be chosen carefully. The date picked will depend on the number of shareholders and the complexity of sending the notice. State statutes usually place restrictions on the record date as well.

In states following the Model Business Corporation Act, the record date may be fixed by the directors as directed in the bylaws of the corporation. However, the record date cannot be more than seventy days before the annual meeting.

The bylaws of the corporation typically prescribe the exact method for determining the record date. Following is an example of a bylaw paragraph regarding the record date.

EXAMPLE: Fixing Record Date

For the purpose of determining shareholders entitled to notice of or to vote at any meeting of shareholders or any adjournment thereof, the Board of Directors may provide that the stock transfer books shall be closed for a stated period but not to exceed, in any case, ___ days. If the stock transfer books shall be closed for the purpose of determining shareholders entitled to notice or to vote at a meeting of shareholders, such books shall be closed for at least ___ days immediately preceding such meeting.

Once the record date has been set, the corporation must prepare a list of shareholders entitled to notice of the meeting. This task typically falls to the individual who is responsible for overseeing all stock transfers of the corporation. In the case of a small corporation, this may be the corporate secretary who keeps the stock certificate ledger in the corporate minute book. In larger corporations, on the other hand, this may be a significant task that is delegated to an individual or another company referred to as the **transfer agent.** The transfer agent is responsible for overseeing all transfers of stock, including the surrender of old stock certificates and the issuance of new ones, and for maintaining an up-to-date record of all shareholders.

The list of shareholders entitled to receive notice of the annual meeting must be made available to all shareholders for inspection for a period prior to the annual meeting that is usually prescribed by statute. Under the Model Business Corporation Act, the shareholder list must be available for inspection by any shareholder beginning two business days after notice of the meeting is given and continuing through the time of the meeting.

============== **TERMS** ==============

transfer agent [†] A person or company that acts on behalf of a corporation in carrying out the transfer of its stock from one owner to another and registering the transaction on the corporate records.

Once a record date has been set and a list of shareholders entitled to receive notice has been compiled, the directors, the corporate secretary, or other officer or individual, who is normally designated by the corporation's bylaws, must be sure that proper notice is given to all shareholders entitled to receive notice in compliance with the statutes of the state of domicile and the articles and bylaws of the corporation.

The notice of the meeting typically includes the date, time, and place of the meeting. If the meeting is a special meeting, a purpose for the meeting is usually given, and is often required by state statute or corporate bylaws. The statutes of the state of domicile usually provide guidelines within which the notice of shareholder meetings must be given, and the bylaws of the corporation typically set forth a more precise manner for giving notice.

Section 7.05(a) of the Model Business Corporation Act sets forth the notice requirements for annual shareholder meetings:

(a) A corporation shall notify shareholders of the date, time, and place of each annual and special shareholders' meeting no fewer than 10 nor more than 60 days before the meeting date. Unless this Act or the articles of incorporation require otherwise, the corporation is required to give notice only to shareholders entitled to vote at the meeting.

Figure 7-6 shows a sample notice of annual shareholder meeting.

The secretary of the corporation, or any other individual responsible for the mailing of the notice of annual meeting, will often prepare an affidavit of mailing to evidence the proper mailing of the notice of

---

**NOTICE OF ANNUAL MEETING
OF THE SHAREHOLDERS**

OF THE _____ **CORPORATION**

PLEASE TAKE NOTICE that the ___ Annual Meeting of the Shareholders of the _____ Corporation will be held on the _____ day of _____ , 19___ , at _____ P.M., at the office of the corporation at _____ , for the purpose of electing directors of the corporation and transacting such other business as may properly come before the meeting.

Dated this _____ day of _____ , 19___ .

FIGURE 7-6   Sample Notice of Annual Shareholder Meeting

the annual meeting in a timely manner. Figure 7-7 is an example of an affidavit of mailing of notice of annual shareholder meeting.

Waiver of Notice

Shareholders may waive notice of a meeting if they so choose. Typically, shareholders may waive notice by delivering to the corporation a signed waiver of notice, or by attending the meeting. In small corporations with only a few shareholders, the shareholders often meet without ever sending any formal notice. The shareholders' attendance at the meeting, as well as their waiver of formal notice, should be noted in the minutes of the meeting. A shareholder's attendance at any meeting is generally considered to constitute a waiver of notice, unless at the beginning of the meeting, the shareholder objects to the holding of the meeting or the transaction of business at the meeting. The waiver of notice in Figure 7-8 is a sample form that could be used

---

**AFFIDAVIT OF MAILING OF NOTICE
OF ANNUAL SHAREHOLDERS' MEETING**

OF THE _____ CORPORATION

STATE OF _____)
)SS

COUNTY OF _____)

_____ , being first duly sworn on oath, deposes and says:

I am the Secretary of the _____ Corporation and that on the _____ day of _____ , 19___ , I personally deposited in a post-office box in the City of _____ , State of _____ , each in a postage-paid envelope, one Notice of the Annual Meeting of the Shareholders of the Corporation to each person whose name appears on the annexed list, and to their respective post-office addresses as therein set forth.

                                    _____
                                    Secretary

Subscribed and sworn to before me
this _____ day of _____ , 19___ .

_____
Notary Public

FIGURE 7-7 Sample Affidavit of Mailing of Notice

FIGURE 7-8
Sample Waiver
of Notice

**WAIVER OF NOTICE OF THE ANNUAL MEETING
OF THE SHAREHOLDERS OF THE**

_____**CORPORATION**

    We, the undersigned being all of the shareholders of the above corporation, hereby agree and consent to the annual meeting of the shareholders held on the _____ day of _____ , 19____ , at _____ P.M., at the office of the corporation at _____ , for thes purpose of electing directors of the corporation and all such other business as may lawfully come before said meeting and hereby waive all notice of the meeting and any adjournment thereof. Dated this _____ day of _____ , 19___ .

_____

_____

_____

_____

---

at an annual meeting of the shareholders of a small corporation, when notice of the meeting was not mailed.

Proxies

    A **proxy** is "an authority given by the holder of the stock who has the right to vote it to another to exercise his voting rights."[29] Shareholders who are unable to attend shareholder meetings may vote through the use of a proxy. The term *proxy* is often used both to define the person who will cast the vote in the place of the shareholder, and the document that transfers the voting power to the person voting in place of the shareholder.

    A proxy may be a *general proxy,* which grants the right to vote the shareholder's shares of stock on all matters with limited restrictions, or it may be a *limited proxy,* which is specific to the situation and authorizes the proxy holder to vote the shares on a specific matter in a specific way.

════════════════ ◀ **TERMS** ▶ ════════════════

proxy [†]   Authority given in writing by one shareholder in a corporation to another shareholder to exercise the first shareholder's voting rights.

General proxies are often used by shareholders of small corporations when one shareholder will be unavailable to attend shareholder meetings for an extended period. The shareholder of a closely held corporation may grant the power to vote his or her shares to an individual who is trusted to vote as the shareholder would if he or she were attending the meeting. Figure 7-9 is an example of a proxy conveying general authority to the proxy holder.

Larger, publicly held corporations use limited proxies to solicit the vote of shareholders who will not be attending the shareholder meeting. The officers or directors of the corporation send a **proxy statement** to each shareholder along with the notice of a meeting of the shareholders. The proxy statement describes the matters to be voted on at the meeting in an attempt to give shareholders enough information to make an informed decision. The proxy statement is accompanied by a proxy form for the shareholder to complete and return to the corporation. The shareholder indicates his or her voting preferences on the proxy and returns it to the corporation. The proxy may appoint an officer or director of the corporation to vote as indicated on the proxy form, unless prohibited by state statute. Often, the voting at the meetings of large corporations is merely a formality, as the corporation will receive enough proxy votes prior to the meeting to reach a majority voting consensus.

Rules for the solicitation of proxies and their use by publicly held corporations is discussed in Chapter 9.

Quorum

For an action to be taken at a meeting of the shareholders, (1) a quorum must be present, and (2) a sufficient number of shareholders present must vote in favor of the proposed action. Unless the articles of incorporation provide otherwise, a majority of the votes entitled to be cast typically constitutes a quorum. State statutes usually provide that the articles may prescribe a different quorum within certain limitations. For action to be taken at a meeting, a majority of the votes cast must be in favor of the action, unless some other manner for approving an action is prescribed by statute or set forth in the corporation's articles of incorporation.

=================== TERMS ===================

proxy statement † A statement sent to shareholders whose proxies are being solicited so that they may be voted at an upcoming stockholders' meeting. The statement, whose contents are regulated by the Securities and Exchange Commission, provides shareholders with the information necessary for them to decide whether to give their proxies.

FIGURE 7-9
Sample Proxy

[From *Ohio Corporations*, Copyright © 1984 LCP]

PROXY

The undersigned, recorded as holder or otherwise entitled to exercise the voting rights of _____ shares of the capital stock of _____ (the "Corporation"), hereby revokes any and all proxies either given by the undersigned or dated before the date of this proxy and appoints _____ , _____ , and _____ or any of them in the absence of any one of them, or any one of them in the absence of any two of them, as proxy of the undersigned, with power of substitution, to attend the annual meeting of shareholders of the Corporation to be held _____ and any adjournments thereof and to vote on each matter which may come before such meeting or any adjournment thereof all shares of the Corporation's capital stock which the undersigned is entitled to vote on each such matter as such proxy shall deem appropriate in the proxy's discretion.

Dated: _____

_____
Signature

Voting at Shareholder Meetings

It is generally assumed that each share of stock is entitled to one vote, although corporations with more than one class of stock may include a class of stock that has no voting rights or limited voting rights. Votes are cast by ballot at most formal shareholder meetings, and those ballots, along with the proxies received from shareholders not in attendance, are tallied to determine whether a quorum is present and whether enough votes were received to adopt the proposed resolutions. The ballot used at a shareholder meeting must be in accordance with the provisions of the statutes of the corporation's state of domicile and the corporation's articles and bylaws, and must be in a form that clearly shows the intent of the voting shareholder.

Voting at meetings held by small corporations may be done by a voice vote that is properly noted by the secretary, or other appointed individual, in the minutes of the meeting.

Although it is generally not required by statute, **inspectors of election** are often appointed to oversee the election of directors at the shareholder

TERMS

inspectors of election   Impartial individuals who are often appointed to oversee the election of directors at the shareholder meetings of large corporations.

meetings of large corporations. These inspectors are impartial individuals who are sworn to oversee the election of directors. Inspectors must determine the number of outstanding shares of stock, the presence of a quorum, and the validity of all proxies used. It is the inspectors' duty to count all votes, whether by ballot or proxy, to determine the outcome of the election.

Voting Trusts

To gain voting control of a corporation, a group of shareholders with common interests may decide to form a voting trust. A *voting trust* is an agreement among shareholders and a trustee whereby rights to vote the stock are transferred to the trustee, and all other rights incident to the ownership of the stock are retained by the shareholders. State statutes generally recognize voting trusts as valid, and the following three criteria are often used to identify a true voting trust:

1. A grant of voting rights for an indefinite period of time
2. Acquisition of voting control of the corporation as the common purpose of the shareholders to the trust
3. Voting rights are separated from the other attributes of stock ownership.

The Model Business Corporation Act allows the formation of voting trusts within the guidelines of § 7.30:

> (a) One or more shareholders may create a voting trust, conferring on a trustee the right to vote or otherwise act for them, by signing an agreement setting out the provisions of the trust (which may include anything consistent with its purpose) and transferring their shares to the trustee. When a voting trust agreement is signed, the trustee shall prepare a list of the names and addresses of all owners of beneficial interest in the trust, together with the number and class of shares each transferred to the trust, and deliver copies of the list and agreement to the corporation's principal office.

Subsections (b) and (c) of § 7.30 further provide that a voting trust may not be valid for a period of more than ten years after its effective date, unless extended by the signing of an extension agreement.

Voting Agreements

Shareholders may also seek to gain voting control of a corporation by means of a voting agreement, which is recognized and regulated in the statutes of most states. A *voting agreement* is an agreement among two or more shareholders that provides for the manner in which they will vote their shares for one or more specific purposes.

Election of Directors

The involvement of the shareholder in the corporate affairs is often confined to and dominated by the annual meeting of the shareholders, when the shareholders vote for the directors of the corporation. Annual meetings are held for the purpose of electing directors of the corporation and for any other matters that may require the attention or approval of shareholders.

Straight Voting versus Cumulative Voting

There are two methods of voting for the election of directors: straight voting and cumulative voting. **Cumulative voting** is designed to give the minority shareholder a chance to elect at least one director to the board of directors. Cumulative voting may be required by statute, or it may be permitted by statute if the articles of incorporation require that cumulative voting be permitted.

When straight voting is the method used for electing the directors of the corporation, each share of stock may cast a vote for the number of directors that are to be elected to the board of directors. For example, if the board of directors is to consist of three individuals, a shareholder voting under the straight method, who owns 100 shares in the corporation, could cast 100 votes for Candidate 1, 100 votes for Candidate 2, and 100 votes for Candidate 3. If cumulative voting were used, the shareholder would have the same total number of votes to cast (300), but could choose to vote all 300 shares for Candidate 1 if desired, thereby granting the shareholder a better chance of getting at least one director of his or her choice elected to the board of directors.

Other Acts Requiring Shareholder Approval

In addition to electing the directors of the corporation, shareholders typically vote to ratify acts of the directors taken during the past

---

TERMS

cumulative voting [†]   A method of voting for corporate directors under which each shareholder is entitled to cast a number of votes equal to the number of shares he or she owns times the number of directors to be elected, with the option of giving all one's votes to a single candidate or of distributing them among two or more as the shareholder wishes. The effect of cumulative voting is to ensure minority representation on a Board of Directors.

year, and vote on any other business that might require shareholder approval, such as amendment of the articles of incorporation, issuance of stock, acquisitions and mergers involving the corporation, sale of corporate assets outside the normal course of business, or dissolution of the corporation. The state statutes or the articles of incorporation or bylaws of the corporation may set forth other or different actions that also require shareholder approval.

TABLE 7-2 ACTS THAT TYPICALLY REQUIRE SHAREHOLDER APPROVAL

- Election of Directors
- Adoption of Amendment of Bylaws
- Amendment of Articles of Incorporation
- Issuance of Corporate Stock
- Mergers and Acquisitions
- Sale of Corporate Assets Outside the Normal Course of Business
- Dissolution of the Corporation

Minutes of Shareholder Meetings

Just as it is important that minutes be taken at every meeting of the board of directors, accurate minutes of shareholder meetings are crucial. Minutes of the shareholder meetings are typically taken and signed by the secretary of the corporation, who then places them in the corporate minute book, along with a copy of the notice of the meeting that was sent to all shareholders, any waivers of notice received from the shareholders, any proxies received, and any other documents pertaining to the meeting. Figure 7-10 is an example of minutes of an annual shareholder meeting.

Unanimous Consents of Shareholders

The Model Business Corporation Act, and the statutes of most states, allow shareholders to take action without a meeting through means of a written consent signed by all shareholders entitled to vote on the action. For small corporations, this written consent or "unanimous writing of the shareholders in lieu of meeting" has become an invaluable tool for approving matters that require shareholder consent, especially matters that require attention between the regularly scheduled shareholder meetings.

**MINUTES OF
ANNUAL MEETING OF SHAREHOLDERS**

OF THE _____ CORPORATION

The annual meeting of the Shareholders of the _____
Corporation was held on _____ , at the registered
office of the corporation at _____ .

_____ presided as chairman of the meeting,
and _____ acted as its secretary.

The secretary reported that the notice of meeting of the annual
shareholders' meeting was mailed in accordance with state statute and with
the articles and bylaws of the corporation, and that the notice of meeting
and affidavit of mailing were filed in the corporate minute book of the
corporation.

The following shareholders were present in person:

_____

_____

_____

_____ .

The following shareholders were present by proxy:

_____

_____ .

It was determined that at least _____% of the shareholders were present,
and the meeting was called to order.

The reports of the president, secretary, and treasurer were presented to
the shareholders, received, and filed in the corporate minute book.

The chairman then called for the election of the directors of the
corporation.

Upon motion duly made, seconded, and carried, the following persons
were elected to the board of directors, to serve as director of the
Corporation until their successors are elected at the next annual meeting
and qualify:

_____

_____

_____

_____ .

FIGURE 7-10   Sample Minutes of Annual Shareholder Meeting

> There being no further business before the meeting, it was, on motion duly made, seconded, and unanimously carried, adjourned.
>
> _____
Secretary

FIGURE 7-10 *(continued)*

In recent years, revisions to the Model Business Corporation Act and many state statutes make it clear that the approved action may be evidenced by more than one document, making it even easier to obtain the consent of a large number of shareholders within a relatively short time period. For example, if there are ten shareholders of a corporation, the corporate secretary can now send out ten identical consents, one to each shareholder, to be signed and returned, instead of having one document that must be circulated to all ten shareholders for signature.

Figure 7-11 shows a sample unanimous written consent of the shareholders in lieu of an annual meeting.

When conducting a thorough review of a corporate minute book, you should answer the following questions:

Incorporation Documents

- What is the exact name of the corporation?

- What was the corporation's date of incorporation?

- What is the corporation's registered office address, and who is the registered agent?

- How many shares of stock of each type is the corporation authorized to issue?

- Is the corporation in compliance with any statutory incorporation formalities concerning publication of notice of incorporation or filing notice of incorporation at the county level?

- Has the corporation received Certificates of Authority to Transact Business in any foreign state in which it transacts business?

- Does the minute book contain other pertinent incorporation documentation required by the statutes of the corporation's state of domicile?

Corporate Bylaws

- Are the procedures in the bylaws for holding annual and special shareholder and director meetings being complied with by the corporation?

**UNANIMOUS WRITING IN LIEU
OF ANNUAL MEETING OF THE SHAREHOLDERS**

OF THE _____ **CORPORATION**

The undersigned, being all of the shareholders of _____ (the "Corporation"), hereby adopt the following resolutions in lieu of holding an annual meeting of the sole shareholders, effective the _____ day of _____ , 19___ .

RESOLVED, that the following persons are hereby elected to the board of directors, to serve as directors of the Corporation until their successors are elected at the next annual meeting and qualify:

_____

_____

_____

_____ .

FURTHER RESOLVED, that the acts of the directors on behalf of the corporation for the past fiscal year are hereby ratified, affirmed, and approved.

_____

_____

_____

FIGURE 7-11   Sample Unanimous Writing in Lieu of Annual Shareholder Meeting

- How many directors are required under the bylaws? Does the corporation currently have the requisite number of directors?

- If the fiscal year end is set forth in the bylaws of the corporation, is it correct?

- Are other procedures for managing the corporation's affairs, as set forth in the bylaws, being complied with?

Corporate Minutes

- Are there any missing minutes (for example, minutes not prepared for a certain year or years)?

- Are there any missing signatures (for example, all elected directors must sign unanimous writings of the board of directors)?

- Have resolutions made by the board of directors or shareholders been carried through?

Stock Certificates

- Are the certificates, subscription agreements, and ledgers consistent with each other?

- Are all stock certificates signed and in place?

- Is there a record of the location of all stock certificates not kept in the minute book?

§ 7.9 Restrictions on Transfer of Shares of Corporate Stock

The freedom to transfer corporate stock without restrictions has always been considered a basic shareholder right. However, recognizing the value of limited restrictions on the transfer of stock under certain conditions, the courts have found that "restrictions may be imposed for the mutual convenience and protection of the parties, so long as such restrictions are not unreasonable and do not constitute an impairment of the stockholder's contractual rights."[30]

This section focuses on the restrictions placed on stock transfers by shareholder agreements and considerations in drafting shareholder agreements. The section concludes with a look at other restrictions that may be placed on share transfers.

Shareholder Agreements Restricting Stock Transfers

The shareholders of a corporation may desire to place certain restrictions on the transfer of shares to protect their status in the corporation and to monitor the inclusion of new shareholders in the corporation. Shareholders of a close corporation may wish to have the option to purchase shares of a withdrawing shareholder before the shares are sold to an outsider. Also, shareholders looking toward the future may desire to insure a market for their stock when they decide to sell.

Restrictions on the transfer of stock may be placed in the articles of incorporation, in the bylaws of the corporation, or in a separate shareholder agreement, or *buy-sell agreement,* as it may be called. Restrictions on the transfer of stock of statutory close corporations may also be prescribed by the close corporation act or close corporation provisions of the business corporation act of the company's state of domicile.

Agreements Granting Option to Purchase Stock

Shareholder agreements that give the corporation or shareholders of the corporation the option to purchase shares of any shareholder upon the happening of a specified event are the least restrictive type of agreement. This sort of agreement does not obligate the shareholders to purchase the shares of a selling shareholder, nor does it guarantee a market for a shareholder who desires to sell his or her shares.

Shareholders of statutory close corporations may be granted, by statute, the option of purchasing the shares of selling shareholders before those shares are sold to third parties. Under the Close Corporation Supplement to the Model Business Corporation Act, a shareholder desiring to sell stock in a close corporation who obtains an offer to purchase the shares for cash from an eligible third person must first offer the shares to the corporation, pursuant to statute, upon the same terms as the offer. However, the Close Corporation Supplement provides that this restriction does not apply to transfers within the corporation. More specifically, shareholders are free to sell their shares to any of the following without restriction:

1. The corporation or to any other holder of the same class or series of shares
2. Members of the shareholder's immediate family or a trust whose beneficiaries are members of the shareholder's immediate family
3. An executor or administrator upon the death of a shareholder
4. A trustee or receiver as the result of a bankruptcy, insolvency, dissolution, or similar proceeding brought by or against a shareholder.

The restrictions also do not apply to transfers of stock that have been approved in writing by all holders of the corporation's shares that have voting rights, or to transfers resulting from a merger or share exchange, a pledge as loan collateral that does not grant voting rights, or the termination of the corporation's status as a statutory close corporation.

The shareholders of corporations that are not subject to statutory restrictions such as those in the Close Corporation Supplement may adopt similar provisions in the articles of incorporation of the corporation, in the corporate bylaws, or in a separate agreement executed by the corporation and all shareholders.

Agreements Mandating the Purchase of Stock

This type of agreement among the shareholders obligates the corporation or other shareholders to purchase the shares of a deceased or withdrawing shareholder upon the happening of a particular event, at a pre-established price. This type of agreement guarantees a market for the shares of a shareholder who wishes to withdraw from the corporation, upon certain conditions.

Statutory provisions mandating the transfer of stock in any regard are rare. Although the Close Corporation Supplement to the Model Business Corporation Act contains provisions for the compulsory purchase of shares after the death of a shareholder, it is clearly stated that that particular section of the Supplement applies only to statutory close corporations that elect so to provide in their articles of incorporation.[31] Section 14(a) of the Close Corporation Supplement, if adopted, provides that "the executor or administrator of the estate of a deceased shareholder may require the corporation to purchase or cause to be purchased all (but not less than all) of the decedent's shares or to be dissolved."

Considerations in Drafting Shareholder Agreements

The shareholder agreement, or buy-sell agreement, need not be exclusively for the optional or mandatory purchase for shares. It may be a hybrid of these two types of agreements, giving shareholders the option to purchase shares of a withdrawing shareholder under certain circumstances and mandating purchase under other circumstances.

Events Triggering Agreement

The events that trigger a buy-sell agreement will vary, depending on the purpose and intent of the shareholders. Buy-sell agreements may be triggered by any of the following events:

1. Death of a shareholder
2. Retirement of a shareholder-employee
3. Disability of a shareholder-employee
4. Proposed sale by any shareholder to a third party.

Purchase Price

The purchase price found in buy-sell agreements that mandate the purchase of stock of a shareholder upon the happening of a specific event is often the most important element in the agreement. The agreement rarely sets a specific price for the stock purchase, but rather specifies a formula for determining the price of the stock. Determining the price of stock of a closely held corporation can be very difficult, because it is impossible to determine a "market value" for stock which, in effect, has no market.

Often the shareholders will agree on a price per share in a supplement to the buy-sell agreement. This supplement is then updated periodically, with the most recent supplement providing the price in effect in the event the agreement is activated. The corporation may use the book value of the stock or the best offer of a third party to determine the price. Other formulas may be used so long as the formula is agreed upon by all shareholders in the buy-sell agreement.

Insurance Funding

Shareholders usually recognize that the mandated buyout of a deceased shareholder could impose a severe financial hardship on the corporation, so they seek to cover that loss by purchasing life insurance on the life of major shareholders. The proceeds of the life insurance policy can then be used to purchase the deceased's shares of stock from the estate.

Other Restrictions on Share Transfers

Corporate shareholders may find it necessary or desirable to place restrictions on the transfer of corporate stock for reasons other than monitoring the ownership of the corporation and ensuring a market for the corporation's stock. For example, shareholders of S corporations may have to place restrictions on the transfer of corporate stock to remain in compliance with the S corporation requirements. Large corporations and publicly held corporations may find it necessary to restrict the transfer of corporate shares in order to comply with securities regulations.

In any event, any restriction on the transfer of shares of stock must be considered reasonable and generally must be approved by all shareholders of the corporation. In addition, the specific restriction must be located on the face or reverse of the stock certificate of any affected shares.

§ 7.10 Shareholder Actions

There are three general types of shareholder lawsuits:

1. Individual shareholder actions
2. Representative actions
3. Derivative actions.

The nature of and requirements for each of these types of actions are discussed briefly in this section.

Individual Actions

An individual shareholder who is injured by an action of the corporation may bring suit against the corporation for damages. An individual shareholder may maintain a suit against a corporation in much the same way as any other individual would. Generally, individual actions are brought only when the individual shareholder alleges that the action committed by the corporation is a direct fraud on the individual shareholder and that such wrongs do not affect the other shareholders. However, the same action that causes injury to the individual plaintiff may also affect a substantial number of other shareholders.

Representative Actions

Representative actions are actions in which the parties are "too numerous to be joined, one party or a few being permitted to sue on behalf of all."[32] The representative action is typically brought by a shareholder on behalf of the shareholder and his or her entire class of shareholders against the corporation.

The derivative action is sometimes also referred to as a representative action, because it is brought by an individual who represents the corporation's interest in the suit. However, it is important to distinguish between the derivative suit and the representative suit as those terms are used in this text. Under our definition of a representative suit, the cause of action belongs personally to the shareholder and the class that the shareholder represents. In derivative actions, discussed below, the cause of action belongs to the corporation itself.

Derivative Actions

A shareholder's *derivative action* has been defined as "an action brought by one or more stockholders of a corporation to enforce a corporate right or remedy a wrong to the corporation in cases where the corporation,

TERMS

representative action   Action brought by a shareholder on behalf of the shareholder and his or her entire class of shareholders against the corporation.

because it is controlled by the wrongdoers or for other reasons, fails and refuses to take appropriate action for its own protection."[33]

Because the corporation is a separate entity, it is possible that the entity could sustain damages at the expense of its shareholders. Shareholders may prosecute derivative lawsuits on behalf of the corporation to protect their own interests in the corporation, especially if they feel that the directors of the corporation are not acting with the corporation's best interests in mind. The derivative action is distinguished from other types of shareholder lawsuits in that the cause of action belongs to the corporation, not to the individual shareholder or shareholders. The following must generally be present for a stockholder in a corporation to maintain a derivative action[34]:

1. Some action or threatened action of the managing board of directors or trustees of the corporation which is beyond the authority conferred on them by their charter or other source of organization

2. Such a fraudulent transaction, completed or contemplated by the acting managers, in connection with some other party, or among themselves, or with other shareholders, as will result in serious injury to the corporation, or to the interests of the other shareholders

3. Action by the board of directors, or a majority of them, in their own interest, destructive of the corporation itself, or of the rights of the other shareholders

4. Action by the majority of shareholders themselves in oppressively and illegally pursuing a course in the name of the corporation, which is in violation of the rights of the other shareholders, and which can only be restrained by the aid of a court of equity.

Many states have enacted legislation in an attempt to alleviate unnecessary litigation. Many states' statutes require shareholders to make a good faith attempt to prompt the corporation to take action in its own behalf to prevent or remedy the injustice that the shareholders are seeking to cure, before a derivative action may be commenced. Section 7.42 of the Model Business Corporation Act, which is typical of such statutory provisions, sets forth strict requirements for the commencement of derivative suits:

§ 7.42 DEMAND

No shareholder may commence a derivative proceeding until:
    (1) a written demand has been made upon the corporation to take suitable action; and
    (2) 90 days have expired from the date the demand was made unless the shareholder has earlier been notified that the demand has

been rejected by the corporation or unless irreparable injury to the corporation would result by waiting for the expiration of the 90 day period.

§ 7.11 The Role of the Legal Assistant in Organizational Corporate Matters

Whether the paralegal works in a law firm or in a corporation, the paralegal will often be asked to assist the attorney and the corporate client in complying with statutory requirements for corporate formalities. This can include extensive research to ascertain the rights, duties, and potential for personal liability of the corporation's officers, directors, and shareholders. Statutory research may also be necessary to insure that the formalities for director and shareholder annual and special meetings and elections are being complied with.

Maintenance of the corporate minute books is a task often assigned to a paralegal. The paralegal may also be asked to draft letters to all corporate clients, reminding them of the statutory annual meeting requirements and the annual meeting requirements established by the articles of incorporation or bylaws of the corporation. The paralegal frequently follows up with each client by drafting and sending out notices of annual meetings and preparing minutes for the minute book, or by drafting unanimous writings in lieu of meetings of the board of directors of the corporation and seeing to their execution.

Corporate minute book maintenance may be considered a low priority in a busy law firm. However, as discussed in Chapter 5, failure to maintain current corporate records and follow corporate formalities can be a factor that contributes to piercing the corporate veil.

§ 7.12 Resources

By far the most important resource in working with corporate organizational matters is the statutes of the state of domicile. The corporate paralegal should be so familiar with state statutes that he or she can quickly locate statutory provisions regarding the organizational formalities that must be complied with by corporations.

Another good resource is the state-specific corporate procedure manuals that are available for every state. One good state-specific series is the *Practice Systems Library* published by the Lawyers Cooperative Publishing Company.

Review Questions

1. Where does a committee get its authority? Who is ultimately responsible for the acts of the committee?

2. What are the three types of duties a director owes to the corporation?

3. If a board of directors, exercising due care, makes a poor business decision that results in a substantial financial loss to the corporation, can the shareholders of the corporation look to the directors' personal assets to recover their damages? What if one director withheld information from the other directors and personally benefited from the decision?

4. Albert is on the board of directors of Acme Sailboard Company, Inc. As the result of a contract dispute, Acme Sailboard Company, Inc. and Albert are both named in a lawsuit brought by one of their suppliers. If Albert is found at the trial to be innocent of any wrongdoing, who is responsible for paying his attorney's fees and legal expenses? What if it is determined at trial that there has been an illegal conversion of funds by Albert that resulted in the lawsuit?

5. Can a corporation incorporated under a state following the Model Business Corporation Act consist of one individual who is an officer, director, and shareholder?

6. Must all corporations have a board of directors?

7. Who typically elects the officers of the corporation?

8. Under the Model Business Corporation Act, what is the minimum number of votes required to pass a resolution of the shareholders if 1,000 shares of the corporation's stock have been issued?

9. If the shareholders of a corporation feel that their stock has lost its value due to the mismanagement and/or misconduct of the corporation's officers and directors, what if any recourse do they have?

10. Who typically benefits when cumulative voting for the directors of a corporation is allowed?

Notes

[1] 8B AM. JUR. 2d *Corporations* § 1483 (1985).

[2] *Id.* § 1507.

[3] 1984 Revised Model Business Corporation Act § 8.25(e)(1).

[4] *Id.* § 8.25(e)(2).

[5] *Id.* § 8.25(e)(3).

[6] *Id.* § 8.25(e)(4).

[7] *Id.* § 8.25(e)(5).

[8] *Id.* § 8.25(e)(6).

[9] *Id.* § 8.25(e)(7).

[10] *Id.* § 8.25(e)(8).

[11] 18B AM. JUR. 2d *Corporations* § 1689 (1985).

[12] *Id.* § 1689.

[13] *Id.* § 1695.

[14] *Id.* § 1699.

[15] 1984 Revised Model Business Corporation Act § 8.30(a)(1).

[16] *Id.* § 8.30(a)(2).

[17] *Id.* § 8.30(a)(3).

[18] 18B AM. JUR. 2d *Corporations* § 1711 (1985).

[19] *Id.* § 1703.

[20] *Id.* § 1700.

[21] 1984 Revised Model Business Corporation Act § 8.03.

[22] 18B AM. JUR. 2d *Corporations* § 1419 (1985).

[23] 1984 Revised Model Business Corporation Act § 8.09.

[24] *Id.* § 8.09.

[25] *Id.* § 8.22(a).

[26] *Id.* § 8.20(b).

[27] 18B AM. JUR. 2d *Corporations* § 1342 (1985).

[28] 1984 Revised Model Business Corporation Act § 7.01.

[29] 18A AM. JUR. 2d *Corporations* § 1069 (1985).

[30] *Id.* § 683.

[31] Close Corporation Supplement to the Model Business Corporation Act § 14(a).

[32] 19 AM. JUR. 2d *Corporations* § 2244 (1985).

[33] *Id.* § 2250.

[34] *Id.* § 2260.

CHAPTER 8

THE CORPORATE FINANCIAL STRUCTURE

Introduction

Three main concerns must be addressed regarding a corporation's financial structure: (1) its ability to raise and maintain the level of capital necessary to operate the business, (2) the distribution of earnings and profits to its shareholders, and (3) the division of its assets upon dissolution. This chapter explores many of the options available to the incorporators or directors of a corporation when deciding which vehicle(s) will best raise capital for the corporation and distribute profits to the corporation's shareholders, in a manner that is equitable and beneficial to both the corporation and its shareholders. The distribution of assets upon dissolution of a corporation is discussed in Chapter 12.

Paralegals are not responsible for advising corporate clients on the financial structure of their organizations. Nevertheless, a basic understanding of the corporation's financial structure will be of great benefit to paralegals, who are often responsible for drafting articles of incorporation, minutes, and other corporate documents that are affected by the manner in which the financial structure of the corporation is designed.

This chapter begins with a general discussion of the capitalization of a corporation. Next, it focuses on equity financing, including par value of stock, the consideration given in exchange for stock of the corporation, and the issuance of stock. The focus then shifts to the redemption of equity shares, dividends, and stock splits. This chapter concludes with an examination of debt financing.

§ 8.1 Capitalization of the Corporation

Before a corporation can begin transacting business, it must have capital with which to work. The *capital* of a corporation is generally considered to be all of the corporation's assets, although the term is sometimes used more narrowly to define only the portion of the corporation's assets that is utilized for operation of the corporation's business.[1] The directors of a corporation typically rely on loans from shareholders, loans from third parties, and the issuance of equity and debt securities to raise the initial capital for the corporation. Subsequent to the formation of the corporation, income generated by the business of the corporation is also a major source of capital. **Equity securities** are shares of stock in the corporation that are sold to shareholders, and **debt securities** represent loans to the corporation, or other interests that must be repaid. Capital generated by the issuance of equity securities is often referred to as *equity capital;* the issuance of debt securities generates *debt capital.*

Some of the advantages of issuing equity securities include the fact that the amount invested by shareholders does not have to be repaid, and **dividends** typically need not be paid to shareholders when the corporation is not earning a profit. As opposed to debt financing, the issuance of equity securities maintains a lower debt/equity ratio for the corporation, which increases the corporation's attractiveness to creditors and potential creditors and lowers the risk of insolvency. In addition, the corporation is not required to expend large sums of money on interest payments, as is usually the case with debt financing. One disadvantage of selling equity securities is the fact that the current shareholders' control over the corporation may be diluted.

Although debt capital must be repaid, debt financing offers several advantages to the corporation. Most importantly, the control of the existing shareholders is not diluted by the issuance of debt securities. Also, the issuance of debt securities, as opposed to equity securities, offers certain tax advantages to the corporation, as the payment of interest on debt securities is generally tax-deductible as an expense, whereas dividends paid to equity shareholders are not.

Some of the disadvantages of debt financing include the fact that interest must generally be paid on the securities, whether or not the corporation has any income for a particular period. Also, too high a debt/equity ratio in a corporation may hinder the corporation's ability to obtain short-term loans and may increase the likelihood of insolvency.

TERMS

equity securities   Securities that represent an ownership interest in the corporation.

debt securities   Securities that represent loans to the corporation, or other interests that must be repaid.

dividend [†]   A payment made by a corporation to its stockholders, either in cash (a cash dividend), in stock (a stock dividend), or out of surplus earnings.

The corporation's capital typically consists of a mixture of debt and equity capital, and it is usually a function of the incorporators or the board of directors to determine the best debt/equity mixture and the best sources for the required capital. One significant factor in that decision is the possible impact of the federal Securities Act of 1933, the Securities and Exchange Act of 1934, and the securities acts of the corporation's state of domicile. Although most small stock issuances are exempt from registration under these acts, certain stock issuances are regulated by the Securities and Exchange Commission, and it is important to be aware of the effect these acts will have on any potential stock issuances. Securities regulations and exemptions are discussed in Chapter 9.

Directors may also be limited, in a very practical sense, by the types of financing available to the corporation. Corporations engaging in high-risk ventures may be forced to rely more heavily on equity financing to raise funds, because debt financing can be difficult to obtain. Lenders are much more willing to finance low-risk ventures. Other available means of raising capital for a corporation include sale and leaseback arrangements and employee stock ownership plans (ESOPs). ESOPs are discussed in Chapter 14.

§ 8.2 Equity Financing

Equity financing involves the issuance of shares of stock of the corporation in exchange for cash or other consideration that will become corporate capital. Equity securities must be authorized in the corporation's articles of incorporation and are usually designated as common or **preferred stock**. The sale of stock is noted in the corporation's books by a debit to the assets column (usually cash) and a credit to the capital account column (or shareholder equity column, as it is sometimes referred to). See Figure 8-1.

The usual method of equity financing is the issuance of common stock in exchange for cash. However, many variations are available. The issuance of equity securities means granting certain rights to the

---

TERMS

preferred stock[†] Corporate stock that is entitled to a priority over other classes of stock, usually common stock, in distribution of the profits of the corporation (i.e., dividends) and in distribution of the assets of the corporation in the event of dissolution or liquidation.

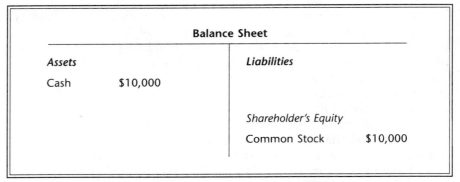

FIGURE 8-1   Balance Sheet Depicting Issuance of $10,000 in Common Stock

individuals who have given consideration for those securities. Those rights generally include the shareholder's proportionate right in the corporation with respect to the earnings, assets, and management of the corporation. Unlike debt security holders, the holders of equity securities are not guaranteed a return on their investment in the corporation, and therefore place at risk their entire investment in the equity securities.

The rest of this section focuses on defining authorized and issued stock of a corporation and the two most common types of equity financing—common stock and preferred stock.

Authorized and Issued Stock

When a corporation is formed, the articles of incorporation must set forth the number and type of shares the corporation is authorized to issue and any other information required by statute. These shares are referred to as the **authorized shares**. Following is a sample provision from the articles of incorporation for a corporation that has authorized only one class of stock.

EXAMPLE: Authorized Stock

The authorized stock of the corporation shall consist of 10,000 shares of Class A Common Stock, without par value.

TERMS

authorized shares   Total number of shares, provided for in the articles of incorporation, that the corporation is authorized to issue.

Dividends

Surviving a Law Firm Merger

The "mergermania" of the 1980s and early 1990s has certainly not bypassed the legal profession. The past decade has seen law firm mergers and acquisitions at a rate never before experienced by the industry. The escalating expenses associated with practicing law, fierce competition, and the need for specialists are just some of the reasons for the record number of law firm mergers and acquisitions in recent years. If you work for a law firm for any substantial length of time, chances are that you will experience a law firm merger or breakup.

Paralegals are rarely involved in merger negotiations or decisions regarding mergers. However, the law firm merger or breakup affects everyone in the law firm. Depending on the terms and conditions, the effects of a merger or law firm breakup on the paralegal can mean minor changes in daily work habits, drastic changes in work responsibilities, or even the loss of a job.

The breakup of of a law firm has often been compared to a divorce, and even a "friendly" divorce can be a very emotional and tense event for everyone involved. Uncertainty reigns as soon as the first rumor of a merger or breakup is heard, and it can cause chaos in the law firm. There are, however, a few simple rules that you can use for surviving a law firm merger or breakup.

1. *Do not believe every rumor you hear, and do not spread gossip.* Although rumors regarding law firm breakups or mergers are usually founded in some truth, a merger is not final until all the papers are signed and an announcement is made. If you hear rumors that concern you, it is best to talk to someone who is in a position to know the truth.

Although law firm management may be reluctant to talk about a merger that is in the negotiation process, they should realize that rumors can be very damaging to law firm morale and even to their negotiations. Management is often eager to squelch rumors by coming forth with the truth.

Further, do not feed the rumors by gossiping about what you hear or what you may speculate. If you need to talk to someone about your feelings regarding the merger or breakup, it may be better to talk to someone outside the law firm, someone who will keep any information regarding a potential merger in the strictest confidence.

2. *Do not assume the worst.* A law firm merger or breakup does not necessarily mean unemployment. Even if the firm you work for will no longer be in existence, there is always a good chance that your employment will be continued by the attorneys you work for, even if it is at a different law firm.

3. *Determine your chain of command.* If the firm you are employed by is breaking up or merging, the first thing you should do is determine who you report to, and who can answer any difficult questions you may have.

4. *Ask for concise rules regarding the release of any information or files to attorneys or other personnel who are leaving the firm.* The question of who is entitled to take certain files and client lists can be a very tough ethical question, but it is not your responsibility. If anyone asks you for files or information and you are not sure whether you should turn over the information, *refer them to your superior.* Do not let a friendship within the firm compromise your ethics or your position.

5. *Be considerate and cooperative.* Do not forget that you are not facing the merger dilemma alone. Tensions are always high in the face of uncertainty and, even if your job is secure, others may not be so fortunate. A kind word or an offer of assistance in finding a new job are always appreciated and may be repaid sometime in the future.

6. *Do not make any quick decisions regarding your future plans.* If you are placed in a new position, or even a new law firm, give it a chance before you decide on the future of your career. Keep in mind that the transition period is always the most difficult, and if you make it through the transition, you may find that the merger has actually worked to your advantage.   ▐▐▐

Once consideration has been received for shares of stock and the shares have been delivered to the shareholders, they are considered to be **issued and outstanding shares.** Shares of stock remain issued and outstanding until they are reacquired, redeemed, converted, or canceled.

The board of directors may not issue equity shares in excess of the authorized shares. If the directors deem it appropriate to increase the number of authorized shares, the articles of incorporation must be amended to provide for the increased number of authorized shares. Such an amendment usually requires shareholder approval.

The articles of incorporation generally must set forth the preferences, limitations, and relative rights of each class of authorized shares before any shares of that class are issued. Although shareholder approval is typically required for amendments to the articles of incorporation concerning the authorized shares of the corporation, the Model Business Corporation Act provides that the board of directors may be granted the right, in the articles of incorporation, to amend the corporation's articles of incorporation without shareholder approval to set forth the rights, preferences, and limitations of any new class of stock. This right does not apply to any class of stock of which there are issued and outstanding shares. Not all state statutes allow this much power to be vested in the board of directors, and it is important that the proper state statutes be consulted with regard to requirements for authorizing new classes of shares of stock. In addition to the articles of incorporation, rights and preferences granted to certain classes of common stock typically must be set forth on the face of the stock certificates of each class, pursuant to statute.

Statutory Requirements for Authorized Stock

Statutory requirements for the authorized stock of a corporation vary greatly. The Model Business Corporation Act (MBCA) grants corporations the opportunity to creatively structure the authorized stock

---

TERMS

issued and outstanding shares   Authorized shares of authorized stock of a corporation that have been issued to shareholders.

of the corporation to meet its specific needs and the needs of its share-holders and investors. The MBCA gives corporations the freedom to authorize classes of stock with a number of differing rights and preferences, provided that the number of each class of shares is set forth in the corporation's articles of incorporation, along with a distinguishing designation for each class of stock if more than one class is authorized.

Most states follow the Model Business Corporation Act in requiring that the authorized stock of a corporation include one or more classes of shares that have unlimited voting rights and one or more classes of shares that together are entitled to receive the net assets of the corporation upon dissolution. These two stock characteristics are commonly found in one class of shares, as is required in many states. These two widely accepted requirements guarantee that at all times there will be shareholders that have the voting rights necessary to take any required corporate actions, and that the corporation will always have shareholders who are entitled to receive the net assets of the corporation, should the corporation dissolve. It is important to note that shares of stock including these two fundamental rights must at all times be issued, not just authorized.

In addition to the foregoing requirements, the Model Business Corporation Act sets forth in § 6.01(c) a sample of some of the rights and preferences that may be designated to shares of stock:

(c) The articles of incorporation may authorize one or more classes of shares that:
(1) have special, conditional, or limited voting rights, or no right to vote, except to the extent prohibited by this Act;
(2) are redeemable or convertible as specified in the articles of incorporation (i) at the option of the corporation, the share-holder, or another person or upon the occurrence of a designated event; (ii) for cash, indebtedness, securities, or other property; (iii) in a designated amount or in an amount determined in accordance with a designated formula or by reference to extrinsic data or events;
(3) entitle the holders to distributions calculated in any manner, including dividends that may be cumulative, noncumulative, or partially cumulative;
(4) have preference over any other class of shares with respect to distributions, including dividends and distributions upon the dissolution of the corporation.

The list set forth in § 6.01(c) is not exhaustive, and not all these rights and preferences are allowed in every state. It is important to consult the statutes of the corporation's state of domicile to determine what the specific state requirements are for authorizing corporate stock.

Drafting Considerations

When drafting the articles of incorporation to specify the initial authorized shares, the immediate and future capital requirements of the corporation must be taken into consideration, as well as the control of the corporation, state and federal securities regulations, the potential market for sale of the stock, and any state taxation or filing fees that may be based on the authorized shares of the corporation. Many states, including Delaware, base an initial incorporation tax on the authorized capital stock of the corporation.

The Model Business Corporation Act no longer uses the term *preferred stock*. However, the Act specifically provides that many of the characteristics commonly found in preferred stock may be found in certain classes of stock, whatever they may be called. For purposes of this discussion, we distinguish between common and preferred stock and discuss the characteristics commonly associated with those types of stock, keeping in mind that those characteristics may be assigned to any class of stock, regardless of what it is labeled.

Common Stock

The ownership of almost all corporations is represented, at least in part, by stock referred to as *common stock*. In the event no designation is made in the articles of incorporation, the authorized stock is considered to be common stock if only one class is authorized. In almost every event, and certainly when common stock is the only stock issued, common stockholders will have unlimited voting rights and will be entitled to receive the net assets of the corporation upon its dissolution.

Classes of Common Stock

The articles of incorporation may authorize more than one class of common stock, with different rights and preferences as set forth in the articles of incorporation. Common stock may also be issued in series in some states. In any event, all shares of common stock within the same class and series are entitled to identical rights.

Common stock may be issued in classes to certain groups with common interests to assure their representation on the board of directors. For example, the articles of incorporation may provide that Class A common stock may elect three directors, and Class B common stock may elect two directors to the board.

Voting Rights

Unless otherwise indicated in the articles of incorporation, holders of common stock are entitled to one vote per share of stock owned. Other voting rights may be prescribed in the articles of incorporation, and this is commonly done when there is more than one class of common stock of the corporation.

The initial shareholders of a corporation may, at times, consent to the subsequent issue of nonvoting common stock to new shareholders. The issue of nonvoting stock can be used to raise capital for the corporation without diluting the management power of the existing shareholders. The corporation may, for example, be authorized to issue Class A common stock that is entitled to one vote per share, and Class B common stock that is not entitled to vote. Following is a sample provision for the articles of incorporation that authorizes two classes of stock, one with voting rights and one without voting rights.

EXAMPLE: Authorized Shares

The authorized capital stock of this corporation shall consist of one million shares of Class A Common Stock, without par value, and one million shares of Class B Common Stock, without par value.

Each shareholder of Class A Common Stock shall be entitled to one (1) vote per share.

Each shareholder of Class B Nonvoting Common Stock shall have no voting rights except those prescribed by statute for both voting and nonvoting shareholders.

In the following case, the court upheld the right of the corporation to issue nonvoting stock, but granted certain shareholders the right of rescission because they were not given notice as to the nonvoting characteristic of the stock, as required by statute.

Liquidation Rights

Unless otherwise prescribed by the articles of incorporation, the shareholders of the corporation's common stock will be entitled to the net assets of the corporation upon dissolution. Shareholders will divide the net assets in proportion to their share ownership.

Preferred Stock

Preferred stock is "stock which enjoys certain limited rights and privileges (usually dividend and liquidation priorities) over other outstanding

HAMPTON
v.
TRI-STATE FINANCE CORP.
Colorado Court of Appeals
495 P.2d 566 (Colo. App.1972)
Smith, Judge

Plaintiffs-appellees are holders of Class B common stock of the Tri-State Finance Corporation. Plaintiffs' complaint in the district court against Tri-State Corporation and its directors alleged in essence that the corporation refused to allow voting by Class B stockholders at an annual meeting of the corporation.

Article IV of the articles of incorporation of Tri-State Finance Corporation, at all times pertinent hereto, read:

"The authorized capital stock of this corporation shall consist of one million shares of common stock ... divided into the following classes:

"Class A—shall consist of one hundred thousand (100,000) shares of the par value of $1.00 per share and each shareholder of said Class A stock shall be entitled to one (1) vote per share.

"Class B—shall consist of nine hundred thousand (900,000) shares of the par value of $1.00 per share ... . The common stock Class A and common stock Class B shall be identical in all respects except that the holders of common stock Class B shall have no voting power for any purpose whatsoever and the holders of common stock Class A shall to the exclusion of the holders of common stock Class B have full voting powers for all purposes ... ."

Plaintiffs alleged that the above voting restriction applicable to Class B stock denies its holders the voting rights guaranteed by Colorado statute; and that the entire voting restriction is therefore void. Plaintiffs also maintained that because Class B stock certificates were issued without the restriction or notice thereof printed upon the certificates, as required by [Colo. Rev. Stat. §] 31-4-8 [(1963)], the restrictions could not be enforced.

Tri-State answered, admitting their failure to comply with [Colo. Rev. Stat. §] 31-4-8, but alleged actual notice to most of the Class B stockholders. They suggested rescission as the remedy for those Class B stockholders not having actual notice of the voting restrictions at the time of the purchase of their Class B shares. Plaintiffs moved for summary judgment which, after argument, was granted by the district court, ruling as follows:

"The Court concludes, as a matter of law, that the provisions in the Articles of Incorporation and in the Amendment to the Articles of Incorporation concerning the voting powers and restrictions on voting powers are null and void because they would deprive the Class B shareholders of their statutory right to vote on certain matters as provided by [Colo. Rev. Stat. §] 31-3-8, and their constitutional right under Article XV, Section 9 of the State Constitution.

"The Court also concludes, as a matter of law, that the failure to comply with [§] 31-4-8(2) re Restrictions, is fatal to the defendants' contention that Class B shareholders are not entitled to vote since it is admitted that their certificates contain no notice of restrictions and were issued subsequent to the Amendment of the Articles of Incorporation." ...

In the case at hand, we must assume that the parties intended to act within the law and did not intend to restrict unlawfully the Class B stockholders' right to vote. Article IV of the articles of incorporation should be construed so as to give it validity under the statutes. The portions of Article IV that purport to exceed statutory authority are void, but all voting restrictions not contrary to the statutes are valid. This construction most nearly effects the result originally intended by the parties, as evidenced by the articles, and does not amount to an amendment or reformation of that document.

Plaintiffs argue that any denial of voting rights to one class of common stock in an election for directors of a corporation violates public policy.

We disagree. The intention of the Legislature is evident from the use of the language, "whether or not entitled to vote thereon by the provisions of the articles of incorporation of the corporation," indicating those instances where it is mandatory that all stockholders vote despite restrictions contained in the articles. ... There is no such language concerning election of directors. ...

The parties agree that [Colo. Rev. Stat. §] 31-4-8(2) has been violated. It reads as follows:

"(2) Every certificate representing shares issued by a corporation which is authorized to issue shares of more than one class shall set forth upon the face or back of the certificate, or shall state that the corporation will furnish to any shareholder upon request and without charge, a full statement of the designations, preferences, limitations, and relative rights of the shares of each class authorized to be issued ... ."

[Colo. Rev. Stat. §] 31-4-8 makes no provision as to the consequences of a violation of the statute. It does not require that the certificate carry the exact restrictions on the certificate, but only that the shareholder be informed by the certificate that upon request the corporation will furnish him with information as to classes of stock and their various restrictions. The purpose of the statute is to ensure that a purchaser of stock has notice of voting restrictions at the time of purchase.

Where notice has not been given pursuant to [§] 31-4-8, and where actual knowledge cannot be shown by the corporation, we agree that a remedy must exist. ... It is settled that the relationship of stockholders to the corporation is one of contract and that the rights and duties of both parties grow out of that contract, which includes other terms of the articles of incorporation. ... In the absence of fraud, rescission would appear to be the most appropriate remedy. ...

Thus, absent a showing of actual knowledge at the time of purchase, failure to follow [Colo. Rev. Stat. §] 31-4-8 renders the stock contract voidable on the part of the stockholder or, if fraud can be shown, appropriate remedies exist. ...

The judgment is reversed and the case remanded to the district court for further proceedings, not inconsistent with this opinion.

---

stock but which doesn't participate in corporate growth in any significant extent."[2] Preferred stock is distinguished from common stock in that it is entitled to a priority over other stock in the distribution of profits. This preference may include the right to cumulative or noncumulative dividends. The terms of the preferred stock are set forth in the articles of incorporation and on the face of the preferred stock certificate, in accordance with state statute, and the specified terms and provisions serve as a contract between the preferred stockholder and the corporation.

The terms of preferred stock can vary and may be restricted by state statute. Typically, preferred stockholders are granted a dividend preference over the common stockholders in a fixed amount per share or in a certain percentage. Aside from this preference, preferred stockholders may also be granted voting rights, redemption rights, conversion rights, and priority in entitlement to the assets of the corporation on dissolution. Following is a sample provision for the articles of incorporation of a corporation that has authorized common and preferred stock.

The authorized capital stock of this corporation shall consist of one million shares of Common Stock, without par value, and one million shares of Nonvoting Preferred Stock, without par value.

Each shareholder of Common Stock shall be entitled to one (1) vote per share.

The holders of Preferred Stock will be entitled to receive cumulative dividends on an annual basis of twelve percent (12%) of the stated value of the Preferred Stock prior to the distribution of any dividends to the holders of Common Stock. Holders of Common Stock will be entitled to dividends of ten percent (10%) of the surplus remaining, with the balance of such surplus to be distributed to holders of both classes of stock on a participating basis equally without distinction as to class.

Voting Rights

Preferred stock may be issued with voting rights, with limited voting rights, or with no voting rights at all, at the discretion of the board of directors. So long as at least one class of issued stock is granted unlimited voting rights, preferred stock is not required to provide voting rights.

Redemption Rights

Often, when a corporation issues preferred stock, that stock will be issued with provisions that allow the corporation, or the preferred shareholder, the right of redemption at a future date, upon the terms and conditions set forth on the stock certificate or in an agreement between the preferred shareholder and the corporation. Following is a sample articles-of-incorporation provision providing for the redemption of preferred stock.

EXAMPLE: Redemption of Preferred Stock

The preferred stock of the corporation may be redeemed in whole or in part on any date after _____ , 19___ , at the option of the board of directors on not less than _____ days' notice to the preferred stockholders of record. Such stock shall be redeemed by payment in cash of _____ percent (___%) of par value of each share to be redeemed, as well as all accrued unpaid dividends on each such share.

Redemption of equity shares is discussed in more detail in § 8.6 of this chapter.

Conversion of Preferred Stock

The preferred stock rights and preferences, which constitute the contract between the corporation and the preferred shareholder, may include **conversion rights** providing that the issued shares of preferred stock may be converted into common stock at some specific point in time, usually at the shareholder's option. Specific provisions in the articles of incorporation and on the stock certificates, or in a separate agreement between the corporation and the preferred stockholder, should include a conversion rate indicating the number of preferred shares that may be converted into common stock and the number of common shares to be issued in the exchange. In addition, the conversion provisions should include the exact method for the conversion, including the period during which the conversion option may validly be exercised, and any other pertinent information. Following is a sample articles-of-incorporation provision providing for the conversion of preferred stock.

EXAMPLE: Right of Conversion

The holder of any shares of preferred stock of the Corporation may, after the fourth anniversary date of the issuance of such stock, and until such time as may be determined by the Board of Directors, elect to convert such shares of preferred stock to shares of common stock of the Corporation. Upon giving the Corporation ninety (90) days' notice by registered mail of such intent and on surrender at the office of the Corporation of the certificates for such preferred shares, duly endorsed to the Corporation, the shareholder shall be entitled to receive one share of common stock for every share of preferred stock so surrendered.

Priority Rights to Assets upon Dissolution

Preferred stockholders may be granted a specific preference over common stockholders with regard to the assets of the corporation upon its dissolution.

Series of Preferred Shares

Preferred stock may be issued in classes and series to the extent that such issuance is authorized in the corporation's articles of incorporation. A *series* of preferred stock refers to a type of shares within a class of preferred stock. The exact rights and preferences of a series of shares may be set by the board of directors before issuance, without shareholder approval or amendment of the articles of incorporation.

─────────────────────── TERMS ───────────────────────

conversion rights   Rights, often granted to preferred shareholders with the issuance of preferred stock, that allow the preferred stockholders to convert their shares of preferred stock into common stock at some specific point in time, usually at the shareholder's option.

This allows the board of directors to act quickly, to take advantage of market conditions, without having to amend the articles of incorporation. All rights and preferences of shares of stock within a series must be identical.

Factors in Deciding Whether to Issue Preferred Stock

The board of directors or incorporators must take several factors into consideration when deciding whether to authorize preferred stock in the corporation's articles of incorporation. Preferred stock may be used to attract investors who are interested in a more conservative investment that offers a steady income in lieu of growth potential. Other factors to be considered by the board of directors or incorporators include the cost of issuing preferred stock, the risk of capital, the flexibility of the payment obligation, and the permanence of the capital represented.[3]

§ 8.3 Par Value

Par value is the nominal value assigned to shares of stock, which amount is imprinted upon the face of the stock certificate as a dollar value. It is widely accepted that "par value and actual value of issued stock are not synonymous, and there is often a wide disparity between them."[4] This section examines the trend toward eliminating par value and the consideration and accounting requirements for par value stock.

Trend Toward Eliminating Par Value

Traditionally, all stock was assigned a par value, and the statutes of many states still require the use of par value. However, the trend in modern corporate law is to eliminate the par value requirement. Some states provide that a corporation's authorized stock can be without par value or with no par value. However, if no par value is assigned to the stock of a corporation, the authorities in those states will assign a specific par value to the shares of stock for certain purposes, such as taxation and filing fees. The statutes of states following the Model Business Corporation Act do not require that a par value be assigned to the authorized stock of the corporation. However, if a par value is assigned, it must be set forth in the corporation's articles of incorporation.

Consideration for Par Value Stock

If a corporation authorizes par value stock, special consideration must be given to the issuance of that stock with regard to the corporation's accounting. Like stock with no par value, par value stock may be issued for any price deemed adequate by the board of directors, with one exception: the consideration received must be at least equal to the par value of the shares issued. For instance, 100 shares of $10 par value common stock could be issued at a price of $5,000 if the board deems it adequate consideration. However, in no event could the board of directors issue the shares of stock for less than $1,000.

Shares issued for less than the par value, which may be the case when consideration is in a form other than cash, are considered **watered shares**, and the shareholder receiving them may be liable to the corporation for the difference between the amount paid and the par value of the shares received. However, the imposition of liability on the shareholders of a corporation for purchase of watered shares, in the absence of fraud or misrepresentation, is becoming a rare event. The Model Business Corporation Act provides only that "[a] purchaser from a corporation of its own shares is not liable to the corporation or its creditors with respect to the shares except to pay for the consideration for which the shares were authorized to be issued."[5]

Accounting for Par Value Stock

Generally, when a corporation receives consideration for the issuance of par value stock, the total amount of the par value of the issued stock is considered **stated capital**. Any amount received in excess of the par value of the shares is considered **capital surplus**. Often, any amount received by the corporation that is considered stated capital must be maintained by the corporation. The issuance of stock without par value allows the directors of the corporation greater flexibility in manipulating the available capital surplus to provide for greater dividends and the redemption of issued stock.[6] If the authorized stock of a corporation is without par value, directors are frequently allowed to

TERMS

watered shares[†]   Shares of stock issued by a corporation as paid-up stock but which have in fact been issued without any consideration or for inadequate consideration.

stated capital   The total of the par values of all shares of stock that a corporation has issued, plus the total consideration paid for its no-par stock.

capital surplus[†]   Such surplus as a corporation may have over and above its earned surplus.

make their own determination as to what part of the consideration received is stated capital and what part is capital surplus. (See Figure 8-2.)

Because the par value amount typically represents only the *minimum* amount that shares may be issued for, and because a high par value may tie up the funds of the corporation, most corporations in states that require par value opt to assign a very nominal amount of par value. Another reason for the frequent use of a nominal par value is that some state authorities employ the par value of stock as part of a taxation formula, with corporations being taxed on the par value of authorized or issued stock of the corporation. Par value may also be a factor in determining state filing fees.

§ 8.4 Consideration for Shares of Stock

Unless the right is granted to the shareholders under statute or the articles of incorporation, the board of directors is typically responsible for the issuance of stock for adequate consideration. This really involves two issues. First, the board must determine a fair value at which the stock should be issued; then they must determine the adequacy of the consideration. Obviously, if the consideration is in the form of cash, the second part of that task is simple.

The price per share of stock for the initial issue of shares is determined by the amount of capital required to begin the business, the number of initial investors, and the number of shares to be issued. For example, if it is determined that a corporation requires $50,000 to begin business, and five initial investors are all willing to invest $10,000, the number and price of the authorized and issued shares will be determined accordingly. The corporation may decide to issue 50,000 shares of common stock at $1.00 per share, or the board may decide to issue 5 shares at $10,000 per share. For ease in transferring stock, it is advisable to put a lower price on the shares of stock. For example, if a shareholder in this example wished to sell half of his or her shares, it would be much easier to transfer 5,000 $1.00 shares than half of a single $10,000 share.

Placing a value on subsequent issues of stock is a more difficult matter. Obviously, stock cannot be priced too high, or it will not sell. On the other hand, if the stock price is too low, it will dilute the interest of the current stockholders by bringing down the per-share value. Also, shares of stock that are issued within a relatively short time period generally must be sold for the same price. If the shares of stock to be issued are par value stock, the consideration must be at least equal to the par value of the shares issued.

**Balance Sheet of a Corporation after Issuance of 10,000
Shares of Common Stock, $1.00 par value**

Assets		Liabilities
Cash	$10,000	
		Shareholder's Equity
		Common Stock
		Stated Capital: $10,000
		Capital Surplus: 0

**Balance Sheet of a Corporation after Issuance of 10,000
Shares of Common Stock, $.50 par value**

Assets		Liabilities
Cash	$10,000	
		Shareholder's Equity
		Common Stock
		Stated Capital: $5,000
		Capital Surplus: 5,000

FIGURE 8-2 Balance Sheets Contrasting Different Treatment of Stated Capital
and Capital Surplus

Historically, restrictions were placed on the type of consideration
that could be accepted by the board of directors for shares of equity
stock. Statutes generally restricted the use of promissory notes, the rendering of future services, and other types of contracts that called for
payment or performance at some time in the future. The intent behind
this restriction was to ensure that the corporation had enough immediate capital with which to operate its business. Many states still place
some restrictions on the form of consideration that may be accepted for
the issuance of stock.

The tendency of modern corporate law is to allow any consideration deemed adequate by the board of directors for the payment of
shares of stock. Under the Model Business Corporation Act, consideration for shares of stock may be in the form of "any tangible or intangible
property or benefit to the corporation."[7] This may include cash, promissory notes, services performed on behalf of the corporation, contracts

for services to be performed on behalf of the corporation, or other securities of the corporation. It is typically left to the discretion of the board of directors to determine the adequacy of consideration. Obviously, if the board of directors decides to accept promissory notes, or other contracts for future benefit to the corporation, there must be an adequate mix of cash or other immediate rewards that gives the corporation the needed initial funds. When a corporation receives valid consideration for shares, the shares are issued and considered to be fully paid and nonassessable.

§ 8.5   Issuance of Stock

Typically, the first shares of stock of a corporation are issued at the first meeting of the board of directors. This is often done by executing or ratifying **stock subscription agreements** that were received before or immediately after incorporation of the business, with the issuance of stock certificates in exchange for the agreed-upon consideration. The right to issue shares of stock is generally granted to the board of directors. However, the statutes of many states allow the shareholders to reserve that power in the articles of incorporation if desired. If the shareholders of the corporation have preemptive rights, the existing shareholders must be given the opportunity to exercise their rights prior to the issuance of any additional shares of stock.

Shares of issued stock are usually represented by stock certificates, as may be required by state statute, the articles of incorporation or bylaws of the corporation, or both. However, in many instances, stock issued under a valid agreement but without the formal stock certificate has been found to be a valid issue of stock.

Stock Certificates

Although the Model Business Corporation Act prescribes the minimum form and content for stock certificates, it also allows corporations to issue stock without the formality of a stock certificate, so long as the information prescribed for stock certificates is included in a written

---

TERMS

stock subscription agreement   Agreement to purchase a specific number of shares of a corporation.

statement sent to the shareholder within a reasonable time after the issue or transfer of the shares without a certificate.[8] Section 6.25(b) of the Model Business Corporation Act prescribes the requirements for stock certificates, as follows:

> (b) At a minimum each share certificate must state on its face:
>   (1) the name of the issuing corporation and that it is organized under the law of this state;
>   (2) the name of the person to whom issued; and
>   (3) the number and class of shares and the designation of the series, if any, the certificate represents.

See Figure 8-3.

The Model Business Corporation Act also requires, as do most states, that the stock certificates contain a summary of the designations, relative rights, preferences, and limitations applicable to the class of shares which the certificate represents when the corporation is authorized to

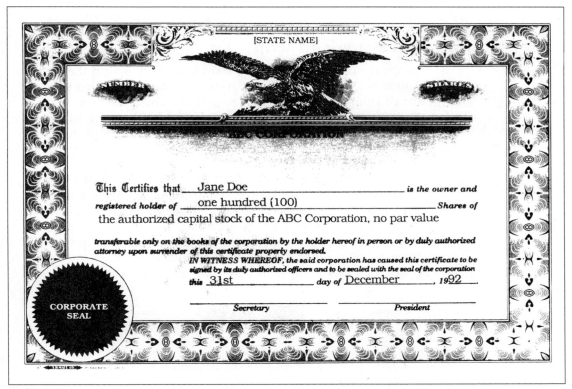

FIGURE 8-3 Sample Common Stock Certificate. (Certificate compliments of A.R. Maul Co., Minneapolis, Minn.)

issue more than one class or series of shares. The Model Business Corporation Act further allows the corporation to provide the pertinent information regarding share classes and series rights and preferences to shareholders upon request, so long as the stock certificate "conspicuously state[s] on its front or back that the corporation will furnish the shareholder this information on request in writing without charge."[9]

Stock certificates must generally be signed by two officers of the corporation, typically the president or chief executive officer and the secretary or assistant secretary.

Lost or Destroyed Stock Certificates

Lost stock certificates can usually be replaced if the shareholder submits an affidavit affirming that the certificate was lost or destroyed. The new stock certificate is typically issued with an indication that it is a "duplicate" stock certificate.

Fractional Shares and Scrip

At times, because of various stock transactions involving the transfer or issuance of shares of stock, a shareholder may be entitled to own an amount of shares of stock that is represented by a fraction. For instance, the corporation may declare a **stock dividend** of one share for every 10 shares that are issued and outstanding. In that event, a shareholder holding 15 shares would be entitled to receive 1.5 more shares of stock.

A corporation may issue a fractional share, which is entitled to voting and all rights incident to stock ownership, or it may issue a **scrip**. A scrip is an instrument that represents the right to receive a fraction of a share. This instrument is freely transferable, but it does not include voting rights or other rights associated with stock ownership. Scrip is often issued with a provision that it must be combined with other fractional shares of stock and exchanged for a whole share or shares of stock

---

TERMS

stock dividend[†]   A dividend paid by a corporation in the stock of the corporation.

scrip[†]   A certificate of a right to receive something. In certain circumstances, instead of money, governments issue scrip that may be redeemed for money. Corporations issue scrip representing fractional shares of stock that, when accumulated in sufficient number, may be exchanged for stock.

within a prescribed time period. If the exchange is not completed within the time prescribed, the scrip becomes void.

§ 8.6 Redemption of Equity Shares

Redemption refers to the repurchase by a corporation of its own shares of stock. Often, a corporation's preferred stock will be issued with provisions that allow the corporation the right of redemption at a future date, upon the terms and conditions set forth on the stock certificate or in an agreement between the preferred stockholder and the corporation. This may be of particular interest to corporations when the market interest rate is declining, or when the corporation expects substantial profits in the near future, because redemption of preferred stock allows the corporation to terminate its obligations to pay fixed dividends on the stock. In a close corporation, rights of redemption allow shareholders to withdraw from participation in the corporation without forfeiting their investment.

Redemption may be at the option of the corporation, the shareholder, or a third party. Shares redeemable at the option of the corporation are often referred to as *callable shares;* the option of a shareholder to redeem shares is sometimes referred to as a *put.* The price paid to redeem shares is set in the articles of incorporation or by a formula prescribed in the articles of incorporation.

Treasury shares are shares of stock that were previously issued by the corporation but later reacquired. Reacquired shares may be subject to special accounting treatment, although the Model Business Corporation Act has eliminated any special treatment of treasury shares in recent years, stating merely that "corporation may acquire its own shares and shares so acquired constitute authorized but unissued shares."[10] Several states, however, require that treasury shares be accounted for under a special status as issued but not outstanding shares. Shares that are issued but not outstanding have no voting rights, and they are not counted in any necessary determinations of the number of outstanding shares of the corporation.

================================== TERMS ==================================

treasury shares[†]   Corporate stock that has been issued to shareholders and paid for in full, and has later been repurchased or otherwise reacquired by the corporation.

§ 8.7 Dividends

Once the business of the corporation has net earnings, the profits of the corporation are usually distributed to the appropriate shareholders, in an equitable manner, in the form of dividends. A *dividend* is considered to be a payment to the stockholders of a corporation as a return on their investment. Generally, recurring dividends are paid on a more or less regular basis in the ordinary course of business without reducing the stockholders' equity or their position to enjoy future returns from the corporation. These dividends are payable out of the surplus or profits of the corporation, and may be in the form of cash, stock, or other property of the corporation.

This section investigates the availability of funds for dividends and the different types of dividends. It also discusses the declaration of dividends and the shareholders' right to receive dividends after they have been declared.

Availability of Funds for Dividends

It is generally accepted that dividends may be paid only out of the profits of the corporation. This principle has been upheld in courts numerous times, as it has been found that "[g]enerally, the net earnings or surplus of a going corporation constitute the proper fund for the payment of dividends, whether on its common stock or preferred stock, and dividends cannot, as a rule, legally be declared and paid out of the capital of the corporation."[11] Dividends are normally payable out of the surplus or profits of a corporation, and it is usually within the discretion of the corporation's directors to decide whether to reinvest the corporation's profits in the corporation or to distribute the profits to the corporation's shareholders.

Newer and smaller, closely held corporations may opt for the declaration of minimal dividends and keep the profits in the corporation to expand its business and increase the value of its stock. Often, the shareholders of these smaller corporations are also employees of the corporation and receive their share of the earnings of the corporation in the form of salaries.

On the other hand, larger, publicly held corporations may find it necessary to declare and pay dividends consistently at a rate attractive to potential investors who are looking for stock investments with steady income potential. These corporations may seek alternative ways to declare dividends when the profits of the corporation do not support a cash distribution at the time dividends are typically paid. The corporation may declare a stock dividend, or it may borrow funds for the stock dividends. The matter of dividend declaration is consistently addressed in state statutes. Under the Model Business Corporation Act, dividends are prohibited if their payment would cause the corporation to be unable to pay its debts as they become due in the usual course of business, or if the corporation's total assets would be less than the sum of its total liabilities plus the amount that would be needed to satisfy the preferential rights, upon dissolution, of the shareholders whose preferential rights are superior to those receiving the distribution, if the corporation were to be dissolved at the time of the distribution.[12] These tests to determine the availability of funds vary by state.

Types of Dividends

Dividends may be paid in several forms. The most common types consist of cash, stock, or other property.

Cash

The majority of corporate dividends are cash dividends. In its simplest form, the cash dividend merely divides the profits of the corporation and distributes the profits, in cash, to the shareholders of the corporation pursuant to the terms of the shares of stock that have been issued.

Stock Dividends

At times, stock dividends may be distributed in lieu of cash. An issue of stock dividends involves the authorization and issuance of new stock to existing shareholders on a pro-rata basis. Because stock dividends make no demands on the funds of a corporation, they are not regulated by statute to the extent that cash dividends are regulated.

So as not to unfairly dilute the shares of one class of stock, shareholders of one class of shares may not be issued shares of another class in a stock dividend, unless the articles of incorporation so provide, or unless, prior to declaration of the stock dividend, no shares of the class to be distributed as a dividend have been issued. Although the corporation issues additional stock, it continues with the same assets and liabilities. The declaration of a stock dividend has the effect of allowing the portion of surplus capital represented by the new stock to be transferred to the permanent capital account of the corporation.

Because the issued shares of the corporation are increased, and all shareholders receive a proportionate amount of shares in the event of a stock dividend, shareholders receiving stock dividends are, in effect, no better off than they were prior to the stock distribution. The stock dividend effectively lowers the price of the issued stock to reflect the value of the corporation.

Other Property

On occasion, dividends may be in a form other than cash or the corporation's stock. These dividends might be any property owned by the corporation, including the stock of another corporation.

Declaration of Dividends

The corporation generally has no legal obligation to pay an undeclared dividend to the shareholders. However, once a dividend is declared, it becomes a debt payable to the shareholders, and the shareholders of the corporation have the legal remedies available to creditors to collect the dividend as declared.

Dividend Preferences

Dividends that are payable, by virtue of contract, to one class of shareholders in priority over another class of shareholders are often referred to as *preferred* or *preferential* dividends.[13] Preferred stockholders generally have a right to priority over other shareholders in the receipt of dividends. Although corporations typically pay consistent dividends to preferred stockholders at regular intervals, preferred stockholders do not have the right to dividends when there is no corporate profit or surplus earnings to justify the dividends. Courts have found in several instances that a "corporation cannot make a valid contract to pay dividends otherwise than from profits, and an agreement to pay such dividends out of capital is unlawful and void."[14]

Cumulative Dividends

Courts have held in several instances that the "omission of a dividend on either the preferred or the common stock of a corporation for any year, because net earnings which will permit the payment of a dividend are lacking, deprives such stock of all right to a share of profits for that year, unless the contract provides for the cumulation of dividends on such stock."[15] The exception to this general rule arises when the contract between the preferred shareholder and the corporation provides for the cumulation of dividends. If the preferred shareholders have a cumulative right to the dividends, dividends omitted in one year generally must be paid the next year before dividends are paid on the shares of common stock.

Authority to Declare Dividends

The authority to declare dividends generally rests with the board of directors, with the exception of stock dividends, which may require shareholder approval. Dividends are generally approved by board of director resolution and declared as a formal act of the corporation. The following items are generally considered when drafting resolutions for the declaration of corporate dividends[16]:

- Kind of dividend to be declared
  — cash
  — stock
  — property
  — scrip

- Whether the dividend is being paid from an appropriate fund

- Class or series of stock on which the dividend is being declared

- Whether the dividend is regular or extraordinary

- The cash amount or value of the dividend

- Formal declaration of the dividend by the board of directors, which distinguishes the date the dividend is declared from the date the dividend is to be paid

- Declaration of the dividend as payable to registered owners of stock, as listed on the corporate books, as of a specified date

Right to Receive Dividends

When a dividend is declared, the declaration includes a date on which all shareholders of record will be entitled to dividends. Once the declaration has been made, those individuals have a right to those dividends, as specified by contract and the declaration. Typically, if no date is declared to determine the shareholders of record entitled to a dividend, the record date is considered the date on which the declaration is made.

Directors are generally under no obligation to declare a dividend in the corporation and may often decide that it is in the company's best interest to reinvest the surplus and profits in the business. The corporation is not under an obligation to pay dividends unless a dividend is declared. Although the courts generally abide by the discretion of the board of directors regarding the declaration of dividends, when the rights of minority shareholders or preferred shareholders are being infringed upon, the courts may intervene. The courts have held many times that the "rights of holders of preferred stock to dividends will be enforced in equity against the corporation in accordance with the terms of the contract."[17]

In addition, if the evidence shows that the board of directors is wrongfully withholding dividends from the profits of the corporation from minority shareholders, a court of equity may order the board of directors to declare a dividend out of surplus profits.

§ 8.8 Stock Splits

Although **stock splits** increase the issued number of shares, they are not considered stock dividends. Stock splits are a common vehicle for lowering the price of a corporation's stock. Stock splits are especially frequent among publicly held corporations with stock that has appreciated significantly, to the point where the price per share may appear prohibitive to the small investor. The effect of a stock split is to "split" the value of each share of stock into smaller denominations. For example, if a corporation's stock appreciates to the point where it is valued at the price of $100 per share, the board of directors may declare a two-for-one split and issue two $50 shares for each outstanding $100 share.

It is important to recognize the difference between a stock split and a stock dividend. Although stock splits increase the number of outstanding shares of a corporation that represent its capital, the actual amount of capital and surplus remain unchanged. A stock dividend, on the other hand, represents a transfer of earnings or profits to the capital of the corporation, together with a distribution of additional shares, which represents the addition of the earnings or profits to the corporation's capital.

§ 8.9 Debt Financing

Debt financing refers to obtaining capital through loans to the corporation, which must be repaid with interest upon the terms agreed to by contract between the corporation and lender or the holder of the

---

TERMS

stock split[†]   The act of a corporation in replacing some or all of its outstanding stock with a greater number of shares of lesser value.

TABLE 8-1 EQUITY FINANCING vs. DEBT FINANCING

Equity	Debt
Represents an ownership in the company	Represents a loan of capital to the company that must be repaid
Payment of dividends to shareholders is usually optional	Periodic payment of interest to debt holders is usually mandatory
Dividends paid on shares of stock are not tax deductible	Interest paid on debt financing is tax deductible
Issuance of stock maintains a lower debt/equity ratio for the corporation	Too high a debt/equity ratio in a corporation increases the likelihood of insolvency
Issuance of equity securities may dilute the current shareholder's control over the corporation	Incurring debt financing usually does not affect the current shareholders' control over the corporation

debt securities. Debt financing refers to anything from a simple loan, represented by a promissory note, to the issuance of debt securities in the form of bonds. Short-term capital can often be acquired by bank loans, either secured or unsecured. Intermediate and long-term debt capital is often acquired through the issuance of debt securities, including bonds and debentures.

Because of the significant tax (and nontax) advantages of raising capital through the issuance of bonds or other debt obligations, the board of directors often decides to maximize the use of debt financing. The interest paid to bondholders is generally deductible as a corporate expense, whereas dividends paid on shares of stock of the corporation are not deductible.

In this section, we look at the authority required to obtain debt financing on behalf of a corporation. We then focus on the two most common types of debt financing: bank loans and bonds.

Authority for Debt Financing

The board of directors usually decides what type of debt capital must be acquired to suit the corporation's needs. This capital can be raised in the form of short-term, intermediate-term, or long-term financing, or any combination of the foregoing. One of the most significant factors influencing the directors' decision as to which type of debt financing to obtain involves the state and federal securities regulations that must be complied with under certain circumstances. Securities matters are discussed in Chapter 9.

The board of directors generally has the power to obtain debt financing on behalf of the corporation, although in some instances this power may be granted to the shareholders of the corporation in the articles of incorporation or state statutes. The amount of bonded indebtedness that a corporation can incur may be limited under the corporation's articles of incorporation or statute.

Bank Loans

The terms of corporate bank loans are established in the loan agreements between the bank and the corporation. The loan can be for a specific term, or it can be in the form of a line of credit, on which the corporation can draw from time to time when additional cash is required. Depending on the corporation's credit rating, it may be able to obtain unsecured bank loans, but most corporate bank loans are secured, with the corporation pledging collateral to the bank, which will be executed or foreclosed on by the bank in the event of default.

Bonds

Bonds can be issued so as to grant the bondholder a wide variety of rights. The rights of bondholders are defined by the terms of the bond contract between the corporation and the bondholder. However, the status of the bondholder differs from that of the stockholder, in that the relationship of the bondholder to the corporation is more that of a creditor than an owner. Bondholders generally have no voting rights. Bonds are usually long-term secured debt instruments payable to the bearer, with interest, upon the terms indicated on the bond. Many bonds are *coupon bonds* that have detachable coupons, which may be presented to the corporation at prescribed intervals for interest payments.

Bonds that represent an unsecured loan to the corporation are referred to as *debentures* or *simple debentures.*

Bonds, or the contracts representing the agreement between the corporation and the bondholder, typically include the face value of the bond, the date when the principal repayment is due (the *maturity date*), and the terms for payment of interest, usually a fixed rate payable in periodic installments until the bond matures. Bonds may be issued for face value, or at a discount or premium.

Discounted Bonds

A debt obligation that bears no interest or interest at a lower-than-current-market rate is usually issued at less than its face amount—that is, at a discount. If bonds are issued at a discount, the difference between the issue price and the face value is deductible by the corporation over the life of the bonds. The discount is considered a form of interest for use of the funds received.

Premium Bonds

If the current market rate is higher than the interest rate on the debt security, the bonds may be issued at a premium. Any amount received for the bond which is over the face value on the bond is considered a premium.

Bonds are typically issued with accompanying bond contracts and indenture agreements setting forth the entire agreement between the corporation and the bondholder. The bond contract sets forth the terms for payment of interest on the bond, the maturity date of the bond, and any applicable conversion or redemption rights.

Conversion Rights

Bonds are often issued with *conversion rights*—the right of the bondholder to convert the bond to stock of the corporation at a set price at some time in the future. Investors who want initially to enjoy a higher income, with the potential to participate in appreciation, may find it desirable to purchase bonds with conversion rights. Basic conversion terms are typically set forth on the face of the bond, with further information in the accompanying bond contract. Bonds often have limitations within which the bondholder must exercise conversion rights, if they are to be exercised at all.

Redemption

Debt securities are often issued with a redemption right granted to the corporation. The right of redemption allows the corporation to buy back its securities on terms specified by the bond agreement. Often the corporation must notify the bondholder of its decision to exercise its right of redemption, and there is often a specified time after notice within which the conversion rights must be exercised.

Review Questions

1. The owners of A & S Marketing, Inc. need financing to expand their business. A & S has only three shareholders and few assets. However, they do have a marketing plan for substantial, sustained growth in revenue. What type of financing may be most beneficial to the owners of A & S Marketing, Inc.? Why?

2. What are some of the factors to be considered when deciding on the authorized stock of a corporation?

3. The articles of incorporation of the Jerry Corporation authorize "10,000 shares of stock, no par value." No further information is given in the articles. Are these shares of common stock or preferred stock?

4. What two widely accepted requirements must be granted to shareholders under the Model Business Corporation Act?

5. Are all common stockholders always granted voting rights?

6. What are redemption rights?

7. What are conversion rights?

8. What are some possible drawbacks to issuing stock with a par value?

9. What information is typically required to be included on stock certificates?

10. The authorized stock of Rob's Boatworks, Inc. is 10,000 shares of common stock, $1.00 par value. If Rob's Boatworks issues 1,000 shares to Bud Peterson for $800, what term is used to describe Mr. Peterson's shares? What are the possible consequences to Mr. Peterson?

Notes

[1] 18A AM. JUR. 2d *Corporations* § 431 (1985).

[2] *Id.* § 438.

[3] *Id.*

[4] 18A AM. JUR. 2d *Corporations* § 452 (1985).

[5] 1984 Revised Model Business Corporation Act § 6.22.

[6] 18A AM. JUR. 2d *Corporations* § 453 (1985).

[7] 1984 Revised Model Business Corporation Act § 6.21(c).

[8] *Id.* § 6.26.

9 *Id.* § 6.25(c).

10 *Id.* § 6.31.

11 18A AM. JUR. 2d *Corporations* § 1185 (1985).

12 1984 Revised Model Business Corporation Act § 6.40(c).

13 18B AM. JUR. 2d *Corporations* § 1175 (1985).

14 *Id.* § 1185.

15 *Englander v. Osborne*, 261 Pa. 366, 104 A. 614, 6 ALR 800 (1918).

16 18B AM. JUR. 2d *Corporations* § 1207 (1985).

17 *Id.* § 1283.

CHAPTER 9

PUBLIC CORPORATIONS AND SECURITIES REGULATIONS

Introduction

Securities regulation of public corporations is a very complex topic that is often treated separately from the law of corporations. However, because many corporate paralegals spend a significant portion of their time working with matters related to securities, and because this topic is generally not addressed in separate paralegal texts, this chapter gives a brief overview of the effect of securities regulation on public corporations. It discusses certain aspects of the public corporation, including the distinction between public and closely held corporations, and then examines the markets in which securities are traded, the Securities and Exchange Commission, the federal regulations imposed by the Securities Act of 1933 and the Securities and Exchange Act of 1934, and state securities regulations or "blue sky laws." This chapter concludes with a look at the paralegal's role in working with securities matters and discusses the resources available in this area.

§ 9.1 The Public Corporation

Although public corporations represent only a small percentage of all corporations in the United States, their enormous economic impact in this country is immeasurable. During 1992, the profits of the top 100 industrial public corporations in the United States exceeded $71 billion.[1]

In contrast to the closely held corporation, the public corporation has a public market for its shares, regardless of the size of the corporation. During 1990, one out of every four adults in the United States was a shareholder of a public corporation.[2] Also unlike the securities of closely held corporations, securities that are offered and traded publicly are subject to federal securities regulations. Any securities offered, sold, or delivered through any means of interstate commerce (including the United States Postal Service) are considered to be part of a **public offering**, and must first be registered in accordance with the Securities Act of 1933 and any applicable state securities regulations. When a corporation decides to sell its securities to the public, it is often referred to as *going public*, and the first offering of a corporation's securities to the public is often referred to as the **initial public offering**.

Initial public offerings were very popular during the 1980s, with record numbers of corporations going public. The early 1990s have sustained that growth. During 1992, the value of initial public stock offerings was over $88 billion.[3] See Figure 9-1. Although the second half of the decade may not match the magnitude of the initial public offerings of recent years, initial public offerings are sure to be of great consequence into the next century.

The decision to go public with a corporation is typically made by the directors and principal shareholders of a corporation, with the advice of their attorneys and accountants. Going public with a corporation has significant ramifications for the company's future as well as the future stake of its shareholders.

The most obvious advantage to going public is the increased availability of capital, which can be acquired through the sale of stock, and the potential increase in the availability of future capital because of the corporation's ability to offer investors a security that is liquid and has an ascertainable market value. Public corporations also may have an advantage over closely held corporations when it comes to hiring and retaining qualified personnel. The public corporation may be able to offer the added incentive of stock options, bonuses, and other incentives. In addition, the corporation that goes public often has the advantage of gaining national exposure for itself and its products or services.

When making the decision to go public, there also are considerable disadvantages that must be weighed, including the fact that the current shareholders of the corporation will experience a certain loss of control, especially in matters requiring shareholder approval. The cost of going public and complying with the federal and state securities regulations that are imposed on public corporations can be significant. Also, the federal and state reporting regulations to which public corporations are

───────────────── **TERMS** ─────────────────

public offering[†]   Securities offered for sale to the public at a particular time by a corporation or by government.

initial public offering   The first offering of a corporation's securities to the public.

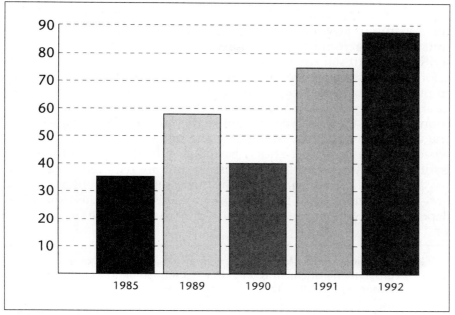

FIGURE 9-1 Total New Securities Issued by Corporations—Common and Preferred Stock in Billions of Dollars

subject require disclosure to shareholders regarding the corporation's financial condition and its management and business operation. These regulations can impose a significant burden on a corporation, both financially and on the time of the corporation's management.

After the decision to go public is made, an agreement is entered into between the issuer of the securities and the underwriter for the initial public offering. The *issuer of securities* is any person who issues or proposes to issue securities, including one who promotes the sale of a corporation not yet in existence.[4] The **underwriter** is any person or organization that purchases securities from an issuer, with a view to distribution of those securities, or any person who offers or sells, or participates in the offer or sale for an issuer, of any security.[5] Large financial institutions and brokers typically serve as underwriters, who purchase the securities from the issuer and in turn sell those securities to dealers for resale.

TERMS

underwriter With regard to securities offerings, any person or organization that purchases securities from an issuer with a view to distributing them, or any person who offers or sells or participates in the offer or sale for an issuer of any security.

The issuers and underwriters agree to the terms and details of their relationship in an underwriting agreement. The issuer may enter into underwriting agreements with more than one underwriter. The underwriters agree to sell the securities on a "firm commitment" or "best-efforts" basis. If the underwriters give a firm commitment, they commit to purchasing an agreed-upon amount of securities of the corporation at an agreed-upon price; the resale of those securities becomes the responsibility of the underwriters. Unlike the firm commitment, whereby the underwriter assumes the risk for the sale of the securities, underwriters selling on a best-efforts basis are obligated to use their best efforts to sell the securities of the issuer, but are required to take and pay for only those securities that they may sell to the public. When a best-efforts arrangement is made, the proceeds paid to the issuers will depend on the amount of securities sold by the underwriters.

SIDEBAR

After a decision is made to go public with a corporation, one of the first steps taken by corporate management is often to enter into an underwriting agreement with one or more underwriters for the sale of the corporation's stock.

§ 9.2 Securities and Securities Markets

When a corporation goes public, it is offering shares of the corporation to the public in the form of securities. Those securities are then traded on a market.

Definition of Securities

The **securities** offered when a corporation goes public are usually in the form of stocks, bonds, or debentures. However, securities can take

TERMS

securities[†] Certificates that represent a right to share in the profits of a company or in the distribution of its assets, or in a debt owed by a company or by the government. (EXAMPLES: stocks; bonds; notes with interest coupons; any registered security.) What is and is not a "security" differs to some degree under different statutes, for EXAMPLE, the securities acts, the Bankruptcy Code, the Uniform Commercial Code, and the Internal Revenue Code. Generally speaking, however, under most legislation, a security is an instrument of a type commonly dealt in on securities exchanges or in similar markets and is commonly recognized as a means of investment.

Dividends

The Paralegal As an "Insider"

Suppose that one of your first duties in your new paralegal position is to organize the file of the XYZ Corporation, a publicly held corporation, and to assemble information to be discussed at an upcoming board of directors' meeting. On review of the XYZ Corporation's preliminary financial statements, you notice that the XYZ Corporation has had a surprisingly good year. The financial forecast for the upcoming year also looks very good. With this in mind, you decide that it might be fun to buy some stock in the XYZ Corporation, just 100 shares or so.

Is this a smart move? Should you be congratulated, or sent to prison? According to the Securities and Exchange Commission, you may be guilty of *insider trading,* a criminal offense punishable by fine or imprisonment. Individuals who are in a position to obtain information on a corporation that is not generally available to the public and who use that information to their unfair advantage are considered to be guilty of insider trading.

In recent years, the SEC has spent considerable time and effort on detecting and prosecuting violators of the insider trading rules. Although most of this time and attention has been focused on the "big guys" on Wall Street, the SEC has also expanded its efforts to include lawyers and law firm personnel. Lawyers found to be in violation of the rules under the Securities Exchange Act are subject to sanctions under state bar association disciplinary rules, in addition to possible criminal prosecution and civil lawsuits

brought by shareholders. The Model Code of Professional Responsibility Disciplinary Rule 4-101, which has been adopted by many states, requires that an attorney shall not knowingly reveal a client's confidences or secrets or use such information to his or her advantage. Further, Disciplinary Rule 4-101 provides that an attorney must use such care as is necessary to prevent his or her employees from disclosing confidential information concerning a client, or from acting on that confidential information to their advantage.

Because the penalties for insider trading can be imposed on members of a law firm's staff, most law firms that represent publicly held corporations have written policies that must be adhered to by all office personnel. Effective law firm policies regarding trading in the securities of corporations represented by the firm serve to educate the firm's personnel about the potential risks involved in such trading. Such policies often place restrictions on trading in the securities of a corporation that the law firm represents by all individuals who may even appear to have access to inside information.

The best policy for you, as a paralegal who may be in doubt as to whether you are at risk of violating insider trading rules, is to cease any trading in the securities of corporations represented by the law firm, at least until you have had a chance to talk with a securities attorney within the firm who can advise you of your potential risks.   ▮▮▮

---

on many different forms. In *SEC v. W. J. Howey Co.*, 328 U.S. 293 (1946), the Supreme Court found that the sale of individual rows of orange trees in conjunction with a service contract for maintenance of the trees and the marketing of their crop involved a "security." The test used by the Supreme Court to detect a security was whether "the person invests his money in a common enterprise and is led to expect profits solely from the efforts of the promoter or a third party." Several types of instruments are generally recognized as securities under federal regulations, including

> any note, stock, treasury stock, bond, debenture, evidence of indebtedness, certificate of interest or participation in any profit-sharing agreement, collateral-trust certificate, preorganization certificate or subscription, transferable share, investment contract, voting-trust certificate, certificate of deposit for a security, fractional undivided interest in oil, gas, or other mineral rights, or, in general, any interest or instrument commonly known as a "security," or any certificate of interest or participation in, temporary or interim certificate for, receipt for, guarantee of, or warrant or right to subscribe to or purchase, any of the foregoing.[6]

Markets

After a decision is made to take a corporation public, the decision must be made as to the best vehicle to trade the corporation's securities. The securities of a publicly held corporation may be traded at a stock **exchange** or **over the counter**. Trading on either of these types of markets is not confined to stock, but may also include bonds and many other types of securities, both corporate and governmental.

Both stock exchanges and over-the-counter markets are subject to significant federal regulation, and the type of market chosen for trading will depend upon the circumstances surrounding the securities offering.

Generally, over-the-counter trading has been subject to less stringent regulation than trading on exchanges. However, the regulation of the Securities Exchange Act of 1934 applies to over-the-counter trading, and the Securities Exchange Commission (SEC) has authority over both types of trading.

In addition to the regulations imposed directly by the Securities and Exchange Commission, both the exchanges and the over-the-counter markets are self-regulating to a certain extent. The exchanges, such as the New York Stock Exchange (NYSE), have regulated themselves since before the formation of the SEC, and continue to do so by imposing rules relating to the transactions on their exchanges as well as

---

TERMS

exchange[†]   A place of business where the marketing of securities is conducted; a stock exchange; a securities exchange.

over the counter   Securities market that has no actual physical location; the market consists of transactions that take place through a series of computer networks among broker-dealers.

rules relating to the members of the exchanges. The Securities and Exchange Act of 1934 provides for the formation of self-regulating "national securities associations" of over-the-counter markets, such as the National Association of Securities Dealers (the NASD).

Soon after a decision is made by corporate management to go public with the corporation, a decision must be made as to where to trade the stock of the corporation—on an exchange or over the counter.

Exchanges

An exchange is considered to be

any organization, association, or group of persons, whether incorporated or unincorporated, which constitutes, maintains, or provides a market place or facilities for bringing together purchasers and sellers of securities or for otherwise performing with respect to securities the functions commonly performed by a stock exchange as that term is generally understood, and includes the market place and the market facilities maintained by such exchange.[7]

The largest stock exchange in the United States is the New York Stock Exchange. The market value of the sales and exchanges on the New York Stock Exchange in 1992 exceeded $2 trillion.[8]

Securities traded on an exchange are traded on the floor of an exchange by members of the exchange. When trading securities on a stock exchange, only a registered firm acting as a specialist for a particular stock may act as a dealer for that stock on the floor of the exchange. Any other stock broker wishing to buy or sell that particular security must act through the designated specialist for that security.

Over-the-Counter Markets

Over-the-counter markets differ from exchanges in that they are not represented by actual physical locations. Over-the-counter transactions take place through a series of computer networks, among broker-dealers. Unlike securities traded on an exchange, more than one firm may act as a broker-dealer for any particular security.

NASDAQ, which was created in 1971, is an electronic automated quotation system for selected over-the-counter securities which has gained in popularity in recent years. With NASDAQ, dealers can insert, and instantaneously update, bid and asked quotations for certain securities that are traded over the counter. In 1993 more than 4,600 companies were listed on NASDAQ.[9] In 1994 NASDAQ actually surpassed the NYSE in the number of shares traded on its exchange [10] (Figure 9-2.)

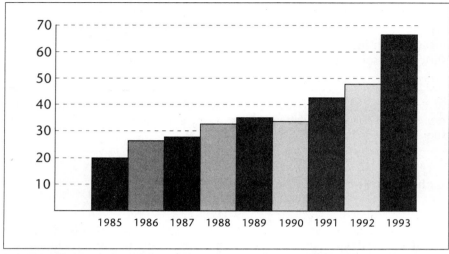

FIGURE 9-2   Annual Trading Volume on NASDAQ—Shares in Billions

§ 9.3 The Securities and Exchange Commission

Prior to enactment of the Securities Exchange Act of 1934, the only federal regulation of securities was under the jurisdiction of the Federal Trade Commission. The enactment of the Securities Exchange Act of 1934 created the **Securities and Exchange Commission** (SEC). The SEC is headed by five presidential appointees, each appointed for five years. Not more than three of the members of the SEC may be of the same political party.

The SEC does not have the authority to rule upon what securities may be issued. However, it does have the authority to impose disclosure requirements upon corporations that are offering securities to the public, through enforcement of the Securities Act of 1933, which relates to the initial registration and issuance of securities through means of interstate commerce, and the Securities Exchange Act of 1934, which relates to ongoing public disclosures by publicly held corporations and requires registration of all over-the-counter brokers and dealers of securities and stock exchanges.

TERMS

Securities and Exchange Commission [†]   The agency that administers and enforces federal statutes relating to securities, including the Securities Act of 1933 and the Securities Exchange Act.

§ 9.4 Federal Regulation of Securities Offerings Under the Securities Act of 1933

Underlying the attempt to regulate securities is the generally accepted belief that "absent some type of governmental control in the area of the issuance of and transactions in securities, some opportunistic and often unscrupulous issuers and dealers in securities will defraud naive or unsophisticated purchasers."[11] Initial attempts to protect investors were at the state level, with the enactment of state statutes to regulate securities offered within each state. The **Securities Act of 1933** (the Securities Act) was the first significant federal legislation to be passed. It was intended to protect the investor through the imposition of disclosure and anti-fraud requirements on corporations issuing securities through means of interstate commerce.

The SEC may prevent the distribution of securities if the disclosure requirements of the Securities Act are not complied with. Further, material misstatements in the disclosure documents or noncompliance with the anti-fraud provisions of the Securities Act may subject the issuer of the securities to civil liabilities or even criminal sanctions. The most significant provisions of the Securities Act for the corporation that is going public are the requirements for registering the securities to be offered to the public and for using prospectuses for the sale of all registered securities.

SIDEBAR

Unless otherwise exempt under the Securities Act of 1933, all securities offered for sale to the public must first be registered with the SEC.

Part I of the registration statement consists of a propsectus that contains pertinent information concerning the corporation, the issuer, and the underwriters. This information will become public information.

Securities Registration

Prior to the issuance of any securities through interstate commerce, the issuer must file a registration statement with the SEC. The intended purpose of the registration statement is to disclose the information necessary to allow investors to make an informed decision.

TERMS

Securities Act of 1933[†] The federal statute regulating the issuance and sale of securities to the public.

Section 5 of the Securities Act contains the major provisions regarding the registration of securities. Section 5(a) prohibits the sale and delivery of unregistered securities.

> Section 5. (a) Unless a registration statement is in effect as to a security, it shall be unlawful for any person, directly or indirectly—
> (1) to make use of any means or instruments of transportation or communication in interstate commerce or of the mails to sell such security through the use or medium of any prospectus or otherwise; or
> (2) to carry or cause to be carried through the mails or in interstate commerce, by any means or instruments of transportation, any such security for the purpose of sale or for delivery after sale.

The registration statement is filed electronically in the form prescribed by the SEC. Form S-1 (see Figure 9-3) is commonly used. However, several other forms are prescribed for certain types of registrations.

The registration statement consists of two parts. Part I is the prospectus, which must be furnished to all purchasers of the corporation's securities. Part II consists of additional information required by the SEC, which will become available for inspection at the office of the SEC, including information with respect to the securities being offered for sale, the corporation, the issuer, and the underwriters. The information required by the registration statement is set forth in Schedule A of the Securities Act (see Figure 9-4).

The registration statement is filed with the SEC and must be accompanied by a filing fee that is equal to one-fiftieth of one percent of the maximum aggregate price at which the securities are proposed to be offered. There is a minimum fee of $100. The registration statement is considered to be filed, but not effective, on the date it is received by the SEC with the proper fee.

The registration statement is effective twenty days from the date of filing with the SEC, unless an accelerated date is requested by the issuer and granted by the SEC. If any amendment to the registration statement is filed prior to its effective date, the date of filing is deemed to be the date on which the amendment was filed, unless the amendment was ordered or approved by the SEC. The SEC has the power to accelerate the effective date and generally will do so, provided that the issuer has submitted all necessary information and acts quickly to furnish the SEC with any different or additional information requested. The SEC also has the power to delay the effective date of any registration statement that is "on its face incomplete or inaccurate in any material respect,"[12] by refusing to permit the registration statement to become effective until after it has been amended in accordance with a notice served upon the issuer not later than ten days after the filing of the registration statement. If, after the effective date of the registration

FIGURE 9-3
SEC Form S-1

OMB APPROVAL	
OMB Number:	3235-0065
Expires:	May 31, 1994
Estimated average burden hours per response . 1258.00	

UNITED STATES
SECURITIES AND EXCHANGE COMMISSION
Washington, D.C. 20549

FORM S-1

REGISTRATION STATEMENT UNDER THE SECURITIES ACT OF 1933

_____
(Exact name of registrant as specified in its charter)

_____
(State or other jurisdiction of incorporation or organization)

_____
(Primary Standard Industrial Classification Code Number)

_____
(I.R.S. Employer Identification Number)

_____
(Address, including zip code, and telephone number,
including area code, of registrant's principal executive offices)

_____
(Name, address, including zip code, and telephone number,
including area code, of agent for service)

_____
(Approximate date of commencement of proposed sale to the public)

If any of the securities being registered on this Form are to be offered on a delayed or continuous basis pursuant to Rule 415 under the Securities Act of 1933 check the following box: ☐

Calculation of Registration Fee

Title of Each Class of Securities to be Registered	Amount to be Registered	Proposed Maximum Offering Price Per Unit	Proposed Maximum Aggregate Offering Price	Amount of Registration Fee

SEC 870 (8/91) 1 of 5

statement, it appears to the SEC that the registration statement includes any untrue statements of material fact, or omits to state any material fact required to be stated therein, the SEC may issue a _stop order_ suspending the effectiveness of the registration statement until such time as the registration statement has been amended in accordance with the stop order.

After the registration statement has been filed, a waiting period begins and lasts until the registration statement is effective. During this waiting period, securities may be offered for sale, but they may not actually be sold until the registration statement becomes effective. During the waiting period, preliminary prospectuses may be used to offer for sale securities that will be sold after the effective date of the registration

FIGURE 9-4
Securities Act
of 1933,
Schedule A

SCHEDULE A

(1) The name under which the issuer is doing or intends to do business;

(2) the name of the State or other sovereign power under which the issuer is organized;

(3) the location of the issuer's principal business office, and if the issuer is a foreign or territorial person, the name and address of its agent in the United States authorized to receive notice;

(4) the names and addresses of the directors or persons performing similar functions, and the chief executive, financial and accounting officers, chosen or to be chosen if the issuer be a corporation, association, trust or other entity; of all partners, if the issuer be a partnership; and of the issuer, if the issuer be an individual; and of the promoters in the case of a business to be formed, or formed within two years prior to the filing of the registration statement;

(5) the names and addresses of the underwriters;

(6) the names and addresses of all persons, if any, owning of record or beneficially, if known, more than 10 per centum of any class of stock of the issuer, or more than 10 per centum in the aggregate of the outstanding stock of the issuer as of a date within 20 days prior to the filing of the registration statement;

(7) the amount of securities of the issuer held by any person specified in paragraphs (4), (5), and (6) of this schedule, as of a date within 20 days prior to the filing of the registration statement, and, if possible, as of one year prior thereto, and the amount of the securities, for which the registration statement is filed, to which such persons have indicated their intention to subscribe;

(8) the general character of the business actually transacted or to be transacted by the issuer;

(9) a statement of the capitalization of the issuer, including the authorized and outstanding amounts of its capital stock and the proportion thereof paid up, the number and classes of shares in which such capital stock is divided, par value thereof, or if it has no par value, the stated or assigned value thereof, a description of the respective voting rights, preferences, conversion and exchange rights, rights to dividends, profits, or capital of each class, with respect to each other class, including the retirement and liquidation rights or values thereof;

(10) a statement of the securities, if any, covered by options outstanding or to be created in connection with the security to be offered, together with the names and addresses of all persons, if any, to be allotted more than 10 per centum in the aggregate of such options;

(11) the amount of capital stock of each class issued or included in the shares of stock to be offered;

(12) the amount of the funded debt outstanding and to be created by the security to be offered, with a brief description of the date, maturity, and character of such debt, rate of interest, character of amortization provisions, and the security, if any, therefor. If substitution of any security is permissible, a summarized statement of the conditions under which such substitution is permitted. If substitution is permissible without notice, a specific statement to that effect;

(13) the specific purposes in detail and the approximate amounts to be devoted to such purposes, so far as determinable, for which the security to be offered is to supply funds, and if the funds are to be raised in part from other sources, the amounts thereof and the sources thereof, shall be stated;

(14) the remuneration, paid or estimated to be paid, by the issuer or its predecessor, directly or indirectly, during the past year and ensuing year to (a) the directors or persons performing similar functions, and (b) its officers and other persons, naming them wherever such remuneration exceeded $25,000 during any such year;

(15) the estimated net proceeds to be derived from the security to be offered;

(16) the price at which it is proposed that the security shall be offered to the public or the method by which such price is computed and any variation therefrom at which any portion of such security is proposed to be offered to any persons or classes of persons, other than the underwriters, naming them or specifying the class. A variation in price may be proposed prior to the date of the public offering of the security, but the Commission shall immediately be notified of such variation;

(17) all commissions or discounts paid or to be paid, directly or indirectly, by the issuer to the underwriters in respect of the sale of the security to be offered. Commissions shall include all cash, securities, contracts, or anything else of value, paid, to be set aside, disposed of, or understandings with or for the benefit of any other persons in which any underwriter is interested, made, in connection with the sale of such security. A commission paid or to be paid in connection with the sale of such security by a person in which the issuer has an interest or which is controlled by, or under common control with, the issuer shall be deemed to have been paid by the issuer. Where any such commission is paid, the amount of such commission paid to each underwriter shall be stated;

statement. After the registration statement becomes effective, the securities may be sold through use of a prospectus.

SIDEBAR

The effective date of the registration statement is twenty days after it is filed, unless the effective date is accelerated or delayed by the SEC.

FIGURE 9-4
(continued)

(18) the amount or estimated amounts, itemized in reasonable detail, of expenses, other than commissions specified in paragraph (17) of this schedule, incurred or borne by or for the account of the issuer in connection with the sale or the security to be offered or properly chargeable thereto, including legal, engineering, certification, authentication, and other charges;

(19) the net proceeds derived from any security sold by the issuer during the two years preceding the filing of the registration statement, the price at which such security was offered to the public, and the names of the principal underwriters of such security;

(20) any amount paid within two years preceding the filing of the registration statement or intended to be paid to any promoter and the consideration for any such payment;

(21) the names and addresses of the vendors and the purchase price of any property, or good will, acquired or to be acquired, not in the ordinary course of business, which is to be defrayed in whole or in part from the proceeds of the security to be offered, the amount of any commission payable to any person in connection with such acquisition, and the name or names of such person or persons, together with any expense incurred or to be incurred in connection with such acquisition, including the cost of borrowing money to finance such acquisition;

(22) full particulars of the nature and extent of the interest, if any, of every director, principal executive officer, and of every stockholder holding more than 10 per centum of any class of stock or more than 10 per centum in the aggregate of the stock of the issuer, in any property acquired, not in the ordinary course of business of the issuer, within two years preceding the filing of the registration statement or proposed to be acquired at such date;

(23) the names and addresses of counsel who have passed on the legality of the issue;

(24) dates of and parties to, and the general effect concisely stated of every material contract made, not in the ordinary course of business, which contract is to be executed in whole or in part at or after the filing of the registration statement or which contract has been made not more than two years before such filing. Any management contract or contract providing for special bonuses or profit-sharing arrangements, and every material patent or contract for a material patent right, and every contract by or with a public utility company or an affiliate thereof, providing for the giving or receiving of technical or financial advice or service (if such contract may involve a charge to any party thereto at a rate in excess of $2,500 per year in cash or securities or anything else of value), shall be deemed a material contract;

(25) a balance sheet as of a date not more than ninety days prior to the date of the filing of the registration statement showing all of the assets of the issuer, the nature and cost thereof, whenever determinable, in such detail and in such form as the Commission shall prescribe (with intangible items segregated), including any loan in excess of $20,000 to any officer, director, stockholder or person directly or indirectly controlling or controlled by the issuer, or person under direct or indirect common control with the issuer. All the liabilities of the issuer in such detail and such form as the Commission shall prescribe, including surplus of the issuer showing how and from what sources such surplus was created, all as of a date not more than ninety days prior to the filing of the registration statement. If such statement be not certified by an independent public or certified accountant, in addition to the balance sheet required to be submitted under this schedule, a similar detailed balance sheet of the assets and liabilities of the issuer, certified by an independent public or certified accountant, of a date not more than one year prior to the filing of the registration statement, shall be submitted;

(26) a profit and loss statement of the issuer showing earnings and income, the nature and source thereof, and the expenses and fixed charges in such detail and such form as the Commission shall prescribe for the latest fiscal year for which such statement is available and for the two preceding fiscal years, year by year, or, if such issuer has been in actual business for less than three years, then for such time as the issuer has been in actual business, year by year. If the date of the filing of the registration statement is more than six months after the close of the last fiscal year, a statement from such closing date to the latest practicable date. Such statement shall show what the practice of the issuer has been during the three years or lesser period as to the character of the charges, dividends or other distributions made against its various surplus accounts, and as to depreciation, depletion, and maintenance charges, in such detail and form as the Commission shall prescribe, and if stock dividends or avails from the sale of rights have been credited to income, they shall be shown separately with a statement of the basis upon which the credit is computed. Such statement shall also differentiate between any recurring and non-recurring income and between any investment and operating income. Such statement shall be certified by an independent public or certified accountant;

(27) if the proceeds, or any part of the proceeds, of the security to be issued is to be applied directly or indirectly to the purchase of any business, a profit and loss statement of such business certified by an independent public or certified accountant, meeting the requirements of paragraph (26) of this schedule, for the three preceding fiscal years, together with a balance sheet, similarly certified, or such business, meeting the requirements of paragraph (25) of this schedule of a date not more than ninety days prior to the filing of the registration statement or at the date such business was acquired by the issuer if the business was acquired by the issuer more than ninety days prior to the filing of the registration statement;

(28) a copy of any agreement or agreements (or, if identical agreements are used, the forms thereof) made with any underwriter, including all contracts and agreements referred to in paragraph (17) of this schedule;

Prospectus Requirements

The **prospectus**, which constitutes part I of the registration statement, contains disclosures required by the SEC, including information

TERMS

prospectus † A statement published by a corporation that provides information concerning stock or other securities it is offering for sale to the

FIGURE 9-4
(continued)

(29) a copy of the opinion or opinions of counsel in respect to the legality of the issue, with a translation of such opinion, when necessary, into the English language;

(30) a copy of all material contracts referred to in paragraph (24) of this schedule, but no disclosure shall be required of any portion of any such contract if the Commission determines that disclosure of such portion would impair the value of the contract and would not be necessary for the protection of investors;

(31) unless previously filed and registered under the provisions of this title, and brought up to date, (a) a copy of its articles of incorporation, with all amendments thereof and of its existing by-laws or instruments corresponding thereto, whatever the name, if the issuer be a corporation; (b) copy of all instruments by which the trust is created or declared, if the issuer is a trust; (c) a copy of its articles of partnership or association and all other papers pertaining to its organization, if the issuer is a partnership, unincorporated association, joint-stock company, or any other form of organization; and

(32) a copy of the underlying agreements or indentures affecting any stock, bonds, or debentures offered or to be offered.

In case of certificates of deposit, voting trust certificates, collateral trust certificates, certificates of interest or shares in unincorporated investment trusts, equipment trust certificates, interim or other receipts for certificates, and like securities, the Commission shall establish rules and regulations requiring the submission of information of a like character applicable to such cases, together with such other information as it may deem appropriate and necessary regarding the character, financial or otherwise, of the actual issuer of the securities and/or the person performing the acts and assuming the duties of depositor or manager.

regarding the corporation, its assets, its officers and directors, and other information material to the business of the corporation. It must be furnished to the purchaser of the securities after the securities have been registered with the SEC.

Section 5(b) of the Securities Act prohibits the use of any prospectus to sell securities, unless the prospectus meets the requirements of the Securities Act, and it prohibits the sale of securities without a prospectus.

(b) It shall be unlawful for any person, directly or indirectly—
   (1) to make use of any means or instruments of transportation or communication in interstate commerce or of the mails to carry or transmit any prospectus relating to any security with respect to which a registration statement has been filed under this title, unless such prospectus meets the requirements of section 10; or
   (2) to carry or cause to be carried through the mails or in interstate commerce any such security for the purpose of sale or for delivery after sale, unless accompanied or preceded by a prospectus that meets the requirements of subsection (a) of section 10.

Notwithstanding this rule, a preliminary prospectus without the offering price and related information may be used by the issuer of securities during the waiting period to inform prospective buyers of the nature of the securities to be sold. Prospectuses used before the effective date of a registration statement are often called **red herring prospectuses**

TERMS

public. The contents of a prospectus are regulated by the Securities Exchange Commission.

red herring prospectus Preliminary prospectus that may be used after the filing, but prior to the effective date, of the registration statement. Contains

because, pursuant to Regulation § 229.501(c)(8), they are required to contain the following legend on the outside front cover in red ink:

> Information contained herein is subject to completion or amendment. A registration statement relating to these securities has been filed with the Securities and Exchange Commission. These securities may not be sold nor may offers to buy be accepted prior to the time the registration statement becomes effective. This prospectus shall not constitute an offer to sell or the solicitation of an offer to buy nor shall there be any sale of these securities in any State in which such offer, solicitation or sale would be unlawful prior to registration or qualification under the securities laws of any such state.

The red herring prospectus must specifically state that sales may not be made until the effective date of the registration statement.

SIDEBAR

Also commonly used during the waiting period, to announce a securities offering and to disseminate certain information regarding the offering, are **tombstone ads**. Tombstone advertisements are not considered to be prospectuses and are not subject to the requirements set forth for prospectuses in the Rules to the Securities Act. However, they must follow certain guidelines and contain certain legends prescribed by the rules. Tombstone ads are frequently found in the business section of major newspapers and are surrounded by a thick black border, which accounts for their name. Figure 9-5 shows a tombstone ad.

§ 9.5 Exemptions from the Registration Requirements of the Securities Act of 1933

Not all securities and transactions involving securities are subject to the registration requirements of the Securities Act. An issue of securities may be exempt from registration because of either the type or class of the securities, or the specific transaction involving the securities.

TERMS

a legend on the front cover in red ink stating specifically that no securities may be sold until the registration statement becomes effective.

tombstone ads   Ads surrounded by a heavy black border and commonly placed in newspapers to announce a securities offering and disseminate certain information regarding the offering.

TABLE 9-1 MAJOR PROVISIONS OF THE SECURITIES ACT OF 1933

- Securities that are issued through interstate commerce must be registered by filing a registration statement with the Securities and Exchange Commission (§ 5(a))
- Prospectuses, which are used to solicit sales of securities, must be approved by the Securities and Exchange Commission (§ 5(b))
- Every person who signs or contributes information to the registration statement has a duty to provide complete and accurate information (§ 11)
- Fraudulent conduct with respect to the sale or offer to sell securities is prohibited (§ 17)

FIGURE 9-5
Tombstone
Advertisement

1,875,000 Shares

BRAUNS

FASHIONS CORPORATION

Common Stock

Price $7 Per Share

This announcement is neither an offer to sell nor a solicitation of offers to buy any of these securities. The offering is made only by the Prospectus, copies of which may be obtained in any State in which this announcement is circulated from only such of the undersigned or other dealers or brokers as may lawfully offer these securities in such State.

Piper, Jaffray & Hopwood
Incorporated

Wessels, Arnold & Henderson

A.G. Edwards & Sons, Inc.   Advest, Inc.   William Blair & Company   J. C. Bradford & Co.

Cowen & Company   Dain Bosworth   First Albany Corporation   Furman Selz
Incorporated   Incorporated

Kemper Securities Group, Inc.   Ladenburg, Thalmann & Co. Inc.

Legg Mason Wood Walker   McDonald & Company   Raymond James & Associates, Inc.
Incorporated   Securities, Inc.

The Robinson-Humphrey Company, Inc.   Tucker Anthony   Wheat First Butcher & Singer
Incorporated   Capital Markets

Robert W. Baird & Co.   The Chicago Corporation   First of Michigan Corporation
Incorporated

Stifel, Nicolaus & Company   Cleary Gull Reiland & McDevitt Inc.
Incorporated

Craig-Hallum, Inc.   John G. Kinnard and Company
Incorporated

March 31, 1992

Exemption from the registration requirements of the Securities Act does not guarantee exemption from the other provisions of the Securities Act or related securities regulations, especially the anti-fraud provisions. In addition, the issuer of securities that qualify under one of the exemptions may not be required to *register* the securities, but may be required to file other disclosure documentation with the SEC.

Exempted Securities

Section 3 of the Securities Act specifies certain classes of securities that are exempted from the registration provisions of the Act. Some of the securities exempted by this section include:

1. Certain securities issued or guaranteed by the United States or state or local governments
2. Certain securities issued or guaranteed by banks
3. Industrial development bonds
4. Short-term commercial paper, including certain notes, drafts, or bills of exchange
5. Securities of nonprofit issuers
6. Securities issued by certain savings and loan associations, building and loan associations, cooperative banks, homestead associations, or similar institutions
7. Interests in railroad equipment trusts
8. Certificates issued by receivers, trustees, or debtors in possession in a case under Title 11 of the United States Code (the Bankruptcy Code), with the approval of the court
9. Insurance or endowment policies, annuity contracts, and optional annuity contracts
10. Certain securities exchanged by the issuer when no commission or other remuneration is paid or given for soliciting such exchange
11. Securities that are sold only to residents of a single state or territory if the issuer is both a resident of and doing business within that state or territory.

In addition, Section 3(b) of the Securities Act gives the SEC authority to exempt other classes of securities from its rules and regulations, provided that the aggregate amount of the issue does not exceed $5 million. Section 3(c) gives the SEC that same authority with regard to securities issued by a small business investment company under the Small Business Investment Act of 1958.

Exemptions for Offerings Involving Limited Dollar Amounts

Section 3(b) of the Securities Act allows the SEC to exempt certain offerings from the registration requirements of the Act when the securities to be offered involve a relatively small dollar amount. Regulations A and D adopted by the SEC set forth the various conditions that must be met to qualify for this exemption.

Under Regulation A, the securities and the issuers must meet several criteria. A securities offering must not exceed $1.5 million in any twelve-month period. The issuer must file an offering statement, consisting of a notification, offering circular, and exhibits, with the SEC's regional office in the region in which the corporation's principal business activities are conducted. Regulation A registrations also permit a simplified registration with the SEC. This simplified registration procedure allows the financial statements required for filing with the SEC to be in a simplified format and unaudited. In addition, issuers that have registered under Regulation A need not file periodic reports with the SEC unless the issuers have more than $5 million in assets and more than 500 shareholders.

Regulation D establishes Rules 504, 505, and 506, which provide further conditions for exemptions from the registration requirements of the Securities Act. Rule 504 provides exemption from registration pursuant to the following conditions:

1. The sale of securities must not exceed $1 million in a twelve-month period.
2. There are no restrictions on the number of the purchasers of the securities under this exemption.
3. Securities exempted pursuant to Regulation D may not be offered through any form of general solicitation or general advertising.
4. A Form D notice must be filed with the SEC headquarters within fifteen days after the first sale of securities under this rule.

Rule 504 is available to all applicable issuer offerings other than an offering by a reporting company or an investment company.

Rule 505 offers exemption from registration pursuant to the following conditions:

1. The issuer may not sell securities totaling more than $5 million in any twelve-month period.
2. The issuer must file financial statements as specifically required by Rule 505.
3. The offering may not be made by means of a general solicitation or general advertising.

4. There is no restriction on the number of accredited investors to which the issuer may sell its securities.

5. The issuer may sell securities to no more than thirty-five non-accredited investors.

6. The issuer must make an effort to ensure that the purchase of its securities are for investment purposes only (not for resale).

7. Fifteen days after the first sale in the offering, the issuer must file a notice of sales on Form D.

An *accredited investor,* as defined in the Securities Act, includes:

1. Certain savings and loan associations

2. Certain private business development companies

3. Certain nonprofit organizations described in § 501(c)(3) of the Internal Revenue Code

4. Directors, executive officers, or general partners of the issuer of the securities being offered or sold, or any director, executive officer, or general partner of a general partner of that issuer

5. Individuals with a net worth, or joint net worth with that person's spouse, that at the time of the purchase exceeds $1 million

6. Individuals who have an income in excess of $200,000 in each of the two most recent years, or joint income with that person's spouse in excess of $300,000 in each of those years, and has a reasonable expectation of reaching the same income level in the current year

7. Certain trusts with total assets in excess of $5 million

8. Entities in which all of the equity owners are accredited investors.

Rule 506 provides the same dollar limits as Rule 505, but requires that the nonaccredited purchasers must have sufficient knowledge and experience. In essence, the securities may be offered only to investors of a certain level of sophistication.

Intrastate Offering Exemptions

Section 3(a)(11) of the Securities Act offers an exemption, commonly referred to as the *intrastate offering exemption,* for corporations that issue securities only within the state in which they are located and doing business. To qualify for the intrastate offering exemption, the issuer must meet the following conditions:

1. The issuer must be a corporation incorporated in the state in which it is making the offering.

2. The issuer must carry out a significant amount of its business in that state.

3. The issuer must make offerings and sales only to residents of that state.

The issuer has an obligation to ensure that each investor who purchases shares of the corporation is a resident of the state of the offering. If the corporation sells shares to investors who are not residents, or if residents resell their shares to nonresidents within nine months of the date the offering is completed, the issuer may lose the right to use the exemption. For this reason, the intrastate offering exemption is often used for relatively small offerings to a limited number of investors.

Exempted Transactions

Section 4 of the Securities Act sets forth certain transactions that are exempt from the registration requirements of the Act, including transactions by persons other than the issuer, underwriter, or dealer; private offerings; certain dealer transactions; certain broker transactions; transactions involving offers or sales of certain promissory notes; and transactions involving accredited investors. The discussion in this following section focuses on the transaction exemptions most commonly used.

Transactions by Persons Other Than Issuers, Underwriters, and Dealers

This exemption ordinarily permits investors to make casual sales of their securities holdings without registration. Transactions that are a part of the scheme of distribution do not qualify under this exemption, which is available only for routine trading transactions.

Exemption for Private Offerings (Private Placements)

Section 4(2) of the Securities Act provides an exemption from the registration requirements of the Act for the issuance of securities, by the issuer, that do not involve any "public offering." Exactly what is meant by *public offering* remains unclear. The SEC has reported that "[w]hether a transaction is one not involving any public offering is essentially a question of fact and necessitates a consideration of all surrounding circumstances, including such factors as the relationship between the offerees, and the issuer, the nature, scope, size, type and manner of the offering."[13] However, sales to employees and those who have access to information about the corporation generally are not considered to be public offerings, and thus qualify for the private placement exemption. To qualify for this exemption, the offering may not be made by public solicitation or general advertising, and the sale of the securities must generally be to individuals who have sufficient knowledge of the corporation to make an informed decision, or are able to bear the risk. The purchasers must have access to the type of information normally provided in a prospectus and must agree not to resell or distribute the securities. Another consideration of this exemption is the sophistication of the purchasers of the securities.

Exemptions for Offerings to Accredited Investors

The § 4(6) exemption provides further exemptions from registration for transactions involving offers and sales of securities by any issuer solely to one or more "accredited investors," as that term is defined in the Act, under certain conditions.

§ 9.6 Antifraud Provisions of the Securities Act

Antifraud provisions are found throughout the Securities Act of 1933. The prohibited acts or practices addressed in those provisions are not limited to the common law concept of fraud, but also include acts and practices that tend to be fraudulent in nature, such as the publication of misstatements or half-truths, devices directed toward market manipulation, and improper touting of securities being offered for sale.[14] These provisions, for jurisdictional reasons, apply to acts involving use of facilities of interstate commerce, the mails, or facilities of the registered National Securities Exchange.[15] The antifraud provisions of the Securities Act are of specific concern to the issuer and all other parties signing or otherwise responsible for the information contained in the registration statement.

Section 11

Every person who signs or contributes information to the registration statement has a duty to provide complete and accurate information. Failure to do so may provide the purchaser of securities with a cause of action under § 11 of the Securities Act for any damages stemming from the purchase of securities for which an inaccurate or misleading registration statement was filed. Section 11(a) of the Securities Act specifies when a purchaser may sue and who may be sued in conjunction with a registration statement containing untrue or misleading information:

Section 11. (a) In case any part of the registration statement, when such part became effective, contained an untrue statement of a material fact or omitted to state a material fact required to be stated therein or necessary to make the statements therein not misleading, any person acquiring such security (unless it is proved that at the time of such acquisition he knew of such untruth or omission) may, either at law or in equity, in any court of competent jurisdiction, sue—

(1) every person who signed the registration statement;

(2) every person who was a director of (or person performing similar functions) or partner in, the issuer at the time of the filing of the part of the registration statement with respect to which his liability is asserted;

(3) every person who, with his consent, is named in the registration statement as being or about to become a director, person performing similar functions, or partner;

(4) every accountant, engineer, or appraiser, or any person whose profession gives authority to a statement made by him, who has with his consent been named as having prepared or certified any part of the registration statement, or as having prepared or certified any report or valuation which is used in connection with the registration statement, with respect to the statement in such registration statement, report, or valuation, which purports to have been prepared or certified by him;

(5) every underwriter with respect to such security.

Obviously, it is not possible for every individual named in § 11(a) to be personally knowledgeable about the truth and validity of every statement in the registration statement. For that reason, the Securities Act provides several defenses to the liabilities in § 11. Section 11(b) provides that no persons, other than the issuer, shall be liable as provided therein if they can prove that: (1) they had resigned from the positions causing their relationships with the issuer; (2) if the registration statement became effective without their knowledge, they advised the SEC upon becoming aware of such fact, and they gave reasonable public notice that the registration statement became effective without their knowledge; or (3) they had, after reasonable investigation, reasonable ground to believe and did believe, the information to be true and accurate. This is referred to as the *due diligence* defense. Corporate directors and others who participate in preparing and filing registration statements and prospectuses relating to domestic securities are required to have made a reasonable investigation of all material facts before they may avail themselves of the statutory defense of due diligence.

SIDEBAR

Issuers, corporate directors, accountants, attorneys, underwriters, and all individuals who sign a registration statement containing untrue statements are in danger of being held liable for damages under § 11 of the Securities Act of 1933.

Section 17

Section 17 of the Securities Act is much broader in its scope than § 11. It prohibits fraudulent conduct with respect to securities transactions, and pertains to the sale of, or an offer to sell, securities, not to their purchase.

> Section 17. (a) It shall be unlawful for any person in the offer or sale of any securities by the use of any means or instruments of transportation or communication in interstate commerce or by the use of the mails, directly or indirectly —
> (1) to employ any device, scheme, or artifice to defraud, or
> (2) to obtain money or property by means of any untrue statement of a material fact or any omission to state a material fact necessary in order to make the statements made, in the light of the circumstances under which they were made, not misleading, or
> (3) to engage in any transaction, practice, or course of business which operates or would operate as a fraud or deceit upon the purchaser.
> (b) It shall be unlawful for any person, by the use of any means or instruments of transportation or communication in interstate commerce or by the use of the mails, to publish, give publicity to, or circulate any notice, circular, advertisement, newspaper, article, letter, investment service, or communication which, though not purporting to offer a security for sale, describes such security for a consideration received or to be received, directly or indirectly, from an issuer, underwriter, or dealer, without fully disclosing the receipt, whether past or prospective, of such consideration and the amount thereof.
> (c) The exemptions provided in section 3 shall not apply to the provisions of this section.

§ 9.7 Federal Regulations Imposed on Public Corporations Under the Securities Exchange Act of 1934

Whereas the Securities Act of 1933 deals primarily with the registration of initial issues of securities, the **Securities Exchange Act of 1934** (Exchange Act) pertains to dealings in securities subsequent to their initial issue and to ongoing reporting requirements. The aim of the Exchange Act is to protect securities investors and the general public by

TERMS

Securities Exchange Act of 1934 The federal statute that empowers the Securities and Exchange Commission to regulate securities exchanges.

regulating securities exchanges and markets, by providing information regarding the issuance of securities to persons who buy and sell securities, by preventing fraud in securities trading and manipulation of the markets, and by protecting the national credit by controlling the amount of such credit that may be used in the securities market.[16]

With regard to publicly traded corporations, the Exchange Act contains provisions requiring registration with the exchange on which the securities are traded. In addition, the Exchange Act contains provisions requiring periodic reporting to the exchanges and the SEC, and provisions regulating the use of proxies. The Exchange Act also contains several anti-fraud provisions that affect the public corporation and its officers, directors, and principal shareholders. Securities exchanges and brokers and dealers are also regulated under the Exchange Act.

Registration Under the Exchange Act

In addition to the registration requirements of the Securities Act, § 12(a) of the Exchange Act requires that every nonexempt security that is traded on a national securities exchange must be registered with that exchange. All exchanges in the United States must be registered with the SEC as a national securities exchange unless exempt from the registration requirements by the SEC because of a limited volume of trading. Section 12(a) of the Exchange Act provides:

> Section 12. (a) It shall be unlawful for any member, broker, or dealer to effect any transaction in any security (other than an exempted security) on a national securities exchange unless a registration is effective as to such security for such exchange in accordance with the provisions of this title and the rules and regulations thereunder.

A security is registered by filing an application with the appropriate exchange, with duplicate originals submitted to the SEC as required. The application contains information regarding the issuer, the corporation, and the securities to be traded. In addition, copies of corporate documents, including articles of incorporation and certain material contracts, may be required to supplement the application. The registration of the security on the exchange is generally effective thirty days after the filing of the application with the exchange and the SEC.

In addition to the issuers of securities actively traded on a national exchange, § 12(g)(1) requires registration with the SEC by every issuer that is engaged in interstate commerce, or in a business affecting interstate commerce, or whose securities are traded by use of the mails or any means or instrumentality of interstate commerce, if the corporation has total assets exceeding $1 million and a class of securities held by 750 or more persons.

Individuals who are responsible for certain portions of the registration statement generally cannot be held liable for untrue statements in other parts of the registration statement beyond the scope of their duty.

Periodic Reporting Requirements

Every issuer of securities that have been registered pursuant to § 12 of the Exchange Act is subject to the periodic reporting requirements of § 13 of the Act. Issuers who are not nominally subject to the registration requirements of the Exchange Act, but have filed a registration statement with the SEC pursuant to the Securities Act, also become subject to the reporting requirements of the Exchange Act. Corporations that do not have an active registration statement filed with the SEC, but are otherwise subject to the reporting requirements of the Exchange Act, may be required to file a special registration statement to activate those reporting requirements.

Section 13 of the Exchange Act requires issuers to make periodic disclosures electronically, on forms prescribed by the SEC, in accordance with the Act. The issuer of securities that are registered on a national securities exchange is required to file duplicate originals of such disclosure forms with the exchange.

Failure to comply with the disclosure requirements of the Exchange Act can leave the public corporation liable for damages to injured parties in some instances. False reporting may subject the issuers to criminal liability.

The periodic reports required of publicly held corporations are the 10-K, the 10-Q, and the 8-K.

The 10-K Report

Annual **10-K reports** must be filed with the SEC by every issuer subject to the reporting requirements of the Exchange Act. The Form 10-K must be filed electronically with the SEC within ninety days after the end of the corporation's fiscal year. The information that must be included in the 10-K report is similar to that required for the initial registration statement filed by the corporation, and includes detailed information as to the nature of the registrant's business and significant changes therein during the previous fiscal year, as well as a summary of

---

TERMS

10-K report[†] The annual report that the Securities and Exchange Commission requires of publicly held corporations.

its operation for the last five fiscal years, or for the life of the registrant if less than five years, and for any additional fiscal years necessary to keep the summary from being misleading.[17] The annual 10-K report also includes identification of principal securities holders of the corporation and any transactions involving the transfer of significant percentages of the securities of the corporation. Parts I and II of the 10-K report consist of information that is typically included in the annual report to shareholders, and much of the information required by the 10-K report is often provided by reference to that information in the annual report to shareholders, which is submitted for filing with the 10-K.

The 10-Q Report

Registrants that are required to file 10-K (annual) reports must also file **10-Q quarterly reports**. The 10-Q contains financial information regarding the registrant, the registrant's capitalization and stockholders' equity, and the registrant's sale of unregistered securities during the reporting period. Quarterly reports must be filed for the first three quarters of a corporation's fiscal year, with information concerning the fourth quarter being included in the corporation's annual report. The Form 10-Q must be filed with the SEC within forty-five days of the close of the quarter.

Much of the information required on the 10-Q reports is identical to the information included in the corporation's quarterly reports to shareholders. Hence, it is often incorporated in the 10-Q reports by reference.

Form 8-K

Form 8-K must be completed and filed electronically by the issuer of registered securities when certain pertinent information contained in the registration statement of the issuer changes. Generally, within ten days after the close of the month in which any of the events requiring reporting occur, a Form 8-K must be filed. Typical of the events that require filing of a Form 8-K are changes in control of the registrant, acquisition or disposition of a significant amount of assets (other than in the normal course of business), nonroutine legal proceedings, changes

---

TERMS

10-Q quarterly reports   Quarterly report that must be filed with the SEC by all corporations that are required to file 10-K reports.

Form 8-K   Form that must be filed with the SEC by the issuer of registered securities when certain pertinent information contained in the registration statement of the issuer changes.

in securities of the registrant or modification of the rights of holders of securities, any material default with respect to senior securities, any increase or decrease in outstanding securities of the registrant, and any grants or extensions of options with respect to the purchase of securities of the registrant or of its subsidiaries, if such options relate to an amount of securities exceeding 5 percent of the outstanding securities of the class to which they belong. The Form 8-K, which is provided by the SEC, includes a complete list of events that trigger 8-K filing requirements.

Liability for Short-Swing Profits

Because of their advantageous position and the availability of inside information to a corporation's officers, directors, and principal shareholders, the Exchange Act imposes specific reporting requirements for shareholders falling into these categories. Section 16 of the Exchange Act provides that any profits realized from the purchase and sale (or sale and purchase) of the equity securities of a corporation by its officers, directors, or 10 percent or more shareholders in any period of less than six months normally shall inure to and be recoverable by the issuer. Profits made by an insider on the purchase and sale of securities within a six-month period are often referred to as **short-swing profits**.

Section 16(a) of the Exchange Act specifically provides that a statement setting forth the beneficial ownership of the securities must be filed by "every person who is directly or indirectly the beneficial owner of more than 10 percentum of any class of any equity security (other than an exempted security) which is registered pursuant to section 12 of this title, or who is a director or an officer of the issuer of such security." The statement must be filed with the SEC and the exchange on which the securities are registered, on the effective date of the registration statement or at the time of registration of the securities on the exchange. Additional reports are required within ten days after the close of each calendar month if there has been a change in such ownership during the month.

Section 16(b) specifically prohibits short-swing profits as follows:

(b) For the purpose of preventing the unfair use of information which may have been obtained by such beneficial owner, director, or officer by reason of his relationship to the issuer, any profit realized by him from any purchase and sale, or any sale and purchase, of any

---

TERMS

---

short-swing profits [†]   A profit made on the sale of corporate stock held for less than six months. Such profits are generally available only to investors who possess insider information.

equity security of such issuer (other than an exempted security) within any period of less than six months, unless such security was acquired in good faith in connection with a debt previously contracted, shall inure to and be recoverable by the issuer ... .

Although the stated purpose of this requirement is to prevent the unfair use of inside information, it is not necessary to prove actual use of inside information to impose short-swing liability.

Proxy Regulations

The Exchange Act also regulates the content and use of **proxies** and **proxy statements** by public corporations. As discussed in Chapter 7, proxies may be used to register the vote of a shareholder not in attendance at a shareholder meeting. The proxy statement contains the information required by the SEC to be given to stockholders in conjunction with the solicitation of a proxy. The purpose of the proxy statement is to give the shareholder adequate information to make a decision regarding the use of the proxy.

Generally, any corporation that is subject to the registration requirements of the Securities Act or the Exchange Act is subject to proxy requirements of the Exchange Act. Section 14(a) of the Exchange Act specifically provides that it is unlawful to solicit proxies "in contravention of such rules and regulations as the Commission may prescribe as necessary or appropriate in the public interest or for the protection of investors." The proxy statement must disclose certain material facts concerning the matters on which shareholders are being asked to vote. Rules 14a-1 through 14b-1 under the Exchange Act set forth the specific requirements for soliciting proxies, including the filing of proxy statements with the SEC.

Rule 14a-3 provides, among other things, that no solicitations shall be made unless those solicitations are accompanied by a proxy statement containing the information required by the SEC. Rule 14a-3 further provides that proxy solicitation by management relating to an annual meeting at which directors are to be elected must be accompanied by an annual report disclosing certain information regarding the company,

---

TERMS

proxy[†]   Authority given in writing by one shareholder in a corporation to another shareholder to exercise the first shareholder's voting rights.

proxy statements[†]   A statement sent to shareholders whose proxies are being solicited so that they may be voted at an upcoming stockholders' meeting. The statement, whose contents are regulated by the Securities and Exchange Commission, provides shareholders with the information necessary for them to decide whether to give their proxies.

including annual financial statements for the latest fiscal year. All required reports must be set forth in the manner prescribed by the rules.

Rule 14a-4 sets forth, among other things, the exact format to be followed for the proxy form.

Rule 14a-5 sets forth the exact manner for the presentation of information in a proxy statement.

Rule 14a-6 provides for the filing of the proxy statement with the SEC. Generally, statements filed under § 14 must be filed electronically. However, certain preliminary proxy materials and information statements for which confidential treatment has been requested must be submitted in paper format. The preliminary proxy statement, proxy form, and all other pertinent materials must be filed with the SEC at least ten days prior to the mailing of the proxies. Rule 14a-6 further provides that definitive proxy statements must be filed with the SEC as of the date those proxy statements are furnished to the security holders.

Pursuant to Rule 14a-8 of the Exchange Act, eligible shareholders that follow specified procedures may notify the corporation's management of the shareholder's intent to present a proposal for action at an upcoming meeting of the shareholders, to be put to a vote. In that event, the corporation must set forth the proposal in its proxy statement. Also pursuant to Rule 14a-8, the corporate management must allow the shareholder to include in the proxy statement a statement of no more than 500 words supporting his or her proposal. By following the procedures under Rule 14a-8, disgruntled shareholders have a chance to present and support a proposal for a shareholder vote, even if the management is in opposition.

Antifraud Provisions Under the Exchange Act

Section 10(b) of the Exchange Act, regarding the prohibition of manipulative and deceptive devices, is the Act's principal anti-fraud provision. It is very broad and applies to both the sale and purchase of securities. Section 10(b) deems it unlawful for any person to use or employ any "manipulative or deceptive device or contrivance in contravention of such rules and regulations as the Commission may prescribe as necessary or appropriate in the public interest or for the protection of investors." The primary fraud-control rule adopted under § 10(b) of the Exchange Act is Securities Exchange Act Rule 10b-5:

RULE 10b-5. EMPLOYMENT OF MANIPULATIVE AND DECEPTIVE DEVICES

It shall be unlawful for any person, directly or indirectly, by the use of any means or instrumentality of interstate commerce, or the mails, or of any facility of any national securities exchange,
(1) to employ any device, scheme, or artifice to defraud,

(2) to make any untrue statement of a material fact or to omit to state a material fact necessary in order to make the statements made, in light of the circumstances under which they were made, not misleading, or

(3) to engage in any act, practice, or course of business which operates or would operate as a fraud or deceit upon any person,

in connection with the purchase or sale of any security.

The general nature of Rule 10b-5 allows its imposition on several types of securities cases, including market manipulation, insider trading, corporate misstatements, and corporate mismanagement.

One of the most infamous applications of Rule 10b-5 has been in deciding insider trading cases. Although there is no specific mention of **insider trading** within § 10(b) of the Exchange Act or Rule 10b-5, the majority of cases regarding the fraudulent nature of acts of insiders have been decided under § 10(b) and Rule 10b-5. One purpose of the Exchange Act was to outlaw the use of inside information by corporate officers and principal stockholders for their own financial advantage and to the detriment of uninformed public security holders.[18]

Insiders are generally considered to be individuals who have access to information intended to be available only for a corporate purpose and not for the personal benefit of anyone. Courts have found that the "Exchange Act and the Rule impose upon an insider the duty to speak and to make full disclosure in those circumstances in which silence would constitute fraud."[19] It has been found that Rule 10b-5 makes it unlawful for an insider to purchase the stock of a minority stockholder without disclosing material facts affecting the value of the stock, when such facts are known to the insider by virtue of his or her inside position.[20] When material information concerning the corporation is released, insiders must wait until the news can be widely disseminated before the insider buys or sells shares of equity securities of the corporation based on that information.

Although the rule against insider trading generally does not apply between insiders, parties to a transaction involving the transfer of stock of public corporations must have the same information. For example, failure or refusal of a majority of the board of directors of a corporation to disclose to the remaining directors information pertinent to a proposed stock issue constitutes fraud under § 10(b) of the Exchange Act and SEC Rule 10b-5 thereunder.

TERMS

insider trading [†]   A transaction in the stock of a corporation by a director, officer, or other insider, buying and selling on the basis of information obtained by her through her position in the company. Insider trading is regulated by the Securities Exchange Act.

Since 1984 the SEC has been developing an electronic filing system known as EDGAR (Electronic Data Gathering, Analysis, and Retrieval). As of 1996, most filings under the Securities Act and the Securities and Exchange Act are required to be made electronically under the EDGAR System. The EDGAR system is intended to streamline the process of preparing and submitting filings with the SEC by replacing paper filings.

The EDGAR system receives filings, verifies filer identification and checks that required information is present. In addition, it stores information and disseminates corporate disclosure data.

Preparing electronic SEC filings—EDGARizing documents—can be a cumbersome process. Typically, the following steps are involved.

1. Filers must gain access to the EDGAR system by completing a Form ID and obtaining the appropriate security codes to identify and verify transmissions. In order to gain access to the EDGAR system, filers must also establish a method of fee payment which typically involves wiring filing fees to the SEC with prearranged codes in advance to the filing.

2. The submission is prepared pursuant to SEC regulations.

3. The document is EDGARized. The document must be specially formatted in compliance with Regulation S-T and the *Edgar Filing Handbook* issued by the SEC. At times, an outside service is contracted to EDGARize filings and electronically submit them to the SEC.

4. The filing is transmitted.

5. EDGAR returns an acceptance or suspension message, either through E-Mail or the United States Mail, depending on the pre-arrangements made.

6. Corrected filings are made if necessary.

EDGAR filings are governed primarily by Regulation S-T and the *Edgar Filing Handbook*.

§ 9.8 State Securities Regulations— Blue Sky Laws

Decades before the adoption of the federal Securities Act and Exchange Act, there was an attempt to regulate securities at the state level. These state statutes regulating securities were an attempt to "stop the sale of stock in fly-by-night concerns, visionary oil wells, distant gold mines, and other like, fraudulent exploitations."[21] The term **blue sky laws,** which is commonly used to refer to state statutes regulating securities, was derived from an early Supreme Court case, in which the Court found that the legislative purpose of the acts were aimed at "speculative schemes which have no more basis than so many feet of blue sky."[22]

Blue sky laws act in concert with the federal securities acts and are considered to be valid so long as they do not conflict with the pertinent federal acts.

Most blue sky laws require the registration of securities and of brokers or dealers dealing in securities. They regulate the sale and purchase of securities within the state of domicile through anti-fraud provisions relating to securities transactions.

It is clear that blue sky laws apply to intrastate sales of securities of a domestic corporation, but several other common circumstances raise the question of jurisdiction. Clearly, blue sky laws do not apply to transactions that occur entirely outside the state, even if residents of the state are purchasers of the securities. However, blue sky laws do apply to securities sold by foreign corporations within the state. Courts have generally found that "if a blue sky law requires registration of a security before it may be offered for sale in the state, or before solicitation with respect to such security lawfully may be made in the state, there must be compliance with such requirements even though the issuance of the stock and transfer of the title thereto is to take place entirely in a foreign state."[23]

Blue sky laws vary from state to state, and the laws of any state where a contract for the sale of securities is entered into or executed must be consulted. Most states have adopted, at least to a significant extent, the Uniform Securities Act, approved by the Conference of Commissioners on Uniform State Laws and the American Bar Association in 1956. Recognizing the general success of the 1956 Act, yet also a need to update the licensing and registration procedures, the Act was amended in 1988. As of July 1, 1990, six states had adopted the most recent version of the Uniform Act—the Uniform Securities Act (1985) with 1988 amendments.[24]

TERMS

blue sky laws [†]   State statutes intended to prevent fraud in the sale of securities. The term derives from investors who are "dumb enough to buy blue sky."

§ 9.9 State Regulation of Stock Offerings

Blue sky laws typically require the registration of securities of public corporations at the state level (in addition to the federal requirements). Under the Uniform Securities Act, the issuer is required to register the securities by one of three means, depending on the "demonstrated degree of stability of the registrant and the information available to prospective investors by reason of a registration statement having been filed with the Securities and Exchange Commission under the Securities Act of 1933."[25]

Registration by Filing

Registration by filing is a new procedure under the 1988 amendments to the Uniform Securities Act, which is available to issuers that have filed a registration statement under the Securities Act and have been actively engaged in business operations in the United States for at least three years prior to that filing. The issuer desiring to register by filing must also meet several other criteria set forth by state statute. Registration by filing is accomplished by submitting the following to the state securities authority with the appropriate filing fee:

1. A statement demonstrating eligibility for registration by filing
2. The name, address, and form of organization of the issuer
3. With respect to a person on whose behalf a part of the offering is to be made in a nonissuer distribution: name and address; the amount of securities of the issuer held by the person as of the date of the filing of the registration statement; and a statement of the reasons for making the offering
4. A description of the security being registered
5. A copy of the latest prospectus filed with the registration statement under and satisfying the requirements of § 10 of the Securities Act of 1933.

Registration by Coordination

The procedures for registration by coordination, available under the statutes of states following the Uniform Securities Act, are available for any securities for which a registration statement has been filed under the Securities Act. The procedures for registration by coordination are similar to those of registration by filing. Because issuers registering by coordination need not be established corporations that have been transacting business in the United States for several years, slightly more information is required to be filed with this type of registration.

Registration by Qualification

Registration by qualification is available to the issuer of any securities. Registration by qualification is the type of registration that must be completed by corporations that are not required to file a registration statement under the Securities Act, but are required to register at the state level. This is the most complex type of registration, and it requires the most information to be filed at the state level, because there is no available copy of a prospectus filed with the SEC.

Exemptions

As with federal registration requirements, there are many exemptions from state registration requirements. The exemptions for each individual state are found in that state's statutes. Often, the securities may be exempt from registration because of either the type or class of the securities, or the specific transaction involving the securities. Exemption from the registration requirements of the state securities regulations does not guarantee exemption from the other provisions of the regulations.

§ 9.10 State Securities Regulations—Antifraud Provisions

State statutes typically prohibit fraudulent activities connected with the offer, sale, and purchase of securities, as do the similar antifraud provisions found in the Securities Act and the Exchange Act. The antifraud provisions of the Uniform Securities Act are found in §§ 501 through 505. Section 505, which parallels Rule 10b-5 of the Securities Act, reads as follows:

§ 501. OFFER, SALE, AND PURCHASE.

In connection with an offer to sell, sale, offer to purchase, or purchase, of a security, a person may not, directly or indirectly:
(1) employ a device, scheme, or artifice to defraud;

(2) make an untrue statement of a material fact or omit to state a material fact necessary in order to make the statements made not misleading, in light of the circumstances under which they are made; or

(3) engage in an act, practice, or course of business that operates or would operate as a fraud or deceit upon a person.

The Uniform Securities Act also contains provisions prohibiting market manipulation; regulating the transactions of investment advisors; and prohibiting misleading filings and unlawful representation concerning licensing, registration, or exemption.

§ 9.11 The Role of the Paralegal

The paralegal is often involved in all aspects of the public securities offering and in complying with the ongoing federal reporting requirements for public corporations.

Initial Public Offerings

Once a decision to go public has been made, a date for filing the registration statement is usually agreed upon by the corporation's directors, its attorneys, and the underwriters. All plans for the public offering depend on that target date, and it is usually crucial that the registration statement be filed on time. For that reason, work on securities offerings often must be completed within very tight time constraints.

The following is a sample timeline for a public stock offering. This timeline is by no means all-inclusive; rather, it is intended to demonstrate the ordinary sequence of the main events leading to a public stock offering.

Week 1 Organizational meeting attended by corporate management, corporate counsel, underwriters, underwriters' counsel, and corporation's accountants. Schedule is decided on, as well as format for registration statement.
Preliminary agreement with underwriters.

Week 2 Circulate first draft of registration statement and underwriting agreement for comments and revisions.
Begin corporate "housekeeping" to make sure financial and corporate records are in order.

Week 3 Due diligence work; drafting and revision of registration statement and underwriting agreement.

Week 4 Continue work on drafting and revision of registration statement and underwriting agreement.

Week 5 Registration statement and underwriting agreement sent to printer.

Week 6 Review proofs of registration statement and underwriting agreement from printer.

Week 7 Meeting of the board of directors to discuss and approve registration statement and other matters related to public offering.

Week 8 Finalize and file registration statement.
Submit press release regarding offering to appropriate papers.
File appropriate documents with NASD.
Begin work to comply with blue sky requirements.

Weeks 8–10 Review comments from SEC.
Prepare amendments to registration statement, if necessary.
Negotiations on price of stock to be offered.
Registration statement becomes effective.
Commence offering.
File copies of prospectuses with SEC, including price.
Closing with corporation and underwriters after price of stock has been set and offering has commenced.

Week 11 Continue work on blue sky requirements.
Set schedule to comply with periodic reporting requirements.

The paralegal may be assigned the task of collecting the necessary information and drafting certain sections of the registration statement and prospectus. Collecting all of the necessary information to complete the registration statement under the Securities Act of 1933 can be a monumental task. The information gathered to prepare the registration statement required under the Securities Act can also be used to complete the necessary documentation under the Exchange Act and the pertinent blue sky laws.

Registration statements are usually printed by a legal or financial printer. The paralegal is often responsible for coordinating the printing of the registration statement and the prospectuses and assisting with the proofreading of those documents.

Periodic Reporting Requirements

Paralegals are also very often involved in the process of complying with the periodic reporting requirements of the Exchange Act, and often must draft the reports for the attorneys' approval, see to their filing, or both. It is important for the paralegal or other assigned individual to keep track of the required filing dates for periodic reporting requirements, to assure that all 10-K, 10-Q, and 8-K reports are filed in a timely manner.

Another area in which the legal assistant often participates is in researching the blue sky laws of the pertinent states, to determine the procedures that must be followed in each of the applicable states. Complying with blue sky laws often involves thorough research into the statutes of several states.

Confidentiality

Keeping a client's confidentiality is very important in every aspect of a paralegal's work, but it is absolutely crucial when dealing with publicly held corporations. Leaks from a law firm that might appear to be harmless can actually lead to serious consequences, including fluctuation in the price of the corporation's stock. In some cases, it may not only be unethical for a paralegal to divulge information about a corporate client to the press or other outsiders, but it may also be in violation of federal statutes.

Law firms typically have strict policies with regard to divulging information regarding any corporate clients to the press or any outsider. Typically, all requests for information regarding a client should be directed to an attorney who is responsible for the client's affairs, and no one else will be permitted to pass on any information regarding a client without permission, even information that may seem quite inconsequential.

§ 9.12 Resources

As discussed in this chapter, the primary sources of law regarding securities regulations are the Securities Act of 1933, 15 U.S.C. § 77a *et seq.,* the Securities Exchange Act of 1934, 15 U.S.C. § 78a *et seq.,* and the rules and regulations that accompany these acts. State statutes must also be consulted for the pertinent blue sky laws.

Looseleaf services that include the federal securities laws, rules, forms, and decisions are often a more user-friendly source of securities laws. The *Federal Securities Law Reporter,* published by Commerce Clearing House, is one such source.

One of the best resources for information on securities regulations is the office of the Securities and Exchange Commission, which has a wealth of information available. Most of this information is available free of charge or at a very minimal cost. Copies of the most current versions of the securities acts and the pertinent rules and regulations can be obtained by contacting the SEC at the following address, or by calling:

Superintendent of Documents
Government Printing Office
Washington, D.C. 20402-9325
(202) 512-1800
(202) 512-1716 (fax)

Review Questions

1. What are some of the advantages and disadvantages of taking a privately held corporation public?

2. Describe the differences between a firm commitment underwriting agreement and a best-efforts underwriting agreement.

3. What are the two general requirements of § 5 of the Securities Act of 1933 with regard to securities that are offered or sold through any means of interstate commerce?

4. What is a "red herring" prospectus?

5. May accountants and attorneys and others who contribute information and sign a registration statement be found liable for damages due to misstatements made therein?

6. What is the due diligence defense? To whom is the due diligence defense available?

7. If an issuer of securities has filed a registration statement under the Securities Act of 1933, is it necessary to register under the Exchange Act of 1934?

8. What is the purpose of Form 8-K?

9. What are short-swing profits?

10. What is the definition and the origin of the term "blue sky laws"?

11. As a 20 percent shareholder in a publicly owned corporation, Jane has decided to sell her shares. What special requirements must she comply with because she owns such a large stake in the company?

Notes

[1] The Reference Press, *The American Almanac Statistical Abstract of the United States: 1994–1995,* 114th ed. at 870 (Austin, Texas 1994).

[2] Information Please Almanac Atlas & Yearbook 1991. 44th ed. Houghton Mifflin, 1991, at 47.

[3] The Reference Press, *The American Almanac Statistical Abstract of the United States: 1994–1995,* 114th ed. at 811 (Austin, Texas 1994).

[4] Securities Act of 1933 § 2(4), 15 U.S.C. § 77b(4).

[5] *Id.* § 2(11), 15 U.S.C. § 77b(11).

[6] *Id.* § 2(1), 15 U.S.C. § 77b(1).

[7] Securities Exchange Act of 1934 § 3(a)(1), 15 U.S.C. § 78c(a)(1).

[8] United States Bureau of the Census, Statistical Abstract of the United States: 1994. 114th ed. Washington, D.C., 1991 at 812.

[9] The Reference Press, *The American Almanac Statistical Abstract of the United States: 1994–1995,* 114th ed. at 816 (Austin, Texas 1994).

[10] *The Economist,* "Trading Places," March 25, 1996, p. 84

[11] 69 AM. JUR. 2d (Rev.) *Securities Regulation—Federal* § 1 (1993).

[12] Securities Act of 1933 § 8(b), 15 U.S.C. § 77.

[13] United States Securities and Exchange Commission Release No. 4552 (Nov. 6, 1962).

[14] 69 AM. JUR. 2d (Rev.) *Securities Regulation—Federal* § 460 (1993).

[15] *Id.* § 5.

[16] *Id.* § 301.

[17] *Id.* § 617.

[18] Speed v. Transamerica Corp., 99 F. Supp. 808 (D. Del. 1951).

[19] Connelly v. Balkwill, 174 F. Supp. 49 (N.D. Ohio 1959), *aff'd.* 279 F.2d 685.

[20] 69 AM. JUR. 2d *Securities Regulation—Federal* § 1528 (1993).

[21] Hall v. Geiger-Jones Co., 242 U.S. 539 (1917).

[22] *Id.*

[23] 69 AM. JUR. 2d *Securities Regulation—State* § 1 (1993).

[24] Colorado, Maine, Nevada, New Mexico, Rhode Island, and Vermont have adopted the Uniform Securities Act with the 1988 amendments.

[25] 69 AM. JUR. 2d *Securities Regulation—State* § 25 (1985).

CHAPTER 10

MERGERS, ACQUISITIONS, AND OTHER CHANGES TO THE CORPORATE STRUCTURE

Introduction

Mergers and acquisitions have been a hot topic since the late 1980s, when news about megamergers, leveraged buyouts, and hostile takeovers made the headlines almost daily and the number of completed mergers and acquisitions reached all-time highs. The year 1989 set a new record with 3,752 mergers and acquisitions in the United States that were valued at over $5 million. The total value of those transactions was $316.8 billion.[1] Activity has not slowed in the 1990s to the extent some had predicted. There were over 3,400 merger and acquisition transactions valued at over $5 million during each year 1990 through 1992.[2]

Mergers and acquisitions are of great consequence to our economy, the stock markets, and corporate directors and shareholders.

This chapter looks at some of the different types of corporate amalgamations that are specifically provided for by statute and discusses the procedures for approving and effecting those types of transactions. It also discusses the acquisition of corporate assets and stock and the procedures for approving and completing acquisition transactions. We then examine the procedures and requirements for amending the articles of incorporation, which is often an integral part of mergers and acquisitions. After a brief look at the definitions of *reorganization* and certain types of reorganizations, the focus turns to the paralegal's role in merger and acquisition work.

§ 10.1 Statutory Mergers and Share Exchanges

State statutes generally set forth requirements for certain types of corporate amalgamations, including mergers, share exchanges, and consolidations. Unions that are provided for by statute are typically referred

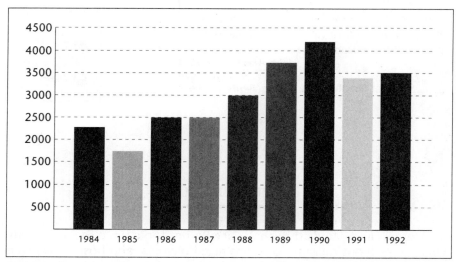

FIGURE 10-1   Number of Mergers in the United States over $5 Million in Value

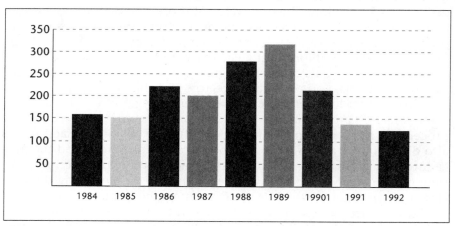

FIGURE 10-2   Total Value of Mergers in the United States over $5 Million (in Billions of Dollars)

to as **statutory mergers**. Statutory mergers and share exchanges may be between domestic corporations, or domestic and foreign corporations,

---

TERMS

statutory merger   Merger that is provided for by statute.

provided that the transaction is permitted by the statutes of the state of domicile of each corporation.

Under the statutes of states following the Model Business Corporation Act, two types of transactions involving the combination of corporations are addressed: the merger and the share exchange. This section focuses on the flexible mergers and share exchanges provided for in the Model Business Corporation Act. We then briefly discuss *consolidations,* another type of corporate amalgamation provided for by the statutes of some states. We also review the state and federal laws affecting statutory mergers and share exchanges.

Mergers

A **merger** is a combination of two or more corporations whereby one of the corporations survives (the surviving corporation) and absorbs one or more other corporations (the merging corporations), which cease to exist. Mergers have the effect of transferring all assets, liabilities, and obligations of the merging corporation to the surviving corporation alone.

Section 11.06(a) of the Model Business Corporation Act sets forth the effect of a merger:

§ 11.06 EFFECT OF MERGER OR SHARE EXCHANGE

(a) When a merger takes effect:
   (1) every other corporation party to the merger merges into the surviving corporation and the separate existence of every corporation except the surviving corporation ceases;
   (2) the title to all real estate and other property owned by each corporation party to the merger is vested in the surviving corporation without reversion or impairment;
   (3) the surviving corporation has all liabilities of each corporation party to the merger;
   (4) a proceeding pending against any corporation party to the merger may be continued as if the merger did not occur or the surviving corporation may be substituted in the proceeding for the corporation whose existence ceased;
   (5) the articles of incorporation of the surviving corporation are amended to the extent provided in the plan of merger; and

---

TERMS

---

merger † The combining of one of anything with another or others; the absorption of one thing by another; a disappearing into something else.

(6) the shares of each corporation party to the merger that are to be converted into shares, obligations, or other securities of the surviving or any other corporation or into cash or other property are converted, and the former holders of the shares are entitled only to the rights provided in the articles of merger or to their rights under chapter 13.

Chapter 13 of the Model Business Corporation Act concerns dissenter's rights, which is discussed in more detail in § 10.2 of this chapter.

There are numerous reasons for merging two or more corporations. A statutory merger is one means often employed to achieve the acquisition of one corporation by another. The management and owners of two corporations of relatively similar size and status may decide that there are business advantages to be had by the combined operation of their two corporations. Also, related corporations may merge to decrease the paperwork, taxes, and other expenses associated with maintaining two separate corporate entities.

The shareholders of the merging corporation generally receive shares of the surviving corporation in exchange for their shares and become shareholders of the surviving corporation. However, § 11.01 of the Model Business Corporation Act and the statutes of most states specifically permit the shares of the merging corporation to be converted into "shares, obligations, or other securities of the surviving or any other corporation or into cash or other property in whole or part." This provision allows the surviving corporation to pay cash as all or part of the consideration given to the merging corporation, so long as the terms are agreed to in the plan of merger.

In mergers involving a surviving corporation owned by the majority shareholders of the merging corporation, the majority shareholders may seek to eliminate the interests of the minority shareholders in the merging corporation by means of a merger in which the minority shareholders are forced either to take cash in consideration for their shares, or to dissent and seek appraisal. The shareholder's right to dissent is discussed in more detail in § 10.2 of this chapter. This type of transaction is sometimes called a *freeze-out* or *take-out,* and may be found invalid in certain jurisdictions, especially if the merger has no clear business purpose other than elimination of the minority shareholders. The management and majority shareholders owe a duty to the corporation and to the minority shareholders to enter into transactions only to promote the best interests of the corporation and all its shareholders, including the minority shareholders.

There are many variations from the simple statutory merger whereby one unrelated corporation merges into another. Some of the more common deviations from that design are upstream mergers, downstream mergers, triangle mergers, and reverse triangle mergers.

Dividends

Mickey Mouse and the Mega Merger

Here's a trivia question: Who is Steamboat Willie, and how does he affect your life? Answer: Steamboat Willie was the very first animated Mickey Mouse cartoon, and he affects the movies you watch, the television you view, and even the newspapers you read.

Even Walt Disneys could not possibly have imagined the impact he would have on media and entertainment when he first put his pen to Mickey Mouse over sixty years ago. In 1995, the Disney Corporation's merger with Capital Cities/ABC Inc. became the biggest mega-merger in history. After the deal, Disney became a conglomerate with annual revenues predicted at over $19 billion, an annual cash flow of over $4.6 billion, and over 85,000 employees. Disney owns three movie companies, eleven TV stations with 228 TV affiliates, twenty-one radio stations, four cable networks, newspapers in thirteen states, and two additional publishing companies. Disney is a part of our lives.

Although the Disney/Capital Cities/ABC mega-merger is to date the largest, it has had company in recent years. Market dominance has been the motivation behind most of the mega-mergers throughout the 1990s, and they can be found in nearly every major market in the United States in recent years.

Joining the Disney deal in the media and entertainment industry is the Time/Warner Communications deal, estimated at $13.9 billion.

The financial services sector has seen two huge mega-mergers in the past decade: Chemical Bank's merger with Chase Manhattan, estimated at $10 billion, and First Union's merger with First Fidelity Bancorp, estimated at $5.4 billion.

The leading health care industry merger in recent years was the Upjohn/Sweden's Pharmacia merger, estimated at $6 billion.

The consumer goods industry mergers has been lead by Kimberly-Clark's $7 billion acquisition of Scott Paper.

Experts who felt that the 1980s were the decade of the mega-merger are being proven wrong, as the mega-mergers of the mid 1990s surpass almost everyone's expectations. The United States merger volume in the first quarter of 1995 totaled $73.2 billion, the highest first-quarter figure since 1989.[1] The volume of mergers for all of 1995 is expected to reach $329 billion, just short of 1988's record of $335 billion. The full impact of these mega-mergers on consumers and on the public in general remains to be seen. Some fear a reduction in competition in many sectors. Many are concerned over the lack of diversity in the media.

One immediate affect is increased activity and work for investment bankers, financial advisors, accountants, and—especially—attorneys and paralegals who specialize in mergers and acquisitions. As demonstrated in the following chapter, mergers are very involved, time consuming projects. Mega-mergers can keep hundreds of individuals extremely busy from the time they are conceived until long after they have been closed.

[1] An Old-Fashioned Feeding Frenzy, *Businessweek,* May 1, 1995, at 34.

Mergers Between Subsidiaries and Parents

Mergers may take place between a parent and a subsidiary corporation. When the subsidiary corporation merges into its parent corporation, it is referred to as an **upstream merger**. Upstream mergers may be eligible for a short-form merger under statute, whereby the statutory merger requirements are simplified because of the relationship between the two corporations. Shareholder approval of the subsidiary corporation is not required when the parent corporation owns at least 90 percent of the outstanding stock of the subsidiary, as the minority shareholders do not have sufficient voting power to block the merger.

Mergers whereby the parent corporation is merged into a subsidiary are referred to as **downstream mergers**.

Triangle Mergers

The **triangle merger** involves three corporations: a parent corporation, a subsidiary of the parent corporation, and a target corporation. In a triangle merger, the parent corporation forms a subsidiary and funds it with sufficient cash or shares of stock to perform a merger with the target corporation, which is merged into the subsidiary corporation. Both the parent and the subsidiary are surviving corporations in a triangle merger.

Reverse Triangle Mergers

A **reverse triangle merger** is also a three-way merger. Its distinction from the triangle merger is that in the reverse triangle merger the subsidiary is merged into the target corporation. The end result is the survival of the parent corporation and the target corporation, which will become a new subsidiary. The survival of the target corporation may be important when it is a special type of corporation that is difficult to form, or when the target corporation being acquired is a party to nonassignable contracts.

TERMS

upstream merger   Merger whereby a subsidiary corporation merges into its parent.

downstream merger   Merger whereby a parent corporation is merged into a subsidiary.

triangle merger   Merger involving three corporations, whereby a corporation forms a subsidiary corporation and funds it with sufficient cash or shares of stock to perform a merger with the target corporation, which is merged into the subsidiary. The parent corporation and the subsidiary corporation both survive a triangle merger.

reverse triangle merger   Three-way merger whereby a subsidiary corporation is merged into the target corporation. The end result is the survival of the parent corporation and the target corporation, which becomes a new subsidiary.

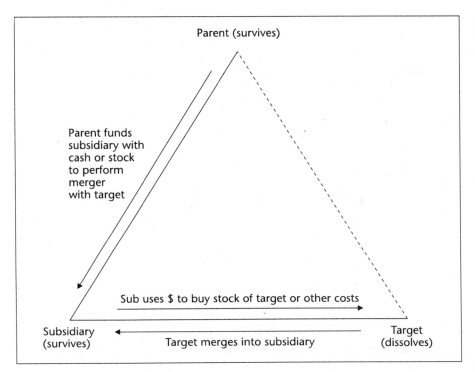

FIGURE 10-3
Triangle
Mergers

The same result achieved by a reverse triangle merger may be achieved by a share exchange of the type permitted by § 11.02 of the Model Business Corporation Act. Unlike the merger, the end result of a share exchange is the survival of both corporations, one that becomes a parent and the other a subsidiary.

Share Exchanges

A **share exchange** is a transaction whereby one corporation (the acquiring corporation) acquires all of the outstanding shares of one or more classes or series of another corporation (the target corporation) by an exchange that is compulsory on the shareholders of the target corporation. The shareholders of the target corporation may receive shares of stock in the acquiring corporation, shares of stock in a third

---

TERMS

share exchange Transaction whereby one corporation acquires all of the outstanding shares of one or more classes or series of another corporation by an exchange that is compulsory on the shareholders of the target corporation.

FIGURE 10-4
Reverse
Triangle
Mergers

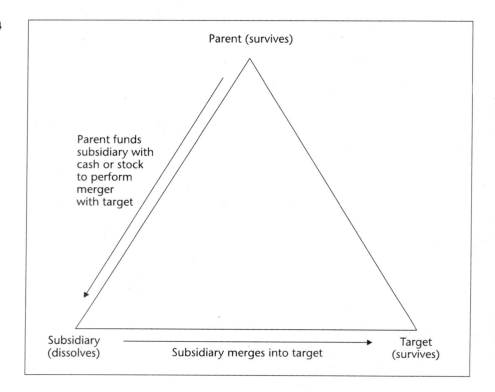

corporation, or cash in consideration for their shares. In this type of transaction, both the acquiring and the target corporation survive, with the target corporation becoming a subsidiary of the acquiring corporation. Section 11.06(b) of the Model Business Corporation Act sets forth the effect of a share exchange:

> (b) When a share exchange takes effect, the shares of each acquired corporation are exchanged as provided in the plan, and the former holders of the shares are entitled only to the exchange rights provided in the articles of share exchange or to their rights under chapter 13.

Consolidations

A **consolidation** involves the merger of two or more corporations into a newly formed corporation and the subsequent disappearance

---

TERMS

consolidation[†]   A joining together of separate things to make one thing; an amalgamation.

of the merging corporations. Although the statutes of many states still allow such consolidations, the Model Business Corporation Act no longer provides for a statutory consolidation, because it is almost always advantageous for one of the merging corporations to survive. The same result obtained in a consolidation may be obtained by a statutory merger involving the merger of two corporations into a corporation formed for the purpose of acting as the surviving corporation of the transaction.

Celotex Corporation v. Pickett demonstrates the importance of the type of transaction used to combine businesses. It is pointed out that in a merger transaction all debts, liabilities, and duties of the merging corporation are transferred to the surviving corporation.

State and Federal Laws Affecting Statutory Mergers and Share Exchanges

Research must be conducted throughout the merger or share exchange transaction to assure that all state and federal laws are being complied with. All parties to a merger or share exchange are typically subject to the statutes of their state of domicile. State statutes typically prescribe the following:

1. Requirements for the plan of merger or plan of exchange
2. The method for adopting a plan of merger or plan of exchange
3. Requirements for articles of merger or articles of share exchange
4. Requirements for filing the articles of merger or articles of share exchange
5. Provisions regarding the effect of the merger or share exchange
6. Provisions for short-form mergers
7. Provisions for dissenting shareholder rights.

A foreign corporation that is being merged into a domestic corporation may also be subject to the laws of the state of domicile of the surviving corporation. Corporations whose shares are being acquired subject to a share exchange typically must be domestic corporations.

In addition to the applicable state statutes regarding statutory mergers and share exchanges, compliance must be made with any federal securities regulations and blue sky laws applicable to mergers and share exchanges, as well as the Internal Revenue Code and pertinent provisions of the federal and state antitrust laws. Under the Hart-Scott-Rodino Antitrust Improvements Act of 1976, the Federal Trade Commission and the Antitrust Division of the Department of Justice have the authority to review certain merger and acquisition transactions prior

CELOTEX CORPORATION
v.
PICKETT
Supreme Court of Florida
490 So. 2d 35 (Fla. 1986)
May 8, 1986
Ehrlich, Justice

We have for our review a decision of the First District Court of Appeal reported as *Celotex Corp. v. Pickett*, 459 So. 2d 375 ... .

The facts relevant for our review here are that the respondent husband (Pickett) was employed in a Jacksonville shipyard from 1965 through June 1968, where as part of his employment as an insulator of ships, he extensively used Philip Carey asbestos cement. Pickett developed severe lung problems, due to the devastating effects on the human body which result from exposure to asbestos. The Picketts sued, on the grounds of negligence and strict liability, several defendants including the petitioner (Celotex) in its capacity as the corporate successor to Philip Carey. Finding that Philip Carey was negligent in placing "defective" asbestos-containing insulating products on the market which caused Pickett's injuries, the jury awarded compensatory damages of $500,000 to Pickett and $15,000 to his wife. The jury also determined that Philip Carey had acted so as to warrant **punitive damages** in the amount of $100,000 against Celotex. Celotex's appeal of the imposition of punitive damages formed the basis for the First District's opinion below which affirmed the award.

The threshold question involved here is the legal status of Celotex as the successor to Philip Carey. The district court opinion set forth the following background:

The Philip Carey Corporation was begun in 1888 and subsequently merged with Glen Alden Corporation in 1967. Thereafter, Philip Carey merged with another Glen Alden subsidiary, Briggs Manufacturing Company, and became known as Panacon Corporation. Celotex purchased Glen Alden's controlling interest in 1972 and later purchased the remaining shares of Panacon and merged it into Celotex.

The effect of this merger, as correctly recognized by the First District, is controlled by [Fla. Stat. §] 607.231(3) ... (1983), which reads:

(c) Such surviving or new corporation shall have all the rights, privileges, immunities and powers, and shall be subject to all of the duties and liabilities, of a corporation organized under this chapter.

Celotex has admitted that it is liable, because of the merger, for the compensatory damages awarded to the Picketts. The sole and narrow issue before us here is whether punitive damages were properly assessed against petitioner, the surviving corporation in a statutory merger.

Celotex, however, maintains that the trial court and the district court below misapplied our prior decisions by holding Celotex liable for punitive damages, when Philip Carey, not Celotex, as the "real wrongdoer." Celotex also claims that imposition of punitive damages against Celotex, simply because it is the statutory successor of Philip Carey, contravenes the purpose of such damages in Florida, We disagree with both contentions. ...

TERMS

punitive damages [†] Damages that are awarded over and above compensatory damages or actual damages because of the wanton, reckless, or malicious nature of the wrong done by the plaintiff. Such damages bear no relation to the plaintiff's actual loss and are often called exemplary damages, because their purpose is to make an example of the plaintiff to discourage others from engaging in the same kind of conduct in the future.

Celotex seeks here to characterize its liability as "vicarious," ... since, according to it, Philip Carey/Panacon is the "real wrongdoer" and there is no evidence of fault by Celotex. We disagree with this characterization. Because of its merger agreement with Panacon, whereby "all debts, liabilities and duties" of Panacon are enforceable against Celotex, and because of the effect of Section 607.231(3), the liability imposed upon Celotex is direct, not vicarious. Liability for the reckless misconduct of Philip Carey/Panacon legally continues to exist within, and under the name of, Celotex. ...

Further, corporations are in a very real sense, "molders of their own destinies" in acquisition transactions, with the full panoply of corporation transformations at their disposal. When a corporation, such as Celotex here, voluntarily chooses a formal merger, it will take the "bad will" along with the "good will." ... We will not allow such an acquiring corporation to "jettison inchoate liabilities into a never-never land of transcorporate limbo." *Wall v. Owens-Corning Fiberglass Corp.*, 602 F. Supp. 252, 255 (N.D. Tex. 1985). ...

We approve the decision of the First District Court of Appeal.

It is so ordered.

to their closing to determine whether there may be any potential antitrust violations stemming from the transaction. Each party subject to this Act must file a Notification and Report Form for Certain Mergers and Acquisitions, which sets forth information regarding the operation and proposed transaction of the parties.

§ 10.2 Statutory Merger and Share Exchange Procedures

The procedures followed for completing statutory mergers and share exchanges will depend on the type of transaction and the parties involved. Obviously, mergers between related parties will involve less negotiation and due diligence than those between unrelated parties. Likewise, mergers or share exchanges involving publicly owned corporations can be much more complex than those involving smaller, closely held corporations.

This section begins with an investigation of some of the procedures common to all types of mergers and share exchanges, including negotiations and the letter of intent. Next it focuses on details necessary to perform a statutory merger, such as the plan of merger and the articles of merger. After examining the documents necessary to the exchange of shares, the section concludes with discussions of due diligence work, closings, and postclosing matters.

Negotiations and Letter of Intent

The first step in the merger or share exchange process of two unrelated parties generally involves meetings and preliminary negotiations between the parties. The parties involved must agree on the general terms and conditions of the transaction and all significant issues involving the proposed merger or share exchange.

If successful, negotiations often lead to a letter of intent. The **letter of intent** is a short document, often just a few pages in length, entered into between the proposed parties to a transaction to set forth their preliminary understandings and intent with regard to the transaction. The letter of intent may contain several contingencies, including a specific date by which a formal agreement must be entered into. The letter of intent demonstrates the seriousness of the parties to go to the next step in the process, which involves entering into a plan of merger or plan of exchange.

Plan of Merger

A **plan of merger**, which is required by statute, sets forth the terms of the agreement between the parties in detail. Specific requirements for the plan of merger, which is sometimes referred to as an "agreement and plan of merger," are contained in the statutes of most states. Following is § 11.01(b) of the Model Business Corporation Act, which sets forth the requirements for the plan of merger as follows:

(b) The plan of merger must set forth:
 (1) the name of each corporation planning to merge and the name of the surviving corporation into which each other corporation plans to merge;
 (2) the terms and conditions of the merger; and
 (3) the manner and basis of converting the shares of each corporation into shares, obligations, or other securities of the surviving or any other corporation or into cash or other property in whole or in part.

TERMS

letter of intent[†] A letter memorializing a preliminary understanding between two or more persons, written by one of them to the other (or others) to serve as a basis for the formal agreement they intend to execute.

plan of merger Document required by state statute that sets forth the terms of the agreement between the two merging parties in detail.

Section 11.01 further states that the plan of merger may contain an amendment to the articles of incorporation of the surviving corporation, and any other provisions relating to the merger.

Following is a list of items often included in an agreement and/or plan of merger:

- Date of agreement

- Name and authorized capitalization of each original corporation

- Name, purpose, location of the principal office, number of directors, and capital stock of the surviving corporation

- Method and rate of exchange for converting shares of the merging corporation into shares of the surviving corporation

- Provisions acknowledging the transfer of the rights, property, and liabilities of the merging corporation to the surviving corporation

- Recital that each board of directors believes it to be in the best interest of its respective corporation that the merger take place

- Provisions for submitting the plan of merger to the shareholders of each corporation for approval, as necessary

- Amendments to the articles of incorporation of the surviving corporation

- Provisions for amending the bylaws of the surviving corporation

- Provisions for dissolving the merging corporation

- Names and addresses of the directors of the surviving corporation

- Treatment of outstanding stock options, if any

- Restrictions on transactions outside the normal course of business by either corporation prior to the effective date of the merger

- Provisions for corporate distributions during the period prior to the effective date of the merger

- Provisions for possible abandonment of the merger prior to the completion thereof by the directors of either corporation

- Provisions for filing the articles of merger or share exchange with the appropriate state office, as required by statute

- Closing and effective date of the merger.

In addition, the plan of merger includes specific information (usually in the form of schedules or exhibits) regarding the business status of each corporation involved, including the corporation's financial status, assets, pending litigation, employees, and all matters that might affect the business or earning potential of the corporation.

Director and Shareholder Approval of the Plan of Merger

With the possible exception of upstream mergers, the plan of merger must be approved by the board of directors and shareholders of each corporation that will be a party to the plan of merger, pursuant to state statutes. Class voting and special voting requirements unique to the plan of merger are often required. Under the Model Business Corporation Act, when shareholder approval is required for a plan of merger, the following procedures must be used:

1. The board of directors must recommend the plan to the shareholders, unless the board determines that it should make no recommendation and communicates the basis for its determination to the shareholders with the plan. Reasons for not rendering a recommendation may include a conflict of interest or other special circumstances.[3] The board may condition its submission of the proposed plan on any basis.[4]

2. Each shareholder, whether or not entitled to vote, must be notified of the shareholder meeting pursuant to statute. The notice must state that the purpose of the meeting is to consider the plan of merger, and it must contain or be accompanied by a summary of the plan.[5]

3. Unless otherwise provided by state statutes, the articles of incorporation, or the board of directors, the plan must be approved by each voting group entitled to vote separately on the plan. Approval of each voting group is given by the majority vote of all votes within each voting group.[6] A **voting group**, as defined by § 1.40 of the Model Business Corporation Act, is:

> all shares of one or more classes or series that under the articles of incorporation or this Act are entitled to vote and be counted together collectively on a matter at a meeting of shareholders. All shares entitled by the articles of incorporation or this Act to vote generally on the matter are for that purpose a single voting group.

4. Separate voting by voting groups is required if the plan contains a provision that, if contained in a proposed amendment to the articles of incorporation, would require action by one or more separate voting groups on the proposed amendment pursuant to statute.[7]

───────────────── **TERMS** ─────────────────

voting group Shareholders that are entitled, as a group, to vote separately at shareholder meetings on certain matters.

Under the Model Business Corporation Act, as in most states, approval of the shareholders of the surviving corporation is not required under certain circumstances when the position and rights of the shareholders of the surviving corporation are not significantly affected by the merger. This allows the board of directors acting on behalf of large, publicly held corporations to acquire several corporations or merge several corporations into the corporation, without the formality of a shareholder meeting to approve each merger. The following paragraphs are examples of board of director and shareholder resolutions approving plans of merger.

EXAMPLE: Resolution of Directors Authorizing Merger into
Another Corporation

Resolved, that the plan of merger this day proposed to the board, pursuant to which this corporation will transfer to _____ [other corporation], a corporation organized and existing under the laws of the State of _____ , all of the assets, tangible and intangible, of this corporation as they exist on _____ , 19___ , subject to the liabilities of this corporation, in the manner and to the extent set forth in the draft agreement heretofore presented and read to this meeting, be and the same hereby is ratified, approved, and adopted.[8]

EXAMPLE: Stockholders' Resolution Adopting Merger
Agreement

Whereas, the board of directors of this corporation has approved an agreement of merger at a meeting of the directors duly held at the corporation's _____ _____ [principal/executive office] at _____ [address], on _____ , 19___ , and ordered that the agreement be submitted to the shareholders for approval at this meeting as provided by law;

Resolved, that the shareholders of this corporation hereby ratify, adopt, and approve the agreement of merger dated _____ , 19___ , and direct the secretary of the corporation to insert a copy of such agreement in the minute book of the corporation immediately following the minutes of this meeting.

Further resolved, that the officers of this corporation are hereby authorized and directed to execute all documents and take such further action as may be deemed necessary or advisable to implement this resolution.[9]

Dissenting Shareholders

Shareholders entitled to vote on a plan of merger may be granted the right to dissent under the statutes of the corporation's state of domicile. A shareholder's *right to dissent* refers to the right to object to certain extraordinary actions being taken by the corporation and to obtain payment of the fair value of the shares held by the dissenting shareholder from the corporation. Under the Model Business Corporation Act, any shareholder who is entitled to vote on a plan of merger, or shareholders of subsidiaries that are merged with the parent in an up-stream merger, have the right to dissent. Other events, including consummation of a plan of exchange and amendment of the articles of incorporation, that materially and adversely affect the rights of shareholders will also entitle shareholders to the right to dissent. Certain statutory formalities, including the submission of a written notice of intent to demand payment, must be followed by the dissenting shareholder in order to exercise their right to payment.

When the dissenting shareholder challenges the fair value placed on his or her shares by the corporation, an appraisal proceeding may be commenced. An appraisal proceeding involves judicial appraisal of the fair value of the stock of the dissenting shareholders. Figure 10-5 is an example of a notice that may be given to the corporation by a dissenting shareholder to demand the fair market value of his or her shares upon merger.

Articles of Merger

After the plan of merger has been adopted pursuant to statute, **articles of merger** must be filed with the Secretary of State or other appropriate state authority. (See appendix A for a Secretary of State directory.) Under § 11.05 of the Model Business Corporation Act, the articles of merger must set forth:

1. The plan of merger
2. A statement that shareholder approval of the plan was not required, if that is the case
3. A statement regarding the approval of the plan of merger by the shareholders, including the number of votes voted for and against the merger in each voting group, if shareholder approval was necessary.

Figure 10-6 shows an example of articles of merger between two domestic corporations.

Plan of Exchange

Procedures for a **plan of exchange** are set forth in the Model Business Corporation Act and the statutes of several states that have followed

---

TERMS

articles of merger   Document filed with the Secretary of State or other appropriate authority to effect a merger.

plan of exchange   Document required by state statute that sets forth the terms of the agreement between the parties to a statutory share exchange.

**DEMAND BY DISSENTING STOCKHOLDER FOR
FAIR MARKET VALUE OF SHARES ON
MERGER OF CORPORATION**

**STATEMENT OF FAIR MARKET VALUE
OF SHARES**

To: _____ [corporation]

_____ [address]

The shareholders of this corporation, at a _____ [special] meeting held on _____ , 19___ , at its principal executive office at _____ [address], purported to approve an agreement providing for the merger of the corporation with _____ [constituent corporation], a _____ [state] corporation.

Notice of the purported approval by the shareholders was mailed to the undersigned on _____ , 19___ , and _____ [30] days have not yet expired since the date of mailing of the notice, and the undersigned has not approved such proposed merger.

The undersigned is the holder of record of _____ [number] shares of _____ [common] stock of _____ [corporation], evidenced by Certificate No. _____. These shares were voted against the merger.

The undersigned hereby makes written demand for the payment to him of the fair market value of such shares as of _____ , 19___ , being the date prior to the first announcement of the terms of the proposed merger.

The undersigned hereby states that _____ dollars ($_____) per share is the fair market value of such shares as of the date prior to the first announcement of the terms of the proposed merger.

The undersigned hereby submits to the corporation at its principal executive office the certificate for such shares with respect to which the undersigned makes this demand, in order that the certificate may be stamped or endorsed with the statement that such shares are dissenting shares and thereupon returned to him at the address stated below.

Dated _____ , 19___.[10]

[Signature and address]

FIGURE 10-5 Sample Demand by Dissenting Stockholder

the Model Act closely. Section 11.02(b) of the Model Business Corporation Act, which follows, sets forth the requirements for a plan of exchange:

ARTICLES OF MERGER OR CONSOLIDATION—
DOMESTIC CORPORATIONS

Pursuant to the provisions of _____ [cite statute], the undersigned corporations have adopted the following articles of _____ [merger or consolidation] for the purpose of combining the undersigned corporations:

The following plan of _____ [merger or consolidation] was approved by the stockholders of each of the undersigned corporations in the manner prescribed by statute: _____ [insert copy of plan].

As to each of the undersigned corporations, the number of shares outstanding, and the designation and number of outstanding shares of each class entitled to vote as a class on such plan, as are follows:

		Entitled to Vote as a Class	
Name of Corporation	Number of Shares Outstanding	Designation of Class	Number of Shares
_____	_____	_____	_____
_____	_____	_____	_____
_____	_____	_____	_____

As to each of the undersigned corporations, the total number of shares voted for and against such plan, respectively, and, as to each class entitled to vote thereon as a class, the number of shares of such class voted for and against such plan, respectively, are as follows:

Number of Shares

Entitled to Vote as a Class

Name of Corporation	Total Voted For	Total Voted Against	Class	Voted For	Voted Against
_____	_____	_____	_____	_____	_____
_____	_____	_____	_____	_____	_____
_____	_____	_____	_____	_____	_____

Dated: _____.[11]

[Signatures]

[Seals]

FIGURE 10-6   Sample Articles of Merger or Consolidation (Domestic Corporations)

(b) The plan of exchange must set forth:
   (1) the name of the corporation whose shares will be acquired and the name of the acquiring corporation;
   (2) the terms and conditions of the exchange;

(3) the manner and basis of exchanging the shares to be acquired for shares, obligations, or other securities of the acquiring or any other corporation or for cash or other property in whole or part.

As with a plan of merger, the plan of exchange may also contain any other provisions relating to the transaction.

Following is a list of items often included in a plan of exchange:

- Date of agreement

- Name and authorized capitalization of each original corporation

- Recital that each board of directors believes it to be in the best interest of its respective corporation that the share exchange take place

- Provisions for the method of exchanging the shares of the target corporation for shares of the acquiring corporation and for continuing the target corporation as a subsidiary of the acquiring corporation

- Name, purposes, location of the principal offices, number of directors, and capital stock of the acquiring corporation and the subsidiary corporation after the exchange

- Amendments to the articles of incorporation of each corporation, reflecting the share exchange

- Provisions for amending the bylaws of each corporation, as necessary

- Treatment of outstanding stock options, if any

- Restrictions on transactions outside the normal course of business by either corporation prior to the effective date of the share exchange

- Provisions for corporate distributions during the period prior to the effective date of the share exchange, if desired

- Provisions for submitting the plan of exchange to the shareholders of each corporation for approval, as necessary

- Agreement regarding the inspection of books, records, and other property of each corporation

- Provisions for possible abandonment of the plan of exchange prior to the completion thereof by the directors of either corporation

- Provisions for filing the articles of share exchange with the appropriate state office, as required by statute

- Closing and effective date of the share exchange.

In addition, the plan of exchange may include schedules and exhibits setting forth the specific assets and liabilities of each corporation, and any other information relevant to the business of each corporation, including pending or threatened litigation.

Director and Shareholder Approval of the Plan of Exchange

The statutory requirements for approving a plan of exchange are substantially the same as those for approving a plan of merger. State statutes generally require that the plan be recommended by the board of directors and approved by the shareholders of the corporation. In addition, the Model Business Corporation Act provides that "separate voting by voting groups is required on a plan of share exchange by each class or series of shares included in the exchange, with each class or series constituting a separate voting group."[12]

Dissenting Shareholders

The share exchange, if properly approved by a majority of the shareholders pursuant to statute, is binding on all shareholders. However, shareholders who dissent from the share exchange may have the right to obtain payment for their shares and withdraw from the corporation. Shareholders entitled to vote on a plan of exchange are granted the same right to dissent that is prescribed for shareholders entitled to vote on a plan of merger.

Articles of Share Exchange

After the plan of exchange has been adopted pursuant to statute, the **articles of share exchange** must be filed with the Secretary of State or other appropriate state authority, generally in the same manner prescribed for articles of merger (discussed above). The statutes of the state of domicile will dictate the contents of the articles of share exchange. Under the Model Business Corporation Act, the articles of share exchange must set forth:

1. The plan of share exchange
2. A statement regarding the approval of the plan of exchange by the shareholders, including the number of votes voted for and against the exchange in each voting group.[13]

TERMS

articles of share exchange   Document filed with the Secretary of State or other appropriate state authority to effect a share exchange.

The share exchange generally becomes effective as the effective date of the articles.

The following states have adopted corporate statutes with share exchange provisions that are comparable to the Revised Model Business Corporation Act:

Alaska	Kentucky	South Carolina
Arkansas	Michigan	Tennessee
Florida	Montana	Utah
Georgia	Mississippi	Virginia
Illinois	New Hampshire	Washington
Indiana	North Carolina	Wisconsin
Iowa	Oregon	Wyoming

Due Diligence and Preclosing Matters

Although the plan of merger or plan of exchange sets forth specific information regarding the business and financial condition of each corporation, the parties to a merger or share exchange and their professional representatives must use due diligence to ascertain the validity of the statements in the plan. *Due diligence* refers to the standard of care that must be exercised by each responsible party, and *due diligence work* refers to the investigation done to ascertain the validity of statements made in an agreement prior to closing.

In a statutory merger or share exchange transaction, due diligence work often involves a thorough review of the documentation supporting the information in the plan of merger or plan of exchange, as well as possible on-site investigations to see and inspect the real estate, buildings, assets, and inventory involved in the transaction, and also to inspect corporate books and records that are too cumbersome to photocopy or remove from the corporate offices. Due diligence work can be very time-consuming, and it often involves the legal assistants working on the transaction, who work on producing the documentation requested by the other party or parties to the transaction and on collecting and reviewing the documentation requested on behalf of the corporate client.

Usually, the plan of merger or share exchange is used to produce a checklist of documentation that must be produced by each party prior to closing. In addition to the corporate clients involved in a merger, accountants and other parties may also be responsible for producing documents. Figure 10-7 is an excerpt from a sample checklist used to assure that all documents are prepared, exchanged, reviewed, and approved before the closing of the merger or share exchange.

**AGREEMENT OF MERGER BETWEEN
CORPORATION A AND CORPORATION B**

PROPOSED CLOSING DATE JUNE 20, 1997

Document/Page Reference	Resp. Party	Received or Prepared	Approved or Submitted
Corporation A Articles of Incorporation/ Page 3, Para. 2	Corp. A		
Corporation A Corporate Bylaws (Certified) Page 3, Para. 3	Corp. A		
Corporation A Corporate Minutes 1990 through Present Date/Page 3, Para. 4	Corp. A		
Corporation B Articles of Incorporation/ Page 3, Para. 2	Corp. B		
Corporation B Corporate Bylaws (Certified) Page 3, Para. 3	Corp. B		
Corporation B Corporate Minutes 1990 through Present Date/ Page 3, Para. 4	Corp. B		
Lease to 2348 Elm Street Exhibit A	Corp. B		
Lease to 3484 Maple Street Exhibit A	Corp. B		
Title to 390 Main Street Exhibit A	Corp. A		
Agreement with ABC Mfg. Exhibit B	Corp. A		
Agreement with Acme Plastics/Exhibit B	Corp. A		

FIGURE 10-7 Sample Document Preparation Checklist

The list of documents that must be exchanged and reviewed prior to closing can be very extensive, and may include the following:

- Proof of corporate existence and good standing of each corporation

- Copies of all documents typically included in corporate minute books, including articles of incorporation and any amendments thereto, bylaws, and minutes of the board of directors and shareholder meetings

- Copies of stock ledgers and stock certificates
- Financial statements for each corporation
- Tax returns for each corporation and results of any tax audits
- Leases and/or titles to all real property that is owned and/or leased by each corporation
- Lists of all equipment and personal property at each location occupied by each corporation
- All paperwork concerning any patents, trademarks, and copyrights pending or owned by each corporation
- Copies of all employment and noncompetition agreements to which each corporation is a party
- Descriptions of all employee benefits, including the names of all employees entitled thereto
- Certified Uniform Commercial Code searches for each corporation
- Copies of any loan agreements to which each corporation is a party
- Lists of accounts payable for each corporation
- Lists of accounts receivable for each corporation
- Copies of all material contracts to which each corporation is a party
- Customer lists
- Vendor lists
- Copies of pleadings in any pending litigation.

The documents that must be produced and reviewed will vary depending on the type of transaction and the relationship of the parties. If the transaction being contemplated is a merger between parent and subsidiary corporations, much of the information required for the transaction will be available to the parties in the normal course of business, and many of the documents in the preceding list will be irrelevant.

Due diligence work also involves ascertaining whether any outside parties may be required to give consent to any part of the transaction. All agreements to which the merging or target corporation is a party must be reviewed to determine whether consent of the other party to the agreement must be obtained before assigning the contract to the surviving or acquiring corporation. For example, if a merging corporation is a tenant under a lease, the landlord's consent will probably be required to transfer the lease to the acquiring corporation. If consent must be obtained, it should be requested promptly to ensure that it is received before closing.

Closing the Statutory Merger or Share Exchange Transaction

The agreement and plan of merger or share exchange typically set forth a date and time for closing the transaction. At the closing, the shares of stock will change hands, assignments and transfers of contracts and real and personal property will be made, and any cash, or contractual obligations to pay out cash at a future date, will be paid out. The key officers from each corporation, the legal team for each corporation, and any other individuals who may be required to sign closing documents usually attend the closing.

The closing is typically conducted by executing and exchanging all documents referred to in the agreement and plan of merger or share exchange, as well as any supplemental documents necessary to effect the transfers referred to therein. A closing agenda is typically prepared from the plan of merger or plan of exchange and the checklist used in accumulating and reviewing the documents. Each party is responsible for preparing or producing certain documents required for the closing, as specified in the agenda. Legal assistants who have been instrumental in getting the transaction to the closing table are often involved in the actual closing, and are usually responsible for seeing that each document is properly executed and that the proper parties are given copies. This may be no small task in complex transactions that could literally involve several boxes of documents.

Merger Closings

Following is a list of some of the types of documents typically required for closing a merger transaction:

1. Articles of merger, including any necessary articles of amendment to the articles of incorporation
2. Instruments assigning and transferring the appropriate shares of stock of each corporation
3. New stock certificates representing stock ownership pursuant to the plan of merger
4. Deeds or other instruments assigning or transferring any real property
5. Bills of sale or other instruments assigning or transferring any equipment, motor vehicles, or other personal property
6. Assignments or other instruments assigning or transferring any patents, trademarks, or copyrights
7. Instruments assigning or transferring bank accounts
8. Legal opinions of transfer agents

9. Legal opinions of attorneys for each party

10. Notices or filings required by the Securities and Exchange

11. Officers Commission (SEC) certificates

12. Certified copies of board of director and shareholder resolutions approving the transaction

13. Announcements to shareholders and/or employees, if necessary.

Share Exchange Closings

Closings of share exchange transactions are very similar to merger closings, with more emphasis placed on documents transferring the ownership of the target corporation. Following is a list of some of the items that may be required for closing a share exchange transaction:

1. Articles of share exchange, including amendments to the articles of the target corporation and the acquiring corporation, as needed

2. Instruments transferring the appropriate shares of stock of each corporation

3. New stock certificates representing the ownership of the acquiring corporation and the target corporation, which will become a subsidiary

4. Any necessary assignments

5. Legal opinions of attorneys for each party

6. Any notices required by the SEC or blue sky laws

7. Officers' certificates

8. Certified copies of board of director and shareholder resolutions approving the transaction.

Postclosing Matters

After the closing, there are typically several matters that still need to be attended to in order to finalize the transaction. Most of these tasks involve notification of interested parties of the merger or share exchange and filings at the county or state level, or with the SEC. Some of the steps that may be required after the closing of a statutory merger or statutory share exchange include the following:

1. Filing the articles of merger or share exchange (if not done prior to closing) and any amendments to the articles of incorporation required by the transaction

2. Organizing new corporate minute books and stock ledgers

3. Filing any deeds transferring real estate

4. Changing title on motor vehicles, as necessary
5. Sending copies of any lease assignments to the proper landlords or tenants
6. Filing any Uniform Commercial Code documents
7. Any filings required by the SEC or blue sky laws.

§ 10.3 Asset and Stock Acquisitions

In addition to statutory mergers and share exchanges, there are several other means of combining or acquiring corporations. This section discusses nonstatutory transactions involving the acquisition of corporate assets and stock.

The discussion in this section concerns nonstatutory corporate acquisitions that are completed through the purchase of all or substantially all of the assets or outstanding shares of stock of a corporation. Although asset acquisitions and stock acquisitions may have an economic effect that is very similar to that of statutory mergers and acquisitions, there are significant differences. Courts have held that "the mere purchase by, and transfer to, one corporation of the property and franchises of another corporation, or the purchase by one corporation of the stock of another corporation, is not a consolidation of the two corporations."[14]

This section focuses on asset acquisition and stock acquisition of closely held corporations and the advantages and disadvantages of each type of transaction. It also examines the state and federal laws affecting statutory mergers and stock exchanges.

Asset Acquisitions

One means of acquiring the business of a corporation is to purchase all, or substantially all, of its assets. In *asset acquisitions,* the acquiring corporation purchases all of the assets of the target corporation, leaving the target corporation a mere corporate shell to be dissolved. This type of transaction has the advantage of permitting the buyers to know exactly what they are getting. The fact that the acquiring corporation will generally not be held liable for any future liabilities and obligations of the target corporation may also be a very important advantage.

TABLE 10-1   LARGEST MERGERS IN THE UNITED STATES
EACH YEAR 1988–1994

Year	Company	Acquirer	Value (in billions of dollars)
1994	Lockheed	Martin Marietta	$10.0
1993	McCaw Cellular	AT&T	$12.6
1991	NCR	AT&T	$ 7.4
1990	MCA	Matsushita	$ 6.5
1989	Warner Communications	Time	$13.9
1988	RJR Nabisco	Kohlberg Kravis Roberts	$24.9
1987	Standard Oil	British Petroleum	$ 7.9
1986	Beatrice	Kohlberg Kravis Roberts	$ 6.2
1985	Hughes Aircraft	General Motors	$ 5.0
1984	Gulf Oil	Chevron	$13.3

No corporate mergers or acquisitions in excess of $2.0 billion were reported during 1992.

However, the necessity of identifying each specific asset being acquired can prove to be much more cumbersome than a stock acquisition.

Stock Acquisitions

A *stock acquisition transaction* involves the purchase of all or substantially all of the outstanding stock of a corporation, either by an individual, a group of individuals, or, more commonly, another corporation. The target corporation generally becomes a subsidiary of the acquiring corporation, or it is merged into the acquiring corporation.

One advantage of this type of purchase is the simplification in transferring the corporation from one individual or group of individuals to another. Instead of transferring each asset owned by the corporation, the ownership of the corporation itself is transferred to the new owner or owners. Disadvantages include the fact that the acquiring corporation will be responsible for all debts and liabilities of the corporation being acquired, even those that have an unknown or undisclosed value at the time of closing. Another disadvantage is that the acquiring corporation may have to deal with several individual shareholders.

Barring any share transfer restrictions on shares of stock, shareholders of closely held or publicly held corporations may sell their shares of stock at will. However, most stock acquisitions that involve the purchase of substantially all of the stock of a corporation must involve a consensus of the shareholders. Obviously, substantially all of the shares of a corporation may not be purchased unless the holders of those shares all agree to sell their stock.

State and Federal Laws Affecting Asset and Stock Acquisitions

Although the procedures for asset and stock purchases are not set forth in state statutes, certain aspects of these transactions, such as shareholder approval of the sale of a corporation's assets, are subject to state law. The statutes of the state of domicile of each party to the transaction must be consulted to be sure that all statutory requirements are complied with. In addition, certain asset or stock acquisition transactions may trigger SEC or blue sky law reporting requirements and the antitrust provisions found in the Hart-Scott-Rodino Act.

An asset acquisition sale may also be subject to the provisions of Article 6 of the Uniform Commercial Code, which provides for notification to creditors in the event of a bulk transfer of assets. However, in 1989 the National Conference of Commissioners on Uniform State Laws recommended the repeal of Article 6, stating that they believe "that modern commercial and legal reality no longer supports the need for regulation of bulk sales." State statutes should be consulted to determine if any provisions of Article 6, or any bulk sales, bulk transfer, or fraudulent conveyance laws are in effect in the pertinent state or states that would affect the proposed transaction.

§ 10.4 Asset and Stock Acquisition Procedures

Unlike statutory mergers and share exchanges, there are no specific statutory procedures to be followed for asset and stock acquisitions. The procedures to be followed for each of these types of transactions vary greatly depending on the type of transaction and the parties involved. Procedures for acquiring the assets of a corporation focus much more on the identification and transfer of the assets; stock acquisitions focus more on the entire corporate entity represented by the shares of stock.

Often, the decision as to whether a transaction should involve the purchase of a corporation's stock or the corporation's assets is made only after a preliminary agreement has been made by the corporations for one to buy out the other. The decision is made based upon the implications of tax laws to all parties involved.

This section looks at the procedures for completing transactions involving asset and stock acquisitions of closely held corporations. First it considers the negotiations involved in those types of transactions. Next it examines the asset purchase agreement and its approval by the shareholders of the target corporation. It then focuses on requirements for an agreement for the purchase and sale of all, or substantially all, of the outstanding stock of a corporation. This section concludes with a discussion of the due diligence and preclosing work involved in asset and stock acquisitions and the closing and postclosing matters concerning acquisitions.

Negotiations and Letter of Intent

The first step in the asset purchase or stock purchase procedures is often very similar to that involved with mergers or share exchanges. Preliminary negotiations, which involve meetings between the two parties and their legal counsel, generally commence with the aim of entering into a preliminary agreement and signing a letter of intent. Price, terms, and the format of the acquisition of the corporation all must be agreed upon before an agreement can be entered into.

Asset Purchase Agreement

An asset purchase agreement specifically sets forth the agreement between the parties with regard to the purchase of all or substantially all of the assets of one corporation by another, based on the letter of intent or preliminary agreement entered into between the parties. The asset purchase agreement must set forth very specifically all the assets that are to be purchased by the acquiring corporation, as well as the terms for the disposition of any debts or liens related to those assets. Following is a list of items often included in an asset purchase agreement:

- Names and other identification of the parties

- Description of the property and assets subject to the agreement

- The nature and amount of the consideration to be paid for the assets
- Terms for assuming any debts and liabilities
- Acts required of the seller, including the delivery of the instruments of transfer
- Agreement regarding the inspection of books, records, and property of the selling corporation
- Warranties of the seller, including the authority to enter into the agreement, the accuracy and completeness of the books and records, title to the property and assets being acquired, and the care and preservation of the property and assets
- Indemnification of the buyer
- Buyer's right to use seller's name
- Remedies in the event of a default by either party
- Governing law
- Date of the agreement
- Signature of all parties involved
- The date, time, and place of closing.

The sale of all or substantially all of the assets of a corporation requires shareholder approval of the target corporation. The Model Business Corporation Act provides for the sale of assets, other than in the regular course of business, as follows:

> (a) A corporation may sell, lease, exchange, or otherwise dispose of all, or substantially all, of its property (with or without the good will), otherwise than in the usual and regular course of business, on the terms and conditions and for the consideration determined by the corporation's board of directors, if the board of directors proposes and its shareholders approve the proposed transaction.[15]

The statutory procedures for obtaining shareholder approval for the sale of all, or substantially all, of the assets of a corporation are usually very similar to those prescribed for the approval of statutory mergers and share exchanges because, in effect, the business of the corporation as it has existed will terminate upon the sale of its assets. The statutes of the state of domicile of the target corporation should always be consulted to be sure that the exact procedures for obtaining shareholder approval are followed. Shareholders of the target corporation almost always have the right to dissent. Figure 10-8 is an example of a stockholders' written consent approving the sale of all or substantially all assets of the corporation.

**STOCKHOLDERS' WRITTEN CONSENT
APPROVING SALE OF ALL OR SUBSTANTIALLY
ALL ASSETS**

Whereas, at a _____ [regular or special] meeting of the board of directors of _____ [corporation] held on _____, 19___ , the board duly passed the following resolution authorizing the sale, conveyance, exchange, and transfer of all or substantially all of the property and assets of the corporation to _____ [purchasing corporation]: _____ [set forth board's resolution].

[If principal terms of transaction and nature and amount of consideration are not specified in board's resolution, add the following: Whereas, the principal terms of the transaction and the nature and amount of the consideration of the sale, conveyance, exchange, and transfer authorized by the board at such meeting are as follows: _____];

Resolved, that the undersigned shareholders, and each of them, hereby approve and consent to the principal terms of the transaction and the nature and amount of the consideration, and the resolutions of the board as set forth above.

In witness whereof, each of the undersigned has signed his or her name and the date of signing and the number of shares of the corporation entitled to vote held by him or her _____ [of record] on such date.

Name	Signature	Date of Execution	Number of Shares
_____	_____	_____	_____
_____	_____	_____	_____
_____	_____	_____	_____ 16

FIGURE 10-8 Sample Stockholders' Consent to Acquisition

Stock Purchase Agreement

In a stock purchase agreement, the purchaser accepts all of the rights and obligations incident to ownership of the stock of the target corporation. It is not necessary to specify the exact assets and liabilities of the selling corporation. Each selling shareholder must be in agreement with the terms of the purchase of the stock and enter into the stock purchase agreement. Special warranties regarding the corporation and its financial and legal status are typically given by the officers of the corporation. Common provisions in a stock purchase agreement include the following:

- Names and other identification of the parties

- Price for purchase of stock

- Method of payment
- Seller's representations regarding the authority to sell the stock being purchased
- Seller's warranty that all securities laws have been and will be complied with to the date of the contemplated transaction
- Disclosure of any pending litigation against the selling corporation
- Seller's warranties as to the good standing of the corporation, its authorized, issued, and outstanding stock, and its financial condition
- Buyer's representations with regard to its ability to finance the purchase of the stock
- The agreement between the acquiring and selling corporations with regard to the payment of any tax liability of the corporation or to be incurred as a result of the sale of the stock
- Covenants not to compete of certain officers and key employees of the corporation
- A general release of the seller from any future liability incurred by the selling corporation
- The date, location, and method of closing
- Execution of all parties.

Due Diligence and Preclosing Matters

The due diligence and preclosing procedures for asset and stock purchases are very similar to those involved in statutory mergers and share exchanges. The asset purchase transaction focuses more on the specific assets being purchased, whereas the stock purchase transaction involves all aspects of the corporation whose shares are being purchased, with specific attention to details involving any potential future liability of the target corporation. The majority of the due diligence work in an asset or share acquisition transaction is done by the acquiring corporations' representatives and legal counsel. The purchase agreement is used to produce a checklist of documents to be prepared, accumulated, and reviewed in much the same way as the checklist for mergers and share exchange documents is prepared.

Closing the Asset or Stock Acquisition Transaction

The procedures for closing an acquisition transaction are usually very similar to those discussed for mergers and share exchanges. The parties in attendance and the documents executed and exchanged will vary depending on the type of transaction.

In an asset purchase transaction, the purchasers and representatives of the selling corporation with authority to sign on behalf of the corporation must be present. In a share purchase, any shareholders selling their stock, who have not presigned the necessary documents, must be in attendance.

Asset Acquisition Closing

Following is a list of some of the documents that might be included in a closing agenda for an asset acquisition:

1. Certified checks, wire transfer documentation, and/or promissory notes representing the consideration being given for the assets
2. Certified copies of the resolutions of the board of directors and shareholders of the selling corporation approving the transaction
3. Deeds or other instruments assigning or transferring any real property
4. Bills of sale or other instruments assigning or transferring any equipment, motor vehicles, or other personal property, including inventory
5. Assignments or other instruments transferring any patents, trademarks, or copyrights
6. Assignments or other instruments assigning any loans on the real or personal property being purchased
7. Documents assigning the name of the corporation, if applicable
8. Instruments assigning or transferring bank accounts
9. Legal opinions of attorneys for each party
10. Notices or filings required by the SEC
11. Officers' certificates
12. Assignments of accounts receivable and payable.

Stock Acquisition Closing

Following is a list of some of the types of documents that may be included in the closing agenda for a stock acquisition transaction:

1. Instruments assigning and transferring the appropriate shares of stock of each corporation
2. New stock certificates representing stock ownership pursuant to the agreement for purchase of shares

3. Legal opinions of transfer agents
4. Legal opinions of attorneys for each party
5. Any required consents or approvals
6. Notices or filings required by the SEC
7. Officers' certificates.

The transfer of real and personal property, as well as loans, contracts, and other agreements entered into by the corporation, will depend on the circumstances. In the event of a stock purchase transaction, when the corporation whose shares are being sold will retain its name, it may not be necessary to prepare and execute assignments for all real and personal property, because the *corporation* is the owner and will remain the owner after the sale; only the shareholders have changed. However, the sale of all or substantially all of the stock of a corporation will probably require an assignment in many instances. Bank loans, for instance, may require an assignment, and usually permission, because the ownership of the corporation that has entered into the loan agreement is changing. In any event, the terms of all agreements to which the selling corporation is a party should be reviewed to be sure that all such transfers and assignments are ready for execution prior to closing.

Postclosing Matters

As with the statutory merger or share exchange, there are always several items that require attention after the closing of an asset or stock acquisition transaction. Following is a list of some of the tasks that may need to be completed after the closing of an asset acquisition:

1. Deeds or other instruments assigning or transferring any real property must be filed at the proper county office.
2. Copies of any loan assignments must be sent to any interested third party.
3. If the name of any corporation involved in the transaction must be changed, the proper articles of amendment must be filed.
4. Copies of instruments assigning or transferring bank accounts must be sent to interested third parties.
5. Any reporting requirements of the SEC or state securities authorities must be complied with.

Following is a list of some of the types of documents and tasks that may require attention after the closing of a stock acquisition transaction:

1. New stock certificates must be prepared (if not done at closing).

2. Any reporting requirements of the SEC or state securities authorities must be complied with.

3. Notification to insurance companies of any insurance policies that have been assigned must be completed.

§ 10.5 Amendments to Articles of Incorporation

Many of the transactions discussed previously in this chapter require amendments to the articles of incorporation of one or more corporations. Under the Model Business Corporation Act, "A corporation may amend its articles of incorporation at any time to add or change a provision that is required or permitted in the articles of incorporation or to delete a provision not required in the articles of incorporation."[17] Generally, whenever any of the information contained in the original articles of incorporation changes, the articles of incorporation must be amended in accordance with the statutes of the corporation's state of domicile.

Approval of the Articles of Amendment

The statutes of the state of domicile provide the necessary procedures for approving and filing amendments to the articles of incorporation. In general, any amendments that affect the rights or position of the shareholders in any way must be approved by the shareholders.

Amendments Not Requiring Shareholder Approval

Although shareholder approval is generally required to amend a corporation's articles of incorporation, the incorporators or board of directors have the authority to amend the articles under certain circumstances. The incorporators or the board of directors of the corporation are generally authorized to amend the articles of incorporation prior to the issuance of shares of stock of the corporation. Under the Model Business Corporation Act, "If a corporation has not yet issued shares, its incorporators or board of directors may adopt one or more amendments to the corporation's articles of incorporation."[18]

The statutes of the state of a corporation's domicile may also expressly provide certain circumstances under which the board of directors may amend the articles of incorporation *after* issuance of the corporation's shares. The type of amendments typically permitted in this manner are routine amendments that will not affect the rights of the shareholders, or amendments required by law, such as the termination of statutory close corporation status if such status is terminated by operation of law.

Amendments Requiring Shareholder Approval

For amendments that require shareholder approval, the method of obtaining approval is often very similar to that required for approving a statutory merger or plan of exchange. Under the Model Business Corporation Act, when shareholder approval is required for an amendment to the articles of incorporation, these procedures must be followed:

1. The board of directors must recommend the amendment to the shareholders, unless the board determines that it should make no recommendation and communicates the basis for its determination to the shareholders with the amendment.[19] Reasons for not rendering a recommendation may include a conflict of interest or other special circumstances.[20] The board may condition its submission of the proposed amendment on any basis.[21]

2. Each shareholder, whether or not entitled to vote, must be notified of the shareholder meeting pursuant to statute. The notice must state that the purpose of the meeting is to consider the proposed amendment, and it must contain or be accompanied by a copy or summary of the amendment.[22]

3. Unless the articles of incorporation or the board of directors require a greater vote or a vote by voting groups, the amendment to be adopted must be approved by a majority of the votes entitled to be cast on the amendment by any voting group with respect to which the amendment would create dissenters' rights, and the votes generally required by statute with regard to every other voting group entitled to vote on the amendment.[23]

The Model Business Corporation Act further sets forth the conditions under which voting on amendments by voting groups is required. Generally, the holders of the outstanding shares of a class are entitled to vote as a separate voting group on a proposed amendment if the rights of that class of shareholder would be affected by the proposed amendment.

Right to Dissent

A shareholder may be entitled to dissent from, and obtain payment of the fair value of his or her shares due to, the amendment of the corporation's articles of incorporation. Section 13.02(4) of the Model Business Corporation Act specifies the sort of amendment from which a shareholder is entitled to dissent:

(4) an amendment of the articles of incorporation that materially and adversely affects rights in respect of a dissenter's shares because it:
  (i) alters or abolishes a preferential right of the shares;
  (ii) creates, alters, or abolishes a right in respect of redemption, including a provision respecting a sinking fund for the redemption or repurchase, of the shares;
  (iii) alters or abolishes a preemptive right of the holder of the shares to acquire shares or other securities;
  (iv) excludes or limits the right of the shares to vote on any matter, or to cumulate votes, other than a limitation by dilution through issuance of shares or other securities with similar voting rights; or
  (v) reduces the number of shares owned by the shareholder to be a fraction of a share if the fractional share so created is to be acquired for cash under section 6.04.

Articles of Amendment

The document amending the articles of incorporation is typically called the **articles of amendment** or the *certificate of amendment*. The requirements for the articles of amendment are set by state statute. In general, the amendment must include the information required by statute, and it must be filed in the office where the original articles of incorporation are filed. (See appendix A for a Secretary of State directory.) Any state requirements for county filing and publishing articles of incorporation generally apply to amendments of the articles of incorporation as well. Section 10.06 of the Model Business Corporation Act sets forth the requirements for the contents of the articles of amendment:

§ 10.06. ARTICLES OF AMENDMENT

A corporation amending its articles of incorporation shall deliver to the secretary of state for filing articles of amendment setting forth:
(1) the name of the corporation;
(2) the text of each amendment adopted;
(3) if an amendment provides for an exchange, reclassification, or cancellation of issued shares, provisions for implementing the amendment if not contained in the amendment itself;
(4) the date of each amendment's adoption;
(5) if an amendment was adopted by the incorporators or board of directors without shareholder action, a statement to that effect and that shareholder action was not required;
(6) if an amendment was approved by the shareholders;

TERMS

articles of amendment Document filed with the Secretary of State or other appropriate state authority to amend a corporation's articles of incorporation.

> (i) the designation, number of outstanding shares, number of votes entitled to be cast by each voting group entitled to vote separately on the amendment, and number of votes of each voting group indisputably represented at the meeting;
>
> (ii) either the total number of votes cast for and against the amendment by each voting group entitled to vote separately on the amendment or the total number of undisputed votes cast for the amendment by each voting group and a statement that the number cast for the amendment by each voting group was sufficient for approval by that voting group.

Restated Articles of Incorporation

Most state statutes grant corporations the right to restate their articles of incorporation at any time. So long as the restated articles contain no amendments that require shareholder approval, shareholder approval is generally not required merely to restate the articles. If any amendments in the restated articles of incorporation do require shareholder approval, the restated articles must be approved by the shareholders in the manner prescribed by law. Restated articles are generally filed in the same manner as articles of amendment.

§ 10.6 Reorganizations

The term *reorganization* is often used to describe any types of change to the corporate structure, including mergers and acquisitions. Reorganizations often involve financially distressed corporations, as demonstrated by the following commonly used court definition of the term:

> It is not ordinarily the combination of several existing corporations, but is simply the carrying out by proper agreements and legal proceedings of a business plan or scheme for winding up the affairs of, or foreclosing a mortgage or mortgages upon, the property of insolvent corporations, and the organization of a new corporation to take over the property and business of the distressed corporation.[24]

The Internal Revenue Service (IRS) has its own definitions of corporate reorganizations, including statutory mergers and share exchanges, to determine whether a particular reorganization is tax-free.

Type A Transactions

A statutory merger or consolidation is considered by the IRS to be a Type A transaction.

Type B Transactions

The exchange of voting shares between two corporations is considered by the IRS to a Type B transaction.

Type C Transactions

A Type C reorganization is the acquisition of substantially all of the properties of another corporation in exchange solely for shares of the acquiring corporation.

Type D Transactions

A Type D transaction is a transaction whereby one corporation transfers all or part of its assets to another corporation which it controls.

Type E Transactions

Type E transactions are changes to the capital structure of the corporation that involve amendments to the articles of incorporation. These types of transactions are referred to as *recapitalizations*.

Type F Transactions

Mere change in identity, form, or place of organization of one corporation, however effected, is considered a Type F transaction.

Type G Transactions

A Type G transaction is one in which a transfer is made by a corporation of all or part of its assets to another corporation in a Title 11 (federal Bankruptcy Act) or similar case. This type of transaction only applies if, in pursuance of the plan, stock or securities of the corporation to which the assets are transferred are distributed in a transaction that qualifies under 26 U.S.C. §§ 354, 355, or 356.

§ 10.7 The Paralegal's Role in Mergers and Acquisitions

Paralegals are essential members of most merger and acquisition teams. While the attorneys may be negotiating the details of the merger or acquisition agreement—often until the final documents are signed at the closing table—the paralegals are often responsible for preparing the necessary supplementary documents on behalf of the client, collecting and reviewing the necessary documents from other parties, and preparing for the closing. The paralegal is often instrumental in organizing and conducting the closing of the transaction and in completing the follow-up work after closing. If the paralegal is working on the legal team that represents the seller of assets or shares of stock in a transaction, he or she may directly assist the corporate client at their offices to assemble information required by the buyers.

Paralegals are often brought in to work on a merger or acquisition after an agreement has been reached. The first step in the paralegal's involvement is a thorough review of the agreement so the paralegal can become familiar with the parties involved and the substance of the transaction. From the agreement, a checklist or agenda can be completed. The checklist should include all the documents that will be drafted or reviewed prior to or at the closing, along with a reference as to who is responsible for preparing or producing the document. It should also include any actions that must be taken by any party to the agreement prior to closing. Once this checklist has been prepared, copies should be circulated to all parties involved in the transaction or all parties who are in any way responsible for producing documents or materials prior to or at closing.

It is often the responsibility of the paralegal to draft several of the necessary corporate documents, possibly including corporate resolutions, amendments to articles of incorporation, and assignments. These documents are then reviewed by the attorney and sent to the corporate client for approval and signature. It is advisable to get preclosing approval by the other party on as many documents as possible to expedite the closing process.

At the same time documents are being drafted and information gathered, they are also being requested and collected from the other parties for review by the attorney and corporate client. The paralegal is often responsible for ensuring that the documents arrive in time to be reviewed prior to closing, and possibly for summarizing longer documents to save the time of the attorney and client, who will undoubtedly be busy with other aspects of the transaction.

Prior to the closing, all documents should be assembled so that they are readily available. With the multitude of documents often required to close mergers and acquisitions, organization is crucial. Often documents are arranged by responsible party, or in groups, such as real estate assets, equipment and machinery, etc. Other times, they may be assembled in the order of their reference in the agreement between the parties, so that the agreement can be reviewed and each document executed in order at the closing table. Whatever order is chosen, sufficient copies should be made for each party involved, usually with one or two extra sets. These documents are usually placed in labeled file folders, numbered and indexed as they are drafted or received at the office. This system also allows for good organization at the closing, when the paralegal may be responsible for seeing that each document is signed by the proper individual or individuals and witnessed and notarized (if necessary), and that each copy is delivered to the appropriate person. The paralegal also often has responsibility for several of the postclosing matters that must be attended to, including assembling copies of all closing documents and making *closing books,* which are often bound and sent to each party involved in the transaction.

Many corporate paralegals work in the mergers and acquisitions area and find it very exciting work. It is also very demanding work that requires exceptional organizational skills, attention to detail, and the ability to work under a certain amount of stress.

Review Questions

1. What is the difference between a consolidation and a merger?

2. What is the final relationship between two corporations who were parties to a share exchange?

3. What is a "surviving" corporation in a merger transaction?

4. What type of mergers might not require shareholder approval of both parties under certain circumstances?

5. If the sole shareholder of Diane's Auto Parts, Inc., which holds the stock of 95 percent of the D.G. Auto Parts Corporation, decides to merge the two corporations together, with Diane's Auto Parts, Inc. being the surviving corporation, what type of merger would it be? Why are the requirements for shareholder approval different for this type of merger? Why are approval requirements different for upstream mergers?

6. What is a letter of intent?

7. Are there statutory requirements for the contents of an agreement for asset acquisition?

8. What constitutes due diligence work?

9. Suppose that the shareholders of Kate's Household Products, Inc. are interested in acquiring one of their biggest suppliers, Nixon Chemical Corporation, but they are concerned about past problems that Nixon Chemical

has had with toxic waste disposal. What type of acquisition might be the most beneficial to Kate's Household Products, Inc.?

10. What are some possible disadvantages of acquiring an auto dealer, or a corporation that owns several pieces of real estate, through an asset acquisition rather than a stock acquisition transaction?

Notes

[1] The Reference Press, *The American Almanac Statistical Abstract of the United States: 1994–1995,* 114th ed. at 855 (Austin, Texas 1994).

[2] *Id.*

[3] 1984 Revised Model Business Corporation Act § 11.03(b).

[4] *Id.* § 11.03(c).

[5] *Id.* § 11.03(d).

[6] *Id.* § 11.03(e).

[7] *Id.* § 11.03(f)(1).

[8] 6B Am. Jur. *Legal Forms* 2d (Rev.) § 74:2692 (1994).

[9] *Id.* § 74:2796.

[10] *Id.* § 74:2800.

[11] *Id.* § 74:2842.

[12] 1984 Revised Model Business Corporation Act § 11.03(f)(2).

[13] *Id.* § 11.05.

[14] 19 Am. Jur. 2d *Corporations* § 2512 (1985).

[15] 1984 Revised Model Business Corporation Act § 12.02.

[16] 6 Am. Jur. *Legal Forms* 2d (Rev.) § 74:2315 (1981).

[17] 1984 Revised Model Business Corporation Act § 10.01.

[18] *Id.* § 10.05.

[19] *Id.* § 10.03(b)(1).

[20] *Id.* § 10.03(b)(1).

[21] *Id.* § 10.03(c).

[22] *Id.* § 10.03(d).

[23] *Id.* § 10.03(e).

[24] 19 Am. Jur. 2d *Corporations* § 2514 (1985).

CHAPTER 11

QUALIFICATION OF A FOREIGN CORPORATION

Introduction

The state or jurisdiction of the corporation's charter or incorporation is considered to be the corporation's state of domicile, regardless of where the company is physically located or transacts the majority of its business. A corporation is considered to be a **foreign corporation** in every state or jurisdiction other than its state of domicile.

This chapter examines the factors to be considered when deciding whether foreign corporation qualification is necessary. Next, it examines the qualification requirements typically imposed by state statutes, followed by a discussion of what is required to maintain the good standing of a foreign corporation and to withdraw it from doing business in a foreign state. After a brief discussion regarding foreign corporation name registration, this chapter concludes with a look at the paralegal's role in qualifying foreign corporations and the resources available to assist in that area.

§ 11.1 Determining When Foreign Corporation Qualification Is Necessary

A corporation does not legally exist beyond the boundaries of its state of domicile and must therefore be granted permission, or *qualify,* to do business with the proper authorities of any state, other than its state of domicile, in which it transacts business. When a corporation is

TERMS

foreign corporation [†]   A corporation incorporated under the laws of one state, doing business in another.

formed or when an existing corporation expands, a decision must be made as to where the corporation must qualify to do business as a foreign corporation. An examination of the corporation's business must be made and research must be done on any state in which there is potential for business to be transacted. The following factors must be considered when deciding whether it is necessary to qualify a corporation to do business in a particular foreign state:

1. The extent, duration, and nature of the corporation's involvement in the foreign state
2. The foreign state's statutory interpretation of what does, or does not, constitute transacting business in that state
3. The cost of qualification and the penalties for transacting business in the foreign state without authority.

State Long-Arm Statutes and Jurisdiction over Foreign Corporations

Whenever a corporation transacts business in a state other than its state of domicile, it subjects itself to the jurisdiction of the courts of that other state for any causes of action arising from the corporation's activities in that state. State **long-arm statutes** give the courts of each state personal jurisdiction over corporations that voluntarily go into that state for the purpose of transacting business. The defendant corporation need not be physically present in a foreign state for the courts of that state to render a binding judgment against it, but it must have minimum contacts within the state. In many instances courts have required that "to subject a defendant to a judgment in personam, if he be not present within the territory of the forum, he have certain minimum contacts with it such that the maintenance of the suit does not offend 'traditional notions of fair play and substantial justice.' "[1] Because corporations are subject to the jurisdiction of the courts in any state in which they transact business, in addition to qualifying or registering to do business as a foreign corporation, they must provide an agent to receive service of process in the foreign state in accordance with the laws of the foreign state.

═══════════════════ **TERMS** ═══════════════════

long-arm statutes [†]   State statutes providing for substituted service of process on a nonresident corporation or individual. Long-arm statutes permit a state's courts to take jurisdiction over a nonresident if he or she has done business in the state (provided the minimum contacts test is met), or has committed a tort or owns property within the state.

Dividends

Corporate Service Companies to the Rescue

Even the experienced corporate paralegal can feel lost when dealing with foreign states and countries. Even if you have mastered all the ins and outs of the state requirements for incorporating or qualifying foreign corporations in your state and a few neighboring states, it is virtually impossible to keep track of appropriate fees, forms, and technicalities in every jurisdiction.

Don't give up hope; there's help. Corporate service companies—which can be found throughout the United States—may offer the expertise or service you need for dealing with corporations in foreign states. Many of these are centered in Delaware, although some of the bigger service companies have offices in nearly every state. So, if you work in Texas and need a same-day UCC search in the Oregon Secretary of State's office, a corporate service company may be able to help.

Corporate service companies offer numerous services. Their two major functions are performing corporate filings at the office of the Secretary of State and similar offices and acting as registered agent for foreign corporations. For example, if you are in Missouri and have a client who wishes to incorporate in Delaware, the corporate service company can assist you in preparing the required documentation, filing the documentation, and then acting as the registered agent for service of process in the state of Delaware.

Other services offered by corporate service companies include:

- Preparing and filing incorporation documents
- Preparing and filing foreign corporation qualification documents
- Filing miscellaneous corporate documents at state and county levels
- Performing UCC filings and searches
- Searching court records
- Performing motor vehicle searches
- Performing various real estate searches and filings.

Corporate service companies cannot provide the services listed above without the assistance of corporate paralegals or those who hire them to perform the tasks. If you hire a corporate service company to perform an incorporation in a foreign state, you will still need to provide them with all of the information required for incorporating in that state. What the service company can do for you is to let you know what information is required, to put it into the proper format, and then to file it for you.

You can usually locate a corporate service company by looking in the telephone directory, or by scanning advertising in various legal publications.   ▮▮▮▮

Statutory Requirements for Qualification of Foreign Corporations

Exactly what does, or does not, constitute transacting business in each state is defined by the state's code or statutes. Typically, the state statutes list a number of activities that do not constitute transacting business, but remain silent on exactly what does constitute transacting business. Most states have adopted a modified version of § 15.01 of the Model Business Corporation Act, which reads:

(a) A foreign corporation may not transact business in this state until it obtains a certificate of authority from the secretary of state.

(b) The following activities, among others, do not constitute transacting business within the meaning of subsection (a):

(1) maintaining, defending, or settling any proceeding;

(2) holding meetings of the board of directors or shareholders or carrying on other activities concerning internal corporate affairs;

(3) maintaining bank accounts;

(4) maintaining offices or agencies for the transfer, exchange, and registration of the corporation's own securities or maintaining trustees or depositories with respect to those securities;

(5) selling through independent contractors;

(6) soliciting or obtaining orders, whether by mail or through employees or agents or otherwise, if the orders require acceptance outside this state before they become contracts;

(7) creating or acquiring indebtedness, mortgages, and security interests in real or personal property;

(8) securing or collecting debts or enforcing mortgages and security interests in property securing the debts;

(9) owning, without more, real or personal property;

(10) conducting an isolated transaction that is completed within 30 days and that is not one in the course of repeated transactions of a like nature;

(11) transacting business in interstate commerce.

(c) The list of activities in subsection (b) is not exhaustive.

Although the list set forth in this statute section is helpful, determining whether qualification as a foreign corporation is necessary still is usually a judgment call. One test that may be applied when making the determination is whether the corporation is engaging in regular and continuous business in the foreign state in question. This test has been applied by several state courts and was recently upheld in federal court as well. In the following case, the Georgia Court of Appeals held that the plaintiff did not need to qualify in Georgia as a foreign corporation prior to the commencement of the lawsuit in Georgia, because it qualified under the isolated transaction exception to the foreign corporation qualification requirement. However, the court also cautions that the question of whether foreign corporation qualification is necessary must be decided on a case-by-case basis, taking all factors into consideration.

Consequences of Not Qualifying As a Foreign Corporation

When making a determination as to whether to qualify to do business in a particular state, the consequences of not qualifying must be

WINSTON CORPORATION
v.
PARK ELECTRIC COMPANY
Court of Appeals of Georgia, Division No. 3
126 Ga. App. 489, 191 S.E.2d 340,
90 A.L.R.3d 929 (1972)
May 24, 1972
Clark, Judge

Park Electric Company filed suit on November 5, 1970, against Winston Corporation for a debt covering labor and material furnished as an electrical contractor in the completion of a nursing home construction project.

An answer was filed denying any obligation together with a counter-claim alleging a breach of the "contractual obligation and duty to the defendant to perform the electrical and related work incident to the construction of said nursing home." After discovery proceedings, including interrogatories from both parties and cross examination of Joseph Herman Park, Winston amended its answer on October 19, 1971, to aver that the plaintiff was a foreign corporation which had transacted business in Georgia without first having procured a qualification certificated required by [Ga.] Code Ann. § 22-1401 and therefore had failed to perform a condition precedent to the bringing of this suit. ...

Thereafter Winston filed its motion for summary judgment on the basis of the foregoing. ...

This motion for summary judgment was denied. A certificate for immediate review brings this case to this court.

The salient facts establish that prior to April 1969, Park, a resident of Cleveland, Tennessee, had conducted an electrical contracting business as a sole proprietorship. Resulting from a subcontract with Diversified Engineering & Sales Corporation on a Tennessee shopping center, he next made another subcontract with Diversified. This was in 1968 and provided for him to do the electrical work for the King's Inn Nursing Home in Atlanta which was to be constructed by Diversified for Winston. Upon default by Diversified, Winston as owner found it necessary for completion

of the construction to assume the contract and function of its general contractor. Comparatively little electrical work had been completed to that date under the 1968 subcontract although Park had material and equipment on the site. This take-over was in April 1969 with Park testifying he had thereafter as an individual proprietorship completed the original 1968 subcontract.

Park Electric Company, plaintiff in this action, had been organized as a Tennessee corporation on March 7, 1969 with its charter authorizing it to conduct the same type of business as had been done by Park as an individual proprietorship. ... Although the record includes an affidavit by Winston's vice president as to the number of plaintiff's employees, the extensive amount of electrical work done by the plaintiff corporation, and that plaintiff corporation transacted business at the nursing home site more or less continuously for a period of six months beginning in April 1969, it is obvious that much of this referred to the work done by Park individually rather than to his corporation. ... After Winston's amendment of October 19, 1971, wherein had been raised the defense of plaintiff being an unqualified foreign corporation doing business in Georgia, the Tennessee corporation was qualified in Georgia on October 27, 1971. The belated qualification application recites "Park Electric Company is not presently doing business in the State of Georgia and does not at this time intend to do business in the State of Georgia hereafter; however, the corporation did do business in the State of Georgia in 1969 and this filing is to qualify for past business transacted." Winston contends this belated qualification to be ineffective because [Ga.] Code Ann. § 22-1421(b) expressly provides that "no foreign corporation that under this Code is required to obtain a certificate of authority shall be permitted to maintain any action, suit or proceeding in any court of this State unless before commencement of the action it shall have obtained such a certificate." ...

The basic question for determination by this court is whether under Ch. 22-14 of the Annotated Code the Tennessee corporation was required under these facts to qualify to do business in Georgia prior to commencement of its suit. Held:

"Whether a foreign corporation is doing business in the sense required for any particular purpose is a question dependent primarily upon the facts and circumstances of each particular case considered in the light of the purposes and language of the pertinent statute or statues involved." ...

The portion of our Corporation Code with which we are involved is § 22-1401(b)(11) which provides that a foreign corporation shall not be considered to be transacting business in this state and therefore is relieved of qualifying where it is "Conducting an isolated transaction not in the course of a number of repeated transactions of like nature." ...

"In most jurisdictions it has been held that single or isolated transactions do not constitute doing business within the meaning of such statutes, although they are a part of the very business for which the corporation is organized to transact, if the action of the corporation in engaging therein indicated no purpose of continuity of conduct in that respect." 20 C.J.S. *Corporations* § 1830, page 48. ...

Applying the C.J.S. principle to the facts and circumstances of this particular case in the light of our statute, we find that where an individual was in Georgia completing a subcontract as a sole proprietor and after incorporation of his business completed the performance of the contract as an individual and in connection therewith undertook additional work in the name of his foreign corporation without any intention of doing any further business in Georgia other than the "isolated transaction," that the foreign corporation was relieved by the terms of subparagraph 11 of the Code Ann. § 22-1401(b) of

qualifying in Georgia before commencement of this suit.

Because this is the first time this issue of law has been brought to the Georgia appellate courts, able counsel for appellant has asked this court to provide guidance as to interpretation of the words "isolated transaction" as applied to construction contracts. A counselor would have no difficulty in advising his client that the South Carolina corporation which crosses the Savannah River to construct an outhouse obviously would not have to qualify whereas the building corporation which enters Georgia to build a multi-story office or apartment building would have to qualify despite its contract being a single transaction. ...

Considering the complexity of the problem, particularly when one must recognize that the levels of activity vary according to whether the foreign corporation is being taxed or being subjected to service of process or being denied access to a court which may be its sole forum for redress, we submit the pragmatic solution is: the question of "doing business" is to be considered a matter of fact to be resolved on an ad hoc or case-by-case basis and not by application of a mechanical rule. ...

Even though Park Electric Co. had a number of employees in Georgia and did considerable work over a substantial period of time in our state, these activities were all in relation to a single contract with no intention to engage in repeated transactions of a like nature. This case is within the "isolated transaction" exception of our Corporation Code. Therefore plaintiff was lawfully in court to sue on the single contract as an isolated transaction without prior qualification as a non-resident corporation. ...

Judgment affirmed.

considered. Penalties for transacting business in a foreign state without first qualifying vary from state to state. One of the most severe consequences is that the corporation usually is prohibited from commencing legal action to enforce contracts in the foreign state in question. This penalty is enforced under state **door-closing statutes**, which provide that a corporation doing business in the state without the necessary authority is precluded from maintaining an action in that state. Foreign corporations that transact business without the proper authority also may be subject to substantial fines. Although it is often unclear whether a corporation is considered to be transacting business in a particular state, when in doubt it is usually in the best interests of the corporation to qualify.

Following is Minnesota Statutes Ann. § 303.20, which provides the consequences of transacting business in the State of the Minnesota without a Certificate of Authority. Many states have similar statutes.

§ 303.20 FOREIGN CORPORATION MAY NOT MAINTAIN ACTION UNLESS LICENSED

No foreign corporation transacting business in this state without a certificate of authority shall be permitted to maintain an action in any court in this state until such corporation shall have obtained a certificate of authority; nor shall an action be maintained in any court by any successor or assignee of such corporation on any right, claim, or demand arising out of the transaction of business by such corporation in this state until a certificate of authority to transact business in this state shall have been obtained by such corporation or by a corporation which has acquired all, or substantially all, of its assets. If such assignee shall be a purchaser without actual notice of such violation by the corporation, recovery may be had to an amount not greater than the purchase price. This section shall not be construed to alter the rules applicable to a holder in due course of a negotiable instrument.

The failure of a foreign corporation to obtain a certificate of authority to transact business in this state does not impair the validity of any contract or act of such corporation, and shall not prevent such corporation from defending any action in any court of this state.

Any foreign corporation which transacts business in this state without a certificate of authority shall forfeit and pay to this state a penalty, not exceeding $1,000, and an additional penalty, not exceeding $100, for each month or fraction thereof during which it shall continue to transact business in this state without a certificate of authority therefor. Such penalties may be recovered in the district court of any county in which such foreign corporation has done business or has property or has a place of business, by an action, in the name of the state, brought by the attorney general.

TERMS

door-closing statute State statute providing that a corporation doing business in the state without the necessary authority is precluded from maintaining an action in that state.

§ 11.2 Rights, Privileges, and Responsibilities of a Foreign Corporation

Except where otherwise specified by state statute, qualified foreign corporations have the same, but no greater, rights and privileges as domestic corporations. As a general rule, a qualified foreign corporation may transact all of the business conferred by its own charter and the laws of its state of domicile, unless those laws are in conflict with the laws of the foreign state. The foreign corporation also is subject to many of the same duties and restrictions applicable to domestic corporations in the foreign state. However, most state statutes provide that the laws of the state of domicile shall govern over all matters concerning the internal affairs of the corporation.

§ 11.3 Qualification Requirements

Although the requirements for qualifying to do business vary from state to state, in general, the corporation must obtain a **certificate of authority** or similar document from the proper state authority before it begins transacting business in that state. For ease of explanation, we refer to the certificate of authority and all similar documents, whatever they are called, as the "certificate of authority" throughout the rest of this chapter. Usually the Secretary of State's corporate division has jurisdiction over all foreign corporations doing business in the state. However, in some states the agency with jurisdiction is the Corporation Commission or a similar agency. For ease in explanation, we refer to the state agency with jurisdiction over foreign corporations as the "Secretary of State" throughout the rest of this chapter.

Qualification requirements are usually the same for all types of corporations, including not-for-profit corporations and professional corporations. However, some of the fees and forms required by the Secretary of State may vary for these different types of corporations. The foreign state's statutes and the appropriate Secretary of State must be consulted to make sure that all requirements are met for these special types of corporations.

TERMS

certificate of authority   Certificate issued by Secretary of State or similar state authority granting a foreign corporation the right to transact business in that state.

Application for Certificate of Authority

The certificate of authority is obtained by filing an application, along with any other required documents, with the Secretary of State in the foreign state. Many states require that the application be made on a form prescribed by their offices. It is important to consult the Secretary of State of the foreign state and the foreign state's statutes or code to be sure that all application requirements have been complied with. Most states have adopted a version of § 15.03 of the Model Business Corporation Act, which sets forth the requirements for the application for certificate of authority:

§ 15.03. APPLICATION FOR CERTIFICATE OF AUTHORITY

(a) A foreign corporation may apply for a certificate of authority to transact business in this state by delivering an application to the secretary of state for filing. The application must set forth:
  (1) The name of the foreign corporation or, if its name is unavailable for use in this state, a corporate name that satisfies the requirements of section 15.06;
  (2) the name of the state or country under whose law it is incorporated;
  (3) its date of incorporation and period of duration;
  (4) the street address of its principal office;
  (5) the address of its registered office in this state and the name of its registered agent at that office; and
  (6) the name and usual business addresses of its current directors and officers.
(b) The foreign corporation shall deliver with the completed application a certificate of existence (or a document of similar import) duly authenticated by the secretary of state or other official having custody of corporate records in the state or country under whose law it is incorporated.

Figure 11-1 is a sample of an application for certificate of authority form that may be used in states following the Model Business Corporation Act.

The application often must be accompanied by a *certificate of existence* or **certificate of good standing** from the state of domicile and a filing fee. Some states require that the application be recorded at the county level in the foreign state, and some states require publication of

certificate of good standing   Also sometimes referred to as a certificate of existence. Certificate issued by the Secretary of State or other appropriate state authority proving the incorporation and good standing of the corporation in that state.

**APPLICATION FOR CERTIFICATE OF
AUTHORITY OF**

_____

The undersigned corporation hereby makes application for a Certificate of Authority to Transact Business in the State of _____ , pursuant to the provisions of § _____ of the _____ Business Corporation Act.

1. The name of the corporation is: _____ .

2. The name that the corporation desires to use in your state, if its name is unavailable for use in this state, is _____ . .

3. This corporation is incorporated under the laws of the state of _____ _____ , and is currently in good standing, as evidenced by the attached Certificate of Good Standing.

4. The corporation was incorporated on _____ , 19___ , and its period of duration is _____ .

5. The street address of the corporation's principal office is _____ .

6. The address of the corporation's registered office in this state and the name of its registered agent at that office are _____ .

7. The names and usual business addresses of the corporation's current directors and officers are as follows:

Name   Title   Address

_____   _____   _____

_____   _____   _____

_____   _____   _____

_____   _____   _____

Dated this _____ day of _____ , 19___ .

_____

By _____

Its _____

FIGURE 11-1   Sample Application for Certificate of Authority

the application or a notice of the application in a legal newspaper in the county where the registered office is located within the foreign state. (See Appendix G for a listing of states that have county filing or publication requirements.)

A thorough review of the pertinent state statutes, as well as any information available from the Secretary of State, must be made to assure that all application procedures are properly followed.

Foreign Name Requirements

Again, each state has its own requirements that must be met with respect to the names of foreign corporations. These name requirements can be found in the state statutes, or they may be obtained by contacting the Secretary of State of the foreign state. In general, most states require that the corporate name be available and that the corporate name meet the same requirements set for the names of domestic corporations incorporated in that state.

Mandatory Inclusions

Corporate names must clearly indicate that the corporation is a corporate entity, not an individual or partnership. State statutes typically require that the names of foreign corporations include one of the following words or abbreviations:

Corporation	Corp.
Limited	Ltd.
Incorporated	Inc.
Company	Co.

If the name of the corporation does not include a word or abbreviation that is required by the foreign state's statutes, the Secretary of State will usually allow the corporation to add one of the required words or abbreviations to its name for use in the foreign state in order to comply with this requirement.

Name Availability

Each state requires that the name of the foreign corporation be available for use in the foreign state. For example, if AB Johnson Corporation, a Minnesota corporation, decides to do business in Wisconsin, it must first make sure that its name is not already in use in Wisconsin and that no deceptively similar name is in use. If there is already a Wisconsin corporation by the name of AB Johnson Corporation, or even AB Johnson Company, there is a conflict.

Several different ways are prescribed by law to get around this problem. Many states allow the addition of a distinguishing word or words to the name of the foreign corporation for use in the foreign state. Following the preceding example, AB Johnson Corporation, the Minnesota corporation, might be able to qualify to do business in Wisconsin under the name of "AB Johnson Corporation, a Minnesota Corporation," or a similar name. In such an event, the foreign corporation must use this full name designation for all of its transactions within the foreign state.

Another common solution to the problem of an unavailable name is to obtain permission to use the name from the corporation or entity with a similar name. Most states that allow this option also require that the established corporation or entity change its name to a distinguishable name. This is sometimes possible if the existing corporation with the conflicting name is dormant or if the holders of the name wish to sell their right to use the name.

Finally, many states allow foreign corporations to adopt an available fictitious name for use in their state if the company's name is unavailable. A fictitious name is simply a different name that the foreign corporation uses for all its business transactions within the foreign state. Often, it is a name similar to its own name, but distinguishable from the conflicting name of the established corporation or entity.

The state's statutes or code should be consulted for further details of the options available in each foreign state. Most states provide a service that allows you to call the Secretary of State's office to check on the availability of the corporation's name.[2] This is a preliminary check and does not guarantee that the name will be available when the application for certificate of authority is filed. (See Appendix A for a Secretary of State directory.)

Corporate Name Reservation

Often, the only way to assure that a name will be available before submitting an application for certificate of authority is to reserve the name with the Secretary of State of the foreign state. Most state statutes provide that an available name may be reserved for a period of up to 120 days, at a minimal cost. This is usually done by submitting the appropriate name reservation form to the Secretary of State with the correct filing fee. Some states will accept a letter requesting the reservation, and a few will reserve an available name over the telephone.[3]

Registered Agent and Registered Office

Foreign corporations must appoint and maintain a **registered agent** and registered office in each state in which they are qualified to do

═══════════════ TERMS ═══════════════

registered agent Individual appointed by a corporation to receive service of process on behalf of the corporation and perform such other duties as

business. The registered office must be an actual physical location in the foreign state where service of process may be made personally on an individual who is authorized to accept service on behalf of the corporation. The registered agent usually must be a resident of the foreign state, a domestic corporation, or qualified foreign corporation. The registered agent must be appointed by the foreign corporation to receive service of process on behalf of the corporation. In many instances the state statutes provide that if no registered agent is appointed and serving, the Secretary of State of the foreign state is authorized to accept service on behalf of the foreign corporation. Thus, a foreign corporation often has an officer or employee in each foreign state who acts as the registered agent for that state. Other times, a professional registered agent is appointed. There are corporation service companies that will act as a registered agent for foreign corporations in each foreign state. These services can be appointed, for a fee, to provide a registered office address and an agent to accept service for corporations in each state.

§ 11.4 Amending the Certificate of Authority

Although each state's statutes define when it is necessary to amend the certificate of authority, typically whenever any significant information that was included in the original certificate changes, an application for amended certificate of authority must be completed and filed. The same filing requirements that cover the application for certificate of authority in each state are generally applied to any amendments. The Model Business Corporation Act provides that whenever the authorized foreign corporation changes its corporate name, the period of its duration, or the state or country of its incorporation, an application for amended certificate of authority must be filed.[4]

Whenever any change in information concerning service of the foreign corporation in the foreign state occurs, such as a change in the registered agent or office in the state, the Secretary of State must be notified immediately, either by an amended application for certificate of authority, or by other means prescribed by the foreign state's

---

TERMS

may be necessary. Registered agents may be required in the corporation's state of domicile and in each state in which the corporation is qualified to transact business.

statutes. Again, a thorough review of the state statutes or code of the foreign state must be made to be sure that all requirements are met.

§ 11.5 Maintaining the Good Standing of the Foreign Corporation

A corporation may continue to transact business as a foreign corporation as long as it continues to meet the requirements of the foreign state, including timely filing of any required reports and the payment of all required fees and taxes. Most Secretaries of State require annual reports from every domestic and qualified foreign corporation.[5] This is usually done on forms generated by the office of the Secretary of State and sent to the principal office or registered office of the corporation, to be completed and returned within a prescribed time period. Many states require that the reports be filed with an annual fee, either a flat fee or a fee based upon the amount of business transacted within the foreign state.

Although these forms are generated by the Secretary of State, it is the responsibility of the corporation to be aware of the annual reporting requirements in each state in which it transacts business and to see that the reports are filed in a timely manner. The Secretary of State must be contacted immediately if the corporation does not receive an annual report form to be completed when prescribed by law. Failure to file an annual report may have severe consequences, such as an additional fee or a fine, and even loss of good standing in the state.

Often, any state taxes that are payable by the qualified foreign corporation are included in the fee paid to the Secretary of State. In some instances, however, a separate tax report may be required by a separate tax authority within the foreign state. Again, it is the responsibility of the corporation to see that all necessary tax reporting is completed in a timely manner.

§ 11.6 Withdrawing from Doing Business As a Foreign Corporation

When a corporation dissolves or ceases to do business in any state in which it is qualified, and there are no plans to recommence business in that state in the near future, it is beneficial for the corporation to withdraw from doing business so that the corporation no longer will be subject to annual reporting, registered office, registered agent, and taxation requirements in the foreign state. The procedures for withdrawing from doing business as a foreign corporation are set by state statute and generally involve obtaining a certificate of withdrawal from the Secretary of State of the foreign state. Under the Model Business Corporation Act, the qualified foreign corporation may not withdraw from the foreign state until it obtains a certificate of withdrawal from that Secretary of State.

The certificate of withdrawal is obtained by filing an application for withdrawal with the Secretary of State. MBCA § 15.20(b) sets forth the requirements for the application for withdrawal:

> (b) A foreign corporation authorized to transact business in this state may apply for a certificate of withdrawal by delivering an application to the secretary of state for filing. The application must set forth:
>
> (1) the name of the foreign corporation and the name of the state or country under whose law it is incorporated;
>
> (2) that it is not transacting business in this state and that it surrenders its authority to transact business in this state;
>
> (3) that it revokes the authority of its registered agent to accept service on its behalf and appoints the secretary of state as its agent for service of process in any proceeding based on a cause of action arising during the time it was authorized to transact business in this state;
>
> (4) a mailing address to which the secretary of state may mail a copy of any process served on him under subdivision (3); and
>
> (5) a commitment to notify the secretary of state in the future of any change in its mailing address.

Most states provide a form to be completed and filed with the Secretary of State. Others prescribe instructions in the state statutes that must be followed. It is important to familiarize yourself with the state statutes on withdrawing from doing business in the state you are concerned with and to be certain all requirements, such as county recording and publication, are complied with.

§ 11.7 Registration of a Corporate Name

Several states provide that a foreign corporation that is not doing business in the state may register its name with the state, in lieu of qualifying to do business. This is very useful to corporations that may commence doing business in a particular state at some time in the future, but would like to reserve their names for an extended period of time. It is also useful to corporations that want to use their names in a state but are not considered to be transacting business in that state under the statutes of that state.

The name to be registered must be available for use in that foreign state and, in most instances, must comply with the requirements set for names of foreign corporations who are applying for a certificate of authority. The name of the foreign corporation typically is registered for renewable one-year periods.

§ 11.8 The Role of the Legal Assistant

The role of the legal assistant in working with foreign corporations must be defined by the legal assistant, the responsible attorney, and the client. In general, with the exception of providing the client with legal advice, the legal assistant can perform almost all the services required to qualify a foreign corporation, see that it remains in good standing, or withdraw the foreign corporation from doing business in the foreign state. In some instances, the legal assistant will work closely with the corporate secretary to assist in complying with the necessary requirements imposed on foreign corporations. In other instances, the corporate secretary may not be so closely involved, and the legal assistant and responsible attorney will see to these matters, while keeping the corporate client informed.

More specifically, in the qualification process, the legal assistant can locate the pertinent state statutes and any other available information to help the attorney and client make a decision on the necessity of qualifying as a foreign corporation. From there, the legal assistant can obtain the necessary paperwork from the Secretary of State and assist the client with completing and filing of these documents. The legal assistant should also check to see that any county recording, publishing, and other detail requirements are complied with. Following is a checklist that could assist the paralegal with the foreign corporation qualification process.

FOREIGN CORPORATION QUALIFICATION CHECKLIST

☐ Locate and review copy of pertinent state statutes relating to the necessity of qualifying as a foreign corporation to make sure that qualification is really necessary.

☐ Review statutes relevant to qualification requirements in foreign state, including any publication requirements, county recording requirements, or other requirements unique to that foreign state.

☐ Contact Secretary of State of foreign state to check name availability in foreign state and request all forms necessary for qualifying as a foreign corporation, including application for corporate name reservation, when appropriate, and application for certificate of authority. Also request up-to-date fee schedule and any printed information and instructions for qualifying as a foreign corporation in that state.

☐ Contact tax authority of foreign state, if separate from Secretary of State, to request information on taxation of foreign corporations.

☐ Resolve any name conflicts, if applicable.

☐ Decide on registered agent and registered office and contact corporation service company, if necessary.

☐ When information and forms are received from Secretary of State of foreign state, complete necessary forms and send to client for review and signature.

☐ Obtain certificate of good standing or certificate of existence and certified copy of articles or certificate of incorporation, when necessary, from Secretary of State of state of domicile.

☐ Submit application for certificate of authority to proper state authority, along with any of the following that may be required:
— Any additional copies of the certificate of authority that may be required
— A current certificate of existence or certificate of good standing from the state of domicile
— A certified copy of the corporation's articles or certificate of incorporation
— The appropriate filing fee
— Separate documents appointing registered agent
— Any other documents required by the state statutes or Secretary of State of the foreign state.

☐ Make sure any publication requirements are complied with.

☐ Make sure any county recording requirements are complied with.

☐ Re-check statutes of foreign state to make sure that all qualification requirements have been met and to see when first annual report will be due, if applicable.

The legal assistant will often perform similar tasks involved in amending the certificate of authority and in withdrawing the foreign corporation from each state when necessary. Another important task that the legal assistant can perform is to keep track of all necessary annual reporting requirements and see that the annual report of each foreign corporation is completed and filed in a timely manner.

§ 11.9 Resources

The primary resources for paralegals working with foreign corporations are the state statutes and secretaries of state of the foreign states. In certain circumstances, corporation service companies can be most helpful and efficient.

State Statutes

It is important that the Business Corporation Act or similar act for each foreign state be carefully reviewed for every state in which the corporate client may be considered a foreign corporation. If the statutes of the foreign state are not readily available, sometimes a special pamphlet including the Business Corporation Act may be ordered from the publisher of the statutes. In other instances, the Business Corporation Act may be available from the Secretary of State at a minimal cost.

Secretaries of State

Many Secretary of State offices provide printed pamphlets or other forms of information regarding foreign corporations. Most of this information is free of charge and may be obtained by writing to or calling the Secretary of State of the appropriate state. (See Appendix A for a Secretary of State directory.)

Corporation Service Companies

Corporation service companies will assist you with almost all aspects of services for foreign corporations. These services can help you complete all the necessary paperwork to qualify a foreign corporation and see that it is filed correctly. In addition, the services can act as a registered agent for a foreign corporation in any foreign state in the country. Using these services involves paying a third party to perform work on behalf of the corporate client. However, they are usually quick and convenient.

Review Questions

1. Assume that Quality Liquor Company has its main office in your home state, where it transacts the majority of its wholesale liquor business. Recently, Quality Liquor has been taking orders from a neighboring state. It has begun sending its sales people into the state in an attempt to increase its business. Assuming that the neighboring state follows the Model Business Corporation Act, does Quality Liquor need to qualify as a foreign corporation in that state? What if Quality Liquor were to set up a branch office in the neighboring state?

2. What are door-closing statutes as they relate to foreign corporations?

3. Explain why a foreign corporation that is qualified in a foreign state may not be able to transact all of the same business in the foreign state that it is authorized to transact in its state of domicile.

4. Assume that it is your responsibility to qualify your corporate client, Alex Enterprises, in a foreign state that has adopted the Model Business Corporation Act. Will there be a problem getting a certificate of authority issued under the name "Alex Enterprises"? What are the possible solutions to this problem?

5. What is a fictitious name, and why is it used?

6. What is the purpose of a registered agent in a foreign state?

7. Why do so many states require that the registered office address used in their state not be a post office box?

8. Assume that you represent a foreign corporation that is qualified in a state that has adopted the Model Business Corporation Act. What steps must be taken when the corporation amends its articles of incorporation to change its authorized shares of stock? What steps must be taken when the corporation amends its articles of incorporation to change its corporate name?

9. Under what circumstances might it be beneficial for a corporation to register its name in a foreign state?

Notes

1 International Shoe Co. v. Washington, 326 U.S. 310, 66 S. Ct. 154, 90 L. Ed 95 (1945).

2 The states of Connecticut, Maine, Nebraska, New York, Washington, Wisconsin, and Wyoming will not check the availability of a corporate name over the telephone.

[3] The states of Delaware, Georgia, and Wisconsin will reserve corporate names over the telephone.

[4] 1984 Revised Model Business Corporation Act § 15.04.

[5] Alaska, Connecticut, and New Mexico all have biennial reporting requirements for foreign corporations. New York, Pennsylvania, South Carolina, and Texas currently have no annual reporting requirements (other than any possible tax reporting that may be required).

CHAPTER 12

CORPORATE DISSOLUTION

Introduction

Corporations are given life by the statutes of their state of domicile, and that life must be terminated in accordance with those statutes. Although articles of incorporation can generally provide for a date or an event upon the happening of which the corporation will be dissolved, most corporations exist perpetually and must be dissolved when there is no further reason for their existence. The **dissolution of a corporation** generally refers to the termination of the legal existence of the corporation. However, as discussed in § 12.1, the corporate existence continues after dissolution for certain purposes.

Corporations are dissolved for many reasons, including bankruptcy or insolvency, the cessation of the business of the corporation, the sale of all or substantially all of the assets of the corporation, or the death of key shareholders, directors, or officers. Extensive planning involving the corporation's management, board of directors, attorneys, and accountants is usually necessary to execute the dissolution, winding up, and liquidation of the corporation in the manner most beneficial to the shareholders of the corporation.

In addition to dissolving in accordance with the statutes of its state of domicile, the corporation is required to surrender its certificate of authority to transact business in any state in which it is qualified to transact business and to file the appropriate forms and returns with the Internal Revenue Service. The statutes regarding corporate dissolution vary considerably from state to state. Every state requires, at a minimum, that one document be filed with the Secretary of State, or other appropriate state authority, notifying the state of the dissolution. Other

---

TERMS

dissolution of corporation [†] The termination of a corporation's existence and its abolishment as an entity.

common statutory provisions include requirements for obtaining and filing good-standing certificates from all state tax authorities, publishing notice in a legal newspaper of the corporation's intent to dissolve, and a second and final filing with the state after all corporate debts have been paid and all assets distributed. There are also significant differences in state statutes for obtaining director and shareholder approval of the corporate dissolution.

This chapter examines the procedures under the Model Business Corporation Act to effect the most common type of dissolution, the voluntary dissolution. It also investigates administrative dissolution and involuntary dissolution by the state of domicile, the shareholders of the corporation, and the creditors of the corporation. The chapter concludes with a brief discussion of the role of the paralegal in dissolving a corporation.

§ 12.1 Voluntary Dissolution

The most common type of corporate dissolution is the **voluntary dissolution**, which is approved by the directors and shareholders of the corporation. The procedures followed for voluntarily dissolving a corporation depend on the statutes of the state of domicile, but generally involve obtaining the appropriate approval from the directors and shareholders, filing articles of dissolution or another appropriate document with the proper state authority, and winding up the affairs of the corporation by liquidating its assets, paying the creditors' claims, and distributing the balance to the shareholders.

Board of Director and Shareholder Approval of Dissolution

The voluntary dissolution of a corporation must be approved by at least a majority of the corporation's shareholders in most instances. Under certain circumstances, the incorporators or initial board of directors of the corporation may act to dissolve a corporation.

TERMS

voluntary dissolution Dissolution that is approved by the directors and shareholders of the corporation.

Dividends

The Ethical Paralegal

The word *ethics* refers to the code of moral principles and standards of behavior for persons in professions. *Legal ethics* is the code of conduct among lawyers that governs their moral and professional duties toward one another, toward their clients, and toward the courts. Legal ethics begins with the attorney, but does not end there. Paralegals are also bound to act in an ethical manner in the performance of their duties.

Paralegals are bound to the ethical guidelines prescribed by the American Bar Association and the state bar association of the state in which they work. These rules and codes dictate conduct in matters such as soliciting clients, contacting adverse parties, protecting client confidences, establishing and sharing legal fees, and several other areas. In addition, both the National Federation of Paralegal Associations and the National Association of Legal Assistants have published paralegal ethics codes and guidelines that paralegals must follow.

There are certain areas of legal ethics that are of special concern to the paralegal. Paralegals must always act in an ethical manner and abide by the rules of conduct governing the unauthorized practice of law, confidentiality, conflicts of interest, and misrepresentation.

1. *Unauthorized Practice of Law.* Corporate paralegals must be careful to avoid charges of the unauthorized practice of law. As a general rule, the paralegal who works under the supervision of an attorney is safe from these charges. Another rule that must be followed by the corporate paralegal is *don't give legal advice to clients.* Although paralegals can advise clients as to how the law reads or what legal procedures must be followed, you must be certain not to cross the line and advise them how to act.

2. *Confidentiality.* Corporate paralegals must be certain to keep client information strictly confidential. This is doubly important for paralegals who work with publicly-held corporations, securities, and mergers and acquisitions.

3. *Conflicts of Interest.* A conflict of interest may arise when there is a variance between the interests of the parties in a fiduciary relationship. Because attorneys act in a fiduciary capacity toward their clients, they must be sure that they have no other interests that conflict—or even appear to conflict—with the interests of their clients. Paralegals are bound by similar rules of conduct. A potential for a conflict of interest may arise when paralegals have personal interest in their corporate clients or in corporations or individuals who are considered to be adverse parties in litigation with corporate clients. A corporate paralegal should always divulge any information concerning a matter that may give even the appearance of a conflict of interest. If in doubt, always ask the responsible attorney.

4. *Misrepresentation.* Paralegals must be careful not to give out any false or misleading information to clients, opposing parties, opposing parties' counsel, or especially to the courts.

Specific rules and guidelines for ethical paralegal behavior can be found in the following:

- 1977 The Affirmation of Professional Responsibility of the National Federation of Paralegal Associations
- 1993 The National Federation of Paralegal Associations Model Code of Ethics and Professional Responsibility
- 1975 The National Association of Legal Assistants Code of Ethics and Professional Responsibility
- 1984 Model Standards and Guidelines for Utilization of Legal Assistants of the National Association of Legal Assistants

Dissolution Prior to Commencement of Business

If a decision is made to dissolve a corporation before it commences doing business or before it issues stock, a streamlined method for dissolution is generally provided by statute. The dissolution of a corporation that has not issued stock may be approved by the incorporators or the initial board of directors, if one was named in the articles of incorporation. The Model Business Corporation Act provides the method for dissolving a corporation by the incorporators or board of directors in § 14.01:

§ 14.01. DISSOLUTION BY INCORPORATORS OR INITIAL DIRECTORS

A majority of the incorporators or initial directors of a corporation that has not issued shares or has not commenced business may dissolve the corporation by delivering to the secretary of state for filing articles of dissolution that set forth:

(1) the name of the corporation;
(2) the date of its incorporation;
(3) either (i) that none of the corporation's shares has been issued or (ii) that the corporation has not commenced business;
(4) that no debt of the corporation remains unpaid;
(5) that the net assets of the corporation remaining after winding up have been distributed to the shareholders, if shares were issued; and
(6) that a majority of the incorporators or initial directors authorized the dissolution.

When a corporation has not commenced business, it will typically have no debts to satisfy and no assets to distribute. Unless there are other statutory requirements in the state of domicile, the dissolution process can generally be satisfied merely by filing the articles of dissolution as prescribed by statute. Articles of dissolution are discussed further in this section.

Dissolution Subsequent to Commencement of Business

After the corporation has commenced business or after shares of stock of the corporation have been issued, its dissolution must be approved by the shareholders of the corporation pursuant to statute. The statutes of the state of domicile may set forth special requirements for obtaining shareholder approval, which are often similar to the requirements for approving a merger or share exchange (discussed in Chapter 10). Shareholders are generally not granted the right to dissent in the event of a dissolution. However, courts may prohibit dissolutions that are aimed at freezing out the minority shareholders of the corporation if the board of directors and majority shareholders are not acting in good faith. It has been held that "majority stockholders cannot vote to discontinue the business of the corporation for the purpose of turning it over to another corporation and excluding minority stockholders from participating therein."[1] The Model Business Corporation Act sets forth the requirements for approving a voluntary corporate dissolution in § 14.02:

§ 14.02. DISSOLUTION BY BOARD OF DIRECTORS AND SHAREHOLDERS

(a) A corporation's board of directors may propose dissolution for submission to the shareholders.

(b) For a proposal to dissolve to be adopted:

    (1) the board of directors must recommend dissolution to the shareholders unless the board of directors determines that because of conflict of interest or other special circumstances it should make no recommendation and communicates the basis for its determination to the shareholders; and

    (2) the shareholders entitled to vote must approve the proposal to dissolve as provided in subsection (e).

(c) The board of directors may condition its submission of the proposal for dissolution on any basis.

(d) The corporation shall notify each shareholder, whether or not entitled to vote, of the proposed shareholders' meeting in accordance with § 7.05. The notice must also state that the purpose, or one of the purposes, of the meeting is to consider dissolving the corporation.

(e) Unless the articles of incorporation or the board of directors (acting pursuant to subsection (c)) require a greater vote or a vote by voting groups, the proposal to dissolve to be adopted must be approved by a majority of all the votes entitled to be cast on that proposal.

Following are sample resolutions that might be passed by the board of directors and by the shareholders of a corporation, respectively, to approve the dissolution of the corporation.

EXAMPLE: Directors' Resolution to Dissolve Corporation—Submission of Proposition to Stockholders[2]

Resolution of the board of directors of _____ [name of corporation], adopted on _____ , 19___.

Whereas, this corporation has entirely ceased to do the business for which it was formed and organized; and whereas, all indebtedness has been paid, and it appears to be to the best interests of the stockholders that it should be dissolved, its business terminated, and its remaining assets distributed among the stockholders, or otherwise disposed of according to law;

Resolved, that in the opinion of this board of directors it is advisable to dissolve this corporation forthwith, and that a meeting of the stockholders be held at its office at _____ [address], on _____ , 19___ , at _____ o'clock, for the purpose of voting upon the proposition that the corporation be forthwith dissolved.

Further resolved, that unless notice of such meeting be waived by all the stockholders, the secretary shall cause notice of such meeting to be both published and served as prescribed by law.

Further resolved, that the president or vice president and secretary execute a certificate showing the adoption of these resolutions and setting forth the proceedings of the meeting of stockholders, and that they also attest the written consent of the stockholders that the corporation be dissolved, and execute and verify all statements required by law to dissolve the corporation.

Further resolved, that the president or vice president and the secretary cause such certificate and consent to be filed in the office of the Secretary of State of the State of _____ , together with a duly verified statement of the names and residences of the members of the existing board of directors and of the names and residences of the officers of the corporation, and all certificates and waivers of all notices required by law, and that the officers and board of directors of the corporation take such further action as may be required to effectuate the dissolution of the corporation and wind up its business affairs.

EXAMPLE: Stockholders' Resolution—Election to Dissolve Corporation— Approval and Adoption of Directors' Resolution[3]

Whereas, a special meeting of the stockholders of _____ [name of corporation] was held at the principal office of the corporation at _____ [address], on _____ , 19___ , and

Whereas, the secretary of the corporation reported that _____ shares of the outstanding capital stock of the corporation were represented in person or by proxy, being _____ percent (_____%) of the total stock outstanding; and

Whereas, the secretary presented the resolution that had been adopted at a meeting of the board of directors held on _____ , 19___ , which resolution provided that the corporation go into liquidation, dispose of its assets, wind up its affairs, be dissolved, and the charter thereof be surrendered and canceled;

After full consideration of the directors' resolution and on motion duly made and seconded, the stockholders have:

Resolved, that _____ [name of corporation], a corporation chartered by the State of _____ , be completely liquidated at the earliest practicable date, that all debts of the corporation be paid and the remaining cash together with securities owned, or the cash realized from the sale thereof, be distributed pro rata to its stockholders prior to _____ , 19___ , and that all other assets of the corporation be disposed of as soon as practicable and the proceeds therefrom, after payment of any remaining liabilities, be distributed pro rata to the stockholders upon surrender by the stockholders to the corporation of all the outstanding stock thereof.

Resolved further, that the officers of the corporation be authorized and directed to take immediate steps to complete the liquidation of the corporation so that its assets or the proceeds therefrom can be distributed to its stockholders prior to _____ , 19___ , and that promptly thereafter steps be taken to surrender the charter and franchise of the corporation to the State of _____ and to dissolve the corporation.

Resolved further, that the corporation cease the transaction of all business as of this date, except such as may be necessary or incidental to the complete liquidation thereof and the winding up of its affairs, including the payment of any obligations of the corporation now outstanding and any expenses incident to the liquidation thereof.

Articles of Dissolution and Notice of Intent to Dissolve

In states following the Model Business Corporation Act, the first and only filing required with the Secretary of State, or other appropriate state authority, is the **articles of dissolution**. (See Table 12-1 for individual state requirements.) After the articles of dissolution are filed, the corporate existence continues, but the corporation is considered to be a "dissolved corporation" and may continue its business only for the purpose of winding up its affairs. The Model Business Corporation Act sets forth the requirements for articles of dissolution in § 14.03:

§ 14.03. ARTICLES OF DISSOLUTION

(a) At any time after dissolution is authorized, the corporation may dissolve by delivering to the secretary of state for filing articles of dissolution setting forth:
  (1) the name of the corporation;
  (2) the date dissolution was authorized;
  (3) if dissolution was approved by the shareholders:
    (i) the number of votes entitled to be cast on the proposal to dissolve; and
    (ii) either the total number of votes cast for and against dissolution or the total number of undisputed votes cast for dissolution and a statement that the number cast for dissolution was sufficient for approval.
  (4) If voting by voting groups was required, the information required by subparagraph (3) must be separately provided for each voting group entitled to vote separately on the plan to dissolve.
(b) A corporation is dissolved upon the effective date of its articles of dissolution.

The articles of dissolution must be submitted with the appropriate filing fee in accordance with state statute. Figure 12-1 shows sample articles

TERMS

articles of dissolution Document filed with the Secretary of State or other appropriate state authority to dissolve the corporation.

FIGURE 12-1
Sample
Articles of
Dissolution

ARTICLES OF DISSOLUTION
OF

_____

Pursuant to _____ [statute], as amended, the undersigned, does hereby state the following as the Articles of Dissolution of said Corporation.

I.

The name of the corporation is _____ .

II.

The authorized stock of the corporation consists of 10,000 shares of Class A Common Stock, without par value, 5,000 of which are issued and outstanding. At a meeting of the shareholders held on _____ , 19___ , at the registered office of the corporation, a resolution to dissolve the corporation effective _____ , 19___ , was passed by unanimous vote of all 5,000 issued and outstanding shares of the corporation.

Dated: _____ , 19___ .

By _____

_____

Subscribed and sworn to before me
this _____ day of _____ , 19___ .

_____
Notary Public

of dissolution that may be appropriate in states following the Model Business Corporation Act.

In several jurisdictions that deviate from the Model Business Corporation Act in this regard, a notice of intent to dissolve must be filed with the Secretary of State or other appropriate state authority prior to the winding-up process. The articles of dissolution are generally filed in these jurisdictions only after all the corporation's debts have been paid, including any tax liabilities, and all the corporation's assets have been distributed. Figure 12-2 is a sample notice of intent to dissolve. In addition to requiring that the notice of intent to dissolve be filed with the Secretary of State, statutes often require that the notice be published in a legal newspaper in the county in which the registered office of the corporation is located, pursuant to state statute.

TABLE 12-1 STATE CORPORATE DISSOLUTION STATUTES

State	Corporate Dissolution Statute	Document(s) Filed at State Level to Dissolve Corporation
Alabama	Ala. Code § 10-2B–14.03	Articles of Dissolution[4]
Alaska	Alaska Stat. § 10.06.620, *et seq.*	Statement of Intent to Dissolve and Articles of Dissolution
Arizona	Ariz. Rev. Stat. Ann. § 10-084(d), *et seq.*	Statement of Intent to Dissolve and Articles of Dissolution
Arkansas	Ark. Stat. Ann. § 4-27-1403	Articles of Dissolution
California	Cal. Corp. Code § 1903, *et seq.*	Statement of Intent to Dissolve and Articles of Dissolution
Colorado	Colo. Bus. Corp. Act § 7-114-103	Articles of Dissolution
Connecticut	Conn. Gen. Stat. § 33-376(d), (e)	Articles of Dissolution
Delaware	Del. Code Ann. tit. 8 § 275	Articles of Dissolution
District of Columbia	D.C. Code Ann. § 29-378(4), *et seq.*	Statement of Intent to Dissolve and Articles of Dissolution[5]
Florida	Fla. Stat. § 607.1403	Articles of Dissolution
Georgia	Ga. Code Ann. § 14-2-1403, *et seq.*	Notice of Intent to Dissolve and Articles of Dissolution[6]
Hawaii	Hawaii Rev. Stat. § 415-84(5), *et seq.*	Statement of Intent to Dissolve and Articles of Dissolution
Idaho	Idaho Code § 30-1-92	Articles of Dissolution
Illinois	805 Ill. Comp. Stat. § 5/12.20	Articles of Dissolution
Indiana	Ind. Code § 23-1-45-3	Articles of Dissolution
Iowa	Iowa Code § 490.1403	Articles of Dissolution
Kansas	Kan. Stat. Ann. § 17-6804(b)	Certificate of Dissolution
Kentucky	Ky. Rev. Stat. Ann. § 271B.14-030	Articles of Dissolution
Louisiana	La. Rev. Stat. Ann. § 12:148	Certificate of Dissolution[7]

TABLE 12-1 *(continued)*

State	Corporate Dissolution Statute	Document(s) Filed at State Level to Dissolve Corporation
Maine	Me. Rev. Stat. Ann. tit. 13-A § 1103(D), *et seq.*	Notice of Intent to Dissolve and Articles of Dissolution
Maryland	Md. Corps. & Ass'ns Code Ann. § 3-406, *et seq.*	Articles of Dissolution
Massachusetts	Mass. Gen. Laws Ann. ch. 56B, § 100(c), (d)	Articles of Dissolution
Michigan	Mich. Comp. Laws § 450.1803(2), *et seq.*	Articles of Dissolution
Minnesota	Minn. Stat. 302A.723	Notice of Intent to Dissolve and Articles of Dissolution
Mississippi	Miss. Code Ann. § 79-4-14.03	Articles of Dissolution
Missouri	Mo. Rev. Stat. § 351.468	Articles of Dissolution
Montana	Mont. Code Ann. § 35-1-933	Articles of Dissolution
Nebraska	Neb. Rev. Stat. § 21-2083(4)	Statement of Intent to Dissolve and Articles of Dissolution
Nevada	Nev. Rev. Stat. § 78.580	Certified copy of Resolution to Dissolve
New Hampshire	N.H. Rev. Stat. Ann. § 293-A:14.03	Articles of Dissolution
New Jersey	N.J. Rev. Stat. § 14A:12-4(6), *et seq.*	Certificate of Dissolution
New Mexico	N.M. Stat. Ann. § 53-16-3(D), *et seq.*	Statement of Intent to Dissolve and Articles of Dissolution
New York	N.Y. Bus. Corp. Law § 1003, *et seq.*	Certificate of Dissolution
North Carolina	N.C. Gen. Stat. § 55-14-03	Articles of Dissolution
North Dakota	N.D. Cent. Code § 10-19.1-108, *et seq.*	Statement of Intent to Dissolve and Articles of Dissolution
Ohio	Ohio Rev. Code Ann. § 1701.86(F), *et seq.*	Articles of Dissolution

TABLE 12-1 *(continued)*

State	Corporate Dissolution Statute	Document(s) Filed at State Level to Dissolve Corporation
Oklahoma	Okla. Stat. tit. 18 § 1096(D)	Articles of Dissolution
Oregon	Or. Rev. Stat. § 60.631	Articles of Dissolution
Pennsylvania	Pa. Cons. Stat. tit. 15 § 1977	Articles of Dissolution
Rhode Island	R.I. Gen. Laws § 7-1.1-77(4), *et seq.*	Statement of Intent to Dissolve and Articles of Dissolution
South Carolina	S.C. Code Ann. § 33-14-103	Articles of Dissolution
South Dakota	S.D. Codified Laws Ann. § 47-7-5.1	Articles of Dissolution
Tennessee	Tenn. Code Ann. § 48-24-103	Articles of Dissolution
Texas	Tex. Bus. Corp. Act arts. 6.06, 6.07	Statement of Intent to Dissolve and Articles of Dissolution
Utah	Utah Code Ann. § 16-10a-1403	Articles of Dissolution
Vermont	Vt. Stat. Ann. tit. 11A § 14-03	Articles of Dissolution
Virginia	Va. Code § 13.1-743	Articles of Dissolution
Washington	Wash. Rev. Code Ann. § 23B.14.030	Articles of Dissolution
West Virginia	W.Va. Code § 31-1-126(d), *et seq.*	Plan of Distribution, Statement of Intent to Dissolve, and Articles of Dissolution
Wisconsin	Wis. Stat. § 180.1403	Articles of Dissolution
Wyoming	Wyo. Stat. § 17-16-1403	Articles of Dissolution

Winding Up and Liquidation

After the dissolved corporation has filed its articles or notice of dissolution, it will begin the process of winding up its affairs and liquidating. The statutes of virtually every state provide for the complete

FIGURE 12-2
Sample Notice
of Intent to
Dissolve

NOTICE OF INTENT TO DISSOLVE

_____

Pursuant to _____ [statute], the undersigned hereby
provides the following notice of intent to dissolve _____
to the Secretary of State.

I.

The name of the corporation is _____.

II.

On _____ , 19___ , a meeting of the shareholders of the corporation was
held at the principal office of the corporation. At that meeting a resolution was
unanimously adopted by all of the shareholders to begin a voluntary dissolution
of the Corporation, effective _____ , 19___.

III.

The board of directors of the corporation is hereby authorized to take any
and all actions necessary to wind up the business of the corporation, and
distribute the corporation's assets in accordance with statute.

Dated: _____.

_____

By _____
Its _____

Subscribed and Sworn to before me
this _____ day of _____ , 1992.

_____
Notary Public

---

and orderly winding up of the affairs of dissolved corporations and
for the protection of the creditors and shareholders of liquidating corporations.[8] In § 14.05, the Model Business Corporation Act lists the following activities that may be appropriate to wind up the affairs of a
corporation and liquidate its business:

1. Collection of assets
2. Disposition of properties that will not be distributed in kind to
   shareholders
3. Discharge or making provision for discharge of liabilities of the
   corporation
4. Distribution of remaining property among shareholders according
   to their interests

5. Every other act necessary to wind up and liquidate the business and affairs of the corporation.

The **liquidation** of a corporation refers to the "winding up of the affairs of the corporation by reducing its assets, paying its debts, and apportioning the profit or loss."[9] Depending on the provisions of the pertinent state statutes, corporations may be liquidated either before or after they are dissolved. Figure 12-3 is a sample plan of liquidation that might be adopted by the board of directors and shareholders of a dissolving corporation.

Voluntary dissolutions in jurisdictions that follow the Model Business Corporation Act are typically nonjudicial dissolutions, although, under certain circumstances, the court may supervise the liquidation of a corporation that is voluntarily dissolving. The statutes of other jurisdictions may require judicial liquidation or offer incentives to corporations to choose judicial liquidations.

Notice to Creditors

As a part of the winding up and liquidation process, state statutes may require that the creditors of the corporation be given notice and that they must be allowed to submit claims to the corporation for payment of any debt owed by the corporation. Often notification must be sent to each individual creditor, and notice must be given to the public, or both.

Corporations domiciled in states following the Model Business Corporation Act are given guidelines to follow for notifying creditors of known claims, and for notifying the public in the event there are any unknown claims against the corporation. Section 14.06 of the Model Business Corporation Act provides that "A dissolved corporation may dispose of the claims against it by following the procedure described in this section." Corporations following the procedures of this section must notify known creditors in writing of the dissolution at any time after the effective date of the dissolution. The notice must include the following:

1. A description of the information that must be included in a claim

2. A mailing address to which the claim may be sent

═══════════════ TERMS ═══════════════

liquidation [†] The winding up of a corporation, partnership, or other business enterprise upon dissolution by converting the assets to money, collecting the accounts receivable, paying the debts, and distributing the surplus if any exists.

FIGURE 12-3
Sample Plan
of Liquidation

PLAN OF LIQUIDATION

WHEREAS, the Board of Directors and Shareholders have approved the dissolution, winding up, and liquidation of the corporation pursuant to _____ [statute]; and

WHEREAS, it is the desire of the directors and shareholders to adopt a plan of liquidation to provide for the liquidation and winding up of the corporation.

NOW, THEREFORE, the following plan is hereby adopted:

1. The officers of the corporation are hereby authorized and directed to wind up the affairs of the corporation, collect its assets, and pay or provide for the payment of the corporation's debts and liabilities.

2. As soon as may be reasonably practicable, the officers of the corporation shall transfer all its remaining property (subject to all its remaining liabilities) to the corporation stockholders, in proportion to their stock ownership, in cancellation of their shares.

3. As soon as may be reasonably practicable, the officers of the corporation shall cause it to be dissolved.

Dated this _____ day of _____, 19___.

By: _____
Its: _____

3. The deadline, which may not be fewer than 120 days from the effective date of the written notice, by which the dissolved corporation must receive the claim

4. A statement that the claim will be barred if not received by the deadline.

Figure 12-4 shows a sample notice to creditors that might be used in compliance with state statutes modeled after the Model Business Corporation Act.

Distributions to Shareholders

As a part of the winding-up and liquidation process, the assets remaining after the debts of the corporation have been paid must be distributed to the shareholders of the dissolved corporation. The assets may be reduced to cash prior to distribution, or they may be distributed in kind. The shareholders will receive a pro-rata portion of the assets of the corporation, based on the number of shares owned by them and

NOTICE TO THE CREDITORS OF

_____

The directors and shareholders of the above corporation have adopted a resolution to voluntarily dissolve the corporation pursuant to _____ [statute].

1. Any claims against the assets of the corporation must be made in writing and include the amount of the claim, the basis of the claim, and the date on which the claim originated.

2. The claim must be sent, by U.S. Mail, to the registered office address of the corporation at _____ .

3. The deadline for submitting claims to this corporation is _____ , 19___ [no sooner than 120 days from the effective date of this notice].

4. Any claims not received by the corporation on or prior to the above deadline will be barred.

Dated this _____ day of _____ , 19___ .

_____
Secretary

FIGURE 12-4
Sample Notice to Creditors

the rights of each particular class of shares. Preferred shareholders may have a priority right to the distribution of assets upon the dissolution of a corporation.

Postdissolution Claims

Under the Model Business Corporation Act, claims against a dissolved corporation are barred if the claimant was given proper notice but did not submit a claim to the dissolved corporation by the deadline. The claim may also be barred if the claim is rejected by the corporation and the claimant does not commence a proceeding to enforce the claim within 90 days from the effective date of the rejection notice. Also under the Model Business Corporation Act, if the dissolving corporation does not give notice to creditors or publish a notice of dissolution, it is not entitled to the protection from future claims that is afforded to a dissolving corporation that gives proper notice.

Although statutes are typically very clear with regard to the means for disposing of known claims against a dissolving corporation, the dissolving corporation may also be liable for certain subsequent claims by unknown claimants. For this reason, the corporate existence continues beyond dissolution for certain purposes.

State statutes differ in their treatment of postdissolution claims. The Model Business Corporation Act provides that the dissolved corporation remains liable for claims for five years after it publishes a notice of its dissolution and request for presentation of any claims against the corporation. The notice must be published in a newspaper in the county where the principal office of the dissolved corporation is located, and it must describe the information that must be included in a claim against the dissolved corporation and the means for presenting that claim. In addition, the notice must include a statement that a claim against the corporation will be barred unless a proceeding to enforce the claim is commenced within five years after publication of the notice.[10] The Model Business Corporation Act further provides that, if a corporation publishes notice of dissolution pursuant to statute, the claims of the following individuals are barred after five years of the date of the publication, unless a proceeding to enforce the claim is commenced within that time period:

1. Claimants who do not receive written notice pursuant to statute
2. Claimants whose claims are timely sent to the dissolved corporation but not acted on
3. Claimants whose claims are contingent or based on an event occurring after the effective date of the dissolution.

Valid claims may be enforced against the undistributed assets of the dissolved corporation, or against a shareholder of the dissolved corporation to the extent of the shareholder's share of the distribution upon the corporation's liquidation. Shareholders may not be held liable in excess of their distribution received upon dissolution of the corporation. Claims of creditors that do not receive proper notice are not barred by statute. The statutes of several states provide dissolving corporations with the option of giving notice to creditors. However, if the dissolving corporation does not give proper notice to creditors it will be liable to its creditors for a substantially longer time. For example, under the General Corporation Law of Delaware, if notice is given to creditors pursuant to statute, any claims against the corporation are barred after three years. This protection from claims presented after three years is not available to the shareholders of corporations that do not give notice pursuant to the statutes. In the following case, the court found that the defendant corporation was not liable to the petitioner for injuries sustained as the result of a defective product that was manufactured by the defendant, a corporation which had dissolved seven years prior to the injury.

Tax Considerations

The dissolving corporation's attorneys often work closely with its in-house accountants or with an independent certified public accountant to dissolve the corporation in the manner that is the most advantageous,

HUNTER
v.
FORT WORTH CAPITAL CORPORATION
Supreme Court of Texas
620 S.W.2d 547, 20 A.L.R.4th 399 (Tex. 1981)
July 15, 1981

The question is whether Theodore Moeller can recover damages against the former shareholders of Hunter-Hayes Elevator Company (Hunter-Hayes) for post-dissolution injuries resulting from the negligence of the company. The trial court rendered summary judgment for the shareholders. The court of civil appeals reversed the judgment and remanded the cause for trial. 608 S.W.2d 352. We reverse the judgment of the court of civil appeals and affirm the judgment of the trial court.

In 1960, Hunter-Hayes installed an elevator in a building under construction in Fort Worth, Texas. The company inspected and serviced the elevator until February 1, 1964, when it transferred its assets to Dover Corporation for 25,000 shares of Dover preferred stock. Hunter-Hayes then changed its name to H.H. Hunter Corporation and distributed the shares of Dover stock among its shareholders. On March 11, 1964, H.H. Hunter Corporation (formerly Hunter-Hayes) was issued a certificate of dissolution by the Secretary of State.

Approximately eleven years later, on May 13, 1975, Theodore Moeller was permanently injured when the elevator fell on him. At the time of the accident, Moeller was working in the elevator pit, which is located in the bottom of the elevator shaft, at the direction of his employer, Dover Elevator Company. The elevator fell when a valve in the elevator pit allegedly came apart, allowing its hydraulic system to lose fluid.

Theodore Moeller sued the former shareholders of Hunter-Hayes and others to recover damages for his personal injuries. He alleged causes of action based on negligence and strict liability. The other defendants filed cross-actions against the shareholders, seeking contribution and indemnity. In his suit against the shareholders, Moeller alleged his injuries were proximately caused by the negligent installation, inspection, and maintenance of the elevator by Hunter-Hayes. He also alleged the shareholders were personally liable to him, to the extent of the assets they received on dissolution, under the "trust fund theory."

In response, the shareholders moved for a summary judgment. They alleged Moeller's action and the cross-actions against them were barred because they were not brought within three years after the company dissolved as required by Article 7.12 of the Texas Business Corporation Act. The trial court granted the motion and severed all causes of action against the shareholders so that it could render a final and appealable judgment. ... The court of civil appeals reversed the judgment and remanded the cause for trial. The court of civil appeals held that Article 7.12 was vitiated in this cause by the "trust fund theory."

Article 7.12, which is derived from Section 105 of the Model Business Corporation Act, provides:

Survival of Remedy
After Dissolution

A. The dissolution of a corporation ... shall not take away or impair any remedy available to or against such corporation, its officers, directors, or shareholders, for any right or claim existing, or any liability incurred, prior to such dissolution ... .

Article 7.12 provides statutory remedies for pre-dissolution claims only and thus is in the nature of a survival statute. Moeller's cause of action did not accrue until he was injured more than eleven years after the company dissolved. ... Consequently, Moeller cannot recover against the shareholders for his post-dissolution claim against the corporation, unless his suit is authorized by some other statute or legal theory. ...

At common law, dissolution terminated the legal existence of a corporation. Once dissolved, the corporation could neither sue nor be sued, and all legal proceedings in which it was a party abated. ...

To alleviate the harsh effects of the common law on creditors, an equitable doctrine evolved.

This doctrine provided that when the assets of a dissolved corporation are distributed among its shareholders, a creditor of the dissolved corporation may pursue the assets on the theory that in equity they are burdened with a lien in his favor. ... This doctrine is often referred to as the "trust fund theory." Actually, the equitable doctrine has a much broader application. The trust fund theory applies whenever the assets of a dissolved corporation are held by any third party, including corporate officers and directors, so long as the assets are traceable and have not been acquired by a bona fide purchaser. ...

We agree with defendant that extension of the trust fund theory to cover plaintiff's claim would mean that the corporation could never completely dissolve but would live on indefinitely through its shareholders. We do not believe that this result would be in accordance with the spirit of the laws governing the dissolution of corporations. ...

We reverse the judgment of the court of civil appeals and affirm the judgment of the trial court.

with regard to taxes, to its shareholders. The dissolving corporation must notify the Internal Revenue Service by filing a Form 966 (see Figure 12-5) together with a certified copy of the resolution or plan of liquidation within thirty days of adoption of the liquidation plan. In addition, the distributions of the liquidating corporation must be reported on Forms 1096 and 1099.

Revocation of Dissolution

Because the dissolution of a corporation is such a final step, the statutes of most states provide for the revocation of dissolution proceedings. The revocation of a dissolution typically must be approved by the directors and shareholders of a corporation in the same manner in which the dissolution was approved. The Model Business Corporation Act provides that a corporation may revoke its dissolution within 120 days after its effective date.[11]

Articles of revocation of dissolution or some other, similar document typically must be filed with the Secretary of State to revoke the dissolution of a corporation. Section 14.04(c) of the Model Business Corporation Act sets forth the requirements for the articles of revocation of dissolution:

(c) After the revocation of dissolution is authorized, the corporation may revoke the dissolution by delivering to the secretary of state for filing articles of revocation of dissolution, together with a copy of its articles of dissolution, that set forth:
(1) the name of the corporation;
(2) the effective date of the dissolution that was revoked;
(3) the date that the revocation of dissolution was authorized;

FIGURE 12-5
IRS Form 966

O   966   FEDERAL   1,895

Form **966**

(Rev. January 1993)
Department of the Treasury
Internal Revenue Service

Corporate Dissolution or Liquidation

(Required under section 6043(a) of the Internal Revenue Code)

OMB No. 1545-0041
Expires 1-31-96

Please type or print

Name of corporation

Employer identification number

Number, street, and room or suite no. (If a P.O. box number, see instructions below.)

Check type of return

☐ 1120   ☐ 1120L
☐ 1120-IC-DISC   ☐ 1120S
☐ Other ▶

City or town, state, and ZIP code

1 Date incorporated

2 Place incorporated

3 Type of liquidation

☐ Complete   ☐ Partial

4 Date resolution or plan or complete or partial liquidation was adopted

5 Service Center where corporation filed its immediately preceding tax return

6 Last month, day, and year of immediately preceding tax year

7a Last month, day, and year of final tax year

7b Was corporation's final tax return filed as part of a consolidated income tax return? If "Yes," complete 7c, 7d, and 7e.

☐ Yes   ☐ No

7c Name of common parent

7d Employer Identification Number of Common Parent

7e Service Center where consolidated return was filed

	Common	Preferred
8 Total number of shares outstanding at time of adoption of plan or liquidation		
9 Date(s) of any amendments to plan of dissolution		
10 Section of the Code under which the corporation is to be dissolved or liquidated . . .		
11 If this return concerns an amendment or supplement to a resolution or plan, enter the date the previous Form 966 was filed		

Attach a certified copy of the resolution or plan and all amendments or supplements not previously filed.

Under penalties of perjury, I declare that I have examined this return, including accompanying schedules and statements, and to the best of my knowledge and belief it is true, correct, and complete.

▶

Signature of officer   Title   Date

Instructions

Paperwork Reduction Act Notice.—We ask for the information on this form to carry out the Internal Revenue laws of the United States. You are required to give us the information. We need it to ensure that you are complying with these laws and to allow us to figure and collect the right amount of tax.

The time needed to complete and file this form will vary depending on individual circumstances. The estimated average time is:

Recordkeeping . . . . 5 hr., 1 min.

Learning about the law or the form . . . . 6 min.

Preparing and sending the form to the IRS . . . . 11 min.

If you have comments concerning the accuracy of these time estimates or suggestions for making this form more simple, we would be happy to hear from you. You can write to both the **Internal Revenue Service,** Washington, DC 20224, Attention: IRS Reports Clearance Officer, T.FP; and the **Office of Management and Budget,** Paperwork Reduction Project (1545-0041), Washington, DC 20503. **DO NOT** send the tax form to either of these offices. Instead, see **When and Where To File** below.

Who Must File.—A corporation must file Form 966 if its adopts a resolution or plan to dissolve the corporation or liquidate any of its stock. Exempt organizations are not required to file Form 966. These organizations should see the Instructions for Form 990 or 990-PF.

When and Where To File.—File Form 966 within 30 days after the resolution or plan is adopted to dissolve the corporation or liquidate any of its stock. If the resolution or plan is amended or supplemented after Form 966 is filed, file another Form 966 within 30 days after the amendment or supplement is adopted. The additional form will be sufficient if the date the earlier form was filed is entered on line 11 and a certified copy of the amendment or supplement is attached. Include all information required by Form 966 that was not given in the earlier form.

File Form 966 with the Internal Revenue Service Center where the corporation is required to file its income tax return.

Distribution of Property.—A corporation must recognize gain or loss on the distribution of its assets in the complete liquidation of its stock. For purposes of determining gain or loss, the distributed assets are valued at fair market value. Exceptions to this rule apply to liquidation of a subsidiary and to a distribution that is made pursuant to a plan of reorganization.

Address.—Include the suite, room, or other unit number after the street address. If mail is not delivered to the street address and the corporation has a P.O. box, enter the box number instead of the street address.

Signature.—The return must be signed and dated by the president, vice president, treasurer, assistant treasurer, chief accounting officer, or any other corporate officer (such as tax officer) authorized to sign. A receiver, trustee, or assignee must sign and date any return required to be filed on behalf of a corporation.

Cat. No. 17053B   Form **966** (Rev 1-93)

---

(4) if the corporation's board of directors (or incorporators) revoked the dissolution, a statement to that effect;

(5) if the corporation's board of directors revoked a dissolution
authorized by the shareholders, a statement that revocation
was permitted by action by the board of directors alone pursuant to that authorization; and

(6) if shareholder action was required to revoke the dissolution,
the information required by section 14.03(a)(3) or (4).

The Model Business Corporation Act further provides that the revocation of dissolution is effective upon the effective date of the articles of revocation of dissolution, and that it relates back to the effective date of the dissolution as if the dissolution had never occurred.

§ 12.2 Involuntary Dissolution

Whereas most corporate dissolutions are voluntary, under certain circumstances a corporation may be forced into dissolving by the state in which it is domiciled, by shareholders of the corporation, or by unsatisfied creditors of the corporation. State statutes generally require that **involuntary dissolutions** be accomplished through judicial proceedings. However, the statutes of several states that have adopted the provisions of the Model Business Corporation Act in this regard provide for an administrative dissolution by the Secretary of State or other appropriate state official, without the necessity of a judicial proceeding.

Administrative Dissolution

A corporation's life is granted to it by the state and that life may be taken away by the state. It has been held that "[c]orporate privileges may be withdrawn by a state if they are abused or misemployed."[12] In an **administrative dissolution**, the state of the corporation's domicile dissolves the corporation. The corporation forfeits its right to exist, usually by failing to pay income taxes, failing to file annual reports, or failing to provide a registered agent or office in compliance with state statutes.

Although state statutes provide several different grounds for dissolution of a corporation by its state of domicile, the corporation is generally given several opportunities to rectify the situation that creates the grounds for involuntary dissolution. Section 14.20 of the Model Business Corporation Act sets forth the grounds for administrative dissolution in states patterned on the Model Act:

TERMS

involuntary dissolution   Dissolution that is not approved by the board of directors or share holders of a corporation, often initiated by creditors of an insolvent corporation.

administrative dissolution   Dissolution of a corporation by the state of the corporation's domicile, usually for failing to pay income taxes or file annual reports.

§ 14.20. GROUNDS FOR ADMINISTRATIVE DISSOLUTION

The secretary of state may commence a proceeding under section 14.21 to administratively dissolve a corporation if:

(1) the corporation does not pay within 60 days after they are due any franchise taxes or penalties imposed by this Act or other law;

(2) the corporation does not deliver its annual report to the secretary of state within 60 days after it is due;

(3) the corporation is without a registered agent or registered office in this state for 60 days or more;

(4) the corporation does not notify the secretary of state within 60 days that its registered agent or registered office has been changed, that its registered agent has resigned, or that its registered office has been discontinued; or

(5) the corporation's period of duration stated in its articles of incorporation expires.

The fact that one or more of the grounds for involuntary dissolution exists does not automatically dissolve the corporation. Specific statutory procedures must be followed for involuntary dissolution of a corporation. Typically, notice must be given to the corporation, and the corporation will have a prescribed time period within which to rectify the offending situation. Under the Model Business Corporation Act, the Secretary of State must serve the corporation with written notice and the corporation must be given sixty days after service of the notice to correct the grounds for dissolution to the reasonable satisfaction of the Secretary of State. If the grounds for dissolution are not corrected within that sixty-day period, the Secretary of State may administratively dissolve the corporation by signing and filing a certificate of dissolution. Any corporation that has been administratively dissolved may continue its existence only for the purpose of winding up and liquidating its business and affairs.

Even after the corporation has been administratively dissolved, statutes typically provide a time period within which the corporation may be reinstated. However, once a corporation is dissolved, it may lose the right to use its name in the state, and that name may be taken by another corporation. In order for a corporation to be reinstated, its corporate name must be available, or it must use a different name. Section 14.22(a) of the Model Business Corporation Act provides for the reinstatement of a corporation following an administrative dissolution:

(a) A corporation administratively dissolved under section 14.21 may apply to the secretary of state for reinstatement within two years after the effective date of dissolution. The application must:

(1) recite the name of the corporation and the effective date of the administrative dissolution;

(2) state that the ground or grounds for dissolution either did not exist or have been eliminated;

(3) state that the corporation's name satisfies the requirements of section 4.01; and

(4) contain a certificate from the [taxing authority] reciting that all taxes owed by the corporation have been paid.

If the reinstatement is determined by the Secretary of State to be effective, it relates back to the effective date of the administrative dissolution, and the corporation resumes its business as if the administrative dissolution had never occurred. In the following case, the court found that a court proceeding initiated by a corporation that had been administratively dissolved, and later reinstated, was valid, even though the corporation was dissolved at the time the proceeding was initiated.

Judicial Dissolutions

Judicial dissolutions are supervised by the proper court. Although in some instances the shareholders and directors of a dissolving corporation will request judicial supervision over a voluntary dissolution, judicial dissolutions are usually involuntary. Judicial proceedings for dissolutions are usually initiated by a petition of the state attorney general, by minority shareholders, or by an unsatisfied creditor. After it is determined that grounds for a judicial dissolution exist, the court may enter a decree dissolving the corporation and directing the commencement of the winding up of the corporation's affairs and the liquidation of its assets.

The court in which the judicial proceedings are brought often appoints a receiver to manage the business and affairs of the corporation during the winding up process. This court-appointed receiver typically has all the rights and powers assigned by the court to sell and dispose of the assets of the corporation and to distribute the remaining assets of the corporation to the shareholders as directed by the court.

Judicial Proceedings by State Authority

State statutes usually provide for involuntary dissolution of corporations by judicial proceedings at the behest of the attorney general or other appropriate state authority. Under the Model Business Corporation Act, the court may dissolve a corporation in a proceeding by the attorney general if it is found that the corporation obtained its articles of incorporation through fraud or the corporation has continued to exceed or abuse the authority conferred upon it by law.[13]

Judicial Proceedings by Shareholders

Although statutes generally require the consensus of a majority of the shareholders to dissolve a corporation, a corporation may be dissolved

REGAL PACKAGE LIQUOR
v.
J.R.D., Inc.
466 N.E.2d 409 (Ill. App. Ct. 1984)
July 17, 1984
Welch, Presiding Justice

This **interlocutory appeal** ... is taken from an order of the circuit court of St. Clair County. The following question of law was identified for our review: Can a reinstated corporation maintain a forcible entry and detainer action based on a real estate installment contract entered into by the corporation while dissolved, if the action was filed when the corporation was dissolved? We hold that it can, if the action was brought within certain time limits.

The question presented by this appeal involves a dissolved corporation which is "reinstated." Reinstatement of a corporation refers to a procedure which follows the involuntary dissolution of a corporation for failure to file annual reports or pay fees. ... That procedure should be distinguished from the revocation of voluntary dissolution proceedings ... and the vacation of an order of dissolution under section 82 of the Business Corporation Act of 1983, (ch. 32, para. 157.82), which concerns fraudulent practices or excessive authority of business corporations. By the language of its order, the trial court has limited our inquiry to the situation in which a corporation is dissolved for failure to file annual reports or pay fees and is reinstated after entering into a real estate contract and bringing a forcible entry and detainer action based on that contract. ...

Normally, upon the dissolution of a corporation, it is no longer able to maintain an action, absent a statutory exception, and all matters pending at the time of the dissolution abate. ... A dissolved corporation may institute an action within two years of dissolution (Ill. Rev. Stat. 1983, ch. 32, para. 157.94), even if its reinstatement occurs after the expiration of the applicable limitations period. ... It may even institute an action more than two years after its dissolution as long as it is reinstated within the appropriate limitations period. ... In the latter instance, reinstatement retroactively restores the status of the corporation. For the purpose of commencing and maintaining suit, it "is as though the corporation were never under any legal disability." ...

A more difficult question is whether that reinstatement also validates contracts entered into during the period of corporate dissolution. The wording of the Business Corporation Act of 1933 provides no obvious answer. ... Section 82a ... governing reinstatement, does not say that reinstatement retroactively validates corporate actions undertaken during the period of dissolution. Neither does it prohibit reinstatement from having such an effect. That provision is simply silent on the question before us. ...

The purpose of those provisions of the Business Corporation Act of 1983 relating to corporate reports and fees are for the benefit of the State and public. It would not serve that purpose to allow those provisions to be used as a defense to an action brought by a delinquent corporation to enforce a contract. As a result, we decide that reinstatement of a dissolved corporation pursuant to section 82a of the Business Corporation Act of 1933 relates back to the date of dissolution, in general, so as to validate corporate contracts entered into during the interim.

For the foregoing reasons, this cause is remanded to the circuit court of St. Clair County for further proceedings consistent with this opinion.

REMANDED

TERMS

interlocutory appeal [†] An appeal of a ruling or order with respect to a question that, although not determinative of the case, must be decided for the case to be decided.

by judicial proceedings brought by minority shareholders under certain circumstances. Some of the grounds set forth in state statutes for the judicial dissolution of a corporation by minority shareholders include insolvency of the corporation, corporate mismanagement or deadlock, and oppressive conduct by the controlling shareholders. It has been held that "even if there is no explicit statutory authority for dissolution of a corporation upon the petition of a minority stockholder, such relief is available as a matter of judicial sponsorship."[14] Section 14.30(2) of the Model Business Corporation Act sets forth the grounds for shareholder-initiated judicial dissolution in states following the Model Act:

> The [name or describe court or courts] may dissolve a corporation: ...
> (2) in a proceeding by a shareholder if it is established that:
>   (i)   the directors are deadlocked in the management of the corporate affairs, the shareholders are unable to break the deadlock, and irreparable injury to the corporation is threatened or being suffered, or the business and affairs of the corporation can no longer be conducted to the advantage of the shareholders generally, because of the deadlock;
>   (ii) the directors or those in control of the corporation have acted, are acting, or will act in a manner that is illegal, oppressive, or fraudulent;
>   (iii) the shareholders are deadlocked in voting power and have failed, for a period that includes at least two consecutive annual meeting dates, to elect successors to directors whose terms have expired; or
>   (iv) the corporate assets are being misapplied or wasted.

Judicial Proceedings by Creditor

At times, corporations that are in severe financial trouble may continue to transact business despite having several judgments filed against them. Creditors may be unable to collect on their judgments if the corporation has insufficient liquid assets. For this reason, the statutes of most states provide for the involuntary dissolution of a corporation in a proceeding initiated by the corporation's creditors. The Model Business Corporation Act provides that the court may dissolve a corporation in a proceeding initiated by a creditor if the creditor's claim has been reduced to judgment, the execution on the judgment is returned unsatisfied, and the corporation is insolvent; or if the corporation has admitted in writing that the creditor's claim is due and owing and the corporation is insolvent.[15]

Buyouts and Other Alternatives to Involuntary Dissolutions

The Model Business Corporation Act further provides that, under certain circumstances, when a shareholder has brought a petition for judicial dissolution, for any of the reasons given under § 14.30(2), the corporation or one or more of the other shareholders may elect to purchase all of the shares of the petitioning shareholder for their fair value. Election to purchase the shares of the petitioning shareholders in lieu of corporate dissolution under the Model Business Corporation Act is subject to many restrictions and conditions designed to protect the interests of the petitioning shareholders. The statutes of several states contain provisions similar to those of the Model Business Corporation Act, which recognize the fact that restructuring a corporation or buying out disgruntled shareholders is often a better alternative than the dissolution of a deadlocked corporation or a corporation that is otherwise unable to operate as presently structured.

§ 12.3 The Role of the Legal Assistant in Dissolving Corporations

Corporate dissolution and liquidation often involve the corporation's attorney, an assisting paralegal, and an accountant. The attorney and paralegal work with the client to see that all statutory formalities are complied with, while the accountant advises the client regarding the income tax aspects of dissolving and liquidating a corporation and the necessary tax filings.

The paralegal can assist with all aspects of the dissolution process, including drafting the plans of dissolution and liquidation and the resolutions of the board of directors and shareholders approving the plan. The paralegal may also be responsible for drafting the articles of dissolution or other documents required for filing in the state of domicile, as well as drafting and publishing notices to the creditors of the dissolving corporation. The corporate paralegal often works directly with the client to obtain necessary information regarding the corporation's assets, liabilities, and creditors. The paralegal also may assist the corporate client with the distribution of assets by drafting deeds, assignments, and other instruments of transfer.

§ 12.4 Resources

The most valuable resource for information regarding corporate dissolutions is the statutes of the state of the corporation's domicile. Provisions for corporate dissolutions are typically found in the Business

Corporation Act or similar act adopted by the state of domicile. See § 5.8 of this text for a list of state corporation statutes. Federal income taxation information concerning corporate dissolutions and liquidations may be found in the Internal Revenue Code at § 331 *et seq.*

Review Questions

1. Suppose that Ann, Bob, and Christie are all incorporators of the ABC Corporation. Dennis and Elaine are elected directors and all five are to become shareholders of the new corporation. Before shares of stock are actually issued, the five investors decide to form a limited liability company instead. Bob has taken on responsibility for dissolving the corporation. Who must approve the dissolution? What if shares of stock had been issued?

2. What are the duties of the individual or individuals who are responsible for winding up the affairs of a dissolving corporation?

3. In states following the Model Business Corporation Act, what documentation must be filed with the Secretary of State?

4. Does the corporate existence dissolve upon the filing of the articles of dissolution in states following the Model Business Corporation Act? If not, for what purpose(s) is the corporate existence extended?

5. Under the Model Business Corporation Act, what notice of liquidation must be given to the creditors of a corporation?

6. What possible recourse does a minority shareholder have when the corporate management is deadlocked?

7. To what extent may the shareholders of a dissolved corporation be held liable for the debts of the corporation incurred prior to dissolution?

8. Suppose that the ABC Corporation is administratively dissolved on January 1, 1992, for failure to file annual reports in compliance with the statutes of its state of domicile. On June 30, the ABC Corporation eliminates the grounds for its dissolution to the satisfaction of the Secretary of State and becomes reinstated. Could the shareholders of the ABC Corporation be held personally liable for obligations incurred on behalf of the corporation on March 15, on the grounds that the corporation did not legally exist?

9. In a state following the Model Business Corporation Act, can a creditor of a dissolved corporation who has received proper notice collect on that claim six months after the notice was received?

Notes

1 19 AM. JUR. 2d *Corporations* § 2752 (1985).

2 6B AM. JUR. 2d *Legal Forms* 2d § 74:3001 (1994).

3 *Id.* § 3025.

4 Articles of Dissolution are filed with probate judge.

5 Articles of Dissolution are filed with mayor.

6 Notice of Intent to Dissolve must be published.

7 Certificates are required from the Department of Revenue and Taxation and the Department of Labor certifying that all fees, charges, taxes, etc., have been paid.

8 19 AM. JUR. 2d *Corporations* § 2828 (1985).

9 *Id.* § 2733 (1985).

10 1984 Revised Model Business Corporation Act § 14.07(b).

11 *Id.* § 14.04(a).

12 19 AM. JUR. 2d *Corporations* § 2788 (1985).

13 1984 Revised Model Business Corporation Act § 14.30(1).

14 19A AM. JUR. 2d *Corporations* § 2758 (1985).

15 1984 Revised Model Business Corporation Act § 14.30(3).

CHAPTER 13

EMPLOYEE
BENEFIT PLANS

> *Driving the interest in ESOPs is a concern in American industry about becoming more entrepreneurial.*
>
> **Frederick M. Rumack**
> **Buck Consultants Inc.**

Introduction

The salary paid to employees by a corporation accounts for only a portion of their total compensation. Employers also compensate their employees with a mixture of other benefits, some of which are mandated by law, such as Social Security and workers' compensation, and some of which the employer may elect to offer to compensate its employees and entice new employees. There are a wide variety of employee benefit plans that employers may elect to adopt, including pension plans and welfare benefit plans.

Plans that meet with certain requirements of the Internal Revenue Code (IRC) and qualify for special tax treatment are referred to as **qualified plans**. Because of the frequent passage of legislation that favors qualified plans, the number and value of qualified plans have been increasing significantly in recent years. As of the end of 1990, nearly 77 million people in this country were participants in private pension plans, and nearly $99 billion annual in contributions were made to those plans.[1] Approximately 71 percent of all employees were participants in employer-sponsored health insurance plans.[2]

§ 13.1 Qualified Plans

In addition to compensating valuable employees and enticing new employees, qualified plans offer several unique benefits to both the employer and the employee.

TERMS

qualified plan Retirement plan that meets with certain requirements of the Internal Revenue Code and qualifies for special tax treatment.

Qualified pension plans offer tax incentives to employers by allowing a tax deduction for the employers' contributions to qualified plans. In addition, investment income earned on contributions is tax-free until it is distributed to plan participants.

Tax benefits to the qualified pension plan participant include deferred income tax payments: No income tax is payable on the contribution to the plan, only on the benefit received from it in the future. Under certain circumstances, income tax payable on the benefits received from a qualified plan may also be deferred.

Qualified welfare benefit plans allow the employer a tax deduction for certain health and welfare benefits they offer to their employees. In addition, in many instances, employees may be allowed to pay for their portion of welfare benefits with pre-tax dollars.

§ 13.2   Laws Governing Qualified Plans

Qualified plans are subject to the restrictions and requirements set forth in the Internal Revenue Code (IRC) §§ 401–418E, and the **Employee Retirement Income Security Act of 1974 (ERISA)**, which is the main act regulating qualified plans.

Employee Retirement Income Security Act of 1974 (ERISA)

ERISA was adopted in 1974 to protect the participants and beneficiaries of employee benefit plans—a growing population of individuals in the United States—in response to congressional findings that "employee benefit plans substantially affect interstate commerce, federal tax revenues, and the national public interest, as well as the continued well-being and security of millions of employees and their beneficiaries."[3]

The provisions of ERISA govern most pension and welfare benefit plans, including those that are not *qualified* plans under the Internal Revenue Code. This means that even certain plans that are not allowed special income tax treatment may be subject to the provisions of ERISA, which establish:

═══════════════════ **TERMS** ═══════════════════

Employee Retirement Income Security Act of 1974 (ERISA) [†]   A federal statute that protects employee pensions by regulating pension plans maintained by private employers, the way in which such plans are funded, and their vesting requirements. ERISA has important tax implications for both employers and employees.

Dividends

An ESOP Fable

Once upon a time, corporate management decided to do something nice for corporate employees. Management wanted to reward its employees for their hard work and to give their employees incentive to produce more. So management gave their employees stock in the corporation through an employee stock ownership plan (ESOP).

This made corporate employees very happy, and they worked harder and harder. They knew that the harder they worked, the more profitable their corporation would become, and the more valuable their stock would be. Workers also enjoyed their ability to have a say in the management of the corporation through the voting of their stock. Although they were usually not able to effect any major changes in the corporation, they felt that they had an outlet to express their opinions.

Corporate management soon found that not only did ESOPs make corporate employees happy, but it made the IRS happy too. Corporate management found that they gained a significant income tax savings through use of the ESOP. In addition to other income tax benefits, they were able to deduct dividends paid on all shares of stock owned by the ESOP.

Corporate management also discovered that the ESOP was a good vehicle for raising capital for the corporation. ESOPs can be used to borrow money from a lending institution to purchase stock from the corporation, and it qualifies for a tax break on interest paid on the loan. Thus, the corporation receives cash from the ESOP, the ESOP receives stock from the corporation, and the money is borrowed from the bank at a low interest rate. This also made corporate management happy.

Retiring corporate management of closely held corporations were also happy, because now they had a market for their stock when they decided to retire. The ESOP became a market for the stock of retiring employees as well. Finally, corporate management found that the ESOP was good protection from hostile corporate takeovers. By putting a substantial amount of the stock of the corporation in the hands of the friendly corporate employees, corporate raiders could not obtain the requisite amount of stock to take over the corporation. Delaware state law provides that hostile bidders must buy 85 percent of the stock of a corporation. Therefore, if 15 percent or more of the stock of a Delaware corporation is in the hands of an ESOP, a hostile takeover cannot be completed.

All of these things made corporate management very happy.

The moral of this story is: "Be nice to your employees, and your employees (and the IRS) will be nice to you."   ▐▐

- Reporting and disclosure requirements

- Minimum participation requirements

- Minimum vesting requirements

- Minimum funding requirements for certain pension plans.

In addition, ERISA imposes fiduciary duties on fiduciaries of employee benefit plans, and it gives employees the ability to enforce their rights in federal court.

Internal Revenue Code

For a plan to receive special income taxation treatment, it must be qualified under the Internal Revenue Code (IRC). The IRC protects employees covered by employee benefit plans by providing tax incentives for corporations that comply with IRC provisions that establish rules for participation, coverage, vesting, and other matters concerning the funding and administration of employee benefit plans.

Other Laws

In addition to ERISA, some of the recent changes to the IRC involving qualified plans include the Tax Equity and Fiscal Responsibility Act of 1982 (TEFRA), the Deficit Reduction Act of 1984 (DEFRA), the Retirement Equity Act of 1984 (REA), and the Omnibus Budget Reconciliation Act of 1993, which imposed numerous rules affecting plans adopted by small employers. The Tax Reform Act of 1986 (TRA 1986), the Single Employer Pension Plan Amendments Act of 1986 (SEPPAA), and the Pension Protection Act of 1987 (PPA) also amended several of the rules with regard to qualified plans. As illustrated by the number of acts listed here, qualified plans are frequently the target of new legislation. The new legislation often means that employers must amend their qualified plans in order to realize their full benefit.

§ 13.3 Elements of a Qualified Plan

The terms and conditions of a qualified plan will depend on the type of plan and the specific plan provisions. However, generally all types of qualified plans have some common elements. Qualified plans usually are adopted by an employer who acts as the sponsor of the plan. Qualified plans are administered by a plan administrator for the benefit of the plan participants or their beneficiaries.

The Sponsor

The **sponsor** of a qualified plan is typically a corporate employer. However, a partnership or even a self-employed individual may act

---

TERMS

sponsor   In ERISA terms, an employer who adopts a qualified plan for the exclusive benefit of the sponsor's employees and/or their beneficiaries.

as a plan sponsor. In addition, under certain circumstances, unions, associations, or similar groups may act as plan sponsors. A sponsor must adopt a qualified plan for the exclusive benefit of the sponsor's employees or their beneficiaries.

The Plan

The plan that is adopted by the sponsor must be a written document that includes the minimum provisions required for qualified plans by law. The plan or its significant provisions must be communicated to the sponsor's employees. The plan must be communicated to employees through use of a summary plan description. This is a document that is furnished to participants and beneficiaries and written in a manner that can be understood by the average plan participant. This simplified version of the plan provisions that affect the plan participants is often distributed to employees in booklet form.

TABLE 13-1 REQUIREMENTS FOR SUMMARY PLAN DESCRIPTION UNDER ERISA § 102

The Summary Plan Description must contain the following information:

- Name of the Plan
- Type of Administration
- Name and Address of Person Designated as Agent for Service of Legal Process
- Name and Address of Plan Administrator
- Names, Titles, and Addresses of any Trustees
- Description of Relevant Provisions of any Applicable Collective Bargaining Agreement
- Eligibility Requirements for Plan Participation
- Eligibility Requirements for Receiving Plan Benefits
- Description of Provisions Providing for Nonforfeitable Pension Benefits
- Circumstances which May Result in Disqualification, Ineligibility, or Denial or Loss of Benefits
- Source of Financing of the Plan
- Identity of any Organization through which Benefits Are Provided
- Date of End of Plan Year; and Whether Records are Kept on Plan or Calendar Year
- Claims Procedures
- Remedies Available for Redress of Denied Claims

The Plan Administrator

Qualified plans may be administered and managed by one or more individuals who are considered to be fiduciaries of the plan. The plan sponsor or trustee may act as the administrator, or the administrator may be a professional plan administrator or investment manager. **Plan administrators** are generally responsible for calculating and processing all contributions to and distributions from the plan, and for all other aspects of plan administration. The specific duties assigned to the plan administrator are typically set forth in the plan document or in a supplement thereto.

The Plan Participants

The terms of the plan document determine who may participate in the plan. **Plan participants** are generally any employees of the sponsor who meet certain minimum requirements set forth in the plan in compliance with ERISA.

§ 13.4 ERISA and IRC Requirements Common to All Types of Qualified Plans

The plan requirements under ERISA and the IRC are numerous, and depend on the type of qualified plan and, in some instances, the plan sponsor. This section discusses some of the fundamental requirements that typically apply to all types of qualified plans. In general, ERISA provides that the qualified plan must be permanent, must be in writing, and must be for the exclusive benefit of the sponsor's employees. In addition, ERISA sets forth minimum coverage requirements that apply to most plans.

TERMS

plan administrator   Individual or entity responsible for calculating and processing all contributions to and distributions from a qualified plan, and for all other aspects of plan administration.

plan participant   Employees who meet with certain minimum requirements to participate in a qualified plan.

Plan Must Be Established for the Exclusive Benefit of Employees

Qualified plans must be established for the exclusive benefit of employees or their beneficiaries. The plan participants usually may choose their beneficiaries freely. However, if the provisions of the plan so specify, the choice of beneficiaries may be limited. For a plan to be qualified under IRC § 401(a), it must be "impossible, at any time prior to the satisfaction of all liabilities with respect to employees and their beneficiaries under the trust, for any part of the corpus or income to be ... diverted to purposes other than for the exclusive benefit of his employees or their beneficiaries." Plan sponsors are prohibited from removing funds from a qualified plan trust for their own use.

Minimum Coverage and Participation Requirements

Qualified plans must meet certain minimum participation standards set forth in the IRC or ERISA, or the plan will lose its qualified status. Qualified plans generally set forth the minimum requirements that must be satisfied before an employee may participate in the plan.

The current minimum participation rules established under IRC § 401(a)(26) state that the plan must, for each day of the plan year, benefit the lesser of (1) fifty employees of the employer, or (2) 40 percent or more of all employees of the employer. This means that, for a 100-employee corporation to pass the test, it must benefit at least forty employees (40 percent) every day of each year that the plan is in effect. A 1,000-employee corporation must benefit at least 50 employees to pass this test. Certain employees, such as those who have not met minimum age and service requirements established by the plan, may be disregarded for purposes of this calculation. Nonresident aliens and certain employees who are covered by a collective bargaining agreement may also be disregarded for coverage calculation purposes.

With few exceptions, the conditions of participation set forth in the plan must not be greater than those set forth in the IRC. The IRC conditions state that a plan cannot require, as a condition of participation, that any employee complete a period of service extending beyond the later of the following dates: (1) the date he or she reaches 21, or (2) the date on which he or she completes one year of service.[4] Therefore, all full-time employees over the age of 21 who have completed at least one year of service have usually met the minimum participation conditions.

Exemptions from the Provisions of ERISA

Not all plans are subject to the provisions of ERISA. Government plans, certain plans of nonprofit corporations, workers' compensation, unemployment and certain disability plans, and unfunded excess benefit plans are among those that are exempt.[5]

§ 13.5 Qualified Pension Plans

Qualified pension plans are qualified plans that are designed to provide retirement income to participants. Benefits may be paid in a lump sum or in the form of an annuity. Disbursements from qualified pension plans are typically not made until the participant retires, reaches retirement age, becomes disabled, or terminates employment with the sponsoring employer.

Contributions made to the qualified pension plan are held in a trust where the funds are managed until they are fully distributed.

Qualified pension plans generally fall into one of two broad categories: the defined benefit plan or the defined contribution plan. At times, an employer may adopt both a defined benefit plan and a defined contribution plan and design them to complement each other.

Contributions

Qualified plan contributions are made to the plan by the plan sponsor, the plan participant, or both. The amount of the contribution is established in accordance with the provisions of the plan, but is limited by provisions of the IRC.[6] Contributions to qualified plans are subject to several different limitations imposed by law, including limitations based on the total amount of the contribution per employee, and the total amount of compensation of each employee which may be considered when calculating the contribution. In addition, contributions to qualified plans must be made in accordance with special rules that prohibit discrimination in favor of highly paid employees. Contributions

---

TERMS

qualified plan contributions Contributions made to a qualified plan by the sponsor, participants, or third parties. Limitations on the amount of contributions are set forth in the Internal Revenue Code.

are deductible if made to qualified plans so long as they are reasonable compensation for services actually rendered to the contributing employer, and so long as the contribution does not exceed statutory limits.

Limits on Benefits and Contributions to Qualified Pension Plans

Plan contributions must not exceed limits established in IRC § 415 for the limitation year. If contributions are made in excess of the IRC § 415 limits, the plan may become disqualified, which can have severe consequences for plan sponsors and participants. If a plan is deemed to be disqualified, contributions made to the plan become taxable, as well as the income earned by the trust holding the assets.

The Trust

The contributions made to the plan are generally held in a **qualified plan trust** that is managed by trustees, who are appointed by the plan sponsors in the plan document or a supplement thereto. The contributions will be invested by the trustees or others who are designated to manage the trust assets. So long as the pension plan remains "qualified," the trust will pay no income tax on the income of its assets.

Benefits

Accrued Benefit Rules

Qualified pension plans generally must meet certain accrued benefit requirements established by the IRC and ERISA. With regard to a defined benefit plan, the term **accrued benefits** refers to the participant's annual benefit, starting at normal retirement age, or the actuarial equivalent of such benefit. With regard to a defined contribution plan, the term *accrued benefit* refers to the balance in an employee's account.[7] ERISA provides that qualified plans generally may not be amended to reduce the accrued benefit provisions.

TERMS

qualified plan trust   Trust managed by trustees who are appointed by the qualified plan sponsors to manage the assets of the qualified plan.

accrued benefits   The plan participant's annual benefit, starting at normal retirement age, or the actuarial equivalent of such benefit.

Vesting

Qualified plans must meet certain vesting requirements set forth in ERISA § 203. **Vesting** refers to the participant's nonforfeitable right to receive the benefit. To comply with ERISA's minimum vesting standards, qualified plans must:

1. Provide that the employee's right to the normal retirement benefit is nonforfeitable upon the attainment of normal retirement age
2. Provide that the employee's right in the accrued benefit derived from the employee's own contributions is nonforfeitable
3. Comply with the minimum vesting provisions set forth in ERISA § 203(a)(2).

ERISA § 203(a)(2) provides that any employee who has at least five years of service with the employer has a nonforfeitable right to 100 percent of the employee's accrued benefit derived from employer contributions. In the alternative, a plan may provide for vesting on the following schedule:

Years of Service	Nonforfeitable Percentage
3	20%
4	40%
5	60%
6	80%
7 or more	100%

Top-Heavy Plans

If a plan primarily favors officers, directors, stockholders, partners, or other key employees, it is considered to be "top-heavy." Top-heavy plans must comply with certain vesting, benefits, and contribution rules for nonkey employees that are prescribed in ERISA specifically for top-heavy plans. Defined benefit plans are considered to be top-heavy if more than 60 percent of the accrued benefits are for the key employees. Defined contribution plans are considered to be top-heavy when more than 60 percent of the aggregate of the account balances is for key employees.

TERMS

---

vesting   The nonforfeitable right that a retirement plan participant acquires to receive benefits accrued.

Distributions

Distributions are made from the plan to the plan participants or their beneficiaries in accordance with the terms and provisions of the plan. **Qualified plan distributions** are usually made at the time of the participant's retirement, death, or termination from the plan sponsor's employment. ERISA § 206 provides that plan provisions of qualified pension plans must provide that benefit payments will begin in the year following the latest of the following events (unless the plan participant elects otherwise):

1. The date the participant reaches the age of 65 (or the normal retirement age set forth in the plan)
2. The date the participant reaches the tenth anniversary of plan participation
3. The date of the participant's termination of service.

Distributions from qualified plans are usually taxable when they are paid out. Distributions made prior to retirement age may be subject to additional excise tax. Plan participants may be allowed to roll over distributions from one qualified pension plan to another. For example, an employee who receives a distribution from a qualified pension plan may be able to roll over that distribution by investing it in an individual retirement account or another qualified plan within sixty days, and defer the income tax owing on the distribution until it is withdrawn from the new plan.

Defined Benefit Plans

As the name implies, **defined benefit plans** are those in which the benefit payable to the participant or the participant's beneficiaries is definitely determinable from a benefit formula set forth in the plan. Contributions to defined benefit plans are based on the amount that will eventually be paid out to the participant, not on the income or profits of the corporation. Benefits are generally calculated by a formula that takes into consideration the employees' years of service and their salaries.

TERMS

qualified plan distributions Distributions made to qualified plan participants or their beneficiaries from a qualified retirement plan trust, usually on the retirement, death, or termination of employment of the plan participant.

defined benefit plans Qualified plans in which the benefit payable to the participant is definitely determinable from a benefit formula set forth in the plan.

Benefits payable from qualified defined benefit plans are limited by the provisions of IRC § 415(b)(1), which states in part that benefits exceed the limitations allowed under that section if they are greater than the lesser of (a) $120,000, or (b) 100 percent of the participant's average compensation for his or her high three years. For example, to meet the requirements of IRC § 415(b)(1), an employee who made an average of $150,000 per year for the last three years of employment could not receive over $120,000 (80 percent of his or her average salary). The benefit payable to an employee who averaged $50,000 per year for the last three years of employment could not exceed $50,000 (100 percent of his or her average salary). The $120,000 limit is subject to indexing for inflation. $120,000 is the correct figure for 1995.

Most defined benefit pension plans provide for the payment of benefits to employees over a period of years, usually for life, after retirement.[8] Pension plan contributions may be made by employers, employees, and third parties. The actual contribution to be made to the plan is typically calculated by an **actuary** or by use of actuarial tables. The basis for contributions to qualified pension plans must be established in the plan, and the contributions must meet the funding requirements of ERISA, which are designed to insure that funds in the pension plan trust will be adequate to meet the plan's obligation to pay benefits as defined in the pension plan.

The amount of investment income generated by the pension trust's assets will not affect the benefit payable to the participant of a defined benefit pension plan. The amount of investment income (or loss) may, however, affect the amount of the contribution required each year to maintain adequate assets in the pension trust.

The pension plan's provisions determine when a participant's benefits commence. A qualified pension plan must provide *retirement* benefits to its participants, but the plan determines when payment of those retirement benefits will commence, within certain limitations set forth in ERISA § 206(a). See § 13.5 of this text dealing with distributions. Distributions from a qualified pension plan may be either in a lump sum or by distribution of an **annuity policy**.

The benefits payable under the pension plan must be calculated in a reasonable manner. The most common formulas for providing benefits for qualified pension plans include the fixed benefit formula, the unit benefit formula, and the variable benefit formula:[9]

TERMS

actuary[†]   A person whose profession is calculating insurance risk from a statistical point of view as, for EXAMPLE, the appropriate premium cost of a particular fire insurance policy.

annuity policy[†]   An insurance policy that provides for or pays an annuity.

The **fixed benefit formula** provides participants with a definite percentage of their income. For example, benefits could be 35 percent of the employee's average compensation during the last five years of employment.

The **unit benefit formula** provides participants with a unit of pension for each year of credited service. The unit may be either a percentage of compensation or a stated dollar amount.

The **variable benefit formula** provides participants with benefits that are related to the market value of the trust assets or are tied to a recognized cost of living index.

Annuity Plans

Annuity plans are a type of defined benefit pension plan with no trust. When annuity plans are used, contributions to the pension plan are used to purchase retirement annuities directly from an insurance company. Although annuity contracts are not "trusts," annuity contracts held by an insurance company are treated as qualified trusts, and the person holding the contract is treated as the trustee.[10]

Defined Contribution Plans

Defined contribution plans establish an individual account for each participant and provide benefits based solely on the amount contributed to the participant's account. They are often designed to allow the plan participants, and beneficiaries of the participants, to share in the profits of the corporation.

TERMS

---

fixed benefit formula   Formula for calculating pension plan benefits that provides participant with a definite percentage of their income.

unit benefit formula   Formula for calculating the benefits payable under a pension plan that provides participants with a unit of pension for each year of credited service.

variable benefit formula   A formula used to calculate benefits payable under a pension plan that provides participants with benefits that are related to the market value of the trust assets or are tied to a recognized cost of living index.

annuity plan   Type of qualified plan that does not involve a qualified plan trust. Contributions to an annuity plan are used to buy annuity policies directly from an insurance company.

defined contribution plan   Qualified plan that establishes individual accounts for each plan participant and provides benefits based solely on the amount contributed to the participants' accounts.

Contributions to participants' accounts, which may be made by the employer, the employee, or a third party, are determined by a formula prescribed in the plan, which may be based on any or all of the following: the corporation's profits, the salary of the participant, and/or the contributions made to the plan by the participant. Each participant's account is credited with the participant's share of the contribution pursuant to the terms of the plan.

Contributions to qualified defined contribution plans are limited by the provisions of IRC § 415(c)(1), which states in part that annual contributions to qualified defined contribution plans exceed the limits allowed under that section if the annual contribution is greater than the lesser of: (1) $30,000 (or, if greater, one-quarter of the dollar limitations in effect under subsection (b)(1)(A), or (2) 25 percent of the participant's compensation. The dollar amount referred to under subsection (b)(1)(A) is the dollar amount limit placed on the benefits receivable under defined benefit plans, which is currently $120,000. Following is an example of a calculation to determine the maximum amount that can be contributed to the account of a defined contribution participant who has an annual salary of $100,000.

Pursuant to IRC § 415(c)(1), the contribution may be no greater than the *lesser* of the following:

(A) $30,000 (or, if greater, one-quarter of the dollar limitations in effect under subsection (b)(1)(A) which is currently $120,000 (in 1995)).

$\frac{1}{4}$ of $120,000 = $30,000.

Because $\frac{1}{4}$ of the subsection (b)(1)(A) figure equals the $30,000 limit, $30,000 is the figure to use for subsection (A) of this section.

(B) 25 percent of the participant's compensation.

25% of $100,000 = $25,000.

The lesser of the figures calculated from (A) and (B) is $25,000, so the annual contribution to the defined contribution plan in this instance may not exceed $25,000.

Plan contributions are retained in a qualified plan trust and income earned through investment of the plan assets is credited to each account, generally in the same proportion as plan contributions. The benefit payable to the participant or the participant's beneficiaries is calculated based upon contributions to the participant's account and any income, expenses, gains, losses, and forfeitures attributable to the participant's account.

Contributions made by the employer to the plan will be vested pursuant to a schedule set forth in the plan, which must comply with the requirements of ERISA. Contributions made by employees are 100 percent vested as of the date of the contribution.

Distributions are made from the defined contribution plan pursuant to plan provisions and the provisions of ERISA § 206(a).

Profit-Sharing Plans

The **profit-sharing plan** is the most common type of qualified defined contribution plan. The profit-sharing plan is a type of deferred compensation plan whereby contributions are typically made to the account of the individual participants based on the profits of the corporation for the previous fiscal year. Employer contributions are often calculated as a percentage of the corporation's profits. However, the plan may provide that the board of directors has the discretion to set the annual contribution. The employer's contribution is generally credited to the account of each profit-sharing plan participant based on a formula that takes into consideration each participant's income as a fraction of the total income of all participants.

A profit-sharing plan offers the employer the flexibility to reduce or omit contributions to the plan during years of adversity. At the same time, it can increase employee motivation by giving employees an added benefit when the corporation does well.

401(k) Provisions and Plans

IRC § 401(k) provides for qualified cash or deferred arrangements whereby employees may elect to defer a certain percentage of their compensation each year to provide for their own retirement benefits. Salary deferrals are considered to be employer contributions and are not taxable to employees until distributed. 401(k) provisions are often found within profit sharing plans that provide for matching contributions by the employer (as permitted by IRC § 401(m)) and discretionary profit sharing contributions (also by the employer). Participants are always 100 percent vested in their plan benefits to the extent that those benefits are attributed to salary deferrals. Plans that contain only 401(k) provisions are sometimes referred to as **401(k) plans**. To receive favorable tax treatment 401(k) plans must not discriminate in favor of highly compensated individuals with regard either to eligibility to participate in the plan or to the actual deferrals made.

TERMS

profit-sharing plan [†]   An arrangement or plan under which the employees participate in the profits of the company that employs them. There are various types of profit-sharing plans. Most are regulated by the federal government under the Employee Retirement Income Security Act. All profit-sharing plans involve significant tax implications.

401(k) plan   Type of savings plan, established for the benefit of employees, which allows employees to elect to receive annual contributions in cash or as a contribution to a 401(k) plan that will defer income tax on the contribution.

Money Purchase Pension Plans

The **money purchase pension plan** is a defined contribution pension plan whereby the employer contributes a fixed amount based on a formula, set forth in the plan, that is based on the employee's salary. The money purchase pension plan is a defined contribution plan, because the employer's contribution is allocated to individual accounts on behalf of the employees and because the benefit received depends on the amount contributed to each account. However, it also resembles a defined benefit plan, because the employer is obligated to contribute to the plan each year and the amount of the contribution is not discretionary, and because the amount of the contributions to the plan each year is not dependent on any profits made by the corporation.

Benefit payments under a money purchase pension plan generally commence with the employee's retirement, as defined in the plan, or at age $70\frac{1}{2}$.

Target Benefit Plan

Similar to the money purchase pension plan, the **target benefit plan** has many features of both a defined benefit plan and a defined contribution plan. It is considered to be a defined contribution plan. Like a defined benefit plan, contributions to the target benefit plan are based on the amount of the fixed retirement benefit for each participant. However, the target benefit plan is also similar to the defined contribution plan, in that the actual amount distributed to the participant depends on the value of the assets of the participant's account at the time of retirement.

Stock Bonus Plans

The **stock bonus plan** is similar to the profit-sharing plan in design. As with the profit-sharing plan, the employer has the discretion to

---

TERMS

money purchase pension plan   Defined contribution pension plan whereby the employer contributes a fixed amount based on a formula set forth in the plan that is based on the employee's salary.

target benefit plan   Type of qualified plan that has many characteristics of both a defined benefit plan and a defined contribution plan. Contributions are based on the amount of the fixed retirement for each participant. However, the amount distributed to plan participants will depend on the value of the assets in the participant's account at the time of retirement.

stock bonus plan   Type of defined contribution plan, similar to the profit-sharing plan, in which the main investment is the employer's stock.

set the amount of the plan contribution each year. However, unlike the profit-sharing plan, the main investment of the stock bonus plan is in the employer's stock. Contributions to the plan may be in the form of cash or the corporation's stock, and distributions to the retiring or terminating employee are in the form of the corporation's stock. If the stock being distributed is not publicly traded, the plan participant is granted the option of receiving cash instead of shares of stock, at a fair price according to a formula established in the plan. Stock bonus plans allow plan participants to own equity in the corporation without committing the corporation to a large cash outlay each year for plan contributions.

Employee Stock Ownership Plans

An **employee stock ownership plan (ESOP)** is designed to give partial ownership of the corporation to the employees of the corporation. ESOPs are generally established by completing the following steps (see Figure 13-1):

1. A contribution is made to the employee stock ownership trust (ESOT). This contribution may be either profits from the corporation, or it may be in the form of a loan. Lenders and borrowers involved in loan transactions may enjoy beneficial tax treatment.
2. The money in the ESOT is used to purchase stock of the corporation. This stock may be newly issued shares of the corporation, or it may be the shares of major stockholders of the corporation who wish to sell some of those shares to the company's employees.
3. Stock (or the cash equivalent of the shares of stock held in the name of each employee) is distributed to the employees upon their termination, retirement, or other event specified in the plan.

ESOPs offer many unique advantages to both the employer and the plan participant. Instead of being a drain on the cash reserves of the corporation, the ESOP can actually aid the employer in raising cash. This occurs when a corporate employer establishes an ESOP and then borrows money from a bank or other financial institution to fund the ESOT. The borrowed cash can then be loaned to the ESOT, and the ESOT in turn invests the cash in newly issued stock of the corporation. The result to the corporation is that it has more issued and outstanding stock and more

═══════════════ **TERMS** ═══════════════

employee stock ownership plan (ESOP)   Qualified plan designed to give partial ownership of the corporation to the employees.

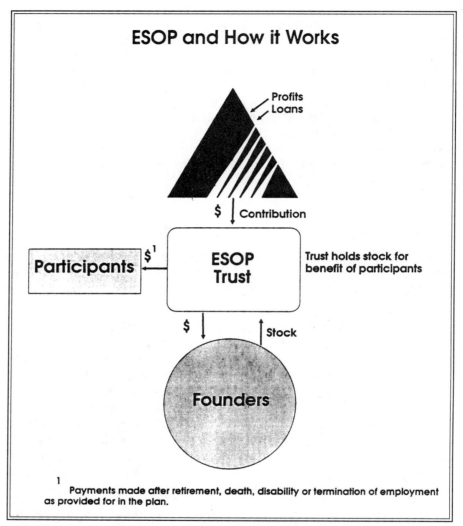

FIGURE 13-1 How an ESOP Works (Graphics courtesy of Dennis Bowman, Parsinen, Bowman & Levy)

cash on hand. The result to the plan participants is that they own an equity interest in the corporation that employs them. See Figure 13-2. ESOPs have also been used to thwart hostile takeover attempts by distributing stock to employees of the corporation in an amount sufficient to prevent the aggressor from obtaining a controlling interest. As with the stock bonus plan, plan participants may receive distributions in the form of stock of the corporation, or they may opt to have the corporation purchase their stock for a fair price.

FINANCING THROUGH AN ESOP

Once a company establishes an ESOP, several possibilities exist. In a common arrangement, the company can finance an acquisition or expansion through an ESOP.

INITIAL TRANSACTION

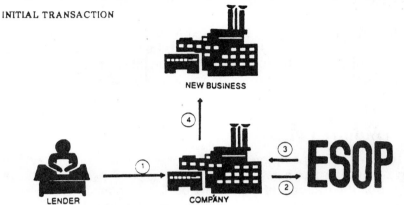

1. Lender loans money to company.
2. Company loans money to ESOP.
3. ESOP uses money to purchase company stock.
4. Company uses money to purchase new business.

SUBSEQUENT TRANSACTION

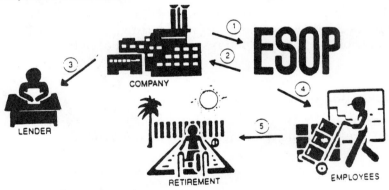

1. Company makes annual contribution to ESOP.
2. ESOP pays down loan from company.
3. Company pays down loan to lender with pre-tax dollars.
4. ESOP allocates stock to employees' accounts.
5. When the employee retires, the stock is usually sold back to the company. New employees join the company and begin accumulating stock.

FIGURE 13-2 Financing Through an ESOP (Graphics courtesy of Dennis Bowman, Parsinen, Bowman & Levy)

Integrated Plans

Both defined benefit and defined contribution plans may be integrated with Social Security. **Integrated plans** consider the employer's contribution to Social Security on behalf of a participant or the participant's Social Security benefit, when calculating the amount of contribution or the amount of benefit to be received by the participant from the plan.

Qualified plans that are integrated with Social Security benefits may provide benefits favoring highly compensated employees so long as the plan complies with the rules that limit the disparity above and below the integration level and provide for minimum benefits for all employees.[11]

Self-Employed Plans

In general, any employer may adopt a qualified employee benefit plan, including partnerships and self-employed persons, who often adopt qualified **Keogh plans**. Contributions are made to the plan by the employer, the employee, or both. Self-employed plans, or *Keogh plans* as they are often referred to, are a type of qualified plan available to self-employed individuals. For purposes of the Keogh plan, the self-employed person is considered to be an employer. Self-employed persons and partnerships are usually allowed to adopt the same type of qualified plans available to corporations. However, Keogh plans are subject to special rules regarding coverage, vesting, distribution, limitations on contributions and deductions, and taxation of retirement payouts.

Individual Retirement Accounts

Individual retirement accounts, or *IRAs* as they are commonly called, are a special type of retirement account that offers tax benefits

---

TERMS

integrated plan   Type of retirement plan that is integrated with the employer's contribution to Social Security on behalf of the participant.

Keogh plan   Qualified plan that may be adopted by self-employed individuals.

individual retirement account (IRA) [†]   Under the Internal Revenue Code, individuals who are not included in an employer-maintained retirement plan may deposit money (up to an annual maximum amount set by the Code) in an account for the purchase of retirement annuities. No tax is paid on income deposited to an IRA, and the proceeds are taxable only when they are withdrawn.

to self-employed individuals and to employees who are not active participants in a retirement plan maintained by their employer. Currently, individuals may contribute the lesser of $2,000 or an amount equal to the compensation included in the individual's gross income for a taxable year. That amount is increased to $2,250 for individuals who are married if their spouses have no compensation. The amount contributed to an IRA is treated as an income tax deduction for federal income tax purposes.

Distributions from an IRA cannot begin before the participant attains the age of 59½, or the tax benefits of the IRA will be lost and the participant will be subject to a tax penalty upon withdrawal of funds from the IRA.

§ 13.6 Nonqualified Pension Plans

Qualified plans are not the only type of pension or profit-sharing plans available. Plan sponsors may determine that their needs would be better met by an unqualified plan—that is, a plan that is not required to comply with all of the rules established for qualified plans. Nonqualified plans often take the form of an agreement between the employer and the employer's executives or otherwise highly compensated individual employees. Nonqualified plans are subject to much less regulation than qualified plans; however, they do not enjoy the same tax benefits as qualified plans.

Plan sponsors who wish to discriminate in favor of highly compensated employees often choose to adopt a nonqualified plan because nonqualified plans are not subject to the nondiscrimination, funding, participation, and vesting requirements of qualified plans. In addition, there are no benefit limits for nonqualified plans and there are fewer reporting requirements. Although nonqualified plans are not subject to the extensive regulation imposed upon qualified plans, they are governed by a number of Internal Revenue Code provisions that apply to both qualified and nonqualified plans, including certain portions of §§ 83 and 451 of the Internal Revenue Code.

Simplified employee pension plans, or *SEPs,* are an alternative to qualified plans and are often used by small businesses and self-employed

---

TERMS

simplified employee pension plan (SEP) Alternative to qualified plan, often used by small employers and self-employed individuals, that offers income tax breaks and simplified administration.

individuals. The SEP is an individual retirement account or annuity that must satisfy certain requirements under the IRC. Specifically, the plan must satisfy certain participation requirements; it must not discriminate in favor of key employees; it must permit withdrawals; and contributions must be made pursuant to a written allocation formula. SEPs have the advantage of offering simplified administration and certain tax breaks. Employer contributions to a SEP are deductible to the employer. The employee must include the contribution on his or her income tax return, but may deduct up to the lesser of $22,500 or 15 percent of his or her compensation.

§ 13.7 Employee Welfare Benefit Plans

An **employee welfare benefit plan** is defined as "any plan, fund, or program ... maintained for the purpose of providing for its participants or their beneficiaries, through the purchase of insurance or otherwise, (A) medical, surgical, or hospital care or benefits, or benefits in the event of sickness, accident, disability, death or unemployment, or vacation benefits, apprenticeship or other training programs, or day care centers, scholarship funds, or prepaid legal services. ... "[12] Most welfare benefit plans are plans offered to employees that include benefits such as medical, life, and dental insurance. A single welfare benefit plan may include one or several types of benefits.

Welfare benefit plans are subject to most of the same requirements that apply to qualified pension plans under ERISA and the IRC, including coverage requirements and non-discrimination requirements. See Figure 13-3.[13]

Welfare Benefits

The most popular welfare benefit is health insurance. In addition, welfare plans may offer such benefits as dental insurance, long and short term disability benefits, and life insurance.

TERMS

employee welfare benefit plan An employee benefit plan that provides participants with welfare benefits such as medical, disability, life insurance, dental, and death benefits. A welfare benefit plan may provide benefits either entirely or partially through insurance coverage.

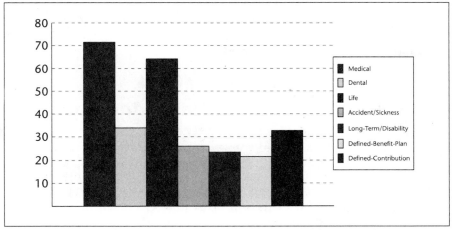

FIGURE 13-3   Percentage of Employers Offering Certain Welfare Benefits During 1992

Section 125 Cafeteria Plans

Cafeteria plans are a special type of welfare benefit plan that offer participants a choice of benefits. This type of plan is designed to cut costs to the employer and offer only the desired benefits to the participant. Benefits offered under cafeteria plans usually include health insurance (possibly more than one option), as well as dependent care reimbursement accounts and medical expense reimbursement accounts.

Funding

The simplest form of welfare benefit plan is the plan that consists only of insurance that is paid directly by the employer for the benefit of the employee, often with contributions made by the employee through salary reduction agreements. These welfare benefit plans are fully insured and typically no trust is involved. Unlike qualified pension plans, certain qualified welfare plans may be funded through the employer's general account. Typically a trust is not required.

Voluntary Employee Benefit Association (VEBA)

A Voluntary Employees Benefit Association (VEBA) is a special type of tax exempt welfare benefit plan trust that provides for the payment of life, sick, accident, or other benefits to the members of such association, their dependents, or their beneficiaries under IRC § 501(c)(9). This type of trust receives contributions from the employer and holds the contribution until welfare benefits are purchased for or on behalf of the employee.

§ 13.8 Qualified Plan Adoption and IRS Approval

When employers adopt qualified plans, they want to be assured that the plans will be considered "qualified" and that the tax benefits associated with qualified plans will be available. The employer can attain that assurance by submitting the qualified plan to the Internal Revenue Service to obtain a favorable **determination letter**, which states that the plan has been reviewed by the Internal Revenue Service and that it complies with the requirements for a qualified plan.

Each employee considered to be an interested party must be notified that an application for a favorable determination letter is to be made. After notice has been given, the employer must file a Form 5300 (see Figure 13-4) or other applicable form with the IRS. The Form 5300, which is printed by the IRS, is used to request determination letters for the qualification of defined benefit and defined contribution plans. The Form 5300 and accompanying instructions may be obtained by contacting the nearest IRS office.

In addition to the Form 5300, the following must be submitted to the IRS to complete the application:

1. A User Fee for Employee Plan Determination Letter Request (Form 8717) and the appropriate user fee
2. A copy of the plan
3. Any other information requested on the Form 5300 or by the IRS.

Employers may cut down on the time required to receive a favorable determination by adopting a master or prototype plan. A *master* or *prototype*

TERMS

determination letter [†]   A letter issued by the IRS in response to a taxpayer's inquiry as to the tax implications of a given transaction. A determination letter that advises concerning the tax exemption status of a charitable organization is often referred to as a "501(c)(3) letter," after the section of the Internal Revenue Code that sets forth the criteria for such an exemption.

< 5300 >
< Rev 2/90 >
Department of the Treasury
Internal Revenue Service

Application for Determination for Employee Benefit Plan

(Under sections 401(a) and 501(a) of the Internal Revenue Code)

OMB No. 1545-0197
Expires 1-31-93
For IRS Use Only
File folder number ▶
Case number ▶

File page 1 of Form 5300 in duplicate.
Note: *User fee must be attached to this application. (See Instruction B—What To File).*
The information provided herein will be read by computer. Therefore page 1 must be typed (except the signature). Please enter information exactly as requested and only in the space provided. Do not type in areas that are shaded.
Review the Procedural Requirements Checklist before submitting this application.

1a Name of plan sponsor (employer if single-employer plan) < >
1b Employer identification number < >
Address (number and street) < >
1c Employer's tax year ends-Enter N/A or (MM)
City < > State < > ZIP code < >
1d Telephone number ( )

2 Person to be contacted if more information is needed. (See Specific Instructions.) (If same as 1a, leave blank.) (Complete even if Power of Attorney is attached):
Name < >
Address (number and street) < >
City < > State < > ZIP code < > Telephone number ( )

3a Determination requested for (enter applicable number(s) at left and fill in required information). (See Specific Instructions.)
< > Enter 1 for Initial Qualification—Date plan signed . . . . ______
< > Enter 2 for Amendment after initial qualification—Is plan restated? . . . Yes < > No < >
Date amendment signed ______ Date amendment effective ______
< > Enter 3 for Affiliated Service Group status (section 414(m))—Date effective ______
< > Enter 4 for Leased Employee Status
< > Enter 5 for Partial termination—Date effective ______
b Has the plan received a determination letter? If "Yes," submit a copy of the latest letter . . . Yes < > No < >
c Have interested parties (as defined in Treasury Regulation section 1.7476-1) been given the required notification of this application? . . . . Yes < > No < >
d Does the plan have a cash or deferred arrangement, or employee or matching contributions (section 401(k) or (m))? . . . . Yes < > No < >

4a Name of Plan: < >
< > **b** Enter plan number (3 digits) ______ **d** Enter date plan effective (MMDDYY)
< > **c** Enter date plan year ends (MMDD) < > **e** Enter number of participants in plan

5a If this is a defined benefit plan, enter the appropriate number in box at left.
< > Enter 1 for unit benefit — Enter 3 for flat benefit
Enter 2 for fixed benefit — Enter 4 for other (Specify) ______
b If this is a defined contribution plan, enter the appropriate number in box at left.
< > Enter 1 for profit sharing — Enter 4 for target benefit
Enter 2 for stock bonus — Enter 5 for other (Specify) ______
Enter 3 for money purchase

6a Is the employer a member of an affiliated service group?
< > Enter 1 if "Yes" — Enter 2 if "No" — Enter 3 if "Not Certain"
b Is the employer a member of a controlled group of corporations or a group of trades or businesses under common control?
< > Enter 1 if "Yes" — Enter 2 if "No"

7 Enter type of plan:
< > Enter 1 if governmental plan or church plan not subject to ERISA
Enter 2 if multiple employer plan (described in section 413(c)). Enter number of participating employers. ______
Enter 3 if other

Under penalties of perjury, I declare that I have examined this application, including accompanying statements, and to the best of my knowledge and belief, it is true, correct, and complete. **Both copies of this page must be signed.**

Signature ▶ **Title ▶** **Date ▶**

Instructions are separate. See page 1 for Paperwork Reduction Act Notice. Form **5300** (Rev. 2-90)

FIGURE 13-4 IRS Form 5300, Application for Determination for Employee Benefit Plan

plan is designed for the purpose of being adopted by several employers. These plans may have special preapproval status that will expedite the IRS's review.

§ 13.9 Annual Reporting Requirements and Disclosure Requirements

Although qualified plans are typically not subject to taxation, they must file annual reports with the Internal Revenue Service. These annual reports provide the Internal Revenue Service with information concerning the plan, the plan benefits, plan participants, and coverage. In addition, qualified plans are required to provide plan participants with a summary of the annual reports.

Form 5500

All qualified employee benefit plans are required to file a Form 5500 annually. Smaller plans may file an abbreviated Form 5500R. Form 5500R filers must file a Form 5500C (which requires more information than a Form 5500R) at least every third year. Single participant plans may file a simplified, one-page Form 5500-EZ. Form 5500s must be filed with the Internal Revenue Service within seven months after the close of the plan year. Substantial penalties may be assessed for plans that do not file or file delinquently.

The reporting requirements for larger pension plans may be quite extensive, and include a full audit of the plan by an independent auditor.

Summary Annual Reports

Plans that are required to file a Form 5500 or 5500C must provide plan participants with a summary of the annual report that has been filed. Filers of the Form 5500R need only make a copy of the form available to participants.

§ 13.10 The Role of the Paralegal in Working with Qualified Plans

Paralegals are often involved in drafting qualified plans and supplementary documents, and in submitting the application for a determination letter to the IRS. Pension plans and other employee benefit plans can be very lengthy documents; many are between fifty and 100 pages long. For that reason, many law firms purchase prepared employee benefit plans from services that prepare them commercially. In that event, the attorney or paralegal completes a detailed form containing the pertinent information regarding the desired qualified plan, and the service prepares the documents as specified. Even though these documents are not prepared within the law firm, the law firm will be responsible for their content, and they must be read carefully. In some instances, plans that have been prepared by commercial services may qualify for a special submission status to the IRS that will expedite the determination letter. Other law firms, with more extensive word processing capabilities, may choose to prepare the required plan documents internally.

Once the qualified plan and related documents have been prepared, the legal assistant often attends to the notice that must be given to employees, and to submitting the application for a determination letter to the Internal Revenue Service. The paralegal may also be requested to draft the corporate client's board of director resolutions approving and adopting the employee benefit plan.

With the new legislation that continues to be introduced regarding qualified plan requirements, there has been extensive work in this area for paralegals in recent years. Much of this work involves adopting new qualified plans and terminating or amending existing qualified plans to comply with new requirements.

§ 13.11 Resources

Qualified plans are all subject to the requirements set forth in Internal Revenue Code §§ 401–418E, and any amendments thereto. Paralegals working in the qualified plan area should thus become familiar with the pertinent requirements of the Internal Revenue Code. The Internal Revenue Service is also a good source for information and for the forms required to request determination letters. The IRS has toll-free telephone numbers within each of its districts that can be used to request the pertinent forms and instructions.

Other information regarding qualified plan requirements, that may be easier to read, can be found in several sources within the law library, including *Pension Coordinator,* by RIA; *Pension & Profit Sharing,* by Prentice Hall; *Pension Plan Guide,* by CCH; and *Pension Reporter,* by BNA. Assistance in drafting plans and summary plan descriptions may be found in many of the form books discussed in previous chapters.

Review Questions

1. How can an employer be certain that an employee benefit plan will be considered a qualified plan by the IRS?

2. Under the current minimum participation rules, what is the minimum number of employees that must benefit from a qualified plan if the plan sponsor (employer) has 500 employees?

3. When is an employee's contribution to a plan considered to be fully vested?

4. Under the provisions of ERISA, could a qualified plan participant ever be ineligible to receive benefits until after his or her 65th birthday? If so, under what circumstances?

5. What are integrated plans?

6. In what ways do target benefit plans resemble typical defined benefit plans? In what way do they resemble typical defined contribution plans?

7. What unique benefit does an ESOP offer to the employer?

8. If Andrews Electronics wants to adopt an employee benefit plan that will pay its employees a specific amount upon their retirement, what type of plan would the company most likely want to adopt?

9. Suppose the management of Gregory Tool & Die Company decides that they would like to offer an employee benefit plan that would allow their employees to share in the corporation's profits and pay a benefit to the employees upon retirement or termination from the corporation. Management is uncertain about the future of the corporation, but they would like to base the contributions upon its earnings and profits. What type of plan might Gregory Tool & Die elect to adopt?

10. The owners of Gabrielle Foods would like to adopt an employee benefit plan that would encourage their employees to save money for retirement. They are willing to pay up to a certain amount per employee, per year, provided that the employee invests an equal amount of his or her pretax income. What type of plan might the owners of Gabrielle Foods adopt?

Notes

[1] The Reference Press, *The American Almanac Statistical Abstract of the United States: 1994–1995,* 114th ed. at 587 (Austin, Texas 1994).

[2] *Id.* § 673.

[3] 60A AM. JUR. 2d *Pensions and Retirement Funds* § 1.

[4] IRC § 401(a)(1).

[5] ERISA § 4(b).

[6] IRC § 415.

[7] IRC § 411(a)(7).

[8] 60A AM. JUR. 2d *Pensions and Retirement Funds* § 16.

[9] AM. JUR. *Legal Forms Federal Tax Guide* § 133-E-25.

[10] IRC § 401(f).

[11] IRC § 401(e).

[12] ERISA § 3.

[13] The Reference Press, *The American Almanac Statistical Abstract of the United States: 1994–1995*, 114th ed. at 673 (Austin, Texas 1994).

CHAPTER 14

EMPLOYMENT AGREEMENTS

CHAPTER OUTLINE

Introduction

Most individuals employed in the United States are employees at will. That is, they are hired by an employer for agreed-upon compensation, and they can be dismissed at the employer's discretion, with or without cause. However, many corporations in the United States require at least some of their employees to enter into employment agreements. An **employment agreement** sets forth the rights and obligations of both the employer and employee with regard to the employee's employment. Corporations frequently enter into employment agreements with their top executives, but they may also enter into employment agreements with other key employees, especially in the sales and technical areas. Often corporations require entire classes of employees to enter into employment agreements as a condition of employment. Corporations may have simple employment agreements that they require their employees to enter into before commencing work, or the terms may be negotiated with potential key employees prior to hiring. The employment agreement is typically drafted by the attorneys for the employer, often with the assistance of a paralegal.

This chapter investigates special considerations for both the employer and the employee when entering into an employment agreement. It then focuses on the drafting of the employment agreement, first with a discussion of some general considerations, then with an examination of specific provisions that are often included in employment agreements, and a sample employment agreement. This chapter concludes with a look at the paralegal's role in drafting employment agreements and resources to aid in that drafting.

TERMS

employment agreement Agreement entered into between an employer and an employee to set forth the rights and obligations of each party with regard to the employee's employment.

§ 14.1 Special Considerations for the Employer

Some of the benefits to the employer of employment agreements are apparent. An employer who enters into an employment agreement with an individual is reasonably assured of hiring and retaining the services of that individual as an employee for a specific period of time. Although the employer cannot compel employees to continue their employment against their will, employees who have entered into employment agreements for a specified time period may be more reluctant than others to terminate their employment before the expiration of the agreement's term, for fear of appearing unprofessional to other potential employers, among other things.

The continued employment of an employee means that the employer will not be forced to search for another individual to fill the position for the duration of the agreement—a task that can be both time-consuming and costly. Also, the person being hired will not be working for the competition. This can be a particular benefit to the employer when hiring individuals with unique experience or knowledge in a very competitive business. Although complete certainty can never exist when the human element is involved, employment agreements offer decidedly more certainty than employment at will.

Another benefit to the employer entering into an employment agreement is that the employee's actions, both during the term of employment and after, may be restricted to protect the employer's confidentiality, trade secrets, and work products. Employment agreements may include provisions restricting the future employment and actions of the employee and protecting the trade secrets, patents, and work product of the employer.

The contractual nature of the employment agreement may also result in drawbacks to the employer. For instance, it may be difficult to dismiss an employee who has an employment agreement. Even if the employee does not work out as well as planned, because of lack of performance, personality conflicts, or some other reason, the employer may be considered to be in breach of contract if the employee is terminated before the expiration of the agreement's term. The terms of an employment agreement frequently provide that the employee's employment may be terminated before expiration of the contract only "with cause," and cause for dismissing an employee may be difficult to prove.

Even if the employee performs as expected, the compensation provided for in the employment agreement may result in a hardship to the employer if the employer's business or profits do not meet projections. An employment agreement may require the employer to compensate the employee at a certain level even when the employer's business is performing poorly or losing money.

§ 14.2 Special Considerations for the Employee

Although an employment agreement may initially seem to be for the primary benefit of the employer, it also offers several potential benefits to the employee. Most importantly, it usually assures the employee of continued employment for a definite period of time for definite compensation. This may be a significant benefit when unemployment is high, either in general or in the specific field of the employee's expertise. The employee with an employment agreement that sets a definite term and definite compensation can also usually be assured of receiving that compensation, regardless of the condition of the employer's business. The employment agreement may also formalize certain benefits, incentives, or rewards that will become a future obligation of the employer to be awarded to the employee upon completion of certain deadlines or the attainment of specific goals.

Disadvantages to the employee include the facts that the employee must typically commit to a position that may not live up to the employee's expectations, and that the employee's obligations may extend beyond the term of the employment. The employee may be required to restrict his or her future employment or actions pursuant to the employment agreement. However, restrictions on future activities must be "reasonable" to be enforceable.

§ 14.3 Drafting the Employment Agreement

An employment agreement is considered to be a binding contract between the employee and the employer, and it must contain all of the elements of a valid contract, including an offer and acceptance, a meeting of minds, and the exchange of consideration. The discussion of employment agreements in this chapter is limited to written employment agreements. This section first discusses the items that must be agreed upon and included in employment agreements. It then examines more closely some of the most important provisions that are commonly included in employment agreements.

A corporation that routinely hires several new employees per year may have a standard employment agreement that each new employee is requested to sign before commencing employment. In that event, the attorney for the corporation typically drafts a "master" agreement, and the corporation tailors it as necessary to suit the particular circumstances surrounding the employment of each new employee. A smaller corporation may find it necessary to draft unique employment agreements for its executives and for key personnel.

In any event, certain key elements must be agreed to by both parties and must be included in each employment agreement for the agreement to be enforceable and for it to attain the desired results. The following checklist sets out some of the items that should be agreed to and included in any employment agreement.[1]

- ☐ Identification of parties.
  - — Employer.
  - — Employee.
- ☐ Term of agreement.
- ☐ Place where agreement is to be performed.
- ☐ Duties of employee.
  - — Hours of employment.
  - — Best efforts to be devoted to employment.
  - — Maintaining outside job or interest.
- ☐ Working facilities.
- ☐ Maintaining trade secrets.
- ☐ Inventions and patents.
  - — Discovery in course of employment.
  - — Use of employer's facilities.
  - — Relation of discovery to employer's business.
- ☐ Compensation.
  - — Wages, salary, or commission.
  - — Overtime work or night differential.
  - — Pay while unable to work because of illness.
  - — Effect of termination or noncompletion of employment.
- ☐ Special compensation plans.
  - — Deferred compensation.
  - — Percentage of sales or profits.
  - — Incentive bonus.
  - — Profit sharing.
  - — Stock options.
  - — Pension and retirement plans.
- ☐ Expense account.
  - — Travel.

— Meals.
— Lodging.
☐ Covenant not to compete after leaving employment.
— Length of time.
— Geographical limitations.
— Irreparable harm suffered by employer.
— Hardship not greater than necessary on employee.
— Agreement not injurious to public interest.
☐ Employee benefits.
— Life and disability insurance.
— Medical insurance.
— Dental insurance.
— Worker's compensation.
☐ Termination of employment.
☐ Right of either party to terminate on proper notice.
☐ Discharge of employee for cause.
☐ Remedies for breach.
— Liquidated damages.
☐ Arbitration of disputes.
☐ Vacations and holidays.
☐ Assignability of contract by employer or employee.
☐ Modification, renewal, or extension of agreement.
☐ Complete agreement in written contract.
☐ Law to govern interpretation of agreement.
☐ Effective date of agreement.
☐ Signatures.
☐ Date(s) of signing.

Term of the Agreement

The term of the agreement should be specifically set forth in the agreement. Often a specific time period, such as one year, is set forth, and the agreement is made renewable with the mutual consent of both parties. If the employment agreement does not specify a definite term of employment, the employer may have the discretion to terminate the employee at will. Likewise, the employee may have the option of terminating the agreement at any time.

EXAMPLE: *Term of Employment*

The term of this agreement shall be a period of _____ years, commencing _____ [date], and terminating _____ [date], subject, however, to prior termination as provided in this agreement. At the expiration date of _____

[date], this agreement shall be considered renewed for regular periods of one year, provided neither party submits a notice of termination.[2]

Description of Duties

The duties and obligations of the employee should be set forth with a certain degree of specificity. Although it would be impossible to set forth every duty and obligation that might possibly be expected of the employee during the term of the employment agreement, the position should be defined well enough to give both the employer and employee a reasonable understanding of the work the employee will be expected to perform and the authority the employee will be granted in accordance with the position. In addition to a description of specific duties, this section of the agreement should include the agreed-upon hours of employment, and a statement that the employee will devote his or her best efforts to the satisfactory performance of the position's duties.

EXAMPLE: Duties of Employee

Employee will serve employer faithfully and to the best of _____ [his or her] ability under the direction of the board of directors of employer. Employee will devote all of _____ [his or her] time, energy, and skill during regular business hours to such employment. Employee shall perform such services and act in such executive capacity as the board of directors of employer shall direct.[3]

EXAMPLE: Best Efforts

Employee agrees that [he or she] will at all times faithfully, industriously, and to best of [his or her] ability, experience, and talents, perform all of the duties that may be required of and from employee pursuant to the express and implicit terms of this agreement, to the reasonable satisfaction of employer.[4]

Covenant Not to Compete

Covenants not to compete, which restrict the future employment and actions of the employee, are commonly found in employment agreements. The purpose behind these covenants is to prevent the employee

---

TERMS

covenant not to compete[†]   A provision in an employment contract in which the employee promises that, upon leaving the employer, she will not engage in the same business, as an employee or otherwise, in competition with her former employer. Such a covenant, which is also found in partnership agreements and agreements for the sale of a business, must be reasonable with respect to its duration and geographical scope.

Dividends

How Much Does a CEO Make?

Unless you are a professional baseball player or a superstar, it is hard not to be impressed by the salaries earned by chief executive officers in this country. According to a 1995 *BusinessWeek* survey,[1] the salaries plus bonuses of the top-twenty-paid CEOs ranged from $726,000 to $12,042,000. Taking long-term compensation (usually in the form of stock options) into consideration, their total compensation packages for 1994 ranged from $8,905,000 to $25,928,000! Charles Lock, Chief Executive Officer of Morton International made the top of the list this year with his 1994 compensation of $25,928,000, replacing Michael Eisner, chairman of Walt Disney Co.—who topped the list last year with a 1993 compensation package of $203,010,590![2] Eisner's 1994 salary fell to a paltry $10,657,000.

One reason for these incredible salaries is the competition among corporations to lure top CEOs. If the CEO you want is making $2 million working for your competitor, he or she surely will not be lured away for less than $3 million. Blame for escalating CEO salaries is also being placed on the boards of directors of corporations who must approve the salaries. Often, a CEO pay raise is coupled with a pay raise for the directors of the corporation.

Although shareholders of these publicly held corporations vote for the directors, and the directors approve the salaries of the CEOs, for years most shareholders have been unconcerned or unaware of the extent to which their CEOs were being compensated. Recently, however, salaries of the top CEOs have been published in many prominent United States magazines, such as *Forbes, Fortune, Newsweek,* and *BusinessWeek*. In many instances, shareholders have become angry because of poor returns on their investments and excessive salaries at the top. In some instances shareholders have watched the price of their stock drop, the amount and frequency of their dividends decrease, and the salaries of their CEOs soar. The anger of these shareholders has not gone unheeded. New SEC proxy rules give shareholders more information with regard to executive pay and more power to act. Annual reports of the corporation must disclose the salary, bonuses, and other compensation received by the officers of the corporation.

In 1993, President Clinton and Congress sought to combat runaway executive compensation by passing a $1,000,000 cap on the corporate income tax deduction that may be taken for an executive's pay. According to some, the effect of that bill has been to increase the pay of many of the lower paid executives to exactly $1,000,000!

Another effect of shareholder outrage in recent years over poor performance of CEOs in relation to their pay has been to link performance more closely to pay. Almost without exception, the compensation package of most CEOs in the *BusinessWeek* salary survey included stock bonuses and stock options. The average CEO has a vested interest in increasing the value of the corporation's stock. In fact, the twenty-five top holders of nonexercised stock option holders in the *BusinessWeek* survey averaged $49,952,076!

On the other hand, CEOs whose compensation packages depend greatly on the value of the stock of their corporations may find their compensation lagging in years where the corporation's stock does not perform. For example, the 1994 salary and bonus for Charles Sanford, CEO of Bankers Trust dropped 29.9 percent from his 1993 compensation package due to poor stock performance. Deryck Maughan of Salomon Brothers saw his compensation package decline 87 percent from 1993 to 1994 due to an upheaval within his corporation which devalued its stock. Even with their pay cuts, Sanford and Maughan will probably survive a poor year or two. Their 1994 salaries were $3.95 million and $1 million, respectively.[3]

---

[1] CEO Pay: Ready for Takeoff, *BusinessWeek,* April 24, 1995, 88.
[2] That Eye-Popping Executive Pay—Is Anybody Worth This Much?, *BusinessWeek,* April 25, 1994.
[3] Deliver—or Else, *BusinessWeek,* March 27, 1995, 36.

---

from leaving one employer, from which he or she has gained significant experience and knowledge, and taking that experience and knowledge to the employer's competition.

Because covenants not to compete restrict the free actions and future employment of the employee, there are limitations on their enforcement. Under the common law of England, covenants not to compete were considered agreements in restraint of a man's right to exercise his trade or calling, and thus were considered void as against public policy.[5] However, the modern view of noncompetition clauses is that an "anticompetitive covenant supported by consideration and ancillary to a lawful contract is enforceable if reasonable and consistent with public interest."[6]

The test of reasonableness depends on the facts of the case. Generally, an agreement not to compete is considered reasonable if it is restricted to a specific time period and a specific geographical location. For instance, an agreement not to work for the competition for the rest of the employee's life anywhere in the United States would not be enforceable. Although exactly what is considered reasonable will depend on the circumstances of the particular case, the following characteristics are often assigned to anticompetition covenants that are considered to be reasonable and enforceable:

1. The covenant is legal in the state in which it is to be executed. (Covenants not to compete may be subject to state statutes that deal specifically with anticompetition covenants.)
2. The covenant is supported by sufficient consideration.
3. The restriction is reasonably necessary to protect some legitimate interest of the employer.
4. The restriction is not contrary to public interests.
5. The covenant applies to only a limited geographical location.
6. The covenant is applicable for only a limited time period.

Another consideration with regard to covenants not to compete is that they are considered unethical, or even illegal in some instances, for certain professionals such as doctors or lawyers. The following example would generally be found to be a reasonable covenant not to compete.

EXAMPLE: Noncompetition with Former Employer

Employee agrees that for a period of _____ [one year] after termination of _____ [his or her] employment with employer in any manner, whether with or without cause, employee will not, within the state of _____ , directly or indirectly engage in the business of _____ [employer's business] or in any business competitive with employer for a period of _____ [one year] from such termination of employment. Directly or indirectly engaging in the business of _____ [employer's business] or in any competitive business shall include, but not be limited to, engaging in business as owner, partner, or agent, or as employee of any person, firm, corporation, or other entity engaged in such business, or in being interested directly or indirectly in any such business conducted by any person, firm, corporation, or other entity.[7]

In the following case, involving a noncompetition clause in a television weatherman's employment agreement, the agreement was found valid primarily because it was for only a limited time period and a limited geographical location.

BECKMAN
v.
COX BROADCASTING CORPORATION
Supreme Court of Georgia
250 Ga. 127, 296 S.E.2d 566 (1982)
October 27, 1982

From 1962 until June 3, 1982, appellant Beckman was employed by Cox Broadcasting Corporation (Cox) as a meteorologist and "television personality," appearing primarily on Cox's affiliate, WSB-TV. In April, 1981, Beckman entered into a five-year contractual agreement with WXIA-TV, a competitor of Cox, to commence working for WXIA as a meteorologist and "television personality" when his contract with Cox expired on July 1, 1982. Cox was made aware of Beckman's plans and in July, 1981, Cox filed a petition for declaratory judgment, [Ga.] Code Ann. § 110-1101, seeking a determination that the restriction against competition in its employment agreement with Beckman was valid. This restriction provides: "Employee shall not, for a period of one hundred-eighty (180) days after the end of the Term of Employment, allow his/her voice or image to be broadcast 'on air'

by any commercial television station whose broadcast transmission tower is located within a radius of thirty-five (35) miles from Company's offices at 1601 West Peachtree Street, N.E., Atlanta, Georgia, unless such broadcast is part of a nationally broadcast program." Following a hearing the trial court dismissed the action finding there was no evidence to conclude either that WXIA-TV would require Beckman to violate the restrictive covenant or that Beckman would violate the covenant. Therefore, the trial court determined, Cox had not presented a justifiable controversy.

On June 16, 1982, Beckman formally demanded to be released from the restrictive covenant in his contract. When Cox refused Beckman filed this declaratory judgment action to ascertain the validity of the restrictive covenant under Georgia law.

The trial court found that the employment contract with WXIA-TV does not require Beckman to appear "on-air" during the first six months of his employment; that Beckman, under the terms of this agreement, is rendering "substantial duties and services to WXIA-TV" for which he is being compensated; that during the term of Beckman's employment with Cox, WSB-TV spent in excess of a million dollars promoting "Beckman's name, voice and image as an individual television personality and as part of WSB-TV's Action News Team," that Beckman is one of the most recognized "television personalities" in the Atlanta area; that television viewers select a local newscast, to a certain degree, based on their "appreciation of the personalities appearing on the newscast"; and that local television personalities "are strongly identified in the minds of television viewers with the stations upon which they appear." The trial court also found that in March, 1982, WSB-TV instituted a "transition plan" to reduce the impact Beckman's departure would have on the station's image. As part of this transition plan Beckman was removed from one of the two nightly WSB-TV news programs. Additionally, WSB-TV undertook an extensive promotional campaign, featuring both Beckman and his replacement as members of the "Action News Team." This transition plan contemplated the gradual phasing out of Beckman from the "Action News Team." The station projected that Beckman would then be "off the air" in the Atlanta market for six months, permitting WSB-TV to diminish its association with Beckman in the public's mind and providing the viewing public an opportunity to adjust to Beckman's replacement.

The trial court concluded that to permit Beckman to appear "on air" in the Atlanta area during the first six months of his contract with WXIA-TV would "disrupt the plans and ability of WSB-TV to adjust successfully to the loss of a well-known personality that it has heavily promoted before it must begin competing with that personality in the same marketplace." The trial court also determined that WSB-TV would be injured by allowing a competitor to take advantage of the popularity of a television personality which WSB-TV had expended great sums to promote before WSB-TV had time to compensate for the loss of that personality. The trial court further found that WSB-TV has a legitimate and protectable interest in the image which it projects to the viewing public.

While the trial court concluded the damage to WSB-TV would be great if Beckman were

permitted to compete against it within the proscribed six months, the court reasoned that Beckman would suffer little harm if the covenant was enforced against him. The trial court found that Beckman is currently employed, without loss of remuneration, and that, based on the testimony of expert witnesses at trial, "Beckman will not suffer substantial damage or loss of recognition and popularity solely as a result of being off the air during the first 180 days of his five year contract with WXIA-TV."

The trial court ruled that the restrictive covenant is valid under Georgia law as it is reasonable and definite with regard to time and territory and is otherwise reasonable considering the interest of Cox to be protected and the impact on Beckman.

Beckman appeals this decision in Case No. 39176. ...

(1) Case No. 39176. Beckman concedes the covenant not to compete is reasonable with regard to the time and territorial restrictions, but urges that it is otherwise unreasonable in that it is broader than is necessary for Cox's protection. ...

A covenant not to compete, being in partial restraint of trade, is not favored in the law, and will be upheld only when strictly limited in time, territorial effect, the capacity in which the employee is prohibited from competing and when it is otherwise reasonable. ... In determining whether a covenant is reasonably limited with regard to these factors, the court must balance the interest the employer seeks to protect against the impact the covenant will have on the employee, factoring in the effect of the covenant on the public's interest in promoting competition and the freedom of individuals to contract. ... The evidence supports the trial court's finding that WSB-TV has a significant interest in the image of its television station which it has created, in large measure, by promoting those individuals who appear on behalf of the station, whether as newscasters ... or "television personalities." This interest is entitled to protection. We further agree with the trial court that WSB-TV would be greatly harmed by Beckman's appearance on a competing station prior to the completion of WSB-TV's transition plan.

Beckman argues, however, that the detrimental impact of the restrictive covenant on him outweighs the need to protect the interests of WSB-TV. ... While the evidence is not without conflict, the trial court's finding that a six month absence from the air will not substantially damage Beckman's popularity or recognition among the public is well-supported by the record.

... [W]e conclude that for a limited time and in a narrowly restricted area, WSB-TV is entitled to prevent Beckman from using the popularity and recognition he gained as a result of WSB-TV's investment in the creation of his image so that WSB-TV may protect its interest in its own image by implementing its transition plan. We find that the restrictive covenant in this case is reasonably tailored to that end. ... We agree with the trial court that the restrictive covenant in this case is valid. ...

Judgment affirmed.

Inventions and Patents

Often an employment agreement between an employer and its research or technical staff includes a provision that assigns any inventions of the employee, and subsequent patents on those inventions, to the employer. Unless inventions are assigned to the employer by the employee, or some special circumstances exist, the employer generally has no right to the employee's inventions. Any assignment of inventions must include provisions that define exactly which inventions are covered under the assignment. The assignment may specifically exclude any inventions by the employee during his or her own time that are unrelated to the employee's work for the employer. The employee may also specifically exempt from this assignment prior inventions that he or she brings to the employer.

EXAMPLE: *Employer to Have Ownership of Employee's Inventions*

All ideas, inventions, and other developments or improvements conceived or reduced to practice by employee, alone or with others, during the term of this employment agreement, whether or not during working hours, that are within the scope of employer's business operations or that relate to any of employer's work or projects, shall be the exclusive property of employer. Employee agrees to assist employer, at its expense, to obtain patents on any such patentable ideas, inventions, and other developments, and agrees to execute all documents necessary to obtain such patents in the name of employer.[8]

In the following case, involving a device to train airplane pilots, the court found that an assignment of inventions between the employee and the employer was valid and binding and that the employer was entitled to the patent on the employee's invention.

CUBIC CORPORATION
v.
MARTY
185 Cal. App. 3d 438,
229 Cal. Rptr. 828 (1996)
August 27, 1986
Staniforth, Associate Judge

William B. Marty, Jr., appeals a judgment awarding Cubic Corporation $34,102 for Marty's breach of an invention agreement signed when he began his employment with Cubic, awarding the patent to the invention to Cubic and enjoining Marty from exploiting any rights under the patent or using or disclosing Cubic's confidential information to others.

FACTS

When Marty became a Cubic employee in December 1976, he signed an invention and secrecy agreement (hereafter the Agreement) which provided in pertinent part that the employee agreed:

"To promptly disclose to Company all ideas, processes, inventions, improvements, developments and discoveries coming within the scope of Company's business or related to Company's products or to any research, design, experimental or production work carried on by Company, or to any problems specifically assigned to Employee, conceived alone or with others during this employment, and whether or not conceived during regular working hours. All such ideas, processes, trademarks, inventions, improvements, developments and discoveries shall be the sole and exclusive property of Company, and Employee assigns and hereby agrees to assign his entire right, title and interest in and to the same to Company."

The agreement also provided the employee would cooperate in obtaining a patent on any such inventions and would not disclose any of Cubic's records, files, drawings, documents or equipment from Cubic without prior written consent. Under the agreement, Cubic promised to pay all expenses in connection with obtaining a patent, pay the employee a $75 cash bonus upon the employee's execution of the patent application and an additional $75 if a patent was obtained.

In mid-May 1977, Marty came up with an idea for an electronic warfare simulator (EWS), a device for training pilots in electronic warfare. Marty's invention had advantages over current training methods which involved the use of very expensive, security-risky, mimic radars. He developed a block diagram in May 1977 and in June 1977 a manuscript describing his invention.

He showed both the diagram and manuscript to Minton Kronkhite of Cubic, representing it might be a new product which Cubic could add to its product for training pilots, the ACMR (air combat maneuvering range). ... Kronkhite thought Marty's invention was a good idea and passed along the manuscript to Hubert Kohnen, another Cubic employee involved with the ACMR. Kohnen also thought the idea was good. He assumed it was another product for the ACMR since Marty had suggested his invention responded to some of the things Kohnen had been talking about. Kohnen made some technical comments on the manuscript. ...

Cubic funded an internal project to study Marty's invention. Marty used a Cubic computer programmer to help design necessary circuitry. Marty's background in microprocessors was weak.

Based on the developed invention, Cubic submitted a proposal to the Navy for Marty's invention under Kohnen's name. Kohnen told Marty if they got a program from the Navy, Marty would be made the program manager. Cubic did get a government program to study Marty's invention and Marty was made program manager. Marty was also given a more than average raise.

In June 1978, Marty, without telling Cubic, applied for a patent on his invention. The patent was issued in December 1979. Marty's patent attorney forwarded a copy of the patent to Cubic and offered to discuss giving Cubic a license under the patent. Cubic took the position the patent belonged to them under the Agreement Marty had signed. Cubic offered to reimburse

Marty's expenses in obtaining the patent if he assigned the patent to Cubic. Marty refused. Cubic told Marty his continued employment at Cubic was contingent on his assigning the patent. Marty continued to refuse and was terminated from his employment at Cubic in early 1980.

Cubic filed a complaint against Marty seeking declaratory relief as to ownership of the patent and alleging breach of contract, confidential relationship and trust, interference with prospective economic advantage and specific enforcement of the secrecy and invention agreement. Marty cross-complained for wrongful discharge, breach of contract, fraudulent misrepresentation, breach of confidential disclosure, copyright infringement, defamation and injunction.

The trial court awarded the patent to Cubic and $34,102 in damages resulting from a government withhold on a Cubic contract (subject to a credit to Marty if and when the amount was recovered from the government). The court also enjoined Marty from exploiting any rights under the patent and from using or disclosing to others confidential information owned by Cubic in specific documents. ...

Marty contends the Agreement was not specifically enforceable because there was inadequate consideration to support a promise to convey the invention to Cubic.

Civil Code section 3391 provides in pertinent part:

> Specific performance cannot be enforced against a party to a contract in any of the following cases:
> "1. If he has not received an adequate consideration for the contract;
> "2. If it is not, as to him, just and reasonable ... ."

The adequacy of consideration is to be determined in light of the conditions existing at the time a contract is made.

Marty argues the only consideration for the Agreement was a "token" bonus of $150. He argues his employment could not have been the consideration for the Agreement because Cubic hired him before he signed the Agreement.

The evidence shows that on the Monday mornings when new employees were scheduled to begin working at Cubic, they attended an orientation session at which employee benefits were explained. The new hires completed insurance and medical forms as well as the secrecy and invention agreement. Cubic required all new employees to sign the secrecy and invention agreement.

The evidence also shows during the course of his employment, in part because of his invention, Marty was given a substantial raise in salary and made a program manager.

This evidence supports the trial court's conclusion the Agreement was a condition of employment and that the employment was adequate consideration for the Agreement. ...

Marty also contends the court erred in awarding damages of $34,102 which represents a government withhold on a Cubic design contract. ...

Marty's wrongful assertion of ownership caused the government withhold and therefore he was liable for that sum unless and until the government paid it to Cubic.

The judgment is affirmed.

Trade Secrets

Another common type of restrictive covenant found in employment agreements restricts the divulgence of an employer's trade secrets. A *trade secret* has been defined as "any formula, pattern, device or compilation of information which is used in one's business and which gives him an opportunity to obtain an advantage over competitors who do not know it or use it."[9] This covenant may extend for a period of time beyond the term of the employment agreement, but it must be reasonable to be enforceable, and it generally loses any effect once the covered trade secrets have become common knowledge. The employment agreement usually also covers confidentiality in a general way, preventing the employee from divulging information to the press, the public, or the competition without permission.

EXAMPLE: Trade Secrets

Employee shall not at any time or in any manner, either directly or indirectly, divulge, disclose or communicate to any person, firm, corporation, or other entity in any manner whatsoever any information concerning any matters affecting or relating to the business of employer, including without limitation, any of its customers, the prices it obtains or has obtained from the sale of, or at which it sells or has sold, its products, or any other information concerning the business of employer, its manner of operation, its plans, processes, or other data without regard to whether all of the above-stated matters will be deemed confidential, material, or important, employer and employee specifically and expressly stipulating that as between them, such matters are important, material, and confidential and gravely affect the effective and successful conduct of the business of employer, and employer's good will, and that any breach of the terms of this section shall be a material breach of this agreement.[10]

EXAMPLE: Trade Secrets After Termination of Employment

All of the terms of [section with regard to maintaining employer's trade secrets] of this agreement shall remain in full force and effect for the period of _____ years after the termination of employee's employment for any reason, and during such ____-year period, employee shall not make or permit the making of any public announcement or statement of any kind that _____ [he or she] was formerly employed by or connected with employer.[11]

Compensation

Provisions regarding compensation should address the areas of wages, salary, or commission, special incentives, overtime work or night differential, and sick pay.

EXAMPLE: Compensation of Employee

Employer shall pay employee, and employee shall accept from employer, in full payment for employee's services under this agreement, compensation at the rate of _____ dollars ($___) per ___ [year], payable twice a month on the ___ [number] and ___ [number] days of each month while this agreement shall be in force.

Employer shall reimburse employee for all necessary expenses incurred by employee while traveling pursuant to employer's directions.[12]

Employee Benefits

Provision should be made in the employment agreement to describe the benefits to which the employee is entitled. This may be done either by describing each benefit in detail, or merely by stating that the employee will be entitled to any employee benefits which the employer maintains for workers in similar positions.

EXAMPLE: Participation in Other Employer Benefits

Employee shall be entitled to and shall receive all other benefits and conditions of employment available generally to other employees of employer employed at the same level and responsibility of employee pursuant to employer plans and programs, including by way of illustration, but not by way of limitation, group health insurance benefits, life insurance benefits, profit-sharing benefits, and pension and retirement benefits.[13]

Termination of Employment

Termination of the employee's employment prior to expiration of the term of the employment agreement may be grounds for a breach-of-contract action, either on behalf of the employer or the employee, if the agreement is so structured. An employment agreement often includes provisions allowing for the employee's termination upon notice given by either party, with or without cause. Although this type of loosely structured agreement affords maximum flexibility to both parties, it provides little certainty of continued employment.

Another commonly used employment agreement provision allows the employee to terminate the contract prior to its expiration upon certain specified conditions. This type of agreement generally allows the employer to terminate the employee only "with cause." Special care must be given to define the cause for which the employee may be terminated.

EXAMPLE: Termination

A. This agreement may be terminated by either party on _____ days' written notice to the other. If employer shall so terminate this agreement, employee shall be entitled to compensation for _____ days.

B. In the event of any violation by employee of any of the terms of this agreement, employer may terminate employment without notice and with compensation to employee only to the date of such termination.

C. It is further agreed that any breach or evasion of any of the terms of this agreement by either party will result in immediate and irreparable injury to the other party and will authorize recourse to injunction and/or specific performance, as well as to all other legal or equitable remedies to which such injured party may be entitled under this agreement.[14]

Arbitration of Disputes

Because even the most carefully drafted employment agreement is subject to interpretation, litigation often results when problems arise between the employee and employer. To curb potential legal fees and to resolve disputes expeditiously, both parties to an employment agreement often agree in advance to submit any disputes to binding arbitration.

EXAMPLE: Arbitration

Any differences, claims, or matters in dispute arising between employer and employee out of or connected with this agreement shall be submitted by them to arbitration by the American Arbitration Association or its successor and the determination of the American Arbitration Association or its successor shall be final and absolute. The arbitrator shall be governed by the duly promulgated rules and regulations of the American Arbitration Association or its successor, and the pertinent provisions of the laws of the state of _____ , relating to arbitration. The decision of the arbitrator may be entered as a judgment in any court in the state of _____ or elsewhere.[15]

Vacations

The employment agreement should include language defining the employer's policy as it pertains to the employee with regard to vacations.

EXAMPLE: Vacations

During the term of this agreement, the employee shall be entitled to _____ days of paid vacation per year. Employer and employee shall mutually agree upon the time for such vacation.

Assignability of Contract

An employment agreement is typically not an assignable contract, especially on the part of the employee. However, the contract may be assignable by the employer under certain circumstances that involve a merger or acquisition.

EXAMPLE: Assumption and Assignability of Agreement—Employer's Merger, Consolidation, etc.

The rights and duties of employer and employee under this agreement shall not be assignable by either party except that this agreement and all rights under this agreement may be assigned by employer to any corporation or other business entity that succeeds to all or substantially all of the business of employer through merger, consolidation, corporate reorganization, or by acquisition of all or substantially all of the assets of employer and which assumes employer's obligations under this agreement.[16]

Amendment or Renewal of Agreement

The employment agreement should contain the agreed-upon provisions for amending and renewing the agreement.

EXAMPLE: Modification of Agreement

Any modification of this agreement or additional obligation assumed by either party in connection with this agreement shall be binding only if evidenced in writing signed by each party or an authorized representative of each party.[17]

Date and Signatures

The employment agreement should be dated and signed by both the employee and an authorized representative of the employer prior to the commencement of the employee's employment. Certain employment agreements may require the approval of the employer's board of directors or designated officers.

§ 14.4 Sample Employment Agreement

The sample agreement in Figure 14-1 incorporates many of the clauses previously discussed in this chapter. Of course, any actual agreement must be drafted with the needs of the particular situation and client in mind.

[From 7A AM. JUR. *Legal Forms* 2d (Rev.)
§ 99:21 (19___)]

EMPLOYMENT OF EXECUTIVE—SALARY PLUS CASH EQUIVALENT TO STOCK DIVIDENDS— RETIREMENT BENEFITS

Agreement made, effective as of _____ [date], by and between _____ , a corporation duly organized and existing under the laws of the State of _____ , with a place of business at _____ [address], City of _____ , County of _____ , State of _____ , hereinafter referred to as employer, and _____ of _____ [address], City of _____ , County of _____ , State of _____ , hereinafter referred to as employee.

RECITALS

The parties recite and declare:

A. Employer desires to hire employee because of employee's vast business experience and expertise in _____ [specify business of employer].

B. Employee desires to be employed by employer in the executive capacity described below.

For the reasons set forth above, and in consideration of the mutual covenants and promises of the parties set forth in this agreement, employer and employee agree as follows:

SECTION ONE
EMPLOYMENT

Employer employs employee on the terms and conditions stated in this agreement to perform _____ [designate generally services employee is to perform], and employee agrees to perform such services for employer on the terms and conditions stated in this agreement.

SECTION TWO
TERM OF EMPLOYMENT

The term of employee's employment shall be _____ years commencing _____ [date]. Continued employment of employee by employer after _____ [date] shall be for the term and on the conditions agreed to by the parties prior to the expiration of this agreement.

SECTION THREE
COMPENSATION

A. Employer shall pay employee an annual salary of _____ dollars ($_____), payable monthly, on the _____ [number] day of each month, commencing _____ [date].

FIGURE 14-1
(continued)

B. In addition to the compensation stated in Paragraph A of this section, employer shall pay employee on _____ [date], and annually thereafter, for the term of this agreement, a sum equal to dividends payable on _____ [number] shares of the present authorized _____ [class] stock of employer to the extent that dividends are declared for that year. If employer declares a stock, rather than a cash dividend, employee shall receive in cash an amount equal to the fair market value of the stock dividend payable on _____ [number] shares. The fair market value of the stock dividends shall be _____ [if stock traded on exchange, the closing market price on the date of the stock dividend; or, if stock not openly traded, determined by mutual agreement of the parties; or, if that fails, by arbitration as provided for in Section Eight of this agreement]. If there is a stock split, the number of shares on which employee shall receive dividends shall increase on a basis proportionate with the stock split.

SECTION FOUR
RETIREMENT BENEFITS

If employee remains in the employ of employer until employee reaches the age of _____ years, employer shall pay employee or _____ [his or her] heirs or designated beneficiary _____ dollars ($_____) per month for _____ [number] years certain. Employer shall also pay employee, but not a designated beneficiary or employee's heirs or legatees, _____ dollars ($_____) after the term certain for so long as employee shall live.

SECTION FIVE
DEATH BENEFITS

If employee remains in the employ of employer continuously until employee's death, employer will pay to employee's designated beneficiary, or in lieu of a designated beneficiary, employee's heirs, a monthly income of _____ dollars ($_____) for _____ years.

SECTION SIX
EMPLOYER'S OBLIGATION ON ITS
TERMINATING EMPLOYEE'S EMPLOYMENT

If, during the term of this agreement, employer terminates this agreement for any reason, employer shall nevertheless continue the payments provided for in this agreement for the above-stated term so long as employee does not engage in gainful employment for another employer or enter into self-employment. If employee engages in gainful employment for another employer or enters into self-employment during the remaining term of this employment agreement, employer will pay employee [one-half] of the monthly payments designated in this agreement.

SECTION SEVEN
EMPLOYER'S OBLIGATION ON TERMINATION OF
EMPLOYMENT BY EMPLOYEE

If, during the term of this agreement, employee should fail or refuse to perform the services contemplated by this agreement, or should be unable to perform such services, or should engage in gainful employment with another employer, employer's obligation to make the payments provided in

FIGURE 14-1
(continued)

this agreement shall cease, but employer shall pay the additional compensation based on dividends declared on employer's stock to employee under Section Three of this agreement on a pro-rata basis for the number of months employee has been in the employ of employer for which no payment equal to such dividends has been paid.

SECTION EIGHT
ARBITRATION

Any differences, claims, or matters in dispute arising between employer and employee out of or connected with this agreement shall be submitted by them to arbitration by the American Arbitration Association or its successor and the determination of the American Arbitration Association or its successor shall be final and absolute. The arbitrator shall be governed by the duly promulgated rules and regulations of the American Arbitration Association or its successor, and the pertinent provisions of the laws of the State of _____ , relating to arbitration. The decision of the arbitrator may be entered as a judgment in any court of the State of _____ or elsewhere.

SECTION NINE
ATTORNEY'S FEES

In the event that any action is filed in relation to this agreement, the unsuccessful party in the action shall pay to the successful party, in addition to all the sums that either party may be called on to pay, a reasonable sum for the successful party's attorney's fees.

SECTION TEN
GOVERNING LAW

It is agreed that this agreement shall be governed by, construed, and enforced in accordance with the laws of the State of _____ .

SECTION ELEVEN
ENTIRE AGREEMENT

This agreement shall constitute the entire agreement between the parties and any prior understanding or representation of any kind preceding the date of this agreement shall not be binding upon either party except to the extent incorporated in this agreement.

SECTION TWELVE
MODIFICATION OF AGREEMENT

Any modification of this agreement or additional obligation assumed by either party in connection with this agreement shall be binding only if evidenced in writing signed by each party or an authorized representative of each party.

SECTION THIRTEEN
NOTICES

Any notice provided for or concerning this agreement shall be in writing and be deemed sufficiently given when sent by certified or registered mail if

FIGURE 14-1
(continued)

sent to the respective address of each party as set forth at the beginning of this agreement.

SECTION FOURTEEN
PARAGRAPH HEADINGS

The titles to the paragraphs of this agreement are solely for the convenience of the parties and shall not be used to explain, modify, simplify, or aid in the interpretation of the provisions of this agreement.

In witness whereof, each party to this agreement has caused it to be executed at _____ [place of execution] on the date indicated below.

[Signatures and date(s) of signing]

[Title of person representing corporation]

§ 14.5 The Role of the Paralegal in Drafting Employment Agreements

Although they may not give legal advice with regard to the employment agreement and other employment matters, paralegals are often involved in every aspect of collecting the information necessary to draft an employment agreement, drafting the agreement, obtaining the signatures, and obtaining approval from the corporation's board of directors when necessary.

When a corporate client requests an attorney to prepare an employment agreement on its behalf, the first step is to collect the pertinent information from the client. The use of an employment agreement worksheet, such as the one shown in Figure 14-2, to gather all pertinent information can be very effective. This worksheet illustrates the types of information that must be gathered from the corporate client before drafting an employment agreement. After gathering the pertinent information from the client, the paralegal can draft the employment agreement, under the supervision of an attorney, and see to its proper execution.

Typically, employment agreements entered into with officers or executives of a corporation are approved by a simple resolution of the board of directors, either by a unanimous written consent or at a regular board meeting. The paralegal can also see to it that the employment agreement is properly approved.

FIGURE 14-2
Employment
Agreement
Worksheet

EMPLOYMENT AGREEMENT WORKSHEET

Identification of parties

Employer _____
Address _____
_____

Employee _____
Address _____
_____

Term of agreement

Number of years _____
Automatically renewable _____

Position

Title _____
Supervisor _____

Duties of employee

_____
_____
_____
_____

Hours of employment _____
Compensation

Salary or commission _____
Rate of pay _____
Scheduled pay periods _____
Overtime compensation _____
Sick pay _____

Vacations and holidays

_____

Employee benefits

Benefits that the employee is entitled to

_____
_____
_____
_____
_____

Date on which employee becomes entitled to benefits

_____

Expense account

_____
_____

FIGURE 14-2
(continued)

Covenant not to compete after leaving employment

Length of time _____
Geographical location _____
_____

Termination of employment

Right of either party to terminate after giving notice

_____
_____

Right of employee to terminate agreement _____
Conditions _____
_____

Right of employer to terminate agreement _____
Conditions _____
_____

§ 14.6 Resources

Numerous form books are available to aid in drafting employment agreements, including AM. JUR. *Forms* 2d, *Nichols Cyclopedia of Legal Forms Annotated, Rabkin & Johnson Current Legal Forms,* and *West's Legal Forms, Second Edition.* In addition, state statutes should be consulted with regard to any covenants not to compete included in the employment agreement. Statutes of certain states include provisions that specifically restrict the use of such covenants.

Review Questions

1. What is employment "at will"?

2. May the employee's actions be restricted even after termination of employment?

3. What possible recourse might an employee have if he or she is unfairly demoted?

4. Why were covenants not to compete void under the common law of England? What is the modern view toward covenants not to compete?

5. Suppose that Alex is hired as a salesperson for the Miles Medical Supply Corporation, a regional medical supplies corporation that sells directly to hospitals in the Midwest. Before Alex commences employment, he is required to sign an employment agreement that specifically provides that he will not sell medical supplies for any competing business within the United States for a period of 10 years after leaving his employment. Five years after termination of Alex's employment with Miles Medical Supply, he is unable to find work in the Midwest, so he relocates to Florida, where he takes a management position with a national medical supply company. Could Miles Medical Supply prevail in a suit against Alex for damages due to his breach of contract? Why or why not?

6. If an employment agreement remains silent on the issue, is the employer necessarily entitled to all inventions of the employee while the employee is working for the employer?

7. Are the rights and obligations of either the employee or employer under an employment agreement ever assignable? If so, under what conditions?

Notes

[1] 7A Am. Jur. *Legal Forms* 2d (Rev.) § 99:13 (1981).

[2] *Id.* § 99:15.

[3] *Id.* § 99:22.

[4] *Id.* § 99:23.

[5] Annotation, *Anticompetitive Covenants,* 60 A.L.R.4th 965 (1986).

[6] *Id.*

[7] 7A Am. Jur. *Legal Forms* 2d (Rev.) § 99:271 (1981).

[8] *Id.* § 99:292.

[9] *Restatement of Torts* § 757, comment (1985).

[10] 7A Am. Jur. *Legal Forms* 2d (Rev.) § 99:15 (1981).

[11] *Id.* § 99:15.

[12] *Id.* § 99:15.

[13] *Id.* § 99:238.

[14] *Id.* § 99:15.

[15] *Id.* § 99:21.

[16] *Id.* § 99:301.

[17] *Id.* § 99:15.

CHAPTER 15

COMPUTERS AND CORPORATE LAW

The real danger is not that computers will begin to think like men, but that men will begin to think like computers.

— *Sydney Harris*

Introduction

Every paralegal working in the United States must be somewhat familiar with computers. Paralegals use computers to perform their tasks, as well as to interact with clients, state and federal agencies, and other law firms. This chapter discusses the computer applications with which a paralegal working in the corporate law area is likely to come in contact.

A detailed discussion of the computer hardware and software technology that is currently available is impractical, for two reasons. First, it does the paralegal little good to become familiar with systems that he or she may never work with. Second, computer technology is developing so rapidly that information that could be written in this chapter about specific computer technology could be out of date by the time this book makes it to the shelf. Therefore, this chapter begins with a brief discussion of the use of computers in law firms and then focuses on some of the uses of computers by paralegals working in the corporate law area. Our overview of computers and corporate law concludes with a brief summary of some possible future trends in law office automation.

§ 15.1 Computers in the Law Firm

Law firms are automated to varying degrees. Some smaller firms may utilize only automated word processing and billing systems. Other fully automated law firms may have computerized filing systems, time and billing systems, accounting systems, word processing systems, calendar control, and numerous other types of systems (see Figure 15-1).

It is becoming common practice for attorneys, paralegals and office support staff to have computers in their offices or work stations. According to the 1995 Survey of Automation in Smaller Law Firms conducted by the American Bar Associations Legal Technology Resource

FIGURE 15-1
Juris is an integrated system that performs all law office functions and can be customized to the needs of the law firm. (Courtesy of Juris, Incorporated)

Center,[1] 87 percent of the nearly 2,000 smaller law firms and 2,000 individual lawyers report that they use a personal computer at work and that they are poised to broaden their communications capabilities through electronic mail (e-mail), on-line services, CD-ROM technology and computerized legal research. Often, all computers within a law firm are part of a network that allows staff members to share their work and resources. Paralegals may utilize their terminals to produce short documents, track their time and work load, and perform legal research. They may communicate with other individuals in the office via e-mail systems in their office.

Although computer use throughout law firms can be very diverse, even the paralegal with little or no computer experience need not feel apprehensive about working with computers in a new law firm. Contemporary computers are usually very user-friendly and nonintimidating. Simple functions can be learned on most computer systems in a matter of moments. Often the computer software includes instructions that allow the paralegal to train himself or herself.

Time and Billing

Paralegals employed in a law firm that practices corporate law will almost always be required to keep an accounting of their time for billing purposes. Numerous software packages are available that are designed for the specific task of keeping track of the time spent by attorneys and paralegals on specific files and producing bills (see Figure 15-2). The paralegal may be required to input time directly into the computer system or to act through a secretary or data processor.

One new application of computer technology to timekeeping is the use of portable hand-held recording devices into which attorneys and paralegals may dictate their time and a brief billing description. Some of these devices have the capability of being downloaded directly onto the law firm's billing system.

File Management

In many law firms, the process of opening a file begins with data entry into a computerized file management system. Often, information regarding the client will be input into the computer system to generate a new file. The input data can then be sorted as directed and numerous types of reports generated. These reports might include all of the law firm's new files, new clients, attorney and paralegal assignments, or any other information that has been entered with each new file.

TIMEKEEPER ANALYSIS REPORT

Juris, Samples & Samples

REPORT DATE 01/01/99   TIMEKEEPER ANALYSIS   PAGE 1
REPORT NUMBER JP062-000025
SORTED BY TIMEKEEPER   PRINTED BY SMGR
RANGE SELECTED: BEG OF FILE TO END OF FILE

TIMEKEEPER	PERIOD	TOTAL HOURS	N.B. HOURS	---- BILLABLE ----		BILLED AMOUNT	BILLED RATE	FEES RECEIVED	---- UNBILLED ----	
				HOURS	AMOUNT				HOURS	AMOUNT
Esther M. Bradberry	MTD	32.05	.00	32.05	3,044.75	3,712.63		760.01	1.50	142.50
	YTD	32.05	.00	32.05	3,044.75	3,712.63	80	760.01		
Cynthia Lee Cole	MTD	24.35	.00	24.35	1,863.75	2,671.34		471.27	8.40	630.00
	YTD	24.35	.00	24.35	1,863.75	2,671.34	89	471.27		
James A. Martin	MTD	9.75	.00	9.75	926.25	1,502.50		284.01	3.25	308.75
	YTD	9.75	.00	9.75	926.25	1,502.50	95	284.01		
Michael J. Ryan	MTD	8.60	.00	8.60	688.00	1,354.14		426.45	.00	.00
	YTD	8.60	.00	8.60	688.00	1,354.14	87	426.45		
Grant C. Tyler	MTD	6.50	.00	6.50	610.00	1,393.68		221.21	2.50	250.00
	YTD	6.50	.00	6.50	610.00	1,393.68	88	221.21		
FINAL TOTALS	MTD	81.25		81.25		10,634.31		2,162.95		1,331.25
	MTD		.00		7,132.75				15.65	
	YTD	81.25		81.25		10,634.31		2,162.95		
	YTD		.00		7,132.75		86			

FIGURE 15-2 Timekeeper information provides a database from which analytical reports can be developed. (Courtesy of Juris, Incorporated)

The file management system can also be used to track and retrieve the file when necessary. At the appropriate time, the file will be given a "closed" designation on the system.

Case Management

Law firms of all sizes and types may use computerized case management systems to track assignments within the office. Attorney and paralegal assignments and crucial deadlines may be tracked through the use of case management systems that are usually monitored by paralegal managers, managing attorneys, and office administrators.

Case management programs can offer the following applications:

- Calendars are tracked and viewed on screen or printed
- Personal diary and "to do" lists are produced
- Case ledgers and financial information are prepared and kept current
- Conflict of interest checks are performed
- Time tracking is performed on a case-by-case basis
- Important deadlines are tracked

In addition to assisting with the smooth performance of law firm functions, proper use of case management technology can actually reduce the cost of legal malpractice insurance for some law firms.

Law Firms on the Internet

The Internet and the World Wide Web have gained increasing popularity with the legal profession in recent years. Attorneys and paralegals have found several new uses for the Web, including new resources for legal news, networking, and marketing.

Several legal newsletters and magazines for the legal professional have gone on-line in recent years. These newsletters and magazines contain much of the information that is included in the traditional legal periodicals. These on-line newsletters and magazines offer the advantage of being current and accessible. Some of these resources offer news about developments in case law and other developments concerning specific areas of law, as well as several cross references for further research.

Many attorneys and paralegals have taken advantage of the networking advantages offered by the Internet. The bulletin boards on the Web offer a way to come in contact with potential contacts in your field, as well as potential clients. There are several sites on the Internet specifically for the use of the legal professional. The National Federation of Paralegal Associations ("NFPA"), Lexis, West Publishing, and the Federal

Government all have Web Sites. Each of these sites offers a variety of information for attorneys and paralegals.

Attorneys are increasingly using the Internet for marketing purposes. By January 1995, an estimated 200 law firms had put up Web pages, with more coming on-line every day.[2] Several attorneys and law firms advertise and offer their services over the Internet. Some offer limited free advice and services over the Web to attract new potential clients.

TABLE 15-1   DIRECTORY TO POPULAR LEGAL SITES ON THE WEB

- The National Federation of Paralegal Associations
  http://www.paralegals.org
- Lexis Counsel Connect
  http://www.counsel.com/
- West Publishing Co.
  http://www.westpub.com
- Federal Government
  http://www.fedworld.gov/

TABLE 15-2   ADVANTAGES AND DISADVANTAGES TO MARKETING ON THE NET

Advantages	Disadvantages
The Net has the potential to reach over 30 million computer users.	Your target market may not be heavy Net users.
The Net offers immediate feedback to marketing.	Some may not perceive advertising on the Net to be ethical or professional.
Information is available 24 hours per day, seven days per week.	Advertising on the Net can be very costly.

§ 15.2 Computer Use by Paralegals Working in the Corporate Area

Corporate paralegals use a variety of computer applications. More and more corporate law-specific software is available each year to make the tasks performed by corporate paralegals simpler and easier to perform. Because document drafting is an integral part of any corporate paralegal's job, word processing is an important computer application for corporate paralegals. Corporate paralegals also frequently make use of various computer research applications, document retrieval, calendar control, and docket systems. Paralegals who work in corporate legal departments may utilize software designed to assist the corporate secretary. Finally, many corporate paralegals are making use of the new technology within state agencies that allows access to their information through computer interfacing.

Word Processing

Word processing is an essential part of any law firm that practices corporate law. Word processing software is used to produce all types of corporate documents, agreements and correspondence.

Word processing software allows the attorney or paralegal to produce lengthy documents in an incredibly short amount of time. Often, law firms have one or more centralized word processing departments where all lengthy documents are produced. When a routine corporate document is required, the attorney or paralegal will send instructions to the word processing department, usually by completing a form that instructs the word processing department as to which routine document is required, and what the variables are to tailor that document to fit the needs of the particular client. Many lengthy but routine corporate documents, such as articles of incorporation, bylaws, and unanimous writings in lieu of annual meetings, can be generated simply by completing a one-page form that is sent to the word processing department.

In other fully automated law firms, where each attorney and paralegal has a computer terminal that is part of a firm-wide computer network, instructions may be sent to word processing via a computer message. Correspondence and shorter documents may be prepared exclusively by the paralegal or with the aid of the paralegal's secretary. (See Figure 15-3.) In addition to preparing a document, most computerized word processing adds the benefit of storing the document to be retrieved at a later date. Even if you as a paralegal are not expected to perform any word processing duties, it is important to understand the system in place at your law firm so you can decide how best to interact with the word processing department.

The incredible speed and accuracy with which routine corporate documentation can be produced makes it easy to overestimate the abilities of the computer. When document preparation becomes routine, it is important not to become careless or to forget that computers cannot make decisions regarding the appropriateness of a particular document or a particular clause within a document. Careful thought must be

FIGURE 15-3
Paralegals are involved in many varying aspects of word processing within the law firm.

given to every corporate document that is prepared, regardless of how easily and quickly it can be produced. The contents of every document must be given careful consideration and proofread thoroughly to avoid serious mistakes or even claims of malpractice.

Legal Research

New technology of the past decade has changed the very nature of legal research. Legal research resources available in law firms are growing exponentially, while the size of law firm law libraries is shrinking. In some law firms, the vast majority of legal research is done either on-line or on CD-ROM.

Research performed on-line makes use of huge databases available through services such as Lexis and Westlaw, which offer vast libraries of up-to-date statutes, cases, and other information for subscribers who dial in by modem. The information offered on services such as Lexis and Westlaw has expanded from statutes and cases to include treatises, directories, periodicals, financial market information, and just about any other type of information that has been published and is of interest to attorneys or paralegals.

Another resource, which is gaining in popularity, is the use of CD-ROM disks. Statutes, case law, treatises, and directories, as well as libraries of information on particular topics of law, can be purchased through subscriptions which are updated periodically with new disks sent to the law firm.

Virtually every major publication in the legal field is now available either on-line, on CD-ROM, or both. Most major loose-leaf services have either been replaced or supplemented by CD-ROM and on-line services.

Document Retrieval

For paralegals who are working with large corporate clients that are often involved in mergers and acquisitions, document retrieval can be a very time-consuming task. Custom-made software or software designed to aid in complex litigation may be used to index and retrieve the enormous amount of documentation often required to close mergers and acquisitions.

Calendar Control and Docket Systems

Although docket and calendar control systems were originally designed to keep track of important court dates and deadlines, they have a strong appeal for the corporate attorney and paralegal as well. Calendar control systems can remind the corporate attorney and paralegal of dates that are important to the corporate client, including securities filings, annual meetings and notice dates, and annual reporting deadlines. A calendar and docket report can be produced daily, weekly, monthly, or as often as desired to notify corporate attorneys and paralegals of important deadlines that must be met. (See Figure 15-4.)

Software for the Corporate Legal Department

New developments in software include software packages designed specifically for the legal departments of corporate law firms. Software designed for the corporate secretary provides a record system that enables the corporate secretary to store and retrieve information regarding the corporation's officers and directors, articles of incorporation, bylaws, and stock and shareholder data. It also contains a diary system to keep track of dates that are important to the corporation, and it can generate reports that are typically produced by the corporate secretary.

Interfacing with State Agencies

In a law firm that practices corporate law extensively in one or more states, it may be possible to access the databases of certain state agencies. Several Secretary of State offices in this country offer the opportunity to

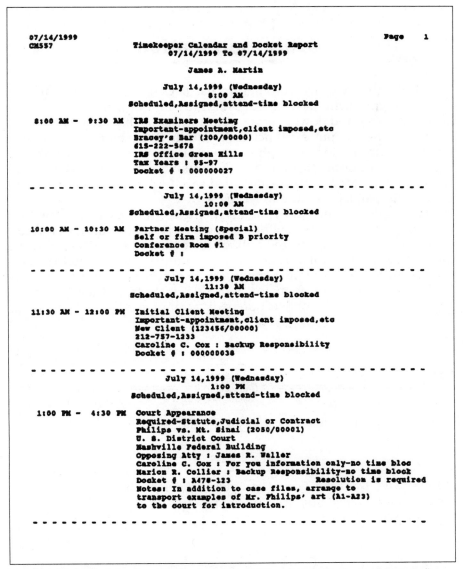

07/14/1999   **Timekeeper Calendar and Docket Report**   Page   1
CM557   07/14/1999 To 07/14/1999

                                        James A. Martin

                                     July 14,1999 (Wednesday)
                                            8:00 AM
                               Scheduled,Assigned,attend-time blocked

   8:00 AM - 9:30 AM   IRS Examiners Meeting
                         Important-appointment,client imposed,etc
                         Bracey's Bar (200/00000)
                         615-222-5678
                         IRS Office Green Hills
                         Tax Years : 95-97
                         Docket # : 000000027

  -
                                     July 14,1999 (Wednesday)
                                            10:00 AM
                               Scheduled,Assigned,attend-time blocked

 10:00 AM - 10:30 AM   Partner Meeting (Special)
                        Self or firm imposed B priority
                        Conference Room #1
                        Docket # :

  -
                                     July 14,1999 (Wednesday)
                                            11:30 AM
                               Scheduled,Assigned,attend-time blocked

 11:30 AM - 12:00 PM   Initial Client Meeting
                        Important-appointment,client imposed,etc
                        New Client (123456/00000)
                        212-757-1233
                        Caroline C. Cox : Backup Responsibility
                        Docket # : 000000038

  -
                                     July 14,1999 (Wednesday)
                                            1:00 PM
                               Scheduled,Assigned,attend-time blocked

   1:00 PM - 4:30 PM   Court Appearance
                         Required-Statute,Judicial or Contract
                         Philips vs. Mt. Sinai (2050/00001)
                         U. S. District Court
                         Nashville Federal Building
                         Opposing Atty : James R. Waller
                         Caroline C. Cox : For you information only-no time bloc
                         Marion R. Collier : Backup Responsibility-no time block
                         Docket # : A478-123   Resolution is required
                         Notes: In addition to case files, arrange to
                         transport examples of Mr. Philips' art (A1-A23)
                         to the court for introduction.

  -

FIGURE 15-4 A Calendar and Docket Report (Courtesy of Juris, Incorporated)

access, through use of a telephone modem, their corporate records with regard to corporate name availability, corporate standing, registered agents, and other corporate information routinely kept on their databases. Information from state agencies may be accessed directly through use of a telephone modem, or it may be part of a commercial database that offers interaction with several states.

§ 15.3 The Future of Law Office Automation

Although law office automation has been growing at an amazing rate throughout the past two decades, the rate of innovation in this area has not slowed down. Future trends will probably include more offices adopting computerized networks and the availability of even more database information through commercial services. New software designed for specific applications is being produced rapidly and becoming less expensive. More software designed specifically for the corporate attorney and paralegal is sure to follow.

Paralegals may benefit from advancing technology in the law firm by being allowed more flexibility on the job. In the past, paralegals were committed to spend the bulk of their time in the office or in the law library. In the future, paralegals may find that new technology used in conjunction with home computers and notebook computers will allow them to perform the majority of their tasks from their homes, or wherever they can carry their notebook computers.

Notes

[1] Survey Says, *Law Office Computing*, October/November 1995, 19.

[2] Woodbury, Carol, Lawyers on the Web, *Law Office Computing*, August/September 1995, 31.

APPENDIX A

SECRETARY OF STATE DIRECTORY

Alabama Secretary of State
Corporation Division
P.O. Box 5616
Montgomery, AL
36103-5616
(334) 242-5324

**Alaska Dept. of Commerce
and Economic Development**
Corporations Section
Floor 9, Alaska State Office
  Building
Juneau, AK 99811
(907) 465-2530

Arizona Corporation Commission
P.O. Box 6019
Phoenix, AZ 85005
(602) 542-3135

Arkansas Secretary of State
Corporations Division
State Capitol Building
Little Rock, AR 72201
(501) 682-3409

California Secretary of State
Corporation Filing Division
1230 J Street
Sacramento, CA 95814
(916) 657-5448

Colorado Secretary of State
1560 Broadway, Suite 200
Denver, CO 80202
(303) 894-2251

Connecticut Secretary of State
Division of Corporations
30 Trinity Street
Hartford, CT 06106
(860) 566-8570

Delaware Secretary of State
Division of Corporations
P.O. Box 898
Dover, DE 19903
(302) 739-3073

District of Columbia
Department of Consumer
  and Regulatory Affairs
614 H Street NW, Room 407
Washington, DC 20001
(202) 727-7283

Florida Department of State
Division of Corporations
P.O. Box 6327
Tallahassee, FL 32314
(904) 488-9000

Georgia Secretary of State
Business Services and Regulation
2 Martin Luther King, Jr. Dr.
Atlanta, GA 30334
(404) 656-2817

**Hawaii Department of Commerce
and Consumer Affairs**
Business Registration Division
P.O. Box 40
Honolulu, HI 96810
(808) 586-2727

Idaho Secretary of State
Statehouse Mail, Room 203
Boise, ID 83720
(208) 334-2300

Illinois Secretary of State
Dept. of Business Services
Howlett Building, 3rd Floor
Springfield, IL 62756
(217) 782-7880

Indiana Secretary of State
Corporations Division
302 West Washington Street,
  Room E018
Indianapolis, IN 46204
(317) 232-6576

Iowa Secretary of State
Division of Corporations
Hoover State Office Building
Des Moines, IA 50319
(515) 281-5204

Kansas Secretary of State
Second Floor, Capitol
  Building
Topeka, KS 66612
(913) 296-4564

**Kentucky Secretary
of State**
Corporations Department
P.O. Box 718
Frankfort, KY 40602-0718
(502) 564-2848

Louisiana Secretary of State
Corporate Division
P.O. Box 94125
Baton Rouge, LA 70804-9125
(504) 925-4704

Maine Secretary of State
Bureau of Corporations,
  Elections and Commissions
State House Station 101
Augusta, ME 04333-0101
(207) 287-4190

**Maryland State Department
of Assessments and Taxation**
301 West Preston Street
Baltimore, MD 21201
(410) 767-8250

**Massachusetts Secretary
of State**
Corporations Division
One Ashburton Place
Boston, MA 02108
(617) 727-9640

**Michigan Department
of Commerce**
Corporation and Securities
  Corporation Department
  Division
546 Mercantile Way
Lansing, MI 48910
(517) 334-6206

Minnesota Secretary of State
Business Services Division
180 State Office Building
St. Paul, MN 55155
(612) 296-2803

Mississippi Secretary of State
Corporate Division
P.O. Box 136
Jackson, MS 39205
(601) 359-1333

Missouri Secretary of State
Corporation Division
Truman Building
P.O. Box 778
Jefferson City, MO 65102
(573) 751-4153

Montana Corporation Bureau
Secretary of State's Office
State Capitol
Helena, MT 59620
(406) 444-2034

**Nebraska Secretary
of State**
State Capitol Building
Lincoln, NE 68509
(402) 471-4079

Nevada Secretary of State
Corporate Division
Capitol Complex
Carson City, NV 89710
(702) 687-5203

**New Hampshire Secretary
of State/Corporations**
204 State House
107 North Main Street
Concord, NH 03301
(603) 271-3246

New Jersey Secretary of State
Division of Commercial
   Recordings
State House
125 West State Street
Trenton, NJ 08625
(609) 530-6400

**New Mexico State
Corporation Commission**
Corporation Department
P.O. Drawer 1269
Santa Fe, NM 87504-1269
(505) 827-4504

New York Department of State
162 Washington Avenue
Albany, NY 12231
(518) 473-2492

North Carolina Secretary of State
Corporations Division
300 North Salisbury Street
Raleigh, NC 27603
(919) 733-4201

North Dakota Secretary of State
State Capitol Building
600 East Boulevard Avenue
Bismarck, ND 58505-0500
(701) 328-4284

Ohio Secretary of State
Division of Corporations
30 East Broad Street, 14th Floor
Columbus, OH 43266-0418
(614) 466-3910

Oklahoma Secretary of State
101 State Capitol
Oklahoma City, OK 73105
(405) 521-3911

Oregon Secretary of State
Corporation Division
255 Capitol Street NE
Salem, OR 97310
(505) 986-2200

**Pennsylvania Department
of State**
Corporation Bureau
308 North Office Building
Harrisburg, PA 17120
(717) 787-1057

Rhode Island Secretary of State
Corporations Division
100 North Main Street
Providence, RI 02903
(401) 277-3040

South Carolina Secretary of State
Corporate Division
P.O. Box 11350
Columbia, SC 29211
(803) 734-2158

South Dakota Secretary of State
Corporate Department
500 East Capitol Street
Pierre, SD 57501
(605) 773-3537

Tennessee Secretary of State
James K. Polk Building,
   18th Floor
Nashville, TN 37243-0306
(615) 741-2286

Texas Secretary of State
Statutory Filings Division
Corporations Section
P.O. Box 13967
Austin, TX 78711-3697
(512) 463-5555

**Utah Corporations and
Commercial Code Division**
P.O. Box 45801
Salt Lake City, UT 84145
(801) 530-4849

**Vermont Secretary of State
Corporations**
109 State Street
Montpelier, VT 05609
(802) 828-2386

**Virginia State Corporation
Commission**
P.O. Box 1197
Richmond, VA 23209
(804) 371-9967

Washington Secretary of State
Corporations Division
505 East Union (MS-PM 21)
Olympia, WA 98504
(360) 753-7115

West Virginia Secretary of State
Corporate Division
139 State Capitol Building
Charleston, WV 25305
(304) 558-8000

Wisconsin Secretary of State
Corporation Division
P.O. Box 7846
Madison, WI 53707
(608) 266-3590

Wyoming Secretary of State
State Capitol Building
Cheyenne, WY 82002
(307) 777-7311

APPENDIX B

UNIFORM PARTNERSHIP ACT

The Uniform Partnership Act has been reprinted through the permission of the National Conference of Commissioners on Uniform State Laws, and copies of the Act may be ordered from them at a nominal cost at 676 North St. Clair Street, Suite 1700, Chicago, Illinois 60611; (312) 915-0195.

UNIFORM PARTNERSHIP ACT

drafted by the

**NATIONAL CONFERENCE
OF COMMISSIONERS ON
UNIFORM STATE LAWS**

and by it

**Approved and Recommended for Enactment in
All the States**

at its

Conference at Washington, D.C.

October 14, 1914

**And Approved by the American
Bar Association
August 18, 1915**

(Edition of 1934)

PREFATORY NOTES

I

The Commissioners on Uniform State Laws

The National Conference of Commissioners on Uniform State Laws was organized in 1892. It is composed of Commissioners deriving their authority from appointment by the Governors of their respective States. The District of Columbia, Alaska, Puerto Rico, Hawaii, and the Philippine Islands also appoint Commissioners. With these added to the 48 States there are 53 jurisdictions represented.

The Commissioners are members of the legal profession and all serve without compensation, but the legislatures of many of the States provide for defraying traveling expenses of their Commissioners in attending meetings.

The Commissioners meet annually in a conference of six days at which most of the States, the District of Columbia, and some of the other jurisdictions mentioned above are represented. At these Conferences the Acts drafted by Committees, assisted in many cases by experts, and under the instructions from the Conference, are carefully considered and discussed section by section by the entire body. Acts are not approved until they have been considered in this manner by at least two, and generally more, annual Conferences. When finally approved and recommended to the several States for adoption, the Acts are also reported to the American Bar Association for its approval before being presented to the States for enactment.

There are now about 53 of the Uniform Laws approved and recommended by the Conference of Commissioners.

The Uniform Negotiable Instruments Law has been adopted in 48 States and the other 5 jurisdictions, making 53 in all. The Bills of Lading Act has been adopted in 29 jurisdictions, the Declaratory Judgments Act in 18, the Fiduciaries Act in 16, the Fraudulent Conveyance Act in 16, the Limited Partnership Act in 20, the Partnership Act in 19, the Proof of Statutes Act in 23, the Reciprocal Transfer Tax Act in 16, the Sales Act in 33, the Stock Transfer Act in 23, the Act Regulating Traffic on Highways in 18, the Veterans Guardianship Act in 32, and the Warehouse Receipts Act in 48.

Many of the States have adopted 20 or more of the Uniform Acts.

II
The Uniform Partnership Act

The Uniform Partnership Act is the result of ten years' consideration by the Conference of Commissioners on Uniform State Laws. The Committee which prepared the Act was assisted at first by Dean James Barr Ames of the Law School of Harvard University as draftsman, and after his death by Dean William Draper Lewis of the Law School of the University of Pennsylvania.

In the fall of 1910 the Committee invited to a Conference, held in Philadelphia, all the teachers of, and writers on, partnerships, besides several other lawyers known to have made a special study of the subject. There was a large attendance. For two days the members of the Committee and their guests discussed the theory on which the proposed act should be drawn. At the conclusion of the discussion the experts recommended that the act be drawn on the aggregate or common law theory, with the modification that the partners be treated as owners of partnership property holding by a special tenancy which should be called tenancy in partnership. (See Section 2 of the Act recommended.) Accordingly, at the meeting of the Conference in the summer of 1911, the Committee reported that, after hearing the discussion of experts, it had voted that Dean Lewis be requested to prepare a draft of a partnership act on the so-called common law theory.

At the National Conferences of the Commissioners in 1912 and 1913 several sessions were devoted to the consideration of the Act, and at the Conference of 1914 the final draft prepared by Dean Lewis was approved and recommended for enactment by the States. The approval of the American Bar Association was given at its meeting on August 18, 1915. The nineteen States which have adopted the Act up to the present time (1934) are the following:

> Alaska, California, Colorado, Idaho, Illinois, Maryland, Massachusetts, Michigan, Minnesota, Nevada, New Jersey, New York, Pennsylvania, South Dakota, Tennessee, Utah, Virginia, Wisconsin, Wyoming.

As to the importance of this Act, the following paragraphs are quoted from the Explanatory Note preceding the pamphlet copy issued in 1915. This note was written by Mr. Walter George Smith of Philadelphia, the Chairman of the Committee which prepared the Act.

> Uniformity of the law of partnerships is constantly becoming more important as the number of firms increases which not only carry on business in more than one state, but have among the members residents of different states.
>
> It is, however, proper here to emphasize the fact that there are other reasons, in addition to the advantages which will result from uniformity, for the adoption of the act now issued by the Commissioners. There is probably no other subject connected with our business law in which a greater number of instances can be found where, in matters of almost daily occurrence, the law is uncertain. This uncertainty is due, not only to conflict between the decisions of different states, but more to the general lack of consistency in legal theory. In several of the sections, but especially in those which relate to the rights of the partner and his separate creditors in partnership property, and to the rights of firm creditors where the personnel of the partnership has been changed without liquidation of partnership affairs, there exists an almost hopeless confusion of theory and practice, making the actual administration of the law difficult and often inequitable.
>
> Another difficulty of the present partnership law is the scarcity of authority on matters of considerable importance in the daily conduct and in the winding up of partnership affairs. In any one state it is often impossible to find an authority on a matter of comparatively frequent occurrence, while not infrequently an exhaustive research of the reports of the decisions of all the states and the federal courts fails to reveal a single authority throwing light on the question. The existence of a statute stating in detail

the rights of the partners inter se during the carrying on of the partnership business, and on the winding up of partnership affairs, will be a real practical advantage of moment to the business world.

> John Hinkley, *Chairman,*
> *Section on Uniform Commercial Acts.*

August 1, 1934.

UNIFORM PARTNERSHIP ACT CONTENTS

Part VI. Dissolution and Winding Up

Part VII. Miscellaneous Provisions

AN ACT TO MAKE UNIFORM THE LAW OF PARTNERSHIPS

(Be it enacted...)

Part I
Preliminary Provisions

1. *Name of Act.* This act may be cited as Uniform Partnership Act.

2. *Definition of Terms.* In this act, "Court" includes every court and judge having jurisdiction in the case.

"Business" includes every trade, occupation, or profession.

"Person" includes individuals, partnerships, corporations, and other associations.

"Bankrupt" includes bankrupt under the Federal Bankruptcy Act or insolvent under any state insolvent act.

"Conveyance" includes every assignment, lease, mortgage, or encumbrance.

"Real property" includes land and any interest or estate in land.

3. *Interpretation of Knowledge and Notice.* (1) A person has "knowledge" of a fact within the meaning of this act not only when he has actual knowledge thereof, but also when he has knowledge of such other facts as in the circumstances shows bad faith.

(2) A person has "notice" of a fact within the meaning of this act when the person who claims the benefit of the notice:

(a) States the fact to such person, or

(b) Delivers through the mail, or by other means of communication, a written statement of the fact to such person or to a proper person at his place of business or residence.

4. *Rules of Construction.* (1) The rule that statutes in derogation of the common law are to be strictly construed shall have no application to this act.

(2) The law of estoppel shall apply under this act.

(3) The law of agency shall apply under this act.

(4) This act shall be so interpreted and construed as to effect its general purpose to make uniform the law of those states which enact it.

(5) This act shall not be construed so as to impair the obligations of any contract existing when the act goes into effect, nor to affect any action or proceedings begun or right accrued before this act takes effect.

5. *Rules for Cases Not Provided for in This Act.* In any case not provided for in this act the rules of law and equity, including the law merchant, shall govern.

Part II
Nature of Partnership

6. *Partnership Defined.* (1) A partnership is an association of two or more persons to carry on as co-owners a business for profit.

(2) But any association formed under any other statute of this state, or any statute adopted by authority, other than the authority of this state, is not a partnership under this act, unless such association would have been a partnership in this state prior to the adoption of this act; but this act shall apply to limited partnerships except in so far as the statutes relating to such partnerships are inconsistent herewith.

7. *Rules for Determining the Existence of a Partnership.* In determining whether a partnership exists, these rules shall apply:

(1) Except as provided by section 16 persons who are not partners as to each other are not partners as to third persons.

(2) Joint tenancy, tenancy in common, tenancy by the entireties, joint property, common property, or part ownership does not of itself establish a partnership, whether such co-owners do or do not share any profits made by the use of the property.

(3) The sharing of gross returns does not of itself establish a partnership, whether or not the persons sharing them have a joint or common right or interest in any property from which the returns are derived.

(4) The receipt by a person of a share of the profits of a business is *prima facie* evidence that he is a partner in the business, but no such inference shall be drawn if such profits were received in payment:

(a) As a debt by installments or otherwise,

(b) As wages of an employee or rent to a landlord,

(c) As an annuity to a widow or representative of a deceased partner,

(d) As interest on a loan, though the amount of payment vary with the profits of the business,

(e) As the consideration for the sale of a good-will of a business or other property by installments or otherwise.

8. *Partnership Property.* (1) All property originally brought into the partnership stock or subsequently acquired by purchase or otherwise, on account of the partnership, is partnership property.

(2) Unless the contrary intention appears, property acquired with partnership funds is partnership property.

(3) Any estate in real property may be acquired in the partnership name. Title so acquired can be conveyed only in the partnership name.

(4) A conveyance to a partnership in the partnership name, though without words of inheritance, passes the entire estate of the grantor unless a contrary intent appears.

Part III
Relations of Partners to Persons Dealing with the Partnership

9. *Partner Agent of Partnership as to Partnership Business.* (1) Every partner is an agent of the partnership for the purpose of its business, and the act of every partner, including the execution in the partnership name of any instrument, for apparently carrying on in the usual way the business of the partnership of which he is a member binds the partnership, unless the partner so acting has in fact no authority to act for the partnership in the particular matter, and the person with whom he is dealing has knowledge of the fact that he has no such authority.

(2) An act of a partner which is not apparently for the carrying on of the business of the partnership in the usual way does not bind the partnership unless authorized by the other partners.

(3) Unless authorized by the other partners or unless they have abandoned the business, one or more but less than all the partners have no authority to:

(a) Assign the partnership property in trust for creditors or on the assignee's promise to pay the debts of the partnership,

(b) Dispose of the good-will of the business,

(c) Do any other act which would make it impossible to carry on the ordinary business of a partnership,

(d) Confess a judgment,

(e) Submit a partnership claim or liability to arbitration or reference.

(4) No act of a partner in contravention of a restriction on authority shall bind the partnership to persons having knowledge of the restriction.

10. *Conveyance of Real Property of the Partnership.*

(1) Where title to real property is in the partnership name, any partner may convey title to such property by a conveyance executed in the partnership name; but the partnership may recover such property unless the partner's act binds the partnership under the provisions of paragraph (1) of section 9, or unless such property has been conveyed by the grantee or a person claiming through such grantee to a holder for value without knowledge that the partner, in making the conveyance, has exceeded his authority.

(2) Where title to real property is in the name of the partnership, a conveyance executed by a partner, in his own name, passes the equitable interest of the partnership, provided the act is one within the authority of the partner under the provisions of paragraph (1) of section 9.

(3) Where title to real property is in the name of one or more but not all the partners, and the record does not disclose the right of the partnership, the partners in whose name the title stands may convey title to such property, but the partnership may recover such property if the partners' act does not bind the partnership under the provisions of paragraph (1) of section 9, unless the purchaser or his assignee, is a holder for value, without knowledge.

(4) Where the title to real property is in the name of one or more or all the partners, or in a third person in trust for the partnership, a conveyance executed by a partner in the partnership name, or in his own name, passes the equitable interest of the partnership, provided the act is one within the authority of the partner under the provisions of paragraph (1) of section 9.

(5) Where the title to real property is in the names of all the partners a conveyance executed by all the partners passes all their rights in such property.

11. *Partnership Bound by Admission of Partner.*
An admission or representation made by any partner concerning partnership affairs within the scope of his authority as conferred by this act is evidence against the partnership.

12. *Partnership Charged with Knowledge of or Notice to Partner.* Notice to any partner of any matter relating to partnership affairs, and the knowledge of the partner acting in the particular matter, acquired while a partner or then present to his mind, and the knowledge of any other partner who reasonably could and should have communicated it to the acting partner, operate as notice to or knowledge of the partnership, except in the case of a fraud on the partnership committed by or with the consent of that partner.

13. *Partnership Bound by Partner's Wrongful Act.* Where, by any wrongful act or omission of any partner acting in the ordinary course of the business of the partnership or with the authority of his copartners, loss or injury is caused to any person, not being a partner in the partnership, or any penalty is incurred, the partnership is liable therefor to the same extent as the partner so acting or omitting to act.

14. *Partnership Bound by Partner's Breach of Trust.* The partnership is bound to make good the loss:

(a) Where one partner acting within the scope of his apparent authority receives money or property of a third person and misapplies it; and

(b) Where the partnership in the course of its business receives money or property of a third person and the money or property so received is misapplied by any partner while it is in the custody of the partnership.

15. *Nature of Partner's Liability.* All partners are liable

(a) Jointly and severally for everything chargeable to the partnership under sections 13 and 14.

(b) Jointly for all other debts and obligations of the partnership; but any partner may enter into a separate obligation to perform a partnership contract.

16. *Partner by Estoppel.* (1) When a person, by words spoken or written or by conduct, represents himself, or consents to another representing him to any one, as a partner in an existing partnership or with one or more persons not actual partners, he is liable to any such person to whom such representation has been made, who has, on the faith of such representation, given credit to the actual or apparent partnership, and if he has made such representation or consented to its being made in a public manner he is liable to such person, whether the representation has or has not been made or communicated to such person so giving credit by or with the knowledge of the apparent partner making the representation or consenting to its being made.

(a) When a partnership liability results, he is liable as though he were an actual member of the partnership.

(b) When no partnership liability results, he is liable jointly with the other persons, if any, so consenting to the contract or representation as to incur liability, otherwise separately.

(2) When a person has been thus represented to be a partner in an existing partnership, or with one

or more persons not actual partners, he is an agent of the persons consenting to such representation to bind them to the same extent and in the same manner as though he were a partner in fact, with respect to persons who rely upon the representation. Where all the members of the existing partnership consent to the representation, a partnership act or obligation results; but in all other cases it is the joint act or obligation of the person acting and the persons consenting to the representation.

17. *Liability of Incoming Partner.* A person admitted as a partner into an existing partnership is liable for all the obligations of the partnership arising before his admission as though he had been a partner when such obligations were incurred, except that this liability shall be satisfied only out of partnership property.

Part IV
Relations of Partners to One Another

18. *Rules Determining Rights and Duties of Partners.* The rights and duties of the partners in relation to the partnership shall be determined, subject to any agreement between them, by the following rules:

(a) Each partner shall be repaid his contributions, whether by way of capital or advances to the partnership property and share equally in the profits and surplus remaining after all liabilities, including those to partners, are satisfied; and must contribute toward the losses, whether of capital or otherwise, sustained by the partnership according to his share in the profits.

(b) The partnership must indemnify every partner in respect of payments made and personal liabilities reasonably incurred by him in the ordinary and proper conduct of its business, or for the preservation of its business or property.

(c) A partner, who in aid of the partnership makes any payment or advance beyond the amount of capital which he agreed to contribute, shall be paid interest from the date of the payment or advance.

(d) A partner shall receive interest on the capital contributed by him only from the date when repayment should be made.

(e) All partners have equal rights in the management and conduct of the partnership business.

(f) No partner is entitled to remuneration for acting in the partnership business, except that a surviving partner is entitled to reasonable compensation for his services in winding up the partnership affairs.

(g) No person can become a member of a partnership without the consent of all the partners.

(h) Any difference arising as to ordinary matters connected with the partnership business may be decided by a majority of the partners; but no act in contravention of any agreement between the partners may be done rightfully without the consent of all the partners.

19. *Partnership Books.* The partnership books shall be kept, subject to any agreement between the partners, at the principal place of business of the partnership, and every partner shall at all times have access to and may inspect and copy any of them.

20. *Duty of Partners to Render Information.* Partners shall render on demand true and full information of all things affecting the partnership to any partner or the legal representative of any deceased partner or partner under legal disability.

21. *Partner Accountable as a Fiduciary.* (1) Every partner must account to the partnership for any benefit, and hold as trustee for it any profits derived by him without the consent of the other partners from any transaction connected with the formation, conduct, or liquidation of the partnership or from any use by him of its property.

(2) This section applies also to the representatives of a deceased partner engaged in the liquidation of the affairs of the partnership as the personal representatives of the last surviving partner.

22. *Right to an Account.* Any partner shall have the right to a formal account as to partnership affairs:

(a) If he is wrongfully excluded from the partnership business or possession of its property by his co-partners,

(b) If the right exists under the terms of any agreement,

(c) As provided by section 21,

(d) Whenever other circumstances render it just and reasonable.

23. *Continuation of Partnership Beyond Fixed Term.* (1) When a partnership for a fixed term or particular undertaking is continued after the termination of such term or particular undertaking without any express agreement, the rights and duties of the partners remain the same as they were at such termination, so far as is consistent with a partnership at will.

(2) A continuation of the business by the partners or such of them as habitually acted therein during the term, without any settlement or liquidation of the partnership affairs, is *prima facie* evidence of a continuation of the partnership.

Part V
Property Rights of a Partner

24. *Extent of Property Rights of a Partner.* The property rights of a partner are (1) his rights in specific partnership property, (2) his interest in the partnership, and (3) his right to participate in the management.

25. *Nature of a Partner's Right in Specific Partnership Property.* (1) A partner is co-owner with his partners of specific partnership property holding as a tenant in partnership.

(2) The incidents of this tenancy are such that:

(a) A partner, subject to the provisions of this act and to any agreement between the partners, has an equal right with his partners to possess specific partnership property for partnership purposes; but he has no right to possess such property for any other purpose without the consent of his partners.

(b) A partner's right in specific partnership property is not assignable except in connection with the assignment of rights of all the partners in the same property.

(c) A partner's right in specific partnership property is not subject to attachment or execution, except on a claim against the partnership. When partnership property is attached for a partnership debt the partners, or any of them, or the representatives of a deceased partner, cannot claim any right under the homestead or exemption laws.

(d) On the death of a partner his right in specific partnership property vests in the surviving partner or partners, except where the deceased was the last surviving partner, when his right in such property vests in his legal representative. Such surviving partner or partners, or the legal representative of the last surviving partner, has no right to possess the partnership property for any but a partnership purpose.

(e) A partner's right in specific partnership property is not subject to dower, curtesy, or allowances to widows, heirs, or next of kin.

26. *Nature of Partner's Interest in the Partnership.* A partner's interest in the partnership is his share of the profits and surplus, and the same is personal property.

27. *Assignment of Partner's Interest.* (1) A conveyance by a partner of his interest in the partnership does not of itself dissolve the partnership, nor, as against the other partners in the absence of agreement, entitle the assignee, during the continuance of the partnership, to interfere in the management or administration of the partnership business or affairs, or to require any information or account of partnership transactions, or to inspect the partnership books; but it merely entitles the assignee to receive in accordance with his contract the profits to which the assigning partner would otherwise be entitled.

(2) In case of a dissolution of the partnership, the assignee is entitled to receive his assignor's interest and may require an account from the date only of the last account agreed to by all the partners.

28. *Partner's Interest Subject to Charging Order.*
(1) On due application to a competent court by any judgment creditor of a partner, the court which entered the judgment, order, or decree, or any other court, may charge the interest of the debtor partner with payment of the unsatisfied amount of such judgment debt with interest thereon; and may then or later appoint a receiver of his share of the profits, and of any other money due or to fall due to him in respect of the partnership, and make all other orders, directions, accounts and inquiries which the debtor partner might have made, or which the circumstances of the case may require.

(2) The interest charged may be redeemed at any time before foreclosure, or in case of a sale being directed by the court may be purchased without thereby causing a dissolution:

(a) With separate property, by any one or more of the partners, or

(b) With partnership property, by any one or more of the partners with the consent of all the partners whose interests are not so charged or sold.

(3) Nothing in this act shall be held to deprive a partner of his right, if any, under the exemption laws, as regards his interest in the partnership.

Part VI
Dissolution and Winding Up

29. *Dissolution Defined.* The dissolution of a partnership is the change in the relation of the partners caused by any partner ceasing to be associated in the carrying on as distinguished from the winding up of the business.

30. *Partnership Not Terminated by Dissolution.*
On dissolution the partnership is not terminated, but continues until the winding up of partnership affairs is completed.

31. *Causes of Dissolution.* Dissolution is caused:

(1) Without violation of the agreement between the partners,

(a) By the termination of the definite term or particular undertaking specified in the agreement,

(b) By the express will of any partner when no definite term or particular undertaking is specified,

(c) By the express will of all the partners who have not assigned their interests or suffered them to be charged for their separate debts, either before or after the termination of any specified term or particular undertaking,

(d) By the expulsion of any partner from the business *bona fide* in accordance with such a power conferred by the agreement between the partners;

(2) In contravention of the agreement between the partners, where the circumstances do not permit a dissolution under any other provision of this section, by the express will of any partner at any time;

(3) By any event which makes it unlawful for the business of the partnership to be carried on or for the members to carry it on in partnership;

(4) By the death of any partner;

(5) By the bankruptcy of any partner or the partnership;

(6) By decree of court under section 32.

32. *Dissolution by Decree of Court.* (1) On application by or for a partner the court shall decree a dissolution whenever:

(a) A partner has been declared a lunatic in any judicial proceeding or is shown to be of unsound mind,

(b) A partner becomes in any other way incapable of performing his part of the partnership contract,

(c) A partner has been guilty of such conduct as tends to affect prejudicially the carrying on of the business,

(d) A partner wilfully or persistently commits a breach of the partnership agreement, or otherwise so conducts himself in matters relating to the partnership business that it is not reasonably practicable to carry on the business in partnership with him,

(e) The business of the partnership can only be carried on at a loss,

(f) Other circumstances render a dissolution equitable.

(2) On the application of the purchaser of a partner's interest under sections 27 and 28:

(a) After the termination of the specified term or particular undertaking,

(b) At any time if the partnership was a partnership at will when the interest was assigned or when the charging order was issued.

33. *General Effect of Dissolution on Authority of Partner.* Except so far as may be necessary to wind up partnership affairs or to complete transactions begun but not then finished, dissolution terminates all authority of any partner to act for the partnership,

(1) With respect to the partners,

(a) When the dissolution is not by the act, bankruptcy or death of a partner; or

(b) When the dissolution is by such act, bankruptcy or death of a partner, in cases where section 34 so requires.

(2) With respect to persons not partners, as declared in section 35.

34. *Right of Partner to Contribution From Co-partners After Dissolution.* Where the dissolution is caused by the act, death or bankruptcy of a partner, each partner is liable to his co-partners for his share of any liability created by any partner acting for the partnership as if the partnership had not been dissolved unless

(a) The dissolution being by act of any partner, the partner acting for the partnership had knowledge of the dissolution, or

(b) The dissolution being by the death or bankruptcy of a partner, the partner acting for the partnership had knowledge or notice of the death or bankruptcy.

35. *Power of Partner to Bind Partnership to Third Persons After Dissolution.* (1) After dissolution a partner can bind the partnership except as provided in Paragraph (3).

(a) By any act appropriate for winding up partnership affairs or completing transactions unfinished at dissolution;

(b) By any transaction which would bind the partnership if dissolution had not taken place, provided the other party to the transaction

(I) Had extended credit to the partnership prior to dissolution and had no knowledge or notice of the dissolution; or

(II) Though he had not so extended credit, had nevertheless known of the partnership prior to dissolution, and, having no knowledge or notice of dissolution, the fact of dissolution had not been advertised in a newspaper of general circulation in the place (or in each place if more than one) at which the partnership business was regularly carried on.

(2) The liability of a partner under Paragraph (1b) shall be satisfied out of partnership assets alone when such partner had been prior to dissolution

(a) Unknown as a partner to the person with whom the contract is made; and

(b) So far unknown and inactive in partnership affairs that the business reputation of the partnership could not be said to have been in any degree due to his connection with it.

(3) The partnership is in no case bound by any act of a partner after dissolution

(a) Where the partnership is dissolved because it is unlawful to carry on the business, unless the act is appropriate for winding up partnership affairs; or

(b) Where the partner has become bankrupt; or

(c) Where the partner has no authority to wind up partnership affairs; except by a transaction with one who

(I) Had an extended credit to the partnership prior to dissolution and had no knowledge or notice of his want of authority; or

(II) Had not extended credit to the partnership prior to dissolution, and, having no knowledge or notice of his want of authority, the fact of his want of authority has not been advertised in the manner provided for advertising the fact of dissolution in Paragraph (1bII).

(4) Nothing in this section shall affect the liability under Section 16 of any person who after dissolution represents himself or consents to another representing him as a partner in a partnership engaged in carrying on business.

36. *Effect of Dissolution on Partner's Existing Liability.* (1) The dissolution of the partnership does not of itself discharge the existing liability of any partner.

(2) A partner is discharged from any existing liability upon dissolution of the partnership by an agreement to that effect between himself, the partnership creditor and the person or partnership continuing the business; and such agreement may be inferred from the course of dealing between the creditor having knowledge of the dissolution and the person or partnership continuing the business.

(3) Where a person agrees to assume the existing obligations of a dissolved partnership, the partners whose obligations have been assumed shall be discharged from any liability to any creditor of the partnership who, knowing of the agreement, consents to a material alteration in the nature or time of payment of such obligations.

(4) The individual property of a deceased partner shall be liable for all obligations of the partnership incurred while he was a partner but subject to the prior payment of his separate debts.

37. *Right to Wind Up.* Unless otherwise agreed the partners who have not wrongfully dissolved the partnership or the legal representative of the last surviving partner, not bankrupt, has the right to wind up the partnership affairs; provided, however, that any partner, his legal representative or his assignee, upon cause shown, may obtain winding up by the court.

38. *Rights of Partners to Application of Partnership Property.* (1) When dissolution is caused in any way, except in contravention of the partnership agreement, each partner, as against his co-partners and all persons claiming through them in respect of their interests in the partnership, unless otherwise agreed, may have the partnership property applied to discharge its liabilities, and the surplus applied to pay in cash the net amount owing to the respective partners. But if dissolution is caused by expulsion of a partner, *bona fide* under the partnership agreement and if the expelled partner is discharged from all partnership liabilities, either by payment or agreement under section 36 (2), he shall receive in cash only the net amount due him from the partnership.

(2) When dissolution is caused in contravention of the partnership agreement the rights of the partners shall be as follows:

(a) Each partner who has not caused dissolution wrongfully shall have,

(I) All the rights specified in paragraph (1) of this section, and

(II) The right, as against each partner who has caused the dissolution wrongfully, to damages for breach of the agreement.

(b) The partners who have not caused the dissolution wrongfully, if they all desire to continue the business in the same name, either by themselves or jointly with others, may do so, during the agreed term for the partnership and for that purpose may possess the partnership property, provided they secure the payment by bond approved by the court, or pay to any partner who has caused the dissolution wrongfully, the value of his interest in the partnership at the dissolution, less any damages recoverable under clause (2aII) of this section, and in like manner indemnify him against all present or future partnership liabilities.

(c) A partner who has caused the dissolution wrongfully shall have:

(I) If the business is not continued under the provisions of paragraph (2b) all the rights of a partner under paragraph (1), subject to clause (2aII), of this section,

(II) If the business is continued under paragraph (2b) of this section the right as against this co-partners and all claiming through them in respect of their interests in the partnership, to have the value of his interest in the partnership, less any damages caused to his co-partners by the dissolution, ascertained and paid to him in cash, or the payment secured by bond approved by the court, and to be released from all existing liabilities of the partnership; but in ascertaining the value of the partner's interest the value of the good-will of the business shall not be considered.

39. *Rights Where Partnership is Dissolved for Fraud or Misrepresentation.*

Where a partnership contract is rescinded on the ground of the fraud or misrepresentation of one of the parties thereto, the party entitled to rescind is, without prejudice to any other right, entitled,

(a) To a lien on, or a right of retention of, the surplus of the partnership property after satisfying the partnership liabilities to third persons for any sum of money paid by him for the purchase of an interest in the partnership and for any capital or advances contributed by him; and

(b) To stand, after all liabilities to third persons have been satisfied, in the place of the creditors of the partnership for any payments made by him in respect of the partnership liabilities; and

(c) To be indemnified by the person guilty of the fraud or making the representation against all debts and liabilities of the partnership.

40. *Rules for Distribution.*

In settling accounts between the partners after dissolution, the following rules shall be observed, subject to any agreement to the contrary:

(a) The assets of the partnership are;

(I) The partnership property,

(II) The contributions of the partners necessary for the payment of all the liabilities specified in clause (b) of this paragraph.

(b) The liabilities of the partnership shall rank in order of payment, as follows:

(I) Those owing to creditors other than partners,

(II) Those owing to partners other than for capital and profits,

(III) Those owing to partners in respect of capital,

(IV) Those owing to partners in respect of profits.

(c) The assets shall be applied in the order of their declaration in clause (a) of this paragraph to the satisfaction of the liabilities.

(d) The partners shall contribute, as provided by section 18 (a) the amount necessary to satisfy the liabilities; but if any, but not all, of the partners are insolvent, or, not being subject to process, refuse to contribute, the other partners shall contribute their share of the liabilities, and, in the relative proportions in which they share the profits, the additional amount necessary to pay the liabilities.

(e) An assignee for the benefit of creditors or any person appointed by the court shall have the right to enforce the contributions specified in clause (d) of this paragraph.

(f) Any partner or his legal representative shall have the right to enforce the contributions specified in clause (d) of this paragraph, to the extent of the amount which he has paid in excess of his share of the liability.

(g) The individual property of a deceased partner shall be liable for the contributions specified in clause (d) of this paragraph.

(h) When partnership property and the individual properties of the partners are in possession of a court for distribution, partnership creditors shall have priority on partnership property and separate creditors on individual property, saving the rights of lien or secured creditors as heretofore.

(i) Where a partner has become bankrupt or his estate is insolvent the claims against his separate property shall rank in the following order:

(I) Those owing to separate creditors,

(II) Those owing to partnership creditors,

(III) Those owing to partners by way of contribution.

41. *Liability of Persons Continuing the Business in Certain Cases.* (1) When any new partner is admitted into an existing partnership, or when any partner retires and assigns (or the representative of the deceased partner assigns) his rights in partnership property to two or more of the partners, or to one or more of the partners and one or more third persons, if the business is continued without liquidation of the partnership affairs, creditors of the first or dissolved partnership are also creditors of the partnership so continuing the business.

(2) When all but one partner retire and assign (or the representative of a deceased partner assigns) their rights in partnership property to the remaining partner, who continues the business without liquidation of partnership affairs, either alone or with others, creditors of the dissolved partnership are also creditors of the person or partnership continuing the business.

(3) When any partner retires or dies and the business of the dissolved partnership is continued as set forth in paragraphs (1) and (2) of this section, with the consent of the retired partners or the representative of the deceased partner, but without any assignment of his right in partnership property, rights of creditors of the dissolved partnership and of the creditors of the person or partnership continuing the business shall be as if such assignment had been made.

(4) When all the partners or their representative assign their rights in partnership property to one or more third persons who promise to pay the debts and who continue the business of the dissolved partnership, creditors of the dissolved partnership are also creditors of the person or partnership continuing the business.

(5) When any partner wrongfully causes a dissolution and the remaining partners continue the business under the provisions of section 38 (2b), either alone or with others, and without liquidation of the partnership affairs, creditors of the dissolved partnership are also creditors of the person or partnership continuing the business.

(6) When a partner is expelled and the remaining partners continue the business either alone or with others, without liquidation of the partnership affairs, creditors of the dissolved partnership are also creditors of the person or partnership continuing the business.

(7) The liability of a third person becoming a partner in the partnership continuing the business, under this section, to the creditors of the dissolved partnership shall be satisfied out of partnership property only.

(8) When the business of a partnership after dissolution is continued under any conditions set forth in this section the creditors of the dissolved partnership, as against the separate creditors of the retiring or deceased partner or the representative of the deceased partner, have a prior right to any claim of the retired partner or the representative of the deceased partner against the person or partnership continuing the business, on account of the retired or deceased partner's interest in the dissolved partnership or on account of any consideration promised for such interest or for his right in partnership property.

(9) Nothing in this section shall be held to modify any right of creditors to set aside any assignment on the ground of fraud.

(10) The use by the person or partnership continuing the business of the partnership name, or the name of a deceased partner as part thereof, shall not of itself make the individual property of the deceased partner liable for any debts contracted by such person or partnership.

42. *Rights of Retiring or Estate of Deceased Partner When the Business is Continued.* When any partner retires or dies, and the business is continued under any of the conditions set forth in section 41 (1, 2, 3, 5, 6), or section 38 (2b), without any settlement of accounts as between him or his estate and the person or partnership continuing the business, unless otherwise agreed, he or his legal representative as against such persons or partnership may have the value of his interest at the date of dissolution ascertained, and shall receive as an ordinary creditor an amount equal to the value of his interest in the dissolved partnership with interest, or, at his option or at the option of his legal representative, in lieu of interest, the profits attributable to the use of his right in the property of the dissolved partnership; provided that the creditors of the dissolved partnership as against the separate creditors, or the representative of the retired or sdeceased partner, shall have priority on any claim arising under this section, as provided by section 41 (8) of this act.

43. *Accrual of Actions.* The right to an account of his interest shall accrue to any partner, or his legal representative, as against the winding up partners or the surviving partners or the person or partnership continuing the business, at the date of dissolution, in the absence of any agreement to the contrary.

Part VII
Miscellaneous Provisions

44. *When Act Takes Effect.* This act shall take effect on the _____ day of _____ one thousand nine hundred and _____.

45. *Legislation Repealed.* All acts or parts of acts inconsistent with this act are hereby repealed.

APPENDIX C

UNIFORM PARTNERSHIP ACT (1994)

[ARTICLE] 1
GENERAL PROVISIONS

SECTION 101. *Definitions.*

In this [Act]:

(1) "Business" includes every trade, occupation, and profession.

(2) "Debtor in bankruptcy" means a person who is the subject of:

    (i) an order for relief under Title 11 of the United States Code or a comparable order under a successor statute of general application; or

    (ii) a comparable order under federal, state, or foreign law governing insolvency.

(3) "Distribution" means a transfer of money or other property from a partnership to a partner in the partner's capacity as a partner or to the partner's transferee.

(4) "Partnership" means an association of two or more persons to carry on as co-owners a business for profit formed under Section 202, predecessor law, or comparable law of another jurisdiction.

(5) "Partnership agreement" means the agreement, whether written, oral, or implied, among the partners concerning the partnership, including amendments to the partnership agreement.

(6) "Partnership at will" means a partnership in which the partners have not agreed to remain partners until the expiration of a definite term or the completion of a particular undertaking.

(7) "Partnership interest" or "partner's interest in the partnership" means all of a partner's interests in the partnership, including the partner's transferable interest and all management and other rights.

(8) "Person" means an individual, corporation, business trust, estate, trust, partnership, association, joint venture, government, governmental subdivision, agency, or instrumentality, or any other legal or commercial entity.

(9) "Property" means all property, real, personal, or mixed, tangible or intangible, or any interest therein.

(10) "State" means a State of the United States, the District of Columbia, the Commonwealth of Puerto Rico, or any territory or insular possession subject to the jurisdiction of the United States.

(11) "Statement" means a statement of partnership authority under Section 303, a statement of denial under Section 304, a statement of dissociation under Section 704, a statement of dissolution under Section 805, a statement of merger under Section 907, or an amendment or cancellation of any of the foregoing.

(12) "Transfer" includes an assignment, conveyance, lease, mortgage, deed, and encumbrance.

SECTION 102. *Knowledge and Notice.*

(a) A person knows a fact if the person has actual knowledge of it.

(b) A person has notice of a fact if the person:

    (1) knows of it;

    (2) has received a notification of it; or

    (3) has reason to know it exists from all of the facts known to the person at the time in question.

(c) A person notifies or gives a notification to another by taking steps reasonably required to inform the other person in ordinary course, whether or not the other person learns of it.

(d) A person receives a notification when the notification:

    (1) comes to the person's attention; or

    (2) is duly delivered at the person's place of business or at any other place held out by the person as a place for receiving communications.

(e) Except as otherwise provided in subsection (f), a person other than an individual knows, has notice, or receives a notification of a fact for purposes of a particular transaction when the individual conducting the transaction knows, has notice, or receives a notification of the fact, or in any event when the fact would have been brought to the individual's attention if the person had exercised reasonable diligence. The person exercises reasonable diligence if it maintains reasonable routines for communicating significant information to the individual conducting the transaction and there is reasonable compliance with the routines. Reasonable diligence does not require an individual acting for the person to communicate information unless the communication is part of the individual's regular duties or the individual has reason to know of the transaction and that the transaction would be materially affected by the information.

(f) A partner's knowledge, notice, or receipt of a notification of a fact relating to the partnership is effective immediately as knowledge by, notice to, or receipt of a notification by the partnership, except in the case of a fraud on the partnership committed by or with the consent of that partner.

SECTION 103. Effect of Partnership Agreement; Nonwaivable Provisions.

(a) Except as otherwise provided in subsection (b), relations among the partners and between the partners and the partnership are governed by the partnership agreement. To the extent the partnership agreement does not otherwise provide, this [Act] governs relations among the partners and between the partners and the partnership.

(b) The partnership agreement may not:

(1) vary the rights and duties under Section 105 except to eliminate the duty to provide copies of statements to all of the partners;

(2) unreasonably restrict the right of access to books and records under Section 403(b);

(3) eliminate the duty of loyalty under Section 404(b) or 603(b)(3), but:

(i) the partnership agreement may identify specific types or categories of activities that do not violate the duty of loyalty, if not manifestly unreasonable; or

(ii) all of the partners or a number or percentage specified in the partnership agreement may authorize or ratify, after full disclosure of all material facts, a specific act or transaction that otherwise would violate the duty of loyalty;

(4) unreasonably reduce the duty of care under Section 404(c) or 603(b)(3);

(5) eliminate the obligation of good faith and fair dealing under Section 404(d), but the partnership agreement may prescribe the standards by which the performance of the obligation is to be measured, if the standards are not manifestly unreasonable;

(6) vary the power to dissociate as a partner under Section 602(a), except to require the notice under Section 601(1) to be in writing;

(7) vary the right of a court to expel a partner in the events specified in Section 601(5);

(8) vary the requirement to wind up the partnership business in cases specified in Section 801(4), (5), or (6); or

(9) restrict rights of third parties under this [Act].

SECTION 104. Supplemental Principles of Law.

(a) Unless displaced by particular provisions of this [Act], the principles of law and equity supplement this [Act].

(b) If an obligation to pay interest arises under this [Act] and the rate is not specified, the rate is that specified in [applicable statute].

SECTION 105. Execution, Filing, and Recording of Statements.

(a) A statement may be filed in the office of [the Secretary of State]. A certified copy of a statement that is filed in an office in another State may be filed in the office of [the Secretary of State]. Either filing has the effect provided in this [Act] with respect to partnership property located in or transactions that occur in this State.

(b) A certified copy of a statement that has been filed in the office of the [Secretary of State] and recorded in the office for recording transfers of real property has the effect provided for recorded statements in this [Act]. A recorded statement that is not a certified copy of a statement filed in the office of the [Secretary of State] does not have the effect provided for recorded statements in this [Act].

(c) A statement filed by a partnership must be executed by at least two partners. Other statements must be executed by a partner or other person authorized by this [Act]. An individual who executes a statement as, or on behalf of, a partner or other person named as a partner in a statement shall personally declare under penalty of perjury that the contents of the statement are accurate.

(d) A person authorized by this [Act] to file a statement may amend or cancel the statement by filing an amendment or cancellation that names the partnership, identifies the statement, and states the substance of the amendment or cancellation.

(e) A person who files a statement pursuant to this section shall promptly send a copy of the statement to every nonfiling partner and to any other person named as a partner in the statement. Failure to send a copy of a statement to a partner or other person does not limit the effectiveness of the statement as to a person not a partner.

(f) The [Secretary of State] may collect a fee for filing or providing a certified copy of a statement. The [officer responsible for] recording transfers of real property may collect a fee for recording a statement.

SECTION 106. Law Governing Internal Relations.

The law of the jurisdiction in which a partnership has its chief executive office governs relations among the partners and between the partners and the partnership.

SECTION 107. Partnership Subject to Amendment or Repeal of [Act].

A partnership governed by this [Act] is subject to any amendment to or repeal of this [Act].

[ARTICLE] 2
NATURE OF PARTNERSHIP

SECTION 201.   *Partnership as Entity.*

A partnership is an entity distinct from its partners.

SECTION 202.   *Formation of Partnership.*

(a)   Except as otherwise provided in subsection (b), the association of two or more persons to carry on as co-owners a business for profit forms a partnership, whether or not the persons intend to form a partnership.

(b)   An association formed under a statute other than this [Act], a predecessor statute, or a comparable statute of another jurisdiction is not a partnership under this [Act].

(c)   In determining whether a partnership is formed, the following rules apply:

(1)   Joint tenancy, tenancy in common, tenancy by the entireties, joint property, common property, or part ownership does not by itself establish a partnership, even if the co-owners share profits made by the use of the property.

(2)   The sharing of gross returns does not by itself establish a partnership, even if the persons sharing them have a joint or common right or interest in property from which the returns are derived.

(3)   A person who receives a share of the profits of a business is presumed to be a partner in the business, unless the profits were received in payment:

(i)   of a debt by installments or otherwise;

(ii)   for services as an independent contractor or of wages of other compensation to an employee;

(iii)   of rent;

(iv)   of an annuity or other retirement or health benefit to a beneficiary, representative, or designee of a deceased or retired partner;

(v)   of interest or other charge on a loan, even if the amount of payment varies with the profits of the business, including a direct or indirect present or future ownership of the collateral, or rights to income, proceeds, or increase in value derived from the collateral; or

(vi)   for the sale of the goodwill of a business or other property by installments or otherwise.

SECTION 203.   *Partnership Property.*

Property acquired by a partnership is property of the partnership and not of the partners individually.

SECTION 204.   *When Property Is Partnership Property.*

(a)   Property is partnership property if acquired in the name of:

(1)   the partnership; or

(2)   one or more partners with an indication in the instrument transferring title to the property of the person's capacity as a partner or of the existence of a partnership but without an indication of the name of the partnership.

(b)   Property is acquired in the name of the partnership by a transfer to:

(1)   the partnership in its name; or

(2)   one or more partners in their capacity as partners in the partnership, if the name of the partnership is indicated in the instrument transferring title to the property.

(c)   Property is presumed to be partnership property if purchased with partnership assets, even if not acquired in the name of the partnership or of one or more partners with an indication in the instrument transferring title to the property of the person's capacity as a partner or of the existence of a partnership.

(d)   Property acquired in the name of one or more of the partners, without an indication in the instrument transferring title to the property of the person's capacity as a partner or of the existence of a partnership and without use of partnership assets, is presumed to be separate property, even if used for partnership purposes.

[ARTICLE] 3
RELATIONS OF PARTNERS TO PERSONS DEALING WITH PARTNERSHIP

SECTION 301.   *Partner Agent of Partnership.*

Subject to the effect of a statement of partnership authority under Section 303:

(1)   Each partner is an agent of the partnership for the purpose of its business. An act of a partner, including the execution of an instrument in the partnership name, for apparently carrying on in the ordinary course the partnership business or business of the kind carried on by the partnership binds the partnership, unless the partner had no authority to act for the partnership in the particular matter and

the person with whom the partner was dealing knew or had received a notification that the partner lacked authority.

(2) An act of a partner which is not apparently for carrying on in the ordinary course the partnership business or business of the kind carried on by the partnership binds the partnership only if the act was authorized by the other partners.

SECTION 302. *Transfer of Partnership Property.*

(a) Partnership property may be transferred as follows:

(1) Subject to the effect of a statement of partnership authority under Section 303, partnership property held in the name of the partnership may be transferred by an instrument of transfer executed by a partner in the partnership name.

(2) Partnership property held in the name of one or more partners with an indication in the instrument transferring the property to them of their capacity as partners or of the existence of a partnership, but without an indication of the name of the partnership, may be transferred by an instrument of transfer executed by the persons in whose name the property is held.

(3) Partnership property held in the name of one or more persons other than the partnership, without an indication in the instrument transferring the property to them of their capacity as partners or of the existence of a partnership, may be transferred by an instrument of transfer executed by the persons in whose name the property is held.

(b) A partnership may recover partnership property from a transferee only if it proves that execution of the instrument of initial transfer did not bind the partnership under Section 301 and:

(1) as to a subsequent transferee who gave value for property transferred under subsection (a)(l) and (2), proves that the subsequent transferee knew or had received a notification that the person who executed the instrument of initial transfer lacked authority to bind the partnership; or

(2) as to a transferee who gave value for property transferred under subsection (a)(3), proves that the transferee knew or had received a notification that the property was partnership property and that the person who executed the instrument of initial transfer lacked authority to bind the partnership.

(c) A partnership may not recover partnership property from a subsequent transferee if the partnership would not have been entitled to recover the property, under subsection (b), from any earlier transferee of the property.

(d) If a person holds all of the partners' interests in the partnership, all of the partnership property vests in that person. The person may execute a document in the name of the partnership to evidence vesting of the property in that person and may file or record the document.

SECTION 303. *Statement of Partnership Authority.*

(a) A partnership may file a statement of partnership authority, which:

(1) must include:

(i) the name of the partnership;

(ii) the street address of its chief executive office and of one office in this State, if there is one;

(iii) the names and mailing addresses of all of the partners or of an agent appointed and maintained by the partnership for the purpose of subsection (b); and

(iv) the names of the partners authorized to execute an instrument transferring real property held in the name of the partnership; and

(2) may state the authority, or limitations on the authority, of some or all of the partners to enter into other transactions on behalf of the partnership and any other matter.

(b) If a statement of partnership authority names an agent, the agent shall maintain a list of the names and mailing addresses of all of the partners and make it available to any person on request for good cause shown.

(c) If a filed statement of partnership authority is executed pursuant to Section 105(c) and states the name of the partnership but does not contain all of the other information required by subsection (a), the statement nevertheless operates with respect to a person not a partner as provided in subsections (d) and (e).

(d) Except as otherwise provided in subsection (g), a filed statement of partnership authority supplements the authority of a partner to enter into transactions on behalf of the partnership as follows:

(1) Except for transfers of real property, a grant of authority contained in a filed statement of partnership authority is conclusive in favor of a person who gives value without knowledge to the contrary, so long as and to the extent that a limitation on that authority is not then contained in another filed statement. A filed cancellation of a limitation on authority revives the previous grant of authority.

(2) A grant of authority to transfer real property held in the name of the partnership contained in a certified copy of a filed statement of partnership authority recorded in the office for recording transfers of that real property is conclusive in favor of a person who gives value without knowledge to the contrary, so long as and to the extent that a certified copy of a filed statement containing a limitation on that authority is not then of record in the office for recording transfers

of that real property. The recording in the office for recording transfers of that real property of a certified copy of a filed cancellation of a limitation on authority revives the previous grant of authority.

(e) A person not a partner is deemed to know of a limitation on the authority of a partner to transfer real property held in the name of the partnership if a certified copy of the filed statement containing the limitation on authority is of record in the office for recording transfers of that real property.

(f) Except as otherwise provided in subsections (d) and (e) and Sections 704 and 805, a person not a partner is not deemed to know of a limitation on the authority of a partner merely because the limitation is contained in a filed statement.

(g) Unless earlier canceled, a filed statement of partnership authority is canceled by operation of law five years after the date on which the statement, or the most recent amendment, was filed with the [Secretary of State].

SECTION 304. Statement of Denial.

A partner or other person named as a partner in a filed statement of partnership authority or in a list maintained by an agent pursuant to Section 303(b) may file a statement of denial stating the name of the partnership and the fact that is being denied, which may include denial of a person's authority or status as a partner. A statement of denial is a limitation on authority as provided in Section 303(d) and (e).

SECTION 305. Partnership Liable for Partner's Actionable Conduct.

(a) A partnership is liable for loss or injury caused to a person, or for a penalty incurred, as a result of a wrongful act or omission, or other actionable conduct, of a partner acting in the ordinary course of business of the partnership or with authority of the partnership.

(b) If, in the course of the partnership's business or while acting with authority of the partnership, a partner receives or causes the partnership to receive money or property of a person not a partner, and the money or property is misapplied by a partner, the partnership is liable for the loss.

SECTION 306. Partner's Liability.

(a) Except as otherwise provided in subsection (b), all partners are liable jointly and severally for all obligations of the partnership unless otherwise agreed by the claimant or provided by law.

(b) A person admitted as a partner into an existing partnership is not personally liable for any partnership obligation incurred before the person's admission as a partner.

SECTION 307. Actions By and Against Partnership and Partners.

(a) A partnership may sue and be sued in the name of the partnership.

(b) An action may be brought against the partnership and any or all of the partners in the same action or in separate actions.

(c) A judgment against a partnership is not by itself a judgment against a partner. A judgment against a partnership may not be satisfied from a partner's assets unless there is also a judgment against the partner.

(d) A judgment creditor of a partner may not levy execution against the assets of the partner to satisfy a judgment based on a claim against the partnership unless:

(1) a judgment based on the same claim has been obtained against the partnership and a writ of execution on the judgment has been returned unsatisfied in whole or in part;

(2) the partnership is a debtor in bankruptcy;

(3) the partner has agreed that the creditor need not exhaust partnership assets;

(4) a court grants permission to the judgment creditor to levy execution against the assets of a partner based on a finding that partnership assets subject to execution are clearly insufficient to satisfy the judgment, that exhaustion of partnership assets is excessively burdensome, or that the grant of permission is an appropriate exercise of the court's equitable powers; or

(5) liability is imposed on the partner by law or contract independent of the existence of the partnership.

(e) This section applies to any partnership liability or obligation resulting from a representation by a partner or purported partner under Section 308.

SECTION 308. Liability of Purported Partner.

(a) If a person, by words or conduct, purports to be a partner, or consents to being represented by another as a partner, in a partnership or with one or more persons not partners, the purported partner is liable to a person to whom the representation is made, if that person, relying on the representation, enters into a transaction with the actual or purported partnership. If the representation, either by the purported partner or by a person with the purported partner's consent, is made in a public manner, the purported partner is liable to a person who relies upon the purported partnership even if the purported partner is not aware of being held out as a partner to the claimant. If partnership liability results, the purported partner is liable with respect to that liability as if the purported partner were a partner. If no partnership liability results, the purported partner is liable with respect to that liability jointly and severally with any other person consenting to the representation.

(b) If a person is thus represented to be a partner in an existing partnership, or with one or more persons not partners, the purported partner is an agent of persons consenting to the representation to bind them to the same extent and in the same manner as if the purported partner were a partner, with respect to persons who enter into transactions in reliance upon the representation. If all of the partners of the existing partnership consent to the representation, a partnership act or obligation results. If fewer than all of the partners of the existing partnership consent to the representation, the person acting and the partners consenting to the representation are jointly and severally liable.

(c) A person is not liable as a partner merely because the person is named by another in a statement of partnership authority.

(d) A person does not continue to be liable as a partner merely because of a failure to file a statement of dissociation or to amend a statement of partnership authority to indicate the partner's dissociation from the partnership.

(e) Except as otherwise provided in subsections (a) and (b), persons who are not partners as to each other are not liable as partners to other persons.

[ARTICLE] 4
RELATIONS OF PARTNERS TO EACH OTHER AND TO PARTNERSHIP

Section 401.   Partner's Rights and Duties.
Section 402.   Distributions in Kind.
Section 403.   Partner's Rights and Duties with Respect to Information.
Section 404.   General Standards of Partner's Conduct.
Section 405.   Actions by Partnership and Partners.
Section 406.   Continuation of Partnership Beyond Definite Term or Particular Undertaking.

SECTION 401.   *Partner's Rights and Duties.*

(a) Each partner is deemed to have an account that is:

(1) credited with an amount equal to the money plus the value of any other property, net of the amount of any liabilities, the partner contributes to the partnership and the partner's share of the partnership profits; and

(2) charged with an amount equal to the money plus the value of any other property, net of the amount of any liabilities, distributed by the partnership to the partner and the partner's share of the partnership losses.

(b) Each partner is entitled to an equal share of the partnership profits and is chargeable with a share of the partnership losses in proportion to the partner's share of the profits.

(c) A partnership shall reimburse a partner for payments made and indemnify a partner for liabilities incurred by the partner in the ordinary course of the business of the partnership or for the preservation of its business or property.

(d) A partnership shall reimburse a partner for an advance to the partnership beyond the amount of capital the partner agreed to contribute.

(e) A payment or advance made by a partner which gives rise to a partnership obligation under subsection (c) or (d) constitutes a loan to the partnership which accrues interest from the date of the payment or advance.

(f) Each partner has equal rights in the management and conduct of the partnership business.

(g) A partner may use or possess partnership property only on behalf of the partnership.

(h) A partner is not entitled to remuneration for services performed for the partnership, except for reasonable compensation for services rendered in winding up the business of the partnership.

(i) A person may become a partner only with the consent of all of the partners.

(j) A difference arising as to a matter in the ordinary course of business of a partnership may be decided by a majority of the partners. An act outside the ordinary course of business of a partnership and an amendment to the partnership agreement may be undertaken only with the consent of all of the partners.

(k) This section does not affect the obligations of a partnership to other persons under Section 301.

SECTION 402.   *Distributions in Kind.*

A partner has no right to receive, and may not be required to accept, a distribution in kind.

SECTION 403.   *Partner's Rights and Duties with Respect to Information.*

(a) A partnership shall keep its books and records, if any, at its chief executive office.

(b) A partnership shall provide partners and their agents and attorneys access to its books and records. It shall provide former partners and their agents and attorneys access to books and records pertaining to the period during which they were partners. The right of access provides the opportunity to inspect and copy books and records during ordinary business hours. A partnership may impose a reasonable charge, covering the costs of labor and material, for copies of documents furnished.

(c) Each partner and the partnership shall furnish to a partner, and to the legal representative of a deceased partner or partner under legal disability:

(1) without demand, any information concerning the partnership's business and affairs reasonably required for the proper exercise of the partner's rights and duties under the partnership agreement or this [Act]; and

(2) on demand, any other information concerning the partnership's business and affairs, except to the extent the demand or the information demanded is unreasonable or otherwise improper under the circumstances.

SECTION 404. *General Standards of Partner's Conduct.*

(a) The only fiduciary duties a partner owes to the partnership and the other partners are the duty of loyalty and the duty of care set forth in subsections (b) and (c).

(b) A partner's duty of loyalty to the partnership and the other partners is limited to the following:

(1) to account to the partnership and hold as trustee for it any property, profit, or benefit derived by the partner in the conduct and winding up of the partnership business or derived from a use by the partner of partnership property, including the appropriation of a partnership opportunity;

(2) to refrain from dealing with the partnership in the conduct or winding up of the partnership business as or on behalf of a party having an interest adverse to the partnership; and

(3) to refrain from competing with the partnership in the conduct of the partnership business before the dissolution of the partnership.

(c) A partner's duty of care to the partnership and the other partners in the conduct and winding up of the partnership business is limited to refraining from engaging in grossly negligent or reckless conduct, intentional misconduct, or a knowing violation of law.

(d) A partner shall discharge the duties to the partnership and the other partners under this [Act] or under the partnership agreement and exercise any rights consistently with the obligation of good faith and fair dealing.

(e) A partner does not violate a duty or obligation under this [Act] or under the partnership agreement merely because the partner's conduct furthers the partner's own interest.

(f) A partner may lend money to and transact other business with the partnership, and as to each loan or transaction the rights and obligations of the partner are the same as those of a person who is not a partner, subject to other applicable law.

(g) This section applies to a person winding up the partnership business as the personal or legal representative of the last surviving partner as if the person were a partner.

SECTION 405. *Actions by Partnership and Partners.*

(a) A partnership may maintain an action against a partner for a breach of the partnership agreement, or for the violation of a duty to the partnership, causing harm to the partnership.

(b) A partner may maintain an action against the partnership or another partner for legal or equitable relief, with or without an accounting as to partnership business, to:

(1) enforce the partner's rights under the partnership agreement;

(2) enforce the partner's rights under this [Act], including:

(i) the partner's rights under Sections 401, 403, or 404;

(ii) the partner's right on dissociation to have the partner's interest in the partnership purchased pursuant to Section 701 or enforce any other right under [Article] 6 or 7; or

(iii) the partner's right to compel a dissolution and winding up of the partnership business under Section 801 or enforce any other right under [Article] 8; or

(3) enforce the rights and otherwise protect the interests of the partner, including rights and interests arising independently of the partnership relationship.

(c) The accrual of, and any time limitation on, a right of action for a remedy under this section is governed by other law. A right to an accounting upon a dissolution and winding up does not revive a claim barred by law.

SECTION 406. *Continuation of Partnership Beyond Definite Term or Particular Undertaking.*

(a) If a partnership for a definite term or particular undertaking is continued, without an express agreement, after the expiration of the term or completion of the undertaking, the rights and duties of the partners remain the same as they were at the expiration or completion, so far as is consistent with a partnership at will.

(b) If the partners, or those of them who habitually acted in the business during the term or undertaking, continue the business without any settlement or liquidation of the partnership, they are presumed to have agreed that the partnership will continue.

[ARTICLE] 5
TRANSFEREES AND CREDITORS OF PARTNER

SECTION 501. *Partner Not Co-Owner of Partnership Property.*

A partner is not a co-owner of partnership property and has no interest in partnership property which can be transferred, either voluntarily or involuntarily.

SECTION 502. Partner's Transferable Interest in Partnership.

The only transferable interest of a partner in the partnership is the partner's share of the profits and losses of the partnership and the partner's right to receive distributions. The interest is personal property.

SECTION 503. Transfer of Partner's Transferable Interest.

(a) A transfer, in whole or in part, of a partner's transferable interest in the partnership:

(1) is permissible;

(2) does not by itself cause the partner's dissociation or a dissolution and winding up of the partnership business; and

(3) does not, as against the other partners or the partnership, entitle the transferee, during the continuance of the partnership, to participate in the management or conduct of the partnership business, to require access to information concerning partnership transactions, or to inspect or copy the partnership books or records.

(b) A transferee of a partner's transferable interest in the partnership has a right:

(1) to receive, in accordance with the transfer, distributions to which the transferor would otherwise be entitled;

(2) to receive upon the dissolution and winding up of the partnership business, in accordance with the transfer, the net amount otherwise distributable to the transferor; and

(3) to seek under Section 801(6) a judicial determination that it is equitable to wind up the partnership business.

(c) In a dissolution and winding up, a transferee is entitled to an account of partnership transactions only from the date of the latest account agreed to by all of the partners.

(d) Upon transfer, the transferor retains the rights and duties of a partner other than the interest in distributions transferred.

(e) A partnership need not give effect to a transferee's rights under this section until it has notice of the transfer.

(f) A transfer of a partner's transferable interest in the partnership in violation of a restriction on transfer contained in the partnership agreement is ineffective as to a person having notice of the restriction at the time of transfer.

SECTION 504. Partner's Transferable Interest Subject to Charging Order.

(a) On application by a judgment creditor of a partner or of a partner's transferee, a court having jurisdiction may charge the transferable interest of the judgment debtor to satisfy the judgment. The court may appoint a receiver of the share of the distributions due or to become due to the judgment debtor in respect of the partnership and make all other orders, directions, accounts, and inquiries the judgment debtor might have made or which the circumstances of the case may require.

(b) A charging order constitutes a lien on the judgment debtor's transferable interest in the partnership. The court may order a foreclosure of the interest subject to the charging order at any time. The purchaser at the foreclosure sale has the rights of a transferee.

(c) At any time before foreclosure, an interest charged may be redeemed:

(1) by the judgment debtor;

(2) with property other than partnership property, by one or more of the other partners; or

(3) with partnership property, by one or more of the other partners with the consent of all of the partners whose interests are not so charged.

(d) This [Act] does not deprive a partner of a right under exemption laws with respect to the partner's interest in the partnership.

(e) This section provides the exclusive remedy by which a judgment creditor of a partner or partner's transferee may satisfy a judgment out of the judgment debtor's transferable interest in the partnership.

[ARTICLE] 6
PARTNER'S DISSOCIATION

Section 601.   Events Causing Partner's Dissociation.

Section 602.   Partner's Power to Dissociate; Wrongful Dissociation.

Section 603.   Effect of Partner's Dissociation.

SECTION 601. Events Causing Partner's Dissociation.

A partner is dissociated from a partnership upon the occurrence of any of the following events:

(1) the partnership's having notice of the partner's express will to withdraw as a partner or on a later date specified by the partner;

(2) an event agreed to in the partnership agreement as causing the partner's dissociation;

(3) the partner's expulsion pursuant to the partnership agreement;

(4) the partner's expulsion by the unanimous vote of the other partners if:

(i) it is unlawful to carry on the partnership business with that partner;

(ii) there has been a transfer of all or substantially all of that partner's transferable interest in the partnership, other than a transfer for security purposes, or a court order charging the partner's interest, which has not been foreclosed;

(iii) within 90 days after the partnership notifies a corporate partner that it will be expelled because it has filed a certificate of dissolution or the equivalent, its charter has been revoked, or its right to conduct business has been suspended by the jurisdiction of its incorporation, there is no revocation of the certificate of dissolution or no reinstatement of its charter or its right to conduct business; or

(iv) a partnership that is a partner has been dissolved and its business is being wound up;

(5) on application by the partnership or another partner, the partner's expulsion by judicial determination because:

(i) the partner engaged in wrongful conduct that adversely and materially affected the partnership business;

(ii) the partner willfully or persistently committed a material breach of the partnership agreement or of a duty owed to the partnership or the other partners under Section 404; or

(iii) the partner engaged in conduct relating to the partnership business which makes it not reasonably practicable to carrry on the business in partnership with the partner;

(6) the partner's:

(i) becoming a debtor in bankruptcy;

(ii) executing an assignment for the benefit of creditors;

(iii) seeking, consenting to, or acquiescing in the appointment of a trustee, receiver, or liquidator of that partner or of all or substantially all of that partner's property; or

(iv) failing, within 90 days after the appointment, to have vacated or stayed the appointment of a trustee, receiver, or liquidator of the partner or of all or substantially all of the partner's property obtained without the partner's consent or acquiescence, or failing within 90 days after the expiration of a stay to have the appointment vacated;

(7) in the case of a partner who is an individual:

(i) the partner's death;

(ii) the appointment of a guardian or general conservator for the partner; or

(iii) a judicial determination that the partner has otherwise become incapable of performing the partner's duties under the partnership agreement;

(8) in the case of a partner that is a trust or is acting as a partner by virtue of being a trustee of a trust, distribution of the trust's entire transferable interest in the partnership, but not merely by reason of the substitution of a successor trustee;

(9) in the case of a partner that is an estate or is acting as a partner by virtue of being a personal representative of an estate, distribution of the estate's entire transferable interest in the partnership, but not merely by reason of the substitution of a successor personal representative; or

(10) termination of a partner who is not an individual, partnership, corporation, trust, or estate.

SECTION 602. *Partner's Power to Dissociate; Wrongful Dissociation.*

(a) A partner has the power to dissociate at any time, rightfully or wrongfully, by express will pursuant to Section 601(1).

(b) A partner's dissociation is wrongful only if:

(1) it is in breach of an express provision of the partnership agreement; or

(2) in the case of a partnership for a definite term or particular undertaking, before the expiration of the term or the completion of the undertaking:

(i) the partner withdraws by express will, unless the withdrawal follows within 90 days after another partner's dissociation by death or otherwise under Section 601(6) through (10) or wrongful dissociation under this subsection;

(ii) the partner is expelled by judicial determination under Section 601(5);

(iii) the partner is dissociated by becoming a debtor in bankruptcy; or

(iv) in the case of a partner who is not an individual, trust other than a business trust, or estate, the partner is expelled or otherwise dissociated because it willfully dissolved or terminated.

(c) A partner who wrongfully dissociates is liable to the partnership and to the other partners for damages caused by the dissociation. The liability is in addition to any other obligation of the partner to the partnership or to the other partners.

SECTION 603. *Effect of Partner's Dissociation.*

(a) If a partner's dissociation results in a dissolution and winding up of the partnership business, [Article] 8 applies; otherwise, [Article] 7 applies.

(b) Upon a partner's dissociation:

(1) the partner's right to participate in the management and conduct of the partnership business terminates, except as otherwise provided in Section 803;

(2) the partner's duty of loyalty under Section 404(b)(3) terminates; and

(3) the partner's duty of loyalty under Section 404(b)(l) and (2) and duty of care under Section 404(c) continue only with regard to matters arising and events occurring before the partner's dissociation, unless the partner participates in winding up the partnership's business pursuant to Section 803.

[ARTICLE] 7
PARTNER'S DISSOCIATION WHEN BUSINESS NOT WOUND UP

Section 701.   Purchase of Dissociated Partner's Interest.

SECTION 701. Purchase of Dissociated Partner's Interest.

(a) If a partner is dissociated from a partnership without resulting in a dissolution and winding up of the partnership business under Section 801, the partnership shall cause the dissociated partner's interest in the partnership to be purchased for a buyout price determined pursuant to subsection (b).

(b) The buyout price of a dissociated partner's interest is the amount that would have been distributable to the dissociating partner under Section 807(b) if, on the date of dissociation, the assets of the partnership were sold at a price equal to the greater of the liquidation value or the value based on a sale of the entire business as a going concern without the dissociated partner and the partnership were wound up as of that date. Interest must be paid from the date of dissociation to the date of payment.

(c) Damages for wrongful dissociation under Section 602(b), and all other amounts owing, whether or not presently due, from the dissociated partner to the partnership, must be offset against the buyout price. Interest must be paid from the date the amount owed becomes due to the date of payment.

(d) A partnership shall indemnify a dissociated partner whose interest is being purchased against all partnership liabilities, whether incurred before or after the dissociation, except liabilities incurred by an act of the dissociated partner under Section 702.

(e) If no agreement for the purchase of a dissociated partner's interest is reached within 120 days after a written demand for payment, the partnership shall pay, or cause to be paid, in cash to the dissociated partner the amount the partnership estimates to be the buyout price and accrued interest, reduced by any offsets and accrued interest under subsection (c).

(f) If a deferred payment is authorized under subsection (h), the partnership may tender a written offer to pay the amount it estimates to be the buyout price and accrued interest, reduced by any offsets under subsection (c), stating the time of payment, the amount and type of security for payment, and the other terms and conditions of the obligation.

(g) The payment or tender required by subsection (e) or (f) must be accompanied by the following:

(1) a statement of partnership assets and liabilities as of the date of dissociation;

(2) the latest available partnership balance sheet and income statement, if any;

(3) an explanation of how the estimated amount of the payment was calculated; and

(4) written notice that the payment is in full satisfaction of the obligation to purchase unless, within 120 days after the written notice, the dissociated partner commences an action to determine the buyout price, any offsets under subsection (c), or other terms of the obligation to purchase.

(h) A partner who wrongfully dissociates before the expiration of a definite term or the completion of a particular undertaking is not entitled to payment of any portion of the buyout price until the expiration of the term or completion of the undertaking, unless the partner establishes to the satisfaction of the court that earlier payment will not cause undue hardship to the business of the partnership. A deferred payment must be adequately secured and bear interest.

(i) A dissociated partner may maintain an action against the partnership, pursuant to Section 405(b)(2)(ii), to determine the buyout price of that partner's interest, any offsets under subsection (c), or other terms of the obligation to purchase. The action must be commenced within 120 days after the partnership has tendered payment or an offer to pay or within one year after written demand for payment if no payment or offer to pay is tendered. The court shall determine the buyout price of the dissociated partner's interest, any offset due under subsection (c), and accrued interest, and enter judgment for any additional payment or refund. If deferred payment is authorized under subsection (h), the court shall also determine the security for payment and other terms of the obligation to purchase. The court may assess reasonable attorney's fees and the fees and expenses of appraisers or other experts for a party to the action, in amounts the court finds equitable, against a party that the court finds acted arbitrarily, vexatiously, or not in good faith. The finding may be based on the partnership's failure to tender payment or an offer to pay or to comply with subsection (g).

SECTION 702. Dissociated Partner's Power to Bind and Liability to Partnership.

(a) For two years after a partner dissociates without resulting in a dissolution and winding up of the partnership business, the partnership, including a surviving partnership under [Article] 9, is bound by an act of the dissociated partner which would have bound the partnership under Section 301 before dissociation only if at the time of entering into the transaction the other party:

(1) reasonably believed that the dissociated partner was then a partner;

(2) did not have notice of the partner's dissociation; and

(3) is not deemed to have had knowledge under Section 303(e) or notice under Section 704(c).

(b) A dissociated partner is liable to the partnership for any damage caused to the partnership arising from an obligation incurred by the dissociated partner after dissociation for which the partnership is liable under subsection (a).

SECTION 703. *Dissociated Partner's Liability to Other Persons.*

(a) A partner's dissociation does not of itself discharge the partner's liability for a partnership obligation incurred before dissociation. A dissociated partner is not liable for a partnership obligation incurred after dissociation, except as otherwise provided in subsection (b).

(b) A partner who dissociates without resulting in a dissolution and winding up of the partnership business is liable as a partner to the other party in a transaction entered into by the partnership, or a surviving partnership under [Article] 9, within two years after the partner's dissociation, only if at the time of entering into the transaction the other party:

(1) reasonably believed that the dissociated partner was then a partner;

(2) did not have notice of the partner's dissociation; and

(3) is not deemed to have had knowledge under Section 303(e) or notice under Section 704(c).

(c) By agreement with the partnership creditor and the partners continuing the business, a dissociated partner may be released from liability for a partnership obligation.

(d) A dissociated partner is released from liability for a partnership obligation if a partnership creditor, with notice of the partner's dissociation but without the partner's consent, agrees to a material alteration in the nature or time of payment of a partnership obligation.

SECTION 704. *Statement of Dissociation.*

(a) A dissociated partner or the partnership may file a statement of dissociation stating the name of the partnership and that the partner is dissociated from the partnership.

(b) A statement of dissociation is a limitation on the authority of a dissociated partner for the purposes of Section 303(d) and (e).

(c) For the purposes of Sections 702(a)(3) and 703(b)(3), a person not a partner is deemed to have notice of the dissociation 90 days after the statement of dissociation is filed.

SECTION 705. *Continued Use of Partnership Name.*

Continued use of a partnership name, or a dissociated partner's name as part thereof, by partners continuing the business does not of itself make the dissociated partner liable for an obligation of the partners or the partnership continuing the business.

[ARTICLE] 8
WINDING UP PARTNERSHIP BUSINESS

SECTION 801. *Events Causing Dissolution and Winding Up of Partnership Business.*

A partnership is dissolved, and its business must be wound up, only upon the occurrence of any of the following events:

(1) in a partnership at will, the partnership's having notice from a partner, other than a partner who is dissociated under Section 601(2) through (10), of that partner's express will to withdraw as a partner, or on a later date specified by the partner;

(2) in a partnership for a definite term or particular undertaking:

(i) the expiration of 90 days after a partner's dissociation by death or otherwise under Section 601(6) through (10) or wrongful dissociation under Section 602(b), unless before that time a majority in interest of the remaining partners, including partners who have rightfully dissociated pursuant to Section 602(b)(2)(i), agree to continue the partnership;

(ii) the express will of all of the partners to wind up the partnership business; or

(iii) the expiration of the term or the completion of the undertaking;

(3) an event agreed to in the partnership agreement resulting in the winding up of the partnership business;

(4) an event that makes it unlawful for all or substantially all of the business of the partnership to be continued, but a cure of illegality within 90 days after notice to the partnership of the event is effective retroactively to the date of the event for purposes of this section;

(5) on application by a partner, a judicial determination that:

(i) the economic purpose of the partnership is likely to be unreasonably frustrated;

(ii) another partner has engaged in conduct relating to the partnership business which makes it not reasonably practicable to carry on the business in partnership with that partner; or

(iii) it is not otherwise reasonably practicable to carry on the partnership business in conformity with the partnership agreement; or

(6) on application by a transferee of a partner's transferable interest, a judicial determination that it is equitable to wind up the partnership business:

(i) after the expiration of the term or completion of the undertaking, if the partnership was for a definite term or particular undertaking at the time of the transfer or entry of the charging order that gave rise to the transfer; or

(ii) at any time, if the partnership was a partnership at will at the time of the transfer or entry of the charging order that gave rise to the transfer.

SECTION 802. Partnership Continues After Dissolution

(a) Subject to subsection (b), a partnership continues after dissolution only for the purpose of winding up its business. The partnership is terminated when the winding up of its business is completed.

(b) At any time after the dissolution of a partnership and before the winding up of its business is completed, all of the partners, including any dissociating partner other than a wrongfully dissociating partner, may waive the right to have the partnership's business wound up and the partnership terminated. In that event:

(1) the partnership resumes carrying on its business as if dissolution had never occurred, and any liability incurred by the partnership or a partner after the dissolution and before the waiver is determined as if dissolution had never occurred; and

(2) the rights of a third party accruing under Section 804(1) or arising out of conduct in reliance on the dissolution before the third party knew or received a notification of the waiver may not be adversely affected.

SECTION 803. Right to Wind Up Partnership Business.

(a) After dissolution, a partner who has not wrongfully dissociated may participate in winding up the partnership's business, but on application of any partner, partner's legal representative, or transferee, the [designate the appropriate court], for good cause shown, may order judicial supervision of the winding up.

(b) The legal representative of the last surviving partner may wind up a partnership's business.

(c) A person winding up a partnership's business may preserve the partnership business or property as a going concern for a reasonable time, prosecute and defend actions and proceedings, whether civil, criminal, or administrative, settle and close the partnership's business, dispose of and transfer the partnership's property, discharge the partnership's liabilities, distribute the assets of the partnership pursuant to Section 807, settle disputes by mediation or arbitration, and perform other necessary acts.

SECTION 804. Partner's Power to Bind Partnership After Dissolution.

Subject to Section 805, a partnership is bound by a partner's act after dissolution that:

(1) is appropriate for winding up the partnership business; or

(2) would have bound the partnership under Section 301 before dissolution, if the other party to the transaction did not have notice of the dissolution.

SECTION 805. Statement of Dissolution.

(a) After dissolution, a partner who has not wrongfully dissociated may file a statement of dissolution stating the name of the partnership and that the partnership has dissolved and is winding up its business.

(b) A statement of dissolution cancels a filed statement of partnership authority for the purposes of Section 303(d) and is a limitation on authority for the purposes of Section 303(e).

(c) For the purposes of Sections 301 and 804, a person not a partner is deemed to have notice of the dissolution and the limitation on the partners' authority as a result of the statement of dissolution 90 days after it is filed.

(d) After filing and, if appropriate, recording a statement of dissolution, a dissolved partnership may file and, if appropriate, record a statement of partnership authority which will operate with respect to a person not a partner as provided in Section 303(d) and (e) in any transaction, whether or not the transaction is appropriate for winding up the partnership business.

SECTION 806. Partner's Liability to Other Partners after Dissolution.

(a) Except as otherwise provided in subsection (b), after dissolution a partner is liable to the other partners for the partner's share of any partnership liability incurred under Section 804.

(b) A partner who, with knowledge of the dissolution, incurs a partnership liability under Section 804(2) by an act that is not appropriate for winding up the partnership business is liable to the partnership for any damage caused to the partnership arising from the liability.

SECTION 807. Settlement of Accounts and Contributions Among Partners.

(a) In winding up a partnership's business, the assets of the partnership, including the contributions of the partners required by this section, must be applied to discharge its obligations to creditors, including, to the extent permitted by law, partners who are creditors. Any surplus must be applied to pay in cash the net amount distributable to partners in accordance with their right to distributions under subsection (b).

(b) Each partner is entitled to a settlement of all partnership accounts upon winding up the partnership business. In settling accounts among the partners, the profits and losses that result from the liquidation of the partnership assets must be credited and charged to the partners' accounts. The partnership shall make a distribution to a partner in an amount equal to any excess of the credits over the charges in the partner's account. A partner shall contribute to the partnership an amount equal to any excess of the charges over the credits in the partner's account.

(c) If a partner fails to contribute, all of the other partners shall contribute, in the proportions in which those partners share partnership losses, the additional amount necessary to satisfy the partnership obligations. A partner or partner's legal representative may recover from the other partners any contributions the partner makes to the extent the amount contributed exceeds that partner's share of the partnership obligations.

(d) After the settlement of accounts, each partner shall contribute, in the proportion in which the partner shares partnership losses, the amount necessary to satisfy partnership obligations that were not known at the time of the settlement.

(e) The estate of a deceased partner is liable for the partner's obligation to contribute to the partnership.

(f) An assignee for the benefit of creditors of a partnership or a partner, or a person appointed by a court to represent creditors of a partnership or a partner, may enforce a partner's obligation to contribute to the partnership.

[ARTICLE] 9
CONVERSIONS AND MERGERS

Section 901. Definitions.
Section 902. Conversion of Partnership to Limited Partnership.
Section 903. Conversion of Limited Partnership to Partnership.
Section 904. Effect of Conversion; Entity Unchanged.
Section 905. Merger of Partnerships.
Section 906. Effect of Merger.
Section 907. Statement of Merger.
Section 908. Nonexclusive.

SECTION 901. *Definitions.*

In this [article]:

(1) "General partner" means a partner in a partnership and a general partner in a limited partnership.

(2) "Limited partner" means a limited partner in a limited partnership.

(3) "Limited partnership" means a limited partnership created under the [State Limited Partnership Act], predecessor law, or comparable law of another jurisdiction.

(4) "Partner" includes both a general partner and a limited partner.

SECTION 902. *Conversion of Partnership to Limited Partnership.*

(a) A partnership may be converted to a limited partnership pursuant to this section.

(b) The terms and conditions of a conversion of a partnership to a limited partnership must be approved by all of the partners or by a number or percentage specified for conversion in the partnership agreement.

(c) After the conversion is approved by the partners, the partnership shall file a certificate of limited partnership in the jurisdiction in which the limited partnership is to be formed. The certificate must include:

(1) a statement that the partnership was converted to a limited partnership from a partnership;

(2) its former name; and

(3) a statement of the number of votes cast by the partners for and against the conversion and, if the vote is less than unanimous, the number or percentage required to approve the conversion under the partnership agreement.

(d) The conversion takes effect when the certificate of limited partnership is filed or at any later date specified in the certificate.

(e) A general partner who becomes a limited partner as a result of the conversion remains liable as a general partner for an obligation incurred by the partnership before the conversion takes effect. If the other party to a transaction with the limited partnership reasonably believes when entering the transaction that the limited partner is a general partner, the limited partner is liable for an obligation incurred by the limited partnership within 90 days after the conversion takes effect. The limited partner's liability for all other obligations of the limited partnership incurred after the conversion takes effect is that of a limited partner as provided in the [State Limited Partnership Act].

SECTION 903. *Conversion of Limited Partnership to Partnership.*

(a) A limited partnership may be converted to a partnership pursuant to this section.

(b) Notwithstanding a provision to the contrary in a limited partnership agreement, the terms and conditions of a conversion of a limited partnership to a partnership must be approved by all of the partners.

(c) After the conversion is approved by the partners, the limited partnership shall cancel its certificate of limited partnership.

(d) The conversion takes effect when the certificate of limited partnership is canceled.

(e) A limited partner who becomes a general partner as a result of the conversion remains liable only as a limited partner for an obligation incurred by the limited partnership before the conversion takes effect. The partner is liable as a general partner for an obligation of the partnership incurred after the conversion takes effect.

SECTION 904. Effect of Conversion; Entity Unchanged.

(a) A partnership or limited partnership that has been converted pursuant to this [article] is for all purposes the same entity that existed before the conversion.

(b) When a conversion takes effect:

(1) all property owned by the converting partnership or limited partnership remains vested in the converted entity;

(2) all obligations of the converting partnership or limited partnership continue as obligations of the converted entity; and

(3) an action or proceeding pending against the converting partnership or limited partnership may be continued as if the conversion had not occurred.

SECTION 905. Merger of Partnerships.

(a) Pursuant to a plan of merger approved as provided in subsection (c), a partnership may be merged with one or more partnerships or limited partnerships.

(b) The plan of merger must set forth:

(1) the name of each partnership or limited partnership that is a party to the merger;

(2) the name of the surviving entity into which the other partnerships or limited partnerships will merge;

(3) whether the surviving entity is a partnership or a limited partnership and the status of each partner;

(4) the terms and conditions of the merger;

(5) the manner and basis of converting the interests of each party to the merger into interests or obligations of the surviving entity, or into money or other property in whole or part; and

(6) the street address of the surviving entity's chief executive office.

(c) The plan of merger must be approved:

(1) in the case of a partnership that is a party to the merger, by all of the partners, or a number or percentage specified for merger in the partnership agreement; and

(2) in the case of a limited partnership that is a party to the merger, by the vote required for approval of a merger by the law of the State or foreign jurisdiction in which the limited partnership is organized and, in the absence of such a specifically applicable law, by all of the partners, notwithstanding a provision to the contrary in the partnership agreement.

(d) After a plan of merger is approved and before the merger takes effect, the plan may be amended or abandoned as provided in the plan.

(e) The merger takes effect on the later of:

(1) the approval of the plan of merger by all parties to the merger, as provided in subsection (c);

(2) the filing of all documents required by law to be filed as a condition to the effectiveness of the merger; or

(3) any effective date specified in the plan of merger.

SECTION 906. Effect of Merger.

(a) When a merger takes effect:

(1) the separate existence of every partnership or limited partnership that is a party to the merger, other than the surviving entity, ceases;

(2) all property owned by each of the merged partnerships or limited partnerships vests in the surviving entity;

(3) all obligations of every partnership or limited partnership that is a party to the merger become the obligations of the surviving entity; and

(4) an action or proceeding pending against a partnership or limited partnership that is a party to the merger may be continued as if the merger had not occurred, or the surviving entity may be substituted as a party to the action or proceeding.

(b) The [Secretary of State] of this State is the agent for service of process in an action or proceeding against a surviving foreign partnership or limited partnership to enforce an obligation of a domestic partnership or limited partnership that is a party to a merger. The surviving entity shall promptly notify the [Secretary of State] of the mailing address of its chief executive office and of any change of address. Upon receipt of process, the [Secretary of State] shall mail a copy of the process to the surviving foreign partnership or limited partnership.

(c) A partner of the surviving partnership or limited partnership is liable for:

(1) all obligations of a party to the merger for which the partner was personally liable before the merger;

(2) all other obligations of the surviving entity incurred before the merger by a party to the merger, but those obligations may be satisfied only out of property of the entity; and

(3) all obligations of the surviving entity incurred after the merger takes effect, but those obligations may be satisfied only out of property of the entity if the partner is a limited partner.

(d) If the obligations incurred before the merger by a party to the merger are not satisfied out of the property of the surviving partnership or limited partnership, the general partners of that party immediately before the effective date of the merger shall contribute the amount necessary to satisfy that party's obligations to the surviving entity, in the manner provided in Section 807 or in the [Limited Partnership Act] of the jurisdiction in which the party was formed, as the case may be, as if the merged party were dissolved.

(e) A partner of a party to a merger who does not become a partner of the surviving partnership or limited partnership is dissociated from the entity, of which that partner was a partner, as of the date the merger takes effect. The surviving entity shall cause the partner's interest in the entity to be purchased under Section 701 or another statute specifically applicable to that partner's interest with respect to a merger. The surviving entity is bound under Section 702 by an act of a general partner dissociated under this subsection, and the partner is liable under Section 703 for transactions entered into by the surviving entity after the merger takes effect.

SECTION 907. Statement of Merger.

(a) After a merger, the surviving partnership or limited partnership may file a statement that one or more partnerships or limited partnerships have merged into the surviving entity.

(b) A statement of merger must contain:

(1) the name of each partnership or limited partnership that is a party to the merger;

(2) the name of the surviving entity into which the other partnerships or limited partnership were merged;

(3) the street address of the surviving entity's chief executive office and of an office in this State, if any; and

(4) whether the surviving entity is a partnership or a limited partnership.

(c) Except as otherwise provided in subsection (d), for the purposes of Section 302, property of the surviving partnership or limited partnership which before the merger was held in the name of another party to the merger is property held in the name of the surviving entity upon filing a statement of merger.

(d) For the purposes of Section 302, real property of the surviving partnership or limited partnership which before the merger was held in the name of another party to the merger is property held in the name of the surviving entity upon recording a certified copy of the statement of merger in the office for recording transfers of that real property.

(e) A filed and, if appropriate, recorded statement of merger, executed and declared to be accurate pursuant to Section 105(c), stating the name of a partnership or limited partnership that is a party to the merger in whose name property was held before the merger and the name of the surviving entity, but not containing all of the other information required by subsection (b), operates with respect to the partnerships or limited partnerships named to the extent provided in subsections (c) and (d).

SECTION 908. Nonexclusive.

This [article] is not exclusive. Partnerships or limited partnerships may be converted or merged in any other manner provided by law.

[ARTICLE] 10
MISCELLANEOUS PROVISIONS

Section 1001. Uniformity of Application and Construction.

Section 1002. Short Title.

Section 1003. Severability.

Section 1004. Effective Date.

Section 1005. Repeals.

Section 1006. Applicability.

Section 1007. Savings Clause.

SECTION 1001. Uniformity of Application and Construction.

This [Act] shall be applied and construed to effectuate its general purpose to make uniform the law with respect to the subject of this [Act] among States enacting it.

SECTION 1002. Short Title.

This [Act] may be cited as the Uniform Partnership Act (1994).

SECTION 1003. Severability Clause.

If any provision of this [Act] or its application to any person or circumstance is held invalid, the invalidity does not affect other provisions or applications of this [Act] which can be given effect without the invalid provision or application, and to this end the provisions of this [Act] are severable.

SECTION 1004. Effective Date.

This [Act] takes effect …

SECTION 1005. Repeals.

Effective January 1, 199__ , the following acts and parts of acts are repealed: [the State Partnership Act as amended and in effect immediately before the effective date of this Act].

SECTION 1006. Applicability.

(a) Before January 1, 199__ , this [Act] governs only a partnership formed:

(1) after the effective date of this [Act], unless that partnership is continuing the business of a dissolved partnership under [Section 41] of the prior Uniform Partnership Act]; and

(2) before the effective date of this [Act], that elects, as provided by subsection (c), to be governed by this [Act].

(b) After January 1, 199__ , this [Act] governs all partnerships.

(c) Before January 1, 199___ , a partnership voluntarily may elect, in the manner provided in its partnership agreement or by law for amending the partnership agreement, to be governed by this [Act]. The provisions of this [Act] relating to the liability of the partnership's partners to third parties apply to limit those partner's liability to a third party who had done business with the partnership within one year preceding the partnership's election to be governed by this [Act], only if the third party knows or has received a notification of the partnership's election to be governed by this [Act].

SECTION 1007. Savings Clause.

This [Act] does not affect an action or proceeding commenced or right accrued before this [Act] takes effect.

APPENDIX D

UNIFORM LIMITED PARTNERSHIP ACT (1976) WITH 1985 AMENDMENTS

The Uniform Limited Partnership Act has been reprinted through the permission of the National Conference of Commissioners on Uniform State Laws, and copies of the Act may be ordered from them at a nominal cost at 676 North St. Clair Street, Suite 1700, Chicago, Illinois 60611; (312) 915-0195.

ARTICLE 9
Foreign Limited Partnerships

ARTICLE 10
Derivative Actions

ARTICLE 11
Miscellaneous

ARTICLE 1
GENERAL PROVISIONS

§ 101. Definitions

As used in this [Act], unless the context otherwise requires:

(1) "Certificate of limited partnership" means the certificate referred to in Section 201, and the certificate as amended or restated.

(2) "Contribution" means any cash, property, services rendered, or a promissory note or other binding obligation to contribute cash or property or to perform services, which a partner contributes to a limited partnership in his capacity as a partner.

(3) "Event of withdrawal of a general partner" means an event that causes a person to cease to be a general partner as provided in Section 402.

(4) "Foreign limited partnership" means a partnership formed under the laws of any state other than this State and having as partners one or more general partners and one or more limited partners.

(5) "General partner" means a person who has been admitted to a limited partnership as a general partner in accordance with the partnership agreement and named in the certificate of limited partnership as a general partner.

(6) "Limited partner" means a person who has been admitted to a limited partnership as a limited partner in accordance with the partnership agreement.

(7) "Limited partnership" and "domestic limited partnership" mean a partnership formed by two or more persons under the laws of this State and having one or more general partners and one or more limited partners.

(8) "Partner" means a limited or general partner.

(9) "Partnership agreement" means any valid agreement, written or oral, of the partners as to the affairs of a limited partnership and the conduct of its business.

(10) "Partnership interest" means a partner's share of the profits and losses of a limited partnership and the right to receive distributions of partnership assets.

(11) "Person" means a natural person, partnership, limited partnership (domestic or foreign), trust, estate, association, or corporation.

(12) "State" means a state, territory, or possession of the United States, the District of Columbia, or the Commonwealth of Puerto Rico.

Comment   The definitions in this section clarify a number of uncertainties in the law existing prior to the 1976 Act, and also make certain changes in such prior law. The 1985 Act makes very few additional changes in Section 101.

Contribution: this definition makes it clear that a present contribution of services and a promise to make a future payment of cash, contribution of property or performance of services are permissible forms for a contribution. Section 502 of the 1985 Act provides that a limited partner's promise to make a contribution is enforceable only when set out in a writing signed by the limited partner. (This result is not dissimilar from that under the 1976 Act, which required all promises of future contributions to be described in the certificate of limited partnership, which was to be signed by, among others, the partners making such promises.) The property or services contributed presently or promised to be contributed in the future must be accorded a value in the partnership agreement or the partnership records required to be kept pursuant to Section 105 and, in the case of a promise, that value may determine the liability of a partner who fails to honor his agreement (Section 502). Section 3 of the 1916 Act did not permit a limited partner's contribution to be in the form of services, although that inhibition did not apply to general partners.

Foreign limited partnership: the Act only deals with foreign limited partnerships formed under the laws of another "state" of the United States (see subdivision 12 of Section 101), and any adopting state that desires to deal by statute with the status of entities formed under the laws of foreign countries must make appropriate changes throughout the Act. The exclusion of such entities from the Act was not intended to suggest that their "limited partners" should not be accorded limited liability by the courts of a state adopting the Act. That question would be resolved by the choice-of-law rules of the forum state.

General partner: this definition recognizes the separate functions of the partnership agreement and the certificate of limited partnership. The partnership agreement establishes the basic grant of management power to the persons named as general partners; but because of the passive role played by the limited partners, the separate, formal step of memorializing that grant of power in the certificate of limited partnership has been preserved to emphasize its importance and to provide notice of the identity of the partnership's general partners to persons dealing with the partnership.

Limited partner: unlike the definition of general partners, this definition provides for admission of limited partners through the partnership agreement alone and does not require identification of any limited partner in the certificate of limited partnership (Section 201). Under the 1916 and the 1976 Acts, being named as a limited partner in the certificate of limited partnership was a statutory requirement and, in most if not all cases, probably also a prerequisite to limited partner status. By eliminating the requirement that the certificate of limited partnership contain the name, address, and capital contribution of each limited partner, the 1985 Act all but eliminates any risk that a person intended to be a limited partner may be exposed to liability as a general partner as a result of the inadvertent omission of any of that information from the certificate of limited partnership, and also dispenses with the need to amend the certificate of limited partnership upon the admission or withdrawal of, transfer of an interest by, or change in the address or capital contribution of, any limited partner.

Partnership agreement: the 1916 Act did not refer to the partnership agreement, assuming that all important matters affecting limited partners would be set forth in the certificate of limited partnership. Under modern practice, however, it has been common for the partners to enter into a comprehensive partnership agreement, only part of which was required to be included or summarized in the certificate of limited partnership. As reflected in Section 201 of the 1985 Act, the certificate of limited partnership is confined principally to matters respecting the partnership itself and the identity of general partners, and other important issues are left to the partnership agreement. Most of the information formerly provided by, but no longer required to be included in, the certificate of limited partnership is now required to be kept in the partnership records (Section 105).

Partnership interest: this definition first appeared in the 1976 Act and is intended to define what it is that is transferred when a partnership interest is assigned.

§ 102. Name

The name of each limited partnership as set forth in its certificate of limited partnership:

(1) shall contain without abbreviation the words "limited partnership";

(2) may not contain the name of a limited partner unless (i) it is also the name of a general partner or the corporate name of a corporate general partner, or (ii) the business of the limited partnership had been carried on under that name before the admission of that limited partner;

(3) may not be the same as, or deceptively similar to, the name of any corporation or limited partnership organized under the laws of this State or licensed or registered as a foreign corporation or limited partnership in this State; and

(4) may not contain the following words [here insert prohibited words].

Comment Subdivision (2) of Section 102 has been carried over from Section 5 of the 1916 Act with certain editorial changes. The remainder of Section 102 first appeared in the 1976 Act and primarily reflects the intention to integrate the registration of limited partnership names with that of corporate names. Accordingly, Section 201 provides for central, state-wide filing of certificates of limited partnership, and subdivisions (3) and (4) of Section 102 contain standards to be applied by the filing officer in determining whether the certificate should be filed. Subdivision (1) requires that the proper name of a limited partnership contain the words "limited partnership" in full. Subdivision (3) of the 1976 Act has been deleted, to reflect the deletion from Section 201 of any requirement that the certificate of limited partnership describe the partnership's purposes or the character of its business.

§ 103. Reservation of Name

(a) The exclusive right to the use of a name may be reserved by:

(1) any person intending to organize a limited partnership under this [Act] and to adopt that name;

(2) any domestic limited partnership or any foreign limited partnership registered in this State which, in either case, intends to adopt that name;

(3) any foreign limited partnership intending to register in this State and adopt that name; and

(4) any person intending to organize a foreign limited partnership and intending to have it register in this State and adopt that name.

(b) The reservation shall be made by filing with the Secretary of State an application, executed by the applicant, to reserve a specified name. If the Secretary of State finds that the name is available for use by a domestic or foreign limited partnership, he [or she] shall reserve the name for the exclusive use of the applicant for a period of 120 days. Once having so reserved a name, the same applicant may not again reserve the same name until more than 60 days after the expiration of the last 120-day period for which that applicant reserved that name. The right to the exclusive use of a reserved name may be transferred to any other person by filing in the office of the Secretary of State a notice of the transfer, executed by the applicant for whom the name was reserved and specifying the name and address of the transferee.

Comment   Section 103 first appeared in the 1976 Act. The 1916 Act did not provide for registration of names.

§ 104. Specified Office and Agent

Each limited partnership shall continuously maintain in this State:

(1) an office, which may but need not be a place of its business in this State, at which shall be kept the records required by Section 105 to be maintained; and

(2) an agent for service of process on the limited partnership, which agent must be an individual resident of this State, a domestic corporation, or a foreign corporation authorized to do business in this State.

Comment   Section 104 first appeared in the 1976 Act. It requires that a limited partnership have certain minimum contacts with its State of organization, i.e., an office at which the constitutive documents and basic financial information is kept and an agent for service of process.

§ 105. Records to be Kept

(a) Each limited partnership shall keep at the office referred to in Section 104(1) the following:

(1) a current list of the full name and last known business address of each partner, separately identifying the general partners (in alphabetical order) and the limited partners (in alphabetical order);

(2) a copy of the certificate of limited partnership and all certificates of amendment thereto, together with executed copies of any powers of attorney pursuant to which any certificate has been executed;

(3) copies of the limited partnership's federal, state and local income tax returns and reports, if any, for the three most recent years;

(4) copies of any then effective written partnership agreements and of any financial statements of the limited partnership for the three most recent years; and

(5) unless contained in a written partnership agreement, a writing setting out:

(i) the amount of cash and a description and statement of the agreed value of the other property or services contributed by each partner and which each partner has agreed to contribute;

(ii) the times at which or events on the happening of which any additional contributions agreed to be made by each partner are to be made;

(iii) any right of a partner to receive, or of a general partner to make, distributions to a partner which include a return of all or any part of the partner's contribution; and

(iv) any events upon the happening of which the limited partnership is to be dissolved and its affairs wound up.

(b) Records kept under this section are subject to inspection and copying at the reasonable request and at the expense of any partner during ordinary business hours.

Comment   Section 105 first appeared in the 1976 Act. In view of the passive nature of the limited partner's position, it has been widely felt that limited partners are entitled to access to certain basic documents and information, including the certificate of limited partnership, any partnership agreement and a writing setting out certain important matters which, under the 1916 and 1976 Acts, were required to be set out in the certificate of limited partnership. In view of the great diversity among limited partnerships, it was thought inappropriate to require a standard form of financial report, and Section 105 does no more than require retention of tax returns and any other financial statements that are prepared. The names and addresses of the general partners are made available to the general public in the certificate of limited partnership.

§ 106. Nature of Business

A limited partnership may carry on any business that a partnership without limited partners may carry on except [here designate prohibited activities].

Comment   Section 106 is identical to Section 3 of the 1916 Act. Many states require that certain regulated industries, such as banking, may be carried on only by entities organized pursuant to special statutes, and it is contemplated that the prohibited activities would be confined to the matters covered by those statutes.

§ 107. Business Transactions of Partner with Partnership

Except as provided in the partnership agreement, a partner may lend money to and transact other business with the limited partnership and, subject to other applicable law, has the same rights and obligations with respect thereto as a person who is not a partner.

Comment   Section 107 makes a number of important changes in Section 13 of the 1916 Act. Section 13, in effect, created a special fraudulent conveyance provision applicable to the making of secured loans by limited partners and the repayment by limited partnerships of loans from limited partners. Section 107 leaves that question to a state's general fraudulent conveyance statute. In addition, Section 107 eliminates the prohibition in Section 13 against a general partner's sharing pro rata with general creditors in the case of an unsecured loan. Of course, other doctrines developed under bankruptcy and insolvency laws may require the subordination of loans by partners under appropriate circumstances.

ARTICLE 2
FORMATION; CERTIFICATE OF LIMITED PARTNERSHIP

§ 201. Certificate of Limited Partnership

(a) In order to form a limited partnership, a certificate of limited partnership must be executed and filed in the office of the Secretary of State. The certificate shall set forth:

(1) the name of the limited partnership;

(2) the address of the office and the name and address of the agent for service of process required to be maintained by Section 104;

(3) the name and the business address of each general partner;

(4) the latest date upon which the limited partnership is to dissolve; and

(5) any other matters the general partners determine to include therein.

(b) A limited partnership is formed at the time of the filing of the certificate of limited partnership in the office of the Secretary of State or at any later time specified in the certificate of limited partnership if, in either case, there has been substantial compliance with the requirements of this section.

Comment The 1985 Act requires far fewer matters to be set forth in the certificate of limited partnership than did Section 2 of the 1916 Act and Section 201 of the 1976 Act. This is in recognition of the fact that the partnership agreement, not the certificate of limited partnership, has become the authoritative and comprehensive document for most limited partnerships, and that creditors and potential creditors of the partnership do and should refer to the partnership agreement and to other information furnished to them directly by the partnership and by others, not to the certificate of limited partnership, to obtain facts concerning the capital and finances of the partnership and other matters of concern. Subparagraph (b), which is based upon the 1916 Act, has been retained to make it clear that existence of the limited partnership depends only upon compliance with this section. Its continued existence is not dependent upon compliance with other provisions of this Act.

§ 202. Amendment to Certificate

(a) A certificate of limited partnership is amended by filing a certificate of amendment thereto in the office of the Secretary of State. The certificate shall set forth:

(1) the name of the limited partnership;

(2) the date of filing the certificate; and

(3) the amendment to the certificate.

(b) Within 30 days after the happening of any of the following events, an amendment to a certificate of limited partnership reflecting the occurrence of the event or events shall be filed:

(1) the admission of a new general partner;

(2) the withdrawal of a general partner; or

(3) the continuation of the business under Section 801 after an event of withdrawal of a general partner.

(c) A general partner who becomes aware that any statement in a certificate of limited partnership was false when made or that any arrangements or other facts described have changed, making the certificate inaccurate in any respect, shall promptly amend the certificate.

(d) A certificate of limited partnership may be amended at any time for any other proper purpose the general partners determine.

(e) No person has any liability because an amendment to a certificate of limited partnership has not been filed to reflect the occurrence of any event referred to in subsection (b) of this section if the amendment is filed within the 30-day period specified in subsection (b).

(f) A restated certificate of limited partnership may be executed and filed in the same manner as a certificate of amendment.

Comment Section 202 of the 1976 Act made substantial changes in Section 24 of the 1916 Act. Further changes in this section are made by the 1985 Act. Paragraph (b) lists the basic events—the addition or withdrawal of a general partner—that are so central to the function of the certificate of limited partnership that they require prompt amendment. With the elimination of the requirement that the certificate of limited partnership include the names of all limited partners and the amount and character of all capital contributions, the requirement of the 1916 and 1976 Acts that the certificate be amended upon the admission or withdrawal of limited partners or on any change in the partnership capital must also be eliminated. This change should greatly reduce the frequency and complexity of amendments to the certificate of limited partnership. Paragraph (c) makes it clear, as it was not clear under Section 24(2)(g) of the 1916 Act, that the certificate of limited partnership is intended to be an accurate description of the facts to which it relates at all times and does not speak merely as of the date it is executed.

Paragraph (e) provides a "safe harbor" against claims of creditors or others who assert that they have been misled by the failure to amend the certificate of limited partnership to reflect changes in any of the important facts referred to in paragraph (b); if the certificate of limited partnership is amended within 30 days of the occurrence of the event, no creditor or other person can recover for damages sustained during the interim. Additional protection is afforded by the provisions of Section 304. The elimination of the requirement that the certificate of limited partnership identify all limited partners and their respective capital contributions may have rendered paragraph (e) an obsolete and unnecessary vestige. The principal, if not the sole, purpose of the paragraph (e) in the 1976 Act was to protect limited partners newly admitted to a partnership from being held liable as general partners when an amendment to the certificate identifying them as limited partners and describing their contributions was not filed contemporaneously with their admission to the partnership. Such liability cannot arise under the 1985 Act because such information is not required to be stated in the certificate. Nevertheless, the 1985 Act retains paragraph (e) because it is protective of partners, shielding them from liability to the extent its provisions apply, and does not create or impose any liability.

Paragraph (f) is added in the 1985 Act to provide explicit statutory recognition of the common practice of restating an amended certificate of limited partnership. While a limited partnership seeking to amend its certificate of limited partnership may do so by recording a restated certificate which incorporates the amendment, that is by no means the only purpose or function of a restated certificate, which may be filed for the sole purpose of restating in a single integrated instrument all the provisions of a limited partnership's certificate of limited partnership which are then in effect.

§ 203. Cancellation of Certificate

A certificate of limited partnership shall be cancelled upon the dissolution and the commencement of winding up of the partnership or at any other time there are no limited partners. A certificate of cancellation shall be filed in the office of the Secretary of State and set forth:

(1) the name of the limited partnership;

(2) the date of filing of its certificate of limited partnership;

(3) the reason for filing the certificate of cancellation;

(4) the effective date (which shall be a date certain) of cancellation if it is not to be effective upon the filing of the certificate; and

(5) any other information the general partners filing the certificate determine.

Comment   Section 203 changes Section 24 of the 1916 Act by making it clear that the certificate of cancellation should be filed upon the commencement of winding up of the limited partnership. Section 24 provided for cancellation "when the partnership is dissolved."

§ 204. Execution of Certificates

(a) Each certificate required by this Article to be filed in the office of the Secretary of State shall be executed in the following manner:

(1) an original certificate of limited partnership must be signed by all general partners;

(2) a certificate of amendment must be signed by at least one general partner and by each other general partner designated in the certificate as a new general partner; and

(3) a certificate of cancellation must be signed by all general partners.

(b) Any person may sign a certificate by an attorney-in-fact, but a power of attorney to sign a certificate relating to the admission of a general partner must specifically describe the admission.

(c) The execution of a certificate by a general partner constitutes an affirmation under the penalties of perjury that the facts stated therein are true.

Comment   Section 204 collects in one place the formal requirements for the execution of certificates which were set forth in Section 2 and 25 of the 1916 Act. Those sections required that each certificate be signed by all partners, and there developed an unnecessarily cumbersome practice of having each limited partner sign powers of attorney to authorize the general partners to execute certificates of amendment on their behalf. The 1976 Act, while simplifying the execution requirements, nevertheless required that an original certificate of limited partnership be signed by all partners and a certificate of amendment by all new partners being admitted to the limited partnership. However the certificate of limited partnership is no longer required to include the name or capital contribution of any limited partner. Therefore, while the 1985 Act still requires all general partners to sign the original certificate of limited partnership, no limited partner is required to sign any certificate. Certificates of amendment are required to be signed by only one general partner, and all general partners must sign certificates of cancellation. The requirement in the 1916 Act that all certificates be sworn was deleted in the 1976 and 1985 Acts as potentially an unfair trap for the unwary (see, e.g., Wisniewski v. Johnson, 223 Va. 141, 286 S.E.2d 223 [1982]); in its place, paragraph (c) now provides, as a matter of law, that the execution of a certificate by a general partner subjects him to the penalties of perjury for inaccuracies in the certificate.

§ 205. Execution by Judicial Act

If a person required by Section 204 to execute any certificate fails or refuses to do so, any other person who is adversely affected by the failure or refusal may petition the [designate the appropriate court] to direct the execution of the certificate. If the court finds that it is proper for the certificate to be executed and that any person so designated has failed or refused to execute the certificate, it shall order the Secretary of State to record an appropriate certificate.

Comment   Section 205 of the 1976 Act changed subdivisions (3) and (4) of Section 25 of the 1916 Act by confining the persons who have standing to seek judicial intervention to partners and to those assignees who were adversely affected by the failure or refusal of the appropriate persons to file a certificate of amendment or cancellation. Section 205 of the 1985 Act reverses that restriction, and provides that any person adversely affected by a failure or refusal to file any certificate (not only a certificate of cancellation or amendment) has standing to seek judicial intervention.

§ 206.   Filing in Office of Secretary of State

(a)   Two signed copies of the certificate of limited partnership and of any certificates of amendment or cancellation (or of any judicial decree of amendment or cancellation) shall be delivered to the Secretary of State. A person who executes a certificate as an agent or fiduciary need not exhibit evidence of his [or her] authority as a prerequisite to filing. Unless the Secretary of State finds that any certificate does not conform to law, upon receipt of all filing fees required by law he [or she] shall:

    (1)   endorse on each duplicate original the word "Filed" and the day, month, and year of the filing thereof;

    (2)   file one duplicate original in his [or her] office; and

    (3)   return the other duplicate original to the person who filed it or his [or her] representative.

(b)   Upon the filing of a certificate of amendment (or judicial decree of amendment) in the office of the Secretary of State, the certificate of limited partnership shall be amended as set forth therein, and upon the effective date of a certificate of cancellation (or a judicial decree thereof), the certificate of limited partnership is cancelled.

Comment   Section 206 first appeared in the 1976 Act. In addition to providing mechanics for the central filing system, the second sentence of this section does away with the requirement, formerly imposed by some local filing officers, that persons who have executed certificates under a power of attorney exhibit executed copies of the power of attorney itself. Paragraph (b) changes subdivision (5) of Section 25 of the 1916 Act by providing that certificates of cancellation are effective upon their effective date under Section 203.

§ 207.   Liability for False Statement in Certificate

If any certificate of limited partnership or certificate of amendment or cancellation contains a false statement, one who suffers loss by reliance on the statement may recover damages for the loss from:

    (1)   any person who executes the certificate, or causes another to execute it on his behalf, and knew, and any general partner who knew or should have known, the statement to be false at the time the certificate was executed; and

    (2)   any general partner who thereafter knows or should have known that any arrangement or other fact described in the certificate has changed, making the statement inaccurate in any respect within a sufficient time before the statement was relied upon reasonably to have enabled that general partner to cancel or amend the certificate, or to file a petition for its cancellation or amendment under Section 205.

Comment   Section 207 changes Section 6 of the 1916 Act by providing explicitly for the liability of persons who sign a certificate as agent under a power of attorney and by confining the obligation to amend a certificate of limited partnership in light of future events to general partners.

§ 208.   Scope of Notice

The fact that a certificate of limited partnership is on file in the office of the Secretary of State is notice that the partnership is a limited partnership and the persons designated therein as general partners are general partners, but it is not notice of any other fact.

Comment   Section 208 first appeared in the 1976 Act, and referred to the certificate's providing constructive notice of the status as limited partners of those so identified therein. The 1985 Act's deletion of any requirement that the certificate name limited partners requires that Section 208 be modified accordingly.

By stating that the filing of a certificate of limited partnership only results in notice of the general liability of the general partners, Section 208 obviates the concern that third parties may be held to have notice of special provisions set forth in the certificate. While this section is designed to preserve by implication the limited liability of limited partners, the implicit protection provided is not intended to change any liability of a limited partner which may be created by his action or inaction under the law of estoppel, agency, fraud or the like.

§ 209.   Delivery of Certificates to Limited Partners

Upon the return by the Secretary of State pursuant to Section 206 of a certificate marked "Filed," the general partners shall promptly deliver or mail a copy of the certificate of limited partnership and each certificate of amendment or cancellation to each limited partner unless the partnership agreement provides otherwise.

Comment This section first appeared in the 1976 Act.

ARTICLE 3
LIMITED PARTNERS

§ 301. Admission of Limited Partners

(a) A person becomes a limited partner:

(1) at the time the limited partnership is formed; or

(2) at any later time specified in the records of the limited partnership for becoming a limited partner.

(b) After the filing of a limited partnership's original certificate of limited partnership, a person may be admitted as an additional limited partner:

(1) in the case of a person acquiring a partnership interest directly from the limited partnership, upon compliance with the partnership agreement or, if the partnership agreement does not so provide, upon the written consent of all partners; and

(2) in the case of an assignee of a partnership interest of a partner who has the power, as provided in Section 704, to grant the assignee the right to become a limited partner, upon the exercise of that power and compliance with any conditions limiting the grant or exercise of the power.

Comment Section 301(a) is new; no counterpart was found in the 1916 or 1976 Acts. This section imposes on the partnership an obligation to maintain in its records the date each limited partner becomes a limited partner. Under the 1976 Act, one could not become a limited partner until an appropriate certificate reflecting his status as such was filed with the Secretary of State. Because the 1985 Act eliminates the need to name limited partners in the certificate of limited partnership, an alternative mechanism had to be established to evidence the fact and date of a limited partner's admission. The partnership records required to be maintained under Section 105 now serve that function, subject to the limitation that no person may become a limited partner before the partnership is formed (Section 201(b)).

Subdivision (1) of Section 301(b) adds to Section 8 of the 1916 Act an explicit recognition of the fact that unanimous consent of all partners is required for admission of new limited partners unless the partnership agreement provides otherwise. Subdivision (2) is derived from Section 19 of the 1916 Act but abandons the former terminology of "substituted limited partner."

§ 302. Voting

Subject to Section 303, the partnership agreement may grant to all or a specified group of the limited partners the right to vote (on a per capita or other basis) upon any matter.

Comment Section 302 first appeared in the 1976 Act, and must be read together with subdivision (b)(6) of Section 303. Although the 1916 Act did not speak specifically of the voting powers of limited partners, it was not uncommon for partnership agreements to grant such powers to limited partners. Section 302 is designed only to make it clear that the partnership agreement may grant such power to limited partners. If such powers are granted to limited partners beyond the "safe harbor" of subdivision (6) or (8) of Section 303(b), a court may (but of course need not) hold that, under the circumstances, the limited partners have participated in "control of the business" within the meaning of Section 303(a). Section 303(c) makes clear that the exercise of powers beyond the ambit of Section 303(b) is not ipso facto to be taken as taking part in the control of the business.

§ 303. Liability to Third Parties

(a) Except as provided in subsection (d), a limited partner is not liable for the obligations of a limited partnership unless he [or she] is also a general partner or, in addition to the exercise of his [or her] rights and powers as a limited partner, he [or she] participates in the control of the business. However, if the limited partner participates in the control of the business, he [or she] is liable only to persons who transact business with the limited partnership reasonably believing, based upon the limited partner's conduct, that the limited partner is a general partner.

(b) A limited partner does not participate in the control of the business within the meaning of subsection (a) solely by doing one or more of the following:

(1) being a contractor for or an agent or employee of the limited partnership or of a general partner or being an officer, director, or shareholder of a general partner that is a corporation;

(2) consulting with and advising a general partner with respect to the business of the limited partnership;

(3) acting as surety for the limited partnership or guaranteeing or assuming one or more specific obligations of the limited partnership;

(4) taking any action required or permitted by law to bring or pursue a derivative action in the right of the limited partnership;

(5) requesting or attending a meeting of partners;

(6) proposing, approving, or disapproving, by voting or otherwise, one of more of the following matters:

(i) the dissolution and winding up of the limited partnership;

(ii) the sale, exchange, lease, mortgage, pledge, or other transfer of all or substantially all of the assets of the limited partnership;

(iii) the incurrence of indebtedness by the limited partnership other than in the ordinary course of its business;

(iv) a change in the nature of the business;

(v) the admission or removal of a general partner;

(vi) the admission or removal of a limited partner;

(vii) a transaction involving an actual or potential conflict of interest between a general partner and the limited partnership or the limited partners;

(viii) an amendment to the partnership agreement or certificate of limited partnership; or

(ix) matters related to the business of the limited partnership not otherwise enumerated in this subsection (b), which the partnership agreement states in writing may be subject to the approval or disapproval of limited partners;

(7) winding up the limited partnership pursuant to Section 803; or

(8) exercising any right or power permitted to limited partners under this [Act] and not specifically enumerated in this subsection (b).

(c) The enumeration in subsection (b) does not mean that the possession or exercise of any other powers by a limited partner constitutes participation by him [or her] in the business of the limited partnership.

(d) A limited partner who knowingly permits his [or her] name to be used in the name of the limited partnership, except under circumstances permitted by Section 102(2), is liable to creditors who extend credit to the limited partnership without actual knowledge that the limited partner is not a general partner.

Comment Section 303 makes several important changes in Section 7 of the 1916 Act. The first sentence of Section 303(a) differs from the text of Section 7 of the 1916 Act in that it speaks of participating (rather than taking part) in the control of the business; this was done for the sake of consistency with the second sentence of Section 303(a), not to change the meaning of the text. It is intended that judicial decisions interpreting the phrase "takes part in the control of the business" under the prior uniform law will remain applicable to the extent that a different result is not called for by other provisions of Section 303 and other provisions of the Act. The second sentence of Section 303(a) reflects a wholly new concept in the 1976 Act that has been further modified in the 1985 Act. It was adopted partly because of the difficulty of determining when the "control" line has been overstepped, but also (and more importantly) because of a determination that it is not sound public policy to hold a limited partner who is not also a general partner liable for the obligations of the partnership except to persons who have done business with the limited partnership reasonably believing, based on the limited partner's conduct, that he is a general partner. Paragraph (b) is intended to provide a "safe harbor" by enumerating certain activities which a limited partner may carry on for the partnership without being deemed to have taken part in control of the business. This "safe harbor" list has been expanded beyond that set out in the 1976 Act to reflect case law and statutory developments and more clearly to assure that limited partners are not subjected to general liability where such liability is inappropriate. Paragraph (d) is derived from Section 5 of the 1916 Act, but adds a condition to the limited partner's liability the requirement that a limited partner must have knowingly permitted his name to be used in the name of the limited partnership.

§ 304. Person Erroneously Believing Himself [or Herself] Limited Partner

(a) Except as provided in subsection (b), a person who makes a contribution to a business enterprise and erroneously but in good faith believes that he [or she] has become a limited partner in the enterprise is not a general partner in the enterprise and is not bound by its obligations by reason of making the contribution, receiving distributions from the enterprise, or exercising any rights of a limited partner, if, on ascertaining the mistake, he [or she]:

(1) causes an appropriate certificate of limited partnership or a certificate of amendment to be executed and filed; or

(2) withdraws from future equity participation in the enterprise by executing and filing in the office of the Secretary of State a certificate declaring withdrawal under this section.

(b) A person who makes a contribution of the kind described in subsection (a) is liable as a general partner to any third party who transacts business with the enterprise (i) before the person withdraws and an appropriate certificate is filed to show withdrawal, or (ii) before an appropriate certificate is filed to show that he [or she] is not a general partner, but in either case only if the third party actually believed in good faith that the person was a general partner at the time of the transaction.

Comment Section 304 is derived from Section 11 of the 1916 Act. The "good faith" requirement has been added in the first sentence of Section 304(a). The provisions of subdivision (2) of Section 304(a) are intended to clarify an ambiguity in the prior law by providing that a person who chooses to withdraw from the enterprise in order to protect himself from liability is not required to renounce any of his then current interest in the enterprise so long as he has no further participation as an equity participant. Paragraph (b) preserves the liability of the equity participant prior to withdrawal by such person from the limited partnership or amendment to the certificate demonstrating that such person is not a general partner to any third party who has transacted business with the person believing in good faith that he was a general partner.

Evidence strongly suggests that Section 11 of the 1916 Act and Section 304 of the 1976 Act were rarely used, and one might expect that Section 304 of the 1985 Act may never have to be used. Section 11 of the 1916 Act and Section 304 of the 1976 Act could have been used by a person who invested in a limited partnership believing he would be a limited partner but who was not identified as a limited partner in the certificate of limited partnership. However, because the 1985 Act does not require limited partners to be named in the certificate, the only situation to which Section 304 would now appear to be applicable is one in which a person intending to be a limited partner was erroneously identified as a general partner in the certificate.

§ 305. Information

Each limited partner has the right to:

(1) inspect and copy any of the partnership records required to be maintained by Section 105; and

(2) obtain from the general partners from time to time upon reasonable demand (i) true and full information regarding the state of the business and financial condition of the limited partnership, (ii) promptly after becoming available, a copy of the limited partnership's federal, state, and local income tax returns for each year, and (iii) other information regarding the affairs of the limited partnership as is just and reasonable.

Comment   Section 305 changes and restates the rights of limited partners to information about the partnership formerly provided by Section 10 of the 1916 Act. Its importance has increased as a result of the 1985 Act's substituting the records of the partnership for the certificate of limited partnership as the place where certain categories of information are to be kept.

Section 305, which should be read together with Section 105(b), provides a mechanism for limited partners to obtain information about the partnership useful to them in making decisions concerning the partnership and their investments in it. Its purpose is not to provide a mechanism for competitors of the partnership or others having interests or agendas adverse to the partnership's to subvert the partnership's business. It is assumed that courts will protect limited partnerships from abuses and attempts to misuse Section 305 for improper purposes.

ARTICLE 4
GENERAL PARTNERS

§ 401. Admission of Additional General Partners

After the filing of a limited partnership's original certificate of limited partnership, additional general partners may be admitted as provided in writing in the partnership agreement or, if the partnership agreement does not provide in writing for the admission of additional general partners, with the written consent of all partners.

Comment   Section 401 is derived from, but represents a significant departure from, Section 9(1)(e) of the 1916 Act and Section 401 of the 1976 Act, which required, as a condition to the admission of an additional general partner, that all limited partners consent and that such consent specifically identify the general partner involved. Section 401 of the 1985 Act provides that the written partnership agreement determines the procedure for authorizing the admission of additional general partners, and that the written consent of all partners is required only when the partnership agreement fails to address the question.

§ 402. Events of Withdrawal

Except as approved by the specific written consent of all partners at the time, a person ceases to be a general partner of a limited partnership upon the happening of any of the following events:

(1) the general partner withdraws from the limited partnership as provided in Section 602;

(2) the general partner ceases to be a member of the limited partnership as provided in Section 702;

(3) the general partner is removed as a general partner in accordance with the partnership agreement;

(4) unless otherwise provided in writing in the partnership agreement, the general partner: (i) makes an assignment for the benefit of creditors; (ii) files a voluntary petition in bankruptcy; (iii) is adjudicated a bankrupt or insolvent; (iv) files a petition or answer seeking for himself [or herself] any reorganization, arrangement, composition, readjustment, liquidation, dissolution, or similar relief under any statute, law, or regulation; (v) files an answer or other pleading admitting or failing to contest the material allegations of a petition filed against him [or her] in any proceeding of this nature; or (vi) seeks, consents to, or acquiesces in the appointment of a trustee, receiver, or liquidator of the general partner or of all or any substantial part of his [or her] properties;

(5) unless otherwise provided in writing in the partnership agreement, [120] days after the commencement of any proceeding against the general partner seeking reorganization, arrangement, composition, readjustment, liquidation, dissolution, or similar relief under any statute, law, or regulation, the proceeding has not been dismissed, or if within [90] days after the appointment without his [or her]

consent or acquiescence of a trustee, receiver, or liquidator of the general partner or of all or any substantial part of his [or her] properties, the appointment is not vacated or stayed or within [90] days after the expiration of any such stay, the appointment is not vacated;

(6) in the case of a general partner who is a natural person,

(i) his [or her] death; or

(ii) the entry of an order by a court of competent jurisdiction adjudicating him [or her] incompetent to manage his [or her] person or his [or her] estate;

(7) in the case of a general partner who is acting as a general partner by virtue of being a trustee of a trust, the termination of the trust (but not merely the substitution of a new trustee);

(8) in the case of a general partner that is a separate partnership, the dissolution and commencement of winding up of the separate partnership;

(9) in the case of a general partner that is a corporation, the filing of a certificate of dissolution, or its equivalent, for the corporation or the revocation of its charter; or

(10) in the case of an estate, the distribution by the fiduciary of the estate's entire interest in the partnership.

Comment Section 402 expands considerably the provisions of Section 20 of the 1916 Act, which provided for dissolution in the event of the retirement, death or insanity of a general partner. Subdivisions (1), (2) and (3) recognize that the general partner's agency relationship is terminable at will, although it may result in a breach of the partnership agreement giving rise to an action for damages. Subdivisions (4) and (5) reflect a judgment that, unless the limited partners agree otherwise, they ought to have the power to rid themselves of a general partner who is in such dire financial straits that he is the subject of proceedings under the National Bankruptcy Code or a similar provision of law. Subdivisions (6) through (10) simply elaborate on the notion of death in the case of a general partner who is not a natural person. Subdivisions (4) and (5) differ from their counterparts in the 1976 Act, reflecting the policy underlying the 1985 revision of Section 201, that the partnership agreement, not the certificate of limited partnership, is the appropriate document for setting out most provisions relating to the respective powers, rights and obligations of the partners inter se. Although the partnership agreement need not be written, the 1985 Act provides that, to protect the partners from fraud, these and certain other particularly significant provisions must be set out in a written partnership agreement to be effective for the purposes described in the Act.

§ 403. General Powers and Liabilities

(a) Except as provided in this [Act] or in the partnership agreement, a general partner of a limited partnership has the rights and powers and is subject to the restrictions of a partner in a partnership without limited partners.

(b) Except as provided in this [Act], a general partner of a limited partnership has the liabilities of a partner in a partnership without limited partners to persons other than the partnership and the other partners. Except as provided in this [Act] or in the partnership agreement, a general partner of a limited partnership has the liabilities of a partner in a partnership without limited partners to the partnership and to the other partners.

Comment Section 403 is derived form Section 9(1) of the 1916 Act.

§ 404. Contributions by General Partner

A general partner of a limited partnership may make contributions to the partnership and share in the profits and losses of, and in distributions from, the limited partnership as a general partner. A general partner also may make contributions to and share in profits, losses, and distributions as a limited partner. A person who is both a general partner and a limited partner has the rights and powers, and is subject to the restrictions and liabilities, of a general partner and, except as provided in the partnership agreement, also has the powers, and is subject to the restrictions, of a limited partner to the extent of his [or her] participation in the partnership as a limited partner.

Comment Section 404 is derived from Section 12 of the 1916 Act and makes clear that the partnership agreement may provide that a general partner who is also a limited partner may exercise all of the powers of a limited partner.

§ 405. Voting

The partnership agreement may grant to all or certain identified general partners the right to vote (on a per capita or any other basis), separately or with all or any class of the limited partners, on any matter.

Comment Section 405 first appeared in the 1976 Act and is intended to make it clear that the Act does not require that the limited partners have any right to vote on matters as a separate class.

ARTICLE 5
FINANCE

§ 501. Form of Contribution

The contribution of a partner may be in cash, property, or services rendered, or a promissory note or other obligation to contribute cash or property or to perform services.

Comment As noted in the comment to Section 101, the explicit permission to make contributions of services expands Section 4 of the 1916 Act.

§ 502. Liability for Contribution

(a) A promise by a limited partner to contribute to the limited partnership is not enforceable unless set out in a writing signed by the limited partner.

(b) Except as provided in the partnership agreement, a partner is obligated to the limited partnership to perform any enforceable promise to contribute cash or property or to perform services, even if he [or she] is unable to perform because of death, disability, or any other reason. If a partner does not make the required contribution of property or services, he [or she] is obligated at the option of the limited partnership to contribute cash equal to that portion of the value, as stated in the partnership records required to be kept pursuant to Section 105, of the stated contribution which has not been made.

(c) Unless otherwise provided in the partnership agreement, the obligation of a partner to make a contribution or return money or other property paid or distributed in violation of this [Act] may be compromised only by consent of all partners. Notwithstanding the compromise, a creditor of a limited partnership who extends credit or otherwise acts in reliance on that obligation after the partner signs a writing which reflects the obligation and before the amendment or cancellation thereof to reflect the compromise, may enforce the original obligation.

Comment Section 502(a) is new; it has no counterpart in the 1916 or 1976 Act. Because, unlike the prior uniform acts, the 1985 Act does not require that promises to contribute cash, property, or services be described in the limited partnership certificate, to protect against fraud it requires instead that such important promises be in a signed writing.

Although Section 17(1) of the 1916 Act required a partner to fulfill his promise to make contributions, the addition of contributions in the form of a promise to render services means that a partner who is unable to perform those services because of death or disability as well as because of an intentional default is required to pay the cash value of the services unless the partnership agreement provides otherwise.

Subdivision (c) is derived from, but expands upon, Section 17(3) of the 1916 Act.

§ 503. Sharing of Profits and Losses

The profits and losses of a limited partnership shall be allocated among the partners, and among classes of partners, in the manner provided in writing in the partnership agreement. If the partnership agreement does not so provide in writing, profits and losses shall be allocated on the basis of the value, as stated in the partnership records required to be kept

pursuant to Section 105, of the contributions made by each partner to the extent they have been received by the partnership and have not been returned.

Comment Section 503 first appeared in the 1976 Act. The 1916 Act did not provide the basis on which partners would share profits and losses in the absence of agreement. The 1985 Act differs from its counterpart in the 1976 Act by requiring that, to be effective, the partnership agreement provisions concerning allocation of profits and losses be in writing, and by its reference to records required to be kept pursuant to Section 105, the latter reflecting the 1985 changes in Section 201.

§ 504. Sharing of Distributions

Distributions of cash or other assets of a limited partnership shall be allocated among the partners and among classes of partners in the manner provided in writing in the partnership agreement. If the partnership agreement does not so provide in writing, distributions shall be made on the basis of the value, as stated in the partnership records required to be kept pursuant to Section 105, of the contributions made by each partner to the extent they have been received by the partnership and have not been returned.

Comment Section 504 first appeared in the 1976 Act. The 1916 Act did not provide the basis on which partners would share distributions in the absence of agreement. Section 504 also differs from its counterpart in the 1976 Act by requiring that, to be effective, the partnership agreement provisions concerning allocation of distributions be in writing, and in its reference to records required to be kept pursuant to Section 105, the latter reflecting the 1985 changes in Section 201. This section also recognizes that partners may choose to share in distributions on a basis different from that on which they share in profits and losses.

ARTICLE 6
DISTRIBUTIONS AND WITHDRAWAL

§ 601. Interim Distributions

Except as provided in this Article, a partner is entitled to receive distributions from a limited partnership before his [or her] withdrawal from the limited partnership and before the dissolution and winding up thereof to the extent and at the times or upon the happening of the events specified in the partnership agreement.

Comment Section 601 first appeared in the 1976 Act. The 1976 Act provisions have been modified to reflect the 1985 changes made in Section 201.

§ 602. Withdrawal of General Partner

A general partner may withdraw from a limited partnership at any time by giving written notice to the other partners, but if the withdrawal violates the partnership agreement, the limited partnership may recover from the withdrawing general partner damages for breach of the partnership agreement and offset the damages against the amount otherwise distributable to him [or her].

Comment   Section 602 first appeared in the 1976 Act, but is generally derived from Section 38 of the Uniform Partnership Act.

§ 603. Withdrawal of Limited Partner

A limited partner may withdraw from a limited partnership at the time or upon the happening of events specified in writing in the partnership agreement. If the agreement does not specify in writing the time or the events upon the happening of which a limited partner may withdraw or a definite time for the dissolution and winding up of the limited partnership, a limited partner may withdraw upon not less than six months' prior written notice to each general partner at his [other] address on the books of the limited partnership at its office in this State.

Comment   Section 603 is derived from Section 16 of the 1916 Act. The 1976 Act provision has been modified to reflect the 1985 changes made in Section 201. This section additionally reflects the policy determination, also embodied in certain other sections of the 1985 Act, that to avoid fraud, agreements concerning certain matters of substantial importance to the partners will be enforceable only if in writing. If the partnership agreement does provide, in writing, whether a limited partner may withdraw and, if he may, when and on what terms and conditions, those provisions will control.

§ 604. Distribution Upon Withdrawal

Except as provided in this Article, upon withdrawal any withdrawing partner is entitled to receive any distribution to which he [or she] is entitled under the partnership agreement and, if not otherwise provided in the agreement, he [or she] is entitled to receive, within a reasonable time after withdrawal, the fair value of his [or her] interest in the limited partnership as of the date of withdrawal based upon his [or her] right to share in distributions from the limited partnership.

Comment   Section 604 first appeared in the 1976 Act. It fixes the distributive share of a withdrawing partner in the absence of an agreement among the partners.

§ 605. Distribution in Kind

Except as provided in writing in the partnership agreement, a partner, regardless of the nature of his [or her] contribution, has no right to demand and receive any distribution from a limited partnership in any form other than cash. Except as provided in writing in the partnership agreement, a partner may not be compelled to accept a distribution of any asset in kind from a limited partnership to the extent that the percentage of the asset distributed to him [or her] exceeds a percentage of that asset which is equal to the percentage in which he [or she] shares in distributions from the limited partnership.

Comment   The first sentence of Section 605 is derived from Section 16(3) of the 1916 Act; it also differs from its counterpart in the 1976 Act, reflecting the 1985 changes made in Section 201. The second sentence first appeared in the 1976 Act, and is intended to protect a limited partner (and the remaining partners) against a distribution in kind of more than his share of particular assets.

§ 606. Right to Distribution

At the time a partner becomes entitled to receive a distribution, he [or she] has the status of, and is entitled to all remedies available to, a creditor of the limited partnership with respect to the distribution.

Comment   Section 606 first appeared in the 1976 Act, and is intended to make it clear that the right of a partner to receive a distribution, as between the partners, is not subject to the equity risks of the enterprise. On the other hand, since partners entitled to distributions have creditor status, there did not seem to be a need for the extraordinary remedy of Section 16(4)(a) of the 1916 Act, which granted a limited partner the right to seek dissolution of the partnership if he was unsuccessful in demanding the return of his contribution. It is more appropriate for the partner to simply sue as an ordinary creditor and obtain a judgment.

§ 607. Limitations on Distribution

A partner may not receive a distribution from a limited partnership to the extent that, after giving effect to the distribution, all liabilities of the limited partnership, other than liabilities to partners on account of their partnership interests, exceed the fair value of the partnership assets.

Comment   Section 607 is derived from Section 16(1)(a) of the 1916 Act.

§ 608. Liability Upon Return of Contribution

(a) If a partner has received the return of any part of his [or her] contribution without violation of the partnership agreement or this [Act], he [or she] is liable to the limited partnership for a period of one year thereafter for the amount of the returned contribution, but only to the extent necessary to discharge the limited partnership's liabilities to creditors who extended credit to the limited partnership during the period the contribution was held by the partnership.

(b) If a partner has received the return of any part of his [or her] contribution in violation of the partnership agreement or this [Act], he [or she] is liable to the limited partnership for a period of six years thereafter for the amount of the contribution wrongfully returned.

(c) A partner receives a return of his [or her] contribution to the extent that a distribution to him [or her] reduces his [or her] share of the fair value of the net assets of the limited partnership below the value, as set forth in the partnership records required to be kept pursuant to Section 105, of his contribution which has not been distributed to him [or her].

Comment   Paragraph (a) is derived from Section 17(4) of the 1916 Act, but the one year statute of limitations has been added. Paragraph (b) is derived from Section 17(2)(b) of the 1916 Act but, again, a statute of limitations has been added.

Paragraph (c) first appeared in the 1976 Act. The provisions of former Section 17(2) that referred to the partner holding as "trustee" any money or specific property wrongfully returned to him have been eliminated. Paragraph (c) in the 1985 Act also differs from its counterpart in the 1976 Act to reflect the 1985 changes made in Sections 105 and 201.

ARTICLE 7
ASSIGNMENT OF PARTNERSHIP INTERESTS

§ 701. Nature of Partnership Interest
A partnership interest is personal property.

Comment   This section is derived from Section 18 of the 1916 Act.

§ 702. Assignment of Partnership Interest
Except as provided in the partnership agreement, a partnership interest is assignable in whole or in part. An assignment of a partnership interest does not dissolve a limited partnership or entitle the assignee to become or to exercise any rights of a partner. An assignment entitles the assignee to receive, to the extent assigned, only the distribution to which the assignor would be entitled. Except as provided in the partnership agreement, a partner ceases to be a partner upon assignment of all his [or her] partnership interest.

Comment   Section 19(1) of the 1916 Act provided simply that "a limited partner's interest is assignable," raising a question whether any limitations on the right of assignment were permitted. While the first sentence of Section 702 recognizes that the power to assign may be restricted in the partnership agreement, there was no intention to affect in any way the usual rules regarding restraints on alienation of personal property. The second and third sentences of Section 702 are derived from Section 19(3)

of the 1916 Act. The last sentence first appeared in the 1976 Act.

§ 703. Rights of Creditor
On application to a court of competent jurisdiction by any judgment creditor of a partner, the court may charge the partnership interest of the partner with payment of the unsatisfied amount of the judgment with interest. To the extent so charged, the judgment creditor has only the rights of an assignee of the partnership interest. This [Act] does not deprive any partner of the benefit of any exemption laws applicable to his [or her] partnership interest.

Comment   Section 703 is derived from Section 22 of the 1916 Act but has not carried over some provisions that were thought to be superfluous. For example, references in Section 22(1) to specific remedies have been omitted, as has a prohibition in Section 22(2) against discharge of the lien with partnership property. Ordinary rules governing the remedies available to a creditor and the fiduciary obligations of general partners will determine those matters.

§ 704. Right of Assignee to Become Limited Partner
(a) An assignee of a partnership interest, including an assignee of a general partner, may become a limited partner if and to the extent that (i) the assignor gives the assignee that right in accordance with authority described in the partnership agreement, or (ii) all other partners consent.

(b) An assignee who has become a limited partner has, to the extent assigned, the rights and powers, and is subject to the restrictions and liabilities, of a limited partner under the partnership agreement and this [Act]. An assignee who becomes a limited partner also is liable for the obligations of his [or her] assignor to make and return contributions as provided in Articles 5 and 6. However, the assignee is not obligated for liabilities unknown to the assignee at the time he [or she] became a limited partner.

(c) If an assignee of a partnership interest becomes a limited partner, the assignor is not released from his [or her] liability to the limited partnership under Sections 207 and 502.

Comment   Section 704 is derived from Section 19 of the 1916 Act, but paragraph (b) defines more narrowly than Section 19 the obligations of the assignor that are automatically assumed by the assignee. Section 704 of the 1985 Act also differs from the 1976 Act to reflect the 1985 changes made in Section 201.

§ 705. Power of Estate of Deceased or Incompetent Partner
If a partner who is an individual dies or a court of competent jurisdiction adjudges him [or her] to be incompetent to manage his [or her] person or his [or

her] property, the partner's executor, administrator, guardian, conservator, or other legal representative may exercise all of the partner's rights for the purpose of settling his [or her] estate or administering his [or her] property, including any power the partner had to give an assignee the right to become a limited partner. If a partner is a corporation, trust, or other entity and is dissolved or terminated, the powers of that partner may be exercised by its legal representative or successor.

Comment Section 705 is derived from Section 21(1) of the 1916 Act. Former Section 21(2), making a deceased limited partner's estate liable for his liabilities as a limited partner was deleted as superfluous, with no intention of changing the liability of the estate.

ARTICLE 8
DISSOLUTION

§ 801. Nonjudicial Dissolution

A limited partnership is dissolved and its affairs shall be wound up upon the happening of the first to occur of the following:

(1) at the time specified in the certificate of limited partnership;

(2) upon the happening of events specified in writing in the partnership agreement;

(3) written consent of all partners;

(4) an event of withdrawal of a general partner unless at the time there is at least one other general partner and the written provisions of the partnership agreement permit the business of the limited partnership to be carried on by the remaining general partner and that partner does so, but the limited partnership is not dissolved and is not required to be wound up by reason of any event of withdrawal if, within 90 days after the withdrawal, all partners agree in writing to continue the business of the limited partnership and to the appointment of one or more additional general partners if necessary or desired; or

(5) entry of a decree of judicial dissolution under Section 802.

Comment Section 801 merely collects in one place all of the events causing dissolution. Paragraph (3) is derived from Sections 9(1)(g) and 20 of the 1916 Act, but adds the 90-day grace period. Section 801 also differs from its counterpart in the 1976 Act to reflect the 1985 changes made in Section 201.

§ 802. Judicial Dissolution

On application by or for a partner the [designate the appropriate court] court may decree dissolution of a limited partnership whenever it is not reasonably practicable to carry on the business in conformity with the partnership agreement.

Comment Section 802 first appeared in the 1976 Act.

§ 803. Winding Up

Except as provided in the partnership agreement, the general partners who have not wrongfully dissolved a limited partnership or, if none, the limited partners, may wind up the limited partnership's affairs; but the [designate the appropriate court] court may wind up the limited partnership's affairs upon application of any partner, his [or her] legal representative, or assignee.

Comment Section 803 first appeared in the 1976 Act, and is derived in part from Section 37 of the Uniform Partnership Act.

§ 804. Distribution of Assets

Upon the winding up of a limited partnership, the assets shall be distributed as follows:

(1) to creditors, including partners who are creditors, to the extent permitted by law in satisfaction of liabilities of the limited partnership other than liabilities for distributions to partners under Section 601 or 604;

(2) except as provided in the partnership agreement, to partners and former partners in satisfaction of liabilities for distributions under Section 601 or 604; and

(3) except as provided in the partnership agreement, to partners first for the return of their contributions and secondly respecting their partnership interests, in the proportions in which the partners share in distributions.

Comment Section 804 revises Section 23 of the 1916 Act by providing that (1) to the extent partners are also creditors, other than in respect of their interests in the partnership, they share with other creditors, (2) once the partnership's obligation to make a distribution accrues, it must be paid before any other distributions of an "equity" nature are made, and (3) general and limited partners rank on the same level except as otherwise provided in the partnership agreement.

ARTICLE 9
FOREIGN LIMITED PARTNERSHIPS

§ 901. Law Governing

Subject to the Constitution of this State, (i) the laws of the state under which a foreign limited partnership is organized govern its organization and internal affairs and the liability of its limited partners, and (ii) a foreign limited partnership may not be denied registration by reason of any difference between those laws and the laws of this State.

Comment Section 901 first appeared in the 1976 Act.

§ 902. Registration

Before transacting business in this State, a foreign limited partnership shall register with the Secretary of State. In order to register, a foreign limited partnership shall submit to the Secretary of State, in duplicate, an application for registration as a foreign limited partnership, signed and sworn to by a general partner and setting forth:

(1) the name of the foreign limited partnership and, if different, the name under which it proposes to register and transact business in this State;

(2) the State and date of its formation;

(3) the name and address of any agent for service of process on the foreign limited partnership whom the foreign limited partnership elects to appoint; the agent must be an individual resident of this State, a domestic corporation, or a foreign corporation having a place of business in, and authorized to do business in, this State;

(4) a statement that the Secretary of State is appointed the agent of the foreign limited partnership for service of process if no agent has been appointed under paragraph (3) or, if appointed, the agent's authority has been revoked or if the agent cannot be found or served with the exercise of reasonable diligence;

(5) the address of the office required to be maintained in the state of its organization by the laws of that state or, if not so required, of the principal office of the foreign limited partnership;

(6) the name and business address of each general partner; and

(7) the address of the office at which is kept a list of the names and addresses of the limited partners and their capital contributions, together with an undertaking by the foreign limited partnership to keep those records until the foreign limited partnership's registration in this State is cancelled or withdrawn.

Comment Section 902 first appeared in the 1976 Act. It was thought that requiring a full copy of the certificate of limited partnership and all amendments thereto to be filed in each state in which the partnership does business would impose an unreasonable burden on interstate limited partnerships and that the information Section 902 required to be filed would be sufficient to tell interested persons where they could write to obtain copies of those basic documents. Subdivision (3) of the 1976 Act has been omitted, and subdivisions (6) and (7) differ from their counterparts in the 1976 Act, to conform these provisions relating to the registration of foreign limited partnerships to the corresponding changes made by the Act in the provisions relating to domestic limited partnerships. The requirement that an application for registration be sworn to by a general partner is simply intended to produce the same result as is provided for in Section 204(c) with respect to certificates of domestic limited partnerships; the acceptance and endorsement by the Secretary of State (or equivalent authority) of an application which was not sworn by a general partner should be deemed a mere technical and insubstantial shortcoming, and should not result in the limited partners' being subjected to general liability for the obligations of the foreign limited partnership (See Section 907(c)).

§ 903. Issuance of Registration

(a) If the Secretary of State finds that an application for registration conforms to law and all requisite fees have been paid, he [or she] shall:

(1) endorse on the application the word "Filed", and the month, day, and year of the filing thereof;

(2) file in his [or her] office a duplicate original of the application; and

(3) issue a certificate of registration to transact business in this State.

(b) The certificate of registration, together with a duplicate original of the application, shall be returned to the person who filed the application or his [or her] representative.

Comment Section 903 first appeared in the 1976 Act.

§ 904. Name

A foreign limited partnership may register with the Secretary of State under any name, whether or not it is the name under which it is registered in its state of organization, that includes without abbreviation the words "limited partnership" and that could be registered by a domestic limited partnership.

Comment Section 904 first appeared in the 1976 Act.

§ 905. Changes and Amendments

If any statement in the application for registration of a foreign limited partnership was false when made or any arrangements or other facts described have changed, making the application inaccurate in any respect, the foreign limited partnership shall promptly file in the office of the Secretary of State a certificate, signed and sworn to by a general partner, correcting such statement.

Comment Section 905 first appeared in the 1976 Act. It corresponds to the provisions of Section 202(c) relating to domestic limited partnerships.

§ 906. Cancellation of Registration

A foreign limited partnership may cancel its registration by filing with the Secretary of State a certificate of cancellation signed and sworn to by a general partner. A cancellation does not terminate the authority of the Secretary of State to accept service of process on the foreign limited partnership with respect to [claims for relief] [causes of action] arising out of the transactions of business in this State.

Comment   Section 906 first appeared in the 1976 Act.

§ 907. Transaction of Business Without Registration

(a) A foreign limited partnership transacting business in this State may not maintain any action, suit, or proceeding in any court of this State until it has registered in this State.

(b) The failure of a foreign limited partnership to register in this State does not impair the validity of any contract or act of the foreign limited partnership or prevent the foreign limited partnership from defending any action, suit, or proceeding in any court of this State.

(c) A limited partner of a foreign limited partnership is not liable as a general partner of the foreign limited partnership solely by reason of having transacted business in this State without registration.

(d) A foreign limited partnership, by transacting business in this State without registration, appoints the Secretary of State as its agent for service of process with respect to [claims for relief] [causes of action] arising out of the transaction of business in this State.

Comment   Section 907 first appeared in the 1976 Act.

§ 908. Action by [Appropriate Official]

The [designate the appropriate official] may bring an action to restrain a foreign limited partnership from transacting business in this State in violation of this Article.

Comment   Section 908 first appeared in the 1976 Act.

ARTICLE 10
DERIVATIVE ACTIONS

§ 1001. Right of Action

A limited partner may bring an action in the right of a limited partnership to recover a judgment in favor if general partners with authority to do so have refused to bring the action or if an effort to cause those general partners to bring the action is not likely to succeed.

Comment   Section 1001 first appeared in the 1976 Act.

§ 1002. Proper Plaintiff

In a derivative action, the plaintiff must be a partner at the time of bringing the action and (i) must

have been a partner at the time of the transaction of which he [or she] complains or (ii) his [or her] status as a partner must have devolved upon him [or her] by operation of law or pursuant to the terms of the partnership agreement from a person who was a partner at the time of the transaction.

Comment   Section 1002 first appeared in the 1976 Act.

§ 1003. Pleading

In a derivative action, the complaint shall set forth with particularity the effort of the plaintiff to secure initiation of the action by a general partner or the reasons for not making the effort.

Comment   Section 1003 first appeared in the 1976 Act.

§ 1004. Expenses

If a derivative action is successful, in whole or in part, or if anything is received by the plaintiff as a result of a judgment, compromise, or settlement of an action or claim, the court may award the plaintiff reasonable expenses, including reasonable attorney's fees, and shall direct him [or her] to remit to the limited partnership the remainder of those proceeds received by him [or her].

Comment   Section 1004 first appeared in the 1976 Act.

ARTICLE 11
MISCELLANEOUS

§ 1101. Construction and Application

This [Act] shall be so applied and construed to effectuate its general purpose to make uniform the law with respect to the subject of this [Act] among states enacting it.

Comment   Because the principles set out in Sections 28(1) and 29 of the 1916 Act have become so universally established, it was felt that the 1976 and 1985 Acts need not contain express provisions to the same effect. However, it is intended that the principles enunciated in those provisions of the 1916 Act also apply to this Act.

§ 1102. Short Title

This [Act] may be cited as the Uniform Limited Partnership Act.

§ 1103. Severability

If any provision of this [Act] or its application to any person or circumstance is held invalid, the invalidity does not affect other provisions or applications of the [Act] which can be given effect without the invalid provision or application, and to this end the provisions of this [Act] are severable.

§ 1104. Effective Date, Extended Effective Date and Repeal

Except as set forth below, the effective date of this [Act] is _____ and the following acts [list existing limited partnership acts] are hereby repealed:

(1) The existing provisions for execution and filing of certificates of limited partnerships and amendments thereunder and cancellations thereof continue in effect until [specify time required to create central filing system], the extended effective date, and Sections 102, 103, 104, 105, 201, 202, 203, 204 and 206 are not effective until the extended effective date.

(2) Section 402, specifying the conditions under which a general partner ceases to be a member of a limited partnership, is not effective until the extended effective date, and the applicable provisions of existing law continue to govern until the extended effective date.

(3) Sections 501, 502 and 608 apply only to contributions and distributions made after the effective date of this [Act].

(4) Section 704 applies only to assignments made after the effective date of this [Act].

(5) Article 9, dealing with registration of foreign limited partnerships, is not effective until the extended effective date.

(6) Unless otherwise agreed by the partners, the applicable provisions of existing law governing allocation of profits and losses (rather than the provisions of Section 503), distributions to a withdrawing partner (rather than the provisions of Section 604), and distributions of assets upon the winding up of a limited partnership (rather than the provisions of

Section 804) govern limited partnerships formed before the effective date of this [Act].

Comment   Subdivisions (6) and (7) did not appear in Section 1104 of the 1976 Act. They are included in the 1985 Act to ensure that the application of the Act to limited partnerships formed and existing before the Act becomes effective would not violate constitutional prohibitions against the impairment of contracts.

§ 1105. Rules for Cases Not Provided for in This [Act]

In any case not provided for in this [Act] the provisions of the Uniform Partnership Act govern.

Comment   The result provided for in Section 1105 would obtain even in its absence in a jurisdiction which had adopted the Uniform Partnership Act, by operation of Section 6 of that act.

§ 1106. Savings Clause

The repeal of any statutory provision by this [Act] does not impair, or otherwise affect, the organization or the continued existence of a limited partnership existing at the effective date of this [Act], nor does the repeal of any existing statutory provision by this [Act] impair any contract or affect any right accrued before the effective date of this [Act].

Comment   Section 1106 did not appear in the 1976 Act. It is included in the 1985 Act to ensure that the application of the Act to limited partnerships formed and existing before the Act becomes effective would not violate constitutional prohibitions against the impairment of contracts.

APPENDIX E

UNIFORM LIMITED LIABILITY COMPANY ACT

[ARTICLE] 1
GENERAL PROVISIONS

SECTION 101. *Definitions.*

In this [Act]:

(1) "Articles of organization" means initial, amended, and restated articles of organization and articles of merger. In the case of a foreign limited liability company, the term includes all records serving a similar function required to be filed in the office of the [Secretary of State] or comparable office of the company's jurisdiction of organization.

(2) "Business" includes every trade, occupation, profession, and other lawful purpose, whether or not carried on for profit.

(3) "Debtor in bankruptcy" means a person who is the subject of an order for relief under Title 11 of the United States Code or a comparable order under a successor statute of general application or a comparable order under federal, state, or foreign law governing insolvency.

(4) "Distribution" means a transfer of money, property, or other benefit from a limited liability company to a member in the member's capacity as a member or to a transferee of the member's distributional interest.

(5) "Distributional interest" means all of a member's interest in distributions by the limited liability company.

(6) "Entity" means a person other than an individual.

(7) "Foreign limited liability company" means an unincorporated entity organized under laws other than the laws of this State which afford limited liability to its owners comparable to the liability under Section 303 and is not required to obtain a certificate of authority to transact business under any law of this State other than this [Act].

(8) "Limited liability company" means a limited liability company organized under this [Act].

(9) "Manager" means a person, whether or not a member of a manager-managed limited liability company, who is vested with authority under Section 301.

(10) "Manager-managed limited liability company" means a limited liability company which is so designated in its articles of organization.

(11) "Member-managed limited liability company" means a limited liability company other than a manager-managed company.

(12) "Operating agreement" means the agreement under Section 103 concerning the relations among the members, managers, and limited liability company. The term includes amendments to the agreement.

(13) "Person" means an individual, corporation, business trust, estate, trust, partnership, limited liability company, association, joint venture, government, governmental subdivision, agency, or instrumentality, or any other legal or commercial entity.

(14) "Principal office" means the office, whether or not in this State, where the principal executive office of a domestic or foreign limited liability company is located.

(15) "Record" means information that is inscribed on a tangible medium or that is stored in an electronic or other medium and is retrievable in perceivable form.

(16) "Signed" includes any symbol executed or adopted by a person with the present intention to authenticate a record.

(17) "State" means a State of the United States, the District of Columbia, the Commonwealth of Puerto Rico, or any territory or insular possession subject to the jurisdiction of the United States.

(18) "Transfer" includes an assignment, conveyance, deed, bill of sale, lease, mortgage, security interest, encumbrance, and gift.

SECTION 102. *Knowledge and Notice.*

(a) A person knows a fact if the person has actual knowledge of it.

(b) A person has notice of a fact if the person:

(1) knows the fact;

(2) has received a notification of the fact; or

(3) has reason to know the fact exists from all of the facts known to the person at the time in question.

(c) A person notifies or gives a notification of a fact to another by taking steps reasonably required to inform the other person in ordinary course, whether or not the other person knows the fact.

(d) A person receives a notification when the notification:

(1) comes to the person's attention; or

(2) is duly delivered at the person's place of business or at any other place held out by the person as a place for receiving communications.

(e) An entity knows, has notice, or receives a notification of a fact for purposes of a particular transaction when the individual conducting the transaction for the entity knows, has notice, or receives a notification of the fact, or in any event when the fact would have been brought to the individual's attention had the entity exercised reasonable diligence. An entity exercises reasonable diligence if it maintains reasonable routines for communicating significant information to the individual conducting the transaction for the entity and there is reasonable compliance with the routines. Reasonable diligence does not require an individual acting for the entity to communicate information unless the communication is part of the individual's regular duties or the individual has reason to know of the transaction and that the transaction would be materially affected by the information.

SECTION 103. Effect of Operating Agreement Nonwaivable Provisions.

(a) Except as otherwise provided in subsection (b), all members of a limited liability company may enter into an operating agreement, which need not be in writing, to regulate the affairs of the company and the conduct of its business, and to govern relations among the members, managers, and company. To the extent the operating agreement does not otherwise provide, this [Act] governs relations among the members, managers, and company.

(b) The operating agreement may not:

(1) unreasonably restrict a right to information or access to records under Section 408;

(2) eliminate the duty of loyalty under Section 409(b) or 603(b)(3), but the agreement may:

(i) identify specific types or categories of activities that do not violate the duty of loyalty, if not manifestly unreasonable; and

(ii) specify the number or percentage of members or disinterested managers that may authorize or ratify, after full disclosure of all material facts, a specific act or transaction that otherwise would violate the duty of loyalty;

(3) unreasonably reduce the duty of care under Section 409(c) or 603(b)(3);

(4) eliminate the obligation of good faith and fair dealing under Section 409(d), but the operating agreement may determine the standards by which the performance of the obligation is to be measured, if the standards are not manifestly unreasonable;

(5) vary the right to expel a member in an event specified in Section 601(5);

(6) vary the requirement to wind up the limited liability company's business in a case specified in Section 801(4) or (5); or

(7) restrict rights of third parties under this [Act], other than managers, members, or their transferees.

SECTION 104. Supplemental Principles of Law.

(a) Unless displaced by particular provisions of this [Act], the principles of law and equity supplement this [Act].

(b) If an obligation to pay interest arises under this [Act] and the rate is not specified, the rate is that specified in [applicable statute].

SECTION 105. Name.

(a) The name of a limited liability company must contain "limited liability company" or "limited company" or the abbreviation "L.L.C.," "LLC," "L.C.," or "LC." "Limited" may be abbreviated as "Ltd.," and "company" may be abbreviated as "Co.".

(b) Except as authorized by subsections (c) and (d), the name of a limited liability company must be distinguishable upon the records of the [Secretary of State] from:

(1) the name of any corporation, limited partnership, or company incorporated, organized or authorized to transact business, in this State;

(2) a company name reserved or registered under Section 106 or 107;

(3) a fictitious name approved under Section 1005 for a foreign company authorized to transact business in this State because its real name is unavailable.

(c) A limited liability company may apply to the [Secretary of State] for authorization to use a name that is not distinguishable upon the records of the [Secretary of State] from one or more of the names described in subsection (b). The [Secretary of State] shall authorize use of the name applied for if:

(1) the present user, registrant, or owner of a reserved name consents to the use in a record and submits an undertaking in form satisfactory to the [Secretary of State] to change the name to a name that is distinguishable upon the records of the [Secretary of State] from the name applied for; or

(2) the applicant delivers to the [Secretary of State] a certified copy of the final judgment of a

court of competent jurisdiction establishing the applicant's right to use the name applied for in this State.

(d) A limited liability company may use the name, including a fictitious name, of another domestic or foreign company which is used in this State if the other company is organized or authorized to transact business in this State and the company proposing to use the name has:

(1) merged with the other company;

(2) been formed by reorganization with the other company; or

(3) acquired substantially all of the assets, including the company name, of the other company.

SECTION 106. Reserved Name.

(a) A person may reserve the exclusive use of the name of a limited liability company, including a fictitious name for a foreign company whose company name is not available, by delivering an application to the [Secretary of State] for filing. The application must set forth the name and address of the applicant and the name proposed to be reserved. If the [Secretary of State] finds that the name applied for is available, it must be reserved for the applicant's exclusive use for a nonrenewable 120-day period.

(b) The owner of a name reserved for a limited liability company may transfer the reservation to another person by delivering to the [Secretary of State] a signed notice of the transfer which states the name and address of the transferee.

SECTION 107. Registered Name.

(a) A foreign limited liability company may register its company name subject to the requirements of Section 1005, if the name is distinguishable upon the records of the [Secretary of State] from company names that are not available under Section 105(b).

(b) A foreign limited liability company registers its company name, or its company name with any addition required by Section 1005, by delivering to the [Secretary of State] for filing an application:

(1) setting forth its company name, or its company name with any addition required by Section 1005, the State or country and date of its organization, and a brief description of the nature of the business in which it is engaged; and

(2) accompanied by a certificate of existence, or a record of similar import, from the State or country of organization.

(c) A foreign limited liability company whose registration is effective may renew it for successive years by delivering for filing in the office of the [Secretary of State] a renewal application complying with subsection (b) between October 1 and December 31 of the preceding year. The renewal application renews the registration for the following calendar year.

(d) A foreign limited liability company whose registration is effective may qualify as a foreign company under its company name or consent in writing to the use of its name by a limited liability company later organized under this [Act] or by another foreign company later authorized to transact business in this State. The registered name terminates when the limited liability company is organized or the foreign company qualifies or consents to the qualification of another foreign company under the registered name.

SECTION 108. Designated Office and Agent for Service of Process.

(a) A limited liability company and a foreign limited liability company authorized to do business in this State shall designate and continuously maintain in this State:

(1) an office, which need not be a place of its business in this State; and

(2) an agent and street address of the agent for service of process on the company.

(b) An agent must be an individual resident of this State, a domestic corporation, another limited liability company, or a foreign corporation or foreign company authorized to do business in this State.

SECTION 109. Change of Designated Office or Agent for Service of Process.

A limited liability company may change its designated office or agent for service of process by delivering to the [Secretary of State] for filing a statement of change which sets forth:

(1) the name of the company;

(2) the street address of its current designated office;

(3) if the current designated office is to be changed, the street address of the new designated office;

(4) the name and address of its current agent for service of process; and

(5) if the current agent for service of process or street address of that agent is to be changed, the new address or the name and street address of the new agent for service of process.

SECTION 110. Resignation of Agent for Service of Process.

(a) An agent for service of process of a limited liability company may resign by delivering to the [Secretary of State] for filing a record of the statement of resignation.

(b) After filing a statement of resignation, the [Secretary of State] shall mail a copy to the designated office and another copy to the limited liability company at its principal office.

(c) An agency is terminated on the 31st day after the statement is filed in the office of the [Secretary of State].

SECTION 111.   Service of Process.

(a) An agent for service of process appointed by a limited liability company or a foreign limited liability company is an agent of the company for service of any process, notice, or demand required or permitted by law to be served upon the company.

(b) If a limited liability company or foreign limited liability company fails to appoint or maintain an agent for service of process in this State or the agent for service of process cannot with reasonable diligence be found at the agent's address, the [Secretary of State] is an agent of the company upon whom process, notice, or demand may be served.

(c) Service of any process, notice, or demand on the [Secretary of State] may be made by delivering to and leaving with the [Secretary of State], the [Assistant Secretary of State], or clerk having charge of the limited liability company department of the [Secretary of State's] office duplicate copies of the process, notice, or demand. If the process, notice, or demand is served on the [Secretary of State], the [Secretary of State] shall forward one of the copies by registered or certified mail, return receipt requested, to the company at its designated office. Service is effected under this subsection at the earliest of:

(1) the date the company receives the process, notice, or demand;

(2) the date shown on the return receipt, if signed on behalf of the company; or

(3) five days after its deposit in the mail, if mailed postpaid and correctly addressed.

(d) The [Secretary of State] shall keep a record of all processes, notices, and demands served pursuant to this section and record the time of and the action taken regarding the service.

(e) This section does not affect the right to serve process, notice, or demand in any manner otherwise provided by law.

SECTION 112.   Nature of Business and Powers.

(a) A limited liability company may be organized under this [Act] for any lawful purpose, subject to any law of this State governing or regulating business.

(b) Unless its articles of organization provide otherwise, a limited liability company has the same powers as an individual to do all things necessary or convenient to carry on its business or affairs, including power to:

(1) sue and be sued, and defend in its company name;

(2) purchase, receive, lease, or otherwise acquire, and own, hold, improve, use, and otherwise deal with real or personal property, or any legal or equitable interest in property, wherever located;

(3) sell, convey, mortgage, grant a security interest in, lease, exchange, and otherwise encumber or dispose of all or any part of its property;

(4) purchase, receive, subscribe for, or otherwise acquire, own, hold, vote, use, sell, mortgage, lend, grant a security interest in, or otherwise dispose of and deal in and with, shares or other interests in or obligations of any other entity;

(5) make contracts and guarantees, incur liabilities, borrow money, issue its notes, bonds, and other obligations, which may be convertible into or include the option to purchase other securities of the limited liability company, and secure any of its obligations by a mortgage on or a security interest in any of its property, franchises, or income;

(6) lend money, invest and reinvest its funds, and receive and hold real and personal property as security for repayment;

(7) be a promoter, partner, member, associate, or manager of any partnership, joint venture, trust, or other entity;

(8) conduct its business, locate offices, and exercise the powers granted by this [Act] within or without this State;

(9) elect managers and appoint officers, employees, and agents of the limited liability company, define their duties, fix their compensation, and lend them money and credit;

(10) pay pensions and establish pension plans, pension trusts, profit sharing plans, share bonus plans, share option plans, and benefit or incentive plans for any or all of its current or former members, managers, officers, employees, and agents;

(11) make donations for the public welfare or for charitable, scientific, or educational purposes; and

(12) make payments or donations, or do any other act, not inconsistent with law, that furthers the business of the limited liability company.

[ARTICLE] 2
ORGANIZATION

SECTION 201.   Limited Liability Company As Legal Entity.

A limited liability company is a legal entity distinct from its members.

SECTION 202. Organization.

(a) One or more persons may organize a limited liability company, consisting of one or more members, by delivering articles of organization to the office of the [Secretary of State] for filing.

(b) Unless a delayed effective date is specified, the existence of a limited liability company begins when the articles of organization are filed.

(c) The filing of the articles of organization by the [Secretary of State] is conclusive proof that the organizers satisfied all conditions precedent to the creation of the organization.

SECTION 203. Articles of Organization.

(a) Articles of organization of a limited liability company must set forth:

(1) the name of the company;

(2) the address of the initial designated office;

(3) the name and street address of the initial agent for service of process;

(4) the name and address of each organizer;

(5) whether the duration of the company is for a specified term and, if so, the period specified;

(6) whether the company is to be manager-managed, and, if so, the name and address of each initial manager; and

(7) whether the members of the company are to be liable for its debts and obligations under Section 303(c).

(b) Articles of organization of a limited liability company may set forth:

(1) provisions permitted to be set forth in an operating agreement; or

(2) other matters not inconsistent with law.

(c) Articles of organization of a limited liability company may not vary the nonwaivable provisions of Section 103(b). As to all other matters, if any provision of an operating agreement is inconsistent with the articles of organization:

(1) the operating agreement controls as to managers, members, and members' transferees; and

(2) the articles of organization control as to persons other than managers, members, and their transferees who rely on the articles to their detriment.

(d) The duration of a limited liability company is at-will unless a term for its duration is specified in its articles of organization.

SECTION 204. Amendment or Restatement of Articles of Organization.

(a) Articles of organization of a limited liability company may be amended at any time by delivering articles of amendment to the [Secretary of State] for filing. The articles of amendment must set forth the:

(1) name of the limited liability company;

(2) date of filing of the articles of organization; and

(3) amendment to the articles.

(b) A limited liability company may restate its articles of organization at any time. Restated articles of organization must be signed and filed in the same manner as articles of amendment. Restated articles of organization must be designated as such in the heading and state in the heading or in an introductory paragraph the limited liability company's present name and, if it has been changed, all of its former names and the date of the filing of its initial articles of organization.

SECTION 205. Signing of Records.

(a) Except as otherwise provided in this [Act], a record to be filed by or on behalf of a limited liability company in the office of the [Secretary of State] must be signed in the name of the company by a:

(1) manager of a manager-managed company;

(2) member of a member-managed company;

(3) person organizing the company, if the company has not been formed; or

(4) fiduciary, if the company is in the hands of a receiver, trustee, or other court-appointed fiduciary.

(b) A record signed under subsection (a) must state adjacent to the signature the name and capacity of the signer.

(c) A person signing a record to be filed under subsection (a) may do so as an attorney-in-fact without any formality. An authorization, including a power of attorney, to sign a record need not be in writing, sworn to, verified, or acknowledged or filed in the office of the [Secretary of State].

SECTION 206. Filing in Office of [Secretary of State].

(a) Articles of organization or any other record authorized to be filed under this [Actl must be in a medium permitted by the [Secretary of State] and must be delivered to the office of the [Secretary of State]. Unless the [Secretary of State] determines that a record fails to comply as to form with the filing requirements of this [Act], and if all filing fees have been paid, the [Secretary of State] shall file the record and send a receipt for the record and the fees to the limited liability company or its representative.

(b) Upon request and payment of a fee, the [Secretary of State] shall send to the requester a certified copy of the requested record.

(c) A record accepted for filing by the [Secretary of State] is effective:

(1) on the date it is filed, as evidenced by the [Secretary of State] maintaining a record of the date and time of the filing;

(2) at the time specified in the record as its effective time; or

(3) on the date and at the time specified in the record if the record specifies a delayed effective date and time.

(d) If a delayed effective date for a record is specified but no time is specified, the record is effective at 12:01 A.M. on that date. A delayed effective date that is later than the 90th day after the record is filed makes the record effective as of the 90th day.

SECTION 207. Correcting Filed Record.

(a) A limited liability company or foreign limited liability company may correct a record filed by the [Secretary of State] if the record contains a false or erroneous statement or was defectively signed.

(b) A record is corrected:

(1) by preparing articles of correction that:

(i) describe the record, including its filing date, or attach a copy of it to the articles of correction;

(ii) specify the incorrect statement and the reason it is incorrect or the manner in which the signing was defective; and

(iii) correct the incorrect statement or defective signing; and

(2) by delivering the corrected record to the [Secretary of State] for filing.

(c) Articles of correction are effective retroactively to the effective date of the record they correct. However, a person who has relied on the uncorrected record and was adversely affected by the correction is not bound by the correction until the articles are filed.

SECTION 208. Certificate of Existence or Authorization.

(a) A person may request the [Secretary of State] to furnish a certificate of existence for a limited liability company or a certificate of authorization for a foreign limited liability company.

(b) A certificate of existence for a limited liability company must set forth:

(1) the company's name;

(2) that it is duly organized under the laws of this State, the date of organization, whether its duration is at-will or for a specified term, and, if the latter, the period specified;

(3) if payment is reflected in the records of the [Secretary of State] and nonpayment affects the existence of the company, that all fees, taxes, and penalties owed to this State have been paid;

(4) whether its most recent annual report required by Section 211 has been filed with the [Secretary of State];

(5) that articles of termination have not been filed; and

(6) other facts of record in the office of the [Secretary of State] which may be requested by the applicant.

(c) A certificate of authorization for a foreign limited liability company must set forth:

(1) the company's name used in this State;

(2) that it is authorized to transact business in this State;

(3) if payment is reflected in the records of the [Secretary of State] and nonpayment affects the authorization of the company, that all fees, taxes, and penalties owed to this State have been paid;

(4) whether its most recent annual report required by Section 211 has been filed with the [Secretary of State];

(5) that a certificate of cancellation has not been filed; and

(6) other facts of record in the office of the [Secretary of State] which may be requested by the applicant.

(d) Subject to any qualification stated in the certificate, a certificate of existence or authorization issued by the [Secretary of State] may be relied upon as conclusive evidence that the domestic or foreign limited liability company is in existence or is authorized to transact business in this State.

SECTION 209. Liability for False Statement in Filed Record.

If a record authorized or required to be filed under this [Act] contains a false statement, one who suffers loss by reliance on the statement may recover damages for the loss from a person who signed the record or caused another to sign it on the person's behalf and knew the statement to be false at the time the record was signed.

SECTION 210. Filing by Judicial Act.

If a person required by Section 205 to sign any record fails or refuses to do so, any other person who is adversely affected by the failure or refusal may petition the [designate the appropriate court] to direct the signing of the record. If the court finds that it is proper for the record to be signed and that a person so designated has failed or refused to sign the record, it shall order the [Secretary of State] to sign and file an appropriate record.

SECTION 211. Annual Report for [Secretary of State].

(a) A limited liability company, and a foreign limited liability company authorized to transact business in this State, shall deliver to the [Secretary of State] for filing an annual report that sets forth:

(1) the name of the company and the State or country under whose law it is organized;

(2) the address of its designated office and the name and address of its agent for service of process in this State;

(3) the address of its principal office; and

(4) the names and business addresses of any managers.

(b) Information in an annual report must be current as of the date the annual report is signed on behalf of the limited liability company.

(c) The first annual report must be delivered to the [Secretary of State] between [January 1 and April 1] of the year following the calendar year in which a limited liability company was organized or a foreign company was authorized to transact business. Subsequent annual reports must be delivered to the [Secretary of State] between [January 1 and April 1] of the following calendar years.

(d) If an annual report does not contain the information required in subsection (a), the [Secretary of State] shall promptly notify the reporting limited liability company or foreign limited liability company and return the report to it for correction. If the report is corrected to contain the information required in subsection (a) and delivered to the [Secretary of State] within 30 days after the effective date of the notice, it is timely filed.

[ARTICLE] 3
RELATIONS OF MEMBERS AND MANAGERS TO PERSONS DEALING WITH LIMITED LIABILITY COMPANY

Section 301.   Agency of Members and Managers.
Section 302.   Limited Liability Company Liable for Member's or Manager's Actionable Conduct.
Section 303.   Liability of Members and Managers.

SECTION 301. Agency of Members and Managers.

(a) Subject to subsections (b) and (c):

(1) each member is an agent of the limited liability company for the purpose of its business;

(2) an act of a member, including the signing of an instrument in the company name, for apparently carrying on in the ordinary course the company's business or business of the kind carried on by the company binds the company, unless the member had no authority to act for the company in the particular matter and the person with whom the member was dealing knew or had notice that the member lacked authority; and

(3) an act of a member which is not apparently for carrying on in the ordinary course the company's business or business of the kind carried on by the company binds the company only if the act was authorized by the other members.

(b) Subject to subsection (c), in a manager-managed limited liability company:

(1) a member is not an agent of the company for the purpose of its business solely by reason of being a member;

(2) each manager is an agent of the company for the purpose of its business;

(3) an act of a manager, including the signing of an instrument in the company name, for apparently carrying on in the ordinary course the company's business or business of the kind carried on by the company binds the company, unless the manager had no authority to act for the company in the particular matter and the person with

whom the manager was dealing knew or had notice that the manager lacked authority; and

(4) an act of a manager which is not apparently for carrying on in the ordinary course the company's business or business of the kind carried on by the company binds the company only if the act was authorized under Section 404(b)(2).

(c) Unless the articles of organization limit their authority, any member of a member-managed limited liability company, or any manager of a manager-managed company, may sign and deliver any instrument transferring or affecting the company's interest in real property. The instrument is conclusive in favor of a person who gives value without knowledge of the lack of the authority of the person signing and delivering the instrument.

SECTION 302. Limited Liability Company Liable for Member's or Manager's Actionable Conduct.

A limited liability company is liable for loss or injury caused to a person, or for a penalty incurred, as a result of a wrongful act or omission, or other actionable conduct, of a member or manager acting in the ordinary course of business of the company or with authority of the company.

SECTION 303. Liability of Members and Managers.

a) Except as otherwise provided in subsection (c), the debts, obligations, and liabilities of a limited liability company, whether arising in contract, tort, or otherwise, are solely the debts, obligations, and liabilities of the company. A member or manager is not personally liable for a debt, obligation, or liability of the company solely by reason of being or acting as a member or manager.

(b) The failure of a limited liability company to observe the usual company formalities or requirements relating to the exercise of its company powers or management of its business is not a ground for imposing personal liability on the members or managers for liabilities of the company.

(c) All or specified members of a limited liability company are liable in their capacity as members for all or specified debts, obligations, or liabilities of the company if:

(1) a provision to that effect is contained in the articles of organization; and

(2) a member so liable has consented in writing to the adoption of the provision or to be bound by the provision.

[ARTICLE] 4
RELATIONS OF MEMBERS TO EACH OTHER AND TO LIMITED LIABILITY COMPANY

Section 401.   Form of Contribution.
Section 402.   Member's Liability for Contributions.

SECTION 401. Form of Contribution.

A contribution of a member of a limited liability company may consist of tangible or intangible property or other benefit to the company, including money, promissory notes, services performed, or other obligations to contribute cash or property, or contracts for services to be performed.

SECTION 402. Member's Liability for Contributions.

(a) A member's obligation to contribute money, property, or other benefit to, or to perform services for, a limited liability company is not excused by the member's death, disability, or other inability to perform personally. If a member does not make the required contribution of property or services, the member is obligated at the option of the company to contribute money equal to that portion of the value of the stated contribution which has not been made.

(b) A creditor of a limited liability company who extends credit or otherwise acts in reliance on an obligation described in subsection (a), and without notice of any compromise under Section 404(c)(5), may enforce the original obligation.

SECTION 403. Member's and Manager's Rights to Payments and Reimbursement.

(a) A limited liability company shall reimburse a member or manager for payments made and indemnify a member or manager for liabilities incurred by the member or manager in the ordinary course of the business of the company or for the preservation of its business or property.

(b) A limited liability company shall reimburse a member for an advance to the company beyond the amount of contribution the member agreed to make.

(c) A payment or advance made by a member which gives rise to an obligation of a limited liability company under subsection (a) or (b) constitutes a loan to the company upon which interest accrues from the date of the payment or advance.

(d) A member is not entitled to remuneration for services performed for a limited liability company, except for reasonable compensation for services rendered in winding up the business of the company.

SECTION 404. Management of Limited Liability Company.

(a) In a member-managed limited liability company:

(1) each member has equal rights in the management and conduct of the company's business; and

(2) except as otherwise provided in subsection (c) or in Section 801(3)(i), any matter relating to the business of the company may be decided by a majority of the members.

(b) In a manager-managed limited liability company:

(1) the managers have the exclusive authority to manage and conduct the company's business;

(2) except as specified in subsection (c) or in Section 801(3)(i), any matter relating to the business of the company may be exclusively decided by the manager or, if there is more than one manager, by a majority of the managers; and

(3) a manager:

(i) must be designated, appointed, elected, removed, or replaced by a vote, approval, or consent of a majority of the members; and

(ii) holds office until a successor has been elected and qualified, unless sooner resigns or is removed.

(c) The only matters of a limited liability company's business requiring the consent of all of the members are:

(1) the amendment of the operating agreement under Section 103;

(2) the authorization or ratification of acts or transactions under Section 103(b)(2)(ii) which would otherwise violate the duty of loyalty;

(3) an amendment to the articles of organization under Section 204;

(4) the compromise of an obligation to make a contribution under Section 402(b);

(5) the compromise, as among members, of an obligation of a member to make a contribution or return money or other property paid or distributed in violation of this [Act];

(6) the making of interim distributions under Section 405(a);

(7) the admission of a new member;

(8) the use of the company's property to redeem an interest subject to a charging order;

(9) the consent to dissolve the company under Section 801(2);

(10) a waiver of the right to have the company's business wound up and the company terminated under Section 802(b);

(11) the consent of members to merge with another entity under Section 904(c)(l); and

(12) the sale, lease, exchange, or other disposal of all, or substantially all, of the company's property with or without goodwill.

(d) Action requiring the consent of members or managers under this [Act] may be taken with or without a meeting. In the event a meeting is otherwise required and a written action in lieu thereof is not prohibited, the written action must be evidenced by one or more consents reflected in a record describing the action taken and signed by all of the members or managers entitled to vote on the action.

(e) A member or manager may appoint a proxy to vote or otherwise act for the member or manager by signing an appointment instrument, either personally or by the member's or manager's attorney-in-fact. An appointment of a proxy is valid for 11 months unless a different time is specified in the appointment instrument. An appointment is revocable by the member or manager unless the appointment form conspicuously states that it is irrevocable and the appointment is coupled with an interest, in which case the appointment is revoked when the interest is extinguished.

SECTION 405. Sharing of and Right to Distributions.

(a) Any distributions made by a limited liability company before its dissolution and winding up must be in equal shares.

(b) A member has no right to receive, and may not be required to accept, a distribution in kind.

(c) If a member becomes entitled to receive a distribution, the member has the status of, and is entitled to all remedies available to, a creditor of the limited liability company with respect to the distribution.

SECTION 406. Limitations on Distributions.

(a) A distribution may not be made if:

(1) the limited liability company would not be able to pay its debts as they become due in the ordinary course of business; or

(2) the company's total assets would be less than the sum of its total liabilities plus the amount that would be needed, if the company were to be dissolved, wound up, and terminated at the time of the distribution, to satisfy the preferential rights upon dissolution, winding up, and termination of members whose preferential rights are superior to those receiving the distribution.

(b) A limited liability company may base a determination that a distribution is not prohibited under subsection (a) on financial statements prepared on the basis of accounting practices and principles that are reasonable in the circumstances or on a fair valuation or other method that is reasonable in the circumstances.

(c) Except as otherwise provided in subsection (e), the effect of a distribution under subsection (a) is measured:

(1) in the case of distribution by purchase, redemption, or other acquisition of a distributional interest in a limited liability company, as of the date money or other property is transferred or debt incurred by the company; and

(2) in all other cases, as of the date the:

(i) distribution is authorized if the payment occurs within 120 days after the date of authorization; or

(ii) payment is made if it occurs more than 120 days after the date of authorization.

(d) A limited liability company's indebtedness to a member incurred by reason of a distribution made in accordance with this section is at parity with the company's indebtedness to its general, unsecured creditors.

(e) Indebtedness of a limited liability company, including indebtedness issued in connection with or as part of a distribution, is not considered a liability for purposes of determinations under subsection (a) if its terms provide that payment of principal and interest are made only if and to the extent that payment of a distribution to members could then be made under this section. If the indebtedness is issued as a distribution, each payment of principal or interest on the indebtedness is treated as a distribution, the effect of which is measured on the date the payment is made.

SECTION 407. Liability for Unlawful Distributions.

(a) A member of a member-managed limited liability company or a member or manager of a manager-managed company who votes for or assents to a distribution made in violation of Section 406, the articles of organization, a written operating agreement, or a signed record is personally liable to the company for the amount of the distribution which exceeds the amount that could have been distributed without violating Section 406, the articles of organization, a written operating agreement, or a signed record if it is established that the member or manager did not perform the member's or manager's duties in compliance with Section 409.

(b) A member of a manager-managed limited liability company who knew a distribution was made in violation of Section 406 is personally liable to the limited liability company, but only to the extent that the distribution received by the member exceeded the amount that could properly have been paid under Section 406.

(c) A member or manager against whom an action is brought under this section may implead in the action all:

(1) other members or managers who voted for or assented to the distribution in violation of subsection (a) and may compel contribution from them; and

(2) members who received a distribution in violation of subsection (b) and may compel contribution from the member in the amount received in violation of subsection (b).

(d) A proceeding under this section is barred unless it is commenced within two years after the distribution.

SECTION 408. Members Right to Information.

(a) A limited liability company shall provide members and their agents and attorneys access to any of its records at reasonable locations specified in the operating agreement. The company shall provide former members and their agents and attorneys access for proper purposes to records pertaining to the period during which they were members. The right of access provides the opportunity to inspect and copy records during ordinary business hours. The company may impose a reasonable charge, limited to the costs of labor and material, for copies of records furnished.

(b) A limited liability company shall furnish to a member, and to the legal representative of a deceased member or member under legal disability:

(1) without demand, information concerning the company's business or affairs reasonably required for the proper exercise of the member's rights and performance of the member's duties under the operating agreement or this [Act]; and

(2) on demand, other information concerning the company's business or affairs, except to the extent the demand or the information demanded is unreasonable or otherwise improper under the circumstances.

(c) A member has the right upon a signed record given to the limited liability company to obtain at the company's expense a copy of any operating agreement in record form.

SECTION 409. General Standards of Member's and Manager's Conduct.

(a) The only fiduciary duties a member owes to a member-managed limited liability company and its other members are the duty of loyalty and the duty of care imposed by subsections (b) and (c).

(b) A member's duty of loyalty to a member-managed limited liability company and its other members is limited to the following:

(1) to account to the company and to hold as trustee for it any property, profit, or benefit derived by the member in the conduct or winding up of the company's business or derived from a use by the member of the company's property, including the appropriation of a company's opportunity;

(2) to refrain from dealing with the company in the conduct or winding up of the company's business as or on behalf of a party having an interest adverse to the company; and

(3) to refrain from competing with the company in the conduct of the company's business before the dissolution of the company.

(c) A member's duty of care to a member-managed limited liability company and its other members in the conduct of and winding up of the company's business is limited to refraining from engaging in grossly negligent or reckless conduct, intentional misconduct, or a knowing violation of law.

(d) A member shall discharge the duties to a member-managed limited liability company and its other members under this [Act] or under the operating agreement and exercise any rights consistently with the obligation of good faith and fair dealing.

(e) A member of a member-managed limited liability company does not violate a duty or obligation under this [Act] or under the operating agreement merely because the member's conduct furthers the member's own interest.

(f) A member of a member-managed limited liability company may lend money to and transact other business with the company. As to each loan or transaction, the rights and obligations of the member are the same as those of a person who is not a member, subject to other applicable law.

(g) This section applies to a person winding up the limited liability company's business as the personal or legal representative of the last surviving member as if the person were a member.

(h) In a manager-managed limited liability company:

(1) a member who is not also a manager owes no duties to the company or to the other members solely by reason of being a member;

(2) a manager is held to the same standards of conduct prescribed for members in subsections (b) through (f);

(3) a member who pursuant to the operating agreement exercises some or all of the rights of a manager in the management and conduct of the company's business is held to the standards of conduct in subsections (b) through (f) to the extent that the member exercises the managerial authority vested in a manager by this [Act]; and

(4) a manager is relieved of liability imposed by law for violation of the standards prescribed by subsections (b) through (f) to the extent of the managerial authority delegated to the members by the operating agreement.

SECTION 410. Actions by Members.

(a) A member may maintain an action against a limited liability company or another member for legal or equitable relief, with or without an accounting as to the company's business, to enforce:

(1) the member's rights under the operating agreement;

(2) the member's rights under this [Act]; and

(3) the rights and otherwise protect the interests of the member, including rights and interests arising independently of the member's relationship to the company.

(b) The accrual, and any time limited for the assertion, of a right of action for a remedy under this section is governed by other law. A right to an accounting upon a dissolution and winding up does not revive a claim barred by law.

SECTION 411. Continuation of Limited Liability Company After Expiration of Specified Term.

(a) If a limited liability company having a specified term is continued after the expiration of the term, the rights and duties of the members and managers remain the same as they were at the expiration of the term except to the extent inconsistent with rights and duties of members and managers of an at-will company.

(b) If the members in a member-managed limited liability company or the managers in a manager-managed company continue the business without any winding up of the business of the company, it continues as an at-will company.

[ARTICLE] 5 TRANSFEREES AND CREDITORS OF MEMBER

Section 501. Member's Distributional Interest.
Section 502. Transfer of Distributional Interest.
Section 503. Rights of Transferee.
Section 504. Rights of Creditor.

SECTION 501. Member's Distributional Interest.

(a) A member is not a co-owner of, and has no transferable interest in, property of a limited liability company.

(b) A distributional interest in a limited liability company is personal property and, subject to Sections 502 and 503, may be transferred in whole or in part.

(c) An operating agreement may provide that a distributional interest may be evidenced by a certificate of the interest issued by the limited liability company and, subject to Section 503, may also provide for the transfer of any interest represented by the certificate.

SECTION 502. Transfer of Distributional Interest.

A transfer of a distributional interest does not entitle the transferee to become or to exercise any rights of a member. A transfer entitles the transferee to receive, to the extent transferred, only the distributions to which the transferor would be entitled. A member ceases to be a member upon transfer of all of the member's distributional interest, other than a transfer for security purposes, or a court order charging the member's distributional interest, which has not been foreclosed.

SECTION 503. Rights of Transferee.

(a) A transferee of a distributional interest may become a member of a limited liability company if and to the extent that the transferor gives the transferee the right in accordance with authority described in the operating agreement or all other members consent.

(b) A transferee who has become a member, to the extent transferred, has the rights and powers, and is subject to the restrictions and liabilities, of a member under the operating agreement of a limited liability company and this [Act]. A transferee who becomes a member also is liable for the transferor member's obligations to make contributions under Section 402 and for obligations under Section 407 to return unlawful distributions, but the transferee is not obligated for the transferor member's liabilities unknown to the transferee at the time the transferee becomes a member and is not personally liable for any obligation of the company incurred before the transferee's admission as a member.

(c) Whether or not a transferee of a distributional interest becomes a member under subsection (a), the transferor is not released from liability to the limited liability company under the operating agreement or this [Act].

(d) A transferee who does not become a member is not entitled to participate in the management or conduct of the limited liability company's business, require access to information concerning the company's transactions, or inspect or copy any of the company's records.

(e) A transferee who does not become a member is entitled to:

(1) receive, in accordance with the transfer, distributions to which the transferor would otherwise be entitled;

(2) receive, upon dissolution and winding up of the limited liability company's business:

(i) in accordance with the transfer, the net amount otherwise distributable to the transferor;

(ii) a statement of account only from the date of the latest statement of account agreed to by all the members;

(3) seek under Section 801(6) a judicial determination that it is equitable to dissolve and wind up the company's business.

(f) A limited liability company need not give effect to a transfer until it has notice of the transfer.

SECTION 504. Rights of Creditor.

(a) On application by a judgment creditor of a member of a limited liability company or of a member's transferee, a court having jurisdiction may charge the distributional interest of the judgment debtor to satisfy the judgment. The court may appoint a receiver of the share of the distributions due or to become due to the judgment debtor and make all other orders, directions, accounts, and inquiries the judgment debtor might have made or which the circumstances may require to give effect to the charging order.

(b) A charging order constitutes a lien on the judgment debtor's distributional interest. The court may order a foreclosure of a lien on a distributional interest subject to the charging order at any time. A purchaser at the foreclosure sale has the rights of a transferee.

(c) At any time before foreclosure, a distributional interest in a limited liability company which is charged may be redeemed:

(1) by the judgment debtor;

(2) with property other than the company's property, by one or more of the other members; or

(3) with the company's property, but only if permitted by the operating agreement.

(d) This [Act] does not affect a member's right under exemption laws with respect to the member's distributional interest in a limited liability company.

(e) This section provides the exclusive remedy by which a judgment creditor of a member or a transferee may satisfy a judgment out of the judgment debtor's distributional interest in a limited liability company.

[ARTICLE] 6
MEMBER'S DISSOCIATION

Section 601.   Events Causing Member's Dissociation.
Section 602.   Member's Power to Dissociate; Wrongful Dissociation.
Section 603.   Effect of Member's Dissociation.

SECTION 601. Events Causing Member's Dissociation.

A member is dissociated from a limited liability company upon the occurrence of any of the following events:

(1) the company's having notice of the member's express will to withdraw upon the date of notice or on a later date specified by the member;

(2) an event agreed to in the operating agreement as causing the member's dissociation;

(3) the member's expulsion pursuant to the operating agreement;

(4) the member's expulsion by unanimous vote of the other members if:

(i) it is unlawful to carry on the company's business with the member;

(ii) there has been a transfer of substantially all of the member's distributional interest, other than a transfer for security purposes, or a court order charging the member's distributional interest, which has not been foreclosed;

(iii) within 90 days after the company notifies a corporate member that it will be expelled because it has filed a certificate of dissolution or the equivalent, its charter has been revoked, or its right to conduct business has been suspended by the jurisdiction of its incorporation, the member fails to obtain a revocation of the certificate of dissolution or a reinstatement of its charter or its right to conduct business; or

(iv) a partnership or a limited liability company that is a member has been dissolved and its business is being wound up;

(5) on application by the company or another member, the member's expulsion by judicial determination because the member:

(i) engaged in wrongful conduct that adversely and materially affected the company's business;

(ii) willfully or persistently committed a material breach of the operating agreement or of a duty owed to the company or the other members under Section 409; or

(iii) engaged in conduct relating to the company's business which makes it not reasonably practicable to carry on the business with the member;

(6) the member's:

(i) becoming a debtor in bankruptcy;

(ii) executing an assignment for the benefit of creditors;

(iii) seeking, consenting to, or acquiescing in the appointment of a trustee, receiver, or liquidator of the member or of all or substantially all of the member's property; or

(iv) failing, within 90 days after the appointment, to have vacated or stayed the appointment of a trustee, receiver, or liquidator of the member or of all or substantially all of the member's property obtained without the member's consent or acquiescence, or failing within 90 days after the expiration of a stay to have the appointment vacated;

(7) in the case of a member who is an individual:

(i) the member's death;

(ii) the appointment of a guardian or general conservator for the member; or

(iii) a judicial determination that the member has otherwise become incapable of performing the member's duties under the operating agreement;

(8) in the case of a member that is a trust or is acting as a member by virtue of being a trustee of a trust, distribution of the trust's entire rights to receive distributions from the company, but not merely by reason of the substitution of a successor trustee;

(9) in the case of a member that is an estate or is acting as a member by virtue of being a personal representative of an estate, distribution of the estate's entire rights to receive distributions from the company, but not merely the substitution of a successor personal representative;

(10) termination of the existence of a member if the member is not an individual, estate, or trust other than a business trust; or

(11) a termination of a member's continued membership in a limited liability company for any other reason.

SECTION 602. Member's Power to Dissociate; Wrongful Dissociation.

(a) A member has the power to dissociate from a limited liability company at any time, rightfully or wrongfully, by express will pursuant to Section 601(1).

(b) A member's dissociation from a limited liability company is wrongful only if:

(1) it is in breach of an express provision of the operating agreement; or

(2) before the expiration of the term of a company having a specified term:

(i) the member withdraws by express will;

(ii) the member is expelled by judicial determination under Section 601(5);

(iii) the member is dissociated by becoming a debtor in bankruptcy; or

(iv) in the case of a member who is not an individual, trust other than a business-trust, or estate, the member is expelled or otherwise dissociated because it willfully dissolved or terminated its existence.

(c) A member who wrongfully dissociates from a limited liability company is liable to the company and to the other members for damages caused by the dissociation. The liability is in addition to any other obligation of the member to the company or to the other members.

(d) If a limited liability company does not dissolve and wind up its business as a result of a member's wrongful dissociation under subsection (b), damages sustained by the company for the wrongful dissociation must be offset against distributions otherwise due the member after the dissociation.

SECTION 603. Effect of Member's Dissociation.

(a) If under Section 801 a member's dissociation from a limited liability company results in a dissolution and winding up of the company's business, [Article] 8 applies. If a member's dissociation from the company does not result in a dissolution and winding up of the company's business under Section 801:

(1) in an at-will company, the company must cause the dissociated member's distributional interest to be purchased under [Article] 7; and

(2) in a company having a specified term:

(i) if the company dissolves and winds up its business on or before the expiration of its specified term, [Article] 8 applies to determine the dissociated member's rights to distributions; and

(ii) if the company does not dissolve and wind up its business on or before the expiration of its specified term, the company must cause the dissociated member's distributional interest to be purchased under [Article] 7 on the date of the expiration of the term specified at the time of the member's dissociation.

(b) Upon a member's dissociation from a limited liability company:

(1) the member's right to participate in the management and conduct of the company's business terminates, except as otherwise provided in Section 803, and the member ceases to be a member and is treated the same as a transferee of a member;

(2) the member's duty of loyalty under Section 409(b)(3) terminates, and

(3) the member's duty of loyalty under Section 409(b)(l) and (2) and duty of care under Section 409(c) continue only with regard to matters arising and events occurring before the member's dissociation, unless the member participates in winding up the company's business pursuant to Section 803.

[ARTICLE] 7
MEMBER'S DISSOCIATION WHEN BUSINESS NOT WOUND UP

Section 701. Company Purchase of Distributional Interest.
Section 702. Court Action to Determine Fair Value of Distributional Interest.
Section 703. Dissociated Member's Power to Bind Limited Liability Company.
Section 704. Statement of Dissociation.

SECTION 701. Company Purchase of Distributional Interest.

(a) A limited liability company shall purchase a distributional interest of a:

(1) member of an at-will limited liability company for its fair value determined as of the date of the member's dissociation if the member's dissociation does not result in a dissolution and winding up of the company's business under Section 801; or

(2) member of a company having a specified term for its fair value determined as of the date of the expiration of the specified term that existed on the member's dissociation if the expiration of the specified term does not result in a dissolution and winding up of the company's business under Section 801.

(b) A limited liability company must deliver a purchase offer to the dissociated member whose distributional interest is entitled to be purchased not later than 30 days after the date determined under subsection (a). The purchase offer must be accompanied by:

(1) a statement of the company's assets and liabilities as of the date determined under subsection (a);

(2) the latest available balance sheet and income statement, if any; and

(3) an explanation of how the estimated amount of the payment was calculated.

(c) If the price and other terms of a purchase of a distributional interest are fixed or are to be determined by the operating agreement, the price and terms so fixed or determined govern the purchase unless the purchaser defaults. In that case the dissociated member is entitled to commence a proceeding to have the company dissolved under Section 801(5)(iv).

(d) If an agreement to purchase the distributional interest is not made within 120 days after the date determined under subsection (a), the dissociated member, within another 120 days, may commence a proceeding against the limited liability company to enforce the purchase. The company at its expense shall notify in writing all of the remaining members, and any other person the court directs, of the commencement of the proceeding. The jurisdiction of the court in which the proceeding is commenced under this subsection is plenary and exclusive.

(e) The court shall determine the fair value of the distributional interest in accordance with the standards set forth in Section 702 together with the terms for the purchase. Upon making these determinations, the court shall order the limited liability company to purchase or cause the purchase of the interest.

(f) Damages for wrongful dissociation under Section 602(b), and all other amounts owing, whether or not currently due, from the dissociated member to a limited liability company, must be offset against the purchase price.

SECTION 702. Court Action to Determine Fair Value of Distributional Interest.

(a) In an action brought to determine the fair value of a distributional interest in a limited liability company, the court shall:

(1) determine the fair value of the interest, considering among other relevant evidence the going concern value of the company, any agreement among some or all of the members fixing the price or specifying a formula for determining value of distributional interests for any purpose, the recommendations of any appraiser appointed by the court, and any legal constraints on the company's ability to purchase the interest;

(2) specify the terms of the purchase, including, if appropriate, terms for installment payments, subordination of the purchase obligation to the rights of the company's other creditors, security for a deferred purchase price, and a covenant not

to compete or other restriction on a dissociated member; and

(3) require the dissociated member to deliver an assignment of the interest to the purchaser upon receipt of the purchase price or the first installment of the purchase price.

(b) After an order to purchase is entered, a party may petition the court to modify the terms of the purchase and the court may do so if it finds that changes in the financial or legal ability of the limited liability company or other purchaser to complete the purchase justify a modification.

(c) After the dissociated member delivers the assignment, the dissociated member has no further claim against the company, its members, officers, or managers, if any, other than a claim to any unpaid balance of the purchase price and a claim under any agreement with the company or the remaining members that is not terminated by the court.

(d) If the purchase is not completed in accordance with the specified terms, the company is to be dissolved upon application under Section 801(5)(iv). If a limited liability company is so dissolved, the dissociated member has the same rights and priorities in the company's assets as if the sale had not been ordered.

(e) If the court finds that a party to the proceeding acted arbitrarily, vexatiously, or not in good faith, it may award one or more other parties their reasonable expenses, including attorney's fees and the expenses of appraisers or other experts, incurred in the proceeding. The finding may be based on the company's failure to make an offer to pay or to comply with Section 701(b).

(f) Interest must be paid on the amount awarded from the determined under Section 701(a) to the date of payment.

SECTION 703. Dissociated Member's Power to Bind Limited Liability Company.

For two years after a member dissociates without the dissociation resulting in a dissolution and winding up of a limited liability company's business, the company, including a surviving company under [Article] 9, is bound by an act of the dissociated member which would have bound the company under Section 301 before dissociation only if at the time of entering into the transaction the other party:

(1) reasonably believed that the dissociated member was then a member;

(2) did not have notice of the member's dissociation; and

(3) is not deemed to have had notice under Section 704.

SECTION 704. Statement of Dissociation.

(a) A dissociated member or a limited liability company may file in the office of the [Secretary of State] a statement of dissociation stating the name of the company and that the member is dissociated from the company.

(b) For the purposes of Sections 301 and 703, a person not a member is deemed to have notice of the dissociation 90 days after the statement of dissociation is filed.

[ARTICLE] 8
WINDING UP COMPANY'S BUSINESS

SECTION 801. Events Causing Dissolution and Winding Up of Company's Business.

A limited liability company is dissolved, and its business must be wound up, upon the occurrence of any of the following events:

(1) an event specified in the operating agreement;

(2) consent of the number or percentage of members specified in the operating agreement;

(3) dissociation of a member of an at-will company, and dissociation of a member of a company having a specified term but only if the dissociation was for a reason provided in Section 601(6) through (10) and occurred before the expiration of the specified term, but the company is not dissolved and required to be wound up by reason of the dissociation:

(i) if, within 90 days after the dissociation, a majority in interest of the remaining members agree to continue the business of the company; or

(ii) the business of the company is continued under a right to continue stated in the operating agreement;

(4) an event that makes it unlawful for all or substantially all of the business of the company to be continued, but any cure of illegality within 90 days

after notice to the company of the event is effective retroactively to the date of the event for purposes of this section;

(5) on application by a member or a dissociated member, upon entry of a judicial decree that:

(i) the economic purpose of the company is likely to be unreasonably frustrated;

(ii) another member has engaged in conduct relating to the company's business that makes it not reasonably practicable to carry on the company's business with that member;

(iii) it is not otherwise reasonably practicable to carry on the company's business in conformity with the articles of organization and the operating agreement;

(iv) the company failed to purchase the petitioner's distributional interest as required by Section 701; or

(v) the managers or members in control of the company have acted, are acting, or will act in a manner that is illegal, oppressive, fraudulent, or unfairly prejudicial to the petitioner;

(6) on application by a transferee of a member's interest, a judicial determination that it is equitable to wind up the company's business:

(i) after the expiration of the specified term, if the company was for a specified term at the time the applicant became a transferee by member dissociation, transfer, or entry of a charging order that gave rise to the transfer; or

(ii) at any time, if the company was at will at the time the applicant became a transferee by member dissociation, transfer, or entry of a charging order that gave rise to the transfer; or

(7) the expiration of a specified term.

SECTION 802. Limited Liability Company Continues After Dissolution.

(a) Subject to subsection (b), a limited liability company continues after dissolution only for the purpose of winding up its business.

(b) At any time after the dissolution of a limited liability company and before the winding up of its business is completed, the members, including a dissociated member whose dissociation caused the dissolution, may unanimously waive the right to have the company's business wound up and the company terminated. In that case:

(1) the limited liability company resumes carrying on its business as if dissolution had never occurred and any liability incurred by the company or a member after the dissolution and before the waiver is determined as if the dissolution had never occurred; and

(2) the rights of a third party accruing under Section 804(a) or arising out of conduct in reliance on the dissolution before the third party knew or received a notification of the waiver are not adversely affected.

SECTION 803. Right to Wind Up Limited Liability Company's Business.

(a) After dissolution, a member who has not wrongfully dissociated may participate in winding up a limited liability company's business, but on application of any member, member's legal representative, or transferee, the [designate the appropriate court], for good cause shown, may order judicial supervision of the winding up.

(b) A legal representative of the last surviving member may wind up a limited liability company's business.

(c) A person winding up a limited liability company's business may preserve the company's business or property as a going concern for a reasonable time, prosecute and defend actions and proceedings, whether civil, criminal, or administrative, settle and close the company's business, dispose of and transfer the company's property, discharge the company's liabilities, distribute the assets of the company pursuant to Section 806, settle disputes by mediation or arbitration, and perform other necessary acts.

SECTION 804. Member's or Manager's Power and Liability As Agent After Dissolution.

(a) A limited liability company is bound by a member's or manager's act after dissolution that:

(1) is appropriate for winding up the company's business; or

(2) would have bound the company under Section 301 before dissolution, if the other party to the transaction did not have notice of the dissolution.

(b) A member or manager who, with knowledge of the dissolution, subjects a limited liability company to liability by an act that is not appropriate for winding up the company's business is liable to the company for any damage caused to the company arising from the liability.

SECTION 805. Articles of Termination.

(a) At any time after dissolution and winding up, a limited liability company may terminate its existence by filing with the [Secretary of State] articles of termination stating:

(1) the name of the company;

(2) the date of the dissolution; and

(3) that the company's business has been wound up and the legal existence of the company has been terminated.

(b) The existence of a limited liability company is terminated upon the filing of the articles of termination, or upon a later effective date, if specified in the articles of termination.

SECTION 806. Distribution of Assets in Winding Up Limited Liability Company's Business.

(a) In winding up a limited liability company's business, the assets of the company must be applied to discharge its obligations to creditors, including members who are creditors. Any surplus must be applied to pay in money the net amount distributable to members in accordance with their right to distributions under subsection (b).

(b) Each member is entitled to a distribution upon the winding up of the limited liability company's business consisting of a return of all contributions which have not previously been returned and a distribution of any remainder in equal shares.

SECTION 807. Known Claims Against Dissolved Limited Liability Company.

(a) A dissolved limited liability company may dispose of the known claims against it by following the procedure described in this section.

(b) A dissolved limited liability company shall notify its known claimants in writing of the dissolution. The notice must:

(1) specify the information required to be included in a claim;

(2) provide a mailing address where the claim is to be sent;

(3) state the deadline for receipt of the claim, which may not be less than 120 days after the date the written notice is received by the claimant; and

(4) state that the claim will be barred if not received by the deadline.

(c) A claim against a dissolved limited liability company is barred if the requirements of subsection (b) are met, and:

(1) the claim is not received by the specified deadline; or

(2) in the case of a claim that is timely received but rejected by the dissolved company, the claimant does not commence a proceeding to enforce the claim within 90 days after the receipt of the notice of the rejection.

(d) For purposes of this section, "claim" does not include a contingent liability or a claim based on an event occurring after the effective date of dissolution.

SECTION 808. Other Claims Against Dissolved Limited Liability Company.

(a) A dissolved limited liability company may publish notice of its dissolution and request persons having claims against the company to present them in accordance with the notice.

(b) The notice must:

(1) be published at least once in a newspaper of general circulation in the [county] in which the dissolved limited liability company's principal office is located or, if none in this State, in which its designated office is or was last located;

(2) describe the information required to be contained in a claim and provide a mailing address where the claim is to be sent; and

(3) state that a claim against the limited liability company is barred unless a proceeding to

enforce the claim is commenced within five years after publication of the notice.

(c) If a dissolved limited liability company publishes a notice in accordance with subsection (b), the claim of each of the following claimants is barred unless the claimant commences a proceeding to enforce the claim against the dissolved company within five years after the publication date of the notice:

(1) a claimant who did not receive written notice under Section 807;

(2) a claimant whose claim was timely sent to the dissolved company but not acted on; and

(3) a claimant whose claim is contingent or based on an event occuring after the effective date of dissolution.

(d) A claim not barred under this section may be enforced:

(1) against the dissolved limited liability company, to the extent of its undistributed assets; or

(2) if the assets have been distributed in liquidation, against a member of the dissolved company to the extent of the member's proportionate share of the claim or the company's assets distributed to the member in liquidation, whichever is less, but a member's total liability for all claims under this section may not exceed the total amount of assets distributed to the member.

SECTION 809.   Grounds for Administrative Dissolution.

The [Secretary of State] may commence a proceeding to dissolve a limited liability company administratively if the company does not:

(1) pay any franchise taxes or penalties imposed by this [Act] or other law within 60 days after they are due;

(2) deliver its annual report to the [Secretary of State] within 60 days after it is due, or

(3) file articles of termination under Section 805 following the expiration of the specified term designated in its articles of organization.

SECTION 810.   Procedure for and Effect of Administrative Dissolution.

(a) If the [Secretary of State] determines that a ground exists for administratively dissolving a limited liability company, the [Secretary of State] shall enter a record of the determination and serve the company with a copy of the record.

(b) If the company does not correct each ground for dissolution or demonstrate to the reasonable satisfaction of the [Secretary of State] that each ground determined by the [Secretary of State] does not exist within 60 days after service of the notice, the [Secretary of State] shall administratively dissolve the company by signing a certification of the dissolution that recites the ground for dissolution and its effective date. The [Secretary of State] shall file the original of the certificate and serve the company with a copy of the certificate.

(c) A company administratively dissolved continues its existence but may carry on only business necessary to wind up and liquidate its business and affairs under Section 802 and to notify claimants under Sections 807 and 808.

(d) The administrative dissolution of a company does not terminate the authority of its agent for service of process.

SECTION 811.   Reinstatement Following Administrative Dissolution.

(a) A limited liability company administratively dissolved may apply to the [Secretary of State] for reinstatement within two years after the effective date of dissolution. The application must:

(1) recite the name of the company and the effective date of its administrative dissolution;

(2) state that the grounds for dissolution either did not exist or have been eliminated;

(3) state that the company's name satisfies the requirements of Section 105; and

(4) contain a certificate from the [taxing authority] reciting that all taxes owed by the company have been paid.

(b) If the [Secretary of State] determines that the application contains the information required by subsection (a) and that the information is correct, the [Secretary of State] shall cancel the certificate of dissolution and prepare a certificate of reinstatement that recites this determination and the effective date of reinstatement, file the original of the certificate, and serve the company with a copy of the certificate.

(c) When reinstatement is effective, it relates back to and takes effect as of the effective date of the administrative dissolution and the company may resume its business as if the administrative dissolution had never occurred.

SECTION 812.   Appeal from Denial of Reinstatement.

(a) If the [Secretary of State] denies a limited liability company's application for reinstatement following administrative dissolution, the [Secretary of State] shall serve the company with a record that explains the reason or reasons for denial.

(b) The company may appeal the denial of reinstatement to the [name appropriate] court within 30 days after service of the notice of denial is perfected. The company appeals by petitioning the court to set aside the dissolution and attaching to the petition copies of the [Secretary of State's] certificate of dissolution, the company's application for reinstatement, and the [Secretary of State's] notice of denial.

(c) The court may summarily order the [Secretary of State] to reinstate the dissolved company or may take other action the court considers appropriate.

(d) The court's final decision may be appealed as in other civil proceedings.

[ARTICLE] 9
CONVERSIONS AND MERGERS

Section 901.   Definitions.
Section 902.   Conversion of Partnership or Limited Partnership To Limited Liability Company.
Section 903.   Effect of Conversion; Entity Unchanged.
Section 904.   Merger of Entities.
Section 905.   Articles of Merger.
Section 906.   Effect of Merger.
Section 907.   [Article] Not Exclusive.

SECTION 901. Definitions.

In this [article]:

(1) "Corporation" means a corporation under [the State Corporation Act], a predecessor law, or comparable law of another jurisdiction.

(2) "General partner" means a partner in a partnership and a general partner in a limited partnership.

(3) "Limited partner" means a limited partner in a limited partnership.

(4) "Limited partnership" means a limited partnership created under [the State Limited Partnership Act], a predecessor law, or comparable law of another jurisdiction.

(5) "Partner" includes a general partner and a limited partner.

(6) "Partnership" means a general partnership under [the State Partnership Act], a predecessor law, or comparable law of another jurisdiction.

(7) "Partnership agreement" means an agreement among the partners concerning the partnership or limited partnership.

(8) "Shareholder" means a shareholder in a corporation.

SECTION 902. Conversion of Partnership or Limited Partnership to Limited Liability Company.

(a) A partnership or limited partnership may be converted to a limited liability company pursuant to this section.

(b) The terms and conditions of a conversion of a partnership or limited partnership to a limited liability company must be approved by all of the partners or by a number or percentage of the partners required for conversion in the partnership agreement.

(c) An agreement of conversion must set forth the terms and conditions of the conversion of the interests of partners of a partnership or of a limited partnership, as the case may be, into interests in the converted limited liability company or the cash or other consideration to be paid or delivered as a result of the conversion of the interests of the partners, or a combination thereof.

(d) After a conversion is approved under subsection (b), the partnership or limited partnership

shall file articles of organization in the office of the [Secretary of State] which satisfy the requirements of Section 203 and contain:

(1) a statement that the partnership or limited partnership was converted to a limited liability company from a partnership or limited partnership, as the case may be;

(2) its former name;

(3) a statement of the number of votes cast by the partners entitled to vote for and against the conversion and, if the vote is less than unanimous, the number or percentage required to approve the conversion under subsection (b); and

(4) in the case of a limited partnership, a statement that the certificate of limited partnership is to be canceled as of the date the conversion took effect.

(e) In the case of a limited partnership, the filing of articles of organization under subsection (d) cancels its certificate of limited partnership as of the date the conversion took effect.

(f) A conversion takes effect when the articles of organization are filed in the office of the [Secretary of State] or at any later date specified in the articles of organization.

(g) A general partner who becomes a member of a limited liability company as a result of a conversion remains liable as a partner for an obligation incurred by the partnership or limited partnership before the conversion takes effect.

(h) A general partner's liability for all obligations of the limited liability company incurred after the conversion takes effect is that of a member of the company. A limited partner who becomes a member as a result of a conversion remains liable only to the extent the limited partner was liable for an obligation incurred by the limited partnership before the conversion takes effect.

SECTION 903. Effect of Conversion; Entity Unchanged.

(a) A partnership or limited partnership that has been converted pursuant to this [article] is for all purposes the same entity that existed before the conversion.

(b) When a conversion takes effect:

(1) all property owned by the converting partnership or limited partnership is vested in the limited liability company;

(2) all debts, liabilities, and other obligations of the converting partnership or limited partnership continue as obligations of the limited liability company;

(3) an action or proceeding pending by or against the converting partnership or limited partnership may be continued as if the conversion had not occurred;

(4) except as prohibited by other law, all of the rights, privileges, immunities, powers, and

purposes of the converting partnership or limited partnership are vested in the limited liability company; and

(5) except as otherwise provided in the agreement of conversion under Section 902(c), all of the partners of the converting partnership continue as members of the limited liability company.

SECTION 904. Merger of Entities.

(a) Pursuant to a plan of merger approved under subsection (c), a limited liability company may be merged with or into one or more limited liability companies, foreign limited liability companies, corporations, foreign corporations, partnerships, foreign partnerships, limited partnerships, foreign limited partnerships, or other domestic or foreign entities.

(b) A plan of merger must set forth:

(1) the name of each entity that is a party to the merger;

(2) the name of the surviving entity into which the other entities will merge;

(3) the type of organization of the surviving entity;

(4) the terms and conditions of the merger;

(5) the manner and basis for converting the interests of each party to the merger into interests or obligations of the surviving entity, or into money or other property in whole or in part; and

(6) the street address of the surviving entity's principal place of business.

(c) A plan of merger must be approved:

(1) in the case of a limited liability company that is a party to the merger, by the members representing the percentage of ownership specified in the operating agreement, but not fewer than the members holding a majority of the ownership or, if provision is not made in the operating agreement, by all the members;

(2) in the case of a foreign limited liability company that is a party to the merger, by the vote required for approval of a merger by the law of the State or foreign jurisdiction in which the foreign limited liability company is organized;

(3) in the case of a partnership or domestic limited partnership that is a party to the merger, by the vote required for approval of a conversion under Section 902(b); and

(4) in the case of any other entities that are parties to the merger, by the vote required for approval of a merger by the law of this State or of the state or foreign jurisdiction in which the entity is organized and, in the absence of such a requirement, by all the owners of interests in the entity.

(d) After a plan of merger is approved and before the merger takes effect, the plan may be amended or abandoned as provided in the plan.

(e) The merger is effective upon the filing of the articles of merger with the [Secretary of State], or at such later date as the articles may provide.

SECTION 905. Articles of Merger.

(a) After approval of the plan of merger under Section 904(c), unless the merger is abandoned under Section 904(d), articles of merger must be signed on behalf of each limited liability company and other entity that is a party to the merger and delivered to the [Secretary of State] for filing. The articles must set forth:

(1) the name and jurisdiction of formation or organization of each of the limited liability companies and other entities that are parties to the merger;

(2) for each limited liability company that is to merge, the date its articles of organization were filed with the [Secretary of State];

(3) that a plan of merger has been approved and signed by each limited liability company and other entity that is to merge;

(4) the name and address of the surviving limited liability company or other surviving entity;

(5) the effective date of the merger;

(6) if a limited liability company is the surviving entity, such changes in its articles of organization as are necessary by reason of the merger;

(7) if a party to a merger is a foreign limited liability company, the jurisdiction and date of filing of its initial articles of organization and the date when its application for authority was filed by the [Secretary of State] or, if an application has not been filed, a statement to that effect; and

(8) if the surviving entity is not a limited liability company, an agreement that the surviving entity may be served with process in this State in any action or proceeding for the enforcement of any liability or obligation of any limited liability company previously subject to suit in this State which is to merge, and for the enforcement, as provided in this [Act], of the right of members of any limited liability company to receive payment for their interest against the surviving entity.

(b) If a foreign limited liability company is the surviving entity of a merger, it may not do business in this State until an application for that authority is filed with the [Secretary of State].

(c) The surviving limited liability company or other entity shall furnish a copy of the plan of merger, on request and without cost, to any member of any limited liability company or any person holding an interest in any other entity that is to merge.

(d) Articles of merger operate as an amendment to the limited liability company's articles of organization.

SECTION 906. Effect of Merger.

(a) When a merger takes effect:

(1) the separate existence of each limited liability company and other entity that is a party to

the merger, other than the surviving entity, terminates;

(2) all property owned by each of the limited liability companies and other entities that are party to the merger vests in the surviving entity;

(3) all debts, liabilities, and other obligations of each limited liability company and other entity that is party to the merger become the obligations of the surviving entity;

(4) an action or proceeding pending by or against a limited liability company or other party to a merger may be continued as if the merger had not occurred or the surviving entity may be substituted as a party to the action or proceeding; and

(5) except as prohibited by other law, all the rights, privileges, immunities, powers, and purposes of every limited liability company and other entity that is a party to a merger become vested in the surviving entity.

(b) The [Secretary of State] is an agent for service of process in an action or proceeding against the surviving foreign entity to enforce an obligation of any party to a merger if the surviving foreign entity fails to appoint or maintain an agent designated for service of process in this State or the agent for service of process cannot with reasonable diligence be found at the designated office. Upon receipt of process, the [Secretary of State] shall send a copy of the process by registered or certified mail, return receipt requested, to the surviving entity at the address set forth in the articles of merger. Service is effected under this subsection at the earliest of:

(1) the date the company receives the process, notice, or demand;

(2) the date shown on the return receipt, if signed on behalf of the company; or

(3) five days after its deposit in the mail, if mailed postpaid and correctly addressed.

(c) A member of the surviving limited liability company is liable for all obligations of a party to the merger for which the member was personally liable before the merger.

(d) Unless otherwise agreed, a merger of a limited liability company that is not the surviving entity in the merger does not require the limited liability company to wind up its business under this [Act] or pay its liabilities and distribute its assets pursuant to this [Act].

(e) Articles of merger serve as articles of dissolution for a limited liability company that is not the surviving entity in the merger.

SECTION 907.   [Article] Not Exclusive.

This [article] does not preclude an entity from being converted or merged under other law.

[ARTICLE] 10
FOREIGN LIMITED LIABILITY COMPANIES

Section 1001. Law Governing Foreign Limited
Liability Companies.

SECTION 1001.   Law Governing Foreign Limited Liability Companies.

(a) The laws of the State or other jurisdiction under which a foreign limited liabiiity company is organized govern its organization and internal affairs and the liability of its managers, members, and their transferees.

(b) A foreign limited liability company may not be denied a certificate of authority by reason of any difference between the laws of another jurisdiction under which the foreign company is organized and the laws of this State.

(c) A certificate of authority does not authorize a foreign limited liability company to engage in any business or exercise any power that a limited liability company may not engage in or exercise in this State.

SECTION 1002.   Application for Certificate of Authority.

(a) A foreign limited liability company may apply for a certificate of authority to transact business in this State by delivering an application to the [Secretary of State] for filing. The application must set forth:

(1) the name of the foreign company or, if its name is unavailable for use in this State, a name that satisfies the requirements of Section 1005;

(2) the name of the State or country under whose law it is organized;

(3) the street address of its principal office;

(4) the address of its initial designated office in this State;

(5) the name and street address of its initial agent for service of process in this State;

(6) whether the duration of the company is for a specified term and, if so, the period specified;

(7) whether the company is manager-managed, and, if so, the name and address of each initial manager; and

(8) whether the members of the company are to be liable for its debts and obligations under a provision similar to Section 303(c).

(b) A foreign limited liability company shall deliver with the completed application a certificate of existence or a record of similar import authenticated by the [Secretary of State] or other official having custody of company records in the State or country under whose law it is organized.

SECTION 1003. Activities Not Constituting Transacting Business.

(a) Activities of a foreign limited liability company that do not constitute transacting business within the meaning of this [article] include:

(1) maintaining, defending, or settling an action or proceeding;

(2) holding meetings of its members or managers or carrying on any other activity concerning its internal affairs;

(3) maintaining bank accounts;

(4) maintaining offices or agencies for the transfer, exchange, and registration of the foreign company's own securities or maintaining trustees or depositories with respect to those securities;

(5) selling through independent contractors;

(6) soliciting or obtaining orders, whether by mail or through employees or agents or otherwise, if the orders require acceptance outside this State before they become contracts;

(7) creating or acquiring indebtedness, mortgages, or security interests in real or personal property;

(8) securing or collecting debts or enforcing mortgages or other security interests in property securing the debts, and holding, protecting, and maintaining property so acquired;

(9) conducting an isolated transaction that is completed within 30 days and is not one in the course of similar transactions of a like manner; and

(10) transacting business in interstate commerce.

(b) For purposes of this [article], the ownership in this State of income-producing real property or tangible personal property, other than property excluded under subsection (a), constitutes transacting business in this State.

(c) This section does not apply in determining the contacts or activities that may subject a foreign limited liability company to service of process, taxation, or regulation under any other law of this State.

SECTION 1004. Issuance of Certificate of Authority.

Unless the [Secretary of State] determines that an application for a certificate of authority fails to comply as to form with the filing requirements of this [Act], the [Secretary of State], upon payment of all filing fees, shall file the application and send a receipt for it and the fees to the limited liability company or its representative.

SECTION 1005. Name of Foreign Limited Liability Company.

(a) If the name of a foreign limited liability company does not satisfy the requirements of Section 105, the company, to obtain or maintain a certificate of authority to transact business in this State, must use a fictitious name to transact business in this State if its real name is unavailable and it delivers to the [Secretary of State] for filing a copy of the resolution of its managers, in the case of a manager-managed company, or of its members, in the case of a member-managed company, adopting the fictitious name.

(b) Except as authorized by subsections (c) and (d), the name, including a fictitious name, of a foreign limited liability company must be distinguishable upon the records of the [Secretary of State] from:

(1) the name of any corporation, limited partnership, or company incorporated, organized, or authorized to transact business in this State;

(2) a company name reserved or registered under Section 106 or 107; and

(3) the fictitious name of another foreign limited liability company authorized to transact business in this State.

(c) A foreign limited liability company may apply to the [Secretary of State] for authority to use in this State a name that is not distinguishable upon the records of the [Secretary of State] from a name described in subsection (b). The [Secretary of State] shall authorize use of the name applied for if:

(1) the present user, registrant, or owner of a reserved name consents to the use in a record and submits an undertaking in form satisfactory to the [Secretary of State] to change its name to a name that is distinguishable upon the records of the [Secretary of State] from the name of the foreign applying limited liability company; or

(2) the applicant delivers to the [Secretary of State] a certified copy of a final judgment of a court establishing the applicant's right to use the name applied for in this State.

(d) A foreign limited liability company may use in this State the name, including the fictitious name, of another domestic or foreign entity that is used in this State if the other entity is incorporated, organized, or authorized to transact business in this State and the foreign limited liability company:

(1) has merged with the other entity;

(2) has been formed by reorganization of the other entity; or

(3) has acquired all or substantially all of the assets, including the name, of the other entity.

(e) If a foreign limited liability company authorized to transact business in this State changes its name to one that does not satisfy the requirements of Section 105, it may not transact business in this State under the name as changed until it adopts a name satisfying the requirements of Section 105 and obtains an amended certificate of authority.

SECTION 1006. Revocation of Certificate of Authority.

(a) A certificate of authority of a foreign limited liability company to transact business in this State may be revoked by the [Secretary of State] in the manner provided in subsection (b) if:

(1) the company fails to:

(i) pay any fees prescribed by law;

(ii) appoint and maintain an agent for service of process as required by this [article]; or

(iii) file a statement of a change in the name or business address of the agent as required by this [articlel; or

(2) a misrepresentation has been made of any material matter in any application, report, affidavit, or other record submitted by the company pursuant to this [article].

(b) The [Secretary of State] may not revoke a certificate of authority of a foreign limited liability company unless the [Secretary of State] sends the company notice of the revocation, at least 60 days before its effective date, by a record addressed to its agent for service of process in this State, or if the company fails to appoint and maintain a proper agent in this State, addressed to the office required to be maintained by Section 108. The notice must identify the cause for the revocation of the certificate of authority. The authority of the company to transact business in this State ceases on the effective date of the revocation unless the foreign limited liability company cures the failure before that date.

SECTION 1007. Cancellation of Authority.

A foreign limited liability company may cancel its authority to transact business in this State by filing in the office of the [Secretary of State] a certificate of cancellation. Cancellation does not terminate the authority of the [Secretary of State] to accept service of process on the company for [claims for relief] arising out of the transactions of business in this State.

SECTION 1008. Effect of Failure to Obtain Certificate of Authority.

(a) A foreign limited liability company transacting business in this State may not maintain an action or proceeding in this State unless it has a certificate of authority to transact business in this State.

(b) The failure of a foreign limited liability company to have a certificate of authority to transact business in this State does not impair the validity of a contract or act of the company or prevent the foreign limited liability company from defending an action or proceeding in this State.

(c) Limitations on personal liability of managers, members, and their transferees are not waived solely by transacting business in this State without a certificate of authority.

(d) If a foreign limited liability company transacts business in this State without a certificate of authority, it appoints the [Secretary of State] as its agent for service of process for [claims for relief] arising out of the transaction of business in this State.

SECTION 1009. Action by [Attorney General].

The [Attorney General] may maintain an action to restrain a foreign limited liability company from transacting business in this State in violation of this [article].

[ARTICLE] 11
DERIVATIVE ACTIONS

SECTION 1101. Right of Action.

A member of a limited liability company may maintain an action in the right of the company if the members or managers having authority to do so have refused to commence the action or an effort to cause those members or managers to commence the action is not likely to succeed.

SECTION 1102. Proper Plaintiff.

In a derivative action for a limited liability company, the plaintiff must be a member of the company when the action is commenced; and:

(1) must have been a member at the time of the transaction of which the plaintiff complains; or

(2) the plaintiff's status as a member must have devolved upon the plaintiff by operation of law or pursuant to the terms of the operating agreement from a person who was a member at the time of the transaction.

SECTION 1103. Pleading.

In a derivative action for a limited liability company, the complaint must set forth with particularity the effort of the plaintiff to secure initiation of the action by a member or manager or the reasons for not making the effort.

SECTION 1104. Expenses.

If a derivative action for a limited liability company is successful, in whole or in part, or if anything is received by the plaintiff as a result of a judgment, compromise, or settlement of an action or claim, the court may award the plaintiff reasonable expenses, including reasonable attorney's fees, and shall direct the plaintiff to remit to the limited liability company the remainder of the proceeds received.

[ARTICLE] 12
MISCELLANEOUS PROVISIONS

SECTION 1201. Uniformity of Application and Construction.

This [Act] shall be applied and construed to effectuate its general purpose to make uniform the law with respect to the subject of this [Act] among States enacting it.

SECTION 1202. Short Title.

This [Act] may be cited as the Uniform Limited Liability Company Act.

SECTION 1203. Severability Clause.

If any provision of this [Act] or its application to any person or circumstance is held invalid, the invalidity does not affect other provisions or applications of this [Act] which can be given effect without the invalid provision or application, and to this end the provisions of this [Act] are severable.

SECTION 1204. Effective Date.

This [Act] takes effect [_____].

SECTION 1205. Transitional Provisions.

(a) Before January 1, 199___, this [Act] governs only a limited liability company organized:

(1) after the effective date of this [Act], unless the company is continuing the business of a dissolved limited liability company under [Section of the existing Limited Liability Company Act]; and

(2) before the effective date of this [Act], which elects, as provided by subsection (c), to be governed by this [Act].

(b) On and after January 1, 199___, this [Act] governs all limited liability companies.

(c) Before January 1, 199___, a limited liability company voluntarily may elect, in the manner provided in its operating agreement or by law for amending the operating agreement, to be governed by this [Act].

SECTION 1206. Savings Clause.

This [Act] does not affect an action or proceeding commenced or right accrued before the effective date of this [Act].

APPENDIX F

EXCERPTS FROM THE MODEL BUSINESS CORPORATION ACT, AS REVISED THROUGH 1994

Reprinted with the permission of Prentice Hall Law & Business.

CHAPTER 13
Dissenters' Rights

CHAPTER 14
Dissolution

CHAPTER 15
Foreign Corporations

CHAPTER 2
INCORPORATION

§ 2.01. Incorporators

One or more persons may act as the incorporator or incorporators of a corporation by delivering articles of incorporation to the secretary of state for filing.

§ 2.02. Articles of Incorporation

(a) The articles of incorporation must set forth:

(1) a corporate name for the corporation that satisfies the requirements of section 4.01;

(2) the number of shares the corporation is authorized to issue;

(3) the street address of the corporation's initial registered office and the name of its initial registered agent at that office; and

(4) the name and address of each incorporator.

(b) The articles of incorporation may set forth:

(1) the names and addresses of the individuals who are to serve as the initial directors;

(2) provisions not inconsistent with law regarding:

(i) the purpose or purposes for which the corporation is organized;

(ii) managing the business and regulating the affairs of the corporation;

(iii) defining, limiting, and regulating the powers of the corporation, its board of directors, and shareholders;

(iv) a par value for authorized shares or classes of shares;

(v) the imposition of personal liability on shareholders for the debts of the corporation to a specified extent and upon specified conditions;

(3) any provision that under this Act is required or permitted to be set forth in the bylaws;

(4) a provision eliminating or limiting the liability of a director to the corporation or its shareholders for money damages for any action taken, or any failure to take any action, as a director, except liability for (A) the amount of a financial benefit received by a director to which he is not entitled; (B) an intentional infliction of harm on the corporation or the shareholders; (C) a violation of section 8.33; or (D) an intentional violation of criminal law; and

(5) a provision permitting or making obligatory indemnification of a director for liability (as defined in section 8.50(5)) to any person for any action taken, or any failure to take any action, as a director, except liability for (A) receipt of a financial benefit to which he is not entitled, (B) an intentional infliction of harm on the corporation or its shareholders, (C) a violation of section 8.33, or (D) an intentional violation of criminal law.

(c) The articles of incorporation need not set forth any of the corporate powers enumerated in this Act.

§ 2.03. Incorporation

(a) Unless a delayed effective date is specified, the corporate existence begins when the articles of incorporation are filed.

(b) The secretary of state's filing of the articles of incorporation is conclusive proof that the incorporators satisfied all conditions precedent to incorporation except in a proceeding by the state to cancel or revoke the incorporation or involuntarily dissolve the corporation.

§ 2.04. Liability for Preincorporation Transactions

All persons purporting to act as or on behalf of a corporation, knowing there was no incorporation under this Act, are jointly and severally liable for all liabilities created while so acting.

§ 2.05. Organization of Corporation

(a) After incorporation:

(1) if initial directors are named in the articles of incorporation, the initial directors shall hold an organizational meeting, at the call of a majority of the directors, to complete the organization of the corporation by appointing officers, adopting bylaws, and carrying on any other business brought before the meeting;

(2) if initial directors are not named in the articles, the incorporator or incorporators shall hold an organizational meeting at the call of a majority of the incorporators:

(i) to elect directors and complete the organization of the corporation; or

(ii) to elect a board of directors who shall complete the organization of the corporation.

(b) Action required or permitted by this Act to be taken by incorporators at an organizational meeting may be taken without a meeting if the action taken is evidenced by one or more written consents describing the action taken and signed by each incorporator.

(c) An organizational meeting may be held in or out of this state.

§ 2.06. Bylaws

(a) The incorporators or board of directors of a corporation shall adopt initial bylaws for the corporation.

(b) The bylaws of a corporation may contain any provision for managing the business and regulating the affairs of the corporation that is not inconsistent with law or the articles of incorporation.

§ 2.07. Emergency Bylaws

(a) Unless the articles of incorporation provide otherwise, the board of directors of a corporation may adopt bylaws to be effective only in an emergency defined in subsection (d). The emergency bylaws, which are subject to amendment or repeal by the shareholders, may make all provisions necessary for managing the corporation during the emergency, including:

(1) procedures for calling a meeting of the board of directors;

(2) quorum requirements for the meeting; and

(3) designation of additional or substitute directors.

(b) All provisions of the regular bylaws consistent with the emergency bylaws remain effective during the emergency. The emergency bylaws are not effective after the emergency ends.

(c) Corporate action taken in good faith in accordance with the emergency bylaws:

(1) binds the corporation; and

(2) may not be used to impose liability on a corporate director, officer, employee, or agent.

(d) An emergency exists for purposes of this section if a quorum of the corporation's directors cannot readily be assembled because of some catastrophic event.

CHAPTER 3
PURPOSES AND POWERS

§ 3.01. Purposes

(a) Every corporation incorporated under this Act has the purpose of engaging in any lawful business unless a more limited purpose is set forth in the articles of incorporation.

(b) A corporation engaging in a business that is subject to regulation under another statute of this state may incorporate under this Act only if permitted by, and subject to all limitations of, the other statute.

§ 3.02. General Powers

Unless its articles of incorporation provide otherwise, every corporation has perpetual duration and succession in its corporate name and has the same powers as an individual to do all things necessary or convenient to carry out its business and affairs, including without limitation power:

(1) to sue and be sued, complain and defend in its corporate name;

(2) to have a corporate seal, which may be altered at will, and to use it, or a facsimile of it, by impressing or affixing it or in any other manner reproducing it;

(3) to make and amend bylaws, not inconsistent with its articles of incorporation or with the laws of this state, for managing the business and regulating the affairs of the corporation;

(4) to purchase, receive, lease, or otherwise acquire, and own, hold, improve, use, and otherwise deal with, real or personal property, or any legal or equitable interest in property, wherever located;

(5) to sell, convey, mortgage, pledge, lease, exchange, and otherwise dispose of all or any part of its property;

(6) to purchase, receive, subscribe for, or otherwise acquire; own, hold, vote, use, sell, mortgage, lend, pledge, or otherwise dispose of; and deal in and with shares or other interests in, or obligations of, any other entity;

(7) to make contracts and guarantees, incur liabilities, borrow money, issue its notes, bonds, and other obligations (which may be convertible into or include the option to purchase other securities of the corporation), and secure any of its obligations by mortgage or pledge of any of its property, franchises, or income;

(8) to lend money, invest and reinvest its funds, and receive and hold real and personal property as security for repayment;

(9) to be a promoter, partner, member, associate, or manager of any partnership, joint venture, trust, or other entity;

(10) to conduct its business, locate offices, and exercise the powers granted by this Act within or without this state;

(11) to elect directors and appoint officers, employees, and agents of the corporation, define their duties, fix their compensation, and lend them money and credit;

(12) to pay pensions and establish pension plans, pension trusts, profit sharing plans, share bonus plans, share option plans, and benefit or incentive plans for any or all of its current or former directors, officers, employees, and agents;

(13) to make donations for the public welfare or for charitable, scientific, or educational purposes;

(14) to transact any lawful business that will aid governmental policy;

(15) to make payments or donations, or do any other act, not inconsistent with law, that furthers the business and affairs of the corporation.

§ 3.03. Emergency Powers

(a) In anticipation of or during an emergency defined in subsection (d), the board of directors of a corporation may:

(1) modify lines of succession to accommodate the incapacity of any director, officer, employee, or agent; and

(2) relocate the principal office, designate alternative principal offices or regional offices, or authorize the officers to do so.

(b) During an emergency defined in subsection (d), unless emergency bylaws provide otherwise:

(1) notice of a meeting of the board of directors need be given only to those directors whom it is practicable to reach and may be given in any practicable manner, including by publication and radio; and

(2) one or more officers of the corporation present at a meeting of the board of directors may be deemed to be directors for the meeting, in order of rank and within the same rank in order of seniority, as necessary to achieve a quorum.

(c) Corporate action taken in good faith during an emergency under this section to further the ordinary business affairs of the corporation:

(1) binds the corporation; and

(2) may not be used to impose liability on a corporate director, officer, employee, or agent.

(d) An emergency exists for purposes of this section if a quorum of the corporation's directors cannot readily be assembled because of some catastrophic event.

§ 3.04. Ultra Vires

(a) Except as provided in subsection (b), the validity of corporate action may not be challenged on the ground that the corporation lacks or lacked power to act.

(b) A corporation's power to act may be challenged:

(1) in a proceeding by a shareholder against the corporation to enjoin the act;

(2) in a proceeding by the corporation, directly, derivatively, or through a receiver, trustee, or other legal representative, against an incumbent or former director, officer, employee, or agent of the corporation; or

(3) in a proceeding by the Attorney General under section 14.30.

(c) In a shareholder's proceeding under subsection (b)(l) to enjoin an unauthorized corporate act, the court may enjoin or set aside the act, if equitable and if all affected persons are parties to the proceeding, and may award damages for loss (other than anticipated profits) suffered by the corporation or another party because of enjoining the unauthorized act.

CHAPTER 4
NAME

§ 4.01. Corporate Name

(a) A corporate name:

(1) must contain the word "corporation," "incorporated," "company," or "limited," or the abbreviation "corp.," "inc.," "co.," or "ltd.," or words or abbreviations of like import in another language; and

(2) may not contain language stating or implying that the corporation is organized for a purpose other than that permitted by section 3.01 and its articles of incorporation.

(b) Except as authorized by subsections (c) and (d), a corporate name must be distinguishable upon the records of the secretary of state from:

(1) the corporate name of a corporation incorporated or authorized to transact business in this state;

(2) a corporate name reserved or registered under section 4.02 or 4.03;

(3) the fictitious name adopted by a foreign corporation authorized to transact business in this state because its real name is unavailable; and

(4) the corporate name of a not-for-profit corporation incorporated or authorized to transact business in this state.

(c) A corporation may apply to the secretary of state for authorization to use a name that is not distinguishable upon his records from one or more of the names described in subsection (b). The secretary of state shall authorize use of the name applied for if:

(1) the other corporation consents to the use in writing and submits an undertaking in form satisfactory to the secretary of state to change its name to a name that is distinguishable upon the records of the secretary of state from the name of the applying corporation; or

(2) the applicant delivers to the secretary of state a certified copy of the final judgment of a court of competent jurisdiction establishing the applicant's right to use the name applied for in this state.

(d) A corporation may use the name (including the fictitious name) of another domestic or foreign corporation that is used in this state if the other corporation is incorporated or authorized to transact business in this state and the proposed user corporation:

(1) has merged with the other corporation;

(2) has been formed by reorganization of the other corporation; or

(3) has acquired all or substantially all of the assets, including the corporate name, of the other corporation.

(e) This Act does not control the use of fictitious names.

§ 4.02. Reserved Name

(a) A person may reserve the exclusive use of a corporate name, including a fictitious name for a foreign corporation whose corporate name is not available, by delivering an application to the secretary of state for filing. The application must set forth the name and address of the applicant and the name proposed to be reserved. If the secretary of state finds that the corporate name applied for is available, he shall reserve the name for the applicant's exclusive use for a nonrenewable 120-day period.

(b) The owner of a reserved corporate name may transfer the reservation to another person by delivering to the secretary of state a signed notice of the transfer that states the name and address of the transferee.

§ 4.03. Registered Name

(a) A foreign corporation may register its corporate name, or its corporate name with any addition required by section 15.06, if the name is distinguishable upon the records of the secretary of state from the corporate names that are not available under section 4.01(b)(3).

(b) A foreign corporation registers its corporate name, or its corporate name with any addition required by section 15.06, by delivering to the secretary of state for filing an application:

(1) setting forth its corporate name, or its corporate name with any addition required by section 15.06, the state or country and date of its incorporation, and a brief description of the nature of the business in which it is engaged; and

(2) accompanied by a certificate of existence (or a document of similar import) from the state or country of incorporation.

(c) The name is registered for the applicant's exclusive use upon the effective date of the application.

(d) A foreign corporation whose registration is effective may renew it for successive years by delivering to the secretary of state for filing a renewal application, which complies with the requirements of subsection (b), between October 1 and December 31 of the preceding year. The renewal application when filed renews the registration for the following calendar year.

(e) A foreign corporation whose registration is effective may thereafter qualify as a foreign corporation under the registered name or consent in writing to the use of that name by a corporation thereafter incorporated under this Act or by another foreign corporation thereafter authorized to transact business in this state. The registration terminates when the domestic corporation is incorporated or the foreign corporation qualifies or consents to the qualification of another foreign corporation under the registered name.

CHAPTER 5
OFFICE AND AGENT

§ 5.01. Registered Office and Registered Agent

Each corporation must continuously maintain in this state:

(1) a registered office that may be the same as any of its places of business; and

(2) a registered agent, who may be:

(i) an individual who resides in this state and whose business office is identical with the registered office;

(ii) a domestic corporation or not-for-profit domestic corporation whose business office is identical with the registered office; or

(iii) a foreign corporation or not-for-profit foreign corporation authorized to transact business in this state whose business office is identical with the registered office.

§ 5.02. Change of Registered Office or Registered Agent

(a) A corporation may change its registered office or registered agent by delivering to the secretary of state for filing a statement of change that sets forth:

(1) the name of the corporation;

(2) the street address of its current registered office;

(3) if the current registered office is to be changed, the street address of the new registered office;

(4) the name of its current registered agent;

(5) if the current registered agent is to be changed, the name of the new registered agent and the new agent's written consent (either on the statement or attached to it) to the appointment; and

(6) that after the change or changes are made, the street addresses of its registered office and the business office of its registered agent will be identical.

(b) If a registered agent changes the street address of his business office, he may change the street address of the registered office of any corporation for which he is the registered agent by notifying the corporation in writing of the change and signing (either manually or in facsimile) and delivering to the secretary of state for filing a statement that complies with the requirements of subsection (a) and recites that the corporation has been notified of the change.

§ 5.03. Resignation of Registered Agent

(a) A registered agent may resign his agency appointment by signing and delivering to the secretary of state for filing the signed original and two exact or conformed copies of a statement of resignation. The statement may include a statement that the registered office is also discontinued.

(b) After filing the statement the secretary of state shall mail one copy to the registered office (if not discontinued) and the other copy to the corporation at its principal office.

(c) The agency appointment is terminated, and the registered office discontinued if so provided, on the 31st day after the day on which the statement was filed.

§ 5.04. Service on Corporation

(a) A corporation's registered agent is the corporation's agent for service of process, notice, or demand required or permitted by law to be served on the corporation.

(b) If a corporation has no registered agent, or the agent cannot with reasonable diligence be served, the corporation may be served by registered or certified mail, return receipt requested, addressed to the secretary of the corporation at its principal office. Service is perfected under this subsection at the earliest of:

(1) the date the corporation receives the mail;

(2) the date shown on the return receipt, if signed on behalf of the corporation; or

(3) five days after its deposit in the United States Mail, as evidenced by the postmark, if mailed postpaid and correctly addressed.

(c) This section does not prescribe the only means, or necessarily the required means, of serving a corporation.

CHAPTER 6
SHARES AND DISTRIBUTIONS

SUBCHAPTER A.
SHARES

§ 6.01. Authorized Shares

(a) The articles of incorporation must prescribe the classes of shares and the number of shares of each class that the corporation is authorized to issue.

If more than one class of shares is authorized, the articles of incorporation must prescribe a distinguishing designation for each class, and, prior to the issuance of shares of a class, the preferences, limitations, and relative rights of that class must be described in the articles of incorporation. All shares of a class must have preferences, limitations, and relative rights identical with those of other shares of the same class except to the extent otherwise permitted by section 6.02.

(b) The articles of incorporation must authorize (1) one or more classes of shares that together have unlimited voting rights, and (2) one or more classes of shares (which may be the same class or classes as those with voting rights) that together are entitled to receive the net assets of the corporation upon dissolution.

(c) The articles of incorporation may authorize one or more classes of shares that:

(1) have special, conditional, or limited voting rights, or no right to vote, except to the extent prohibited by this Act;

(2) are redeemable or convertible as specified in the articles of incorporation (i) at the option of the corporation, the shareholder, or another person or upon the occurrence of a designated event; (ii) for cash, indebtedness, securities, or other property; (iii) in a designated amount or in an amount determined in accordance with a designated formula or by reference to extrinsic data or events;

(3) entitle the holders to distributions calculated in any manner, including dividends that may be cumulative, noncumulative, or partially cumulative;

(4) have preference over any other class of shares with respect to distributions, including dividends and distributions upon the dissolution of the corporation.

(d) The description of the designations, preferences, limitations, and relative rights of share classes in subsection (c) is not exhaustive.

§ 6.02. *Terms of Class or Series Determined by Board of Directors*

(a) If the articles of incorporation so provide, the board of directors may determine, in whole or part, the preferences, limitations, and relative rights (within the limits set forth in section 6.01) of (1) any class of shares before the issuance of any shares of that class or (2) one or more series within a class before the issuance of any shares of that series.

(b) Each series of a class must be given a distinguishing designation.

(c) All shares of a series must have preferences, limitations, and relative rights identical with those of other shares of the same series and, except to the extent otherwise provided in the description of the series, with those of other series of the same class.

(d) Before issuing any shares of a class or series created under this section, the corporation must deliver to the secretary of state for filing articles of amendment, which are effective without shareholder action, that set forth:

(1) the name of the corporation;

(2) the text of the amendment determining the terms of the class or series of shares;

(3) the date it was adopted; and

(4) a statement that the amendment was duly adopted by the board of directors.

§ 6.03. *Issued and Outstanding Shares*

(a) A corporation may issue the number of shares of each class or series authorized by the articles of incorporation. Shares that are issued are outstanding shares until they are reacquired, redeemed, converted, or cancelled.

(b) The reacquisition, redemption, or conversion of outstanding shares is subject to the limitations of subsection (c) of this section and to section 6.40.

(c) At all times that shares of the corporation are outstanding, one or more shares that together have unlimited voting rights and one or more shares that together are entitled to receive the net assets of the corporation upon dissolution must be outstanding.

§ 6.04. *Fractional Shares*

(a) A corporation may:

(1) issue fractions of a share or pay in money the value of fractions of a share;

(2) arrange for disposition of fractional shares by the shareholders;

(3) issue scrip in registered or bearer form entitling the holder to receive a full share upon surrendering enough scrip to equal a full share.

(b) Each certificate representing scrip must be conspicuously labeled "scrip" and must contain the information required by section 6.25(b).

(c) The holder of a fractional share is entitled to exercise the rights of a shareholder, including the right to vote, to receive dividends, and to participate in the assets of the corporation upon liquidation. The holder of scrip is not entitled to any of these rights unless the scrip provides for them.

(d) The board of directors may authorize the issuance of scrip subject to any condition considered desirable, including:

(1) that the scrip will become void if not exchanged for full shares before a specified date; and

(2) that the shares for which the scrip is exchangeable may be sold and the proceeds paid to the scripholders.

SUBCHAPTER B.
ISSUANCE OF SHARES

§ 6.20. *Subscription for Shares Before Incorporation*

(a) A subscription for shares entered into before incorporation is irrevocable for six months unless the subscription agreement provides a longer or shorter period or all the subscribers agree to revocation.

(b) The board of directors may determine the payment terms of subscriptions for shares that were entered into before incorporation, unless the subscription agreement specifies them. A call for payment by the board of directors must be uniform so far as practicable as to all shares of the same class or series, unless the subscription agreement specifies otherwise.

(c) Shares issued pursuant to subscriptions entered into before incorporation are fully paid and nonassessable when the corporation receives the consideration specified in the subscription agreement.

(d) If a subscriber defaults in payment of money or property under a subscription agreement entered into before incorporation, the corporation may collect the amount owed as any other debt. Alternatively, unless the subscription agreement provides otherwise, the corporation may rescind the agreement and may sell the shares if the debt remains unpaid more than 20 days after the corporation sends written demand for payment to the subscriber.

(e) A subscription agreement entered into after incorporation is a contract between the subscriber and the corporation subject to section 6.21.

§ 6.21. Issuance of Shares

(a) The powers granted in this section to the board of directors may be reserved to the shareholders by the articles of incorporation.

(b) The board of directors may authorize shares to be issued for consideration consisting of any tangible or intangible property or benefit to the corporation, including cash, promissory notes, services performed, contracts for services to be performed, or other securities of the corporation.

(c) Before the corporation issues shares, the board of directors must determine that the consideration received or to be received for shares to be issued is adequate. That determination by the board of directors is conclusive insofar as the adequacy of consideration for the issuance of shares relates to whether the shares are validly issued, fully paid, and nonassessable.

(d) When the corporation receives the consideration for which the board of directors authorized the issuance of shares, the shares issued therefor are fully paid and nonassessable.

(e) The corporation may place in escrow shares issued for a contract for future services or benefits or a promissory note, or make other arrangements to restrict the transfer of the shares, and may credit distributions in respect of the shares against their purchase price, until the services are performed, the note is paid, or the benefits received. If the services are not performed, the note is not paid, or the benefits are not received, the shares escrowed or restricted and the distributions credited may be cancelled in whole or part.

§ 6.22. Liability of Shareholders

(a) A purchaser from a corporation of its own shares is not liable to the corporation or its creditors with respect to the shares except to pay the consideration for which the shares were authorized to be issued (section 6.21) or specified in the subscription agreement (section 6.20).

(b) Unless otherwise provided in the articles of incorporation, a shareholder of a corporation is not personally liable for the acts or debts of the corporation except that he may become personally liable by reason of his own acts or conduct.

§ 6.23. Share Dividends

(a) Unless the articles of incorporation provide otherwise, shares may be issued pro rata and without consideration to the corporation's shareholders or to the shareholders of one or more classes or series. An issuance of shares under this subsection is a share dividend.

(b) Shares of one class or series may not be issued as a share dividend in respect of shares of another class or series unless (1) the articles of incorporation so authorize, (2) a majority of the votes entitled to be cast by the class or series to be issued approve the issue, or (3) there are no outstanding shares of the class or series to be issued.

(c) If the board of directors does not fix the record date for determining shareholders entitled to a share dividend, it is the date the board of directors authorizes the share dividend.

§ 6.24. Share Options

A corporation may issue rights, options, or warrants for the purchase of shares of the corporation. The board of directors shall determine the terms upon which the rights, options, or warrants are issued, their form and content, and the consideration for which the shares are to be issued.

§ 6.25. Form and Content of Certificates

(a) Shares may but need not be represented by certificates. Unless this Act or another statute expressly provides otherwise, the rights and obligations of shareholders are identical whether or not their shares are represented by certificates.

(b) At a minimum each share certificate must state on its face:

(1) the name of the issuing corporation and that it is organized under the law of this state;

(2) the name of the person to whom issued; and

(3) the number and class of shares and the designation of the series, if any, the certificate represents.

(c) If the issuing corporation is authorized to issue different classes of shares or different series within a class, the designations, relative rights, preferences, and limitations applicable to each class and the variations in rights, preferences, and limitations determined for each series (and the authority of the board of directors to determine variations for future series) must be summarized on the front or back of each certificate. Alternatively, each certificate may state conspicuously on its front or back that the corporation will furnish the shareholder this information on request in writing and without charge.

(d) Each share certificate (1) must be signed (either manually or in facsimile) by two officers designated in the bylaws or by the board of directors and (2) may bear the corporate seal or its facsimile.

(e) If the person who signed (either manually or in facsimile) a share certificate no longer holds office when the certificate is issued, the certificate is nevertheless valid.

§ 6.26. Shares Without Certificates

(a) Unless the articles of incorporation or bylaws provide otherwise, the board of directors of a corporation may authorize the issue of some or all of the shares of any or all of its classes or series without certificates. The authorization does not affect shares already represented by certificates until they are surrendered to the corporation.

(b) Within a reasonable time after the issue or transfer of shares without certificates, the corporation shall send the shareholder a written statement of the information required on certificates by section C.25(b) and (c), and, if applicable, section 6.27.

§ 6.27. Restriction on Transfer of Shares and Other Securities

(a) The articles of incorporation, bylaws, an agreement among shareholders, or an agreement between shareholders and the corporation may impose restrictions on the transfer or registration of transfer of shares of the corporation. A restriction does not affect shares issued before the restriction was adopted unless the holders of the shares are parties to the restriction agreement or voted in favor of the restriction.

(b) A restriction on the transfer or registration of transfer of shares is valid and enforceable against the holder or a transferee of the holder if the restriction is authorized by this section and its existence is noted conspicuously on the front or back of the certificate or is contained in the information statement required by section 6.26(b). Unless so noted, a restriction is not enforceable against a person without knowledge of the restriction.

(c) A restriction on the transfer or registration of transfer of shares is authorized:

(1) to maintain the corporation's status when it is dependent on the number or identity of its shareholders;

(2) to preserve exemptions under federal or state securities law;

(3) for any other reasonable purpose.

(d) A restriction on the transfer or registration of transfer of shares may:

(1) obligate the shareholder first to offer the corporation or other persons (separately, consecutively, or simultaneously) an opportunity to acquire the restricted shares;

(2) obligate the corporation or other persons (separately, consecutively, or simultaneously) to acquire the restricted shares;

(3) require the corporation, the holders of any class of its shares, or another person to approve the transfer of the restricted shares, if the requirement is not manifestly unreasonable;

(4) prohibit the transfer of the restricted shares to designated persons or classes of persons, if the prohibition is not manifestly unreasonable.

(e) For purposes of this section, "shares" includes a security convertible into or carrying a right to subscribe for or acquire shares.

§ 6.28. Expense of Issue

A corporation may pay the expenses of selling or underwriting its shares, and of organizing or reorganizing the corporation, from the consideration received for shares.

SUBCHAPTER C.
SUBSEQUENT ACQUISITION OF SHARES BY SHAREHOLDERS AND CORPORATION

§ 6.30. Shareholders' Preemptive Rights

(a) The shareholders of a corporation do not have a preemptive right to acquire the corporation's unissued shares except to the extent the articles of incorporation so provide.

(b) A statement included in the articles of incorporation that "the corporation elects to have preemptive rights" (or words of similar import) means that the following principles apply except to the extent the articles of incorporation expressly provide otherwise:

(1) The shareholders of the corporation have a preemptive right, granted on uniform terms and conditions prescribed by the board of directors to provide a fair and reasonable opportunity to exercise the right, to acquire proportional amounts of the corporation's unissued shares upon the decision of the board of directors to issue them.

(2) A shareholder may waive his preemptive right. A waiver evidenced by a writing is irrevocable even though it is not supported by consideration.

(3) There is no preemptive right with respect to:

(i) shares issued as compensation to directors, officers, agents, or employees of the corporation, its subsidiaries or affiliates;

(ii) shares issued to satisfy conversion or option rights created to provide compensation to directors, officers, agents, or employees of the corporation, its subsidiaries or affiliates;

(iii) shares authorized in articles of incorporation that are issued within six months from the effective date of incorporation;

(iv) shares sold otherwise than for money.

(4) Holders of shares of any class without general voting rights but with preferential rights to distributions or assets have no preemptive rights with respect to shares of any class.

(5) Holders of shares of any class with general voting rights but without preferential rights to distributions or assets have no preemptive rights with respect to shares of any class with preferential rights to distributions or assets unless the shares with preferential rights are convertible into or carry a right to subscribe for or acquire shares without preferential rights.

(6) Shares subject to preemptive rights that are not acquired by shareholders may be issued to any person for a period of one year after being offered to shareholders at a consideration set by the board of directors that is not lower than the consideration set for the exercise of preemptive rights. An offer at a lower consideration or after the expiration of one year is subject to the shareholders' preemptive rights.

(c) For purposes of this section, "shares" includes a security convertible into or carrying a right to subscribe for or acquire shares.

§ 6.31. Corporation's Acquisition of Its Own Shares

(a) A corporation may acquire its own shares and shares so acquired constitute authorized but unissued shares.

(b) If the articles of incorporation prohibit the reissue of acquired shares, the number of authorized shares is reduced by the number of shares acquired, effective upon amendment of the articles of incorporation.

(c) The board of directors may adopt articles of amendment under this section without shareholder action and deliver them to the secretary of state for filing. The articles must set forth:

(1) the name of the corporation;

(2) the reduction in the number of authorized shares, itemized by class and series; and

(3) the total number of authorized shares, itemized by class and series, remaining after reduction of the shares.

SUBCHAPTER D.
DISTRIBUTIONS

§ 6.40 Distributions to Shareholders

(a) A board of directors may authorize and the corporation may make distributions to its shareholders subject to restriction by the articles of incorporation and the limitation in subsection (c).

(b) If the board of directors does not fix the record date for determining shareholders entitled to a distribution (other than one involving a purchase, redemption, or other acquisition of the corporation's shares), it is the date the board of directors authorizes the distribution.

(c) No distribution may be made if, after giving it effect:

(1) the corporation would not be able to pay it debts as they become due in the usual course of business; or

(2) the corporation's total assets would be less than the sum of its total liabilities plus (unless the articles of incorporation permit otherwise) the amount that would be needed, if the corporation were to be dissolved at the time of the distribution, to satisfy the preferential rights upon dissolution of shareholders whose preferential rights are superior to those receiving the distribution.

(d) The board of directors may base a determination that a distribution is not prohibited under subsection (c) either on financial statements prepared on the basis of accounting practices and principles that are reasonable in the circumstances or on a fair valuation or other method that is reasonable in the circumstances.

(e) Except as provided in subsection (g), the effect of a distribution under subsection (c) is measured:

(1) in the case of distribution by purchase, redemption, or other acquisition of the corporation's shares, as of the earlier of (i) the date money or other property is transferred or debt incurred by the corporation or (ii) the date the shareholder ceases to be a shareholder with respect to the acquired shares;

(2) in the case of any other distribution of indebtedness, as of the date the indebtedness is distributed; and

(3) in all other cases, as of (i) the date the distribution is authorized if the payment occurs within 120 days after the date of authorization or (ii) the date the payment is made if it occurs more than 120 days after the date of authorization.

(f) A corporation's indebtedness to a shareholder incurred by reason of a distribution made in accordance with this section is at parity with the corporation's indebtedness to its general, unsecured creditors except to the extent subordinated by agreement.

(g) Indebtedness of a corporation, including indebtedness issued as a distribution, is not considered a liability for purposes of determinations under subsection (c) if its terms provide that payment of principal and interest are made only if and to the extent that payment of a distribution to shareholders could then be made under this section. If the indebtedness is issued as a distribution, each payment of principal or interest is treated as a distribution, the effect of which is measured on the date the payment is actually made.

CHAPTER 7
SHAREHOLDERS

SUBCHAPTER A.
MEETINGS

§ 7.01. Annual Meeting

(a) A corporation shall hold a meeting of shareholders annually at a time stated in or fixed in accordance with the bylaws.

(b) Annual shareholders' meetings may be held in or out of this state at the place stated in or fixed in accordance with the bylaws. If no place is stated in or fixed in accordance with the bylaws, annual meetings shall be held at the corporation's principal office.

(c) The failure to hold an annual meeting at the time stated in or fixed in accordance with a corporation's bylaws does not affect the validity of any corporate action.

§ 7.02. Special Meeting

(a) A corporation shall hold a special meeting of shareholders:
(1) on call of its board of directors or the person or persons authorized to do so by the articles of incorporation or bylaws; or
(2) if the holders of at least 10 percent of all the votes entitled to be cast on any issue proposed to be considered at the proposed special meeting sign, date, and deliver to the corporation's secretary one or more written demands for the meeting describing the purpose or purposes for which it is to be held.

(b) If not otherwise fixed under section 7.03 or 7.07, the record date for determining shareholders entitled to demand a special meeting is the date the first shareholder signs the demand.

(c) Special shareholders' meetings may be held in or out of this state at the place stated in or fixed in accordance with the bylaws. If no place is stated or fixed in accordance with the bylaws, special meetings shall be held at the corporation's principal office.

(d) Only business within the purpose or purposes described in the meeting notice required by section 7.05(c) may be conducted at a special shareholders' meeting.

§ 7.03. Court-ordered Meeting

(a) The [name or describe] court of the county where a corporation's principal office (or, if none in this state, its registered office) is located may summarily order a meeting to be held:
(1) on application of any shareholder of the corporation entitled to participate in an annual meeting if an annual meeting was not held within the earlier of 6 months after the end of the corporation's fiscal year or 15 months after its last annual meeting; or
(2) on application of a shareholder who signed a demand for a special meeting valid under section 7.02, if:
(i) notice of the special meeting was not given within 30 days after the date the demand was delivered to the corporation's secretary; or
(ii) the special meeting was not held in accordance with the notice.

(b) The court may fix the time and place of the meeting, determine the shares entitled to participate in the meeting, specify a record date for determining shareholders entitled to notice of and to vote at the meeting, prescribe the form and content of the meeting notice, fix the quorum required for specific matters to be considered at the meeting (or direct that the votes represented at the meeting constitute a quorum for action on those matters), and enter other orders necessary to accomplish the purpose or purposes of the meeting.

§ 7.04. Action Without Meeting

(a) Action required or permitted by this Act to be taken at a shareholders' meeting may be taken without a meeting if the action is taken by all the shareholders entitled to vote on the action. The action must be evidenced by one or more written consents describing the action taken, signed by all the shareholders entitled to vote on the action, and delivered to the corporation for inclusion in the minutes or filing with the corporate records.

(b) If not otherwise fixed under section 7.03 or 7.07, the record date for determining shareholders entitled to take action without a meeting is the date the first shareholder signs the consent under subsection (a).

(c) A consent signed under this section has the effect of a meeting vote and may be described as such in any document.

(d) If this Act requires that notice of proposed action be given to nonvoting shareholders and the action is to be taken by unanimous consent of the voting shareholders, the corporation must give its nonvoting shareholders written notice of the proposed action at least 10 days before the action is taken. The notice must contain or be accompanied by the same material that, under this Act, would have been required to be sent to nonvoting shareholders in a notice of meeting at which the proposed action would have been submitted to the shareholders for action.

§ 7.05. Notice of Meeting

(a) A corporation shall notify shareholders of the date, time, and place of each annual and special shareholders' meeting no fewer than 10 nor more than 60 days before the meeting date. Unless this Act or the articles of incorporation require otherwise, the corporation is required to give notice only to shareholders entitled to vote at the meeting.

(b) Unless this Act or the articles of incorporation require otherwise, notice of an annual meeting need not include a description of the purpose or purposes for which the meeting is called.

(c) Notice of a special meeting must include a description of the purpose or purposes for which the meeting is called.

(d) If not otherwise fixed under section 7.03 or 7.07, the record date for determining shareholders entitled to notice of and to vote at an annual or special shareholders' meeting is the day before the first notice is delivered to shareholders.

(e) Unless the bylaws require otherwise, if an annual or special shareholders' meeting is adjourned to a different date, time, or place, notice need not be given of the new date, time, or place if the new date, time, or place is announced at the meeting before adjournment. If a new record date for the adjourned meeting is or must be fixed under section 7.07, however, notice of the adjourned meeting must be given under this section to persons who are shareholders as of the new record date.

§ 7.06. Waiver of Notice

(a) A shareholder may waive any notice required by this Act, the articles of incorporation, or bylaws before or after the date and time stated in the notice. The waiver must be in writing, be signed by the shareholder entitled to the notice, and be delivered to the corporation for inclusion in the minutes or filing with the corporate records.

(b) A shareholder's attendance at a meeting:

(1) waives objection to lack of notice or defective notice of the meeting, unless the shareholder at the beginning of the meeting objects to holding the meeting or transacting business at the meeting;

(2) waives objection to consideration of a particular matter at the meeting that is not within the purpose or purposes described in the meeting notice, unless the shareholder objects to considering the matter when it is presented.

§ 7.07. Record Date

(a) The bylaws may fix or provide the manner of fixing the record date for one or more voting groups in order to determine the shareholders entitled to notice of a shareholders' meeting, to demand a special meeting, to vote, or to take any other action. If the bylaws do not fix or provide for fixing a record date, the board of directors of the corporation may fix a future date as the record date.

(b) A record date fixed under this section may not be more than 70 days before the meeting or action requiring a determination of shareholders.

(c) A determination of shareholders entitled to notice of or to vote at a shareholders' meeting is effective for any adjournment of the meeting unless the board of directors fixes a new record date, which it must do if the meeting is adjourned to a date more than 120 days after the date fixed for the original meeting.

(d) If a court orders a meeting adjourned to a date more than 120 days after the date fixed for the original meeting, it may provide that the original record date continues in effect or it may fix a new record date.

SUBCHAPTER B.
VOTING

§ 7.20. Shareholders' List for Meeting

(a) After fixing a record date for a meeting, a corporation shall prepare an alphabetical list of the names of all its shareholders who are entitled to notice of a shareholders' meeting. The list must be arranged by voting group (and within each voting group by class or series of shares) and show the address of and number of shares held by each shareholder.

(b) The shareholders' list must be available for inspection by any shareholder, beginning two business days after notice of the meeting is given for which the list was prepared and continuing through the meeting, at the corporation's principal office or at a place identified in the meeting notice in the city where the meeting will be held. A shareholder, his agent, or attorney is entitled on written demand to inspect and, subject to the requirements of section 16.02(c), to copy the list, during regular business hours and at his expense, during the period it is available for inspection.

(c) The corporation shall make the shareholders' list available at the meeting, and any shareholder, his agent, or attorney is entitled to inspect the list at any time during the meeting or any adjournment.

(d) If the corporation refuses to allow a shareholder, his agent, or attorney to inspect the shareholders' list before or at the meeting (or copy the list as permitted by subsection (b)), the [name or describe] court of the county where a corporation's principal office (or, if none in this state, its registered office) is located, on application of the shareholder, may summarily order the inspection or copying at the corporation's expense and may postpone the meeting for which the list was prepared until the inspection or copying is complete.

(e) Refusal or failure to prepare or make available the shareholders' list does not affect the validity of action taken at the meeting.

§ 7.21. Voting Entitlement of Shares

(a) Except as provided in subsections (b) and (c) or unless the articles of incorporation provide otherwise, each outstanding share, regardless of class, is entitled to one vote on each matter voted on at a shareholders' meeting. Only shares are entitled to vote.

(b) Absent special circumstances, the shares of a corporation are not entitled to vote if they are owned, directly or indirectly, by a second corporation, domestic or foreign, and the first corporation owns, directly or indirectly, a majority of the shares entitled to vote for directors of the second corporation.

(c) Subsection (b) does not limit the power of a corporation to vote any shares, including its own shares, held by it in a fiduciary capacity.

(d) Redeemable shares are not entitled to vote after notice of redemption is mailed to the holders and a sum sufficient to redeem the shares has been deposited with a bank, trust company, or other financial institution under an irrevocable obligation to pay the holders the redemption price on surrender of the shares.

§ 7.22. *Proxies*

(a) A shareholder may vote his shares in person or by proxy.

(b) A shareholder may appoint a proxy to vote or otherwise act for him by signing an appointment form, either personally or by his attorney-in-fact.

(c) An appointment of a proxy is effective when received by the secretary or other officer or agent authorized to tabulate votes. An appointment is valid for 11 months unless a longer period is expressly provided in the appointment form.

(d) An appointment of a proxy is revocable by the shareholder unless the appointment form conspicuously states that it is irrevocable and the appointment is coupled with an interest. Appointments coupled with an interest include the appointment of:

(1) a pledgee;

(2) a person who purchased or agreed to purchase the shares;

(3) a creditor of the corporation who extended it credit under terms requiring the appointment;

(4) an employee of the corporation whose employment contract requires the appointment; or

(5) a party to a voting agreement created under section 7.31.

(e) The death or incapacity of the shareholder appointing a proxy does not affect the right of the corporation to accept the proxy's authority unless notice of the death or incapacity is received by the secretary or other officer or agent authorized to tabulate votes before the proxy exercises his authority under the appointment.

(f) An appointment made irrevocable under subsection (d) is revoked when the interest with which it is coupled is extinguished.

(g) A transferee for value of shares subject to an irrevocable appointment may revoke the appointment if he did not know of its existence when he acquired the shares and the existence of the irrevocable appointment was not noted conspicuously on the certificate representing the shares or on the information statement for shares without certificates.

(h) Subject to section 7.24 and to any express limitation on the proxy's authority appearing on the face of the appointment form, a corporation is entitled to accept the proxy's vote or other action as that of the shareholder making the appointment.

§ 7.23. *Shares Held by Nominees*

(a) A corporation may establish a procedure by which the beneficial owner of shares that are registered in the name of a nominee is recognized by the corporation as the shareholder. The extent of this recognition may be determined in the procedure.

(b) The procedure may set forth:

(1) the types of nominees to which it applies;

(2) the rights or privileges that the corporation recognizes in a beneficial owner;

(3) the manner in which the procedure is selected by the nominee;

(4) the information that must be provided when the procedure is selected;

(5) the period for which selection of the procedure is effective; and

(6) other aspects of the rights and duties created.

§ 7.24. *Corporation's Acceptance of Votes*

(a) If the name signed on a vote, consent, waiver, or proxy appointment corresponds to the name of a shareholder, the corporation if acting in good faith is entitled to accept the vote, consent, waiver, or proxy appointment and give it effect as the act of the shareholder.

(b) If the name signed on a vote, consent, waiver, or proxy appointment does not correspond to the name of its shareholder, the corporation if acting in good faith is nevertheless entitled to accept the vote, consent, waiver, or proxy appointment and give it effect as the act of the shareholder if:

(1) the shareholder is an entity and the name signed purports to be that of an officer or agent of the entity;

(2) the name signed purports to be that of an administrator, executor, guardian, or conservator representing the shareholder and, if the corporation requests, evidence of fiduciary status acceptable to the corporation has been presented with respect to the vote, consent, waiver, or proxy appointment;

(3) the name signed purports to be that of a receiver or trustee in bankruptcy of the shareholder and, if the corporation requests, evidence of this status acceptable to the corporation has been presented with respect to the vote, consent, waiver, or proxy appointment;

(4) the name signed purports to be that of a pledgee, beneficial owner, or attorney-in-fact of the shareholder and, if the corporation requests,

evidence acceptable to the corporation of the signatory's authority to sign for the shareholder has been presented with respect to the vote, consent, waiver, or proxy appointment;

(5) two or more persons are the shareholder as cotenants or fiduciaries and the name signed purports to be the name of at least one of the coowners and the person signing appears to be acting on behalf of all the coowners.

(c) The corporation is entitled to reject a vote, consent, waiver, or proxy appointment if the secretary or other officer or agent authorized to tabulate votes, acting in good faith, has reasonable basis for doubt about the validity of the signature on it or about the signatory's authority to sign for the shareholder.

(d) The corporation and its officer or agent who accepts or rejects a vote, consent, waiver, or proxy appointment in good faith and in accordance with the standards of this section are not liable in damages to the shareholder for the consequences of the acceptance or rejection.

(e) Corporate action based on the acceptance or rejection of a vote, consent, waiver, or proxy appointment under this section is valid unless a court of competent jurisdiction determines otherwise.

§ 7.25. Quorum and Voting Requirements for Voting Groups

(a) Shares entitled to vote as a separate voting group may take action on a matter at a meeting only if a quorum of those shares exists with respect to that matter. Unless the articles of incorporation or this Act provide otherwise, a majority of the votes entitled to be cast on the matter by the voting group constitutes a quorum of that voting group for action on that matter.

(b) Once a share is represented for any purpose at a meeting, it is deemed present for quorum purposes for the remainder of the meeting and for any adjournment of that meeting unless a new record date is or must be set for that adjourned meeting.

(c) If a quorum exists, action on a matter (other than the election of directors) by a voting group is approved if the votes cast within the voting group favoring the action exceed the votes cast opposing the action, unless the articles of incorporation or this Act require a greater number of affirmative votes.

(d) An amendment of articles of incorporation adding, changing, or deleting a quorum or voting requirement for a voting group greater than specified in subsection (a) or (c) is governed by section 7.27.

(e) The election of directors is governed by section 7.28.

§ 7.26. Action by Single and Multiple Voting Groups

(a) If the articles of incorporation or this Act provide for voting by a single voting group on a matter, action on that matter is taken when voted upon by that voting group as provided in section 7.25.

(b) If the articles of incorporation or this Act provide for voting by two or more voting groups on a matter, action on that matter is taken only when voted upon by each of those voting groups counted separately as provided in section 7.25. Action may be taken by one voting group on a matter even though no action is taken by another voting group entitled to vote on the matter.

§ 7.27. Greater Quorum or Voting Requirements

(a) The articles of incorporation may provide for a greater quorum or voting requirement for shareholders (or voting groups of shareholders) than is provided for by this Act.

(b) An amendment to the articles of incorporation that adds, changes, or deletes a greater quorum or voting requirement must meet the same quorum requirement and be adopted by the same vote and voting groups required to take action under the quorum and voting requirements then in effect or proposed to be adopted, whichever is greater.

§ 7.28. Voting for Directors; Cumulative Voting

(a) Unless otherwise provided in the articles of incorporation, directors are elected by a plurality of the votes cast by the shares entitled to vote in the election at a meeting at which a quorum is present.

(b) Shareholders do not have a right to cumulate their votes for directors unless the articles of incorporation so provide.

(c) A statement included in the articles of incorporation that "[all] [a designated voting group of] shareholders are entitled to cumulate their votes for directors" (or words of similar import) means that the shareholders designated are entitled to multiply the number of votes they are entitled to cast by the number of directors for whom they are entitled to vote and cast the product for a single candidate or distribute the product among two or more candidates.

(d) Shares otherwise entitled to vote cumulatively may not be voted cumulatively at a particular meeting unless:

(1) the meeting notice or proxy statement accompanying the notice states conspicuously that cumulative voting is authorized; or

(2) a shareholder who has the right to cumulate his votes gives notice to the corporation not less than 48 hours before the time set for the meeting of his intent to cumulate his votes during the meeting, and if one shareholder gives this notice all other shareholders in the same voting group participating in the election are entitled to cumulate their votes without giving further notice.

SUBCHAPTER C. VOTING TRUSTS AND AGREEMENTS

§ 7.30. Voting Trusts

(a) One or more shareholders may create a voting trust, conferring on a trustee the right to vote or otherwise act for them, by signing an agreement setting out the provisions of the trust (which may include anything consistent with its purpose) and transferring their shares to the trustee. When a voting trust agreement is signed, the trustee shall prepare a list of the names and addresses of all owners of beneficial interests in the trust, together with the number and class of shares each transferred to the trust, and deliver copies of the list and agreement to the corporation's principal office.

(b) A voting trust becomes effective on the date the first shares subject to the trust are registered in the trustee's name. A voting trust is valid for not more than 10 years after its effective date unless extended under subsection (c).

(c) All or some of the parties to a voting trust may extend it for additional terms of not more than 10 years each by signing an extension agreement and obtaining the voting trustee's written consent to the extension. An extension is valid for 10 years from the date the first shareholder signs the extension agreement. The voting trustee must deliver copies of the extension agreement and list of beneficial owners to the corporation's principal office. An extension agreement binds only those parties signing it.

§ 7.31. Voting Agreements

(a) Two or more shareholders may provide for the manner in which they will vote their shares by signing an agreement for that purpose. A voting agreement created under this section is not subject to the provisions of section 7.30.

(b) A voting agreement created under this section is specifically enforceable.

§ 7.32. Shareholder Agreements

(a) An agreement among the shareholders of a corporation that complies with this section is effective among the shareholders and the corporation even though it is inconsistent with one or more other provisions of this Act in that it:

(1) eliminates the board of directors or restricts the discretion or powers of the board of directors;

(2) governs the authorization or making of distributions whether or not in proportion to ownership of shares, subject to the limitations in section 6.40;

(3) establishes who shall be directors or officers of the corporation, or their terms of office or manner of selection or removal;

(4) governs, in general or in regard to specific matters, the exercise or division of voting power by or between the shareholders and directors or by or among any of them, including use of weighted voting rights or director proxies;

(5) establishes the terms and conditions of any agreement for the transfer or use of property or the provision of services between the corporation and any shareholder, director, officer or employee of the corporation or among any of them;

(6) transfers to one or more shareholders or other persons all or part of the authority to exercise the corporate powers or to manage the business and affairs of the corporation, including the resolution of any issue about which there exists a deadlock among directors or shareholders;

(7) requires dissolution of the corporation at the request of one or more of the shareholders or upon the occurrence of a specified event or contingency; or

(8) otherwise governs the exercise of the corporate powers or the management of the business and affairs of the corporation or the relationship among the shareholders, the directors and the corporation, or among any of them, and is not contrary to public policy.

(b) An agreement authorized by this section shall be:

(1) set forth (A) in the articles of incorporation or bylaws and approved by all persons who are shareholders at the time of the agreement or (B) in a written agreement that is signed by all persons who are shareholders at the time of the agreement and is made known to the corporation;

(2) subject to amendment only by all persons who are shareholders at the time of the amendment, unless the agreement provides otherwise; and

(3) valid for 10 years, unless the agreement provides otherwise.

(c) The existence of an agreement authorized by this section shall be noted conspicuously on the front or back of each certificate for outstanding shares or on the information statement required by section 6.26(b). If at the time of the agreement the corporation has shares outstanding represented by certificates, the corporation shall recall the outstanding certificates and issue substitute certificates that comply with this subsection. The failure to note the existence of the agreement on the certificate or information statement shall not affect the validity of the agreement or any action taken pursuant to it. Any purchaser of shares who, at the time of purchase, did not have knowledge of the existence of the agreement shall be entitled to rescission of the purchase. A purchaser shall be deemed to have knowledge of the existence of the agreement if its existence is noted on the certificate or information statement for the shares in compliance with this subsection and, if the shares are not represented by a certificate, the information statement is delivered to the purchaser at or prior to the time of purchase of the shares. An action to enforce the right of rescission authorized by this subsection must be commenced within the earlier of 90 days after discovery of the existence of the agreement or two years after the time of purchase of the shares.

(d) An agreement authorized by this section shall cease to be effective when shares of the corporation are listed on a national securities exchange or regularly traded in a market maintained by one or more members of a national or affiliated securities association. If the agreement ceases to be effective for any reason, the board of directors may, if the agreement is contained or referred to in the corporation's articles of incorporation or bylaws, adopt an amendment to the articles of incorporation or bylaws, without shareholder action, to delete the agreement and any references to it.

(e) An agreement authorized by this section that limits the discretion or powers of the board of directors shall relieve the directors of, and impose upon the person or persons in whom such discretion or powers are vested, liability for acts or omissions imposed by law on directors to the extent that the discretion or powers of the directors are limited by the agreement.

(f) The existence or performance of an agreement authorized by this section shall not be a ground for imposing personal liability on any shareholder for the acts or debts of the corporation even if the agreement or its performance treats the corporation as if it were a partnership or results in failure to observe the corporate formalities otherwise applicable to the matters governed by the agreement.

(g) Incorporators or subscribers for shares may act as shareholders with respect to an agreement authorized by this section if no shares have been issued when the agreement is made.

SUBCHAPTER D.
DERIVATIVE PROCEEDINGS

§ 7.40. Subchapter Definitions

In this subchapter:

(1) "Derivative proceeding" means a civil suit in the right of a domestic corporation or, to the extent provided in section 7.47, in the right of a foreign corporation.

(2) "Shareholder" includes a beneficial owner whose shares are held in a voting trust or held by a nominee on the beneficial owner's behalf.

§ 7.41. Standing

A shareholder may not commence or maintain a derivative proceeding unless the shareholder:

(1) was a shareholder of the corporation at the time of the act or omission complained of or became a shareholder through transfer by operation of law from one who was a shareholder at that time; and

(2) fairly and adequately represents the interests of the corporation in enforcing the right of the corporation.

§ 7.42. Demand

No shareholder may commence a derivative proceeding until:

(1) a written demand has been made upon the corporation to take suitable action; and

(2) 90 days have expired from the date the demand was made unless the shareholder has earlier been notified that the demand has been rejected by the corporation or unless irreparable injury to the corporation would result by waiting for the expiration of the 90 day period.

§ 7.43. Stay of Proceedings

If the corporation commences an inquiry into the allegations made in the demand or complaint, the court may stay any derivative proceeding for such period as the court deems appropriate.

§ 7.44. Dismissal

(a) A derivative proceeding shall be dismissed by the court on motion by the corporation if one of the groups specified in subsections (b) or (f) has determined in good faith after conducting a reasonable inquiry upon which its conclusions are based that the maintenance of the derivative proceeding is not in the best interests of the corporation.

(b) Unless a panel is appointed pursuant to subsection (f), the determination in subsection (a) shall be made by:

(1) a majority vote of independent directors present at a meeting of the board of directors if the independent directors constitute a quorum; or

(2) a majority vote of a committee consisting of two or more independent directors appointed by majority vote of independent directors present at a meeting of the board of directors, whether or not such independent directors constituted a quorum.

(c) None of the following shall by itself cause a director to be considered not independent for purposes of this section:

(1) the nomination or election of the director by persons who are defendants in the derivative proceeding or against whom action is demanded;

(2) the naming of the director as a defendant in the derivative proceeding or as a person against whom action is demanded; or

(3) the approval by the director of the act being challenged in the derivative proceeding or demand if the act resulted in no personal benefit to the director.

(d) If a derivative proceeding is commenced after a determination has been made rejecting a demand by a shareholder, the complaint shall allege with particularity facts establishing either (1) that a majority of the board of directors did not consist of independent directors at the time the determination was made or (2) that the requirements of subsection (a) have not been met.

(e) If a majority of the board of directors does not consist of independent directors at the time the determination is made, the corporation shall have the burden of proving that the requirements of sub-section (a) have been met. If a majority of the board of directors consists of independent directors at the time the determination is made, the plaintiff shall have the burden of proving that the requirements of subsection (a) have not been met.

(f) The court may appoint a panel of one or more independent persons upon motion by the corporation to make a determination whether the mainte-nance of the derivative proceeding is in the best interests of the corporation. In such case, the plain-tiff shall have the burden of proving that the require-ments of subsection (a) have not been met.

§ 7.45. Discontinuance or Settlement

A derivative proceeding may not be discontinued or settled without the court's approval. If the court determines that a proposed discontinuance or settle-ment will substantially affect the interests of the cor-poration's shareholders or a class of shareholders, the court shall direct that notice be given to the share-holders affected.

§ 7.46. Payment of Expenses

On termination of the derivative proceeding the court may:

(1) order the corporation to pay the plaintiff's reasonable expenses (including counsel fees) incurred in the proceeding if it finds that the proceeding has resulted in a substantial benefit to the corporation;

(2) order the plaintiff to pay any defendant's rea-sonable expenses (including counsel fees) incurred in defending the proceeding if it finds that the proceed-ing was commenced or maintained without reason-able cause or for an improper purpose; or

(3) order a party to pay an opposing party's rea-sonable expenses (including counsel fees) incurred because of the filing of a pleading, motion or other pa-per, if it finds that the pleading, motion or other paper was not well grounded in fact, after reasonable inquiry, or warranted by existing law or a good faith argument for the extension, modification or reversal of existing law and was interposed for an improper purpose, such as to harass or to cause unnecessary delay or needless increase in the cost of litigation.

§ 7.47. Applicability to Foreign Corporations

In any derivative proceeding in the right of a for-eign corporation, the matters covered by this subchap-ter shall be governed by the laws of the jurisdiction of incorporation of the foreign corporation except for sections 7.43, 7.45 and 7.46.

CHAPTER 8
DIRECTORS AND OFFICERS

SUBCHAPTER A.
BOARD OF DIRECTORS

§ 8.01. Requirements for and Duties of Board of Directors.

(a) Except as provided is [sic] section 7.32, each corporation must have a board of directors.

(b) All corporate powers shall be exercised by or under the authority of, and the business and affairs of the corporation managed under the direction of, its board of directors, subject to any limitation set forth in the articles of incorporation or in an agree-ment authorized under section 7.32.

§ 8.02. Qualifications of Directors

The articles of incorporation or bylaws may pre-scribe qualifications for directors. A director need not be a resident of this state or a shareholder of the cor-poration unless the articles of incorporation or by-laws so prescribe.

§ 8.03. Number and Election of Directors

(a) A board of directors must consist of one or more individuals, with the number specified in or fixed in accordance with the articles of incorporation or bylaws.

(b) If a board of directors has power to fix or change the number of directors, the board may in-crease or decrease by 30 percent or less the number of directors last approved by the shareholders, but only the shareholders may increase or decrease by more than 30 percent the number of directors last ap-proved by the shareholders.

(c) The articles of incorporation or bylaws may establish a variable range for the size of the board of directors by fixing a minimum and maximum num-ber of directors. If a variable range is established, the number of directors may be fixed or changed from time to time, within the minimum and maximum, by the shareholders or the board of directors. After shares are issued, only the shareholders may change the range for the size of the board or change from a fixed to a variable-range size board or vice versa.

(d) Directors are elected at the first annual share-holders' meeting and at each annual meeting there-after unless their terms are staggered under section 8.06.

§ 8.04. Election of Directors by Certain Classes of Shareholders

If the articles of incorporation authorize dividing the shares into classes, the articles may also author-ize the election of all or a specified number of directors by the holders of one or more authorized classes of shares. A class (or classes) of shares entitled to elect one or more directors is a separate voting group for purposes of the election of directors.

§ 8.05. Terms of Directors Generally

(a) The terms of the initial directors of a corporation expire at the first shareholders' meeting at which directors are elected.

(b) The terms of all other directors expire at the next annual shareholders' meeting following their election unless their terms are staggered under section 8.06.

(c) A decrease in the number of directors does not shorten an incumbent director's term.

(d) The term of a director elected to fill a vacancy expires at the next shareholders' meeting at which directors are elected.

(e) Despite the expiration of a director's term, he continues to serve until his successor is elected and qualifies or until there is a decrease in the number of directors.

§ 8.06. Staggered Terms for Directors

If there are nine or more directors, the articles of incorporation may provide for staggering their terms by dividing the total number of directors into two or three groups, with each group containing one half or one-third of the total, as near as may be. In that event, the terms of directors in the first group expire at the first annual shareholders' meeting after their election, the terms of the second group expire at the second annual shareholders' meeting after their election, and the terms of the third group, if any, expire at the third annual shareholders' meeting after their election. At each annual shareholders' meeting held thereafter, directors shall be chosen for a term of two years or three years, as the case may be, to succeed those whose terms expire.

§ 8.07. Resignation of Directors

(a) A director may resign at any time by delivering written notice to the board of directors, its chairman, or to the corporation.

(b) A resignation is effective when the notice is delivered unless the notice specifies a later effective date.

§ 8.08. Removal of Directors by Shareholders

(a) The shareholders may remove one or more directors with or without cause unless the articles of incorporation provide that directors may be removed only for cause.

(b) If a director is elected by a voting group of shareholders, only the shareholders of that voting group may participate in the vote to remove him.

(c) If cumulative voting is authorized, a director may not be removed if the number of votes sufficient to elect him under cumulative voting is voted against his removal. If cumulative voting is not authorized, a director may be removed only if the number of votes cast to remove him exceeds the number of votes cast not to remove him.

(d) A director may be removed by the shareholders only at a meeting called for the purpose of removing him and the meeting notice must state that the purpose, or one of the purposes, of the meeting is removal of the director.

§ 8.09. Removal of Directors by Judicial Proceeding

(a) The [name or describe] court of the county where a corporation's principal office (or, if none in this state, its registered office) is located may remove a director of the corporation from office in a proceeding commenced either by the corporation or by its shareholders holding at least 10 percent of the outstanding shares of any class if the court finds that (1) the director engaged in fraudulent or dishonest conduct, or gross abuse of authority or discretion, with respect to the corporation and (2) removal is in the best interest of the corporation.

(b) The court that removes a director may bar the director from reelection for a period prescribed by the court.

(c) If shareholders commence a proceeding under subsection (a), they shall make the corporation a party defendant.

§ 8.10. Vacancy on Board

(a) Unless the articles of incorporation provide otherwise, if a vacancy occurs on a board of directors, including a vacancy resulting from an increase in the number of directors:

(1) the shareholders may fill the vacancy;

(2) the board of directors may fill the vacancy; or

(3) if the directors remaining in office constitute fewer than a quorum of the board, they may fill the vacancy by the affirmative vote of a majority of all the directors remaining in office.

(b) If the vacant office was held by a director elected by a voting group of shareholders, only the holders of shares of that voting group are entitled to vote to fill the vacancy if it is filled by the shareholders.

(c) A vacancy that will occur at a specific later date (by reason of a resignation effective at a later date under section 8.07(b) or otherwise) may be filled before the vacancy occurs but the new director may not take office until the vacancy occurs.

§ 8.11. Compensation of Directors

Unless the articles of incorporation or bylaws provide otherwise, the board of directors may fix the compensation of directors.

SUBCHAPTER B.
MEETINGS AND ACTION OF THE BOARD

§ 8.20. *Meetings*

(a) The board of directors may hold regular or special meetings in or out of this state.

(b) Unless the articles of incorporation or bylaws provide otherwise, the board of directors may permit any or all directors to participate in a regular or special meeting by, or conduct the meeting through the use of, any means of communication by which all directors participating may simultaneously hear each other during the meeting. A director participating in a meeting by this means is deemed to be present in person at the meeting.

§ 8.21. *Action Without Meeting*

(a) Unless the articles of incorporation or bylaws provide otherwise, action required or permitted by this Act to be taken at a board of directors' meeting may be taken without a meeting if the action is taken by all members of the board. The action must be evidenced by one or more written consents describing the action taken, signed by each director, and included in the minutes or filed with the corporate records reflecting the action taken.

(b) Action taken under this section is effective when the last director signs the consent, unless the consent specifies a different effective date.

(c) A consent signed under this section has the effect of a meeting vote and may be described as such in any document.

§ 8.22. *Notice of Meeting*

(a) Unless the articles of incorporation or bylaws provide otherwise, regular meetings of the board of directors may be held without notice of the date, time, place, or purpose of the meeting.

(b) Unless the articles of incorporation or bylaws provide for a longer or shorter period, special meetings of the board of directors must be preceded by at least two days' notice of the date, time, and place of the meeting. The notice need not describe the purpose of the special meeting unless required by the articles of incorporation or bylaws.

§ 8.23. *Waiver of Notice*

(a) A director may waive any notice required by this Act, the articles of incorporation, or bylaws before or after the date and time stated in the notice. Except as provided by subsection (b), the waiver must be in writing, signed by the director entitled to the notice, and filed with the minutes or corporate records.

(b) A director's attendance at or participation in a meeting waives any required notice to him of the meeting unless the director at the beginning of the meeting (or promptly upon his arrival) objects to holding the meeting or transacting business at the meeting and does not thereafter vote for or assent to action taken at the meeting.

§ 8.24. *Quorum and Voting*

(a) Unless the articles of incorporation or bylaws require a greater number, a quorum of a board of directors consists of:

(1) a majority of the fixed number of directors if the corporation has a fixed board size; or

(2) a majority of the number of directors prescribed, or if no number is prescribed the number in office immediately before the meeting begins, if the corporation has a variable-range size board.

(b) The articles of incorporation or bylaws may authorize a quorum of a board of directors to consist of no fewer than one-third of the fixed or prescribed number of directors determined under subsection (a).

(c) If a quorum is present when a vote is taken, the affirmative vote of a majority of directors present is the act of the board of directors unless the articles of incorporation or bylaws require the vote of a greater number of directors.

(d) A director who is present at a meeting of the board of directors or a committee of the board of directors when corporate action is taken is deemed to have assented to the action taken unless: (1) he objects at the beginning of the meeting (or promptly upon his arrival) to holding it or transacting business at the meeting; (2) his dissent or abstention from the action taken is entered in the minutes of the meeting; or (3) he delivers written notice of his dissent or abstention to the presiding officer of the meeting before its adjournment or to the corporation immediately after adjournment of the meeting. The right of dissent or abstention is not available to a director who votes in favor of the action taken.

§ 8.25. *Committees*

(a) Unless the articles of incorporation or bylaws provide otherwise, a board of directors may create one or more committees and appoint members of the board of directors to serve on them. Each committee must have two or more members, who serve at the pleasure of the board of directors.

(b) The creation of a committee and appointment of members to it must be approved by the greater of (1) a majority of all the directors in office when the action is taken or (2) the number of directors required by the articles of incorporation or bylaws to take action under section 8.24.

(c) Sections 8.20 through 8.24, which govern meetings, action without meetings, notice and waiver of notice, and quorum and voting requirements of the board of directors, apply to committees and their members as well.

(d) To the extent specified by the board of directors or in the articles of incorporation or bylaws, each committee may exercise the authority of the board of directors under section 8.01.

(e) A committee may not, however:

(1) authorize distributions;

(2) approve or propose to shareholders action that this Act requires be approved by shareholders;

(3) fill vacancies on the board of directors or on any of its committees;

(4) amend articles of incorporation pursuant to section 10.02;

(5) adopt, amend, or repeal bylaws;

(6) approve a plan of merger not requiring shareholder approval;

(7) authorize or approve reacquisition of shares, except according to a formula or method prescribed by the board of directors; or

(8) authorize or approve the issuance or sale or contract for sale of shares, or determine the designation and relative rights, preferences, and limitations of a class or series of shares, except that the board of directors may authorize a committee (or a senior executive officer of the corporation) to do so within limits specifically prescribed by the board of directors.

(f) The creation of, delegation of authority to, or action by a committee does not alone constitute compliance by a director with the standards of conduct described in section 8.30.

SUBCHAPTER C.
STANDARDS OF CONDUCT

§ 8.30. General Standards for Directors

(a) A director shall discharge his duties as a director, including his duties as a member of a committee:

(1) in good faith;

(2) with the care an ordinarily prudent person in a like position would exercise under similar circumstances; and

(3) in a manner he reasonably believes to be in the best interests of the corporation.

(b) In discharging his duties a director is entitled to rely on information, opinions, reports, or statements, including financial statements and other financial data, if prepared or presented by:

(1) one or more officers or employees of the corporation whom the director reasonably believes to be reliable and competent in the matters presented;

(2) legal counsel, public accountants, or other persons as to matters the director reasonably believes are within the person's professional or expert competence; or

(3) a committee of the board of directors of which he is not a member if the director reasonably believes the committee merits confidence.

(c) A director is not acting in good faith if he has knowledge concerning the matter in question that makes reliance otherwise permitted by subsection (b) unwarranted.

(d) A director is not liable for any action taken as a director, or any failure to take any action, if he performed the duties of his office in compliance with this section.

§ 8.31. [Reserved]

§ 8.32. [Reserved]

§ 8.33. Liability for Unlawful Distributions

(a) A director who votes for or assents to a distribution made in violation of section 6.40 or the articles of incorporation is personally liable to the corporation for the amount of the distribution that exceeds what could have been distributed without violating section 6.40 or the articles of incorporation if it is established that he did not perform his duties in compliance with section 8.30. In any proceeding commenced under this section, a director has all of the defenses ordinarily available to a director.

(b) A director held liable under subsection (a) for an unlawful distribution is entitled to contribution:

(1) from every other director who could be held liable under subsection (a) for the unlawful distribution; and

(2) from each shareholder for the amount the shareholder accepted knowing the distribution was made in violation of section 6.40 or the articles of incorporation.

(c) A proceeding under this section is barred unless it is commenced within two years after the date on which the effect of the distribution was measured under section 6.40(e) or (g).

SUBCHAPTER D.
OFFICERS

§ 8.40. Required Officers

(a) A corporation has the officers described in its bylaws or appointed by the board of directors in accordance with the bylaws.

(b) A duly appointed officer may appoint one or more officers or assistant officers if authorized by the bylaws or the board of directors.

(c) The bylaws or the board of directors shall delegate to one of the officers responsibility for preparing minutes of the directors' and shareholders' meetings and for authenticating records of the corporation.

(d) The same individual may simultaneously hold more than one office in a corporation.

§ 8.41. Duties of Officers

Each officer has the authority and shall perform the duties set forth in the bylaws or, to the extent consistent with the bylaws, the duties prescribed by the board of directors or by direction of an officer authorized by the board of directors to prescribe the duties of other officers.

§ 8.42. Standards of Conduct for Officers

(a) An officer with discretionary authority shall discharge his duties under that authority:

(1) in good faith;

(2) with the care an ordinarily prudent person in a like position would exercise under similar circumstances; and

(3) in a manner he reasonably believes to be in the best interests of the corporation.

(b) In discharging his duties an officer is entitled to rely on information, opinions, reports, or statements, including financial statements and other financial data, if prepared or presented by:

(1) one or more officers or employees of the corporation whom the officer reasonably believes to be reliable and competent in the matters presented; or

(2) legal counsel, public accountants, or other persons as to matters the officer reasonably believes are within the person's professional or expert competence.

(c) An officer is not acting in good faith if he has knowledge concerning the matter in question that makes reliance otherwise permitted by subsection (b) unwarranted.

(d) An officer is not liable for any action taken as an officer, or any failure to take any action, if he performed the duties of his office in compliance with this section.

§ 8.43. Resignation and Removal of Officers

(a) An officer may resign at any time by delivering notice to the corporation. A resignation is effective when the notice is delivered unless the notice specifies a later effective date. If a resignation is made effective at a later date and the corporation accepts the future effective date, its board of directors may fill the pending vacancy before the effective date if the board of directors provides that the successor does not take office until the effective date.

(b) A board of directors may remove any officer at any time with or without cause.

§ 8.44. Contract Rights of Officers

(a) The appointment of an officer does not itself create contract rights.

(b) An officer's removal does not affect the officer's contract rights, if any, with the corporation. An officer's resignation does not affect the corporation's contract rights, if any, with the officer.

SUBCHAPTER E.
INDEMNIFICATION

§ 8.50. Subchapter Definitions

In this subchapter:

(1) "Corporation" includes any domestic or foreign predecessor entity of a corporation in a merger.

(2) "Director" or "officer" means an individual who is or was a director or officer, respectively, of a corporation or who, while a director or officer of the corporation, is or was serving at the corporation's request as a director, officer, partner, trustee, employee, or agent of another domestic or foreign corporation, partnership, joint venture, trust, employee benefit plan, or other entity. A director or officer is considered to be serving an employee benefit plan at the corporation's request if his duties to the corporation also impose duties on, or otherwise involve services by, him to the plan or to participants in or beneficiaries of the plan. "Director" or "officer" includes, unless the context requires otherwise, the estate or personal representative of a director or officer.

(3) "Disinterested director" means a director who, at the time of a vote referred to in section 8.53(c) or a vote or selection referred to in section 8.55(b) or (c), is not (i) a party to the proceeding, or (ii) an individual having a familial, financial, professional or employment relationship with the director whose indemnification or advance for expenses is the subject of the decision being made, which relationship would, in the circumstances, reasonably be expected to exert an influence on the director's judgment when voting on the decision being made.

(4) "Expenses" includes counsel fees.

(5) "Liability" means the obligation to pay a judgment, settlement, penalty, fine (including an excise tax assessed with respect to an employee benefit plan), or reasonable expenses incurred with respect to a proceeding.

(6) "Official capacity" means: (i) when used with respect to a director, the office of director in a corporation; and (ii) when used with respect to an office, as contemplated in section 8.56, the office in a corporation held by the officer. "Official capacity" does not include service for any other foreign or domestic corporation or any partnership, joint venture, trust, employee benefit plan, or other enterprise.

(7) "Party" means an individual who was, is, or is threatened to be made, a named defendant or respondent in a proceeding.

(8) "Proceeding" means any threatened, pending, or completed action, suit, or proceeding, whether civil, criminal, administrative, arbitrative, or investigative and whether formal or informal.

§ 8.51. *Permissible Indemnification*

(a) Except as otherwise provided in this section, a corporation may indemnify an individual who is a party to a proceeding because he is a director against liability incurred in the proceeding if:

  (1) (i) he conducted himself in good faith; and

    (ii) he reasonably believed:

      (A) in the case of conduct in his official capacity, that his conduct was in the best interests of the corporation; and

      (B) in all other cases, that his conduct was at least not opposed to the best interests of the corporation; and

      (iii) in the case of any criminal proceeding, he had no reasonable cause to believe his conduct was unlawful.

  (2) he engaged in conduct for which broader indemnification has been made permissible or obligatory under a provision of the articles of incorporation (as authorized by section 2.02(b)(5)).

(b) A director's conduct with respect to an employee benefit plan for a purpose he reasonably believed to be in the interests of the participants in, and beneficiaries of, the plan is conduct that satisfies the requirement of subsection (a)(1)(ii)(B).

(c) The termination of a proceeding by judgment, order, settlement, or conviction, or upon a plea of nolo contendere or its equivalent, is not, of itself, determinative that the director did not meet the relevant standard of conduct described in this section.

(d) Unless ordered by a court under section 8.54(a)(3), a corporation may not indemnify a director:

  (1) in connection with a proceeding by or in the right of the corporation, except for reasonable expenses incurred in connection with the proceeding if it is determined that the director has met the relevant standard of conduct under subsection (a); or

  (2) in connection with any proceeding with respect to conduct for which he was adjudged liable on the basis that he received a financial benefit to which he was not entitled, whether or not involving action in his official capacity.

§ 8.52. *Mandatory Indemnification*

A corporation shall indemnify a director who was wholly successful, on the merits or otherwise, in the defense of any proceeding to which he was a party because he was a director of the corporation against reasonable expenses incurred by him in connection with the proceeding.

§ 8.53. *Advance for Expenses*

(a) A corporation may, before final disposition of a proceeding, advance funds to pay for or reimburse the reasonable expenses incurred by a director who is a party to a proceeding because he is a director if he delivers to the corporation:

  (1) a written affirmation of his good faith belief that he has met the relevant standard of conduct described in section 8.51 or that the proceeding involves conduct for which liability has been eliminatd under a provision of the articles of incorporation as authorized by section 2.02(b)(4); and

  (2) his written undertaking to repay any funds advanced if he is not entitled to mandatory indemnification under section 8.52 and it is ultimately determined under section 8.54 or section 8.55 that he has not met the relevant standard of conduct described in section 8.51.

(b) The undertaking required by subsection (a)(2) must be an unlimited general obligation of the director but need not be secured and may be accepted without reference to the financial ability of the director to make repayment.

(c) Authorizations under this section shall be made:

  (1) by the board of directors:

    (i) If there are two or more disinterested directors, by a majority vote of all the disinterested directors (a majority of whom shall for such purpose constitute a quorum) or by a majority of the members of a committee of two or more disinterested directors appointed by such a vote; or

    (ii) if there are fewer than two disinterested directors, by the vote necessary for action by the board in accordance with section 8.24(c), in which authorization directors who do not qualify as disinterested directors may participate; or

  (2) by the shareholders, but shares owned by or voted under the control of a director who at the time does not qualify as a disinterested director may not be voted on the authorization.

§ 8.54. *Court-ordered Indemnification and Advance for Expenses*

(a) A director who is a party to a proceeding because he is a director may apply for indemnification or an advance for expenses to the court conducting the proceeding or to another court of competent jurisdiction. After receipt of an application and after giving any notice it considers necessary, the court shall:

  (1) order indemnification if the court determines that the director is entitled to mandatory indemnification under section 8.52;

  (2) order indemnification or advance for expenses if the court determines that the director is entitled to indemnification or advance for expenses pursuant to a provision authorized by section 8.58(a); or

  (3) order indemnification or advance for expenses if the court determines, in view of all the relevant circumstances, that it is fair and reasonable

(i) to indemnify the director, or

(ii) to advance expenses to the director, even if he has not met the relevant standard of conduct set forth in section 8.51(a), failed to comply with section 8.53 or was adjudged liable in a proceeding referred to in subsection 8.51(d)(1) or (d)(2), but if he was adjudged so liable his indemnification shall be limited to reasonable expenses incurred in connection with the proceeding.

(b) If the court determines that the director is entitled to indemnification under subsection (a)(1) or to indemnification or advance for expenses under subsection (a)(2), it shall also order the corporation to pay the director's reasonable expenses incurred in connection with obtaining court-ordered indemnification or advance for expenses. If the court determines that the director is entitled to indemnification or advance for expenses under subsection (a)(3), it may also order the corporation to pay the director's reasonable expenses to obtain court-ordered indemnification or advance for expenses.

§ 8.55. Determination and Authorization of Indemnification

(a) A corporation may not indemnify a director under section 8.51 unless authorized for a specific proceeding after a determination has been made that indemnification of the director is permissible because he has met the standard of conduct set forth in section 8.51.

(b) The determination shall be made:

(1) if there are two or more disinterested directors, by the board of directors by a majority vote of all the disinterested directors (a majority of whom shall for such purpose constitute a quorum), or by a majority of the members of a committee of two or more disinterested directors appointed by such a vote;

(2) by special legal counsel:

(i) selected in the manner prescribed in subdivision (1); or

(ii) if there are fewer than two disinterested directors, selected by the board of directors (in which selection directors who do not qualify as disinterested directors may participate); or

(3) by the shareholders, but shares owned by or voted under the control of a director who at the time does not qualify as a disinterested director may not be voted on the determination.

(c) Authorization of indemnification shall be made in the same manner as the determination that indemnification is permissible, except that if there are fewer than two disinterested directors or if the determination is made by special legal counsel, authorization of indemnification shall be made by those

entitled under subsection (b)(2)(ii) to select special legal counsel.

§ 8.56. Officers

(a) A corporation may indemnify and advance expenses under this subchapter to an officer of the corporation who is a party to a proceeding because he is an officer of the corporation

(1) to the same extent as a director; and

(2) if he is an officer but not a director, to such further extent as may be provided by the articles of incorporation, the bylaws, a resolution of the board of directors, or contract except for (A) liability in connection with a proceeding by or in the right of the corporation other than for reasonable expenses incurred in connection with the proceeding or (B) liability arising out of conduct that constitutes (i) receipt by him of a financial benefit to which he is not entitled, (ii) an intentional infliction of harm on the corporation or the shareholders, or (iii) an intentional violation of criminal law.

(b) The provisions of subsection (a)(2) shall apply to an officer who is also a director if the basis on which he is made a party to the proceeding is an act or omission solely as an officer.

(c) An officer of a corporation who is not a director is entitled to mandatory indemnification under section 8.52, and may apply to a court under section 8.54 for indemnification or an advance for expenses, in each case to the same extent to which a director may be entitled to indemnification or advance for expenses under those provisions.

§ 8.57. Insurance

A corporation may purchase and maintain insurance on behalf of an individual who is a director or officer of the corporation, or who, while a director or officer of the corporation, serves at the corporation's request as a director, officer, partner, trustee, employee, or agent of another domestic or foreign corporation, partnership, joint venture, trust, employee benefit plan, or other entity, against liability asserted against or incurred by him in that capacity or arising from his status as a director or officer, whether or not the corporation would have power to indemnify or advance expenses to him against the same liability under this subchapter.

§ 8.58. Variation by Corporate Action; Application of Subchapter

(a) A corporation may, by a provision in its articles of incorporation or bylaws or in a resolution adopted or a contract approved by its board of directors or shareholders, obligate itself in advance of the act or omission giving rise to a proceeding to provide indemnification in accordance with section 8.51 or advance funds to pay for or reimburse expenses in accordance with section 8.53. Any such obligatory provision shall be deemed to satisfy the requirements for authorization referred to in section 8.53(c) and in section 8.55(c). Any such provision that obligates the corporation to provide indemnification to the fullest extent permitted by law shall be deemed to obligate the corporation to advance funds to pay for or reimburse expenses in accordance with section 8.53 to the fullest extent permitted by law, unless the provision specifically provides otherwise.

(b) Any provision pursuant to subsection (a) shall not obligate the corporation to indemnify or advance expenses to a director of a predecessor of the corporation, pertaining to conduct with respect to the predecessor, unless otherwise specifically provided. Any provision for indemnification or advance for expenses in the articles of incorporation, bylaws, or a resolution of the board of directors or shareholders of a predecessor of the corporation in a merger or in a contract to which the predecessor is a party, existing at the time the merger takes effect, shall be governed by section 11.06(a)(3).

(c) A corporation may, by a provision in its articles of incorporation, limit any of the rights to indemnification or advance for expenses created by or pursuant to this subchapter.

(d) This subchapter does not limit a corporation's power to pay or reimburse expenses incurred by a director or an officer in connection with his appearance as a witness in a proceeding at a time when he is not a party.

(e) This subchapter does not limit a corporation's power to indemnify, advance expenses to or provide or maintain insurance on behalf of an employee or agent.

§ 8.59. *Exclusivity of Subchapter*

A corporation may provide indemnification or advance expenses to a director or an officer only as permitted by this subchapter.

SUBCHAPTER F.
DIRECTORS' CONFLICTING INTEREST TRANSACTIONS

§ 8.60. *Subchapter Definitions*

In this subchapter:

(1) "Conflicting interest" with respect to a corporation means the interest a director of the corporation has respecting a transaction effected or proposed to be effected by the corporation (or by a subsidiary of the corporation or any other entity in which the corporation has a controlling interest) if:

(i) whether or not the transaction is brought before the board of directors of the corporation for action, the director knows at the time of commitment that he or a related person is a party to the transaction or has a beneficial financial interest in or so closely linked to the transaction and

of such financial significance to the director or a related person that the interest would reasonably be expected to exert an influence on the director's judgment if he were called upon to vote on the transaction; or

(ii) the transaction is brought (or is of such character and significance to the corporation that it would in the normal course be brought) before the board of directors of the corporation for action, and the director knows at the time of commitment that any of the following persons is either a party to the transaction or has a beneficial financial interest in or so closely linked to the transaction and of such financial significance to the person that the interest would reasonably be expected to exert an influence on the director's judgment if he were called upon to vote on the transaction: (A) an entity (other than the corporation) of which the director is a director, general partner, agent, or employee; (B) a person that controls one or more of the entities specified in subclause (A) or an entity that is controlled by, or is under common control with, one or more of the entities specified in subclause (A); or (C) an individual who is a general partner, principal, or employer of the director.

(2) "Director's conflicting interest transaction" with respect to a corporation means a transaction effected or proposed to be effected by the corporation (or by a subsidiary of the corporation or any other entity in which the corporation has a controlling interest) respecting which a director of the corporation has a conflicting interest.

(3) "Related person" of a director means (i) the spouse (or a parent or sibling thereof) of the director, or a child, grandchild, sibling, parent (or spouse of any thereof) of the director, or an individual having the same home as the director, or a trust or estate of which an individual specified in this clause (i) is a substantial beneficiary; or (ii) a trust, estate, incompetent, conservatee, or minor of which the director is a fiduciary.

(4) "Required disclosure" means disclosure by the director who has a conflicting interest of (i) the existence and nature of his conflicting interest, and (ii) all facts known to him respecting the subject matter of the transaction that an ordinarily prudent person would reasonably believe to be material to a judgment about whether or not to proceed with the transaction.

(5) "Time of commitment" respecting a transaction means the time when the transaction is consummated or, if made pursuant to contract, the time when the corporation (or its subsidiary or the entity in which it has a controlling interest) becomes contractually obligated so that its unilateral withdrawal from the transaction would entail significant loss, liability, or other damage.

§ 8.61. *Judicial Action*

(a) A transaction effected or proposed to be effected by a corporation (or by a subsidiary of the corporation or any other entity in which the corporation has a controlling interest) that is not a director's conflicting interest transaction may not be enjoined, set aside, or give rise to an award of damages or other sanctions, in a proceeding by a shareholder or by or in the right of the corporation, because a director of the corporation, or any person with whom or which he has a personal, economic, or other association, has an interest in the transaction.

(b) A director's conflicting interest transaction may not be enjoined, set aside, or give rise to an award of damages or other sanctions, in a proceeding by a shareholder or by or in the right of the corporation, because the director, or any person with whom or which he has a personal, economic, or other association, has an interest in the transaction, if:

(1) directors' action respecting the transaction was at any time taken in compliance with section 8.62;

(2) shareholders' action respecting the transaction was at any time taken in compliance with section 8.63;

(3) the transaction, judged according to the circumstances at the time of commitment, is established to have been fair to the corporation.

§ 8.62. *Directors' Action*

(a) Directors' action respecting a transaction is effective for purposes of section 8.61(b)(1) if the transaction received the affirmative vote of a majority (but no fewer than two) of those qualified directors on the board of directors or on a duly empowered committee of the board who voted on the transaction after either required disclosure to them (to the extent the information was not known by them) or compliance with subsection (b); provided that action by a committee is so effective only if (1) all its members are qualified directors, and (2) its members are either all the qualified directors on the board or are appointed by the affirmative vote of a majority of the qualified directors on the board.

(b) If a director has a conflicting interest respecting a transaction, but neither he nor a related person of the director specified in section 8.60(3)(i) is a party to the transaction, and if the director has a duty under law or professional canon, or a duty of confidentiality to another person, respecting information relating to the transaction such that the director may not make the disclosure described in section 8.60(4)(ii), then disclosure is sufficient for purposes of subsection (a) if the director (I) discloses to the directors voting on the transaction the existence and nature of his conflicting interest and informs them of the character and limitations imposed by that duty before

their vote on the transaction, and (2) plays no part, directly or indirectly, in their deliberations or vote.

(c) A majority (but no fewer than two) of all the qualified directors on the board of directors, or on the committee, constitutes a quorum for purposes of action that complies with this section. Directors' action that otherwise complies with this section is not affected by the presence or vote of a director who is not a qualified director.

(d) For purposes of this section, "qualified director" means, with respect to a director's conflicting interest transaction, any director who does not have either (1) a conflicting interest respecting the transaction, or (2) a familial, financial, professional, or employment relationship with a second director who does have a conflicting interest respecting the transaction, which relationship would, in the circumstances, reasonably be expected to exert an influence on the first director's judgment when voting on the transaction.

§ 8.63. *Shareholders' Action*

(a) Shareholders' action respecting a transaction is effective for purposes of section 8.61(b)(2) if a majority of the votes entitled to be cast by the holders of all qualified shares were cast in favor of the transaction after (1) notice to shareholders describing the director's conflicting interest transaction, (2) provision of the information referred to in subsection (d), and (3) required disclosure to the shareholders who voted on the transaction (to the extent the information was not known by them).

(b) For purposes of this section, "qualified shares" means any shares entitled to vote with respect to the director's conflicting interest transaction except shares that, to the knowledge, before the vote, of the secretary (or other officer or agent of the corporation authorized to tabulate votes), are beneficially owned (or the voting of which is controlled) by a director who has a conflicting interest respecting the transaction or by a related person of the director, or both.

(c) A majority of the votes entitled to be cast by the holders of all qualified shares constitutes a quorum for purposes of action that complies with this section. Subject to the provisions of subsections (d) and (e), shareholders' action that otherwise complies with this section is not affected by the presence of holders, or the voting, of shares that are not qualified shares.

(d) For purposes of compliance with subsection (a), a director who has a conflicting interest respecting the transaction shall, before the shareholders' vote, inform the secretary (or other officer or agent of the corporation authorized to tabulate votes) of the number, and the identity of persons holding or controlling the vote, of all shares that the director knows are beneficially owned (or the voting of which is controlled) by the director or by a related person of the director, or both.

(e) If a shareholders' vote does not comply with subsection (a) solely because of a failure of a director to comply with subsection (d), and if the director establishes that his failure did not determine and was not intended by him to influence the outcome of the vote, the court may, with or without further proceedings respecting section 8.61(b)(3), take such action respecting the transaction and the director, and give such effect, if any, to the shareholders' vote, as it considers appropriate in the circumstances.

Chapter 9 [Reserved]

[Chapter 10, Amendment of Articles of Incorporation and Bylaws, Omitted]

CHAPTER 11
MERGER AND SHARE EXCHANGE

§ 11.01. Merger

(a) One or more corporations may merge into another corporation if the board of directors of each corporation adopts and its shareholders (if required by section 11.03) approve a plan of merger.

(b) The plan of merger must set forth:

(1) the name of each corporation planning to merge and the name of the surviving corporation into which each other corporation plans to merge;

(2) the terms and conditions of the merger; and

(3) the manner and basis of converting the shares of each corporation into shares, obligations, or other securities of the surviving or any other corporation or into cash or other property in whole or part.

(c) The plan of merger may set forth:

(1) amendments to the articles of incorporation of the surviving corporation; and

(2) other provisions relating to the merger.

§ 11.02. Share Exchange

(a) A corporation may acquire all of the outstanding shares of one or more classes or series of another corporation if the board of directors of each corporation adopts and its shareholders (if required by section 11.03) approve the exchange.

(b) The plan of exchange must set forth:

(1) the name of the corporation whose shares will be acquired and the name of the acquiring corporation;

(2) the terms and conditions of the exchange;

(3) the manner and basis of exchanging the shares to be acquired for shares, obligations, or other securities of the acquiring or any other corporation or for cash or other property in whole or part.

(c) The plan of exchange may set forth other provisions relating to the exchange.

(d) This section does not limit the power of a corporation to acquire all or part of the shares of one or more classes or series of another corporation through a voluntary exchange or otherwise.

§ 11.03. Action on Plan

(a) After adopting a plan of merger or share exchange, the board of directors of each corporation party to the merger, and the board of directors of the corporation whose shares will be acquired in the share exchange, shall submit the plan of merger (except as provided in subsection (g)) or share exchange for approval by its shareholders.

(b) For a plan of merger or share exchange to be approved:

(1) the board of directors must recommend the plan of merger or share exchange to the shareholders, unless the board of directors determines that because of conflict of interest or other special circumstances it should make no recommendation and communicates the basis for its determination to the shareholders with the plan; and

(2) the shareholders entitled to vote must approve the plan.

(c) The board of directors may condition its submission of the proposed merger or share exchange on any basis.

(d) The corporation shall notify each shareholder, whether or not entitled to vote, of the proposed shareholders' meeting in accordance with section 7.05. The notice must also state that the purpose, or one of the purposes, of the meeting is to consider the plan of merger or share exchange and contain or be accompanied by a copy or summary of the plan.

(e) Unless this Act, the articles of incorporation, or the board of directors (acting pursuant to subsection (c)) require a greater vote or a vote by voting groups, the plan of merger or share exchange to be authorized must be approved by each voting group entitled to vote separately on the plan by a majority of all the votes entitled to be cast on the plan by that voting group.

(f) Separate voting by voting groups is required:

(1) on a plan of merger if the plan contains a provision that, if contained in a proposed amendment to articles of incorporation, would require action by one or more separate voting groups on the proposed amendment under section 10.04;

(2) on a plan of share exchange by each class or series of shares included in the exchange, with each class or series constituting a separate voting group.

(g) Action by the shareholders of the surviving corporation on a plan of merger is not required if:

(1) the articles of incorporation of the surviving corporation will not differ (except for amendments enumerated in section 10.02) from its articles before the merger;

(2) each shareholder of the surviving corporation whose shares were outstanding immediately before the effective date of the merger will hold the same number of shares, with identical designations, preferences, limitations, and relative rights, immediately after;

(3) the number of voting shares outstanding immediately after the merger, plus the number of voting shares issuable as a result of the merger (either by the conversion of securities issued pursuant to the merger or the exercise of rights and warrants issued pursuant to the merger), will not exceed by more than 20 percent the total number of voting shares of the surviving corporation outstanding immediately before the merger; and

(4) the number of participating shares outstanding immediately after the merger, plus the number of participating shares issuable as a result of the merger (either by the conversion of securities issued pursuant to the merger or the exercise of rights and warrants issued pursuant to the merger), will not exceed by more than 20 percent the total number of participating shares outstanding immediately before the merger.

(h) As used in subsection (g):

(1) "Participating shares" means shares that entitle their holders to participate without limitation in distributions.

(2) "Voting shares" means shares that entitle their holders to vote unconditionally in elections of directors.

(i) After a merger or share exchange is authorized, and at any time before articles of merger or share exchange are filed, the planned merger or share exchange may be abandoned (subject to any contractual rights), without further shareholder action, in accordance with the procedure set forth in the plan of merger or share exchange or, if none is set forth, in the manner determined by the board of directors.

§ 11.04. Merger of Subsidiary

(a) A parent corporation owning at least 90 percent of the outstanding shares of each class of a subsidiary corporation may merge the subsidiary into itself without approval of the shareholders of the parent or subsidiary.

(b) The board of directors of the parent shall adopt a plan of merger that sets forth:

(1) the names of the parent and subsidiary; and

(2) the manner and basis of converting the shares of the subsidiary into shares, obligations, or other securities of the parent or any other corporation or into cash or other property in whole or part.

(c) The parent shall mail a copy or summary of the plan of merger to each shareholder of the subsidiary who does not waive the mailing requirement in writing.

(d) The parent may not deliver articles of merger to the secretary of state for filing until at least 30 days after the date it mailed a copy of the plan of merger to each shareholder of the subsidiary who did not waive the mailing requirement.

(e) Articles of merger under this section may not contain amendments to the articles of incorporation of the parent corporation (except for amendments enumerated in section 10.02).

§ 11.05. Articles of Merger or Share Exchange

(a) After a plan of merger or share exchange is approved by the shareholders, or adopted by the board of directors if shareholder approval is not required, the surviving or acquiring corporation shall deliver to the secretary of state for filing articles of merger or share exchange setting forth:

(1) the plan of merger or share exchange;

(2) if shareholder approval was not required, a statement to that effect;

(3) if approval of the shareholders of one or more corporations party to the merger or share exchange was required:

(i) the designation, number of outstanding shares, and number of votes entitled to be cast by each voting group entitled to vote separately on the plan as to each corporation; and

(ii) either the total number of votes cast for and against the plan by each voting group entitled to vote separately on the plan or the total number of undisputed votes cast for the plan separately by each voting group and a statement that the number cast for the plan by each voting group was sufficient for approval by that voting group.

(b) A merger or share exchange takes effect upon the effective date of the articles of merger or share exchange.

§ 11.06. Effect of Merger or Share Exchange

(a) When a merger takes effect:

(1) every other corporation party to the merger merges into the surviving corporation and the separate existence of every corporation except the surviving corporation ceases;

(2) the title to all real estate and other property owned by each corporation party to the merger is vested in the surviving corporation without reversion or impairment;

(3) the surviving corporation has all liabilities of each corporation party to the merger;

(4) a proceeding pending against any corporation party to the merger may be continued as if the merger did not occur or the surviving corporation may be substituted in the proceeding for the corporation whose existence ceased;

(5) the articles of incorporation of the surviving corporation are amended to the extent provided in the plan of merger; and

(6) the shares of each corporation party to the merger that are to be converted into shares, obligations, or other securities of the surviving or any other corporation or into cash or other property are converted, and the former holders of the shares are entitled only to the rights provided in the articles of merger or to their rights under chapter 13.

(b) When a share exchange takes effect, the shares of each acquired corporation are exchanged as provided in the plan, and the former holders of the shares are entitled only to the exchange rights provided in the articles of share exchange or to their rights under chapter 13.

§ 11.07. Merger or Share Exchange with Foreign Corporation

(a) One or more foreign corporations may merge or enter into a share exchange with one or more domestic corporations if:

(1) in a merger, the merger is permitted by the law of the state or country under whose law each foreign corporation is incorporated and each foreign corporation complies with that law in effecting the merger;

(2) in a share exchange, the corporation whose shares will be acquired is a domestic corporation, whether or not a share exchange is permitted by the law of the state or country under whose law the acquiring corporation is incorporated;

(3) the foreign corporation complies with section 11.05 if it is the surviving corporation of the merger or acquiring corporation of the share exchange; and

(4) each domestic corporation complies with the applicable provisions of sections 11.01 through 11.04 and, if it is the surviving corporation of the merger or acquiring corporation of the share exchange, with section 11.05.

(b) Upon the merger or share exchange taking effect, the surviving foreign corporation of a merger and the acquiring foreign corporation of a share exchange is deemed:

(1) to appoint the secretary of state as its agent for service of process in a proceeding to enforce any obligation or the rights of dissenting shareholders of each domestic corporation party to the merger or share exchange; and

(2) to agree that it will promptly pay to the dissenting shareholders of each domestic corporation party to the merger or share exchange the amount, if any, to which they are entitled under chapter 13.

(c) This section does not limit the power of a foreign corporation to acquire all or part of the shares of one or more classes or series of a domestic corporation through a voluntary exchange or otherwise.

CHAPTER 12
SALE OF ASSETS

§ 12.01. Sale of Assets in Regular Course of Business and Mortgage of Assets

(a) A corporation may, on the terms and conditions and for the consideration determined by the board of directors:

(1) sell, lease, exchange, or otherwise dispose of all, or substantially all, of its property in the usual and regular course of business;

(2) mortgage, pledge, dedicate to the repayment of indebtedness (whether with or without recourse), or otherwise encumber any or all of its property whether or not in the usual and regular course of business; or

(3) transfer any or all of its property to a corporation all the shares of which are owned by the corporation.

(b) Unless the articles of incorporation require it, approval by the shareholders of a transaction described in subsection (a) is not required.

§ 12.02. Sale of Assets Other Than in Regular Course of Business

(a) A corporation may sell, lease, exchange, or otherwise dispose of all, or substantially all, of its property (with or without the good will), otherwise than in the usual and regular course of business, on the terms and conditions and for the consideration determined by the corporation's board of directors, if the board of directors proposes and its shareholders approve the proposed transaction.

(b) For a transaction to be authorized:

(1) the board of directors must recommend the proposed transaction to the shareholders unless the board of directors determines that because of conflict of interest or other special circumstances it should make no recommendation and communicates the basis for its determination to the shareholders with the submission of the proposed transaction; and

(2) the shareholders entitled to vote must approve the transaction.

(c) The board of directors may condition its submission of the proposed transaction on any basis.

(d) The corporation shall notify each shareholder, whether or not entitled to vote, of the proposed shareholders' meeting in accordance with section 7.05. The notice must also state that the purpose, or one of the purposes, of the meeting is to consider the sale, lease, exchange, or other disposition of all, or substantially all, the property of the corporation and contain or be accompanied by a description of the transaction.

(e) Unless the articles of incorporation or the board of directors (acting pursuant to subsection (c)) require a greater vote or a vote by voting groups, the transaction to be authorized must be approved by a majority of all the votes entitled to be cast on the transaction.

(f) After a sale, lease, exchange, or other disposition of property is authorized, the transaction may be abandoned (subject to any contractual rights) without further shareholder action.

(g) A transaction that constitutes a distribution is governed by section 6.40 and not by this section.

CHAPTER 13
DISSENTERS' RIGHTS

SUBCHAPTER A.
RIGHT TO DISSENT AND OBTAIN PAYMENT FOR SHARES

§ 13.01. *Definitions*

In this chapter:

(1) "Corporation" means the issuer of the shares held by a dissenter before the corporate action, or the surviving or acquiring corporation by merger or share exchange of that issuer.

(2) "Dissenter" means a shareholder who is entitled to dissent from corporate action under section 13.02 and who exercises that right when and in the manner required by sections 13.20 through 13.28.

(3) "Fair value," with respect to a dissenter's shares, means the value of the shares immediately before the effectuation of the corporate action to which the dissenter objects, excluding any appreciation or depreciation in anticipation of the corporate action unless exclusion would be inequitable.

(4) "Interest" means interest from the effective date of the corporate action until the date of payment, at the average rate currently paid by the corporation on its principal bank loans or, if none, at a rate that is fair and equitable under all the circumstances.

(5) "Record shareholder" means the person in whose name shares are registered in the records of a corporation or the beneficial owner of shares to the

extent of the rights granted by a nominee certificate on file with a corporation.

(6) "Beneficial shareholder" means the person who is a beneficial owner of shares held in a voting trust or by a nominee as the record shareholder.

(7) "Shareholder" means the record shareholder or the beneficial shareholder.

§ 13.02. *Right to Dissent*

(a) A shareholder is entitled to dissent from, and obtain payment of the fair value of his shares in the event of, any of the following corporate actions:

(1) consummation of a plan of merger to which the corporation is a party (i) if shareholder approval is required for the merger by section 11.03 or the articles of incorporation and the shareholder is entitled to vote on the merger or (ii) if the corporation is a subsidiary that is merged with its parent under section 11.04;

(2) consummation of a plan of share exchange to which the corporation is a party as the corporation whose shares will be acquired, if the shareholder is entitled to vote on the plan;

(3) consummation of a sale or exchange of all, or substantially all, of the property of the corporation other than in the usual and regular course of business, if the shareholder is entitled to vote on the sale or exchange, including a sale in dissolution, but not including a sale pursuant to court order or a sale for cash pursuant to a plan by which all or substantially all of the net proceeds of the sale will be distributed to the shareholders within one year after the date of sale;

(4) an amendment of the articles of incorporation that materially and adversely affects rights in respect of a dissenter's shares because it:

(i) alters or abolishes a preferential right of the shares;

(ii) creates, alters, or abolishes a right in respect of redemption, including a provision respecting a sinking fund for the redemption or repurchase, of the shares;

(iii) alters or abolishes a preemptive right of the holder of the shares to acquire shares or other securities;

(iv) excludes or limits the right of the shares to vote on any matter, or to cumulate votes, other than a limitation by dilution through issuance of shares or other securities with similar voting rights; or

(v) reduces the number of shares owned by the shareholder to a fraction of a share if the fractional share so created is to be acquired for cash under section 6.04; or

(5) any corporate action taken pursuant to a shareholder vote to the extent the articles of incorporation, bylaws, or a resolution of the board

of directors provides that voting or nonvoting shareholders are entitled to dissent and obtain payment for their shares.

(b) A shareholder entitled to dissent and obtain payment for his shares under this chapter may not challenge the corporate action creating his entitlement unless the action is unlawful or fraudulent with respect to the shareholder or the corporation.

§ 13.03. Dissent by Nominees and Beneficial Owners

(a) A record shareholder may assert dissenters' rights as to fewer than all the shares registered in his name only if he dissents with respect to all shares beneficially owned by any one person and notifies the corporation in writing of the name and address of each person on whose behalf he asserts dissenters' rights. The rights of a partial dissenter under this subsection are determined as if the shares as to which he dissents and his other shares were registered in the names of different shareholders.

(b) A beneficial shareholder may assert dissenters' rights as to shares held on his behalf only if:

(1) he submits to the corporation the record shareholder's written consent to the dissent not later than the time the beneficial shareholder asserts dissenters' rights; and

(2) he does so with respect to all shares of which he is the beneficial shareholder or over which he has power to direct the vote.

SUBCHAPTER B.
PROCEDURE FOR EXERCISE OF DISSENTERS' RIGHTS

§ 13.20. Notice of Dissenters' Rights

(a) If proposed corporate action creating dissenters' rights under section 13.02 is submitted to a vote at a shareholders' meeting, the meeting notice must state that shareholders are or may be entitled to assert dissenters' rights under this chapter and be accompanied by a copy of this chapter.

(b) If corporate action creating dissenters' rights under section 13.02 is taken without a vote of shareholders, the corporation shall notify in writing all shareholders entitled to assert dissenters' rights that the action was taken and send them the dissenters' notice described in section 13.22.

§ 13.21. Notice of Intent to Demand Payment

(a) If proposed corporate action creating dissenters' rights under section 13.02 is submitted to a vote at a shareholders' meeting, a shareholder who wishes to assert dissenters' rights (1) must deliver to the corporation before the vote is taken written notice of his intent to demand payment for his shares if the proposed action is effectuated and (2) must not vote his shares in favor of the proposed action.

(b) A shareholder who does not satisfy the requirements of subsection (a) is not entitled to payment for his shares under this chapter.

§ 13.22. Dissenters' Notice

(a) If proposed corporate action creating dissenters' rights under section 13.02 is authorized at a shareholders' meeting, the corporation shall deliver a written dissenters' notice to all shareholders who satisfied the requirements of section 13.21.

(b) The dissenters' notice must be sent no later than 10 days after the corporate action was taken, and must:

(1) state where the payment demand must be sent and where and when certificates for certificated shares must be deposited;

(2) inform holders of uncertificated shares to what extent transfer of the shares will be restricted after the payment demand is received;

(3) supply a form for demanding payment that includes the date of the first announcement to news media or to shareholders of the terms of the proposed corporate action and requires that the person asserting dissenters' rights certify whether or not he acquired beneficial ownership of the shares before that date;

(4) set a date by which the corporation must receive the payment demand, which date may not be fewer than 30 nor more than 60 days after the date the subsection (a) notice is delivered; and

(5) be accompanied by a copy of this chapter.

§ 13.23. Duty to Demand Payment

(a) A shareholder sent a dissenters' notice described in section 13.22 must demand payment, certify whether he acquired beneficial ownership of the shares before the date required to be set forth in the dissenters' notice pursuant to section 13.22(b)(3), and deposit his certificates in accordance with the terms of the notice.

(b) The shareholder who demands payment and deposits his share certificates under section (a) retains all other rights of a shareholder until these rights are cancelled or modified by the taking of the proposed corporate action.

(c) A shareholder who does not demand payment or deposit his share certificates where required, each by the date set in the dissenters' notice, is not entitled to payment for his shares under this chapter.

§ 13.24. Share Restrictions

(a) The corporation may restrict the transfer of uncertificated shares from the date the demand for their payment is received until the proposed corporate action is taken or the restrictions released under section 13.26.

(b) The person for whom dissenters' rights are asserted as to uncertificated shares retains all other rights of a shareholder until these rights are cancelled or modified by the taking of the proposed corporate action.

§ 13.25. Payment

(a) Except as provided in section 13.27, as soon as the proposed corporate action is taken, or upon receipt of a payment demand, the corporation shall pay each dissenter who complied with section 13.23 the amount the corporation estimates to be the fair value of his shares, plus accrued interest.

(b) The payment must be accompanied by:

(1) the corporation's balance sheet as of the end of a fiscal year ending not more than 16 months before the date of payment, an income statement for that year, a statement of changes in shareholders' equity for that year, and the latest available interim financial statements, if any;

(2) a statement of the corporation's estimate of the fair value of the shares;

(3) an explanation of how the interest was calculated;

(4) a statement of the dissenter's right to demand payment under section 13.28; and

(5) a copy of this chapter.

§ 13.26. Failure to Take Action

(a) If the corporation does not take the proposed action within 60 days after the date set for demanding payment and depositing share certificates, the corporation shall return the deposited certificates and release the transfer restrictions imposed on uncertificated shares.

(b) If after returning deposited certificates and releasing transfer restrictions, the corporation takes the proposed action, it must send a new dissenters' notice under section 13.22 and repeat the payment demand procedure.

§ 13.27. After-acquired Shares

(a) A corporation may elect to withhold payment required by section 13.25 from a dissenter unless he was the beneficial owner of the shares before the date set forth in the dissenters' notice as the date of the first announcement to news media or to shareholders of the terms of the proposed corporate action.

(b) To the extent the corporation elects to withhold payment under subsection (a), after taking the proposed corporate action, it shall estimate the fair value of the shares, plus accrued interest, and shall pay this amount to each dissenter who agrees to accept it in full satisfaction of his demand. The corporation shall send with its offer a statement of its estimate of the fair value of the shares, an explanation of how the interest was calculated, and a statement of the dissenter's right to demand payment under section 13.28.

§ 13.28. Procedure if Shareholder Dissatisfied With Payment or Offer

(a) A dissenter may notify the corporation in writing of his own estimate of the fair value of his shares and amount of interest due, and demand payment of his estimate (less any payment under section 13.25), or reject the corporation's offer under section 13.27 and demand payment of the fair value of his shares and interest due, if:

(1) the dissenter believes that the amount paid under section 13.25 or offered under section 13.27 is less than the fair value of his shares or that the interest due is incorrectly calculated;

(2) the corporation fails to make payment under section 13.25 within 60 days after the date set for demanding payment; or

(3) the corporation, having failed to take the proposed action, does not return the deposited certificates or release the transfer restrictions imposed on uncertificated shares within 60 days after the date set for demanding payment.

(b) A dissenter waives his right to demand payment under this section unless he notifies the corporation of his demand in writing under subsection (a) within 30 days after the corporation made or offered payment for his shares.

SUBCHAPTER C.
JUDICIAL APPRAISAL OF SHARES

§ 13.30. Court Action

(a) If a demand for payment under section 13.28 remains unsettled, the corporation shall commence a proceeding within 60 days after receiving the payment demand and petition the court to determine the fair value of the shares and accrued interest. If the corporation does not commence the proceeding within the 60-day period, it shall pay each dissenter whose demand remains unsettled the amount demanded.

(b) The corporation shall commence the proceeding in the [name or describe] court of the county where a corporation's principal office (or, if none in this state, its registered office) is located. If the corporation is a foreign corporation without a registered office in this state, it shall commence the proceeding in the county in this state where the registered office of the domestic corporation merged with or whose shares were acquired by the foreign corporation was located.

(c) The corporation shall make all dissenters (whether or not residents of this state) whose demands remain unsettled parties to the proceeding as in an action against their shares and all parties must be served with a copy of the petition. Nonresidents may be served by registered or certified mail or by publication as provided by law.

(d) The jurisdiction of the court in which the proceeding is commenced under subsection (b) is plenary and exclusive. The court may appoint one or more persons as appraisers to receive evidence and recommend decision on the question of fair value. The appraisers have the powers described in the order appointing them, or in any amendment to it. The dissenters are entitled to the same discovery rights as parties in other civil proceedings.

(e) Each dissenter made a party to the proceeding is entitled to judgment (1) for the amount, if any, by which the court finds the fair value of his shares, plus interest, exceeds the amount paid by the corporation or (2) for the fair value, plus accrued interest, of his after-acquired shares for which the corporation elected to withhold payment under section 13.27.

§ 13.31. Court Costs and Counsel Fees

(a) The court in an appraisal proceeding commenced under section 13.30 shall determine all costs of the proceeding, including the reasonable compensation and expenses of appraisers appointed by the court. The court shall assess the costs against the corporation, except that the court may assess costs against all or some of the dissenters, in amounts the court finds equitable, to the extent the court finds the dissenters acted arbitrarily, vexatiously, or not in good faith in demanding payment under section 13.28.

(b) The court may also assess the fees and expenses of counsel and experts for the respective parties, in amounts the court finds equitable:

(1) against the corporation and in favor of any or all dissenters if the court finds the corporation did not substantially comply with the requirements of sections 13.20 through 13.28; or

(2) against either the corporation or a dissenter, in favor of any other party, if the court finds that the party against whom the fees and expenses are assessed acted arbitrarily, vexatiously, or not in good faith with respect to the rights provided by this chapter.

(c) If the court finds that the services of counsel for any dissenter were of substantial benefit to other dissenters similarly situated, and that the fees for those services should not be assessed against the corporation, the court may award to these counsel reasonable fees to be paid out of the amounts awarded the dissenters who were benefited.

CHAPTER 14
DISSOLUTION

SUBCHAPTER A.
VOLUNTARY DISSOLUTION

§ 14.01. Dissolution by Incorporators or Initial Directors

A majority of the incorporators or initial directors of a corporation that has not issued shares or has not commenced business may dissolve the corporation by delivering to the secretary of state for filing articles of dissolution that set forth:

(1) the name of the corporation;

(2) the date of its incorporation;

(3) either (i) that none of the corporation's shares has been issued or (ii) that the corporation has not commenced business;

(4) that no debt of the corporation remains unpaid;

(5) that the net assets of the corporation remaining after winding up have been distributed to the shareholders, if shares were issued; and

(6) that a majority of the incorporators or initial directors authorized the dissolution.

§ 14.02. Dissolution by Board of Directors and Shareholders

(a) A corporation's board of directors may propose dissolution for submission to the shareholders.

(b) For a proposal to dissolve to be adopted:

(1) the board of directors must recommend dissolution to the shareholders unless the board of directors determines that because of conflict of interest or other special circumstances it should make no recommendation and communicates the basis for its determination to the shareholders; and

(2) the shareholders entitled to vote must approve the proposal to dissolve as provided in subsection (e).

(c) The board of directors may condition its submission of the proposal for dissolution on any basis.

(d) The corporation shall notify each shareholder, whether or not entitled to vote, of the proposed shareholders' meeting in accordance with section 7.05. The notice must also state that the purpose, or one of the purposes, of the meeting is to consider dissolving the corporation.

(e) Unless the articles of incorporation or the board of directors (acting pursuant to subsection (c)) require a greater vote or a vote by voting groups, the proposal to dissolve to be adopted must be approved by a majority of all the votes entitled to be cast on that proposal.

§ 14.03. Articles of Dissolution

(a) At any time after dissolution is authorized, the corporation may dissolve by delivering to the secretary of state for filing articles of dissolution setting forth:

(1) the name of the corporation;

(2) the date dissolution was authorized;

(3) if dissolution was approved by the shareholders:

(i) the number of votes entitled to be cast on the proposal to dissolve; and

(ii) either the total number of votes cast for and against dissolution or the total number of undisputed votes cast for dissolution and a statement that the number cast for dissolution was sufficient for approval.

(4) If voting by voting groups was required, the information required by subparagraph (3) must be separately provided for each voting group entitled to vote separately on the plan to dissolve.

(b) A corporation is dissolved upon the effective date of its articles of dissolution.

§ 14.04. *Revocation of Dissolution*

(a) A corporation may revoke its dissolution within 120 days of its effective date.

(b) Revocation of dissolution must be authorized in the same manner as the dissolution was authorized unless that authorization permitted revocation by action of the board of directors alone, in which event the board of directors may revoke the dissolution without shareholder action.

(c) After the revocation of dissolution is authorized, the corporation may revoke the dissolution by delivering to the secretary of state for filing articles of revocation of dissolution, together with a copy of its articles of dissolution, that set forth:

(1) the name of the corporation;

(2) the effective date of the dissolution that was revoked;

(3) the date that the revocation of dissolution was authorized;

(4) if the corporation's board of directors (or incorporators) revoked the dissolution, a statement to that effect;

(5) if the corporation's board of directors revoked a dissolution authorized by the shareholders, a statement that revocation was permitted by action by the board of directors alone pursuant to that authorization; and

(6) if shareholder action was required to revoke the dissolution, the information required by section 14.03(a)(3) or (4).

(d) Revocation of dissolution is effective upon the effective date of the articles of revocation of dissolution.

(e) When the revocation of dissolution is effective, it relates back to and takes effect as of the effective date of the dissolution and the corporation resumes carrying on its business as if dissolution had never occurred.

§ 14.05. *Effect of Dissolution*

(a) A dissolved corporation continues its corporate existence but may not carry on any business except that appropriate to wind up and liquidate its business and affairs, including:

(1) collecting its assets;

(2) disposing of its properties that will not be distributed in kind to its shareholders;

(3) discharging or making provision for discharging its liabilities;

(4) distributing its remaining property among its shareholders according to their interests; and

(5) doing every other act necessary to wind up and liquidate its business and affairs.

(b) Dissolution of a corporation does not:

(1) transfer title to the corporation's property;

(2) prevent transfer of its shares or securities, although the authorization to dissolve may provide for closing the corporation's share transfer records;

(3) subject its directors or officers to standards of conduct different from those prescribed in chapter 8;

(4) change quorum or voting requirements for its board of directors or shareholders; change provisions for selection, resignation, or removal of its directors or officers or both; or change provisions for amending its bylaws;

(5) prevent commencement of a proceeding by or against the corporation in its corporate name;

(6) abate or suspend a proceeding pending by or against the corporation on the effective date of dissolution; or

(7) terminate the authority of the registered agent of the corporation.

§ 14.06. *Known Claims Against Dissolved Corporation*

(a) A dissolved corporation may dispose of the known claims against it by following the procedure described in this section.

(b) The dissolved corporation shall notify its known claimants in writing of the dissolution at any time after its effective date. The written notice must:

(1) describe information that must be included in a claim;

(2) provide a mailing address where a claim may be sent;

(3) state the deadline, which may not be fewer than 120 days from the effective date of the written notice, by which the dissolved corporation must receive the claim; and

(4) state that the claim will be barred if not received by the deadline.

(c) A claim against the dissolved corporation is barred:

(1) if a claimant who was given written notice under subsection (b) does not deliver the claim to the dissolved corporation by the deadline;

(2) if a claimant whose claim was rejected by the dissolved corporation does not commence a proceeding to enforce the claim within 90 days from the effective date of the rejection notice.

(d) For purposes of this section, "claim" does not include a contingent liability or a claim based on an event occurring after the effective date of dissolution.

§ 14.07. *Unknown Claims Against Dissolved Corporation*

(a) A dissolved corporation may also publish notice of its dissolution and request that persons with claims against the corporation present them in accordance with the notice.

(b) The notice must:

(1) be published one time in a newspaper of general circulation in the county where the dissolved corporation's principal office (or, if none in this state, its registered office) is or was last located;

(2) describe the information that must be included in a claim and provide a mailing address where the claim may be sent; and

(3) state that a claim against the corporation will be barred unless a proceeding to enforce the claim is commenced within five years after the publication of the notice.

(c) If the dissolved corporation publishes a newspaper notice in accordance with subsection (b), the claim of each of the following claimants is barred unless the claimant commences a proceeding to enforce the claim against the dissolved corporation within five years after the publication date of the newspaper notice:

(1) a claimant who did not receive written notice under section 14.06;

(2) a claimant whose claim was timely sent to the dissolved corporation but not acted on;

(3) a claimant whose claim is contingent or based on an event occurring after the effective date of dissolution.

(d) A claim may be enforced under this section:

(1) against the dissolved corporation, to the extent of its undistributed assets; or

(2) if the assets have been distributed in liquidation, against a shareholder of the dissolved corporation to the extent of his pro rata share of the claim or the corporate assets distributed to him in liquidation, whichever is less, but a shareholder's total liability for all claims under this section may not exceed the total amount of assets distributed to him.

SUBCHAPTER B.
ADMINISTRATIVE DISSOLUTION

§ 14.20. *Grounds for Administrative Dissolution*

The secretary of state may commence a proceeding under section 14.21 to administratively dissolve a corporation if:

(1) the corporation does not pay within 60 days after they are due any franchise taxes or penalties imposed by this Act or other law;

(2) the corporation does not deliver its annual report to the secretary of state within 60 days after it is due;

(3) the corporation is without a registered agent or registered office in this state for 60 days or more;

(4) the corporation does not notify the secretary of state within 60 days that its registered agent or registered office has been changed, that its registered agent has resigned, or that its registered office has been discontinued; or

(5) the corporation's period of duration stated in its articles of incorporation expires.

§ 14.21. *Procedure for and Effect of Administrative Dissolution*

(a) If the secretary of state determines that one or more grounds exist under section 14.20 for dissolving a corporation, he shall serve the corporation with written notice of his determination under section 5.04.

(b) If the corporation does not correct each ground for dissolution or demonstrate to the reasonable satisfaction of the secretary of state that each ground determined by the secretary of state does not exist within 60 days after service of the notice is perfected under section 5.04, the secretary of state shall administratively dissolve the corporation by signing a certificate of dissolution that recites the ground or grounds for dissolution and its effective date. The secretary of state shall file the original of the certificate and serve a copy on the corporation under section 5.04.

(c) A corporation administratively dissolved continues its corporate existence but may not carry on any business except that necessary to wind up and liquidate its business and affairs under section 14.05 and notify claimants under sections 14.06 and 14.07.

(d) The administrative dissolution of a corporation does not terminate the authority of its registered agent.

§ 14.22. *Reinstatement Following Administrative Dissolution*

(a) A corporation administratively dissolved under section 14.21 may apply to the secretary of state for reinstatement within two years after the effective date of dissolution. The application must:

(1) recite the name of the corporation and the effective date of its administrative dissolution;

(2) state that the ground or grounds for dissolution either did not exist or have been eliminated;

(3) state that the corporation's name satisfies the requirements of section 4.01; and

(4) contain a certificate from the [taxing authority] reciting that all taxes owed by the corporation have been paid.

(b) If the secretary of state determines that the application contains the information required by subsection (a) and that the information is correct, he shall cancel the certificate of dissolution and prepare a certificate of reinstatement that recites his determination and the effective date of reinstatement, file the original of the certificate, and serve a copy on the corporation under section 5.04.

(c) When the reinstatement is effective, it relates back to and takes effect as of the effective date of the administrative dissolution and the corporation resumes carrying on its business as if the administrative dissolution had never occurred.

§ 14.23. Appeal From Denial of Reinstatement

(a) If the secretary of state denies a corporation's application for reinstatement following administrative dissolution, he shall serve the corporation under section 5.04 with a written notice that explains the reason or reasons for denial.

(b) The corporation may appeal the denial of reinstatement to the [name or describe] court within 30 days after service of the notice of denial is perfected. The corporation appeals by petitioning the court to set aside the dissolution and attaching to the petition copies of the secretary of state's certificate of dissolution, the corporation's application for reinstatement, and the secretary of state's notice of denial.

(c) The court may summarily order the secretary of state to reinstate the dissolved corporation or may take other action the court considers appropriate.

(d) The court's final decision may be appealed as in other civil proceedings.

SUBCHAPTER C.
JUDICIAL DISSOLUTION

§ 14.30. Grounds for Judicial Dissolution

The [name or describe court or courts] may dissolve a corporation:

(1) in a proceeding by the attorney general if it is established that:

(i) the corporation obtained its articles of incorporation through fraud; or

(ii) the corporation has continued to exceed or abuse the authority conferred upon it by law;

(2) in a proceeding by a shareholder if it is established that:

(i) the directors are deadlocked in the management of the corporate affairs, the shareholders are unable to break the deadlock, and irreparable injury to the corporation is threatened or being suffered, or the business and affairs of the corporation can no longer be conducted to the advantage of the shareholders generally, because of the deadlock;

(ii) the directors or those in control of the corporation have acted, are acting, or will act in a manner that is illegal, oppressive, or fraudulent;

(iii) the shareholders are deadlocked in voting power and have failed, for a period that includes at least two consecutive annual meeting dates, to elect successors to directors whose terms have expired; or

(iv) the corporate assets are being misapplied or wasted;

(3) in a proceeding by a creditor if it is established that:

(i) the creditor's claim has been reduced to judgment, the execution on the judgment returned unsatisfied, and the corporation is insolvent; or

(ii) the corporation has admitted in writing that the creditor's claim is due and owing and the corporation is insolvent; or

(4) in a proceeding by the corporation to have its voluntary dissolution continued under court supervision.

§ 14.31. Procedure for Judicial Dissolution

(a) Venue for a proceeding by the attorney general to dissolve a corporation lies in [name the county or counties]. Venue for a proceeding brought by any other party named in section 14.30 lies in the county where a corporation's principal office (or, if none in this state, its registered office) is or was last located.

(b) It is not necessary to make shareholders parties to a proceeding to dissolve a corporation unless relief is sought against them individually.

(c) A court in a proceeding brought to dissolve a corporation may issue injunctions, appoint a receiver or custodian pendente lite with all powers and duties the court directs, take other action required to preserve the corporate assets wherever located, and carry on the business of the corporation until a full hearing can be held.

(d) Within 10 days of the commencement of a proceeding under section 14.30(2) to dissolve a corporation that has no shares listed on a national securities exchange or regularly traded in a market maintained by one or more members of a national securities exchange, the corporation must send to all shareholders, other than the petitioner, a notice stating that the shareholders are entitled to avoid the dissolution of the corporation by electing to purchase the petitioner's shares under section 14.34 and accompanied by a copy of section 14.34.

§ 14.32. Receivership or Custodianship

(a) A court in a judicial proceeding brought to dissolve a corporation may appoint one or more receivers to wind up and liquidate, or one or more custodians to manage, the business and affairs of the corporation. The court shall hold a hearing, after notifying all parties to the proceeding and any interested persons designated by the court, before appointing a receiver or custodian. The court appointing a receiver or custodian has exclusive jurisdiction over the corporation and all of its property wherever located.

(b) The court may appoint an individual or a domestic or foreign corporation (authorized to transact business in this state) as a receiver or custodian. The court may require the receiver or custodian to post bond, with or without sureties, in an amount the court directs.

(c) The court shall describe the powers and duties of the receiver or custodian in its appointing order, which may be amended from time to time. Among other powers:

(1) the receiver (i) may dispose of all or any part of the assets of the corporation wherever located, at a public or private sale, if authorized by the court; and (ii) may sue and defend in his own name as receiver of the corporation in all courts of this state;

(2) the custodian may exercise all of the powers of the corporation, through or in place of its board of directors or officers, to the extent necessary to manage the affairs of the corporation in the best interests of its shareholders and creditors.

(d) The court during a receivership may redesignate the receiver a custodian, and during a custodianship may redesignate the custodian a receiver, if doing so is in the best interests of the corporation, its shareholders, and creditors.

(e) The court from time to time during the receivership or custodianship may order compensation paid and expense disbursements or reimbursements made to the receiver or custodian and his counsel from the assets of the corporation or proceeds from the sale of the assets.

§ 14.33. Decree of Dissolution

(a) If after a hearing the court determines that one or more grounds for judicial dissolution described in section 14.30 exist, it may enter a decree dissolving the corporation and specifying the effective date of the dissolution, and the clerk of the court shall deliver a certified copy of the decree to the secretary of state, who shall file it.

(b) After entering the decree of dissolution, the court shall direct the winding up and liquidation of the corporation's business and affairs in accordance with section 14.05 and the notification of claimants in accordance with sections 14.06 and 14.07.

§ 14.34. Election to Purchase in Lieu of Dissolution

(a) In a proceeding under section 14.30(2) to dissolve a corporation that has no shares listed on a national securities exchange or regularly traded in a market maintained by one or more members of a national or affiliated securities association, the corporation may elect or, if it fails to elect, one or more shareholders may elect to purchase all shares owned by the petitioning shareholder at the fair value of the shares. An election pursuant to this section shall be irrevocable unless the court determines that it is equitable to set aside or modify the election.

(b) An election to purchase pursuant to this section may be filed with the court at any time within 90 days after the filing of the petition under section 14.30(2) or at such later time as the court in its discretion may allow. If the election to purchase is filed by one or more shareholders, the corporation shall, within 10 days thereafter, give written notice to all shareholders, other than the petitioner. The notice must state the name and number of shares owned by the petitioner and the name and number of shares owned by each electing shareholder and must advise the recipients of their right to join in the election to purchase shares in accordance with this section. Shareholders who wish to participate must file notice of their intention to join in the purchase no later than 30 days after the effective date of the notice to them. All shareholders who have filed an election or notice of their intention to participate in the election to purchase thereby become parties to ownership of shares as of the date the first election was filed, unless they otherwise agree or the court otherwise directs. After an election has been filed by the corporation or one or more shareholders, the proceeding under section 14.30(2) may not be discontinued or settled, nor may the petitioning shareholder sell or otherwise dispose of his shares, unless the court determines that it would be equitable to the corporation and the shareholders, other than the petitioner, to permit such discontinuance, settlement, sale, or other disposition.

(c) If, within 60 days of the filing of the first election, the parties reach agreement as to the fair value and terms of purchase of the petitioner's shares, the court shall enter an order directing the purchase of petitioner's shares upon the terms and conditions agreed to by the parties.

(d) If the parties are unable to reach an agreement as provided for in subsection (c), the court, upon application of any party, shall stay the section 14.30(2) proceedings and determine the fair value of the petitioner's shares as of the day before the date on which the petition under section 14.30(2) was filed or as of such other date as the court deems appropriate under the circumstances.

(e) Upon determining the fair value of the shares, the court shall enter an order directing the purchase upon such terms and conditions as the court deems appropriate, which may include payment of the purchase price in installments, where necessary in the interests of equity, provision for security to assure payment of the purchase price and any additional costs, fees, and expenses as may have been awarded, and, if the shares are to be purchased by shareholders, the allocation of shares among them. In allocating petitioner's shares among holders of different classes of shares, the court should attempt to preserve the existing distribution of voting rights among holders of different classes insofar as practicable and may direct that holders of a specific class or classes shall not participate in the purchase. Interest may be allowed at the rate and from the date determined by the court to be equitable, but if the court finds that the refusal of the petitioning shareholder to accept an offer of payment was arbitrary or otherwise not in good faith, no interest shall be allowed. If the court finds that the petitioning shareholder had probable grounds for relief under paragraphs (ii) or (iv) of section 14.30(2), it may award to the petitioning shareholder reasonable fees and expenses of counsel and of any experts employed by him.

(f) Upon entry of an order under subsections (c) or (e), the court shall dismiss the petition to dissolve the corporation under section 14.30, and the petitioning shareholder shall no longer have any rights or status as a shareholder of the corporation, except the right to receive the amounts awarded to him by the order of the court which shall be enforceable in the same manner as any other judgment.

(g) The purchase ordered pursuant to subsection (e), shall be made within 10 days after the date the order becomes final unless before that time the corporation files with the court a notice of its intention to adopt articles of dissolution pursuant to sections 14.02 and 14.03, which articles must then be adopted and filed within 50 days thereafter. Upon filing of such articles of dissolution, the corporation shall be dissolved in accordance with the provisions of sections 14.05 through 07, and the order entered pursuant to subsection (e) shall no longer be of any force or effect, except that the court may award the petitioning shareholder reasonable fees and expenses in accordance with the provisions of the last sentence of subsection (e) and the petitioner may continue to pursue any claims previously asserted on behalf of the corporation.

(h) Any payment by the corporation pursuant to an order under subsections (c) or (e), other than an award of fees and expenses pursuant to subsection (e), is subject to the provisions of section 6.40.

[Subchapter D omitted]

CHAPTER 15
FOREIGN CORPORATIONS

SUBCHAPTER A.
CERTIFICATE OF AUTHORITY

§ 15.01. *Authority to Transact Business Required*

(a) A foreign corporation may not transact business in this state until it obtains a certificate of authority from the secretary of state.

(b) The following activities, among others, do not constitute transacting business within the meaning of subsection (a):

(1) maintaining, defending, or settling any proceeding;

(2) holding meetings of the board of directors or shareholders or carrying on other activities concerning internal corporate affairs;

(3) maintaining bank accounts;

(4) maintaining offices or agencies for the transfer, exchange, and registration of the corporation's own securities or maintaining trustees or depositaries with respect to those securities;

(5) selling through independent contractors;

(6) soliciting or obtaining orders, whether by mail or through employees or agents or otherwise, if the orders require acceptance outside this state before they become contracts;

(7) creating or acquiring indebtedness, mortgages, and security interests in real or personal property;

(8) securing or collecting debts or enforcing mortgages and security interests in property securing the debts;

(9) owning, without more, real or personal property;

(10) conducting an isolated transaction that is completed within 30 days and that is not one in the course of repeated transactions of a like nature;

(11) transacting business in interstate commerce.

(c) The list of activities in subsection (b) is not exhaustive.

§ 15.02. *Consequences of Transacting Business Without Authority*

(a) A foreign corporation transacting business in this state without a certificate of authority may not maintain a proceeding in any court in this state until it obtains a certificate of authority.

(b) The successor to a foreign corporation that transacted business in this state without a certificate of authority and the assignee of a cause of action arising out of that business may not maintain a proceeding based on that cause of action in any court in this state until the foreign corporation or its successor obtains a certificate of authority.

(c) A court may stay a proceeding commenced by a foreign corporation, its successor, or assignee until it determines whether the foreign corporation or its successor requires a certificate of authority. If it so determines, the court may further stay the proceeding until the foreign corporation or its successor obtains the certificate.

(d) A foreign corporation is liable for a civil penalty of $_____ for each day, but not to exceed a total of $_____ for each year, it transacts business in this state without a certificate of authority. The attorney general may collect all penalties due under this subsection.

(e) Notwithstanding subsections (a) and (b), the failure of a foreign corporation to obtain a certificate of authority does not impair the validity of its corporate acts or prevent it from defending any proceeding in this state.

§ 15.03. Application for Certificate of Authority

(a) A foreign corporation may apply for a certificate of authority to transact business in this state by delivering an application to the secretary of state for filing. The application must set forth:

(1) the name of the foreign corporation or, if its name is unavailable for use in this state, a corporate name that satisfies the requirements of section 15.06;

(2) the name of the state or country under whose law it is incorporated;

(3) its date of incorporation and period of duration;

(4) the street address of its principal office;

(5) the address of its registered office in this state and the name of its registered agent at that office; and

(6) the names and usual business addresses of its current directors and officers.

(b) The foreign corporation shall deliver with the completed application a certificate of existence (or a document of similar import) duly authenticated by the secretary of state or other official having custody of corporate records in the state or country under whose law it is incorporated.

§ 15.04. Amended Certificate of Authority

(a) A foreign corporation authorized to transact business in this state must obtain an amended certificate of authority from the secretary of state if it changes:

(1) its corporate name;

(2) the period of its duration; or

(3) the state or country of its incorporation.

(b) The requirements of section 15.03 for obtaining an original certificate of authority apply to obtaining an amended certificate under this section.

§ 15.05. Effect of Certificate of Authority

(a) A certificate of authority authorizes the foreign corporation to which it is issued to transact business in this state subject, however, to the right of the state to revoke the certificate as provided in this Act.

(b) A foreign corporation with a valid certificate of authority has the same but no greater rights and has the same but no greater privileges as, and except as otherwise provided by this Act is subject to the same duties, restrictions, penalties, and liabilities now or later imposed on, a domestic corporation of like character.

(c) This Act does not authorize this state to regulate the organization or internal affairs of a foreign corporation authorized to transact business in this state.

§ 15.06. Corporate Name of Foreign Corporation

(a) If the corporate name of a foreign corporation does not satisfy the requirements of section 4.01, the foreign corporation to obtain or maintain a certificate of authority to transact business in this state:

(1) may add the word "corporation," "incorporated," "company," or "limited," or the abbreviation "corp.," "inc.," "co.," or "ltd.," to its corporate name for use in this state; or

(2) may use a fictitious name to transact business in this state if its real name is unavailable and it delivers to the secretary of state for filing a copy of the resolution of its board of directors, certified by its secretary, adopting the fictitious name.

(b) Except as authorized by subsections (c) and (d), the corporate name (including a fictitious name) of a foreign corporation must be distinguishable upon the records of the secretary of state from:

(1) the corporate name of a corporation incorporated or authorized to transact business in this state;

(2) a corporate name reserved or registered under section 4.02 or 4.03;

(3) the fictitious name of another foreign corporation authorized to transact business in this state; and

(4) the corporate name of a not-for-profit corporation incorporated or authorized to transact business in this state.

(c) A foreign corporation may apply to the secretary of state for authorization to use in this state the name of another corporation (incorporated or authorized to transact business in this state) that is not distinguishable upon his records from the name applied for. The secretary of state shall authorize use of the name applied for if:

(1) the other corporation consents to the use in writing and submits an undertaking in form satisfactory to the secretary of state to change its name to a name that is distinguishable upon the records of the secretary of state from the name of the applying corporation; or

(2) the applicant delivers to the secretary of state a certified copy of a final judgment of a court of competent jurisdiction establishing the applicant's right to use the name applied for in this state.

(d) A foreign corporation may use in this state the name (including the fictitious name) of another domestic or foreign corporation that is used in this state if the other corporation is incorporated or authorized to transact business in this state and the foreign corporation:

(1) has merged with the other corporation;

(2) has been formed by reorganization of the other corporation; or

(3) has acquired all or substantially all of the assets, including the corporate name, of the other corporation.

(e) If a foreign corporation authorized to transact business in this state changes its corporate name to one that does not satisfy the requirements of section 4.01, it may not transact business in this state under the changed name until it adopts a name satisfying the requirements of section 4.01 and obtains an amended certificate of authority under section 15.04.

§ 15.07. Registered Office and Registered Agent of Foreign Corporation

Each foreign corporation authorized to transact business in this state must continuously maintain in this state:

(1) a registered office that may be the same as any of its places of business; and

(2) a registered agent, who may be:

(i) an individual who resides in this state and whose business office is identical with the registered office;

(ii) a domestic corporation or not-for-profit domestic corporation whose business office is identical with the registered office; or

(iii) a foreign corporation or foreign not-for-profit corporation authorized to transact business in this state whose business office is identical with the registered office.

§ 15.08. Change of Registered Office or Registered Agent of Foreign Corporation

(a) A foreign corporation authorized to transact business in this state may change its registered office or registered agent by delivering to the secretary of state for filing a statement of change that sets forth:

(1) its name;

(2) the street address of its current registered office;

(3) if the current registered office is to be changed, the street address of its new registered office;

(4) the name of its current registered agent;

(5) if the current registered agent is to be changed, the name of its new registered agent and the new agent's written consent (either on the statement or attached to it) to the appointment; and

(6) that after the change or changes are made, the street addresses of its registered office and the business office of its registered agent will be identical.

(b) If a registered agent changes the street address of his business office, he may change the street address of the registered office of any foreign corporation for which he is the registered agent by notifying the corporation in writing of the change and signing (either manually or in facsimile) and delivering to the secretary of state for filing a statement of change that complies with the requirements of subsection (a) and recites that the corporation has been notified of the change.

§ 15.09. Resignation of Registered Agent of Foreign Corporation

(a) The registered agent of a foreign corporation may resign his agency appointment by signing and delivering to the secretary of state for filing the original and two exact or conformed copies of a statement of resignation. The statement of resignation may include a statement that the registered office is also discontinued.

(b) After filing the statement, the secretary of state shall attach the filing receipt to one copy and mail the copy and receipt to the registered office if not discontinued. The secretary of state shall mail the other copy to the foreign corporation at its principal office address shown in its most recent annual report.

(c) The agency appointment is terminated, and the registered office discontinued if so provided, on the 31st day after the date on which the statement was filed.

§ 15.10. Service on Foreign Corporation

(a) The registered agent of a foreign corporation authorized to transact business in this state is the corporation's agent for service of process, notice, or demand required or permitted by law to be served on the foreign corporation.

(b) A foreign corporation may be served by registered or certified mail, return receipt requested, addressed to the secretary of the foreign corporation at its principal office shown in its application for a certificate of authority or in its most recent annual report if the foreign corporation:

(1) has no registered agent or its registered agent cannot with reasonable diligence be served;

(2) has withdrawn from transacting business in this state under section 15.20; or

(3) has had its certificate of authority revoked under section 15.31.

(c) Service is perfected under subsection (b) at the earliest of:

(1) the date the foreign corporation receives the mail;

(2) the date shown on the return receipt, if signed on behalf of the foreign corporation; or

(3) five days after its deposit in the United States Mail, as evidenced by the postmark, if mailed postpaid and correctly addressed.

(d) This section does not prescribe the only means, or necessarily the required means, of serving a foreign corporation.

SUBCHAPTER B.
WITHDRAWAL

§ 15.20.   *Withdrawal of Foreign Corporation*

(a) A foreign corporation authorized to transact business in this state may not withdraw from this state until it obtains a certificate of withdrawal from the secretary of state.

(b) A foreign corporation authorized to transact business in this state may apply for a certificate of withdrawal by delivering an application to the secretary of state for filing. The application must set forth:

(1) the name of the foreign corporation and the name of the state or country under whose law it is incorporated;

(2) that it is not transacting business in this state and that it surrenders its authority to transact business in this state;

(3) that it revokes the authority of its registered agent to accept service on its behalf and appoints the secretary of state as its agent for service of process in any proceeding based on a cause of action arising during the time it was authorized to transact business in this state;

(4) a mailing address to which the secretary of state may mail a copy of any process served on him under subdivision (3); and

(5) a commitment to notify the secretary of state in the future of any change in its mailing address.

(c) After the withdrawal of the corporation is effective, service of process on the secretary of state under this section is service on the foreign corporation. Upon receipt of process, the secretary of state shall mail a copy of the process to the foreign corporation at the mailing address set forth under subsection (b).

[Subchapter C omitted]

[Chapter 16, Records and Reports, omitted]

[Chapter 17, omitted]

APPENDIX G

FOREIGN CORPORATION TABLE

Note: Because filing and publication requirements are subject to change, paralegals should always check for the most recent state and local requirements.

State	Publication Required	County Recording Required	Name Registration Available
Alabama	No	No	Yes
Alaska	No	No	Yes
Arizona	Yes	No	No
Arkansas	No	No	Yes
California	No	No	Yes
Colorado	No	No	Yes
Connecticut	No	No	Yes
Delaware	No	No	No
District of Columbia	No	No	No
Florida	No	No	Yes
Georgia	No	No	Yes
Hawaii	No	No	No
Idaho	No	No	Yes
Illinois	No	Yes	Yes
Indiana	No	No	Yes
Iowa	No	No	Yes
Kansas	No	Yes	No
Kentucky	No	Yes	Yes
Louisiana	No	No	No
Maine	No	No	Yes
Maryland	No	No	Yes
Massachusetts	No	No	No
Michigan	No	No	Yes
Minnesota	No	No	No
Mississippi	No	No	Yes
Missouri	No	No	No
Montana	No	No	Yes
Nebraska	No	No	Yes
Nevada	Yes	Yes	Yes
New Hampshire	No	No	Yes

State	Publication Required	County Recording Required	Name Registration Available
New Jersey	No	No	Yes
New Mexico	No	No	Yes
New York	No	Yes	No
North Carolina	No	No	Yes
North Dakota	No	No	No
Ohio	No	No	Yes
Oklahoma	No	No	No
Oregon	No	No	Yes
Pennsylvania	Yes	No	Yes
Rhode Island	No	No	Yes
South Carolina	No	No	Yes
South Dakota	No	No	Yes
Tennessee	No	No	Yes
Texas	No	No	Yes
Utah	No	No	Yes
Vermont	No	No	Yes
Virginia	No	No	Yes
Washington	No	No	Yes
West Virginia	No	Yes	Yes
Wisconsin	No	No	No
Wyoming	No	No	No

APPENDIX H

FORMS

H-1: COMMERCIAL PARTNERSHIP AGREEMENT

H-2: LIMITED PARTNERSHIP AGREEMENT

H-3: LIMITED LIABILITY COMPANY OPERATING AGREEMENT

H-4: CORPORATE BYLAWS

APPENDIX H-1
COMMERCIAL PARTNERSHIP AGREEMENT

[From 14 AM. JUR. 2d *Legal Forms* (Rev)]

Agreement made _____ , 19___ , between _____ , of _____ , City of _____ , County of _____ , State of _____ , and _____ , of _____ , City of _____ , County of _____ , State of _____ , herein referred to as partners.

RECITALS

1. Partners desire to join together for the pursuit of common business goals.

2. Partners have considered various forms of joint business enterprises for their business activities.

3. Partners desire to enter into a partnership agreement as the most advantageous business form for their mutual purposes.

In consideration of the mutual promises contained herein, partners agree as follows:

ARTICLE ONE
NAME, PURPOSE, AND DOMICILE

The name of the partnership shall be _____. The partnership shall be conducted for the purposes of _____ . The principal place of business shall be at _____ , City of _____ , County of _____ , State of _____ , unless relocated by majority consent of the partners.

ARTICLE TWO
DURATION OF AGREEMENT

The term of this agreement shall be for _____ years, commencing on _____ , 19___ , and terminating on _____ , 19___ , unless sooner terminated by mutual consent of the parties or by operation of the provisions of this agreement.

ARTICLE THREE
CLASSIFICATION AND
PERFORMANCE BY PARTNERS

1. Partners shall be classified as active partners, advisory partners, or estate partners.

An active partner may voluntarily become an advisory partner, may be required to become one irrespective of age, and shall automatically become one after attaining the age of _____ years, and in each case shall continue as such for _____ years unless he sooner withdraws or dies.

If an active partner dies, his estate will become an estate partner for _____ years. If an advisory partner dies within _____ years of having become an advisory partner, his estate will become an estate partner for the balance of the _____-year period.

Only active partners shall have any vote in any partnership matter.

At the time of the taking effect of this partnership agreement, all the partners shall be active partners except _____ and _____ , who shall be advisory partners.

2. An active partner, after attaining the age of _____ years, or prior thereto if the _____ [executive committee or as the case may be] with the approval of _____ [two-thirds or as the case may be] of all the other active partners determines that the reason for the change in status is bad health, may become an advisory partner at the end of any calendar month upon giving _____ [number] calendar months' prior notice in writing of his intention so to do. Such notice shall be deemed to be sufficient if sent by registered mail addressed to the partnership at its principal office at _____ [address] not less than _____ [number] calendar months prior to the date when such change is to become effective.

3. Any active partner may at any age be required to become an advisory partner at any time if the _____ [executive committee or as the case may be] with the

approval of _____ [two-thirds or as the case may be] of the other active partners shall decide that such change is for any reason in the best interests of the partnership, provided notice thereof shall be given in writing to such partner. Such notice shall be signed by the _____ [chairman or as the case may be] of the _____ [executive committee or as the case may be] or, in the event of his being unable to sign at such time, by another member of such [executive committee or as the case may be] and shall be served personally upon such partner required to change his status, or mailed by registered mail to his last known address and thereupon such change shall become effective as of the date specified in such notice.

4. Every active partner shall automatically and without further act become an advisory partner at the end of the fiscal year in which his _____ birthday occurs.

5. In the event that an active partner becomes an advisory partner or dies, he or his estate shall be entitled to the following payments at the following times: _____ [enumerate].

Each active partner shall apply all of his experience, training, and ability in discharging his assigned functions in the partnership and in the performance of all work that may be necessary or advantageous to further the business interests of the partnership.

ARTICLE FOUR
CONTRIBUTION

Each partner shall contribute _____ Dollars ($_____) on or before _____ , 19___ , to be used by the partnership to establish its capital position. Any additional contribution required of partners shall only be determined and established in accordance with Article Nineteen herein.

ARTICLE FIVE
BUSINESS EXPENSES

The rent of the buildings where the partnership business shall be carried on, and the cost of repairs and alterations, all rates, taxes, payments for insurance, and other expenses in respect to the buildings used by the partnership, and the wages for all persons employed by the partnership are all to become payable on the account of the partnership. All losses incurred shall be paid out of the capital of the partnership or the profits arising from the partnership business, or, if both shall be deficient, by the partners on a pro rata basis, in proportion to their original contributions, as provided in Article Nineteen.

ARTICLE SIX
AUTHORITY

No partner shall buy any goods or articles or enter into any contract exceeding the value of _____ Dollars ($_____) without the prior consent in writing of the other partners. If any partner exceeds this authority the other partner shall have the option to take the goods or accept the contract on account of the partnership to let the goods remain the sole property of the partner who shall have obligated himself.

ARTICLE SEVEN
SEPARATE DEBTS

No partner shall enter into any bond or become surety, security, bail, or cosigner for any person, partnership, or corporation, or knowingly condone anything whereby the partnership property may be attached or taken in execution, without the written consent of the other partners.

Each partner shall punctually pay his separate debts and indemnify the other partners and the capital and property of the partnership against his separate debts and all expenses relating thereto.

ARTICLE EIGHT
BOOKS AND RECORDS

Books of accounts shall be maintained by the partners, and proper entries made therein of all sales, purchases, receipts, payments, transactions, and property of the partnership, and the books of accounts and all records of the partnership shall be retained at the principal place of business as specified in Article One herein. Each partner shall have free access at all times to all books and records maintained relative to the partnership business.

ARTICLE NINE
ACCOUNTING

The fiscal year of the partnership shall be from _____ [month and day] to _____ [month and day] of each year. On the _____ day of _____ [month], commencing in 19___ , and on the _____ day of _____ [month] in each succeeding year, a general accounting shall be made and taken by the partners of all sales, purchases, receipts, payments, and transactions of the partnership during the preceding fiscal year, and all of the capital property and current liabilities of the partnership. The general accounting shall be written in the partnership account books and signed in each book by each partner immediately after it is completed. After the signature of each partner is entered, each partner shall keep one of the books and shall be bound by every account, except that if any manifest effort is found therein by any partner and shown to the other partners within _____ months after the error shall have been noted by all of them, the error shall be rectified.

ARTICLE TEN
DIVISION OF PROFITS AND LOSSES

Each partner shall be entitled to _____ percent (_____%) of the net profits of the business, and all losses occurring in the course of the business shall be borne in the same proportion, unless the losses are occasioned by the willful neglect or default, and not the mere mistake or error, of any of the partners, in which case the loss so incurred shall be made good by the partner through whose neglect or default the losses shall arise. Distribution of profits shall be made on the _____ day of _____ each year.

ARTICLE ELEVEN
ADVANCE DRAWS

Each partner shall be at liberty to draw out of the business in anticipation of the expected profits any sums that may be mutually agreed on, and the sums are to be drawn only after there has been entered in the books of the partnership the terms of agreement, giving the date, the amount to be drawn by the respective partners, the time at which the sums shall be drawn, and any other conditions or matters mutually agreed on. The signatures of each partner shall be affixed thereon. The total sum of the advanced draw for each partner shall be deducted from the sum that partner is entitled to under the distribution of profits as provided for in Article Ten of this agreement.

ARTICLE TWELVE
SALARY

No partner shall receive any salary from the partnership, and the only compensation to be paid shall be as provided in Articles Ten and Eleven herein.

ARTICLE THIRTEEN
RETIREMENT

In the event any partner shall desire to retire from the partnership, he shall give _____ months' notice in writing to the other partners and the continuing partners shall pay to the retiring partner at the termination of the _____ months' notice the value of the interest of the retiring partner in the partnership. The value shall be determined by a closing of the books and a rendition of the appropriate profit and loss, trial balance, and balance sheet statements. All disputes arising therefrom shall be determined as provided in Article Twenty.

ARTICLE FOURTEEN
RIGHTS OF CONTINUING PARTNERS

On the retirement of any partner, the continuing partners shall be at liberty, if they so desire, to retain all trade names designating the firm name used, and each of the partners shall sign and execute any assignments, instruments, or papers that shall be reasonably required for effectuating an amicable retirement.

ARTICLE FIFTEEN
DEATH OF PARTNER

In the event of the death of one partner, the legal representative of the deceased partner shall remain as a partner in the firm, except that the exercising of the right on the part of the representative of the deceased partner shall not continue for a period in excess of _____ months, even though under the terms hereof a greater period of time is provided before termination of this agreement. The original rights of the partners herein shall accrue to their heirs, executors, or assigns.

ARTICLE SIXTEEN
EMPLOYEE MANAGEMENT

No partner shall hire or dismiss any person in the employment of the partnership without the consent of the other partners, except in cases of gross misconduct by the employee.

ARTICLE SEVENTEEN
RELEASE OF DEBTS

No partner shall compound, release, or discharge any debt that shall be due or owing to the partnership, without receiving the full amount thereof, unless that partner obtains the prior written consent of the other partners to the discharge of the indebtedness.

ARTICLE EIGHTEEN
COVENANT AGAINST REVEALING TRADE SECRETS

No partner shall, during the continuance of the partnership or for _____ years after its determination by any means, divulge to any person not a member of the firm any trade secrets or special information employed in or conducive to the partnership business and which may come to his knowledge in the course of this partnership, without the consent in writing of the other partners, or of the other partners' heirs, administrators, or assigns.

ARTICLE NINETEEN
ADDITIONAL CONTRIBUTIONS

The partners shall not have to contribute any additional capital to the partnership to that required under Article Four herein, except as follows: (1) each partner shall be required to contribute a proportionate share in additional contributions if the fiscal year closes with an insufficiency in the capital account or profits of the partnership to meet current expenses, or (2) the capital account falls below _____ Dollars ($_____) for a period of _____ months.

ARTICLE TWENTY
ARBITRATION

If any differences shall arise between or among the partners as to their rights or liabilities under this agreement, or under any instrument made in furtherance of the partnership business, the difference shall be determined and the instrument shall be settled by _____ [name of arbitrator], acting as arbitrator, and the decision shall be final as to the contents and interpretations of the instrument and as to the proper mode of carrying the provision into effect.

ARTICLE TWENTY-ONE
ADDITIONS, ALTERATIONS OR MODIFICATIONS

Where it shall appear to the partners that this agreement, or any terms and conditions contained herein, are in any way ineffective or deficient, or not expressed as originally intended, and any alteration or addition shall be deemed necessary, the partners will enter into, execute, and perform all further deeds and instruments as their counsel shall advise. Any addition, alteration, or modification shall be in writing, and no oral agreement shall be effective.

In witness whereof, the parties have executed this agreement at _____ [designate place of execution] the day and year first above written.

[Signatures]

APPENDIX H-2
LIMITED PARTNERSHIP AGREEMENT

[From 14 AM. JUR. *Legal Forms* (Rev)]

Agreement of limited partnership made _____, 19___, between _____, of _____ [address], City of _____, County of _____, State of _____, herein referred to as general partner, and _____, of _____ [address], City of _____, County of _____, State of _____, and _____, of _____ [address], City of _____, County of _____, State of _____, both herein referred to as limited partners.

RECITALS

1. General and limited partners desire to enter into the business of _____.
2. General partner desires to manage and operate the business.
3. Limited partners desire to invest in the business and limit their liabilities.

In consideration of the mutual covenants contained herein, the parties agree as follows:

1. *General Provisions.* The limited partnership is organized pursuant to the provisions of _____ [cite statute] of the State of _____, and the rights and liabilities of the general and limited partners shall be as provided therein, except as herein otherwise expressly stated.

2. *Name of Partnership.* The name of the partnership shall be _____, herein referred to as the partnership.

3. *Business of Partnership.* The purpose of the partnership is to engage in the business of _____.

4. *Principal Place of Business.* The principal place of business of the partnership shall be at _____ [address], City of _____, County of _____, State of _____. The partnership shall also have

other places of business as from time to time shall be determined by general partner.

5. *Capital Contribution of General Partner.* General partner shall contribute _____ Dollars ($_____) to the original capital of the partnership. The contribution of general partner shall be made on or before _____, 19___. If general partner does not make his entire contribution to the capital of the partnership on or before that date, this agreement shall be void. Any contributions to the capital of the partnership made at that time shall be returned to the partners who have made the contributions.

6. *Capital Contributions of Limited Partners.* The capital contributions of limited partner shall be as follows:

Name	Amount
_____	$_____
_____	$_____

Receipt of the capital contribution from each limited partner as specified above is acknowledged by the partnership. No limited partner has agreed to contribute any additional cash or property as capital for use of the partnership.

7. *Duties and Rights of Partners.* General partner shall diligently and exclusively apply himself in and about the business of the partnership to the utmost of his skill and on a full-time basis.

General partner shall not engage directly or indirectly in any business similar to the business of the partnership at any time during the term hereof without obtaining the written approval of all other partners.

General partners shall be entitled to _____ days' vacation and _____ days' sick leave in each calendar year, commencing with the calendar year 19___. If general partner uses sick leave or vacation days in a calendar year in excess of the number specified above, the effect on his capital interest and share of the profits and losses of the partnership for that year shall be determined by a majority vote of limited partners.

No limited partner shall have any right to be active in the conduct of the partnership's business, nor have power to bind the partnership in any contract, agreement, promise, or undertaking.

8. *Salary of General Partner.* General partner shall be entitled to a monthly salary of _____ Dollars ($_____) for the services rendered by him. The salary shall commence on _____, 19___, and be payable on the _____ day of each month thereafter. The salary shall be treated as an expense of the operation of the partnership business and shall be payable irrespective of whether or not the partnership shall operate at a profit.

9. *Limitations on Distribution of Profits.* General partner shall have the right, except as hereinafter provided, to determine whether from time to time

partnership profits shall be distributed in cash or shall be left in the business, in which event the capital account of all partners shall be increased.

In no event shall any profits be payable for a period of _____ months until _____ percent (_____%) of those profits have been deducted to accumulate a reserve fund of _____ Dollars ($_____) over and above the normal monthly requirements of working capital. This accumulation is to enable the partnership to maintain a sound financial operation.

10. *Profits and Losses for Limited Partners.* Limited partners shall be entitled to receive a share of the annual net profits equivalent to their share in the capitalization of the partnership.

Limited partners shall each bear a share of the losses of the partnership equal to the share of profits to which each limited partner is entitled. The share of losses of each limited partner shall be charged against the limited partner's capital contribution.

Limited partners shall at no time become liable for any obligations or losses of the partnership beyond the amounts of their respective capital contributions.

11. *Profits and Losses for General Partner.* After provisions have been made for the shares of profits of limited partners, all remaining profits of the partnership shall be paid to general partner. After giving effect to the share of losses chargeable against the capital contributions of limited partners, the remaining partnership losses shall be borne by general partner.

12. *Books of Accounts.* There shall be maintained during the continuance of this partnership an accurate set of books of accounts of all transactions, assets, and liabilities of the partnership. The books shall be balanced and closed at the end of each year, and at any other time on reasonable request of the general partner. The books are to be kept at the principal place of business of the partnership and are to be open for inspection by any partner at all reasonable times. The profits and losses of the partnership and its books of accounts shall be maintained on a fiscal year basis, terminating annually on _____ [month and day], unless otherwise determined by general partner.

13. *Substitutions, Assignments, and Admission of Additional Partners.* General partner shall not substitute a partner in his place, or sell or assign all or any part of his interest in the partnership business, without the written consent of limited partners.

Additional limited partners may be admitted to this partnership on terms that may be agreed on in writing between general partner and the new limited partners. The terms so stipulated shall constitute an amendment to this partnership agreement.

No limited partner may substitute an assignee as a limited partner in his place; but the person or persons entitled by rule or by intestate laws, as the case may be, shall succeed to all the rights of limited partner as a substituted limited partner.

14. *Termination of Interest of Limited Partner, Return of Capital Contribution.* The interest of any limited partner may be terminated by (1) dissolution of the partnership for any reason as provided herein, (2) the agreement of all partners, or (3) the consent of the personal representative of a deceased limited partner and the partnership.

On the termination of the interest of a limited partner there shall be payable to that limited partner, or his estate, as the case may be, a sum to be determined by all partners, which sum shall not be less than _____ times the capital account of the limited partnership as shown on the books at the time of the termination, including profits or losses from the last closing of the books of the partnership to the date of the termination, when the interest in profits and losses terminated. The amount payable shall be an obligation payable only out of partnership assets, and at the option of the partnership, may be paid within _____ years after the termination of the interest, provided that interest at the rate of _____ percent (_____%) shall be paid on the unpaid balance.

15. *Borrowing by Partner.* In case of necessity as determined by a majority vote of all partners, a partner may borrow up to _____ Dollars ($_____) from the partnership. Any such loan shall be repayable at _____ percent (_____%) per year, together with interest thereon at the rate of _____ percent (_____%) per year.

16. *Term of Partnership and Dissolution.* The partnership term commences _____ , 19___ , and shall end on (1) the dissolution of the partnership by operation of law, (2) dissolution at any time designated by general partner, or (3) dissolution at the close of the month following the qualification and appointment of the personal representative of deceased general partner.

17. *Payment for Interest of Deceased General Partner.* In the event of the death of general partner there shall be paid out of the partnership's assets to decedent's personal representative for decedent's interest in the partnership, a sum equal to the capital account of decedent as shown on the books at the time of his death, adjusted to reflect profits or losses from the last closing of the books of the partnership to the day of his death.

18. *Amendments.* This agreement, except with respect to vested rights of partners, may be amended at any time by a majority vote as measured by the interest and the sharing of profits and losses.

19. *Binding Effect of Agreement.* This agreement shall be binding on the parties hereto and their respective heirs, executors, administrators, successors, and assigns.

In witness whereof, the parties have executed this agreement at _____ [designate place of execution] the day and year first above written.

[Signature]

APPENDIX H-3
OPERATING AGREEMENT OF
_____

This Operating Agreement (this "Agreement") of _____ , [Limited Liability Company] [L.L.C.] [LLC], a *[State]* limited liability company (the "Company"), is adopted and entered into by and among _____ and _____ , as members (the "Members", which term includes any other persons who may become members of the Company in accordance with the terms of this Agreement and the Act) and the Company pursuant to and in accordance with the Limited Liability Company Law of the State of *[state],* as amended from time to time (the "Act"). Terms used in this Agreement which are not otherwise defined shall have the respective meanings given those terms in the Act.

The parties agree as follows:

SECTION ONE
NAME

The name of the limited liability company under which it was formed is _____ [Limited Liability Company] [L.L.C.] [LLC].

SECTION TWO
TERM

[Alternative 1:] The Company shall dissolve on _____ *[date]* unless dissolved before such date in accordance with the Act.

[Alternative 2:] The Company shall continue until dissolved in accordance with the Act.

SECTION THREE
MANAGEMENT

Management of the Company is vested in its Members, who will manage the Company in accordance with the Act. Any Member exercising management powers or responsibilities will be deemed to be a manager for purposes of applying the provisions of the Act, unless the context otherwise requires, and that Member will have and be subject to all of the duties and liabilities of a manager provided in the Act. The Members will have the power to do any and all acts necessary or convenient to or for the furtherance of the purposes of the Company set forth in this Agreement, including all powers of Members under the Act.

SECTION FOUR
PURPOSE

The purpose of the Company is to engage in any lawful act or activity for which limited liability companies may be formed under the Act and to engage in any and all activities necessary or incidental to these acts.

SECTION FIVE
MEMBERS

The names and the business, residence or mailing address of the members are as follows:

Name	Address
_____	_____
_____	_____

SECTION SIX
CAPITAL CONTRIBUTIONS

The Members have contributed to the Company the following amounts, in the form of cash, property or services rendered, or a promissory note or other obligation to contribute cash or property or to render services:

Member	Amount of capital Contribution
_____	_____
_____	_____

SECTION SEVEN
ADDITIONAL CONTRIBUTIONS

No member is required to make any additional capital contribution to the Company.

SECTION EIGHT
ALLOCATION OF PROFITS AND LOSSES

The Company's profits and losses will be allocated in proportion to the value of the capital contributions of the Members.

SECTION NINE
DISTRIBUTIONS

Distributions shall be made to the Members at the times and in the aggregate amounts determined by the Members. Such distributions shall be allocated among the Members in the same proportion as their then capital account balances.

SECTION TEN
WITHDRAWAL OF MEMBER

A Member may withdraw from the Company in accordance with the Act.

SECTION ELEVEN
ASSIGNMENTS

A Member may assign in whole or part his or her membership interest in the Company; provided, however, an assignee of a membership interest may not become a Member without the vote or written consent of at least a majority in interest of the Members, other than the Member who assigns or proposes to assign his or her membership interest.

SECTION TWELVE
ADMISSION OF ADDITIONAL MEMBERS

One or more additional Members of the Company may be admitted to the Company with the vote or written consent of a majority in interest of the Members (as defined in the Act).

SECTION THIRTEEN
LIABILITY OF MEMBERS

The members do not have any liability for the obligations or liabilities of the Company, except to the extent provided in the Act.

SECTION FOURTEEN
EXCULPATION OF MEMBER-MANAGERS

A Member exercising management powers or responsibilities for or on behalf of the Company will not have personal liability to the Company or its members for damages for any breach of duty in that capacity, provided that nothing in this Section shall eliminate or limit: (a) the liability of any Member-Manager if a judgment or other final adjudication adverse to him or her establishes that his or her acts or omissions were in bad faith or involved intentional misconduct or a knowing violation of law, or that he or she personally gained in fact a financial profit or other advantage to which he or she was not legally entitled, or that, with respect to a distribution to Members, his or her acts were not performed in accordance with Section _____ of the Act, or (b) the liability of any Member-Manager for any act or omission prior to the date of first inclusion of this paragraph in this Agreement.

SECTION FIFTEEN
GOVERNING LAW

This Agreement shall be governed by, and construed in accordance with, the laws of the State of _____ , all rights and remedies being governed by those laws.

SECTION SIXTEEN
INDEMNIFICATION

To the fullest extent permitted by law, the Company shall indemnify and hold harmless, and may advance expenses to, any Member, manager or other person, or any testator or intestate of such Member, manager or other person (collectively, the "Indemnitees"), from and against any and all claims and demands whatsoever; provided, however, that no indemnification may be made to or on behalf of any Indemnitee if a judgment or other final adjudication adverse to such Indemnitee establishes: (a) that his or her acts were committed in bad faith or were the result of active and deliberate dishonesty and were material to the cause of action so adjudicated, or (b) that he or she personally gained in fact a financial profit or other advantage to which he or she was not legally entitled. The provisions of this section shall continue to afford protection to each Indemnitee regardless of whether he or she remains a Member, manager, employee or agent of the Company.

SECTION SEVENTEEN
TAX MATTERS

The Members of the Company and the Company intend that the Company be treated as a partnership for all income tax purposes, and will file all necessary and appropriate forms in furtherance of that position.

IN WITNESS OF WHICH, the undersigned have duly executed this Agreement as of the _____ day of _____ , 19___.

[THE COMPANY]
By: _____

[Member] _____

[Member] _____

Caution: This model operating agreement is not suitable for use without customization. Legal counsel must take care to prepare an operating agreement that complies with all relevant legislation, rules and regulations adopted in your state, and that reflects the business understanding and intentions of the parties to the transaction. This agreement is merely an example, and may not be appropriate for use in specific transactions.

APPENDIX H-4
CORPORATE BYLAWS

BYLAWS
OF
_____ CORPORATION

ARTICLE I—OFFICES

The principal office of the corporation in the State of _____ shall be located in the _____ of _____ _____ County of _____ .
The corporation may have such other offices, either within or without the state of incorporation, as the board of directors may designate or as the business of the corporation may from time to time require.

ARTICLE II—STOCKHOLDERS

1. ANNUAL MEETING.

The annual meeting of the stockholders shall be held on the _____ day of _____ in each year, beginning with the year 19___ at the hour _____ o'clock ___ M., for the purpose of electing directors and for the transaction of such other business as may come before the meeting. If the day fixed for the annual meeting shall be a legal holiday, such meeting shall be held on the next succeeding business day.

2. SPECIAL MEETINGS.

Special meetings of the stockholders, for any purpose or purposes, unless otherwise prescribed by statute, may be called by the president or by the directors, and shall be called by the president at the request of the holders of not less than _____ percent of all the outstanding shares of the corporation entitled to vote at the meeting.

3. PLACE OF MEETING.

The directors may designate any place, either within or without the state unless otherwise prescribed by statute, as the place of meeting for any annual meeting or for any special meeting called by the directors. A waiver of notice signed by all stockholders entitled to vote at a meeting may designate any place, either within or without the state unless otherwise prescribed by statute, as the place for holding such meeting. If no designation is made, or if a special meeting be otherwise called, the place of meeting shall be the principal office of the corporation.

4. NOTICE OF MEETING.

Written or printed notice stating the place, day, and hour of the meeting and, in case of a special meeting, the purpose or purposes for which the meeting is called, shall be delivered not less than _____ nor more than _____ days before the date of the meeting, either personally or by mail, by or at the direction of the president, or the secretary, or the officer or persons calling the meeting, to each stockholder of record entitled to vote at such meeting. If mailed, such notice shall be deemed to be delivered when deposited in the United States mail, addressed to the stockholder at his address as it appears on the stock transfer books of the corporation, with postage thereon prepaid.

5. CLOSING OF TRANSFER BOOKS OR FIXING OF RECORD DATE.

For the purpose of determining stockholders entitled to notice of or to vote at any meeting of stockholders or any adjournment thereof, or stockholders entitled to receive payment of any dividend, or in order to make a determination of stockholders for any other proper purpose, the directors of the corporation may provide that the stock transfer books shall be closed for a stated period but not to exceed, in any case, _____ days. If the stock transfer books shall be closed for the purpose of determining stockholders entitled to notice of or to vote at a meeting of stockholders, such books shall be closed for at least _____ days immediately preceding such meeting. In lieu of closing the stock transfer books, the directors may fix in advance a date as the record date for any such determination of stockholders, such date in any case to be not more than _____ days and, in case of a meeting of stockholders, not less than _____ days prior to the date on which the particular action requiring such determination of stockholders is to be taken. If the stock transfer books are not closed and no record

date is fixed for the determination of stockholders entitled to notice of or to vote at a meeting of stockholders, or stockholders entitled to receive payment of a dividend, the date on which notice of the meeting is mailed or the date on which the resolution of the directors declaring such dividend is adopted, as the case may be, shall be the record date for such determination of stockholders. When a determination of stockholders entitled to vote at any meeting of stockholders has been made as provided in this section, such determination shall apply to any adjournment thereof.

6. VOTING LISTS.

The officer or agent having charge of the stock transfer books for shares of the corporation shall make, at least _____ days before each meeting of the stockholders, a complete list of the stockholders entitled to vote at such meeting, or any adjournment thereof, arranged in alphabetical order, with the address of and the number of shares held by each, which list, for a period of _____ days prior to such meeting, shall be kept on file at the principal office of the corporation and shall be subject to inspection by any stockholder at any time during usual business hours. Such list shall also be produced and kept open at the time and place of the meeting and shall be subject to the inspection of any stockholder during the whole time of the meeting. The original stock transfer book shall be prima facie evidence as to who are the stockholders entitled to examine such list or transfer books or to vote at the meeting of stockholders.

7. QUORUM.

At any meeting of stockholders, _____ of the outstanding shares of the corporation entitled to vote, represented in person or by proxy, shall constitute a quorum at a meeting of stockholders. If less than said number of the outstanding shares are represented at a meeting, a majority of the shares so represented may adjourn the meeting from time to time without further notice. At such adjourned meeting at which a quorum shall be present or represented, any business may be transacted which might have been transacted at the meeting as originally notified. The stockholders present at a duly organized meeting may continue to transact business until adjournment, notwithstanding the withdrawal of enough stockholders to leave less than a quorum.

8. PROXIES.

At all meetings of stockholders, a stockholder may vote by proxy executed in writing by the stockholder or by his duly authorized attorney in fact. Such proxy shall be filed with the secretary of the corporation before or at the time of the meeting.

9. VOTING.

Each stockholder entitled to vote in accordance with the terms and provisions of the certificate of incorporation and these by-laws shall be entitled to one vote, in person or by proxy, for each share of stock entitled to vote held by such stockholders. Upon the demand of any stockholder, the vote for directors and upon any question before the meeting shall be by ballot. All elections for directors shall be decided by plurality vote; all other questions shall be decided by majority vote except as otherwise provided by the Certificate of Incorporation or the laws of this state.

10. ORDER OF BUSINESS.

The order of business at all meetings of the stockholders shall be as follows:
  a. Roll call.
  b. Proof of notice of meeting or waiver of notice.
  c. Reading of minutes of preceding meeting.
  d. Reports of officers.
  e. Reports of committees.
  f. Election of directors.
  g. Unfinished business.
  h. New business.

11. INFORMAL ACTION BY STOCKHOLDERS.

Unless otherwise provided by law, any action required to be taken at a meeting of the shareholders, or any other action which may be taken at a meeting of the shareholders, may be taken without a meeting if a consent in writing, setting forth the action so taken, shall be signed by all of the shareholders entitled to vote with respect to the subject matter thereof.

ARTICLE III—BOARD OF DIRECTORS

1. GENERAL POWERS.

The business and affairs of the corporation shall be managed by its board of directors. The directors shall in all cases act as a board, and they may adopt such rules and regulations for the conduct of their meetings and the management of the corporation as they may deem proper, not inconsistent with these by-laws and the laws of this state.

2. NUMBER, TENURE, AND QUALIFICATIONS.

The number of directors of the corporation shall be _____. Each director shall hold office until the next annual meeting of stockholders and until his successor shall have been elected and qualified.

3. REGULAR MEETINGS.

A regular meeting of the directors shall be held without other notice than this by-law immediately after, and at the same place as, the annual meeting of stockholders. The directors may provide, by resolution, the time and place for the holding of additional regular meetings without other notice than such resolution.

4. SPECIAL MEETINGS.

Special meetings of the directors may be called by or at the request of the president or any two directors.

The person or persons authorized to call special meetings of the directors may fix the place for holding any special meeting of the directors called by them.

5. NOTICE.

Notice of any special meeting shall be given at least _____ days previously thereto by written notice delivered personally, or by telegram or mailed to each director at his business address. If mailed, such notice shall be deemed to be delivered when deposited in the United States mail so addressed, with postage thereon prepaid. If notice be given by telegram, such notice shall be deemed to be delivered when the telegram is delivered to the telegraph company. The attendance of a director at a meeting shall constitute a waiver of notice of such meeting, except where a director attends a meeting for the express purpose of objecting to the transaction of any business because the meeting is not lawfully called or convened.

6. QUORUM.

At any meeting of the directors, _____ shall constitute a quorum for the transaction of business, but if less than said number is present at a meeting, a majority of the directors present may adjourn the meeting from time to time without further notice.

7. MANNER OF ACTING.

The act of the majority of the directors present at a meeting at which a quorum is present shall be the act of the directors.

8. NEWLY CREATED DIRECTORSHIPS AND VACANCIES.

Newly created directorships resulting from an increase in the number of directors and vacancies occurring in the board for any reason except the removal of directors without cause may be filled by a vote of a majority of the directors then in office, although less than a quorum exists. Vacancies occurring by reason of the removal of directors without cause shall be filled by vote of the stockholders. A director elected to fill a vacancy caused by resignation, death, or removal shall be elected to hold office for the unexpired term of his predecessor.

9. REMOVAL OF DIRECTORS.

Any or all of the directors may be removed for cause by vote of the stockholders or by action of the board. Directors may be removed without cause only by vote of the stockholders.

10. RESIGNATION.

A director may resign at any time by giving written notice to the board, the president, or the secretary of the corporation. Unless otherwise specified in the notice, the resignation shall take effect upon receipt thereof by the board or such officer, and the acceptance of the resignation shall not be necessary to make it effective.

11. COMPENSATION.

No compensation shall be paid to directors, as such, for their services, but by resolution of the board a fixed sum and expenses for actual attendance at each regular or special meeting of the board may be authorized. Nothing herein contained shall be construed to preclude any director from serving the corporation in any other capacity and receiving compensation therefor.

12. PRESUMPTION OF ASSENT.

A director of the corporation who is present at a meeting of the directors at which action on any corporate matter is taken shall be presumed to have assented to the action taken unless his dissent shall be entered in the minutes of the meeting or unless he shall file his written dissent to such action with the person acting as the secretary of the meeting before the adjournment thereof or shall forward such dissent by registered mail to the secretary of the corporation immediately after the adjournment of the meeting. Such right to dissent shall not apply to a director who voted in favor of such action.

13. EXECUTIVE AND OTHER COMMITTEES.

The board, by resolution, may designate from among its members an executive committee and other committees, each consisting of three or more directors. Each such committee shall serve at the pleasure of the board.

ARTICLE IV—OFFICERS

1. NUMBER.

The officers of the corporation shall be a president, a vice-president, a secretary, and a treasurer, each of who shall be elected by the directors. Such other officers and assistant officers as may be deemed necessary may be elected or appointed by the directors.

2. ELECTION AND TERM OF OFFICE.

The officers of the corporation to be elected by the directors shall be elected annually at the first meeting of the directors held after each annual meeting of the stockholders. Each officer shall hold office until his successor shall have been duly elected and shall have qualified or until his death or until he shall resign or shall have been removed in the manner hereinafter provided.

3. REMOVAL.

Any officer or agent elected or appointed by the directors may be removed by the directors whenever in their judgment the best interests of the corporation would be served thereby, but such removal shall be without prejudice to the contract rights, if any, of the person so removed.

4. VACANCIES.

A vacancy in any office because of death, resignation, removal, disqualification, or otherwise may be filled by the directors for the unexpired portion of the term.

5. PRESIDENT.

The president shall be the principal executive officer of the corporation and, subject to the control of the directors, shall in general supervise and control all of the business and affairs of the corporation. He shall, when present, preside at all meetings of the stockholders and of the directors. He may sign, with the secretary or any other proper officer of the corporation thereunto authorized by the directors, certificates for shares of the corporation, any deeds, mortgages, bonds, contracts, or other instruments which the directors have authorized to be executed, except in cases where the signing and execution thereof shall be expressly delegated by the directors or by these by-laws to some other officer or agent of the corporation, or shall be required by law to be otherwise signed or executed; and in general shall perform all duties incident to the office of president and such other duties as may be prescribed by the directors from time to time.

6. VICE-PRESIDENT.

In the absence of the president or in event of his death, inability, or refusal to act, the vice-president shall perform the duties of the president, and when so acting shall have all the powers of and be subject to all the restrictions upon the president. The vice-president shall perform such other duties as from time to time may be assigned to him by the president or by the directors.

7. SECRETARY.

The secretary shall keep the minutes of the stockholders' and of the directors' meetings in one or more books provided for that purpose; see that all notices are duly given in accordance with the provisions of these by-laws or as required; be custodian of the corporate records and of the seal of the corporation; keep a register of the post office address of each stockholder which shall be furnished to the secretary by such stockholder; have general charge of the stock transfer books of the corporation; and in general perform all duties incident to the office of secretary and such other duties as from time to time may be assigned to him by the president or by the directors.

8. TREASURER.

If required by the directors, the treasurer shall give a bond for the faithful discharge of his duties in such sum and with such surety or sureties as the directors shall determine. He shall have charge and custody of and be responsible for all funds and securities of the corporation; receive and give receipts for moneys due and payable to the corporation from any source whatsoever; deposit all such moneys in the name of the corporation in such banks, trust companies, or other depositories as shall be selected in accordance with these by-laws; and in general perform all of the duties incident to the office of treasurer and such other duties as from time to time may be assigned to him by the president or by the directors.

9. SALARIES.

The salaries of the officers shall be fixed from time to time by the directors and no officer shall be prevented from receiving such salary by reason of the fact that he is also a director of the corporation.

ARTICLE V—CONTRACTS, LOANS, CHECKS, AND DEPOSITS

1. CONTRACTS.

The directors may authorize any officer or officers, agent or agents, to enter into any contract or execute and deliver any instrument in the name of and on behalf of the corporation, and such authority may be general or confined to specific instances.

2. LOANS.

No loans shall be contracted on behalf of the corporation and no evidences of indebtedness shall be issued in its name unless authorized by a resolution of the directors. Such authority may be general or confined to specific instances.

3. CHECKS, DRAFTS, ETC.

All checks, drafts, or other orders for the payment of money, notes, or other evidences of indebtedness issued in the name of the corporation shall be signed by such officer or officers, agent or agents of the corporation and in such manner as shall from time to time be determined by resolution of the directors.

4. DEPOSITS.

All funds of the corporation not otherwise employed shall be deposited from time to time to the credit of the corporation in such banks, trust companies, or other depositories as the directors may select.

ARTICLE VI—CERTIFICATES FOR SHARES AND THEIR TRANSFER

1. CERTIFICATES FOR SHARES.

Certificates representing shares of the corporation shall be in such form as shall be determined by the directors. Such certificates shall be signed by the president and by the secretary or by such other officers authorized by law and by the directors. All certificates for shares shall be consecutively numbered or otherwise identified. The name and address of the stockholders, the number of shares and the date of issue, shall be entered on the stock transfer books of the corporation. All certificates surrendered to the corporation for transfer shall be canceled and no new certificate shall be issued until the former certificate for a like number of shares shall have been surrendered and canceled, except that in case of a lost, destroyed, or mutilated certificate a new one may be issued therefor upon such terms and indemnity to the corporation as the directors may prescribe.

2. TRANSFERS OF SHARES.

(a) Upon surrender to the corporation or the transfer agent of the corporation of a certificate for shares duly endorsed or accompanied by proper evidence of succession, assignment, or authority to transfer, it shall be the duty of the corporation to issue a new certificate to the person entitled thereto, and cancel the old certificate; every such transfer shall be entered on the transfer book of the corporation which shall be kept at its principal office.

(b) The corporation shall be entitled to treat the holder of record of any share as the holder in fact thereof, and, accordingly, shall not be bound to recognize any equitable or other claim to or interest in such share on the part of any other person whether or not it shall have express or other notice thereof, except as expressly provided by the laws of this state.

ARTICLE VII—FISCAL YEAR

The fiscal year of the corporation shall begin on the _____ day of _____ in each year.

ARTICLE VIII—DIVIDENDS

The directors may from time to time declare, and the corporation may pay, dividends on its outstanding shares in the manner and upon the terms and conditions provided by law.

ARTICLE IX—SEAL

The directors shall provide a corporate seal which shall be circular in form and shall have inscribed thereon the name of the corporation, the state of incorporation, year of incorporation and the words "Corporate Seal".

ARTICLE X—WAIVER OF NOTICE

Unless otherwise provided by law, whenever any notice is required to be given to any stockholder or director of the corporation under the provisions of these by-laws or under the provisions of the articles of incorporation, a waiver thereof in writing, signed by the person or persons entitled to such notice, whether before or after the time stated therein, shall be deemed equivalent to the giving of such notice.

ARTICLE XI—AMENDMENTS

These by-laws may be altered, amended, or repealed and new by-laws may be adopted by a vote of the stockholders representing a majority of all the shares issued and outstanding, at any annual stockholders' meeting or at any special stockholders' meeting when the proposed amendment has been set out in the notice of such meeting.

GLOSSARY

accrued benefits The plan participant's annual benefit, starting at normal retirement age, or the actuarial equivalent of such benefit.

actual authority [†] In the law of agency, the power of an agent to bind his principal. Although such authority must be granted by the principal to his or her agent, authority will be deemed to have been granted if the principal allows the agent to believe that the agent possesses it. Further, actual authority may be implied from the circumstances and need not be specifically granted.

actuary [†] A person whose profession is calculating insurance risk from a statistical point of view as, for EXAMPLE, the appropriate premium cost of a particular fire insurance policy.

administrative dissolution Dissolution of a corporation by the state of the corporation's domicile, usually for failing to pay income taxes or file annual reports.

affirmative defense A defense that amounts to more than simply a denial of the allegations in the plaintiff's complaint. It sets up new matter which, if proven, could result in a judgment against the plaintiff even if all the allegations of the complaint are true.

aggregate theory Theory regarding partnerships that suggests that a partnership is the totality of the persons engaged in a business rather than a separate entity.

annuity plan Type of qualified plan that does not involve a qualified plan trust. Contributions to an annuity plan are used to buy annuity policies directly from an insurance company.

annuity policy [†] An insurance policy that provides for or pays an annuity.

apparent authority [†] Authority which, although not actually granted by the principal, he or she permits his or her agent to exercise.

arbitration [†] A method of settling disputes by submitting a disagreement to a person (an arbitrator) or a group of individuals (an arbitration panel) for decision instead of going to court. If the parties are required to comply with the decision of the arbitrator, the process is called *binding arbitration;* if there is no such obligation, the arbitration is referred to as *nonbinding arbitration.* Compulsory arbitration is arbitration required by law, most notably in labor disputes.

articles of amendment Document filed with the Secretary of State or other appropriate state authority to amend a corporation's articles of incorporation.

articles of dissolution Document filed with the Secretary of State or other appropriate state authority to dissolve the corporation.

articles of incorporation [†] The charter or basic rules that create a corporation and by which it functions. Among other things, it states the purposes for which the corporation is being organized, the amount of authorized capital stock, and the names and addresses of the directors and incorporators.

articles of merger Document filed with the Secretary of State or other appropriate authority to effect a merger.

articles of organization Document required to be filed with the proper state authority to form a limited liability company.

articles of share exchange Document filed with the Secretary of State or other appropriate state authority to effect a share exchange.

articles of termination Document that must be filed with the proper state authority to dissolve a limited liability company.

assignments of error[†] On appeal, a listing of mistakes of law or mistakes of fact alleged to have been committed by the lower court, which are designated by the party complaining of them as grounds for reversal.

assumed name[†] A fictitious name or an alias.

authorized shares Total number of shares, provided for in the articles of incorporation, that the corporation is authorized to issue.

blue sky laws[†] State statutes intended to prevent fraud in the sale of securities. The term derives from investors who are "dumb enough to buy blue sky."

board of managers Group of individuals who manage the limited liability company. Similar to a corporation's board of directors.

bulletproof statutes With regard to limited liability company statutes, bulletproof statutes are state statutes that are drafted to make it impossible to form a limited liability in that state that complies with the statutes, unless it also complies with the Internal Revenue Code requirement limiting the limited liability company to two corporate characteristics.

bylaws Document which is considered the rules and guidelines for the internal government and control of a corporation. Bylaws prescribe the rights and duties of the shareholders, directors, and officers with regard to management and governance of the corporation.

capital surplus[†] Such surplus as a corporation may have over and above its earned surplus.

certificate of assumed name, trade name, or fictitious name A certificate granted by the proper state authority to an individual or an entity that grants the right to use an assumed or fictitious name for the transaction of business in that state.

certificate of authority Certificate issued by Secretary of State or similar state authority granting a foreign corporation the right to transact business in that state.

certificate of authority to transact business as a foreign limited liability company Certificate issued by the secretary of state, or other appropriate state official, to a foreign limited liability company to allow it to transact business in that state.

certificate of good standing Also sometimes referred to as a certificate of existence. Certificate issued by the Secretary of State or other appropriate state authority proving the incorporation and good standing of the corporation in that state.

charter[†] A corporation's articles of incorporation, together with the laws that grant corporate powers.

common stock[†] Ordinary capital stock in a corporation, the market value of which is based upon the worth of the corporation. Owners of common stock vote in proportion to their holdings, as opposed to owners of other classes of stock that are without voting rights. By contrast, however, common stock earns dividends only after other preferred classes of stock.

consolidation[†] A joining together of separate things to make one thing; an amalgamation.

conversion rights Rights, often granted to preferred shareholders with the issuance of preferred stock, that allow the preferred stockholders to convert their shares of preferred stock into common stock at some specific point in time, usually at the shareholder's option.

counterclaim A cause of action on which a defendant in a lawsuit might have sued the plaintiff in a separate action. Such a cause of action, stated in a separate division of a defendant's answer, is a counterclaim.

covenant not to compete [†] A provision in an employment contract in which the employee promises that, upon leaving the employer, she will not engage in the same business, as an employee or otherwise, in competition with her former employer. Such a covenant, which is also found in partnership agreements and agreements for the sale of a business, must be reasonable with respect to its duration and geographical scope.

cumulative voting [†] A method of voting for corporate directors under which each shareholder is entitled to cast a number of votes equal to the number of shares he or she owns times the number of directors to be elected, with the option of giving all one's votes to a single candidate or of distributing them among two or more as the shareholder wishes. The effect of cumulative voting is to ensure minority representation on a Board of Directors.

debt securities Securities that represent loans to the corporation, or other interests that must be repaid.

defined benefit plans Qualified plans in which the benefit payable to the participant is definitely determinable from a benefit formula set forth in the plan.

defined contribution plan Qualified plan that establishes individual accounts for each plan participant and provides benefits based solely on the amount contributed to the participants' accounts.

deposition [†] The transcript of a witness's testimony given under oath outside of the courtroom, usually in advance of the trial or hearing, upon oral examination or in response to written interrogatories.

derivative action An action brought by one or more stockholders of a corporation to enforce a corporate right or to remedy a wrong to the corporation, when the corporation, because it is controlled by wrongdoers or for other reasons, fails to take action.

determination letter [†] A letter issued by the IRS in response to a taxpayer's inquiry as to the tax implications of a given transaction. A determination letter that advises concerning the tax exemption status of a charitable organization is often referred to as a "501(c)(3) letter," after the section of the Internal Revenue Code that sets forth the criteria for such an exemption.

dissociation The event that occurs when a partner ceases to be associated in the carrying on of the partnership business.

dissolution [†] A breaking up; the separation of a thing into its component parts. With regard to a limited liability company, dissolution refers to the termination of the limited liability company's existence and its abolishment as an entity.

dissolution of corporation [†] The termination of a corporation's existence and its abolishment as an entity.

dividend [†] A payment made by a corporation to its stockholders, either in cash (a cash dividend), in stock (a stock dividend), or out of surplus earnings.

door-closing statute State statute providing that a corporation doing business in the state without the necessary authority is precluded from maintaining an action in that state.

downstream merger Merger whereby a parent corporation is merged into a subsidiary.

Employee Retirement Income Security Act of 1974 (ERISA) [†] A federal statute that protects employee pensions by regulating pension plans maintained by private employers, the way in which such plans are funded, and their vesting requirements. ERISA has important tax implications for both employers and employees.

employee stock ownership plan (ESOP) Qualified plan designed to give partial ownership of the corporation to the employees.

employee welfare benefit plan An employee benefit plan that provides participants with welfare benefits such as medical, disability, life insurance, dental, and death benefits. A welfare benefit plan may provide benefits either entirely or partially through insurance coverage.

employment agreement   Agreement entered into between an employer and an employee to set forth the rights and obligations of each party with regard to the employee's employment.

entity at will   Entity that may be dissolved at the wish of one or more members or owners.

entity theory   Theory that suggests that a partnership is an entity separate from its partners, much like a corporation.

equity securities   Securities that represent an ownership interest in the corporation.

exchange [†]   A place of business where the marketing of securities is conducted; a stock exchange; a securities exchange.

express authority [†]   Authority expressly granted to or conferred upon an agent or employee by a principal or employer.

fictitious name [†]   An artificial name that a person or a corporation adopts for business or professional purposes.

fiduciary duty [†]   A relationship between two persons in which one is obligated to act with the utmost good faith, honesty, and loyalty on behalf of the other. A fiduciary relationship is often loosely but inaccurately considered to be the equivalent of a confidential relationship.

fixed benefit formula   Formula for calculating pension plan benefits that provides participant with a definite percentage of their income.

foreign corporation [†]   A corporation incorporated under the laws of one state, doing business in another.

foreign limited liability company   A limited liability company that is transacting business in any state other than the state of its organization.

Form 8-K   Form that must be filed with the SEC by the issuer of registered securities when certain pertinent information contained in the registration statement of the issuer changes.

401(k) plan   Type of savings plan, established for the benefit of employees, which allows employees to elect to receive annual contributions in cash or as a contribution to a 401(k) plan that will defer income tax on the contribution.

general partner [†]   A partner in an ordinary partnership, as distinguished from a limited partnership. "General partner" is synonymous with "partner."

general partnership [†]   An ordinary partnership, as distinguished from a limited partnership. "General partnership" is synonymous with "partnership."

goodwill [†]   The benefit a business acquires, beyond the mere value of its capital stock and tangible assets, as a result of having a good reputation and the respect of the public. Goodwill is intangible property. However, goodwill is a function only of a going concern, and therefore can be assigned a value for accounting purposes only in connection with the sale of a business that is a going concern.

implied authority [†]   The authority of an agent to do whatever acts are necessary to carry out his or her express authority.

in personam jurisdiction (or *jurisdiction in personam***)** [†]   The jurisdiction a court has over the person of a defendant. It is acquired by service of process upon the defendant or by his or her voluntary submission to jurisdiction. Voluntary submission may be implied from a defendant's conduct within the jurisdiction, for example, by doing business in a state or by operating a motor vehicle within a state (see implied consent statutes). Jurisdiction in personam is also referred to as personal jurisdiction.

individual retirement account (IRA) [†]   Under the Internal Revenue Code, individuals who are not included in an employer-maintained retirement plan may deposit money (up to an annual maximum amount set by the Code) in an account for the purchase of retirement annuities. No tax is paid on income deposited to an IRA, and the proceeds are taxable only when they are withdrawn.

initial public offering The first offering of a corporation's securities to the public.

insider trading [†] A transaction in the stock of a corporation by a director, officer, or other insider, buying and selling on the basis of information obtained by her through her position in the company. Insider trading is regulated by the Securities Exchange Act.

inspectors of election Impartial individuals who are often appointed to oversee the election of directors at the shareholder meetings of large corporations.

integrated plan Type of retirement plan that is integrated with the employer's contribution to Social Security on behalf of the participant.

interlocutory appeal [†] An appeal of a ruling or order with respect to a question that, although not determinative of the case, must be decided for the case to be decided.

interrogatory Written question submitted by one party to a lawsuit to another party in the lawsuit, which must be answered in writing and under oath. The court may also submit written interrogatories upon one or more issues of fact to the jury. The answers to these interrogatories are necessary for a verdict.

involuntary dissolution Dissolution that is not approved by the board of directors or shareholders of a corporation, often initiated by creditors of an insolvent corporation.

issued and outstanding shares Authorized shares of authorized stock of a corporation that have been issued to shareholders.

joint and several liability [†] The liability of two or more persons who enter into an agreement promising, individually and together, to perform some act. Thus, there are joint and several notes, bonds, mortgages, and other contracts.

The legal effect is that if default or breach occurs, the promisee can sue either or both promissors. However, such liability is always based upon express language in the agreement ... or upon language from which severalty can be implied.

joint liability [†] The liability of two or more persons as if they were one person so that, in the absence of statute providing otherwise ... , if one of them is sued the other or others liable with her must be joined as defendants.

Keogh plan Qualified plan that may be adopted by self-employed individuals.

legatee [†] A person who receives personal property as a beneficiary under a will, although the word is often loosely used to mean a person who receives a testamentary gift of either personal property or real property.

letter of intent [†] A letter memorializing a preliminary understanding between two or more persons, written by one of them to the other (or others) to serve as a basis for the formal agreement they intend to execute.

limited liability company A type of non-corporate entity that offers limited liability to its owners, as well as partnership taxation status.

limited liability partnership A form of business organization similar to a partnership but that offers limited liability to its partners.

limited partner A partner in a limited partnership whose liability is limited to the sum she contributed to the partnership as capital; a special partner. A limited partner is not involved in managing or carrying out the business of the partnership.

limited partnership [†] A partnership in which the liability of one or more of the partners is limited to the amount of money they have invested in the partnership.

limited partnership certificate Document required to be filed with the Secretary of State or other appropriate state authority to form a limited partnership.

liquidation † The winding up of a corporation, partnership, or other business enterprise upon dissolution by converting the assets to money, collecting the accounts receivable, paying the debts, and distributing the surplus if any exists.

long-arm statutes † State statutes providing for substituted service of process on a nonresident corporation or individual. Long-arm statutes permit a state's courts to take jurisdiction over a nonresident if he or she has done business in the state (provided the minimum contacts test is met), or has committed a tort or owns property within the state.

manager-managed limited liability company A limited liability company in which the members have agreed to have the company's affairs managed by one or more managers.

member-managed limited liability company A limited liability company in which the members have elected to share the managing of the company's affairs.

merger † The combining of one of anything with another or others; the absorption of one thing by another; a disappearing into something else.

money purchase pension plan Defined contribution pension plan whereby the employer contributes a fixed amount based on a formula set forth in the plan that is based on the employee's salary.

novation † The extinguishment of one obligation by another; a substituted contract that dissolves a previous contractual duty and creates a new one. Novation, which requires the mutual agreement of everyone concerned, replaces a contracting party with a new party who had no rights or obligations under the previous contract.

operating agreement Document that governs the limited liability company. Similar to a corporation's by-laws.

over the counter Securities market that has no actual physical location; the market consists of transactions that take place through a series of computer networks among broker-dealers.

par value † The value of a share of stock or of a bond, according to its face; the named or nominal value of an instrument. The par value and the market value of stock are not synonymous; there is often a wide difference between them. The issuer of a bond is obligated to redeem it at par value upon maturity.

partnership † An undertaking of two or more persons to carry on, as coowners, a business or other enterprise for profit; an agreement between or among two or more persons to put their money, labor, and skill into commerce or business, and to divide the profit in agreed-upon proportions. Partnerships may be formed by entities as well as individuals; a corporation … may be a partner.

partnership at will A partnership formed without a designated date for its termination, or without stating a condition under which the partnership will terminate.

plan administrator Individual or entity responsible for calculating and processing all contributions to and distributions from a qualified plan, and for all other aspects of plan administration.

plan of exchange Document required by state statute that sets forth the terms of the agreement between the parties to a statutory share exchange.

plan of merger Document required by state statute that sets forth the terms of the agreement between the two merging parties in detail.

plan participant Employees who meet with certain minimum requirements to participate in a qualified plan.

preemptive right † The right or privilege of a stockholder of a corporation to purchase shares of a new issue before persons who are not stockholders. This entitlement allows a shareholder to preserve his or her percentage of ownership (i.e., his or her equity) in the corporation.

preferred stock [†] Corporate stock that is entitled to a priority over other classes of stock, usually common stock, in distribution of the profits of the corporation (i.e., dividends) and in distribution of the assets of the corporation in the event of dissolution or liquidation.

preincorporation agreement Agreement entered into between parties setting forth their intentions with regard to the formation of a corporation.

preincorporation transactions Actions taken by promoters or incorporators prior to the actual formation of the corporation.

professional limited liability company Entity similar to a professional corporation, that allows limited liability and partnership taxation status to its members, who must be professionals.

profit-sharing plan [†] An arrangement or plan under which the employees participate in the profits of the company that employs them. There are various types of profit-sharing plans. Most are regulated by the federal government under the Employee Retirement Income Security Act. All profit-sharing plans involve significant tax implications.

promoter [†] A person who organizes a business venture or is a major participant in organizing the venture.

prospectus [†] A statement published by a corporation that provides information concerning stock or other securities it is offering for sale to the public. The contents of a prospectus are regulated by the Securities Exchange Commission.

proxy [†] Authority given in writing by one shareholder in a corporation to another shareholder to exercise the first shareholder's voting rights.

proxy statement [†] A statement sent to shareholders whose proxies are being solicited so that they may be voted at an upcoming stockholders' meeting. The statement, whose contents are regulated by the Securities and Exchange Commission, provides shareholders with the information necessary for them to decide whether to give their proxies.

public offering [†] Securities offered for sale to the public at a particular time by a corporation or by government.

punitive damages [†] Damages that are awarded over and above compensatory damages or actual damages because of the wanton, reckless, or malicious nature of the wrong done by the plaintiff. Such damages bear no relation to the plaintiff's actual loss and are often called exemplary damages, because their purpose is to make an example of the plaintiff to discourage others from engaging in the same kind of conduct in the future.

qualified plan Retirement plan that meets with certain requirements of the Internal Revenue Code and qualifies for special tax treatment.

qualified plan contributions Contributions made to a qualified plan by the sponsor, participants, or third parties. Limitations on the amount of contributions are set forth in the Internal Revenue Code.

qualified plan distributions Distributions made to qualified plan participants or their beneficiaries from a qualified retirement plan trust, usually on the retirement, death, or termination of employment of the plan participant.

qualified plan trust Trust managed by trustees who are appointed by the qualified plan sponsors to manage the assets of the qualified plan.

quorum The minimum number of individuals who must be present or represented at a meeting as a prerequisite to the valid transaction of business.

red herring prospectus Preliminary prospectus that may be used after the filing, but prior to the effective date, of the registration statement. Contains a legend on the front cover in red ink stating specifically that no securities may be sold until the registration statement becomes effective.

registered agent Individual appointed by a corporation to receive service of process on behalf of the corporation and perform such other duties as may be necessary. Registered agents may be required in the corporation's state of domicile and in each state in which the corporation is qualified to transact business.

registered office Office designated by the corporation as the office where process may be served. The Secretary of State or other appropriate state authority must be informed as to the location of the registered office. Corporations are generally required to maintain a registered office in each state in which the corporation is qualified to transact business.

representative action Action brought by a shareholder on behalf of the shareholder and his or her entire class of shareholders against the corporation.

res judicata † Means "the thing (i.e., the matter) has been adjudicated"; the thing has been decided. The principle that a final judgment rendered on the merits by a court of competent jurisdiction is conclusive of the rights of the parties and is an absolute bar in all other actions based upon the same claim, demand, or cause of action.

reverse triangle merger Three-way merger whereby a subsidiary corporation is merged into the target corporation. The end result is the survival of the parent corporation and the target corporation, which becomes a new subsidiary.

scrip † A certificate of a right to receive something. In certain circumstances, instead of money, governments issue scrip that may be redeemed for money. Corporations issue scrip representing fractional shares of stock that, when accumulated in sufficient number, may be exchanged for stock.

Securities Act of 1933 † The federal statute regulating the issuance and sale of securities to the public.

Securities and Exchange Commission † The agency that administers and enforces federal statutes relating to securities, including the Securities Act of 1933 and the Securities Exchange Act.

Securities Exchange Act of 1934 The federal statute that empowers the Securities and Exchange Commission to regulate securities exchanges.

securities † Certificates that represent a right to share in the profits of a company or in the distribution of its assets, or in a debt owed by a company or by the government. (EXAMPLES: stocks; bonds; notes with interest coupons; any registered security.) What is and is not a "security" differs to some degree under different statutes, for EXAMPLE, the securities acts, the Bankruptcy Code, the Uniform Commercial Code, and the Internal Revenue Code. Generally speaking, however, under most legislation, a security is an instrument of a type commonly dealt in on securities exchanges or in similar markets and is commonly recognized as a means of investment.

security † Collateral; a pledge given to a creditor by a debtor for the payment of a debt or for the performance of an obligation. With regard to limited liability companies, certificates representing a right to share in the company's profits or in the distribution of its assets, or in a debt owed by a company or by the government.

share exchange Transaction whereby one corporation acquires all of the outstanding shares of one or more classes or series of another corporation by an exchange that is compulsory on the shareholders of the target corporation.

short-swing profits † A profit made on the sale of corporate stock held for less than six months. Such profits are generally available only to investors who possess insider information.

simplified employee pension plan (SEP) Alternative to qualified plan, often used by small employers and self-employed individuals, that offers income tax breaks and simplified administration.

sole proprietor The owner of a sole proprietorship.

sole proprietorship † Ownership by one person, as opposed to ownership by more than one person, ownership by a corporation, ownership by a partnership, etc.

sponsor In ERISA terms, an employer who adopts a qualified plan for the exclusive benefit of the sponsor's employees and/or their beneficiaries.

state of domicile The home state of a corporation or partnership; the state in which the corporation is incorporated or the partnership is formed.

stated capital The total of the par values of all shares of stock that a corporation has issued, plus the total consideration paid for its no-par stock.

statement of authority A statement filed for public record by the partners of a partnership to expand or limit the agency authority of a partner, to deny the authority or status of a partner or to give notice of certain events such as the dissociation of a partner or the dissolution of the partnership.

statement of denial A statement filed for public record by a partner or other interested party to contradict the information included in a statement of authority.

statute of frauds † A statute, existing in one or another form in every state, that requires certain classes of contracts to be in writing and signed by the parties. Its purpose is to prevent fraud or reduce the opportunities for fraud.

statutory merger Merger that is provided for by statute.

stock bonus plan Type of defined contribution plan, similar to the profit-sharing plan, in which the main investment is the employer's stock.

stock dividend † A dividend paid by a corporation in the stock of the corporation.

stock split † The act of a corporation in replacing some or all of its outstanding stock with a greater number of shares of lesser value.

stock subscription agreement Agreement to purchase a specific number of shares of a corporation.

target benefit plan Type of qualified plan that has many characteristics of both a defined benefit plan and a defined contribution plan. Contributions are based on the amount of the fixed retirement for each participant. However, the amount distributed to plan participants will depend on the value of the assets in the participant's account at the time of retirement.

10-K report † The annual report that the Securities and Exchange Commission requires of publicly held corporations.

10-Q quarterly reports Quarterly report that must be filed with the SEC by all corporations that are required to file 10-K reports.

tenancy in partnership Form of ownership for property held by a partnership, subject to the pertinent statutory provisions regarding partnership property.

tombstone ads Ads surrounded by a heavy black border and commonly placed in newspapers to announce a securities offering and disseminate certain information regarding the offering.

tortious Wrongful. A tortious act subjects the actor to liability under the law of torts. A *tort* is a private or civil wrong for which the legal system provides a remedy in the form of an action for damages.

trade name † The name under which a company does business. The goodwill of a company includes its trade name.

transfer agent [†] A person or company that acts on behalf of a corporation in carrying out the transfer of its stock from one owner to another and registering the transaction on the corporate records.

treasury shares [†] Corporate stock that has been issued to shareholders and paid for in full, and has later been repurchased or otherwise reacquired by the corporation.

triangle merger Merger involving three corporations, whereby a corporation forms a subsidiary corporation and funds it with sufficient cash or shares of stock to perform a merger with the target corporation, which is merged into the subsidiary. The parent corporation and the subsidiary corporation both survive a triangle merger.

underwriter With regard to securities offerings, any person or organization that purchases securities from an issuer with a view to distributing them, or any person who offers or sells or participates in the offer or sale for an issuer of any security.

Uniform Limited Liability Company Act Uniform Act adopted by the National Conference of the Commissions of Uniform State Laws in 1994 to give states guidance when drafting limited liability company statutes.

unit benefit formula Formula for calculating the benefits payable under a pension plan that provides participants with a unit of pension for each year of credited service.

upstream merger Merger whereby a subsidiary corporation merges into its parent.

variable benefit formula A formula used to calculate benefits payable under a pension plan that provides participants with benefits that are related to the market value of the trust assets or are tied to a recognized cost of living index.

vesting The nonforfeitable right that a retirement plan participant acquires to receive benefits accrued.

voluntary dissolution Dissolution that is approved by the directors and shareholders of the corporation.

voting group Shareholders that are entitled, as a group, to vote separately at shareholder meetings on certain matters.

watered shares [†] Shares of stock issued by a corporation as paid-up stock but which have in fact been issued without any consideration or for inadequate consideration.

winding up [†] The dissolution or liquidation of a corporation or a partnership.

writ of mandamus [†] (Latin) Means "we command." A writ issuing from a court of competent jurisdiction, directed to an inferior court, board, or corporation, or to an officer of a branch of government (judicial, executive, or legislative), requiring the performance of some ministerial act. A writ of mandamus is an extraordinary remedy.

INDEX

EIN. *See* Employer
identification number
Employee at will, 491, 495
Employee benefit plans, 219,
461–64
administrators, 464, 466
approval, 487
nonqualified, 462
pension. *See* Pension plans
qualified. *See* Qualified
plans
welfare. *See* Welfare benefit
plans
Employee Retirement Income
Security Act of 1974
(ERISA), 462–63, 466–68.
See also Qualified pension
plans
Employee stock ownership
plans, 297, 463, 477–79
Employee welfare benefit
plans, 461, 482–84
Employees
employment agreements.
See Employment
agreements
highly compensated, 169,
468, 475, 481
key, 470
plan participants, 466
of sole proprietorship, 3, 10
stock ownership, 297, 463,
477–79
termination, 492
Employer identification
number (EIN), 10
Employment, 492, 493, 498,
505–6
Employment agreements, 491
amendment, 507
approval of, 507, 511
as contracts, 493
drafting, 493–507
elements, 494–95
employee considerations,
493
employer considerations,
492–93
form, 494

paralegals and, 511–13
renewal, 507
sample, 507–11
term, 495–96
worksheet, 512–13
Entity at will, 118
Entity theory (partnership),
21
Entrepreneurs, 5
Equity financing, 297–308,
321
Equity securities, 296
ERISA. *See* Employee
Retirement Income
Security Act of 1974
ESOP. *See* Employee stock
ownership plans
Ethics, 75, 435
Event of withdrawal, 104–5
Exchanges (securities), 332,
333, 350
Express authority, 31

F

Federal Bankruptcy Act, 162
Federal Trade Commission,
334
Fictitious name, 422. *See also*
Assumed name
Fiduciary duty, 22
corporate directors, 240,
242–43
corporate officers, 265
employee benefit plans
and, 463
general partners, 81
LLC managers, 132
LLC members, 131
partners, 26–27
Fifth Amendment, 166
File management, 519–20
Filing fees
articles of dissolution, 439
articles of incorporation,
206
certificate of assumed
name, 4, 40
limited partnerships, 84, 89

partnerships, 36, 40
securities registration
statements, 336
stock shares, 302
verification, 231
Financing through ESOP, 479
Fines, 417, 424
Fixed benefit formula, 473
For profit, 18. *See also* Profit
and loss
Foreign corporations, 411, 418
certificate of authority,
418–21, 423–24
cessation of business,
424–25
good standing, 424
name, 421–22, 425–26
nonqualification problems,
414, 416–17
paralegal tasks, 413, 426–28
qualification to do
business, 36, 171, 188,
411–14, 418–24
state requirements, 164,
188, A111–A112
Foreign limited liability
companies, 145–49
Foreign limited partnership,
84, 108
Foreign states, 4
Form 8-K, 352–53
Form 966, 450, 451
Form 1096, 450
Form 1099, 450
Form 2553, 175, 176–77
Form 5300, 484, 485
Form 5500, 486
Form 5500C, 486
Form 5500-EZ, 486
Form 5500R, 486
Form 8717, 484
Form books, 64, 65, 68, 108,
109–10, 152, 156, 181,
232, 487
Form S-1, 336, 337
Form SS-4, 10, 11
Forms, 152
application for certificate of
authority, 419, 420